Learning Microsoft® Office Word 2007

Suzanne Weixel

PEARSON

Prentice
Hall
DDC

ISBN-13: 978-0-13-365690-9
ISBN-10: 0-13-365690-X

2 3 4 5 6 7 8 9 10   11 10 09 08

Table of Contents

Introduction

Microsoft Office Word 2007 is Microsoft's tool for creating professional-looking documents and basic Web pages. Use Word to build the documents that today's information-driven world demands from businesses, governments, schools, and virtually every organization that needs to communicate.

HOW THIS BOOK IS ORGANIZED

■ This book is organized into thirteen lessons:

- **Lesson 1— Word Basics.** This lesson covers the most essential skills required to get up and running with Microsoft Office Word 2007. You learn how to start and exit Word 2007, and how to use the mouse—or other pointing device—and keyboard to navigate and select commands. You explore the main components of the Word 2007 window elements, and how to use them to access the features you need. You also learn how to customize the Word window to suit your needs, and how to use the Help program to get help for Word 2007 features.

- **Lesson 2—Getting Started with Word 2007.** Once you are familiar with the Word 2007 interface, you move on to creating documents. You learn how to type in a document and correct errors, how to save a document so you can open it again in the future, and how to print a document on paper. You learn how to use horizontal and vertical alignment, line spacing, and paragraph spacing, and font formatting to produce professional business documents, including letters, memos, and press releases, as well as how to generate envelopes and labels.

- **Lesson 3—Basic Editing Skills.** In Lesson 3 you build on your knowledge as you practice opening and editing saved documents. You learn how to insert and overwrite text, and how to copy and move text from one location to another. In addition, in this lesson you learn how to manage your documents. You learn to save a document

with a new name or in a new location, and how to work with multiple documents at the same time. You preview and print documents without opening them, and learn how to open a document in read-only mode so that you cannot make inadvertent changes. You also explore document properties and learn how to work with different file types.

- **Lesson 4—Formatting Basics.** In this lesson you expand your knowledge of how to format text, paragraphs, and pages. You start learning how to apply color and highlights to text and how to insert symbols and special characters. Next, you learn about indents, and how to create bulleted and numbered lists. Styles are covered in depth, so you are able to apply styles, select a style set, create styles, modify styles, and remove all formatting. You learn about how to prepare a one-page report by setting margins and page orientation. You learn how to use the AutoFormat as You Type feature. Finally, you are introduced to themes. You learn how to select a theme and how to customize a theme.

- **Lesson 5—Word and the World Wide Web.** Word provides tools for creating new Web page documents and saving existing documents as Web pages. In this lesson you learn to use these tools to create Web pages and Web sites, complete with backgrounds, themes, hyperlinks, and titles. You also learn how to send a Word document as an attachment to an Outlook e-mail message.

Lesson 6—Creating Tables. Tables let you arrange text in neat columns and rows. In Lesson 6 you learn how to create and format a table in any document. You use different methods to insert and draw tables, change the structure of a table, and align a table on a page. You also learn how to apply a style to a table, and to format borders and shading. You even learn how to perform simple calculations in a table.

Lesson 7—Creating Documents with Merge. In this lesson you learn how to merge a Word document with a data source to create form letters, envelopes, labels, directories, and e-mail messages. You create a data source from scratch, and use an existing data source. You learn how to work with merge fields and merge blocks to customize merge documents. You also learn how to edit, filter, and sort a data source.

Lesson 8—Creating and Editing Long Documents. Word 2007 has the tools you need to create and manage long documents. In this lesson you learn how to work with an outline, and how to create sections and new pages when you need them. You learn how to add headers and footers to a document, and how to insert page numbers. You learn about tools for navigating in a long document, such as Document Map, Thumbnails, and Full Screen Reading view, as well as Find and Replace, Bookmarks, and Browse Objects. You use the Track Changes feature and comments to collaborate with others. Finally, you learn how to insert features that help readers locate information, such as footnotes and endnotes, captions, cross-references, tables of contents, tables of figures, tables of authorities, bibliographies, and indexes.

Lesson 9—Desktop Publishing and Automation. In this lesson you explore some of the more advanced features available in Word. You learn how to work with newsletter-style columns and how to add visual excitement to a document with features such as dropped capitals, borders, and shading. You learn how to fine-tune documents for publication by adjusting character spacing, paper size, and controlling text flow, and you identify and correct inconsistent formatting. You learn how to use time-saving features such as building blocks, templates, and macros.

Lesson 10—Graphics. Lesson 10 covers all types of graphics objects including shapes, text boxes, pictures, and WordArt. You learn how to insert and format objects, and how to integrate them with text. The lesson closes by covering how to create graphic or text watermarks.

Lesson 11—Securing Documents. Protecting and securing documents is vital to companies and individuals alike. In this lesson you learn how to protect a document from unauthorized changes, how to apply password protection, and how to assign digital signatures. You also learn how to create and fill out forms.

Lesson 12—Integration. Word 2007 is part of the Microsoft Office Suite of programs, and in Lesson 12 you learn how to integrate documents created with the different Microsoft Office programs. You start by learning how to work with more than one program at a time, and then move on to sharing data. You link and embed Excel and PowerPoint objects in Word documents. You learn how to create SmartArt graphics and charts in a Word document, and how to convert text to a table and a table to text. You learn to use the Research tool to locate information in reference sources or on the World Wide Web, and how to incorporate that information into your Word documents. You share data between programs using Smart Tags and you use an Access data base as a data source for a merge.

Lesson 13—Challenge Exercises. Lesson 13 is comprised of exercises that challenge your knowledge of Word and your critical thinking skills. You create complex documents using data from multiple sources, such as the World Wide Web, Excel workbooks, and PowerPoint presentations. You create Web pages and link them into Web sites. You create multi-page flyers that incorporate text and graphics. You use tables and outlines, Smart Tags and e-mail. You even complete a research project from start to finish.

- Lessons are comprised of short exercises designed for using Microsoft Office Word 2007 in real-life business settings. Each exercise is made up of seven key elements:
  - **Software Skills.** Each exercise starts with a brief overview of the Word tools that you'll be working with in the exercise.
  - **Application Skills.** The objectives are then put into context by setting a scenario.
  - **Terms.** Key terms are included and defined at the start of each exercise, so you can quickly refer back to them. The terms are then highlighted in the text.
  - **Notes.** Concise notes for learning the computer concepts.
  - **Procedures.** Hands-on mouse and keyboard procedures teach all necessary skills.
  - **Application Exercise.** Step-by-step instructions put your skills to work.
  - **On Your Own.** Each exercise concludes with a critical thinking activity that you can work through on your own. In many of these exercises you need to create your own data. The On Your Own sections can be used as additional reinforcement, for practice, or to test skill proficiency.

- Each lesson ends with a **Critical Thinking Exercise** that, as with the *On Your Owns*, requires you to rely on your own skills to complete the task, and a **Curriculum Integration Exercise**, which incorporates Language Arts, Math, Science, or Social Studies content.

- Two **Curriculum Connections** appear in each lesson. These activities involve research on a topic and then using that data in Word. A listing of these activities is included on page xiv.

WORKING WITH DATA AND SOLUTION FILES

As you work through the exercises in this book, you'll be creating, opening, and saving files. You should keep the following instructions in mind:

- For many of the exercises you can use the data files provided on the CD-ROM that comes with this book. The data files are used so that you can focus on the skills being introduced—not on keyboarding lengthy documents. The files are organized by application in the **Datafiles** folders on the CD-ROM.

- When the application exercise includes a file name and a CD icon, you can open the file provided on CD.

- If the exercise includes a CD icon and a keyboard icon, you can choose to work off of either the data file or a file that you created in an earlier exercise.

- Unless the book instructs otherwise, use the default settings for displaying Normal view and Ribbon and Quick Access Toolbar settings. The appearance of your files may look different if the system is set to a screen resolution other than 800 x 600.

- All the exercises instruct you to save the files created or to save the exercise files under a new name.

- When you see _xx in any instructions in this book, it means that you should type an underscore followed by your own initials—not the actual text "_xx". This will help your instructor identify your work.

- You should verify the name of the hard disk or network folder to which files should be saved.

DIRECTORY OF CURRICULUM CONNECTIONS

WHAT'S ON THE CD

The CD contains the following:

- **Data Files** for many of the exercises. This way you don't have to type lengthy documents from scratch.
- **Microsoft® Office 2007 Glossary** includes terms and definitions.
- **Glossary of Business and Financial Terms** used in the workplace, the financial arena, and Learning Microsoft Office Word 2007. Key business terms help you understand the work scenarios.
- **Keyboarding Course** teaches all the keys and includes skill-building drills.
- **Computer Literacy Basics.** These exercises include information on computer care, computer basics, and a brief history of computer.

To Access the Files Included on CD:

1. Insert the *Learning Microsoft Office Word 2007* CD in the CD-ROM drive.
2. Navigate to your CD-ROM drive; right-click [start] / [icon] and choose Explore from the shortcut menu.
3. Navigate to your CD-ROM drive.
4. Right-click the folder that you wish to copy.
5. Navigate to the location where you wish to place the folder.
6. Right-click and choose Paste from the Shortcut menu.

SUPPORT MATERIAL

A complete instructor support package is available with all the tools teachers need:

- **Teacher's Manual** includes teaching tips, hints, and pointers to help teachers maximize classroom presentation time. Includes solution files on CD. (ISBN: 0-13-365691-8)

- **Test Binder** includes both application and concept tests correlated to each lesson in the book. Also includes a pretest, posttest, and final exam. (ISBN: 0-13-365694-2)
- **Solutions Binder** includes printouts of exercise solutions to visually check students' results. Also includes solution files on CD. (ISBN: 0-13-365695-0)

Lesson | 1

Microsoft Office Word 2007 Basics

Exercise | 1

Skills Covered

- ■ Evaluate Word Processing Software
- ■ About Microsoft Office Word 2007
- ■ Conventions Used in this Book
- ■ Use the Mouse
- ■ Use the Keyboard
- ■ Start and Exit Word 2007
- ■ Identify Common Screen Elements

Software Skills Microsoft Office Word 2007 is a word-processing application you can use to prepare many different types of documents. Word 2007 makes it easy to create simple documents such as letters and memos, as well as more complex documents such as newsletters and brochures. You can use Word 2007 with only a keyboard, or with a combination of the mouse—or other pointing device—and the keyboard.

Application Skills You've just been hired as the assistant to the president of Long Shot, Inc., a manufacturing company that produces golf equipment, apparel, and accessories. She has asked you to become familiar with Microsoft Office Word 2007, since the company uses it throughout its business operations. In this exercise, you'll practice using the mouse and the keyboard to start and exit Word 2007, and you will review the screen elements of the Word window so you can use these skills on the job.

TERMS

Compatibility The ability to work with another program or hardware device.

Current document The document currently open and active. Actions and commands will affect the current document.

Default A standard setting or mode of operation.

Elements Menus, icons, and other items that are part of an on-screen interface.

Format Arrange and enhance the contents of a document to improve its appearance.

Hardware Computers, printers, and other devices.

Hyperlink Text or graphics set up to provide a direct connection with a destination location. When you click a hyperlink, the destination is displayed.

I-beam A mouse pointer shape resembling the uppercase letter I.

Icon A picture used to identify an element on-screen, such as a Ribbon button.

Insertion point The flashing vertical line that indicates where the next action will occur in a document or file on-screen.

Menu A list of commands or choices.

Mouse A device that allows you to select items on-screen by pointing at them with the mouse pointer.

Mouse pad A smooth, cushioned surface on which you slide a mouse.

Pointer A marker on your computer screen that moves in response to the movements of a pointing device such as a mouse or touchpad. It indicates where the next action will occur. The pointer changes shape depending on the current action. May be called the mouse pointer.

Pointing device A device such as a mouse or touchpad that allows you to control the movement of a pointer on the screen in order to select items and commands.

Ribbon A screen element that displays buttons for accessing Office features and commands.

Scroll wheel A wheel on some pointing devices used to navigate through a document on-screen.

Software Programs that provide the instructions for a computer or other hardware device.

Software suite A group of software programs sold as a single unit. Usually the programs have common features that make it easy to integrate and share data.

Toolbar A row of buttons used to select features and commands.

Window The area on-screen where a program or document is displayed.

Word processing The act of creating text-based documents.

NOTES

Evaluate Word Processing Software

- There are many **word processing** programs available for use on desktop and networked personal computers.

- They range from basic programs, such as Microsoft WordPad, to full-featured programs, such as Microsoft Office Word 2007.

- Basic programs have minimal features for entering and editing text, while full-featured programs include sophisticated tools for formatting, desktop publishing, and graphics manipulation.

- When evaluating **software** packages, consider the following:
  - Tasks you need to accomplish
  - Cost
  - Ease-of-use
  - Compatibility with other programs you already own
  - Compatibility with your hardware systems

- You can research software programs using the Internet, consulting a magazine or buyer's guide, or by visiting a retailer to talk to a salesperson.

- Some software manufacturers provide trial versions of a program that you can test for a limited number of days.

- Most stores will not let you return software once you open the package. Take the time to make sure you are purchasing the software that best meets your needs.

About Microsoft Office Word 2007

- Microsoft Office Word 2007 is designed to make it easy for you to create, edit, **format**, and distribute word processing documents.

- With Word 2007 you can easily include text and graphics in documents.

- You can transfer data between documents and between different applications running under the Windows operating environment.

- You can even collaborate with others to create and edit documents.

- Word 2007 also provides tools for creating documents for distribution on the Internet, and for keeping your documents secure.

- If you have used previous versions of Microsoft Office Word, you will notice many similarities as well as many new features and enhancements.

- The new user interface is designed to make it easier to access the most commonly used commands. Key new features include:
  - The **Ribbon** replaces traditional menus and toolbars.
  - Preset formatting options are organized into galleries that let you preview how changes will affect your document, and then quickly apply the formatting you want to use.
  - The spelling checker provides consistent functionality across all Office 2007 programs.
  - In addition, there are new **default** file formats based on Extensible Markup Language (XML) for some Office 2007 programs, including Word 2007. The new file formats result in smaller files, improved recovery of damaged files, improved security, and easier integration between different file types.

- Microsoft Office 2007 programs are fully compatible with files created with previous versions.

- If you are using Word 2007 as part of the Microsoft Office 2007 **software suite** of applications, you will find it easy to transfer your knowledge of Word 2007 to any of the other Office programs.

- Microsoft Office Word 2007 can run with either the Microsoft Windows XP or the Microsoft Windows Vista operating system.

- There may be slight differences in the program depending on the operating system you are using.

- For example, features that involve browsing for storage locations are different depending on the operating system. This includes opening and saving a file, and selecting a file to insert.

- In addition, there may be some minor visual differences in the way the program looks on-screen. For example, the colors may differ, and the program Close button may be larger under Windows Vista.

- The procedures in this book assume you are using Microsoft Windows XP. Procedures that may be different on systems using Windows Vista are indicated by notes referring you to ask your instructor for additional information.

Conventions Used in This Book

- The conventions used throughout this book are designed to help you quickly understand the concepts and the skills required to use Word 2007 effectively.

- Procedures for completing a task are documented as follows:

  - Definitions of new words are provided in the Terms section.

  - Concepts are introduced in the Notes section.

  - Actions are listed in the Procedures section.

  - Keyboard shortcut keys (if available) are included next to the task heading.

  - Actions performed using a mouse or other pointing device are numbered on the left, with button icons providing a visual reference.

  - Keystrokes are listed on the right.

    - Keys pressed in sequence are separated by a comma.

    - Keys pressed in combination are separated by a plus sign.

  - The name of the Ribbon group precedes the steps where actions occur.

    ✓ *The width of the program window on your screen affects the way buttons and groups display, which may affect the order in which you select commands. If your screen is narrower than the one in this book, you may have to click a group button to display the commands in that group before you can complete the steps in the procedure. Refer to Exercise 2 for more information on using the Ribbon.*

- Exercise Directions provide step-by-step instructions for applying the new skills.

- Illustrations are included to provide visual support for the text.

- This book assumes you have installed all of the features covered. If necessary, run Word 2007 Setup again to install additional options.

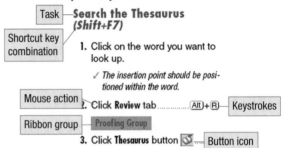

Sample of procedure conventions

Use the Mouse

- Use your **mouse** or other **pointing device** to point to and select commands and features of Microsoft Office Word 2007.

  ✓ *The term mouse is used throughout this book to refer to all types of pointing devices.*

- Other types of pointing devices include a touchpad, trackball, stylus, or pen.

- When you move the mouse or other pointing device on your desk, the **pointer** moves on-screen. For example, when you move a mouse to the left, the mouse pointer moves to the left.

- When you click a button on the device, the program executes a command. For example, when you move the pointer to the Save button and then click, the program saves the current document.

- Clicking a button can also be used to move the **insertion point** to a new location.

- Older mouse devices work by sliding a tracking ball on your desk.

- Newer devices might work using light. Others may use a wireless connection.

- A device such as a mouse may have one, two, or three buttons. Unless otherwise noted, references in this book are to the use of the left button.

- Your device might have a **scroll wheel**. Spin the scroll wheel to move through the file open on your screen.

■ The pointer changes shape depending on the program in use, the object being pointed to, and the action being performed. Common pointer shapes include an arrow (for selecting), an **I-beam** (which indicates location on-screen), and a hand with a pointing finger (to indicate a **hyperlink**).

■ You should use a mouse on a **mouse pad** that is designed specifically to make it easy to slide the mouse on a desk or table.

✓ *You can move the mouse without moving the pointer by picking it up. This is useful if you move the mouse too close to the edge of the mouse pad or desk.*

Use the Keyboard

■ Use your keyboard to type characters, including letters, numbers, and symbols. The keyboard can also be used to access Word commands and features.

■ In addition to the regular text and number keys, computer keyboards have special keys used for shortcuts or for executing special commands.

● Function keys (F1–F12) often appear in a row above the numbers at the top of the keyboard. They can be used as shortcut keys to perform certain tasks.

● Modifier keys (Shift, Alt, Ctrl) are used in combination with other keys or mouse actions to select certain commands or perform actions. In this book, key combinations are shown as: the modifier key followed by a plus sign followed by the other key or mouse action. For example, Ctrl+S is the key combination for saving the current document.

● The Alt key is also used to display KeyTips, which are the keys used to access commands on the Ribbon.

✓ *You learn more about using KeyTips in Exercise 2.*

● The Numeric keys are made up of the 17-key keypad to the right of the main group of keyboard keys on an enhanced keyboard.

✓ *Most laptop and notebook computers integrate the numeric keys into the regular keyboard.*

● When the Num Lock (number lock) feature is on, the keypad can be used to enter numbers. When the feature is off, the keys can be used as directional keys to move the insertion point in the current file.

● The Escape key (Esc) is used to cancel a command.

● Use the Enter key to execute a command or to start a new paragraph when typing text.

● Directional keys are used to move the insertion point.

● Editing keys (Insert, Delete, and Backspace) are used to insert or delete text.

● The Windows key (sometimes called the Winkey or the Windows Logo key) is used alone to open the Windows Start menu, or in combination with other keys to execute certain Windows commands.

● The Application key is used alone to open a shortcut menu, or in combination with other keys to execute certain application commands.

● Some keyboards also have keys for launching a Web browser, or opening an e-mail program.

Start and Exit Word 2007

■ To use Word 2007 you must first start it so it is running on your computer.

■ Use Windows to start Word.

● Select Microsoft Office Word 2007 from the Microsoft Office folder accessed from the Windows All Programs menu.

● If the program has been used recently, or pinned to the Windows Start menu, you can select it directly from the Windows Start menu.

● You can click a program shortcut icon on the desktop or on the Windows Taskbar, if available.

■ When you are done using Word, close it to exit.

Options for starting Microsoft Office Word

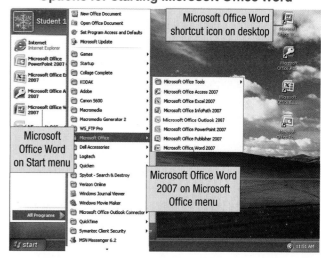

Identify Common Screen Elements

- When Word is running, it displays in a **window** on your screen.

- The following figure identifies **elements** you will find in the Word program window, as well as in the windows of other Microsoft Office programs.

  ✓ *More information about the elements in the Word program window can be found in Exercise 8.*

- Ribbon. Displays buttons for accessing features and commands.

  ✓ *Note that the way items display on the Ribbon may depend on the width of the program window. Refer to Exercise 2 for more information.*

- Ribbon tabs. Used to change the commands displayed on the Ribbon.

- Quick Access Toolbar. A **toolbar** that displays buttons for commonly used commands. You can customize the Quick Access Toolbar to display buttons you use frequently.

- Office button. Click to display a menu of common commands for managing documents and files.

- Program Close button. Used to close the program window. It is one of three buttons used to control the size and position of the program window.

  ✓ *Using the window control buttons is covered in Exercise 3.*

- Pointer. Marks the location of the mouse (or other pointing device) on the screen.

  ✓ *The appearance of the pointer changes depending on the current action.*

- Scroll bar. Used with a mouse to shift the on-screen display up and down or left and right.

- Status bar. Displays information about the current document.

- Document area. The workspace where you enter text, graphics, and other data.

- ScreenTip. Displays information about the element on which the mouse pointer is resting.

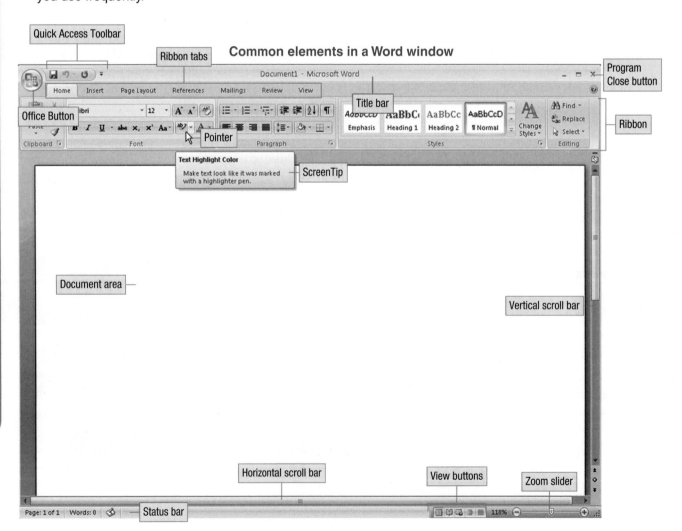

Common elements in a Word window

- Title bar. Displays the program and document names.
- Zoom slider. Used to increase or decrease the size of the document on-screen.

- Help button. Used to start the Word Help system.
  - ✓ Using Help is covered in Exercise 5.
- View buttons. Used to change the document view.
  - ✓ Changing the document view is covered in Exercise 8

Curriculum Connection: Language Arts

Office Applications

The Microsoft Office suite of applications provides the tools you need to prepare documents throughout a business organization. It offers sophisticated and easy-to-use programs that use a common interface and share many tools and features. It is one of the most widely used programs in the world.

Pitch Microsoft Office 2007

Prepare an oral presentation that you could deliver to a company that does not yet use Microsoft Office 2007. Use the presentation to promote the product by including information about the important features that it offers, and how the company would benefit from it. You may want to demonstrate basic features of the software suite in order to illustrate your presentation.

PROCEDURES

Start Microsoft Office Word 2007

1. Click **Start** button
   start / .... Ctrl+Esc
2. Click **All Programs** .... P, ↵Enter
   - ✓ If you are using Windows Vista, the keystrokes for opening the All Programs menu are ↑, ↵Enter
3. Point to the **Microsoft Office** folder icon .... ↓, →
4. Click **Microsoft Office Word 2007** .... ↓, ↵Enter

   OR

1. Click **Start** button
   start / .... Ctrl+Esc
2. Click **Microsoft Office Word 2007** in the list of recently used programs................ ↓, ↵Enter

   OR

- Double-click the **Word** program shortcut icon on the desktop.

Exit Microsoft Office Word 2007

- Click **Program Close** button ☒ at the right end of the Word window's title bar.
  - ✓ If you are using Windows Vista, the Program Close button may look different.

  OR

1. Click **Office Button** ..... Alt+F
2. Click **Exit Word** X
3. Click **Yes** to save changes to the current document............ Y

   OR

   Click **No** to exit without saving .... N

Use the Mouse

Move the pointer:

- **Right** Move mouse to right.
- **Left** Move mouse to left.
- **Up** Move mouse away from you.
- **Down** Move mouse toward you.

Mouse actions:

- **Point to** Move mouse pointer to touch specified element.
- **Click** Point to element then press and release left mouse button.
- **Right-click** Point to element then press and release right mouse button.
- **Double-click** Point to element then press and release left mouse button twice in rapid succession.
- **Drag** Point to element, hold down left mouse button, then move mouse pointer to new location.
  - ✓ Element, or icon representing element, moves with mouse pointer.
- **Drop** Drag element to new location, then release mouse button.

IntelliMouse actions:

- **Scroll** Rotate center wheel backward (toward you) to scroll down, or forward (away from you) to scroll up.
- **Pan** Press center wheel and drag up or down.
- **Auto-Scroll** Click center wheel and move pointer down to scroll down; move pointer up to scroll up.
- **Zoom** Hold down Ctrl and rotate center wheel.

Use the Keyboard

- Press specified key on the keyboard.

For key combinations:

1. Press and hold modifier key(s)........... Ctrl or Alt or ⬆Shift

2. Press combination key.

   ✓ *Remember, key combinations are written with a plus sign between each key. For example,* Ctrl + Esc *means press and hold* Ctrl *and then press* Esc.

EXERCISE DIRECTIONS

1. Start your computer if it is not already on.
2. Move the mouse pointer around the Windows desktop.
3. Point to the Start button.

   ✓ *A ScreenTip displays.*

4. Point to the Recycle Bin icon.
5. Click any icon on the desktop.

   ✓ *The icon is selected.*

6. Right-click the Recycle Bin icon.

   ✓ *A menu is displayed.*

7. Press Esc to cancel the menu.
8. Use the All Programs menu to start Microsoft Office Word 2007.

   ✓ *You may use any method, or ask your instructor which method to use.*

10. Point to each button on the Quick Access Toolbar to see the ScreenTips.

11. Click the Insert tab above the Ribbon to display the Insert commands.
12. Point to the Chart button in the Illustrations group to see the ScreenTip. The window should look similar to Illustration A.
13. Move the mouse pointer over the document window. It changes to an I-beam.
14. Press Alt+F, the shortcut key combination for opening the Office menu.

    ✓ *Notice the KeyTips that display letters over each command. You press the KeyTip letter to select the command with the keyboard. You learn more about KeyTips in Exercise 2.*

15. Press Esc to cancel the menu, and then press Esc again to hide the KeyTips.
16. Exit Word.
17. Click No if a box displays asking if you want to save the changes.

Illustration A

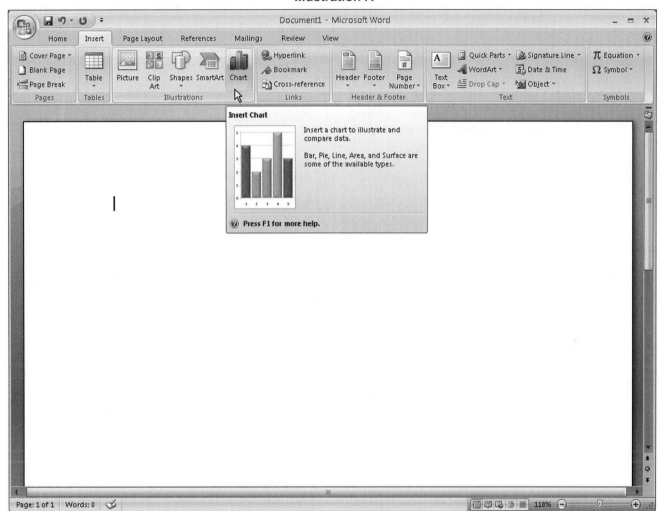

ON YOUR OWN

Part 1

1. Working alone or in a group, make a list of tasks you use a word processing software package to accomplish. For example, the list might include typing and printing letters and envelopes, creating a newsletter, and preparing reports for distribution.

2. Research at least three word processing packages. You can locate information on the Internet, in a magazine, or by calling or visiting a retail store.

3. Compile the following information about each package:

   ■ Does it offer the features you need to accomplish the tasks listed in step 1?

   ■ What is the price?

   ■ What are the system requirements?

   ■ Is it compatible with other programs?

4. Using the information you compiled, make a decision about which software package you think would be the best one to purchase.

5. Prepare an oral report to present your recommendation to your class. Include information from your research to support your decision.

Part 2

1. Practice starting and exiting Word using the mouse.

2. Practice moving the mouse around the Word window to identify different elements.

3. Point to the View buttons.

4. Point to the Close button.

5. Practice changing tabs on the Ribbon.

6. Practice starting and exiting Word using the keyboard.

Exercise | 2

Skills Covered

- About Commands
- About the Ribbon
- Use the Ribbon
- Use Access Keys
- Use the Office Button

- Use the Quick Access Toolbar
- Use a Mini Toolbar
- Use Shortcut Menus
- Use Dialog Box Options
- Use Task Panes

Software Skills To accomplish a task in Word 2007, you must execute a command. You select the commands using buttons, menus, and toolbars. Once you learn to use these tools, you will be able to access the features you need to create documents.

Application Skills To get up to speed using Microsoft Office Word 2007, you want to spend more time exploring the user interface so that you know how to locate and use commands when you need them. In this exercise, you will practice using the Ribbon, the Office Button, and toolbars, selecting menu commands, and choosing options in dialog boxes.

TERMS

Access keys Keystrokes that can be used in place of mouse clicks to select any command.

Command Input that tells the computer which task to execute.

Contextual tab A Ribbon tab that is only available in a certain context or situation.

Dialog box A window in which you select options that affect the way the program executes a command.

Gallery A menu that displays pictures instead of plain text options. Often, the pictures indicate the effect that will result if you select the option.

KeyTip A pop-up letter that identifies the access key(s) for a command.

Live Preview A feature that displays the potential result of applying an editing or formatting change.

ScreenTip A box containing information that is displayed when you rest your mouse pointer on certain screen elements.

Shortcut menu A menu of relevant commands that displays when you right-click an item. Also called a context menu.

Submenu A menu that is displayed when you select a command on another menu.

Task pane A small window that displays additional options and commands for certain features.

Toggle A type of command that can be switched off or on.

NOTES

About Commands

- To accomplish a task in Word 2007, you execute **commands**. For example, Save is the command for saving a document.
- Most commands are available as buttons on the Ribbon.
- A few frequently-used commands such as Save are available on the Quick Access Toolbar.
- Some commands commonly used for file management are listed on the Office menu, which displays when you click the Office Button. For example, that's where you'll find the commands for creating a new file or opening an existing file.
- Sometimes, a list of choices displays when you select a command. The list may be a standard menu, or it may be a **gallery**, which displays pictures instead of plain text descriptions. You click an item in the list to select it.
- If a command requires that you select options to control specifications, a **dialog box** or **task pane** displays when you select the command.
- You use the mouse—or other pointing device—and/or the keyboard to select and execute commands.

About the Ribbon

- The Ribbon is the area where most commands are available.
- The Ribbon is organized into tabs based on activities, such as writing a document or inserting content.
- Each tab is organized into groups based on specific tasks, such as rearranging text or formatting paragraphs.
- In each group there are buttons representing specific commands and tasks.
- **Contextual tabs** —which may be called on-demand tabs—are only available in certain situations. For example, if you select a picture, the Picture Tools tab becomes available. If you deselect the picture, the Picture Tools tab disappears.

- You can minimize the Ribbon to display only the tabs if you want to see more of a document. When you click a tab, the Ribbon expands so you can select a command.

The Ribbon is minimized

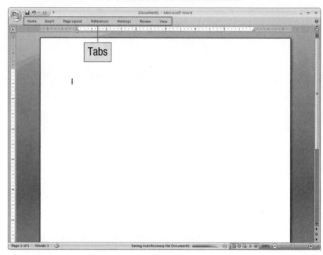

- Note that the way items display on the Ribbon may depend on the width of the program window, or the resolution of your display.
  - If the window is wide enough, or if the resolution is higher, groups expand to display all items.
  - If the window is not wide enough, or if the resolution is lower, groups collapse to a single group button. Click the button to display a menu of commands in the group.
  - The size of icons in a group may vary depending on the width of the window.
- If your program window is not the same size as the one used for the illustrations in this book, the Ribbon on your screen may look different from the one in the figures.

- In addition, the steps you must take to complete a procedure may vary slightly.
  - If your screen is narrower than the one in this book, or if your screen resolution is lower, you may have to click a group button to display the commands in that group before you can complete the steps in the procedure.
  - If your screen is wider, or your resolution higher, you may be able to skip a step for selecting a group button and go directly to the step for selecting a specific command.

The Ribbon in a narrower Word window

Show/Hide group collapses to a group button

The Ribbon in a wider Word window

Show/Hide group expands so all items display

Use the Ribbon

- When you point to a button on the Ribbon, the button is highlighted, and a **ScreenTip** displays information about the command.
- Click the button to select the command.
- Buttons representing commands that are not currently available are dimmed.
- Some buttons are **toggles**; they appear highlighted when active, or "on."
- If there is an arrow on a button, it means that when you click that button a menu or gallery displays so you can make a specific selection.
- Some Ribbon groups have a **dialog box launcher** button.
- Click the dialog box launcher to display a dialog box, task pane, or window where you can select additional options, or multiple options at the same time.
- Sometimes, the entire first row of a gallery displays on the Ribbon.
- You can rest the mouse pointer on a gallery item to see a **Live Preview** of the way your document will look if you select that item.
- You can scroll a gallery on the Ribbon, or click the More button to view the entire gallery.

Ribbon elements on the Home tab

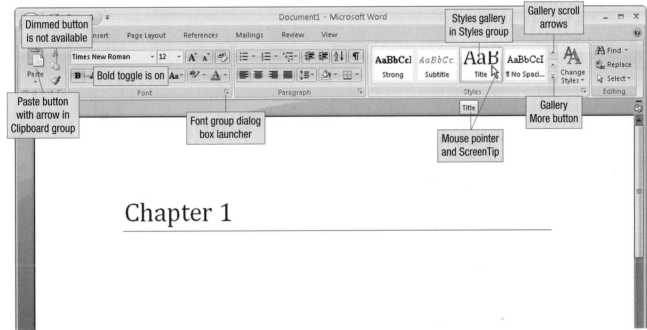

13

Use Access Keys

- Microsoft Office Word 2007 is designed primarily for use with a mouse or other pointing device.
- Many people prefer to select commands using the keyboard. In that case, you can press the Alt key to activate **access keys**.
- When access keys are active, **KeyTips** showing one or more keyboard characters display on the screen over any feature or command that can be selected using the keyboard.
- You press the character(s) shown in the KeyTip to select the command or feature.
- If there is more than one access key for a command, you may press the keys in combination (at the same time) or consecutively (press the first key and then immediately press the next key).
- If a KeyTip is dimmed, the command is not available.
- The KeyTips remain active if you must press additional keys to complete a command.
- Once a command is executed, the KeyTips disappear.
- To continue using the keyboard, you must press the Alt key to activate the access keys again.

  ✓ *People accustomed to the shortcut key combinations in previous versions of Microsoft Office Word will be happy to know that they function in the Microsoft Office Word 2007 program as well. For example, you can still press Ctrl+Shift+F to open the Font dialog box.*

- If you just want to change the selected element using a keyboard, you can press the Alt key to activate the access keys, use the arrow keys to move from one element to another, and then press the Enter key to make a selection.

KeyTips on the Insert tab

KeyTips

Use the Office Button

- Click the Office Button [icon] to display the Office menu, which is a menu of common file management commands.

  ✓ *If you are familiar with previous versions of Word, you may see the similarity between the Office menu and the old File menu.*

- Commands are listed on the left side of the menu.
- Recently used files are listed on the right side of the menu, providing easy access.

  ✓ *You can click the pushpin icon to the right of an item on the recently-used files list to keep that item on the list. Click the icon again when you no longer need the item on the list.*

- To the left of each command is its button icon.
- An arrowhead to the right of the command indicates that the command opens a **submenu** or gallery.

The Office menu

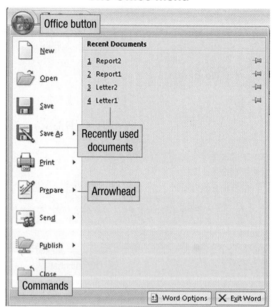

Use the Quick Access Toolbar

- The Quick Access Toolbar is always available in the upper left corner of the program window, no matter which tab displays on the Ribbon.
- To select a command from the Quick Access Toolbar, click its button.
- By default, there are three buttons on the Quick Access Toolbar: Save, Undo, and Repeat. The Repeat button changes to Redo once you use the Undo command.
- The Quick Access Toolbar can be customized in Word 2007.

  ✓ *You learn how to customize the Quick Access Toolbar in Exercise 4.*

The default Quick Access Toolbar

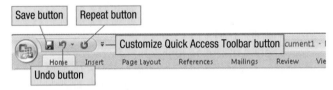

Use a Mini Toolbar

- A Mini toolbar displays when the mouse pointer rests on selected text or data that can be formatted.
- At first, the Mini toolbar is semi-transparent, so you can ignore it if you want.

Transparent Mini toolbar

- When you move the mouse pointer over the Mini toolbar, it becomes opaque.
- Select a command from a Mini toolbar the same way you select a command from the Ribbon.

Opaque Mini toolbar

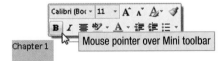

Use Shortcut Menus

- When you right-click almost any element on the screen in Word 2007, a shortcut menu displays.
- Shortcut menus include options relevant to the current item.

  ✓ *Shortcut menus are sometimes called context menus.*

- Click an option on the shortcut menu to select it.
- If you right-click selected data, a Mini toolbar may display in addition to the shortcut menu. The Mini toolbar disappears when you select an option on the menu.

This shortcut menu displays when you right-click the vertical scroll bar

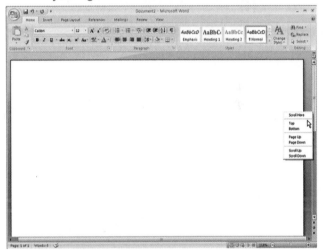

Use Dialog Box Options

- Although many commands are available directly from the Ribbon, when you must provide additional information before executing a command, a dialog box will display. For example, in the Print dialog box, you can specify which pages to print.
- You enter information in a dialog box using a variety of elements.
- To move from one element to another in a dialog box you can click the element with the mouse, or press Tab.
- Some dialog box elements have access keys which are underlined in the element name. Press Alt and the access key to select the element.
- Use the numbers to locate the corresponding element in the following two figures.

List box (1)

- A list of items from which selections can be made. If more items are available than can fit in the space, a scrollbar is displayed.

Palette (2)

- A display, such as colors or shapes, from which you can select an option.

  ✓ *Some Ribbon buttons also open palettes.*

Drop-down list box (3)

- A combination of text box and list box; type your selection in the box or click the drop-down arrow to display the list.

Check box (4)

- A square that you click to select or deselect an option. A check mark in the box indicates that the option is selected.

Command button (5)

- A button used to execute a command. An ellipsis on a command button means that clicking the button opens another dialog box.

Tabs (6)

- Markers across the top of the dialog box that, when clicked, display additional pages of options within the dialog box.

Preview area (7)

- An area where you can preview the results of your selections before executing the commands.

Increment box (8)

- A space where you type a value, such as inches or numbers. Increment arrows beside the box are used to increase or decrease the value with a mouse. Sometimes called a spin box.

Text box (9)

- A space where you type variable information, such as a file name.

Option buttons (10)

- A series of circles, only one of which can be selected at a time. Click the circle you want to select one item or one control in the series.

Print dialog box

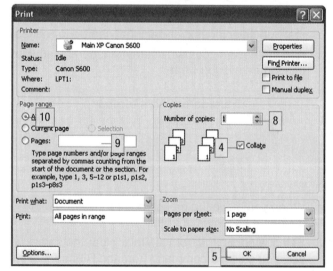

Font dialog box

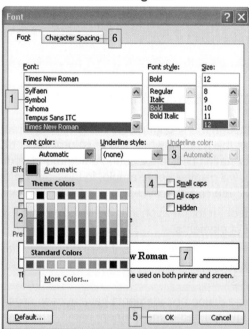

Use Task Panes

- Some commands open a task pane instead of a dialog box. For example, if you select to insert a clip art picture, the Clip Art task pane displays.

- Task panes have some features in common with dialog boxes. For example, some have text boxes in which you type text as well as drop-down list boxes, check boxes, and option buttons.

- You can leave a task pane open while you work, or you can close it to get it out of the way.

- You learn how to accomplish tasks using task panes in the exercise in which that feature is covered. For example, in Exercise 19 you learn to use the Clipboard task pane to move text in a Word document.

The Clip Art task pane

PROCEDURES

Select a Command on the Ribbon

1. Click a tab on the Ribbon............(Alt), access key
2. Click command......access key
   ✓ *If the button you want is not displayed, click the Group button arrow to display additional buttons, and then click the button you want.*
3. If necessary, click option on drop-down menu or gallery......................access key

Hide KeyTips

- Press **Esc**..............................(Esc)
  ✓ *You may need to press (Esc) multiple times.*

Select Screen Elements with the Keyboard

1. Press the **Alt** key..............(Alt)
2. Press arrow keys to move from one element to another..............(↑), (↓), (←), (→)
3. Press **Enter** to select a command........................(↵Enter)

Use the Office Menu

1. Click the **Office Button** ....(Alt)+(F)
2. Click desired command access key
   OR
   a. Click the **Office Button** ....(Alt)+(F)
   b. Click or point to command's submenu arrow..............access key
   c. Click option on submenu...........access key

Select a Command from the Quick Access Toolbar

1. Point to a button.................(Alt)
2. Click button to select..................press number displayed in button's KeyTip

Minimize the Ribbon (Ctrl+F1)

- Double-click the active tab.
  OR
1. Click the **Customize Quick Access Toolbar** button (▾)...........(Alt), (H), (↑), (→), (→),(↵Enter)
2. Click **Minimize the Ribbon**...........(N)
   ✓ *A check mark next to command indicates it is already selected.*

Expand the Ribbon (Ctrl+F1)

- Double-click the active tab.

    ✓ *To expand the Ribbon temporarily, click the active tab once.*

    OR

1. Click the **Customize Quick Access Toolbar** button ▾ .... Alt, H, →, ↑, →, →, ↵Enter
2. Click **Minimize the Ribbon** .... N

Use a Mini Toolbar

1. Select text or data to format.
2. Move mouse pointer over Mini toolbar.
3. Select option on Mini toolbar.

Use a Shortcut Menu

1. Right-click **element** on screen .... Select element, ⇧Shift+F10
2. Click **command** .... access key

    ✓ *If no access keys are available, use arrow keys to select command, then press Enter.*

Use a Dialog Box

1. Click group's **dialog box launcher** button 🗗 .

    ✓ *Some dialog boxes open when you select a command.*

2. Make selections or type text entries in dialog box.

    ✓ *See procedures below.*

3. Click **OK** .... ↵Enter

    ✓ *Sometimes button displays Close, Add, Insert, or Yes in place of OK.*

    OR

    Click **Cancel** to close dialog box without making changes .... Esc

Use Dialog Box Options

Move from one option to the next:

- Click desired option.

    OR

- Press **Tab** key .... Tab⇆

    OR

- Press option's access keys .... Alt+access key

Select from a list box:

- Click desired item .... ↑, ↓, ↵Enter

Select from a drop-down list box:

1. Click **drop-down arrow** .... Alt+access key
2. Click desired item .... ↑, ↓, ↵Enter

Select/deselect check box:

- Click **check box** .... Alt+access key

    ✓ *A check mark indicates box is selected. Repeat action to remove check mark and deselect box.*

Display tabbed pages:

- Click desired **tab** .... Alt+access key

    ✓ *If no access key is displayed, press Ctrl+Tab⇆.*

Use a text box:

1. Click in **text box** .... Alt+access key
2. Type data.

Use an increment box:

1. Click in **increment box** .... Alt+access key
2. Type value.

    OR

    Click **increment arrows** to change value.

Select option button:

- Click **option button** .... Alt+access key

    ✓ *A black dot indicates option is selected. Select alternative option button to change setting.*

Select palette option:

1. Click **palette** drop-down arrow .... Alt+access key

    ✓ *Some palettes are always open. If the palette is open, skip to step 2.*

2. Click desired option .... ↑, ↓, ←, →, ↵Enter

Close a Task Pane

- Click **Close** button ✕ on task pane title bar.

EXERCISE DIRECTIONS

1. Start Word.
2. Click the Office Button 🔘 to open the Office menu using the mouse, and then take note of the available commands.
3. Point to the Print submenu arrow to display the submenu.
4. Click the Office Button or press (Esc) twice to close the menu without making a selection.
5. Press (Alt) and then press (W) to display the View tab using the keyboard.
6. Press (Esc) twice to hide the access key KeyTips.
7. Use the mouse to display the Home tab.
8. Click the Font group dialog box launcher 🔲 to display the Font dialog box.
9. Select Bold in the Font style list box.
10. Select the Superscript check box.
11. Select the Character Spacing tab to show another page of options.
12. Select the Font tab.
13. Open the Underline style drop-down list.
14. Cancel the dialog box without making any of the selected changes.
15. Click the Clipboard group dialog box launcher 🔲 to display the Clipboard task pane.

    ✓ *The Clipboard is a temporary storage area that you use when copying and moving selections. You learn more about it in Exercise 19.*

16. Close the task pane.
17. Click the Customize Quick Access Toolbar button and then click Minimize the Ribbon to minimize the Ribbon so that only the tabs show.
18. Make the Page Layout tab active.
19. Right-click anywhere in the document window to display a shortcut menu and a Mini toolbar.
20. Select the Paragraph command on the shortcut menu.

    ✓ *Note that the Paragraph dialog box includes increment boxes, drop-down lists, and a preview area.*

21. Cancel the dialog box without making any changes.
22. Click the Customize Quick Access Toolbar button and then click Minimize the Ribbon to expand the Ribbon.
23. Click the Page Color command in the Page Background group to open a gallery of colors.
24. Move the mouse pointer across the colors. A live preview displays each color on the page.
25. Click the color purple which is on the right of the row under Standard Colors, to select purple as the page background. The program window should look similar to Illustration A.
26. Click the Office Button and then click Exit Word.
27. Select No in the confirmation dialog box to exit without saving the document.

Illustration A

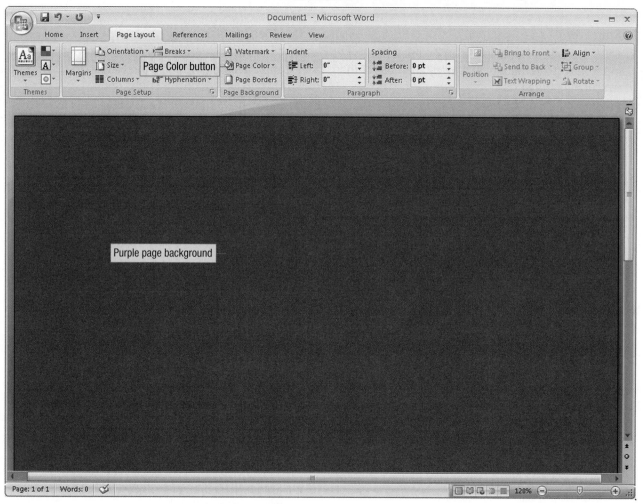

ON YOUR OWN

1. Start Word and explore the Ribbon tabs.
2. Look to see which commands are on each tab, and use ScreenTips to identify commands.
3. Determine if any commands open dialog boxes or galleries.
4. Use any group's dialog box launcher, such as the Page Setup group on the Page Layout tab.
5. If the dialog box has multiple tabbed pages, click each tab. Note the different options available on each tab.
6. Exit Word without saving any changes.

Exercise | 3

Skills Covered

- Use Window Controls
- Zoom
- Scroll

Software Skills Controlling the way Microsoft Office Word 2007 documents are displayed on your computer monitor is a vital part of using the program successfully. For example, you can control the size and position of the program window on-screen, and you can control the size a document is displayed.

Application Skills As you spend more time working with Microsoft Office Word 2007, you'll find that there are many tools that help you do your job more efficiently. In this exercise, you will learn how to maximize, minimize, and restore windows on your screen, and you will experiment with the zoom level. You'll also practice scrolling through a document.

TERMS

Maximize Enlarge a window so it fills the entire screen.

Minimize Hide a window so it appears only as a button on the Windows taskbar.

Restore Return a minimized window to its previous size and position on the screen.

Restore down Return a maximized window to its previous size and position on the screen.

Scroll Shift the displayed area of the document up, down, left, or right.

Taskbar button A button on the Windows Taskbar that represents an open program, document, or group of documents.

Zoom in Increase the size of the document as it is displayed on-screen. This does not affect the actual size of the printed document.

Zoom out Decrease the size of the document as it is displayed on-screen. This does not affect the actual size of the printed document.

NOTES

Use Window Controls

- When you start Microsoft Office Word 2007, the program window opens with a new blank document displayed in Print Layout view.

  ✓ *You learn more about views in Exercise 8.*

- You can control the size and position of the program window.
  - You can **maximize** the window to fill the screen.
  - You can **minimize** the window to a **taskbar button**.
  - You can **restore** a minimized window to its previous size and position.
  - You can **restore down** a maximized window to its previous size and position.

■ There are three ways to control the program window:
- ● Use the Control buttons located on the right end of the title bar.
  - ● [–] Minimize
  - ● [▭] Maximize
  - ● [⊡] Restore Down
    - ✓ *Restore Down is only available in a maximized window.*
- ● Use the Windows' taskbar button shortcut menu.
- ● Use the Program Control icon drop-down menu.

Taskbar button shortcut menu

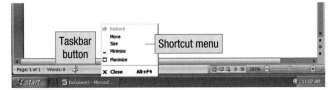

Zoom

■ You can adjust the zoom magnification setting to increase or decrease the size Word uses to display a document on-screen.

■ There are three ways to set the zoom:
- ● The Zoom slider on the right end of the program's status bar

Zoom slider

- ● The commands in the Zoom group of the View tab on the Ribbon

Zoom group

● The Zoom dialog box.

Zoom dialog box

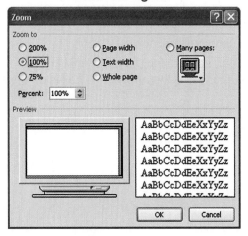

■ **Zoom in** to make the document contents appear larger on screen. This is useful for getting a close look at graphics, text, or data.
- ✓ *When you zoom in, only a small portion of the document will be visible on-screen at a time.*

■ **Zoom out** to make the document contents appear smaller on-screen. This is useful for getting an overall look at a document.

■ You can set the zoom magnification as a percentage of a document's actual size. For example, if you set the zoom to 50%, the program displays the document half as large as the actual, printed document would appear. If you set the zoom to 200%, the program displays the document twice as large as the actual printed file would appear.

■ You can also select from the following preset sizes:
- ● Page width. Word automatically sizes the document so that the width of the page matches the width of the screen. You see the left and right margins of the page.
- ● Text width. Word automatically sizes the document so that the width of the text on the page matches the width of the screen. The left and right margins may be hidden.
- ● Whole page. Word automatically sizes the document so that one whole page is visible on the screen.
- ● Two pages. Word automatically sizes the document so that two pages are visible on the screen.
- ● Many pages. Word automatically sizes the document so that the number of pages you select can all be seen on-screen.
  - ✓ *Some options may not be available, depending on the current view. Options that are not available will appear dimmed.*

23

Scroll

- When there is more text in a window or dialog box than can be displayed on-screen at one time, you must **scroll** to see the hidden parts.
- You can scroll up, down, left, or right.
- You can scroll using the directional keys on the keyboard, or using the arrows and boxes on the scroll bars.

  ✓ *Some pointing devices have scroll wheels that are used to scroll.*

- The size of a scroll box changes to represent the percentage of the document visible on the screen.
- For example, in a very long document, the scroll boxes will be small, indicating that a small percentage of the document is visible. In a short document, the scroll boxes will be large, indicating that a large percentage of the document is visible.

Tools for scrolling in a document

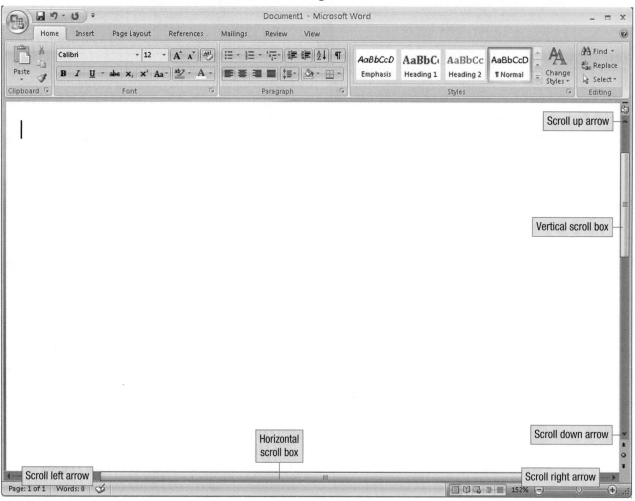

PROCEDURES

Control Windows

Minimize a window: (Alt+Spacebar, N)

- Click the **Minimize** button 　.

OR

1. Right-click the taskbar button.
2. Click **Minimize**............... N

OR

1. Press Alt + Spacebar.
2. Click **Minimize**............... N

Restore a window: (Alt+F5)

- Click the **Restore Down** button 　.

OR

1. Right-click the taskbar button.
2. Click **Restore**............... R

OR

1. Press Alt + Spacebar.
2. Click **Restore**............... R

Maximize a window: (Ctrl+F10)

- Click the **Maximize** button 　.

OR

1. Right-click the taskbar button.
2. Click **Maximize**............... X

OR

1. Press Alt + Spacebar.
2. Click **Maximize**............... X

Adjust Zoom

Use zoom slider to zoom out:

- Drag the slider to the left.

OR

- Click the **Zoom Out** button ⊖.

Use zoom slider to zoom in:

- Drag the slider to the right.

OR

- Click the **Zoom In** button ⊕.

Use Zoom group:

1. Click **View** tab............... Alt + W

   Zoom Group

2. Click desired zoom option button.

   ✓ Available options depend on the view you are using.

Use Zoom dialog box:

1. Click **View tab**............... Alt + W

   Zoom Group

2. Click **Zoom** button 🔍............... Q
3. Click desired zoom option.

OR

   a. Click **Percent increment box**............... Alt + E
   b. Type **percentage**.
4. Click **OK**............... ↵Enter

Scroll

Scroll down:

- Click **scroll down arrow** ▼........ ↓

OR

- Click in **Vertical scroll bar** below Scroll box.

OR

- Drag **Scroll box** down.

OR

- Press **Page Down**............... PgDn

OR

- Spin scroll wheel on mouse toward your palm.

Scroll up:

- Click **scroll up arrow** ▲........... ↑

OR

- Click in **Vertical scroll bar** above Scroll box.

OR

- Drag **Scroll box** up.

OR

- Press **Page Up**............... PgUp

OR

- Spin scroll wheel on mouse away from your palm.

Scroll left:

- Click **scroll left arrow** ◀.......... ←

OR

- Click in **Horizontal scroll bar** to left of Scroll box.

OR

- Drag **Scroll box** left.

Scroll right:

- Click **scroll right arrow** ▶........ →

OR

- Click in **Horizontal scroll bar** to right of Scroll box.

OR

- Drag **Scroll box** right.

EXERCISE DIRECTIONS

1. Start Word.
2. Minimize the Word window.
3. Maximize the Word window.
4. Restore Down the Word window.
5. Maximize the Word window.
6. Click in the document window and type **Restoration Architecture**.

   ✓ *Do not worry about making errors while you type. This is just a practice exercise, and you will not save the document. You learn more about typing in Exercise 8.*

7. Press Enter.
8. Type **12345 Main Street**.
9. Press Enter.
10. Type **Hometown, City 12345**.
11. Set the Zoom to 25%.
12. Set the Zoom to 500%.
13. Scroll the window so that all lines of the address are visible. It should look similar to the document shown in Illustration A.
14. Scroll down to the bottom of the document.
15. Scroll up to the top of the document.
16. Scroll to the right margin.
17. Scroll to the left margin.
18. Set the Zoom to Page Width.
19. Exit Word.
20. When Word prompts you to save the changes, select No.

Illustration A

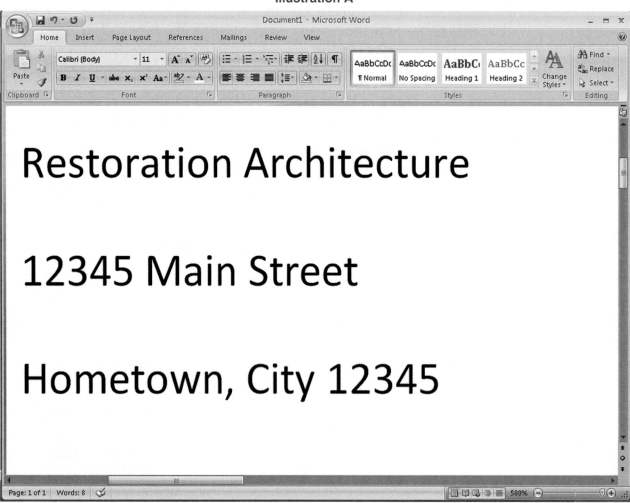

ON YOUR OWN

1. Start Word.
2. Practice maximizing, minimizing, and restoring the Word window, using all three available methods.
3. Click the mouse pointer anywhere in the document window and start typing.

   ✓ You learn more about typing in a Word document in Exercise 8.

4. Try different zoom magnifications to see how they affect the display.
5. Set the zoom very high so you have to scroll down to see the end of the document.
6. Maximize the Word window and set the zoom to Page Width.
7. Exit Word without saving the document.

Exercise | 4

Skills Covered

- About Word Options
- Customize the Quick Access Toolbar
- Set a Default Save Location
- Personalize Your User Name and Initials

Software Skills Microsoft Office Word 2007 is designed to provide quick access to the tools and features that you will need most often. In addition, you can customize the Quick Access Toolbar to display buttons you want to have available at all times. You can also specify a storage location where new documents will be saved by default, and you can personalize the user name and initials that Microsoft Office Word uses to identify you as the author of documents that you create.

Application Skills Now that you are familiar with the Microsoft Office Word 2007 user interface, you would like to customize and personalize the program for your own use. In this exercise, you will practice customizing the Quick Access Toolbar by adding and removing buttons, you will specify a default location for storing documents, and you will learn how to personalize your user name and initials.

TERMS

User Name A name assigned to someone who uses a computer system or program that identifies the user to the system.

NOTES

About Word Options

- You can modify the way Word 2007 executes certain commands and features by customizing settings in the Word Options dialog box.

- The settings in the Word Options dialog box are organized into groups according to the type of command.

- For example, settings that affect the way documents and commands appear on-screen or when printed are in the Display group, and settings that affect the way documents are saved are in the Save group.

- The groups display in a pane on the left side of the Word Options dialog box; you click a group name to display the settings in that group.

The Display settings in the Word Options dialog box

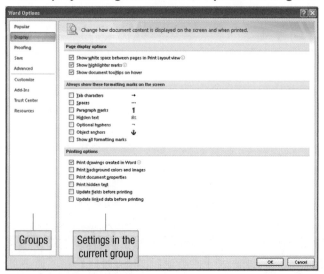

Customize the Quick Access Toolbar

■ As you learned in Exercise 2, by default, the Save, Undo, and Repeat buttons display on the Quick Access Toolbar in the upper left corner of the program window, no matter which tab displays on the Ribbon.

■ You can customize the Quick Access Toolbar by adding and removing buttons for other commands.

■ For example, if you frequently print documents using the default Print settings, you can add the Quick Print button to the Quick Access Toolbar.

✓ *You learn how to print documents in Exercise 9.*

■ Some common buttons display on a menu when you click the Customize Quick Access Toolbar button ⬇.

■ You simply click a button on the menu to add it to the Quick Access Toolbar.

■ If the button does not display in the menu, you can simply locate it on its Ribbon tab, right-click it, and select the command to add it to the Quick Access Toolbar.

■ Alternatively, you can select it from a list of all available commands using the Customize group in the Word Options dialog box.

■ You can also rearrange the order of buttons on the Quick Access Toolbar, and reset the Quick Access Toolbar to its default configuration.

■ Finally, you can choose to display the Quick Access Toolbar below the Ribbon.

The Customize settings in the Word Options dialog box

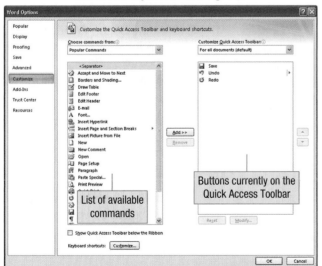

Set a Default Save Location

■ By default, Word 2007 saves documents in the My Documents folder if you are using Windows XP, or the Documents folder if you are using Windows Vista.

■ You can change the default storage location to a different folder or drive using options in the Save group in the Word Options dialog box.

■ You system may have been customized to use a different default save location. For example, files may be saved on a network.

The Save settings in the Word Options dialog box

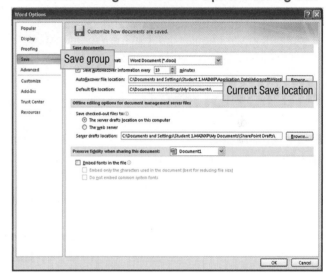

Personalize Your User Name and Initials

- When you set up Microsoft Office Word 2007 on your computer, you enter a user name and initials.

- Word uses this information to identify you as the author of new documents that you create and save, and as the editor of existing documents that you open, modify, and save.

- In addition, your user name is associated with revisions that you make when you use the Track Changes features, and the initials are associated with comments that you insert.

  ✓ *Tracking changes and inserting comments are covered in Exercise 56.*

- You can change the user name and initials using options in the Popular group in the Word Options dialog box.

The Popular settings in the Word Options dialog box

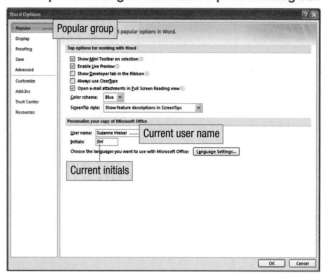

PROCEDURES

Add a Command Button to the Quick Access Toolbar

1. Click the **Customize Quick Access Toolbar** button `▼` .... `Alt`, `H`, `↑`, `→`, `→`, `↵Enter`

2. Click command to add .... `↓`, `↵Enter`

   ✓ *A check mark next to command name indicates it is already on the Quick Access Toolbar.*

   OR

1. Right-click command button to add on Ribbon.

2. Click **Add to Quick Access Toolbar** .... `A`

   OR

1. Click the **Customize Quick Access Toolbar** button `▼` .... `Alt`, `H`, `↑`, `→`, `→`, `↵Enter`

2. Click **More Commands** .... `M`

3. Click the **Choose commands from** drop-down arrow .... `Alt`+`C`

4. Click category of commands .... `↓`, `↵Enter`

   ✓ *Click All commands to display all available commands.*

5. Click command to add .... `Tab⇄`, `↓`

6. Click **Add** .... `Alt`+`A`

7. Click **OK** .... `↵Enter`

Remove a Command Button from the Quick Access Toolbar

1. Click the **Customize Quick Access Toolbar** button `▼` .... `Alt`, `H`, `↑`, `→`, `→`, `↵Enter`

2. Click command to remove .... `↓`, `↵Enter`

   ✓ *No check mark next to command name indicates it is not displayed on the Quick Access Toolbar.*

   OR

1. Right-click command button to remove on Quick Access Toolbar.

2. Click **Remove from Quick Access Toolbar** .... `R`

   OR

1. Click the **Customize Quick Access Toolbar** button `▼` .... `Alt`, `H`, `↑`, `→`, `→`, `↵Enter`

2. Click **More Commands** .... `M`

3. Click the button to remove in the list on the right side of the dialog box ..... `Alt`+`Q`, `Tab⇄`, `↓`

4. Click **Remove** .... `Alt`+`R`

5. Click **OK** .... `↵Enter`

Rearrange Buttons on the Quick Access Toolbar

1. Click the **Customize Quick Access Toolbar** button `▼` .... `Alt`, `H`, `↑`, `→`, `→`, `↵Enter`

2. Click **More Commands** .... `M`

3. Click the button to move in the list on the right side of the dialog box ..... `Alt`+`Q`, `Tab⇄`, `↓`

4. Click **Move Up** button `▲` to move button up list.

   ✓ *Moving a button up the list moves it to the left on the Quick Access Toolbar.*

   OR

   Click **Move Down** button `▼` to move button down list.

   ✓ *Moving a button down the list moves it to the right on the Quick Access Toolbar.*

5. Click **OK** .... `↵Enter`

Reset the Default Quick Access Toolbar

1. Click the **Customize Quick Access Toolbar** button ⊽ .... Alt , H , ↑ , → , → , ↵Enter
2. Click **More Commands** .... M
3. Click **Reset** .... Alt + S

Change the Location of the Quick Access Toolbar

1. Click the **Customize Quick Access Toolbar** button ⊽ .... Alt , H , ↑ , → , → , ↵Enter
2. Click **Show Below the Ribbon** ..... S
   OR
   Click **Show Above the Ribbon** ..... S

Set a Default Save Location

1. Click the **Office Button** 🔘 .... Alt + F
2. Click **Word Options** I
3. Click **Save** .... S
4. Click **Default file location** .... Alt + I
5. Key path to new storage location.
   OR
   a. Click **Browse** button .... Tab↹ , ↵Enter
   b. Navigate to new storage location.
   c. Click **OK** .... ↵Enter
6. Click **OK** .... ↵Enter

Personalize Your User Name and Initials

1. Click the **Office Button** 🔘 .... Alt + F
2. Click **Word Options** I
3. Click **User name** .... Alt + U
4. Key new user name.
5. Click **Initials** .... Alt + I
6. Key new initials.
7. Click **OK** .... ↵Enter

EXERCISE DIRECTIONS

1. Start Word, if necessary.
2. Click the Customize Quick Access Toolbar button and add the Quick Print button to the Quick Access Toolbar.
3. Click the Customize Quick Access Toolbar button and add the Print Preview button to the Quick Access Toolbar
4. Click the Customize Quick Access Toolbar button and then click More Commands to open the Word Options dialog box with the Customize group settings displayed.
5. Display all available commands.
6. Add the Open button to the Quick Access Toolbar.
7. Remove the Quick Print button from the Quick Access Toolbar.
8. Rearrange the buttons on the Quick Access Toolbar into the following order, from left to right: Open, Print Preview, Undo, Redo, Save.
9. Click OK to apply the changes and close the Word Options dialog box.
10. Select to display the Quick Access Toolbar below the Ribbon. The window should look similar to Illustration A.
11. With your instructor's permission, set the default save location to your desktop.
12. Change the default save location back to its previous setting.
13. With your instructor's permission, change your user name to User1 and your initials to U1
14. Change the user name and initials back to their previous settings.
15. Reset the Quick Access Toolbar to its default configuration.
16. Select to display the Quick Access Toolbar above the Ribbon.
17. Exit Word. Do not save the document.

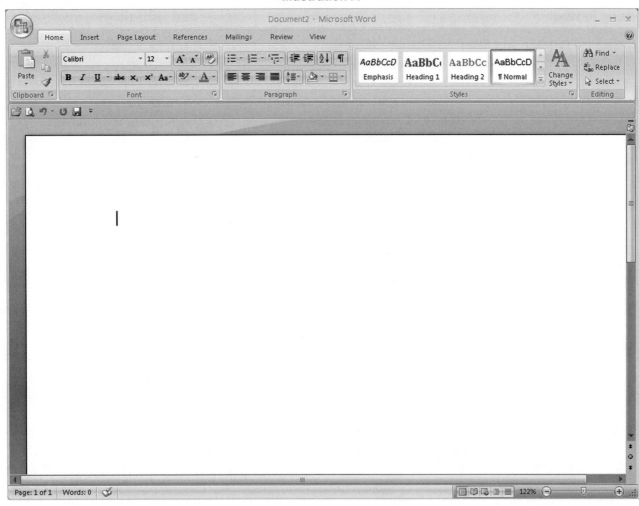

Curriculum Connection: Mathematics

The Cost of Starting a Business

A new business must spend money before it can start earning money. There are overhead costs such as rent and electricity, costs of office supplies, costs of technology, and salaries that must be paid. Smart business owners develop a business plan that itemizes start-up costs. This helps avoid surprises and gives everyone a blueprint to use to meet common goals.

Technology Budget

Imagine you are responsible for purchasing the technology for a new small business. Create a list of items you think you need and how much each item costs. Explain the importance of the items you include in the list.

ON YOUR OWN

1. Start Word and open the Word Options dialog box.
2. Explore the settings available in each group listed in the left pane.
3. Select the Customize group.
4. Click the Choose commands from drop down arrow and review the available command tabs.
5. Select any tab and review the available commands.
6. Select a different tab and review the available commands.
7. Add at least two buttons to the Quick Access Toolbar.
8. Rearrange the order of the buttons on the Quick Access Toolbar.
9. Reset the Quick Access Toolbar to its default configuration.
10. Exit Word without saving any changes.

Exercise | 5

Skills Covered

- Use the Help Program
- Search for Help
- Use the Help Table of Contents
- Recover a Document
- Computer Ethics

Software Skills   Word 2007 comes with Help information that you can access and display in a window while you work. You can search for help on a particular topic, or browse through the Help Table of Contents to find the information you need. The Help program is linked to the Microsoft Office Web site making it easy to locate and access the most current information available.

Application Skills   As a new employee at Restoration Architecture, it's important to learn how to solve problems on your own. In this exercise, you will learn how to use the Help system to answer the questions you may have while working with Microsoft Office Word 2007.

TERMS

AutoRecover   A feature in Microsoft Office Word 2007 that automatically saves open documents at a set interval so that in the event of a system failure the files may be recovered.

Internet   A worldwide network of computers.

NOTES

Use the Help Program

- Use the Help program to search for help topics, access the Help table of contents, or link to additional resources on the Microsoft Office Web site.
- To start Help, click the Help button ⓐ or press F1.

  ✓ *Some keyboards are customized to execute specific commands when you press the function keys. If your keyboard has been customized, you may have to use a different function key to access Help.*

- Some dialog boxes have a Help button ❓ that you can click to go directly to a relevant Help topic.

- Some command button ScreenTips prompt you to press F1 to go directly to a relevant Help topic.
- Help opens in a window which you can keep open while you work.
- By default, the Help Home page displays, listing links to Help categories.
- When the mouse pointer touches a link, it changes to a hand with a pointing finger.
- Click a link to display subcategories or topics in a category, and then click a topic to display the specific Help information.

- Links that have been clicked display in a different color.

  ✓ *If a list of subcategories displays, click a subcategory and then click a topic.*

The Help Home page

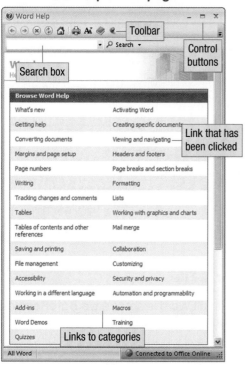

- Under the heading *What do you want to do?*, most Help topic pages list links to content on the page.
- Other links might go to related content on different pages.
- The links are formatted in blue so they stand out from the surrounding text.
- Some words or phrases link to definitions or explanations. These links are formatted in dark red.

  ✓ *Click Show All at the top of a page to display all definitions and explanations within the page text.*

- You can use buttons on the Help window toolbar to control the Help display.

  ✓ *At the bottom of most Help pages there is a question asking if you found the information helpful. *If you are connected to the Internet click Yes, No, or I don't know to display a text box where you can type information that you want to submit to Microsoft.*

- The Help window has control buttons so you can minimize, maximize, restore down, or close it at any time.

Help topic page

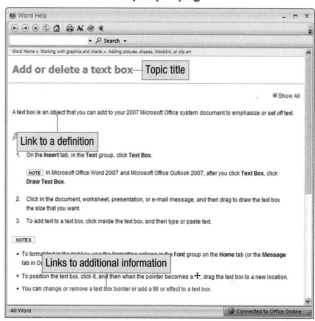

Search for Help

- You can search for a Help topic at any time.
- Simply type the term or phrase for which you want to search in the Search box at the top of the Help window, and then click the Search button.
- A list of topics that contain the term or phrase displays in the Help window.
- Click a topic to display the Help information.
- If you have access to the **Internet**, Help automatically includes information from the Microsoft Office Web site in all searches.

■ You can control where Help searches by selecting an option from the Search drop-down list.

Search for Help

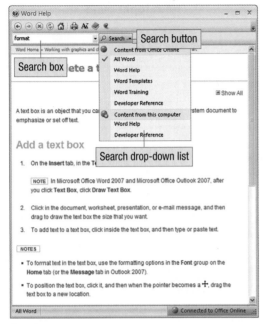

Use the Help Table of Contents

■ The Help Table of Contents is an alternative to the Help Home page.

■ In the Table of Contents, each Help category displays in a list.

■ You can click a category to expand the list to show categories, subcategories, and topics at the same time.

■ Categories have book icons; topics have help button icons.

■ Click a topic to display its Help page in the Help window.

■ The Help Table of Contents opens in a separate pane on the left side of the Help window.

■ Close the Table of Contents pane to display only the Help window.

Use the Help Table of Contents

Recover a File

■ By default Word is set to save **AutoRecover** information every ten minutes.

  ✓ *You can change the AutoRecover interval—or turn it off—using options in the Save group in the Word Options dialog box.*

■ In the event of a system failure, Word will attempt to recover your files based on the most recently saved AutoRecover information.

■ If any damage was done to the file data during the crash, Word will attempt to repair it.

■ When you open the program again, the Document Recovery task pane displays, listing original files, recovered files (if any), and repaired files (if any).

■ Click the drop-down arrow beside a file name to display a list of options for opening the file, saving it with a new name, deleting it, or showing repairs.

- In addition, in the event of a program crash Word will ask if you want to send a report to Microsoft. If you agree to send a report, your computer will log on to the Internet and transmit the information.

Document Recovery task pane

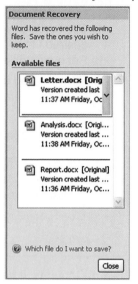

Computer Ethics

- In general, the ethics for computer use should follow the same basic code of ethics for all business and personal conduct.

- In other words, employees and employers should conduct themselves with honesty and integrity, according to legal and corporate policies.

- Most companies and organizations establish corporate computer application policies or rules, as well as policies for using the Internet and e-mail.

- These policies address the legal and social aspects of computer use, and are designed to protect privacy while respecting personal and corporate values, and adhering to federal and local laws.

- Some topics typically covered by corporate computer application policies include:
  - The type of language allowed in documents and messages
  - Permissions for accessing documents and data
  - The amount of time allowed for personal Internet and e-mail use
  - The types of Web sites which may be accessed from corporate computers
  - Storage policies for documents and e-mail
  - The types of programs which may be used on corporate computers

PROCEDURES

Display Help (F1)

1. Click **Microsoft Office Word Help** button ⓦ.
2. Click Help category.
3. Click Help topic.
4. Use links as necessary.

Search for Help

1. Display Help window.
2. Click in **Search** box.
3. Type keyword, topic, or question.
4. Click **Search** button drop-down arrow 🔎 Search ▾.
5. Click location to search.

6. Click **Search** button 🔎 Search .... ←Enter
7. Click topic in Search Results task pane.
8. Use links as necessary.

Use the Help Table of Contents

1. Display Help window.
2. Click **Show Table of Contents** button 📖.
3. Click Help category.
4. Click Help topic.
5. Use links as necessary.
6. Click **Hide Table of Contents** button 📖 to close pane.

Use the Help Toolbar

- Click a button on the toolbar to select that command or feature:
  - Click the **Back** button ⊙ to display the previously viewed page.
  - Click the **Forward** button ⊙ to return to a viewed page.
  - Click the **Stop** button ⊗ to cancel a search.
  - Click the **Refresh** button ⊕ to update the current page.
  - Click the **Home** button 🏠 to display the Help Home page.
  - Click the **Print** button 🖶 to print the current page.

- Click the **Change Font Size** button ![icon] to select an option to change the size of the characters in the Help window.
- Click the **Show Table of Contents** button ![icon] to display the Help table of contents page.
- Click the **Keep on Top** button ![icon] to set the Help window to always display on top of other open windows.

Get Help from a Dialog Box

- In the dialog box, click **Help** button ![icon].

Get Help for a Command

1. Rest mouse pointer on command button on Ribbon.
2. Press **F1**.
3. If necessary, use Help tools to locate specific Help information.

Close Help

- Click **Close** button ![x] on Help window title bar .... [Alt]+[F4]

Recover a File

1. Click drop-down arrow beside desired file in Document Recovery task pane.
2. Click desired option to open, save, or delete file.

   ✓ Steps for saving files are covered later in this book.

   ✓ If you save a repaired file, Word will prompt you to review the repairs before continuing.

EXERCISE DIRECTIONS

1. Start Word, if necessary.
2. Display the Help window.
3. Click What's New.
4. Click Top Tips for Word 2007.
5. Read the information about Startup and Settings.
6. Click the Back button on the Help window toolbar to go back to the list of What's New topics.
7. Search for help topics on selecting.
   - Type **select** in the Search box and then click the Search button.
8. Read the available topics.
9. Click the topic *Select an entire document*.
10. Under the heading *What do you want to do?*, click *Select an entire document by using the mouse*.
11. Read the Help topic.
12. Display the Help Home page.
   - Click the Home button on the Help window toolbar.
13. Click the category *Viewing and navigating*.
14. Click the topic *Zoom in or out of a document, presentation, or worksheet*, and then read the information about how to choose a particular zoom setting.
15. Display the Table of Contents, if necessary.
   - Click the Show Table of Contents button on the Help window toolbar.
16. Click the category *Getting help* to expand it to show topics and subcategories. It should look similar to Illustration A.
17. Click the topic *Work with the Help window*.
18. Close the Table of Contents and then close the Help window.
19. Click the dialog box launcher in the Font group on the Home tab of the Ribbon to display the Font dialog box.
20. Click the Help button in the dialog box to display the related Help topic.
21. Minimize the Help window and cancel the Font dialog box.
22. Click the Insert tab on the Ribbon.
23. Rest the mouse pointer on the Chart button ![icon] to display a ScreenTip.
24. Press F1 to display the related Help topic.
25. Close the Help window.
26. Exit Word. Do not save any changes.

Illustration A

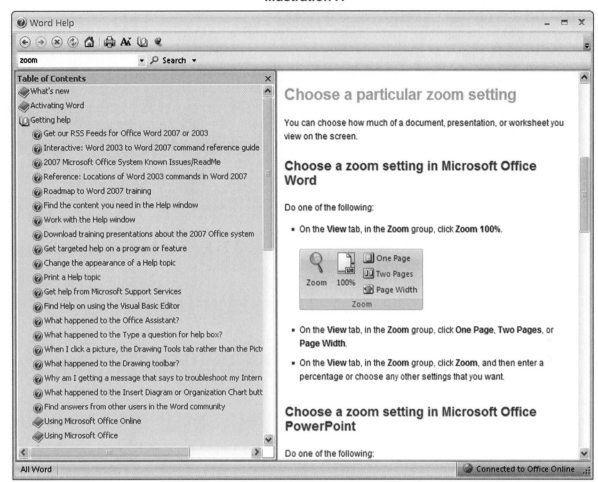

ON YOUR OWN

1. Start Word and display Help.
2. Search for help topics related to saving.
3. Open any topic that sounds interesting.
4. Go back to the Home page.
5. Open the Table of Contents and explore the topics.
6. Open any topic that sounds interesting.
7. Close the Table of Contents and then close the Help window.
8. Use ScreenTips to identify the Format Painter button in the Clipboard group on the Home tab.
9. With the ScreenTip displayed, press F1 to display the relevant Help topic.
10. Continue to explore the help topics as long as you want. When you are done, close the Help window and exit Word. Do not save the document.

Exercise | 6

Critical Thinking

Application Skills   The Marketing Director at Restoration Architecture expects you to be ready to work at full speed tomorrow morning. In this exercise, you will practice the basic skills you have learned in this lesson to start Word, use the keyboard and the mouse, execute commands, zoom in the Word window, customize the Quick Access Toolbar, and use the Help program.

EXERCISE DIRECTIONS

1. Start Word, if necessary.
2. Minimize the Word window.
3. Maximize the Word window.
4. Make the Insert tab of the Ribbon active.
5. Make the View tab of the Ribbon active.
6. Set the zoom to 200%.
7. Make the Home tab of the Ribbon active.
8. Start the Help program and search for information on the Ribbon.
9. Look over the available topics.
10. Select the topic *Can I customize the Ribbon?*.
11. Read the topic.
12. Click the link to the topic *Move the Quick Access Toolbar*, and read that topic.
13. Minimize the Help window.
14. Move the Quick Access Toolbar below the Ribbon.
15. Minimize the Ribbon.
16. Add the New and Open buttons to the Quick Access Toolbar.
17. Arrange the buttons on the Quick Access Toolbar in the following order, from left to right: Open, Save, Redo/Repeat, New, Undo.
18. Restore the Help program window and display the Table of Contents.
19. Expand the topic *Saving and printing*.
20. Expand the topic *Saving*.
21. Display the topic *Save a document*.
22. Read the topic.
23. Hide the Table of Contents. The window should look similar to Illustration A.
24. Close the Help window.
25. Reset the Quick Access Toolbar to its default configuration.
26. Move the Quick Access Toolbar above the Ribbon.
27. Set the zoom to Page Width.
28. Expand the Ribbon.
29. Exit Word. Do not save the changes to the document.

Illustration A

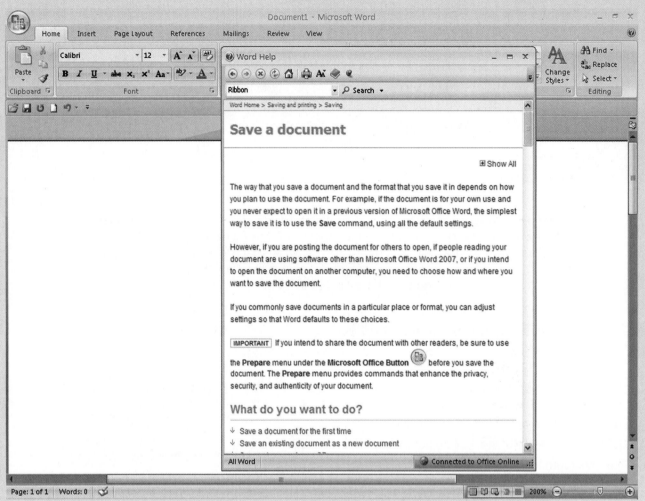

Exercise | 7

Curriculum Integration

Application Skills   Use the information you have learned about Microsoft Office Word 2007 and word processing software to develop an oral presentation convincing others of why they should learn how to use Word 2007.

EXERCISE DIRECTIONS

Start by writing down the reasons someone might need word processing software.

Next, write down features of Word 2007 that you think would be useful for anyone needing word processing software.

Write down other facts that you want to include in the presentation, such as the cost of the software, the type of computer it runs on, and even your personal thoughts about the software.

Review the information to be sure you have included what word processing software is, how you can use it, and why Microsoft Office Word 2007 is a good choice.

Organize the information into a logical order, and then make sure it makes sense when you read it out loud.

You may want to develop a visual aid to show during the presentation, such as a chart showing the different features available in Word 2007, or a picture of the Word 2007 program window.

Practice delivering the presentation. Ask a classmate to listen and to make suggestions on how to improve the presentation.

Make the improvements and practice again.

With your instructor's permission, deliver the presentation to the class.

Lesson | 2

Getting Started with Word 2007

Exercise | 8

Skills Covered

- Start Word
- The Word Window
- Change the Word Window
- Type in a Document
- Correct Errors

- Use Undo, Redo, and Repeat
- Save a New Document
- Close a Document
- Types of Business Documents
- Exit Word

Software Skills   Word is the word processing application included in the Microsoft Office 2007 suite. You use Word to create text-based documents such as letters, memos, reports, flyers, and newsletters. The first step in mastering Word is learning how to start the program and create a document.

Application Skills   You are the office manager at the Michigan Avenue Athletic Club in Chicago, Illinois. A new personal trainer has recently joined the staff, and you must type up a brief biography that will be made available at the club and sent to prospective members. In this exercise, you will start Word, create and save a document, and then exit Word.

TERMS

Business document A professional document used to communicate information within a company, or between one company and another.

Default A standard setting or mode of operation.

Elements Icons, buttons, and other items that are part of an on-screen interface.

Extensible Markup Language (XML) A file format that is compatible across different platforms, provides improved security, and smaller files.

Nonprinting characters Characters such as paragraph marks and tab symbols that are not printed in a document but that can be displayed on the screen.

Paragraph mark A **nonprinting** character inserted in a document to indicate where a paragraph ends.

Personal business document A document used to communicate information between an individual and a company.

Redo The command for reversing the Undo command.

Undo The command for reversing a previous action.

View The way a document is displayed on screen.

Word wrap A feature that causes text to move automatically from the end of one line to the beginning of the next line.

NOTES

Start Word

■ To use Word 2007 you must first start it so it is running on your computer.

■ You use Windows to start Word.

   ✓ *Different methods of starting Microsoft Word 2007 are covered in Exercise 1.*

■ When Word is running, it displays in a window on your screen.

The Word Window

■ Word opens a new, blank document using standard, or **default**, settings. Default settings control features of a new document, such as the margins, the line spacing, the character font, and the font size.

■ Word starts with a new blank document open in Print Layout **view** and displays **elements** for accessing tools and menus to create, edit, format, and distribute a document.

■ Many of the elements in the Word window are the same as those in other Microsoft Office 2007 programs, such as the Ribbon and the Quick Access Toolbar. Other elements are unique to Word.

   ✓ *Word 2007 elements are covered in Exercise 1.*

■ The following illustration identifies elements of the Word window.

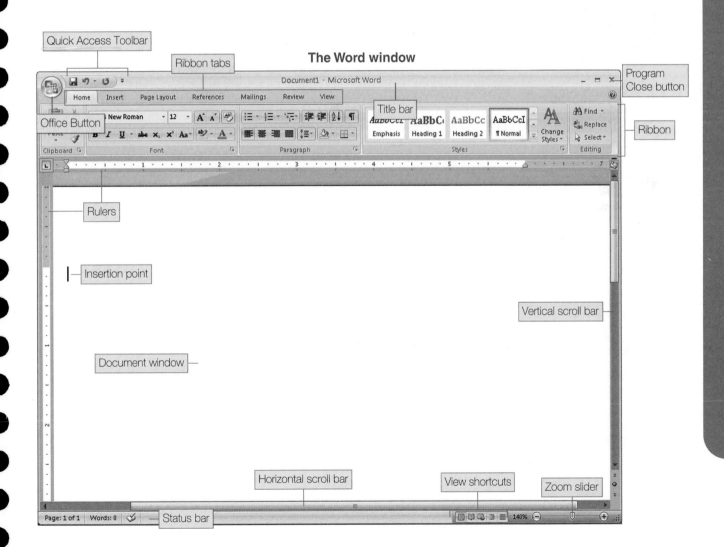

The Word window

Title bar

- Displays the program and document name.

Ribbon

- Displays buttons for accessing features and commands.
- ✓ *Note that the way items display on the Ribbon may depend on the width of the program window. If your program window is wider than the one used in the figures, more or larger buttons may display. If your program window is narrower, fewer or smaller buttons may display. Refer to Exercise 2 for more information.*

Ribbon tabs

- Used to change the commands displayed on the Ribbon.

Office Button

- Click to display a menu of common commands for managing documents and files.

Quick Access Toolbar

- A toolbar that displays buttons for commonly used commands. You can customize the Quick Access Toolbar to display buttons you use frequently.

Rulers

- The horizontal ruler measures the width of the document page; it displays information such as margins, tab stops, and indents.
- The vertical ruler measures the height of the document page.
- ✓ *The vertical ruler displays only in Print Layout view and Print Preview.*
- The rulers may not display by default. You can click the View Ruler button ⬜ above the vertical scroll bar or click the Ruler check box in the Show/Hide group on the View tab of the Ribbon to toggle them on or off.

ScreenTip

- Displays the name of the element on which the mouse pointer is resting.

Insertion point

- A blinking vertical line that displays to the right of the space where characters are inserted in a document.

Document window

- The area where you type document text or insert graphics, tables, or other content.

Scroll boxes

- Used with a mouse to shift the on-screen display up and down or left and right.

Status bar

- Displays information, such as the currently displayed page, currently displayed section, how many pages are in the document, where the insertion point is located, and which mode buttons are active.

Zoom slider

- Used to change the magnification of the document on the screen.

View shortcuts

- Displays buttons used to change to one of five available document views.

Change the Word Window

- You can change the default settings to control whether certain Word elements display while you work.
- You can show or hide rulers.
- You can minimize the Ribbon.

■ You can change views using the View shortcut buttons on the Status bar or the commands in the Document Views group on the View tab of the Ribbon.

- Print Layout view displays a document on-screen the way it will look when it is printed. It is the default view.
- Web Layout view wraps text to fit the window, the way it would on a Web page document.
- Outline view is used to create and edit outlines.
- Full Screen Reading view adjusts the display of text to make it easier to read documents on-screen.
- Draft view can be used for most typing, editing, and formatting, but some formatting does not show on-screen.

Type in a Document

■ By default, the insertion point is positioned at the beginning (left end) of the first line of a new document.

■ You simply begin typing to insert new text.

■ Characters you type are inserted to the left of the insertion point.

■ **Word wrap** automatically wraps the text at the end of a line to the beginning of the next line.

■ When you press (Enter), Word inserts a **paragraph mark** and starts a new paragraph.

■ After you type enough text to fill a page, Word automatically starts a new page.

✓ *Note that Word includes many features designed to make your work easier, such as a spelling checker. These features are often displayed automatically on-screen as colored underlines or buttons. Simply ignore these features for now; you learn to use them later in this book.*

Correct Errors

■ You can delete characters to the left of the insertion point by pressing (←Backspace).

■ You can delete characters to the right of the insertion point by pressing (Del).

■ You can cancel commands before you execute them by pressing (Esc) key or clicking a Cancel button if available.

Use Undo, Redo, and Repeat

■ Use the **Undo** button ⟲ on the Quick Access Toolbar to reverse a single action made in error, such as deleting the wrong word.

■ Use the Undo drop-down list to reverse a series of actions.

- The most recent action is listed at the top of the list; click an action to undo it and all actions above it.

■ Use the **Redo** button ⟳ on the Quick Access Toolbar to reinstate any actions that you reversed with Undo.

■ If the Undo button is dimmed, there are no actions that can be undone.

■ If the Redo button is dimmed, there are no actions that can be redone.

■ Sometimes when there are no actions to redo, the Repeat button ↻ is available in place of Redo. Use Repeat to repeat the most recent action.

Save a New Document

■ As mentioned, Word starts with a new blank document named *Document1* open on-screen.

✓ *Subsequent new documents are named consecutively: Document2, Document3, etc. You will learn more about creating additional new documents in Exercise 9.*

■ If you want to have a file available for future use, you must save it on a removable disk, on an internal fixed disk, or on a network disk.

■ When you save a new document, you must give it a name and select the location where you want it stored.

■ Word automatically adds a period and a file extension to the end of the file name to identify the file type. By default, the file extension is *.docx*, which identifies a document file that is compatible with the **Extensible Markup Language (XML)** format.

✓ *By default, file extensions are not displayed in Windows.*

■ You can select a different file type from the Save as type drop down list, such as the Word .doc type that is compatible with Word versions 97 through 2003.

■ The default storage location for Word documents is My Documents in Windows XP or Documents in Windows Vista.

- You can select a different storage location such as a new folder, a different folder, a disk drive, or a removable device, such as a flash drive plugged into a USB port.
  - Floppy disk drives are usually drives A: and B:. A hard drive is usually drive C:. Additional storage locations are labeled consecutively. For example, a CD-RW or DVD-RW drive may be D, and so on.
- The steps for selecting a storage location in Word 2007 running on Windows Vista are slightly different from those in Word 2007 running on Windows XP.
  - On Windows XP, you can click a common storage location in the Navigation bar on the left side of the Save As dialog box, or select a specific folder or disk drive from the Save in drop-down list.
  - On Windows Vista, you can navigate to a different location using the Address bar, or click Browse Folders to display a Navigation pane where you can click a common location, or use the Folders list.

Save As dialog box in Windows XP

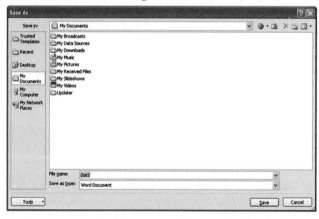

Save As dialog box in Windows Vista

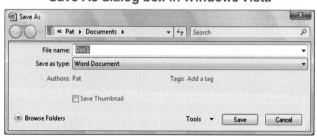

Close a Document

- A document remains open on-screen until you close it.
- Use the program Close button ☒ or the Close command on the Office menu to close a document when you are finished working with it.
  - If multiple documents are open in Word, using the Close button closes the current document only.
  - If only one document is open, using the Close button closes Word, as well.
- If you try to close a document without saving it, Word prompts you to save it.
- You can close a document without saving it if you do not want to keep it for future use or if you are not happy with changes you have made since you last saved the document.

Types of Business Documents

- Some common **business documents** used by most companies include letters, memos, fax covers, invoices, purchase orders, press releases, agendas, reports, and newsletters.
- Certain businesses—or departments within a larger company—may have specialized documents. For example, a law office or legal department produces legal documents such as wills, contracts, and bills of sale.
- In addition, individuals create **personal business documents** such as letters, research papers, and resumes.
- Most business documents have standard formats, which means each type of document includes similar parts. For example, an agenda should always include the following:
  - The meeting start and end time and location
  - The topics to be covered
  - The duration each topic will be discussed
  - The main speakers for each topic
- Throughout this book you learn how to set up and create many types of business documents.

Exit Word

- When you are done using Word, you exit the Word application.
- If you try to exit Word without saving your documents, Word prompts you to do so.
- If you exit Word without closing your saved documents, Word closes them automatically.

PROCEDURES

Start Word

1. Click **Start** button

   `start` / .... Ctrl+Esc

2. Click **All Programs** .... P, ←Enter

3. Point to the **Microsoft Office** folder icon .... ↓, →

4. Click **Microsoft Office Word 2007** .... ↓, ←Enter

   OR

1. Click **Start** button

   `start` / .... Ctrl+Esc

2. Click **Microsoft Office Word 2007** in the list of recently used programs .... ↓, ←Enter

   OR

3. Double-click the Word shortcut icon on the desktop.

Change the Word Window

To show or hide ruler:

■ Click **View Ruler** button above vertical scroll bar.

   OR

1. Click **View** tab .... Alt+W

   Show/Hide Group

2. Click **Ruler** check box .... R

   ✓ A check in the check box indicates the ruler is displayed.

To change the view:

■ Click a View icon on the Status bar:
   ● **Print Layout**
   ● **Full Screen Reading**
   ● **Web Layout**
   ● **Outline**
   ● **Draft**

OR

1. Click **View** tab .... Alt+W

   Document Views Group

2. Click desired view icon:
   ■ **Print Layout** .... P
   ■ **Full Screen Reading** .... F
   ■ **Web Layout** L
   ■ **Outline** .... U
   ■ **Draft** .... E

To Minimize/Expand the Ribbon (Ctrl+F1)

■ Double-click the active tab.

   OR

1. Click the **Customize Quick Access Toolbar** button
   .... Alt, ↑, →, ←Enter

2. Click **Minimize the Ribbon** .... N

   ✓ A check mark next to command indicates it is already selected.

Correct Errors

■ Press **Backspace** ←Backspace to delete character to *left* of insertion point.

■ Press **Delete** Del to delete character to *right* of insertion point.

■ Press **Escape** Esc to cancel command or close dialog box.

   ✓ If available, you may click a Cancel or Close button to close a dialog box without making changes.

Undo the Previous Action (Ctrl+Z)

■ Click **Undo** button on Quick Access Toolbar.

Undo a Series of Actions (Ctrl+Z)

■ Click **Undo** button repeatedly.

   OR

1. Click drop-down arrow to right of **Undo** button.

2. Click any action in the list to undo all previous actions.

Redo the Previous Action

■ Click **Redo** button on Quick Access Toolbar.

Redo a Series of Actions

■ Click **Redo** button repeatedly.

Repeat the Previous Action

■ Click **Repeat** button on Quick Access Toolbar.

Save a New Document (Ctrl+S)

On Windows XP:

1. Click **Save** button on Quick Access Toolbar.

   OR

   Click **Office Button** ...... Alt+F

2. Click **Save** .... S

3. If necessary, click common storage location in the Navigation bar, or click the **Save in** drop-down arrow and select storage location .... Alt+I

   OR

   a. Click **Create New Folder** button.

   b. Type new folder name.

   c. Click **OK** .... ←Enter

4. Select **File name** text
box .... Alt+N

5. Type **file name**.

6. If necessary, click **Save as type**
drop down arrow and select
file type .... Alt+T

7. Click **Save** .... Alt+S

On Windows Vista:

1. Click **Save** button 💾 on Quick
Access Toolbar.

OR

Click **Office Button** 📋 ..... Alt+F

2. Click **Save** .... S

3. If necessary, click Browse
Folders and then use Windows
Vista tools to navigate to
desired storage location.

OR

a. Click **Create New Folder**
button 📁.

b. Type new folder name.

c. Press ↵Enter.

4. Select **File name** text
box .... Alt+N

5. Type **file name**.

6. If necessary, click **Save as type**
drop-down arrow and select
file type .... Alt+T

7. Click **Save** .... Alt+S

Close a Document (Ctrl+W)

■ Click the **Close** button ✖.

OR

1. Click **Office Button** 📋 ..... Alt+F

2. Click **Close** C

3. Click **Yes** to save changes .... Y

OR

Click **No** to close without
saving .... N

Exit Word

■ Click **Close Window** button ✖.

OR

1. Click **Office Button** 📋 ..... Alt+F

2. Click **Exit Word** X

3. Click **Yes** to save changes .... Y

OR

Click **No** to close without
saving .... N

EXERCISE DIRECTIONS

✓ *Note that the Word documents in the exercise illustrations use 11-point Calibri font, unless otherwise noted. Fonts are covered in Exercise 14.*

1. Start Word.

2. Type the first paragraph shown in Illustration A.

✓ *Remember that you do not have to press Enter at the end of each line. Word wrap automatically moves the text to the next line as necessary.*

3. At the end of the paragraph, press ↵Enter to start a new paragraph.

4. Undo the previous action.

✓ *When you execute the Undo command, Word reverses the action of pressing Enter and may also undo some of the typing. Sometimes Word combines actions for the purpose of Undo and Redo. In this case, it considers the typing and pressing Enter one action (called Typing on the Undo ScreenTip, and Typing "area with his family" on the drop-down menu).*

5. Redo the previous action.

✓ *Word redoes the action of pressing Enter.*

6. Type the second paragraph shown in Illustration A.

7. If you make a typing error, press ←Backspace to delete it, and then type the correct text.

✓ *Word marks spelling errors with a red wavy underline, and grammatical errors with a green wavy underline. If you see these lines in the document, proofread for errors.*

8. Change to Web Layout view.

9. Change to Draft view.

10. Change to Full Screen Reading view.

11. Change to Print Layout view.

12. Minimize the Ribbon.

13. Expand the Ribbon.

14. Hide the ruler, if it is currently displayed.

15. Show the ruler.

16. Save the document with the name **08TRAINER_xx**.

✓ *When you see _xx in any instructions in this book, it means that you should type an underscore followed by your own initials—not the actual text "_xx". This will help your instructor identify your work.*

✓ *Ask your instructor where to save the documents you create for use with this book.*

17. Close the document, saving all changes if prompted.

18. Exit Word.

Illustration A

Michigan Avenue Athletic Club is pleased to announce that David Fairmont has joined our staff. David is a licensed personal trainer with extensive experience in cardiovascular health. He holds a master's degree in health management from the University of Vermont in Burlington, Vermont. After graduation, he remained at UVM as an instructor. He recently moved to the Chicago area with his family.

We are certain that David will be a valuable addition to our staff. His skills and experience make him highly qualified and his attitude and personality make him a lot of fun to have around. David is available for private, semi-private, and group sessions. Please contact the club office for more information or to schedule an appointment.

ON YOUR OWN

1. Create a new document in Word.
2. Save the file as **OWD08_*xx***.
3. Type a brief biography about yourself, using at least two paragraphs.
4. Correct errors as necessary.
5. Practice changing from one view to another.
6. Display and hide the rulers.
7. Minimize and expand the Ribbon.
8. Close the document, saving all changes, and exit Word when you are finished.

Skills Covered

- **Create a New Document**
- **Work with Show/Hide Marks**
- **Move the Insertion Point in a Document**
- **Use Click and Type**

- **Save Changes**
- **Print**
- **Preview an Open Document**
- **About Press Releases**

Software Skills   Mastering insertion point movements in Word is necessary to enter and edit text anywhere in a document. You save changes to keep a document up-to-date as you work. When you want to have a hard copy version of a document, you must print it. Preview a document before you print it to make sure there are no errors and that it looks good on the page.

Application Skills   Michigan Avenue Athletic Club has decided to issue a press release announcing the hiring of a new personal trainer. In this exercise, you will create a new document and type the press release. You will practice moving the insertion point around the document and you will align text with the click and type feature. When you have completed the press release, you will save the changes, preview the document, and then print it.

TERMS

Hard copy A document printed on paper.

Horizontal alignment The position of text on a line in relation to the left and right margins.

Insertion point The flashing vertical line that indicates where the next action will occur in a document on-screen.

Media outlet A means of mass communication, such as a newspaper, magazine, television station, radio station, or a Web site.

Press release A short document used to provide information about a company, organization, or event to the media.

NOTES

Create a New Document

- As you learned in Exercise 8, when you start Word it opens and displays a new blank document called *Document1*.
- You can create additional new, blank documents without closing and restarting Word.

✓ *You can also create documents based on templates that contains some text and formatting. You learn how to use templates in Exercise 65.*

- Each new document is named using consecutive numbers, so the second document is *Document2,* the third is *Document3,* and so on until you exit Word or save a file with a new name.

Work with Show/Hide Marks

- When you type in Word you insert nonprinting characters such as spaces, tabs, and paragraph marks along with printing characters such as letters and numbers.

- Displaying nonprinting characters on-screen is helpful because you see where each paragraph ends and if there are extra spaces or unwanted tab characters.

- On-screen, the most common nonprinting characters display as follows:
  - Space: dot (•)
  - Paragraph: paragraph symbol (¶)
  - Tab: right arrow (→)

  ✓ *Other nonprinting characters include optional hyphens and line breaks.*

Display nonprinting marks in a document

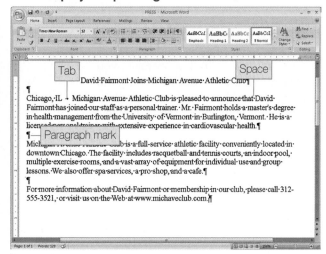

Move the Insertion Point in a Document

- The **insertion point** indicates where text will be inserted or deleted.

- You can move the insertion point anywhere in the existing text with keystrokes or mouse clicks.

- Scrolling to shift the document view does not move the insertion point.

Use Click and Type

- Use the Click and Type feature to position the insertion point anywhere in a blank document to begin typing.

  ✓ *Click and Type cannot be used in Normal view or Outline view.*

- When Click and Type is active, the mouse pointer changes to indicate the **horizontal alignment** of the new text, as follows:

  ✓ *You learn more about horizontal alignment in Exercise 11.*

Text will be flush with the left margin

Text will be centered

Text will be flush with the right margin

The first line of text will be indented .5"

Save Changes

- To keep revisions permanently, you must save changes that you make to a document.

- Saving frequently ensures that no work will be lost if there is a power outage or you experience computer problems.

  ✓ *The Document Recovery feature also helps insure that you won't lose your work in case of a computer failure. Refer to Exercise 5 for more information.*

- Saving replaces the previously saved version of the document with the most recent changes.

Print

- Printing creates a **hard copy** version of a document.
- You can use Quick Print to print the current document with the default settings.
- Use the Print dialog box to change the settings before printing.
- Your computer must be connected to a printer in order to print.

Print dialog box

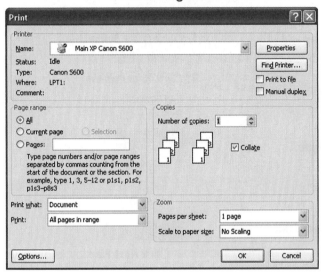

Preview an Open Document

- Use Print Preview to display a document as it will look when printed.
- Print Preview is similar to Print Layout view except that the Print Preview tab of the Ribbon displays.

- The Print Preview tab of the Ribbon displays commands for controlling the Print Preview display and selecting options for printing.

Print Preview tab of the Ribbon

About Press Releases

- Use a **press release** to announce information about your company to **media outlets**.
- For example, you can issue a press release about new products, trends, developments, and even to provide tips or hints.
- The media outlet may provide you with publicity by reporting the information.
- A press release should be no more than one page in length. It should provide the basic facts, details that define why the content is newsworthy, and who to contact for more information.
- The basic parts of a press release include the following:
  - Contact information
  - Headline
  - Location
  - Lead paragraph
  - Additional information and details

Curriculum Connection: Mathematics

Pi

Pi—the ratio of a circumference of a circle to its diameter—has been around since at least 1800 B.C. The ancient Babylonians might not have called it Pi, but they figured its value was about 3, and probably used it to calculate things like the size of a grain storage facility. Nowadays, Pi comes in handy for a wide variety of applications, ranging from designing jet planes to calculating global positioning.

Announcing Pi

Write a press release about a calculation that involves Pi. Explain the calculation and why it is important. (You may want to leave space so that you can hand draw an illustration.) Include background information, as well, such as why Pi is called Pi and who first used the Greek letter Pi (π) as its symbol. Use the Internet and other resources to track down the information.

PROCEDURES

Create a New Document (Ctrl+N)

1. Start Word.
2. Click **Office Button** 🗕 .... Alt+F
3. Click **New** .... N
4. Click **Blank document**.
5. Click **Create** .... ↵Enter

Show or Hide Marks

1. Click **Home** tab .... Alt+H

   Paragraph Group

2. Click **Show/Hide** button ¶ ... 8

To select nonprinting characters to display:

1. Click **Office Button** 🗕 ..... Alt+F
2. Click **Word Options** I
3. Click **Display** .... D
4. Click to select one or more of the following:
   - **Tab characters** .... Alt+T
   - **Spaces** .... Alt+S
   - **Paragraph marks** .... Alt+M
   - **Hidden text** .... Alt+D
   - **Optional hyphens** .... Alt+Y
   - **Object anchors** .... Alt+C
   - **Show all formatting marks** .... Alt+A
5. Click **OK** .... ↵Enter

Insertion Point Movements

To move with the mouse:
- Click mouse pointer in text where you want to position insertion point.

To move with the keyboard:
- One character left .... ←
- One character right .... →
- One line up .... ↑
- One line down .... ↓
- Previous word .... Ctrl+←

- Next word .... Ctrl+→
- Up one paragraph .... Ctrl+↑
- Down one paragraph .... Ctrl+↓
- Beginning of document .... Ctrl+Home
- End of document ... Ctrl+End
- Beginning of line .... Home
- End of line .... End

Use Click and Type

1. Change to Print Layout view.
2. Double-click at location where you want to position insertion point.

To enable Click and Type:

1. Click **Office Button** 🗕 ..... Alt+F
2. Click **Word Options** I
3. Click **Advanced** .... A
4. Click to select **Enable click and type** check box .... Alt+C, Spacebar
5. Click **OK** .... ↵Enter

Save Changes (Ctrl+S)

- Click **Save** button 🖫 on Quick Access Toolbar.

   OR

   a. Click **Office Button** 🗕 .... Alt+F
   b. Click **Save** .... S

Print the Current Document

1. Click **Office Button** 🗕 ..... Alt+F
2. Point to **Print** .... W
3. Click **Quick Print** .... Q

   ✓ This prints the document with the default settings.

Change Print Settings and then Print (Ctrl+P)

1. Click **Office Button** 🗕 ..... Alt+F
2. Click **Print** .... P
3. Select options in Print dialog box
4. Click **OK** .... ↵Enter

Preview a Document

1. Click **Office Button** 🗕 ..... Alt+F
2. Point to **Print** .... W
3. Click **Print Preview** V
4. Select options on Print Preview tab:

   Zoom Group
   - Click desired zoom options

      ✓ See Exercise 3 for information on zooming.

   Preview Group
   - Click **Next Page** 🔲 to display next page .... PgDn
   - Click **Previous Page** 🔲 to display previous page ...... PgUp
   - Click **Close Print Preview** ☒ to close print preview .... Esc

   Print Group
   - Click **Print** 🖨 to display Print dialog box .... Ctrl+P

EXERCISE DIRECTIONS

1. Start Word, if necessary.
2. Create a new document and save it as **09PRESS_xx**.
3. Change to Print Layout view, if necessary.
4. Display all nonprinting characters.
5. Use Click and Type to center the insertion point on the first line of the document.
6. Type the text shown on the first line of Illustration A.

    ✓ Ignore any automatic features that are displayed as underlines or buttons.

7. Press Enter, and then use Click and Type to move the insertion point so it is flush left.

    ✓ When you press Enter to start a new paragraph, the insertion point will still be centered. That's because Word carries formatting such as horizontal alignment forward from one paragraph to the next. You must use Click and Type to change the alignment to flush left.

8. Type the rest of the document shown in Illustration A.

✓ Depending on the default settings on your computer, Word may automatically format the Web address in the last paragraph as a hyperlink by changing the color to blue and applying an underline. If you click the hyperlink, your computer may try to log onto the Internet to locate the site. You can remove the hyperlink by right-clicking on it, then clicking Remove Hyperlink on the shortcut menu.

9. Move the insertion point back to the second sentence in the first paragraph of the press release and delete the text in *Burlington, Vermont*. Do not delete the final period.
10. Move the insertion point between the words *offer* and *spa* in the last sentence of the second paragraph.
11. Type the word **exceptional**.
12. If necessary type a space between the new word *exceptional* and the existing word *spa*.
13. Save the changes you have made to the document.
14. Display the document in Print Preview.
15. Close Print Preview.
16. Print the document with the default settings.
17. Close the document, saving all changes.

Illustration A

David Fairmont Joins Michigan Avenue Athletic Club

Chicago, IL -- Michigan Avenue Athletic Club is pleased to announce that David Fairmont has joined our staff as a personal trainer. Mr. Fairmont holds a master's degree in health management from the University of Vermont in Burlington, Vermont. He is a licensed personal trainer with extensive experience in cardiovascular health.

Michigan Avenue Athletic Club is a full-service athletic facility conveniently located in downtown Chicago. The facility includes racquetball and tennis courts, an indoor pool, multiple exercise rooms, and a vast array of equipment for individual use and group lessons. We also offer spa services, a pro shop, and a cafe.

For more information about David Fairmont or membership in our club, please call 312-555-3521, or visit us on the Web at www.michaveclub.com.

ON YOUR OWN

1. Create a new document in Word.
2. Save the file as **OWD09_xx.**
3. Draft a press release announcing that you are taking a course to learn how to use Microsoft Office 2007.
4. Using Click and Type, center a headline at the top of the document.
5. Using Click and Type, move the pointer back to the flush left or first line indent position to type the rest of the press release. Include information such as your instructor's name, the textbook you are using, and when the course will be completed.
6. Save the changes, and then preview the document to see how it will look when printed. See Illustration A for a sample press release.
7. Print the document.
8. Close the document when you are finished, saving all changes.

Illustration A

Carolyn Johnson Studies Word Processing

Middletown, USA – Carolyn Johnson, a sophomore at Middletown High School, recently started the Word Processing 1 course. The course uses the Learning Microsoft Office 2007 series of books to introduce students to the wonderful world of Word.

In addition to studying the use of Word for word processing, the semester-long course covers the basics of using the Internet and integrating Word with other Office 2007 programs. Ms. Johnson is particularly eager to learn how to create PowerPoint presentations.

There are twenty-one students in the Word Processing 1 course this semester. The teacher, Mr. Hammond, expresses great delight in having Ms. Johnson in class. For more information, contact the Business Education Department at Middletown High School, 555-5500, ext. 233.

Exercise | 10

Skills Covered

- Correct Spelling as You Type
- Correct Grammar as You Type
- Check Spelling and Grammar
- Use the Thesaurus

Software Skills A professional document should be free of spelling and grammatical errors. Word can check the spelling and grammar in a document and recommend corrections.

Application Skills The Marketing Director at Michigan Avenue Athletic Club has asked you to create a mission statement explaining the corporate goals. In this exercise, you will type the statement and then improve it by correcting the spelling and grammar

TERMS

Antonyms Words with opposite meanings.

Mini toolbar A toolbar that displays in the document area when you select text, providing quick, convenient access to common text editing and formatting commands.

Smart tag A feature of most Microsoft Office 2007 programs that lets you perform actions within Word that you would normally have to open another application to accomplish. For example, you can add a person's name and address to an Outlook contact list using a smart tag in Word.

Synonyms Words with the same meaning.

Thesaurus A listing of words with synonyms and antonyms.

NOTES

Correct Spelling as You Type

- By default, Word checks spelling as you type and marks misspelled words with a red, wavy underline.
- Any word not in the Word dictionary is marked as misspelled, including proper names, words with unique spellings, and many technical terms. Word will also mark double occurrences of words.
- You can ignore the wavy lines and keep typing, correct the spelling, or add the marked word to the dictionary.
- There are two ways to correct the error:
  - Delete and replace the misspelled word.

- Right-click the word to display a shortcut menu from which you can select the correctly spelled word, choose to ignore the error, or add the word to the dictionary. If you choose to ignore the word, the wavy underline is removed.

  ✓ *When you right-click a word, Word displays a **Mini toolbar**, which you can ignore. Refer to Exercise 2 for more information on using a Mini toolbar.*

- You can also turn on the Contextual Spelling feature, which applies a wavy blue underline to words that are spelled correctly, but are used in the wrong context.

- For example, if you type *I red the book*, Word underlines the word *red*.
- Right-click a contextual spelling error to select the correct word from the shortcut menu.

  ✓ *Word uses a few other underlines to mark text on-screen, although most are turned off by default. For example, blue wavy underlines also indicate inconsistent formatting and purple dotted lines indicate **smart tags**. You learn about checking for inconsistent formatting in Exercise 92.*

- If the wavy underlines distract you from your work, you can turn off the Check spelling as you type feature.

A misspelled word

This is an example of a mespelled word.

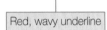
Red, wavy underline

Correct Grammar as You Type

- Word can also check grammar as you type, identifying errors such as punctuation, matching case or tense, sentence fragments, and run-on sentences.
- Word marks grammatical errors with a green, wavy underline.
- Word picks out grammatical errors based on either the Grammar Only style guide or the Grammar and Style style guide.
- As with the spelling checker, you can ignore the green wavy lines and keep typing, or correct the error.
- If the wavy underlines distract you from your work, you can turn off the Check grammar as you type feature.

A grammatical error

This is an example of a grammatical errors.

Green wavy underline

Check Spelling and Grammar

- You can check the spelling and grammar in an entire document or in part of a document.
- To check part of a document, you must first select the section you want checked.
- Word first checks for spelling errors, and then checks for grammatical errors.
- The spelling checker identifies any word not in the Word dictionary as misspelled, including proper names, words with unique spellings, and technical terms.
- When Word identifies a misspelled word, you can correct the spelling, ignore the spelling, or add the word to the dictionary.
- When Word identifies a grammatical mistake, you can accept the suggestion or ignore it.
- To check only the spelling, you can deselect the Check grammar check box in the Spelling and Grammar dialog box or in the Word Options dialog box.

Correct spelling in the Spelling and Grammar dialog box

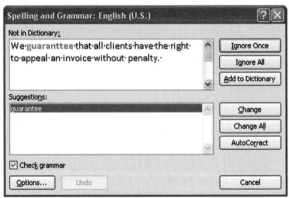

Correct grammar in the Spelling and Grammar dialog box

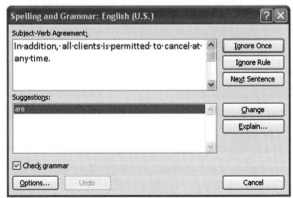

Use the Thesaurus

- Use the **thesaurus** to search for **synonyms**, definitions, and **antonyms** for any word.
- The results of the search display in the Research task pane.
- Click a plus sign to expand the list to show additional words.
- Click a minus sign to collapse the list to hide some words.
- Use the available drop-down list to insert a word from the results list at the current insertion point location, copy it at a different location, or look it up in the thesaurus.
- Use the Back ⊕Back and Forward ⊕ buttons to browse through the content you previously viewed in the research pane.
- By default, Word searches an English thesaurus, but you can select to search different reference sources, including all available reference books, a thesaurus in a different language, or online Web sites such as the Microsoft Encarta encyclopedia.

- A thesaurus can improve your writing by helping you eliminate repetitive use of common words and to choose more descriptive words.

Look up synonyms in the Research task pane

PROCEDURES

Correct Spelling as You Type

1. Right-click word marked with red, wavy underline.
2. Click correctly spelled word on shortcut menu.

   OR
   - Click **I**gnore .... G
   - Click **I**gnore All I
   - Click **A**dd to add word to dictionary .... A

To turn on Contextual Spelling feature:

1. Click **Office Button** 🔘 ...... Alt + F
2. Click **Word Opti**ons I
3. Click **Proofing** .... P
4. Click to select **Use contextual spelling** check box .... Alt + N
5. Click **OK** .... ↵Enter

To turn off Automatic Spelling Checker:

1. Click **Office Button** 🔘 ...... Alt + F
2. Click **Word Opti**ons I

3. Click **Proofing** .... P
4. Click to clear **Check spelling as you type** check box .... Alt + P
5. Click **OK** .... ↵Enter

Correct Grammar as You Type

1. Right-click text marked with green, wavy underline.
2. Click correct grammar option on the shortcut menu.

   OR

   Click **I**gnore Once I

To turn Off Automatic Grammar Checker:

1. Click **Office Button** 🔘 ...... Alt + F
2. Click **Word Opti**ons I
3. Click **Proofing** .... P
4. Click to clear **Mark grammar errors as you type** check box .... Alt + M
5. Click **OK** .... ↵Enter

Select Grammar Style

1. Click **Office Button** 🔘 ...... Alt + F
2. Click **Word Options** I
3. Click **Proofing** .... P
4. Click **Writing Style** drop-down arrow .... Alt + W
5. Click desired style .... ↑ / ↓
6. Click **OK** .... ↵Enter

Check Spelling and Grammar(F7)

1. Position insertion point where you want to start checking.

   ✓ *Word checks document from the insertion point forward.*

   OR

   Select text you want to check.
2. Click **Review** tab .... Alt + R

   Proofing Group
3. Click **Spelling & Grammar** button 🔤 .... S

4. For the first misspelled word, choose from the following options:

- Delete the error and type the correction in the **Not in Dictionary:** text box.
- Click correctly spelled word in **Suggestions list.** .... `Alt`+`N`
- Click **Ignore Once** to continue without changing ...... `Alt`+`I`
- Click **Ignore All** to continue without changing word and without highlighting it anywhere else in document .... `Alt`+`G`
- Click **Add to Dictionary** to add word to dictionary ..... `Alt`+`A`
- Click **Change** .... `Alt`+`C`
- Click **Change All** to change the word everywhere in document .... `Alt`+`L`

5. Repeat step 4 for every misspelled word.

6. For the first grammatical error, choose from the following options:

- Delete the error and type the correction in the *grammatical error:* text box.

  ✓ *The name of the text box changes, depending on the type of error.*

- Click correct grammar in the **Suggestions list.** .... `Alt`+`N`
- Click **Ignore Once** to continue without changing ...... `Alt`+`I`
- Click **Ignore Rule** to continue without changing text and without highlighting error if it occurs anywhere else in document .... `Alt`+`G`
- Click **Next Sentence** to skip highlighted error and continue checking document .... `Alt`+`X`
- Click **Change** .... `Alt`+`C`
- Click **Explain** to display information about grammatical error .... `Alt`+`E`

7. Repeat step 6 for every grammatical error.

8. Click **OK** when Word completes check. .... `↵Enter`

   ✓ *Word may prompt you to check the formatting in your document. Click* Yes *to check the formatting, or* No *to close the prompt without checking the formatting. For more information on checking formatting, refer to Exercise 29.*

Search the Thesaurus (Shift+F7)

1. Click on the word you want to look up.

   ✓ *The insertion point should be positioned within the word.*

2. Click **Review** tab .... `Alt`+`R`

   Proofing Group

3. Click **Thesaurus** button 📖 ...... `E`

   OR

1. Right-click on the word you want to look up.

2. Click **Look Up** on the shortcut menu .... `K`

   OR

1. Click **Review** tab .... `Alt`+`R`

   Proofing Group

2. Click **Thesaurus** button 📖 ...... `E`

3. Type word to look up in **Search for** text box in Research task pane.

4. Click drop-down arrow next to text box that displays current reference source.

5. Click desired reference location.

6. Click **Start searching** button ➡ .... `↵Enter`

Insert a synonym:

1. Position the insertion point where you want to insert the word.

   OR

   Select the word to replace.

2. Move the mouse pointer to touch the synonym in the Research task pane results list.

   ✓ *A drop-down arrow displays.*

3. Click the drop-down arrow to the right of the synonym.

4. Click **Insert** .... `I`

Look up a synonym:

- Click the word in the Research task pane results list.

   OR

1. Move the mouse pointer to touch the word in the Research task pane results list.

   ✓ *A drop-down arrow displays.*

2. Click the drop-down arrow to the right of the synonym.

3. Click **Look Up** .... `L`

Copy a synonym:

1. Move the mouse pointer to touch the word in the Research task pane results list.

   ✓ *A drop-down arrow displays.*

2. Click the drop-down arrow to the right of the synonym.

3. Click **Copy** .... `C`

4. Right-click in the document where you want to insert the copied word.

5. Click **Paste** on the shortcut menu .... `P`

Locate a synonym as you type:

1. Right-click on the word you want to look up.

2. Click **Synonyms** on the shortcut menu .... `Y`

3. Click desired synonym submenu.

EXERCISE DIRECTIONS

1. Start Word, if necessary.
2. Create a new document.
3. Save the file as **10MISSION_xx**.
4. Display paragraph marks.
5. Begin at the top of the screen and type the paragraphs shown in Illustration A, including all the circled errors.
6. As you type, correct the spelling of the word *committed*.

   ✓ *The AutoCorrect feature may automatically correct this word. If it does, continue typing. AutoCorrect is covered in Exercise 11.*

7. As you type, correct the grammar in the first sentence of the second paragraph.

8. Check the spelling and grammar starting at the beginning of the document.
   a. Correct the spelling of the words *personal* and *professional*.
   b. Capitalize the word *Under* at the beginning of the second sentence in the second paragraph.
   c. Ignore all occurrences of the proper name *Chardudutta Saroj*.
   d. Correct the spelling of the word *environment*.
   e. Change the double comma in the middle of the last sentence in the second paragraph to a single comma.
9. Use the Thesaurus to replace the word *hope* in the last sentence.
10. Display the document in Print Preview.
11. Print the document.
12. Close the document, saving all changes.

Illustration A

The Michigan Avenue Athletic Club is comitted to excellence. We encourage our employees and our members to strive for the highest goals, meet all challenges with spirit and enthusiasm, and work hard to achieve personel and professionel harmony.

At MAAC, we respects individuality and value diversity. under the guidance of General Manager Ray Peterson and Exercise Director Charudutta Saroj we hope to provide an enviromnent where people feel comfortable, safe,, and free to pursue their physical fitness goals.

ON YOUR OWN

1. A mission statement is used to define the purpose and goals of a business or organization. Think about your purpose and goals in terms of this class. Consider what you hope to achieve, what you would like to learn, as well as how you want to interact with your instructor and classmates.

2. When you are ready, create a new document in Word.

3. Save the document as **OWD10_xx.**

4. Type your own mission statement for this class in the blank document.

5. Check and correct the spelling and grammar.

6. Use the Thesaurus to improve the wording of your document.

7. Print the document.

8. Ask someone in your class to read the statement and to provide written and oral feedback.

9. Integrate the suggestions into the document.

10. Save your changes, close the document, and exit Word when you are finished.

Exercise | 11

Skills Covered

- Use AutoCorrect
- Select Text in a Document
- Replace Selected Text
- Align Text Horizontally
- Align a Document Vertically
- Line Spacing
- Paragraph Spacing
- About Memos

Software Skills   As you type a document, Word's AutoCorrect feature automatically corrects common spelling errors before you even know you've made them. You must select text in a document in order to edit it or format it. For example, changing the horizontal and vertical alignment can improve the appearance of a document and make it easier to read. Format documents using the right amount of space between lines and paragraphs to make the pages look better and the text easier to read, and to achieve the standard page setup for documents such as memos and letters.

Application Skills   You are an assistant in the personnel department at Whole Grains Bread, a manufacturer of specialty breads and pastries based in Larkspur, California. In this exercise, your supervisor has asked you to type a memo to employees about a new automatic deposit payroll option.

TERMS

AutoCorrect A feature available in most Microsoft Office 2007 programs that automatically corrects common spelling errors as you type.

Caps Lock Keyboard key used to **toggle** uppercase letters with lowercase letters.

Contiguous Next to or adjacent.

Flush Lined up evenly along an edge.

Highlight To apply a colored background to text to call attention to it.

Horizontal alignment The position of text in relation to the left and right page margins.

Leading Line spacing measured in points.

Line spacing The amount of white space between lines of text in a paragraph.

Paragraph spacing The amount of white space between paragraphs.

Select Mark text as the focus of the next action, such as editing or formatting.

Selection bar A narrow strip along the left margin of a page that automates selection of text. When the mouse pointer is in the selection area, the cursor changes to an arrow pointing up and to the right.

Toggle A command that turns a particular mode on and off. Also, to switch back and forth between two modes.

Vertical alignment The position of text in relation to the top and bottom page margins.

NOTES

Use AutoCorrect

- **AutoCorrect** automatically replaces spelling errors with the correct text as soon as you press the spacebar after typing a word.

AutoCorrect dialog box

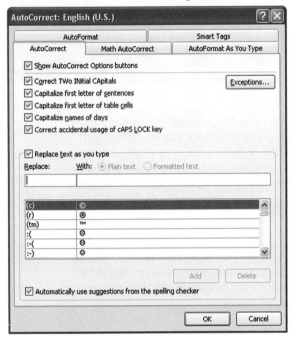

- Word comes with a built-in list of AutoCorrect entries including common typos like *adn* for *and* and *teh* for *the*.

- AutoCorrect can also replace regular characters with symbols, such as the letters *T* and *M* enclosed in parentheses (TM) with the trademark symbol, ™. It will also insert accent marks in words such as café, cliché, crème, and déjà vu.

- By default, AutoCorrect corrects capitalization errors as follows:
  - TWo INitial CApital letters are replaced with one initial capital letter.
  - The first word in a sentence is automatically capitalized.
  - The days of the week are automatically capitalized.
  - Accidental use of the cAPS LOCK feature is corrected if the **Caps Lock** key is set to ON.

- You can add words to the AutoCorrect list. For example, if you commonly misspell someone's name, you can add it to the list.

- You can also set Word to use the spelling checker dictionary to determine if a word is misspelled and to correct it automatically.

- If AutoCorrect changes text that was not incorrect, you can use Undo or the AutoCorrect Options button to reverse the change.

- If you find AutoCorrect distracting, you can disable it.

- The AutoCorrect list is shared among the Microsoft Office programs.

Select Text in a Document

- **Select** text already entered in a document in order to edit it or format it.

- You can select any amount of **contiguous** or non-contiguous text.

  ✓ You can also select non-text characters, such as symbols; nonprinting characters, such as paragraph marks; and graphics, such as pictures.

- By default, selected text appears **highlighted** on screen as black characters on a blue background.

- When you first select text, a transparent Mini toolbar displays. The toolbar will fade away completely if you do not use it.

Selected text is highlighted

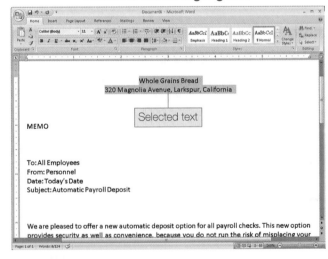

Replace Selected Text

- You can replace selected text simply by typing new text.

- You can delete selected text by pressing Del or ⟵Backspace.

Align Text Horizontally

- **Horizontal alignment** is used to adjust the position of paragraphs in relation to the left and right margins of a page.

  ✓ *You have already used Click and Type to align text horizontally in a document.*

- There are four horizontal alignments:
  - *Left.* Text is **flush** with left margin. The text along the right side of the page is uneven (or ragged). Left is the default horizontal alignment.
  - *Right.* Text is flush with right margin. The text along the left side of the page is uneven (or ragged).
  - *Center.* Text is centered between margins.
  - *Justify.* Text is spaced so it runs evenly along both the left and right margins.
- You can use different alignments in a document.
- Buttons for changing the alignment are available in the Paragraph group on the Home tab of the Ribbon.
- The Center align button is available on the Mini toolbar that displays when you select text.

Horizontally aligned text

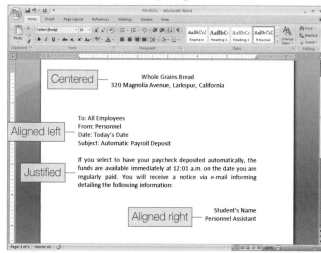

Align a Document Vertically

- **Vertical alignment** is used to adjust the position of all text on a page in relation to the top and bottom margins.
- There are four vertical alignments:
  - *Top:* Text begins below the top margin. Top is the default vertical alignment.
  - *Center:* Text is centered between the top and bottom margins. Centering can improve the appearance of some one-page documents, such as flyers or invitations.
  - *Justified:* Paragraphs are spaced to fill the page between the top and bottom margins. Vertical justification improves the appearance of documents that contain nearly full pages of text.
  - *Bottom:* The last line of text begins just above the bottom margin.

Line Spacing

- **Line spacing** sets the amount of vertical space between lines. By default, line spacing in Word is set to 1.15 lines.
- Line spacing can be measured in either lines (single, double, etc.) or in points.
- When line spacing is measured in points, it is called **leading** (pronounced *ledding*).
  - Increase leading to make text easier to read.
  - Decrease leading to fit more lines on a page.

  ✓ *You should never decrease leading so much that the text is difficult to read.*

- You can set line spacing using the Line spacing button in the Paragraph group on the Home tab of the Ribbon, or in the Paragraph dialog box.

Paragraph Spacing

- **Paragraph spacing** affects space before and after paragraphs.
- The amount of space can be specified in lines or in points. The default paragraph spacing in Word is set to 10 points after each paragraph.
- Use increased paragraph spacing in place of extra returns or blank lines.
- You can set paragraph spacing using the Spacing options in the Paragraph group on the Page Layout tab of the Ribbon, or in the Paragraph dialog box.

About Memos

- A memo, or memoranda, is a business document commonly used for communication within a company.

- Unlike a letter, a memo is not usually addressed to a particular individual and does not include a formal closing.

  ✓ *You will learn about business letters in Exercise 12.*

- Usually, a memo includes the company name, the word memo, the headings To:, From:, Date:, and Subject: and the memo text.

- Line spacing in a memo is usually set to Single, so that no extra space is left between lines.

- One blank line, or spacing equal to one line, is usually used to separate parts of a memo.

- The writer may include his or her name, title, and/or signature at the end of the memo text.

- If someone other than the writer types the memo, that person's initials should be entered below the memo text. In addition, if there is an attachment or an enclosure, the word Attachment or Enclosure should be entered after the text (or the typist's initials).

- Some variations on this memo format include typing headings in all uppercase letters, typing the subject text in all uppercase letters, and leaving additional spacing between memo parts. Also, the word memo may be omitted.

PROCEDURES

Use AutoCorrect

Add words to the AutoCorrect list:
1. Click **Office Button** .... Alt + F
2. Click **Word Options** I
3. Click **Proofing** ...... P
4. Click **AutoCorrect Options** ...... Alt + A
5. Click in **Replace** text box ...... Alt + R
6. Type misspelled word to add.
7. Click in **With** text box .... Alt + W
8. Type correct word.
9. Click **Add** ...... Alt + A
10. Click **OK** ...... ↵Enter

Set AutoCorrect Options:
1. Click **Office Button** ...... Alt + F
2. Click **Word Options** I
3. Click **Proofing** ...... P
4. Click **AutoCorrect Options** ...... Alt + A
5. Select or deselect checkboxes as desired:
   - **Show AutoCorrect options buttons** ...... Alt + H
   - **Correct TWO INitial CApitals** ...... Alt + O
   - **Capitalize first letter of sentences** ...... Alt + S

- **Capitalize first letter of table cells** ...... Alt + C
- **Capitalize names of days** ...... Alt + N
- **Correct accidental usage of cAPS LOCK key** ...... Alt + L
- **Automatically use suggestions from the spelling checker** ...... Alt + G
6. Click **OK** ...... ↵Enter

Disable AutoCorrect:
1. Click **Office Button** ...... Alt + F
2. Click **Word Options** I
3. Click **Proofing** ...... P
4. Click **AutoCorrect Options** ...... Alt + A
5. Click to deselect **Replace text as you type** check box ..... Alt + T
6. Click **OK** ...... ↵Enter

Use AutoCorrect Options button:
1. Click word that was automatically corrected.

   ✓ *A blue rectangle displays below the word.*

2. Rest mouse pointer on **blue rectangle**.

   ✓ *The AutoCorrect Options button displays.*

3. Click **AutoCorrect Options** button ☷ ▾.
4. Select desired option.

   ✓ *The commands change depending on the most recent action.*

Select Using the Keyboard

1. Position insertion point to left of first character to select.
2. Use following key combinations:
   - One character right ...... ⬆Shift + →
   - One character left ...... ⬆Shift + ←
   - One line up ...... ⬆Shift + ↑
   - One line down ...... ⬆Shift + ↓
   - To end of line ...... ⬆Shift + End
   - To beginning of line ...... ⬆Shift + Home
   - To end of document .... ⬆Shift + Ctrl + End
   - To beginning of document .. ⬆Shift + Ctrl + Home
   - Entire document ...... Ctrl + A

Select Using the Mouse

1. Position insertion point to the left of first character to select.
2. Hold down left mouse button.
3. Drag to where you want to stop selecting.
4. Release mouse button.

Mouse Selection Shortcuts

One word:

- Double-click word.

One sentence:

1. Press and hold **Ctrl** .... Ctrl
2. Click in sentence.

One line:

- Click in **selection bar** to the left of the line.

  ✓ *In the selection bar, the mouse pointer changes to an arrow pointing up and to the right* [⬈].

One paragraph:

- Double-click in selection bar to the left of the paragraph you want to select.

Document:

- Triple-click in selection bar.

Select noncontiguous blocks:

1. Select first block.
2. Press and hold **Ctrl** .... Ctrl
3. Select additional block(s).

Cancel a Selection

- Click anywhere in document.

OR

- Press any arrow key .... ↑, ↓, ←, →

Replace Selected Text

1. Select text to replace.
2. Type new text.

OR

Press **Delete** .... Del
to delete selected text.

Align Horizontally

1. Position insertion point in paragraph to align.

OR

Select paragraphs to align.

OR

Position insertion point where you intend to type text.

2. Click **Home** tab .... Alt + H

   Paragraph Group

3. Click alignment button:
   - **Align Text Left** 📄 .... A, L
   - **Center** 📄 .... A, C
   - **Align Text Right** 📄 .... A, R
   - **Justify** 📄 .... A, J

To align text using shortcut key combinations:

- **Align Text Left** .... Ctrl + L
- **Center** .... Ctrl + E
- **Align Text Right** .... Ctrl + R
- **Justify** .... Ctrl + J

To center align text using the Mini toolbar:

1. Select text to align.
2. Move mouse pointer over Mini toolbar.
3. Click **Center** button 📄.

Align Vertically

1. Click **Page Layout** tab ...... Alt + P

   Page Setup Group

2. Click **Page Setup** dialog box launcher button 🔲 .... S, P
3. Click **Layout** tab .... Ctrl + Tab
4. Click **Vertical alignment** drop-down arrow .... Alt + V
5. Select desired alignment: .... ↑, ↓
   - **Top**
   - **Center**
   - **Justified**
   - **Bottom**
6. Click **OK** .... ↵Enter

Set Line Spacing (Ctrl+1, Ctrl+2, Ctrl+5)

1. Position insertion point where text will be typed.

OR

Position insertion point in paragraph to change.

OR

Select paragraph(s) to change.

2. Click the **Home** tab .... Alt + H

   Paragraph Group

3. Click **Line Spacing** button 📄 to display a menu of options .... K

   ✓ *Values on the menu are measured in lines.*

4. Click desired spacing option .... ↑/↓, ↵Enter

To use the Paragraph dialog box:

1. Position insertion point where text will be typed.

OR

Position insertion point in paragraph to change.

OR

Select paragraph(s) to change.

2. Click the **Home** tab .... Alt + H

Paragraph Group

3. Click **Line Spacing**
   button ⊞⊟▾ .... Ⓚ

4. Click **Line Spacing**
   Options .... ⬇ 6x, ⏎Enter

   OR

   Click **Paragraph** group dialog
   box launcher ⊡ .... Ⓟ, Ⓖ

5. Click **Indents and Spacing**
   page tab .... Alt+Ⓘ

6. Click **Line spacing** drop-down
   arrow .... Alt+Ⓝ

7. Select a line spacing
   option: .... ⬆/⬇, ⏎Enter
   - **Single**
   - **1.5 lines**
   - **Double**

   OR

   a. Select a leading
      option: .... ⬆/⬇, ⏎Enter
   - **At least** to set a minimum
     leading.
   - **Exactly** to set an exact
     leading.
   - **Multiple** to specify a percent-
     age by which to increase
     leading.

   b. Click **At** box .... Alt+Ⓐ
   c. Type value in points.

8. Click **OK** .... ⏎Enter

Set Paragraph Spacing

1. Position insertion point where
   text will be typed.

   OR

   Position insertion point in
   paragraph to change.

   OR

   Select paragraph(s) to change.

2. Click the **Home** tab .... Alt+Ⓗ

Paragraph Group

3. Click **Line Spacing** button ⊞⊟▾ to
   display a menu of options ... Ⓚ

   ✓ *Values on the menu are measured
   in lines.*

4. Do one of the following:
   - Click **Add Space Before
     Paragraph** to add 12 points
     before paragraph. .... Ⓑ
   - Click **Add Space After
     Paragraph** to add 12 points
     after paragraph .... Ⓐ
   - Click **Remove Space Before
     Paragraph** .... Ⓑ
   - Click **Remove Space After
     Paragraph** .... Ⓐ

   ✓ *The Remove Space options are
   only available if you have already
   added space.*

To use the Paragraph dialog box:

1. Position insertion point where
   text will be typed.

   OR

   Position insertion point in
   paragraph to change.

   OR

   Select paragraph(s) to change.

2. Click the **Home** tab .... Alt+Ⓗ

Paragraph Group

3. Click **Line Spacing**
   button ⊞⊟▾ .... Ⓚ

4. Click **Line Spacing**
   Options .... ⬇ 6x, ⏎Enter

   OR

   Click **Paragraph** group dialog
   box launcher ⊡ .... Ⓟ, Ⓖ

5. Click **Indents and Spacing**
   page tab .... Alt+Ⓘ

6. Click **Before** text box ...... Alt+Ⓑ

   OR

   Click **After** text box ...... Alt+Ⓕ

7. Type value in points.

   ✓ *By default spacing is in points.
   Type **li** after value to specify lines.*

8. Click **OK** .... ⏎Enter

EXERCISE DIRECTIONS

1. Start Word, if necessary.
2. Create a new document and save it as
   11PAYROLL_xx.
3. Display nonprinting characters, if necessary.
4. Open the AutoCorrect dialog box.
   a. Add the misspelled word **Magonlia** to the
      AutoCorrect list; replace it with the correctly
      spelled **Magnolia**.
   b. Add the misspelled word **personell** to the
      AutoCorrect list; replace it with the correctly
      spelled **personnel**.
   c. Add the two words **pay check** to the AutoCorrect
      list; replace them with the single word **paycheck**.
   d. Select all AutoCorrect option check boxes and
      then click OK to close the dialog box.

5. Set the line spacing in the document to Single.
6. Set the paragraph spacing to 0 points before and
   0 points after.
7. Begin typing the document shown in Illustration A.
   - Type the actual date in place of the text *Today's
     date*.

   ✓ *If Word displays wavy blue underlines under your text,
   right-click the text and click Ignore Rule on the shortcut
   menu.*

   - Type your own name in place of the text
     Student's Name.
   - Type the circled errors exactly as shown in the
     illustration.

   ✓ *Notice that Word automatically corrects the errors.*

   - Press Enter to start new paragraphs and leave
     blank lines as marked on the illustration.

8. After typing the first full paragraph in the memo (ending with the text **your pay check**), set the paragraph spacing to 11 points after.

9. Press Enter to start the next paragraph, leaving the equivalent of one line of blank space.

10. Type the second paragraph, press Enter, and type the first line in the list of information (Date).

11. Change the paragraph spacing back to 0 points after, press Enter, and finish typing the document as shown in Illustration A.

12. Save the document.

13. Horizontally align the text in the document as marked on the illustration.

    a. Select the lines marked for centering.

    b. Center the selected text.

    c. Select the paragraphs marked for justification.

    d. Justify the selected paragraphs.

    e. Select the lines marked for right alignment.

    f. Right-align the selected text.

14. Select the text *New Option* on the *Subject:* line near the top of the document and replace it with the text **Automatic Payroll Deposit**.

15. Check and correct the spelling and grammar in the document. Ignore all proper names.

16. Display the document in Print Preview.

17. Center the document vertically on the page.

18. Justify the document vertically.

19. Print the document.

20. Close the document, saving all changes.

Illustration A

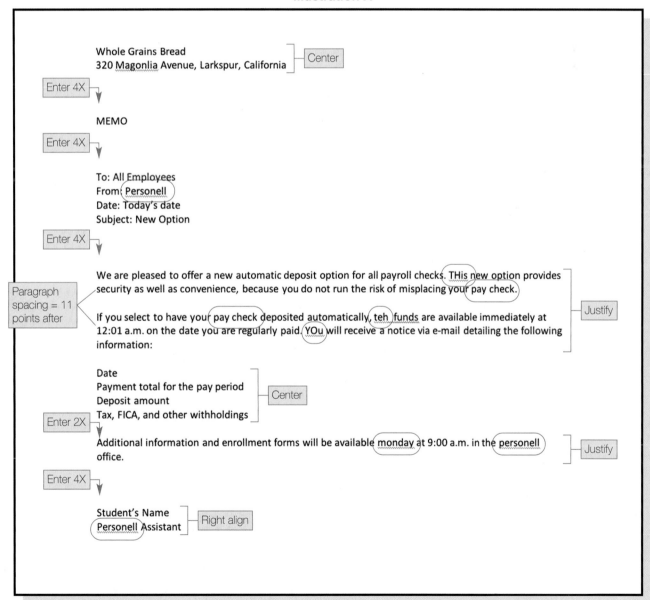

ON YOUR OWN

1. Create a new document in Word.
2. Save the file as **OWD11_xx**.
3. Add words that you commonly misspell to the AutoCorrect list.
4. Type a memo to your instructor introducing yourself. Use correct formatting for a memo, including line and paragraph spacing.
5. In the body of the memo, include your name (try misspelling it to see if AutoCorrect fixes it) and things you think are your strengths and your weaknesses. If you want, include information from the Mission Statement you created in the On Your Own section of Exercise 10.
6. Change the horizontal alignment of some of the text in the memo.
7. Change the vertical alignment of the document.
8. Check the spelling and grammar.
9. Print the document.
10. Ask someone in your class to read the document and offer suggestions.
11. Incorporate the suggestions.
12. Close the document, saving all changes.

Skills Covered

- **Format a Business Letter**
- **Insert the Date and Time**
- **Use Uppercase Mode**
- **Change Case**
- **Create an Envelope**

Software Skills Write business letters as a representative of your employer to communicate with other businesses, such as clients or suppliers, or to communicate with individuals, such as prospective employees. For example, you might write a business letter to request a job quote from a supplier or to inquire about a loan from a bank.

Application Skills You are the assistant to Mr. Frank Kaplan, the Franchise Manager for Whole Grains Bread. He has asked you to type a letter to a franchisee about opening a new shop outside California. In this exercise, you will compose a full-block business letter, and print an envelope for it.

TERMS

Case The specific use of upper- or lowercase letters.

Computer's clock The clock/calendar built into your computer's main processor to keep track of the current date and time.

Delivery address A recipient's address printed on the outside of an envelope.

Field A placeholder for data that might change.

Full block A style of letter in which all lines start flush with the left margin—that is, without a first-line indent.

Inside address The recipient's address typed in the letter above the salutation.

Letterhead Paper with a company's name and address already printed on it.

Modified block A style of letter in which some lines start at the center of the page.

Return address The author's address, typically appearing at the very top of the letter as well as in the upper-left corner of an envelope.

Salutation The line at the start of a letter including the greeting and the recipient's name, such as *Dear Mr. Doe.*

NOTES

Format a Business Letter

- There are different styles of business letters.
  - In a **full-block** business letter, all lines start flush with the left margin.
  - In a **modified-block** business letter, certain lines start at the center of the page.

  ✓ *Modified-block business letters will be covered in Exercise 13.*

- The parts of a business letter are the same regardless of the style.
- Vertical spacing is achieved by inserting blank lines between letter parts, or adjusting the paragraph spacing.

- Refer to the illustration on page 79 to identify the parts of a business letter.
  - **Return address** (may be omitted if the letter is printed on **letterhead** stationery)
  - Date
  - **Inside address**
  - **Salutation**
  - Body
  - Signature line
  - Title line (the job title of the letter writer)
  - Reference initials (the initials of the person who wrote the letter, followed by a slash, followed by the initials of the person who typed the letter)

  ✓ *Whenever you see "yo" as part of the reference initials in an exercise, type your own initials.*

  - Special notations (included only when appropriate):
  - Mail service notation indicates a special delivery method. It is typed in all capital letters, two lines below the date. Typical mail service notations include *CERTIFIED MAIL, REGISTERED MAIL,* or *BY HAND.*
  - Subject notation identifies or summarizes the letter topic. The word *Subject* may be typed in all capital letters or with just an initial capital. It is placed two lines below the salutation.

    ✓ *The word Re (meaning with regard to) is sometimes used in place of the word Subject.*

  - Enclosure or attachment notation indicates whether there are other items in the envelope. It is typed two lines below the reference initials in any of the following styles: *ENC., Enc., Encl., Enclosure, Attachment.*

    ✓ *If there are multiple items, the number may be typed in parentheses following the notation.*

  - Copy notation indicates if any other people are receiving copies of the same letter. It is typed two lines below either the enclosure notation, or reference initials, whichever is last. It may be typed as Copy to:, cc:, or pc: (photocopy) with the name(s) of the recipient(s) listed after the colon.

Insert the Date and Time

- Word can automatically enter today's date into a document.
- When you type the first four letters of the name of the current month, Word prompts you to press Enter to automatically complete the word.

- You can also use the Date and Time dialog box to insert the current date and/or time in a document.
- The inserted date and time are based on your **computer's clock**. A variety of date and time formats are available.
- If you want, you can insert the date and/or time as a **field**, so that they update automatically whenever you save or print the document.

Date and Time dialog box

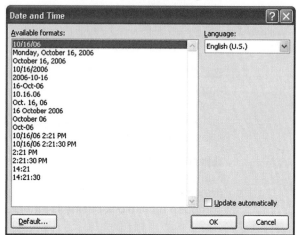

Use Uppercase Mode

- Use uppercase mode to type all capital letters without pressing the Shift key.
- Uppercase mode affects only letter characters.
- When Uppercase mode is on, the Caps Lock indicator on your keyboard is lit.

Change Case

- You can easily change the **case** of selected text in a document using the Change Case button in the Font group on the Home tab of the Ribbon.
- There are five case options:
  - Sentence case: First character in a sentence is uppercase.
  - lowercase: All characters are lowercase.
  - UPPERCASE: All characters are uppercase.
  - Capitalize Each Word: First character in each word is uppercase.
  - tOGGLE cASE: Case is reversed for all selected text.

Create an Envelope

- Use Word's Envelopes and Labels feature to automatically set up an envelope for printing.
- If a letter document is open on-screen, Word picks up the inside address for the envelope's **delivery address**.
- You can type any delivery address as well as a return address.
- You can select to omit the return address if you are printing on an envelope that has the return address pre-printed, or if you plan to use return address labels.
- Before printing an envelope, you should be certain the envelope is correctly inserted in your printer, and that the printer is set to print an envelope.
- Consult your printer's manual or ask your instructor for information on printing envelopes.
- Alternatively, you can print on standard paper to see how the content will display, without using an envelope.

- You can print the envelope immediately or add it to the beginning of the open document and save it to print later.

Envelopes tab of the Envelopes and Labels dialog box

PROCEDURES

Format a Full-Block Business Letter

1. Start 2" from the top of the page.

   ✓ If you are using stationery with a printed letterhead, you may have to adjust the spacing.

2. Insert the date.
3. Leave one blank line and type the mail service notation.
4. Leave three blank lines and type the inside address.
5. Leave a blank line and type the salutation.
6. Leave one blank line and type the subject notation.
7. Leave a blank line and type the letter body.
8. Leave a blank line and type the closing.
9. Leave three blank lines and type the signature line.

10. On the next line, type the title.
11. Starting on the next line, type the lines of the return address.

   ✓ If you are using letterhead stationery, omit the return address.

12. Leave a blank line and type the reference initials.
13. Leave a blank line and type the enclosure notation.
14. Leave a blank line and type the copy notation.

Insert the Date and/or Time

1. Position the insertion point.
2. Type first four characters of name of current month.
3. Press **Enter** .... ↵Enter

OR

1. Click **Insert** tab .... Alt + N

   Text Group

2. Click **Date & Time** .... D
3. Click the desired format.

   ✓ Select Update automatically checkbox if you want date and/or time to update when you save or print document.

4. Click **OK** .... ↵Enter

Use Uppercase Mode

1. Press **Caps Lock** .... Caps Lock
2. Type **text**.

To turn off Uppercase Mode:

- Press **Caps Lock** .... Caps Lock

Change Case

1. Select text to format.
2. Click **Home** tab .... `Alt`+`H`

   Font Group

3. Click **Change Case**
   button `Aa▾` .... `7`
4. Click desired case option:
   - ■ **S**entence case .... `S`
   - ■ **l**owercase .... `L`
   - ■ **U**PPERCASE .... `U`
   - ■ **C**apitalize Each Word .... `C`
   - ■ **t**OGGLE cASE .... `T`

Create an Envelope

1. Click **Mailings** tab .... `Alt`+`M`

   Create Group

2. Click **Envelopes** button `≡` ...... `E`
3. Type **D**elivery address ...... `Alt`+`D`

   ✓ *If inside address is already entered, skip to step 4.*

4. Type **R**eturn address .... `Alt`+`R`
   OR

   Click to select **O**mit
   check box .... `Alt`+`M`

   ✓ *If Omit check box is selected, you cannot type in Return address text box.*

5. Click **P**rint to print
   envelope .... `Alt`+`P`

OR

Click **Add to Document** to add
envelope to document for
printing later .... `Alt`+`A`

To print an envelope added to a document:

1. Open document containing envelope.
2. Click anywhere within the delivery address or return address.

   ✓ *This insures that the envelope is the current page.*

3. Click **Office Button** `≡` ...... `Alt`+`F`
4. Click **P**rint .... `P`
5. Click **Curr**e**nt page** option
   button .... `Alt`+`E`
6. Click **OK** .... `↵Enter`

EXERCISE DIRECTIONS

Create the Letter

1. Start Word, if necessary.
2. Create a new document and save it as **12EXPAND_xx**.
3. Set the line spacing to Single and the paragraph spacing to 0 points before and after.
4. Type the letter shown in Illustration A.

   ✓ *Word may display ScreenTips as you type certain parts of the letter (for example, CERTIFIED MAIL). Simply ignore them and continue typing. If Word displays a wavy blue underline, right-click the text and click Ignore Rule on the shortcut menu.*

   - Press `↵Enter` between parts of the letter to leave blank lines as indicated.

   ✓ *Alternatively, you could adjust the paragraph spacing.*

   - Insert the current date using the MONTH DAY, YEAR format found third from the top in the Date and Time dialog box.

   - Set the date so that it does not update automatically.
   - Use Uppercase mode to type the mail notation, and all occurrences of the company name (**Whole Grains Bread**).

5. Change the case of the company name to Capitalize Each Word.
6. Change the case back to all uppercase.
7. Check and correct the spelling and grammar in the document.

   - Ignore all proper names.

   ✓ *If the document does not fit on one page, you may have inserted too many blank lines. Make sure you have non-printing characters displayed so you can see the paragraph marks, count the marks, and delete any extras.*

8. Save changes to the document.
9. Preview the document.
10. Print the document.

Create the Envelope

1. Create an envelope for the letter.
   - Use the inside address from the letter as the delivery address.
   - Use your name and address as the return address.
2. Add the envelope to the document.
   - When prompted to save the new return address as the default, choose No.

3. Preview the document.
4. Print the envelope only.

   ✓ *Make sure the insertion point is in the return address or delivery address of the envelope, and select to print the current page in the Print dialog box.*

5. Close the document, saving all changes.

Illustration A

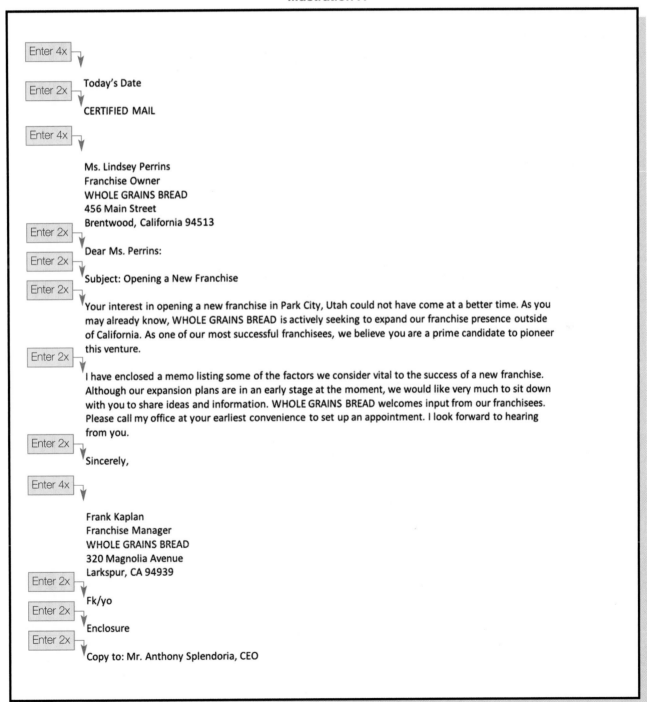

Enter 4x

Today's Date

Enter 2x

CERTIFIED MAIL

Enter 4x

Ms. Lindsey Perrins
Franchise Owner
WHOLE GRAINS BREAD
456 Main Street
Brentwood, California 94513

Enter 2x

Dear Ms. Perrins:

Enter 2x

Subject: Opening a New Franchise

Enter 2x

Your interest in opening a new franchise in Park City, Utah could not have come at a better time. As you may already know, WHOLE GRAINS BREAD is actively seeking to expand our franchise presence outside of California. As one of our most successful franchisees, we believe you are a prime candidate to pioneer this venture.

Enter 2x

I have enclosed a memo listing some of the factors we consider vital to the success of a new franchise. Although our expansion plans are in an early stage at the moment, we would like very much to sit down with you to share ideas and information. WHOLE GRAINS BREAD welcomes input from our franchisees. Please call my office at your earliest convenience to set up an appointment. I look forward to hearing from you.

Enter 2x

Sincerely,

Enter 4x

Frank Kaplan
Franchise Manager
WHOLE GRAINS BREAD
320 Magnolia Avenue
Larkspur, CA 94939

Enter 2x

Fk/yo

Enter 2x

Enclosure

Enter 2x

Copy to: Mr. Anthony Splendoria, CEO

ON YOUR OWN

1. Create a new document in Word.
2. Save the document as **OWD12_xx**.
3. Representing your school or organization, draft a full-block business letter to a local newspaper asking them to include information about upcoming events in a calendar listing. School events might include athletic contests, such as a homecoming football game, club activities, field trips, band and choir concerts, or vacation days. Use proper formatting, including line and paragraph spacing.
4. Insert the current date so that it does not update.
5. In the letter, indicate that you have attached the necessary information and that you are sending a copy to your instructor.
6. Check the spelling and grammar in the document.
7. Print the document.
8. Ask someone in your class to read the letter and provide comments and suggestions.
9. Incorporate the suggestions into the document.
10. Create an envelope for the letter and add it to the document.
11. Print just the envelope.
12. Save your changes, close the document, and exit Word when you are finished.

Exercise | 13

Skills Covered

- ■ **Set Tabs**
- ■ **Format a Modified-Block Business Letter**
- ■ **Shrink One Page**

Software Skills   You use tabs to align text in a document, such as the date in a modified-block business letter. If a letter is just a bit too long to fit on a single page, use *Shrink One Page* to automatically reduce the printed length of a document so it fits on one page.

Application Skills   The Manager of the pro shop at the Michigan Avenue Athletic Club has asked you to type a letter to a supplier regarding an incomplete order. In this exercise, you compose a modified-block business letter using tabs and the Shrink One Page feature.

TERMS

Font A set of characters with a specific size and style.

Tab The measurement of the space the insertion point advances when you press the Tab key.

Tab leader A series of characters inserted along the line between the location of the insertion point when you press the Tab key and the tab stop.

Tab stop The location on a horizontal line to which the insertion point advances when you press the Tab key.

NOTES

Tab stops on the horizontal ruler

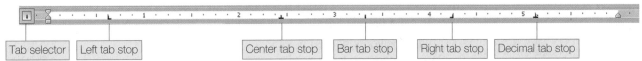

Tab selector | Left tab stop | Center tab stop | Bar tab stop | Right tab stop | Decimal tab stop

Set Tabs

- ■ **Tabs** are used to indent a single line of text.
- ■ Each time you press the Tab key, the insertion point advances to the next set **tab stop**.
- ■ There are five types of tab stops:
    - • Left: Text starts flush left with the tab stop.
    - • Right: Text ends flush right with the tab stop.
    - • Center: Text is centered on the tab stop.
    - • Decimal: Decimal points are aligned with the tab stop.
    - • Bar: A vertical bar is displayed at the tab stop position. Text starts to the right of the bar.
- ■ By default, left tab stops are set every 0.5" on the horizontal ruler.
- ■ You can set any type of tab stop at any point along the ruler.

- To select a tab type, click the Tab selector box at the left end of the ruler until the tab you want to use displays.

  ✓ *Note that after the five tab types display on the Tab selector, the first line indent and hanging indent markers display. Setting indents is covered in Exercise 27.*

- You can use the Tabs dialog box to set precise tab stops.

- You can also select a **tab leader** in the Tabs dialog box.

- You can set tabs before you type new text, for the current existing paragraph, or for selected multiple paragraphs.

- Once you set tabs, the formatting will be carried forward each time you press ⏎Enter key to start a new paragraph.

Tabs dialog box

Format a Modified-Block Business Letter

- A modified-block style letter is set up with all lines starting flush with the left margin except the date, closing, signature, and title lines, which begin at the center point of the page.

  ✓ *The parts of a modified-block style letter are the same as those of a full-block style letter. The special notations are used when appropriate.*

- A left tab stop set at the center point of the page enables you to position the insertion point quickly where you need it.

  ✓ *Using a center tab stop or centered alignment centers the text around the tab stop. You must use a left tab stop in order to position the text to start at the center point of the page.*

Shrink One Page

- Shrink One Page 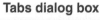 automatically reduces the **font** size and spacing in a document just enough to fit the document on one less page.

- Use Shrink One Page if the last page of a document contains only a small amount of text.

- The command for the Shrink One Page feature is available only in Print Preview mode.

PROCEDURES

Set Tabs

1. Click Tab selector until desired tab type displays.

   ✓ *Each time you click, the tab stop icon on the tab selector changes. Stop when tab stop you want displays.*

2. Position insertion point in paragraph to format.

   OR

   Select paragraphs to format.

3. Click ruler at location where you want to set tab stop.

To set a precise tab stop:

1. Position insertion point in paragraph to format.
   OR
   Select paragraphs to format.

2. Click **Home** tab .... Alt+H

   Paragraph Group

3. Click **Paragraph** dialog box launcher ⬚ .... P, G

4. Click **Tabs** .... Alt+T

5. Click option button for desired tab type:
   - **Left** .... Alt+L
   - **Center** .... Alt+C
   - **Right** .... Alt+R
   - **Decimal** .... Alt+D
   - **Bar** .... Alt+B

6. Click in the **Tab stop position** box .... Alt+T

7. Type precise position.

8. Click **Set** .... Alt+S

9. Repeat steps 5 - 8 to set additional tab stops.

10. Click **OK** .... ⏎Enter

To select a tab leader:

1. Position insertion point in paragraph to format.

   OR

   Select paragraphs to format.

2. Click **Home** tab .... Alt+H

   Paragraph Group

3. Click **Paragraph** dialog box launcher ☐ .... P, G

4. Click **Tabs** .... Alt+T

5. Select existing tab.

   OR

   Set new tab.

6. Click option button for desired tab leader:

   ◼ **1** None .... Alt+1
   ◼ **2** .... Alt+2
   ◼ **3** ------- .... Alt+3
   ◼ **4** ____ .... Alt+4

7. Click **Set** .... Alt+S

8. Repeat steps 5 - 7 to set additional tab stops.

9. Click **OK** .... ↵Enter

To clear a tab stop:

1. Position insertion point in paragraph to format.

   OR

   Select paragraphs to format.

2. Drag tab stop marker off ruler.

   OR

   a. Click **Home** tab .... Alt+H

   Paragraph Group

   b. Click **Paragraph** dialog box launcher ☐ .... P, G

   c. Click **Tabs** .... Alt+T

   d. Select tab stop to clear.

   e. Click **Clear** .... Alt+E

   f. Repeat steps d and e to clear additional tab stops.

   g. Click **OK** .... ↵Enter

To clear all tab stops:

1. Position insertion point in paragraph to format.

   OR

   Select paragraphs to format.

2. Click **Home** tab .... Alt+H

   Paragraph Group

3. Click **Paragraph** dialog box launcher ☐ .... P, G

4. Click **Tabs** .... Alt+T

5. Click **Clear All** .... Alt+A

6. Click **OK** .... ↵Enter

Format a Modified-Block Business Letter

1. Start 2" from top of page

   ✓ If you are using stationery with a printed letterhead, you may have to adjust the spacing.

2. Set left tab stop at 3.25", or at center of page.

   ✓ By default, the page width is set to 6.5", which makes 3.25" the center of the page. If you have a wider or narrower page, you may have to adjust the position of the left tab stop so that it is at the center.

3. Press **Tab** .... Tab⇄

4. Insert date.

5. Leave three blank lines and type inside address.

6. Leave a blank line and type the salutation.

7. Leave a blank line and type the letter body.

8. Leave a blank line.

9. Press **Tab**.

10. Type the closing.

11. Leave three blank lines.

12. Press **Tab**.

13. Type signature line.

14. Move to next line and press **Tab**.

15. Type title line.

16. Leave a blank line and type reference initials.

Shrink One Page

1. Click **Office Button** ☐ ..... Alt+F

2. Point to **Print** .... W

3. Click **Print Preview** V

   Preview Group

4. Click **Shrink One Page** button ☐ .... Alt+P, K

EXERCISE DIRECTIONS

1. Start Word, if necessary.

2. Create a new document and save it as **13ORDER_xx**.

3. Set a left tab stop at the center of the page (by default, 3.25" on the horizontal ruler).

4. Set the paragraph spacing to 0 points before and after, leaving the default 1.15 line spacing unchanged.

5. Type the letter shown in Illustration A.

   ✓ When you type the letter as shown in the illustration, it will not fit on a single page.

   ✓ If Word displays wavy blue underlines, right-click the text and click Ignore Rule on the shortcut menu.

   ● Position the date, closing, signature, and title at the tab stop.

   ● Press the Enter key between parts of the letter as indicated.

   ● Insert the current date using the MONTH DAY, YEAR format found third from the top in the Date and Time dialog box.

   ● Set the date so that it does not update automatically.

6. Check the spelling and grammar and make changes as suggested.

- Ignore all proper names.

7. Display the document in Print Preview.

8. Shrink the document to fit on a single page.

9. Print the document.

10. Close the document, saving all changes.

Illustration A

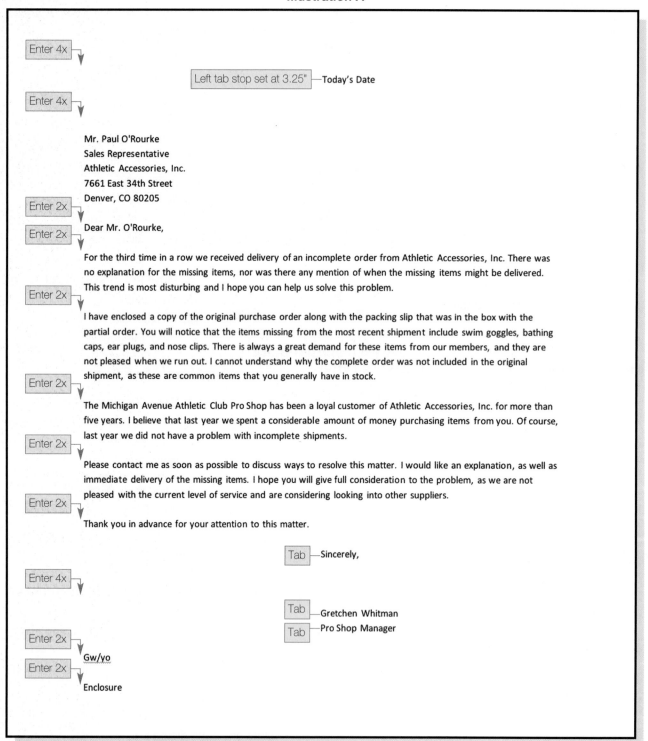

ON YOUR OWN

1. Create a new document in Word.
2. Save the file as **OWD13_xx**.
3. As a representative of a school organization, draft a modified-block business letter to a company that delivers music CDs by mail, telling the company that your organization did not receive the complete order in the last shipment. Use proper formatting including tabs and line and paragraph spacing.
4. List the music CDs that you ordered and indicate which titles were missing in the shipment.
5. Preview the document. Make sure it fits on one page.
6. Print one copy of the document.
7. Ask someone in your class to read the letter and to provide comments and suggestions.
8. Incorporate the suggestions into the document.
9. Close the document, saving all changes.

Skills Covered

- **Format a Personal Business Letter**
- **About Fonts**
- **Change the Font**
- **Change Font Size**
- **Apply Font Styles**
- **Apply Underlines**
- **Create Labels**

Software Skills Write personal business letters to find a job or communicate with businesses such as your bank or your insurance company. For example, you might write a personal business letter to your insurance company to ask about a claim that needs to be paid. The letter serves as a formal record of your inquiry. Use fonts, font sizes, underlines, and font styles to dress up the appearance of a document. Fonts are a basic means of applying formatting to text and characters. They can set a mood, command attention, and convey a message. Printed labels are useful for addressing envelopes that don't fit in your printer, or for creating return address labels.

Application Skills You are interested in obtaining a position as a tour guide for Voyager Travel Adventures. In this exercise, you will create and format a personal business letter asking about job opportunities. You will also create return address labels which you will save in a separate document. Finally, you will create a **resume** to include with the letter.

TERMS

Font A complete set of characters in a specific face, style, and size.

Font face The character design of a font set.

Font size The height of an uppercase letter in a font set.

Font style The slant and weight of characters in a font set.

Resume A document listing information about a person's education, work experience, and interests.

Sans serif A font that has straight edges.

Script A font that looks like handwriting.

Serif A font that has curved or extended edges.

NOTES

Format a Personal Business Letter

- A business letter written on behalf of an individual instead of on behalf of another business is considered a personal business letter.

- A personal business letter includes the same elements as a business letter, minus the title line and reference initials, and plus a return address.

  ✓ If the paper has a letterhead, omit the return address.

- A personal business letter can be full block or modified block.

  - In full block, type the return address following the signature.

  - In modified block, type the return address above the date.

    ✓ For more information on the parts of a business letter, refer to Exercise 12.

About Fonts

- Each **font** set includes upper- and lowercase letters, numbers, and punctuation marks.

- There are three basic categories of **font faces**:
  - **Serif** fonts are easy to read and are often used for document text.

A Serif Font

  - **Sans serif** fonts are often used for headings.

A Sans Serif Font

  - **Script** face fonts are often used to simulate handwriting on invitations or announcements.

A Script Font

- A fourth font category includes decorative fonts, which may have embellishments such as curlicues or double lines designed to dress up or enhance the characters.

A Decorative Font

- Both Microsoft Office and Windows come with built-in fonts; you can install additional fonts.

- You can set the tone of a document by putting thought into the fonts you select.

- More than two or three font faces makes a document look disjointed and unprofessional.

Change the Font

- The default Word 2007 font is Calibri, a sans serif font.

- The current font name displays in the Font box on the Home tab of the Ribbon.

- You can change the font of existing text, or you can select a font before you type new text.

- Click the Font box drop-down arrow in the Font group or on the Mini toolbar to display a menu of all available fonts. The fonts display in alphabetical order, but theme fonts and recently used fonts are listed at the top.

  ✓ *Theme fonts are covered in Exercise 31.*

- To preview how selected text will look in a particular font, rest the mouse pointer on the font name in the Font list.

Font list

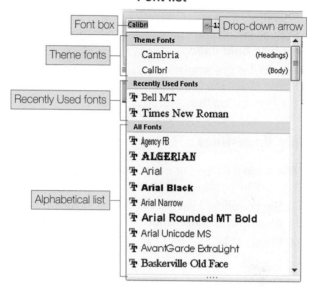

Change Font Size

- **Font size** is measured in points. There are 72 points in an inch.

- The default Word 2007 font size is 11 points.

- The current font size displays in the Font Size box on the Home tab of the Ribbon.

- Click the Font Size drop-down arrow in the Font group or on the Mini toolbar to display a menu of font sizes.

- Alternatively, you can select a font size in the Font dialog box.

- You can also use the Grow Font [A˄] and Shrink Font [A˅] buttons to adjust the font size by one point.

Font size list

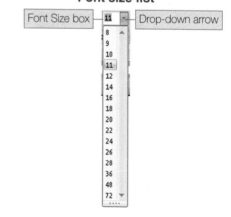

Apply Font Styles

- The most common **font styles** are **bold** B and *italic* I.

- When no style is applied to a font, it is called regular.

- Font styles can be combined for different effects, such as ***bold italic***.

- Font styles are available in the Font group on the Home tab of the Ribbon, on the Mini toolbar, or in the Font dialog box.

Apply Underlines

- There are 17 types of underline styles available in Word, which include:

  - <u>Single</u> (underlines all characters, including non-printing characters such as spaces and tabs)

  - <u>Words</u> <u>only</u>

  - <u>Double</u>

  - Dotted

- Some underlines are available from the Underline drop-down list in the Font group on the Home tab of the Ribbon, or you can select from the complete list in the Font dialog box.

Font dialog box

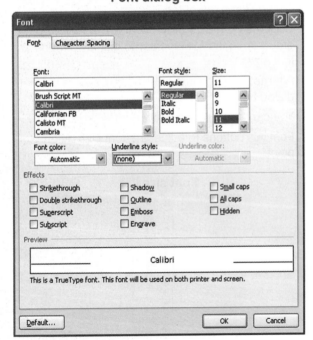

Create Labels

- Use Word's Label feature to create mailing labels, file folder labels, or CD/DVD labels.

- The Label feature automatically sets up a document to print on predefined label types.

- You select the manufacturer and label type loaded in the printer.

- By default, Word creates a full page of labels using the inside address from the current document.

- You can change the default to create labels using the return address or to create a single label.

- You can print the labels or save them in a new document to print later.

  ✓ *A label document is set up as a table. Tables are covered in Lesson 6.*

Labels tab of the Envelopes and Labels dialog box

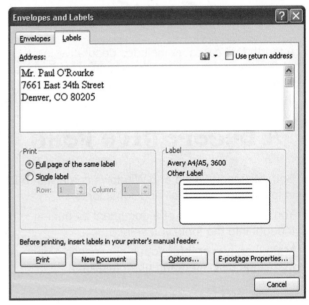

PROCEDURES

Change the Font

1. Select text.

   OR

   Position insertion point where new text will be typed.

2. Click **Font** drop-down arrow on Mini toolbar.

   OR

   a. Click **Home** tab............Alt+H

   Font Group

   b. Click **Font** drop-down arrow ....F, F, ↓

3. Click name of font to apply.

   ✓ *If necessary, scroll down the list to locate desired font.*

   OR

1. Select text.

   OR

   Position insertion point where new text will be typed.

2. Click **Home** tab................Alt+H

   Font Group

3. Click **Font** dialog box launcher ⊡ ....F, N

4. Click **Fon_t** tab................Alt+N

5. Click **Font** box................Alt+F

6. Click font to apply...........↓, ↑

7. Click **OK**................↵Enter

To Preview Selected Text in a Particular Font:

1. Select text.

2. Click **Home** tab................Alt+H

   Font Group

3. Click **Font** drop-down arrow ....F, F, ↓

4. Rest mouse pointer on name of font to preview.............↓, ↑

   ✓ *If necessary, scroll down the list to locate desired font.*

Change Font Size

1. Select text.

   OR

   Position insertion point where new text will be typed.

2. Click **Font Size** drop-down arrow on Mini toolbar.

   OR

   a. Click **Home** tab............Alt+H

   Font Group

   b. Click **Font** drop-down arrow ....F, S, ↓

3. Click font size to apply.

   ✓ *If necessary, scroll down the list to locate desired size.*

   OR

1. Select text.

   OR

   Position insertion point where new text will be typed.

2. Click **Home** tab................Alt+H

   Font Group

3. Click **Font** dialog box launcher ⊡ ....F, N

4. Click **Size** box................Alt+S

5. Click size to apply...........↓, ↑

6. Click **OK**................↵Enter

   ✓ *You can also type desired font size directly into Font Size box, then press Enter. You can even type half sizes, such as 10.5, 12.5, and so on.*

To Preview Selected Text in a Particular Size:

1. Select text.

2. Click **Home** tab................Alt+H

   Font Group

3. Click **Font Size** drop-down arrow ....F, S, ↓

4. Rest mouse pointer on size to preview.............↓, ↑

   ✓ *If necessary, scroll down the list to locate desired size.*

To Increase Font Size by One Point:

1. Select text.

   OR

   Position insertion point where new text will be typed.

2. Click **Grow Font** button A˙ on Mini toolbar.

   OR

   a. Click **Home** tab............Alt+H

   Font Group

   b. Click **Grow Font** button A˙ ....F, G

To Decrease Font Size by One Point:

1. Select text.

   OR

   Position insertion point where new text will be typed.

2. Click **Shrink Font** button A˙ on Mini toolbar.

   OR

   a. Click **Home** tab............Alt+H

   Font Group

   b. Click **Shrink Font** button A˙ ....F, K

Apply Font Styles

1. Select text.

2. Click font style button on Mini toolbar:

   ■ **Bold** B................Ctrl+B

   ■ *Italic* I................Ctrl+I

   OR

1. Select text.

   OR

   Position insertion point where new text will be typed.

2. Click **Home** tab................Alt+H

   Font Group

3. Click font style button

   ■ **Bold** B................1

   ■ *Italic* I................2

OR

1. Select text.

   OR

   Position insertion point where new text will be typed.
2. Click **Home** tab `Alt`+`H`

   Font Group
3. Click **Font** dialog box launcher 🔲 `F`, `N`
4. Click **Font Style** box `Alt`+`Y`
5. Click style to apply `↓`, `↑`
6. Click **OK** `↵Enter`

   ✓ *Repeat steps to remove font style.*

Apply Underlines *(Ctrl+U)*

1. Select text.

   OR

   Position insertion point where new text will be typed.
2. Click **Home** tab `Alt`+`H`

   Font Group
3. Click **Underline** button `U ▾` drop-down arrow `3`
4. Click desired underline style `↓`, `↑`, `↵Enter`

   OR

1. Select text.

   OR

   Position insertion point where new text will be typed.
2. Click **Home** tab `Alt`+`H`

   Font Group
3. Click **Font** dialog box launcher 🔲 `F`, `N`

OR

   a. Click **Underline** button `U ▾` drop-down arrow `3`
   b. Click **More Underlines** `M`
4. Click **Underline Style** box `Alt`+`U`
5. Click style to apply `↓`, `↑`

   ✓ *Click (None) to remove underline.*

6. Click **OK** `↵Enter`

Remove Formatting *(Ctrl+Spacebar)*

1. Select text.

   OR

   Position insertion point within text.
2. Click **Home** tab `Alt`+`H`

   Font Group
3. Click **Clear Formatting** button 🖉 `E`

Create a Single Label

1. Click **Mailings** tab `Alt`+`M`

   Create Group
2. Click **Labels** button 🖺 `L`
3. Type **Address** `Alt`+`A`

   ✓ *If inside address is already entered, skip to step 4.*

4. Click **Single label** option button `Alt`+`N`
5. Click **Options** `Alt`+`O`
6. Select option from **Label vendors** list `Alt`+`V`
7. Select option from **Product number** list `Alt`+`U`

   ✓ *Make sure correct printer and tray information is selected.*

8. Click **OK** `↵Enter`
9. Make sure labels are correctly loaded in printer.
10. Click **Print** `Alt`+`P`

Create Return Address Labels

1. Click **Mailings** tab `Alt`+`M`

   Create Group
2. Click **Labels** button 🖺 `L`
3. Click to select **Use return address** check box `Alt`+`R`
4. Click **Options** `Alt`+`O`
5. Select option from **Label vendors** list `Alt`+`V`
6. Select option from **Product number** list `Alt`+`U`

   ✓ *Make sure correct printer and tray information is selected.*

7. Click **OK** `↵Enter`
8. Make sure labels are correctly loaded in printer.
9. Click **Print** `Alt`+`P`

   OR

   a. Click **New Document** to save labels in a separate document `Alt`+`D`

   ✓ *If prompted to save the return address, click **No** `N`*

   b. Save label document as desired.

EXERCISE DIRECTIONS

Create the Letter

1. Start Word, if necessary.
2. Create a new document and save it as **14REQUEST_xx**.
3. Set the paragraph spacing to 0 points before and after and the line spacing to Single.
4. Type the letter shown in Illustration A.
   - Use the full-block format for the letter.
   - Insert today's date using the Month Date, Year format. Make sure the date will not update automatically.
   - Use the default font and font size.
5. Check the spelling and grammar.

Create the Labels

1. Create return address labels for the document.
   - Use the return address in the document.
   - Create a full page of the same label.
   - If you have labels available, select the label manufacturer and number on the label sheet.
   - If you do not have labels available select Avery 5130.
2. Save the label document as **14LABELS_xx**.

   ✓ Do not save the return address as the default.

3. Preview the new label document.

4. Print the label document.

   ✓ You can print the labels on standard letter-sized paper if you do not have labels available.

5. Close the label document, saving all changes.
6. Close the letter document, saving all changes.

Create the Resume

1. Create a new document and save it as **14RESUME_xx**.
2. Set the line spacing to Single and the paragraph spacing to 0 points before and after.
3. Type the document shown in Illustration B.
4. Apply font formatting, tabs, and alignments as marked.

   ✓ Unless otherwise marked, use the default 11-point Calibri font.

5. Leave one blank line between each section as shown.
6. Preview the **14RESUME_xx** document. If necessary, shrink the document to fit on a single page.
7. Print the document.
8. Close the **14RESUME_xx** document, saving all changes

Curriculum Connection: Language Arts

Alliteration

Alliteration is the repetition of a letter or sound, usually at the beginning of words in a sentence. It is often used in poetry to help people remember a phrase, or just for fun. Some alliterative sentences are even called tongue twisters, because they can be very difficult to say out loud! For example: Peter Piper picked a peck of pickled peppers.

Write with Alliteration

Use alliteration to write a poem, short story, or tongue-twister. Try to include at least five repetitions of a letter or sound. You can even expand the work to include more than one example of alliteration.

Your Street Address
Your City, Your State, Your Postal Code

Today's date

Ms. Maria Sanchez
President
Voyager Travel Adventures
1635 Logan Street
Denver, CO 80205

Dear Ms. Sanchez:

I am writing to inquire about tour leader opportunities at Voyager Travel Adventures. I recently graduated from the state university with a degree in recreational management, and a minor in business administration. I am looking for a position that will challenge my abilities both physically and mentally, and I believe that Voyager Travel Adventures offers just that.

While studying for my degree, I worked as a trip leader for teen adventure tours during the summer and school vacations. I also worked as a lifeguard for the city, and volunteered as a youth counselor at a local outdoor education facility. I believe that my experience and positive outlook on life combined with my knowledge of nature and first aid make me uniquely suited for a job at your company.

I am available to begin work immediately, and would love to schedule an appointment for an interview at your earliest convenience. Please refer to my enclosed resume for additional information.

I look forward to hearing from you soon.

Sincerely,

Your Name

Enc.

Illustration B

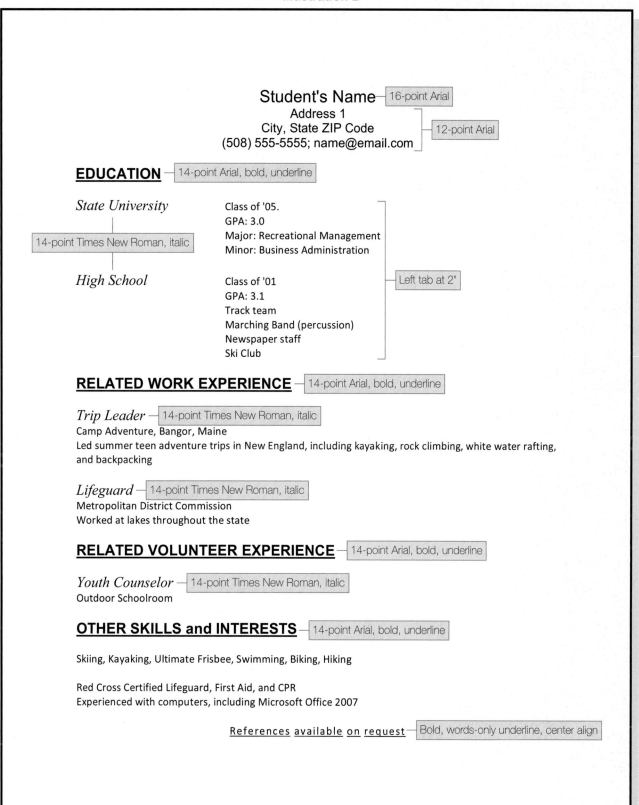

Student's Name —[16-point Arial]
Address 1
City, State ZIP Code —[12-point Arial]
(508) 555-5555; name@email.com

EDUCATION —[14-point Arial, bold, underline]

State University —[14-point Times New Roman, italic]

Class of '05.
GPA: 3.0
Major: Recreational Management
Minor: Business Administration

High School

Class of '01 —[Left tab at 2"]
GPA: 3.1
Track team
Marching Band (percussion)
Newspaper staff
Ski Club

RELATED WORK EXPERIENCE —[14-point Arial, bold, underline]

Trip Leader —[14-point Times New Roman, italic]
Camp Adventure, Bangor, Maine
Led summer teen adventure trips in New England, including kayaking, rock climbing, white water rafting, and backpacking

Lifeguard —[14-point Times New Roman, italic]
Metropolitan District Commission
Worked at lakes throughout the state

RELATED VOLUNTEER EXPERIENCE —[14-point Arial, bold, underline]

Youth Counselor —[14-point Times New Roman, italic]
Outdoor Schoolroom

OTHER SKILLS and INTERESTS —[14-point Arial, bold, underline]

Skiing, Kayaking, Ultimate Frisbee, Swimming, Biking, Hiking

Red Cross Certified Lifeguard, First Aid, and CPR
Experienced with computers, including Microsoft Office 2007

References available on request —[Bold, words-only underline, center align]

ON YOUR OWN

1. Create a new document in Word.
2. Save the file as **OWD14_xx**.
3. Draft a personal business letter. For example, you might write a letter asking about summer job opportunities. If you have a job, you could write to your employer asking to take a vacation day in the coming month. You can also draft a personal letter to a company with whom you do business asking for credit on returned merchandise or to a college asking about application requirements. Record stores, clothing stores, or sporting goods stores are companies you might use.
4. Ask a classmate to review the letter and offer comments and suggestions. Incorporate the comments and suggestions into the document.
5. Create your own return address labels using the return address from your letter, and save them in a separate document with the name **OWD14-2_xx**.
6. Check the spelling and grammar before printing the documents.
7. Save your changes, close all open documents, and exit Word when you are finished

Critical Thinking

Application Skills   You are the manager of the café at Michigan Avenue Athletic Club. On a recent trip to California you ate at a Whole Grains Bread franchise, and you are interested in offering some of their products at your café. In this exercise, you will start by creating a business letter proposing the idea to the sales manager at Whole Grains Bread. Next, you will create an envelope for the letter along with return address labels. Finally, you will create a flyer about the café that you can attach to the letter. You will use alignments and font formatting to make the flyer visually exciting.

EXERCISE DIRECTIONS

Create the Letter

1. Start Word, if necessary.
2. Create a new document and save it as **15PROPOSAL_xx**.
3. Display nonprinting characters.
4. Make sure AutoCorrect is enabled.
5. Set the line spacing to Single and the paragraph spacing to 0 points before and after, and then type the letter in Illustration A exactly as shown, including all circled errors.

    ✓ *Notice that AutoCorrect automatically inserts the accent when you type the word* **café**.

6. Insert the date in the Month Date, Year format so that it does not update automatically.
7. Correct spelling and grammatical errors.
    - Add your name to the dictionary, if necessary.
    - Ignore all proper names.
    - If necessary, correct all spelling errors that AutoCorrect does not automatically change.
8. Search the thesaurus to find an appropriate replacement for the word *variety*.
9. Save the changes you have made to the document.
10. Display the document in Print Preview.
11. Return the document to Print Layout view.

Create an Envelope and Labels

1. Create an envelope for the letter and add it to the document. Omit the return address.
2. Print the envelope and the document.
3. Create return address mailing labels for yourself using the following information:

    Your Name

    Café Manager

    Michigan Avenue Athletic Club

    235 Michigan Avenue

    Chicago, IL 60601

    ✓ *If you have actual labels, use the manufacturer and label number on the package. Otherwise, use Avery 5130.*

4. Save the labels document with the name **15RETURN_xx**.
5. Display the **15RETURN_xx** document in Print Preview, and then print it.

    ✓ *If you do not have labels available, print it on regular paper.*

6. Close all open documents, saving all changes.

Create a Flyer

1. Create a new document.
2. Save the document as **15FLYER_***xx.*
3. Display nonprinting characters.
4. Type the document shown in Illustration B, using the specified alignments, font formatting, and tabs.
5. Check the spelling and grammar in the document.
6. Display the document in Print Preview.
7. If the document is longer than one page, shrink it to fit; if it is shorter than one page, adjust the vertical alignment to improve the appearance, as necessary.
8. Print the document.
9. Share the flyer with a classmate and ask for comments and suggestions.
10. Incorporate the comments and suggestions into the document.
11. Close the document, saving all changes

Illustration A

Today's date —— Insert the date in month, date, year format

Ms. Carol Chen
Sales Manager
Whole Grains Bread
320 Magnolia Avenue
Larkspur, CA 94939

Dear Ms. Chen:

On a recent trip to California I had the good fortune of eating in a Whole Grains Bread restarant. I was quite impressed with the quality and variety of the the food, as well as the atmosphere and the service... The franchise owner gave me your name and address along with the information that you may be interested in expanding outside the california area.

As the managers of an athletic club café that prides itself on ofering healthy yet satisfying food, I is very interested in learning more about the Whole Grains Bread product line. If possible, I would like very much to carry some of your items in our café ALternatively, we may be interested in becoming a frenchise.

I have attached a flyer that we use to advertise specials and events to our members so that you can see some of the items we have now, and how we market them. I think the flyer illustrates the spirit and enthusiesm of our club.

I looks forward to hearing from you soon.

Sincerely,

Your Name
Café Manager

Attachment

Illustration B

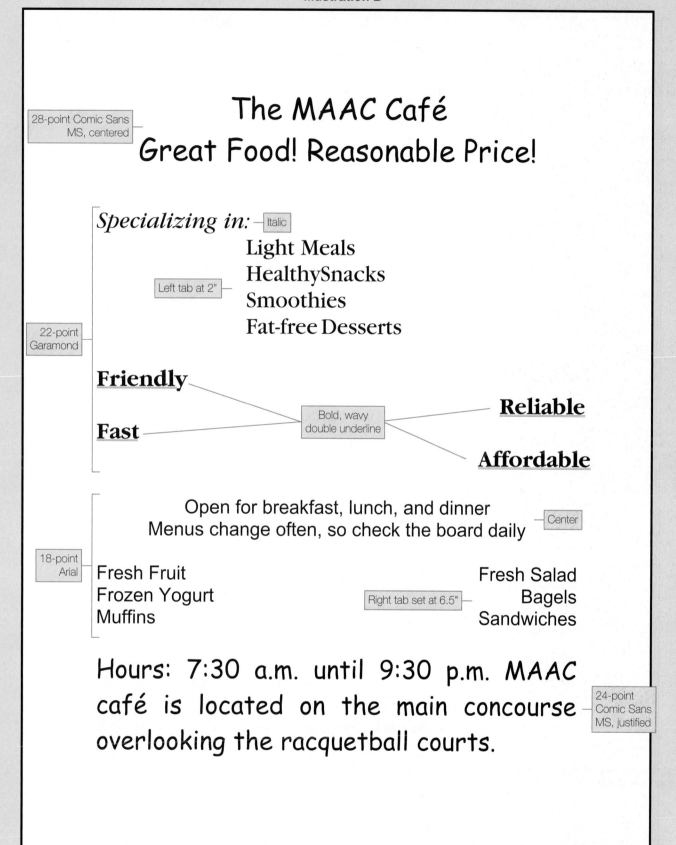

Exercise | 16

Curriculum Integration

Application Skills Use the skills you have learned in Lesson 2 to write a letter to someone you have learned about in your social studies or history class. In the letter, include information that you have learned about the person, such as a particular action that he or she was noted for, the date when the action occurred, and references to other people alive at the same time. If necessary, do additional research. You may use any format for the letter, such as full-block or modified block. (A sample letter is shown in Illustration A.) When appropriate, use font formatting to enhance the document. Create an envelope for the letter and return address labels.

EXERCISE DIRECTIONS

Start Word, if necessary, and create a new document. Save it as **16HISTORY_xx**.

Select to display elements that might help you while you work, such as the rulers and nonprinting characters, and make sure all the features you want to use are enabled, such as AutoCorrect and Check Spelling as you Type.

Set up the letter correctly, based on the format you want to use. Remember to include all parts of the letter and to separate the parts using blank lines. For example, remember to leave 2 inches of space at the top of the page, and to insert today's date.

Correct spelling and grammatical errors as you type, if necessary, and search the thesaurus to find alternatives to common words, such as *go*, *went*, and *said*.

Save the changes you have made to the document.

Display the document in Print Preview.

If necessary, adjust the vertical alignment, or shrink the document to fit on one page.

Create an envelope for the letter and add it to the document. Omit the return address.

Print the document, including the envelope.

Create return address mailing labels for yourself. You do not have to save the labels, but you should print them. If necessary print them on regular paper.

Close all open documents, saving all changes.

Illustration A

Today's date

Mrs. Rosa Parks
Civil Rights Leader
Montgomery, AL

Dear Mrs. Parks:

I recently read the book, <u>*Rosa Parks: My Story*</u>, which is an autobiography of your life. You were an *amazing* and *brave* woman and I admire you very much. I like the way you stood up for your rights as an American and a human being. Or maybe, you sat down for your rights. Your simple action of refusing to give up your seat on the bus on December 1, 1955 inspired a great many people to stand up for their rights, too.

From one small action, numerous larger actions grew. Civil rights activists, including Martin Luther King, rallied around you and started the great bus boycott. Many people endured harassment and intimidation as a result of the Montgomery Bus Boycott for over a year. But it took more than just a loss of revenue to convince the bus company to integrate. It required a decision by the Supreme Court! And it all started because you didn't give up your seat on the bus.

Mrs. Parks, I hope I can live my life as well as you lived yours. I feel inspired by your story to look out for the civil rights of all people. Thanks you for your inspiration.

Sincerely,

Your Name

Mrs. Rosa Parks
Civil Rights Leader
Montgomery, AL

Lesson | 3

Basic Editing Skills

Skills Covered

- **Use Proofreaders' Marks**
- **Open a Saved Document**
- **Insert and Edit Text**

- **Use Overtype Mode**
- **Save a Document with a New Name**

Software Skills When you are ready to revise or improve a document that you've already created and saved, open it again in Word. Use the Save As command to save a copy of the document with a new name or in a new location. For example, you might need to write a letter that is similar to one you wrote earlier. Instead of starting from scratch, you can open the original letter, save it as a new document, then edit it.

Application Skills As the Office Manager for Michigan Avenue Athletic Club, you have decided that you need to revise the press release that you wrote earlier regarding the new personal trainer who has joined the staff. In this exercise, you will open the press release document and save it with a new name. You will then revise the document and save the changes. Finally, you will print the document.

TERMS

Insert mode The method of operation used for inserting new text within existing text in a document. Insert mode is the default.

Overtype mode The method of operation used to replace existing text in a document with new text.

Proofreaders' marks Symbols written on a printed document by a copyeditor or proofreader to indicate where revisions are required.

NOTES

Use Proofreaders' Marks

- Often, you may need to revise a Word document based on a marked-up printed copy of the document. **Proofreaders' marks** on printed documents are written symbols that indicate where to make revisions.

Some common proofreaders' marks

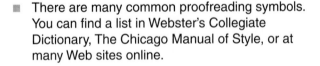

∿∿∿∿	indicates text to be bold.
∧	indicates where new text should be inserted.
⌒	indicates text to be deleted.
¶	indicates where a new paragraph should be inserted.
≡	indicates that a letter should be capitalized.
___ or (ital)	indicates text to be italicized.
(highlight)	indicates text to highlight.
][	indicates text to center.

- There are many common proofreading symbols. You can find a list in Webster's Collegiate Dictionary, The Chicago Manual of Style, or at many Web sites online.

Open a Saved Document

- To revise a Word document that has been saved and closed, open it again in Word.

- You can easily locate recently used files on the right side of the Office menu. Click a file to open it.

- Alternatively, use the Open dialog box to locate any file that you want to open.

- The steps for locating a file to open in Word 2007 running on Windows Vista are slightly different from those in Word 2007 running on Windows XP.

  - On Windows XP, you can click a common storage location in the Places bar on the left side of the Save As dialog box, or select a specific folder or disk drive from the Look in drop-down list.

  - On Windows Vista, you can you can click a common storage location in the Favorite Links list in the Navigation pane, navigate to a different location using the Address bar, or use the Folders list.

  - You can also display a list of shortcuts to recently used files and folder in the Open dialog box.

  ✓ *Recently used documents of all types may be listed on the My Recent Documents menu in Windows. Open the Start menu, click My Recent Documents, then click the document you want to open.*

Open dialog box in Windows XP

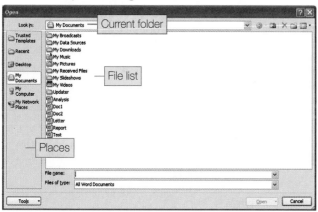

Open dialog box in Windows Vista

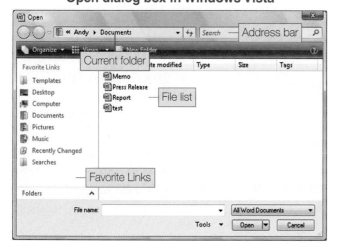

Insert and Edit Text

- By default, you insert new text in a document in **Insert mode**. Existing text moves to the right as you type to make room for new text.

- You can insert text anywhere in a document.

- You can also insert nonprinting characters as you type, including paragraph marks to start a new paragraph (press ↵Enter)), tabs (press Tab↹)), and spaces (press Spacebar)).

Use Overtype Mode

- To replace text as you type, use **Overtype mode**.

- In Overtype mode, existing characters do not shift right to make room for new characters. Instead, new characters replace existing characters as you type, deleting existing characters.

- Most editing should be done in Insert mode, so you do not accidentally type over text that you need.

Save a Document with a New Name

- The Save As command lets you save a copy of a document in a different location or with a different file name.

- Use the Save As command to leave the original document unchanged while you edit the new copy.

- The procedure for saving a document in a different location or with a different file name is slightly different in Windows Vista than in Windows XP.

  ✓ *The Save As command is the same command you use to save a new document for the first time. For more information, refer to Exercise 8.*

PROCEDURES

Open a Saved Document (Ctrl+O)

On Windows XP:
1. Click **Office Button** 🗔 ..... Alt + F
2. Click **Open** .... O
3. If necessary, click common storage location in the Places bar.

   OR

   Click the **Look in** drop-down arrow and select storage location .... Alt + I

   ✓ *Double-click folder or drive name to open it.*

4. Double-click document name to open it.

   OR

   a. Click document name.
   b. Click **Open** .... O

On Windows Vista:
1. Click **Office Button** 🗔 ..... Alt + F
2. Click **Open** .... O
3. If necessary, click Favorite Link location in the Navigation pane,

   OR

   Use other Vista navigation tools to locate stored document.

4. Double-click document name to open it.

   OR

   a. Click document name.
   b. Click **Open** .... O

Open a Recently Saved Document

1. Click **Office Button** 🗔 ..... Alt + F
2. Click document name in Recent Documents list in right pane of File menu .... →, ↓, ↵Enter

   OR

1. Click **Office Button** 🗔 ..... Alt + F
2. Click **Open** .... O
3. Click **My Recent Documents** in the Places bar.
4. Double-click document name to open it.

   OR

   a. Click document name.
   b. Click **Open** .... O

Insert Text

1. Position insertion point to right of character where you want to insert new text.
2. Type new text.

Turn Overtype Mode On or Off

1. Click **Office Button** 🗔 ..... Alt + F
2. Click **Word Options** I
3. Click **Advanced** .... A
4. Click **Use overtype mode** .... Alt + V, Spacebar

   ✓ *A check mark indicates that the mode is on.*

5. Click **OK** .... ↵Enter

Use Overtype Mode

1. Position insertion point to left of first character you want to replace.
2. Type new text.

Save a Document with a New Name or Storage Location

On Windows XP:
1. Click **Office Button** 🗔 ..... Alt + F
2. Click **Save As** .... A
3. If necessary, click common storage location in the Places bar.

   OR

   Click the **Save in** drop-down arrow and select storage location .... Alt + I

   ✓ *Double-click folder or drive name to open it.*

   OR

   a. Click **Create New Folder** button 🖿 .... Alt + 4
   b. Type new folder name.
   c. Click **OK** .... ↵Enter

4. Select current name in **File name** text box .... Alt + N
5. Type new **file name**.
6. Click **Save** .... Alt + S

On Windows Vista:
1. Click **Office Button** 🗔 ..... Alt + F
2. Click **Save As** .... A
3. If necessary, click **Browse Folders** and then use Windows Vista tools to navigate to desired storage location.

   OR

   a. Click **Create New Folder** button 🖿.
   b. Type new folder name.
   c. Press **OK** .... ↵Enter

4. Select current name in **File name** text box .... Alt + N
5. Type new file name.
6. Click **Save** .... Alt + S

EXERCISE DIRECTIONS

1. Start Word, if necessary.
2. Open 17PRESS. This is a version of the press release you worked with in Exercise 9.

   ✓ *If necessary, ask your instructor where this file is located.*

3. Save the file as **17PRESS_xx**.
4. Make the revisions as indicated by the proofreaders' marks in Illustration A.

   a. Insert new text as marked.

   b. Replace text as marked.

   c. Apply font styles as marked.

   d. Insert your own name in place of the text *Your Name*.

5. Check the spelling and grammar.
6. Print the document.
7. Close the document, saving all changes.

Illustration A

ON YOUR OWN

1. Open 🖥OWD13_*xx*, the document you created in the On Your Own section of Exercise 13, or open 💿17LETTER.

2. Save the file as OWD17_*xx*.

3. Make revisions to the document using Insert mode and Overtype mode.

4. Check the spelling and grammar in the document.

5. Print the document.

6. If possible, exchange the printed document with a classmate.

7. Use proofreader's marks to indicate at least three changes to the document. For example, apply font styles or replace text.

8. Retrieve your document and make the changes as marked.

9. Close the document, saving all changes.

Skills Covered

- **Use Split Screen View**
- **Open Multiple Documents at the Same Time**
- **Arrange Documents On-Screen**
- **Compare Documents Side by Side**

Software Skills   Use Split Screen view to see different sections of the same document on-screen at the same time. For example, you may want to see a table of contents at the beginning of a document while you work in a section at the end of the document. Open multiple documents when you need to work with more than one document at a time. For example, if you are planning a meeting, you may need to work with an agenda and a list of attendees at the same time.

Application Skills   As an assistant at the Michigan Avenue Athletic Club, you often have many different tasks to attend to at the same time. Today, the Pro Shop Manager has asked you to modify a letter to a supplier regarding an incomplete order, and the General Manager has asked you to make sure the correct version of a press release about a new personal trainer is sent out. Both managers want the tasks completed as soon as possible, but the letter to the supplier must go out today, while the press release will not be issued until tomorrow. In order to be successful, you must demonstrate productive work habits and attitudes such as dependability and punctuality. You must also stay organized and learn to prioritize your tasks.

In this exercise, you will first open the letter to the supplier and use Split Screen view to make the necessary changes. You will save the changes and print the letter along with an envelope. When the letter is complete, you will move on to the press release. You will arrange all versions of the press release on-screen and select the two you believe are the most accurate. You will then compare the two side by side to determine which is correct. You will then print the correct press release.

TERMS

Active document   The document in which the insertion point is currently located. Commands and actions occur in the active document.

Active pane   The pane in which the insertion point is currently located. Commands and actions occur in the active pane.

Independent scrolling   The ability to scroll a window without affecting the display in other open windows.

Synchronous scrolling   A feature that links the scroll bars in two windows so that when you scroll in one window the other window scrolls as well.

Tile   Arrange windows so they do not overlap on-screen.

NOTES

Use Split Screen View

- Split the screen into two panes so you can see and work in different sections of a single document.
- Word tiles the panes one above the other within the program window, separated by a split bar.
- Each pane has its own scroll bars so you can scroll each section independently from the other.
- Each pane also has its own rulers.
- There is only one Quick Access Toolbar, one title bar, and one Ribbon.
- Commands affect the **active pane**. For example, you can change the zoom in the top pane if it is active without affecting the inactive bottom pane.
- You can switch from one pane to the other to make edits and formatting changes.

Split screen view

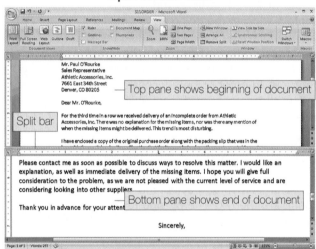

Open Multiple Documents at the Same Time

- You can open multiple Word documents at the same time.
- By default, each open document is represented by a button on the Windows taskbar.
- However, if there is not enough room on the taskbar to show all buttons, they are grouped into one Word button.
- By default, the **active document** is displayed on-screen while other open documents are hidden.

- Only one document can be active at a time. You can identify the active document window by the following:
  - The active document contains the insertion point.
  - The active document window may have a brighter colored border than other open document windows, and the elements on the title bar may be brighter.
  - The active document window is represented by the "pressed in" taskbar button.
- You can change the active document at any time.

Arrange Documents On-Screen

- You can arrange all open documents on-screen at the same time.
- Word **tiles** up to three open documents one above the other.
- If there are more than three open documents, Word fits them on-screen by tiling some of them side by side as well.
- The more open documents there are, the smaller each document window is on-screen. Therefore, editing with more than two documents arranged on-screen may be difficult.
  - ✓ To keep a document from being arranged on-screen with other open documents, minimize it.

Multiple documents tiled on-screen

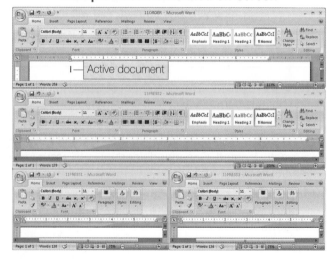

Compare Documents Side by Side

- You can select to compare the active document with another open document by arranging them side by side.

- By default, both windows are set to use **synchronous scrolling**, but you can use **independent scrolling** if you want.

- Changes you make to the view in one window affect the other window as well.

- If the windows move or are resized on the desktop, you can reset their position to side by side.

Compare documents side by side

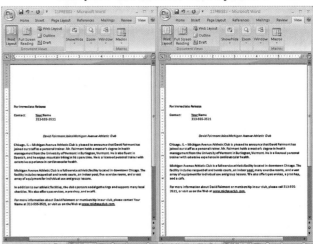

PROCEDURES

Open Split Screen View

- Double-click **Split box** at top of vertical scroll bar.

  ✓ *Split box is the vertical bar above the View Ruler button.*

  OR

1. Click **View** tab................. Alt + W

   Window Group

2. Click **Split** button ▭ .... S

   ✓ *Mouse pointer changes to a resizing pointer and a dark gray bar extends horizontally across the screen.*

3. Click at location where you want to split the screen .... ↑, ↓, ↵Enter

To Change the Active Pane:

- Click on pane to make it active.

To Remove Split Screen View:

- Double-click **Split bar** that divides window.

  ✓ *Split bar is border between the top pane's horizontal scroll bar and the bottom pane's vertical ruler.*

  OR

1. Click **View** tab................. Alt + W

   Window Group

2. Click **Remove Split** button ▭ . S

To Resize Split Screen Panes:

1. Position mouse pointer so it touches **Split bar**.

   ✓ *Pointer changes to a resizing pointer.*

2. Press and hold **left mouse button**.

3. Drag **Split bar** up or down to desired position.

Open Multiple Documents (*Ctrl+O*)

1. Open first document.

2. Open second document.

3. Continue opening documents as desired.

Arrange Multiple Documents on Screen

1. Open all documents.

2. Click **View** tab................. Alt + W

   Window Group

3. Click **Arrange All** button ▤ ..... A

Display Active Document Only

- Click active document's **Maximize** button ▭.

Change the Active Document

1. Click **View** tab................. Alt + W

   Window Group

2. Click **Switch Windows** button ▦ .... W

3. Click name of document to make active .... ↓, ↵Enter

   ✓ *You may also press the number next to the document name.*

   OR

- Click in window of document to make active.

   OR

- Click taskbar button of window to make active.

   ✓ *If there is a group taskbar button, click the button, then click document name.*

   OR

1. Press and hold Alt .... Alt

2. Press Tab↹ .... Tab↹

   ✓ *A window displays previews of each open window.*

3. Press Tab↹ repeatedly to cycle through open windows .... Tab↹

4. Release Alt and Tab↹ when desired window is active.

Compare Documents Side by Side

1. Open both documents.
2. Click **View** tab .... `Alt`+`W`

   Window Group

3. Click **View Side by Side** button `⊞` .... `B`

If more than two documents are open:

1. Make first document to compare active.
2. Click **View** tab .... `Alt`+`W`

   Window Group

3. Click **View Side by Side** button `⊞` .... `B`
4. Click name of second file to compare .... `↓`
5. Click **OK** .... `↵Enter`

Toggle Synchronous/Independent Scrolling:

1. Click **View** tab .... `Alt`+`W`

   Window Group

2. Click **Window** button `⊟` ... `Z`, `W`

   ✓ *The Window group button displays if the active window is too narrow to show all buttons on the Ribbon. If the Window group button does not display, skip step 2.*

3. Click **Synchronous Scrolling** button `⊟↕` .... `V`, `S`

   ✓ *If button is highlighted, synchronous scrolling is set. Click it again to allow independent scrolling.*

Reset Windows:

1. Click **View** tab .... `Alt`+`W`

   Window Group

2. Click **Window** button `⊟` ... `Z`, `W`

   ✓ *The Window group button displays if the active window is too narrow to show all buttons on the Ribbon. If the Window group button does not display, skip step 2.*

3. Click **Reset Window Position** button `⊞↔` .... `T`

Remove side by side arrangement:

1. Open both documents.
2. Click **View** tab .... `Alt`+`W`

   Window Group

3. Click **View Side by Side** button `⊞` .... `B`

EXERCISE DIRECTIONS

Prepare the Letter

1. Start Word, if necessary.
2. Open ⊙ **18ORDER**.
3. Save the file as **18ORDER2_xx**.
4. Change the date to today's date.
5. Display the document in Split Screen view.
6. Adjust the zoom in the top pane to Page Width.
7. Adjust the contents of the top pane to show from the inside address through the first paragraph of the letter.
8. Click in the bottom pane and adjust the zoom to Text Width.
9. Scroll down in the bottom pane until you see the paragraph beginning *Please contact me as soon as possible...*
10. Insert the recipient's name at the beginning of the sentence. Refer to the information in the top pane to make sure you use the correct name and spelling.
11. Edit the text to use correct grammar and punctuation. For example, make sure to include a comma after the name and to change the uppercase **P** at the beginning of the sentence to lowercase. When you have made the changes, your screen should look similar to Illustration A.
12. Remove the split screen.
13. Check the spelling and grammar in the document.
14. Preview the document.
15. Create an envelope for the document and add it to the letter. Omit the return address.
16. Print the document.
17. Close the document, saving all changes.

Prepare the Press Release

1. In Word, open the file ⊙ **18PRESS1**.
2. Open the file ⊙ **18PRESS2**.
3. Open the file ⊙ **18PRESS3**.
4. Arrange all three documents on the screen.
5. Make **18PRESS1** active. This is clearly the oldest of the three. It does not have as much information or detail as the others.
6. Close **18PRESS1** without saving any changes.
7. Arrange the remaining two documents on the screen.
8. Make **18PRESS2** active.
9. Select to compare it side by side with **18PRESS3**.
10. Set the zoom of **18PRESS3** to Text Width. Your screen should look similar to Illustration B.
11. The press releases look similar, but are not exactly the same. Read one and then the other to determine which is more complete.

    ✓ *If necessary, adjust the zoom to increase the size of the text on-screen.*

12. Close the side by side display.
13. Close **18PRESS3** without saving any changes.

14. Save **18PRESS2** as **18FINALPRESS_xx**.

15. Maximize the document. Replace the text *Your Name* with your name in both locations.

16. Check the spelling and grammar in the document.

17. Preview the document.

18. Print the document.

19. Close the document, saving all changes.

Illustration A

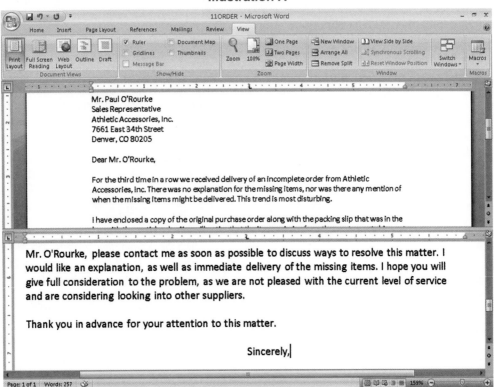

Illustration B

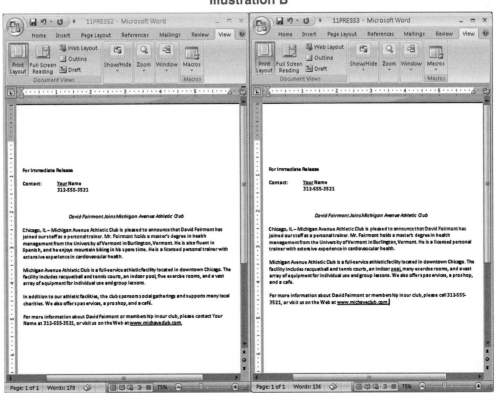

ON YOUR OWN

1. Look around your classroom and note the types of technology that you have available. For example, the hardware may include desktop computers, printers, networks drives, CD-ROM drives, monitors, keyboards, and so on. The software may include the Microsoft Office 2007 programs as well as other programs.

2. In addition, consider how each item is used for a different purpose or to accomplish specific tasks.

3. Create a new document in Word.

4. Save the document as **OWD18_xx**.

5. Create a document listing the available hardware and software and the appropriate use for each item.

   ✓ *For example, you might use an inkjet printer for printing color documents. You might have a floppy disk drive for storing small files that you need to take to a different computer. You use Word to create text-based documents and PowerPoint to create presentations.*

6. Include a heading for the entire document, such as Available Technology, and headings for each category: hardware and software.

7. Use tabs to separate the items on the left from the appropriate tasks on the right.

8. As your list gets longer, use Split Screen View to make sure you don't duplicate items that you have already entered.

9. When you believe the list is complete, check the spelling and grammar and then print the document.

10. Close the document, saving all changes.

11. Get together with a classmate who also completed the assignment.

12. Open both your document and his or her document in Word.

13. Working together, compare the two documents side by side to see if you have missing items, or have incorrect information about appropriate usage.

14. Using a different font or font style, make changes to the documents as necessary.

   ✓ *With the different font, you'll be able to see the information you had originally and the information you added based on your collaboration with a classmate.*

15. Close all open documents, saving all changes.

Exercise | 19

Skills Covered

- Move Text
- Use Cut and Paste
- Use the Clipboard Task Pane
- Use Drag-and-Drop Editing
- Select Paste Formatting Options
- Move a Paragraph

Software Skills   Move text to rearrange a document quickly without retyping existing information. You can move any amount of text, from a single character to an entire page.

Application Skills   The Manager of the café at the Michigan Avenue Athletic Club has asked you to revise an advertising flyer. In this exercise, you will open the existing document and use different methods to rearrange the text.

TERMS

Clipboard A temporary storage area that can hold up to 24 selections at a time.

Cut To delete a selection from its original location and move it to the Clipboard.

Drag-and-drop editing The action of using a mouse to drag a selection from its original location and drop it in a new location.

Paste To insert a selection from the Clipboard into a document.

NOTES

Move Text

- While editing, you may decide you need to move text that is already typed in a document to a new location.
- You can move text within a document or from one document to another.
- Word's move commands can save you from deleting and retyping text.
- Be sure to consider nonprinting characters when you select text to move:
  - Select the space following a word or sentence to move along with text.
  - Select the paragraph mark following a paragraph or line to move paragraph formatting and blank lines with text.
- Use Undo to reverse a move that you make unintentionally.

Use Cut and Paste

- Use the **Cut** and **Paste** commands to move text in a document.
- The Cut command deletes selected text from its original location and moves it to the **Clipboard**.
- The Paste command copies the selection from the Clipboard to the insertion point location.
- The Cut and Paste commands are on the Home tab of the Ribbon.
- You can also access the Cut and Paste commands on a shortcut menu, or with keyboard shortcuts.

Use the Clipboard Task Pane

- Use the Clipboard task pane to access selections for pasting.
- The last 24 items cut or copied display in the Clipboard.
- You can paste or delete one or all of the items.

- You can turn the following Clipboard options off or on (a check mark indicates the option is on):
  - Show Office Clipboard Automatically. Sets the Clipboard task pane to open automatically when you cut or copy a selection.
  - Show Office Clipboard when Ctrl+C pressed twice. Sets Word to display the Clipboard task pane when you press and hold the Ctrl key and then press C on the keyboard twice.
  - Collect Without Showing Office Clipboard. Sets the Clipboard task pane so it does not open automatically when you cut or copy data.
  - Show Office Clipboard Icon on Taskbar. Displays a Clipboard icon at the right end of the taskbar if there are selections on the Clipboard. Double-click the icon to open the task pane.
  - Show Status Near Taskbar When Copying. Displays a ScreenTip with the number of items on the Clipboard when you cut or copy a selection.

Clipboard task pane

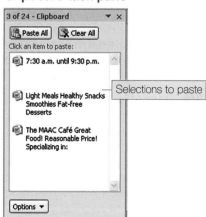

Use Drag-and-Drop Editing

- Use **drag-and-drop editing** to move text with the mouse.
- Drag-and-drop editing is convenient when you can see the text to move and the new location on the screen at the same time.

Select Paste Formatting Options

- By default, when you paste text into a new location, Word displays the Paste Options button 📋.
- Click the Paste Options button to display a list of options for formatting the text in the new location.

Paste Formatting options

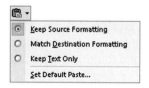

Move a Paragraph

- You can quickly move an entire paragraph up or down in a document.

PROCEDURES

Move Text

1. Select text to move.
2. Press F2 .... F2
3. Position insertion point at new location.
4. Press ↵Enter .... ↵Enter

Use Cut and Paste to Move Text *(Ctrl+X, Ctrl+V)*

1. Select text to move.
2. Click **Home** tab .... Alt+H

Clipboard Group

3. Click **Cut** button ✂ X
   OR
   a. Right-click selection.
   b. Click **Cut** .... T
4. Position insertion point in new location.
5. Click **Paste** button 📋 .... Alt+H, V, P
   OR
   a. Right-click insertion point location.
   b. Click **Paste** .... P

Display the Clipboard Task Pane *(Ctrl+C, C)*

1. Click **Home** tab .... Alt+H

Clipboard Group

2. Click **Clipboard** dialog box launcher 🔲 .... F, O

Paste an Item from the Clipboard

1. Display Clipboard task pane.
2. Position insertion point in new location.

3. Click item to paste.

OR

Click **Paste All** to paste all selections from the Clipboard to the insertion point location.

Set Clipboard Options

1. Display Clipboard task pane.
2. Click **Options** button.
3. Click desired option:
   - **Show Office Clipboard Automatically** .... Ⓐ
   - **Show Office Clipboard when Ctrl+C Pressed Twice** .... Ⓟ
   - **Collect Without Showing Office Clipboard** .... Ⓒ
   - **Show Office Clipboard Icon on Taskbar** .... Ⓣ
   - **Show Status Near Taskbar When Copying** .... Ⓢ

   ✓ *A check mark indicates the option is selected.*

Delete Selections from the Clipboard

1. Display Clipboard task pane.
2. Right-click selection to delete.

3. Click **Delete** on shortcut menu .... Ⓓ

OR

Click **Clear All** to delete all selections from the Clipboard.

Use Drag-and-Drop Editing to Move Text

1. Select text to move.
2. Move mouse pointer anywhere over selected text.
3. Press and hold left mouse button.
4. Drag mouse to position mouse pointer/insertion point at new location.

   ✓ *As you drag, the mouse pointer changes to the move pointer, which is a box with a dotted shadow attached to an arrow 🔲.*

5. Release mouse button to move selection to insertion point location.

Move a Paragraph

1. Position insertion point anywhere within paragraph to move.

OR

Select the paragraphs to move.

2. Do one of the following
   - Press Alt+⇧Shift+↑ to move paragraph(s) up.
   - Press Alt+⇧Shift+↓ to move paragraph(s) down.
3. Repeat step 2 until paragraph is in desired location.

Select Paste Formatting Options

1. Paste text at new location.
2. Click **Paste Options** button 📋.
3. Click an option on the drop-down menu:
   - **Keep Source Formatting** to maintain formatting from original location .... Ⓚ
   - **Match Destination Formatting** to apply existing formatting to new text .... Ⓓ
   - **Keep Text Only** to remove all applied formatting .... Ⓣ
   - **Set Default Paste** to display Word Options dialog box ... Ⓢ

If Paste Options button is not displayed:

1. Click **Office Button** ...... Alt+Ⓕ
2. Click **Word Options** .... Ⓘ
3. Click **Advanced** .... Ⓐ
4. Click **Show Paste Options** Buttons check box ...... Alt+Ⓞ, Ⓞ, Spacebar
5. Click **OK** .... ↵Enter

EXERCISE DIRECTIONS

1. Start Word, if necessary.
2. Open 💿19FLYER.
3. Save the file as **19CAFE_xx**.
4. Revise the document so it resembles the document shown in Illustration A.
   a. Select the line *Great Food! Reasonable Price!*, including the paragraph mark at the end of the line.
   b. Cut the selection to the Clipboard.
   c. Position the insertion point on the blank line following the text *Menus change often, so check the board daily*.
   d. Paste the selection in the new location.

   e. Click the Paste Options button and then click Match Destination Formatting.
   f. Select the four lines beginning with the line on which the text *Fresh Fruit* and *Fresh Salad* are entered. Include the blank line after the list of items.
   g. Press and hold Shift+Alt and then press Up arrow nine times to move the selected paragraphs up on the page.
   h. Select the text *Hours: 7:30 a.m. until 9:30 p.m.*
   i. Drag the selected text and drop it on the blank line below the headline: *The MAAC Café*.
   j. Insert a new blank line after the line with the hours on it that you just moved. The document should look similar to the one in Illustration A.

5. Check the spelling and grammar in the document.
6. Display the document in Print Preview.

7. Print the document.
8. Close the document, saving all changes.

Illustration A

The MAAC Café
Hours: 7:30 a.m. until 9:30 p.m.

Specializing in:

Light Meals
Healthy Snacks
Smoothies
Fat-free Desserts

Fresh Fruit
Frozen Yogurt
Muffins

Fresh Salad
Bagels
Sandwiches

Friendly

Reliable

Fast

Affordable

Open for breakfast, lunch, and dinner
Menus change often, so check the board daily
Great Food! Reasonable Price!

MAAC café is located on the main concourse overlooking the racquetball courts.

ON YOUR OWN

1. Think about how you would create a resume for yourself.

2. Look up information about how to format a resume. You might find the information in a career guidance center, in the library, or on the Internet. You can also ask your instructor or refer to the resume that you typed in Exercise 14.

3. Once you have selected a format, gather the information you would like to include on the resume. For example, you should include the schools you have attended, as well as any volunteer or paid work experience. Be sure to include the dates and locations.

4. You can also include clubs, teams and organizations to which you belong, awards that you have won, certifications that you have received, and any other interests that you have.

5. When you have all of the information you need, create a new document in Word.

6. Save the file as **OWD19_xx**.

7. Based on the format you selected, enter the text to create the resume.

8. Save the changes as you work.

9. Apply formatting to enhance the appearance of the text. For example, use different fonts, font styles, and font sizes.

10. Move text as necessary so that the information in is the correct order and so that it looks good on the page. Make sure it fits on a single page.

11. When you have completed the document, check the spelling and grammar.

12. Print the document.

13. Ask a classmate to review the document and make comments and suggestions.

14. Incorporate the suggestions into the document.

15. Close the document, saving all changes.

Skills Covered

- **Use Copy and Paste**
- **Use Drag-and-Drop Editing to Copy**

Software Skills Copy or move text from one location to another to speed up your work and avoid repetitive typing. You can copy or move any amount of text, from a single character to an entire document.

Application Skills In this exercise, you will copy text to complete the flyer for the Michigan Avenue Athletic Club café.

TERMS

Copy To create a duplicate of a selection.

NOTES

Use Copy and Paste

- Use the Copy and Paste feature to copy existing text from one location in a document and paste it to another location.

- The **Copy** command stores a duplicate of selected text on the Clipboard, leaving the original selection unchanged.

- You can then use the Paste command to paste the selection from the Clipboard to the insertion point location.

- You can access the Copy and Paste commands from the Clipboard group on the Home tab of the Ribbon, a shortcut menu, or with keyboard shortcuts.

- Use the Clipboard task pane to choose which selection to paste into the document.

  ✓ *The same Clipboard used for moving is used for copying. For more information, refer to Exercise 19.*

- Use the Paste Options button to control formatting when copying text just as you use it when moving text.

  ✓ *For more information about the Paste Options button, refer to Exercise 19.*

- You can also use the Clipboard to copy and paste a selection from one document into a different document.

Use Drag-and-Drop Editing to Copy

- Use drag-and-drop editing to copy text with the mouse.

- Drag-and-drop is convenient when you can see the text to copy and the new location on the screen at the same time.

Curriculum Connection: Social Studies

Governor

Every state in the United States of America has a chief executive called a governor. The governor is elected directly by the residents of the state, and is generally responsible for working with the state's legislature to develop new laws and then applying those laws within the state. Many of our presidents were governors first, including George W. Bush (Texas), Bill Clinton (Arkansas), and Ronald Reagan (California).

Write a Letter to Your Governor

Find out who is the governor of your state and then write him or her a personal business letter. You might want to mention an issue that it is important to you, comment on something the governor has done recently, or just tell the governor who you are and why you are writing. Be sure to include the governor's correct name and address, and to set up the letter using the proper format.

PROCEDURES

Use Copy and Paste (Ctrl+C, Ctrl+V)

1. Select text to copy.
2. Click **Home** tab .... Alt + H
   > Clipboard Group
3. Click **Copy** button 🔲 C
   OR
   a. Right-click selection.
   b. Click **C**opy C
4. Position insertion point in new location.
5. Click **Paste** button 🔲 .... Alt + H, V, P
   OR
   a. Right-click insertion point location.
   b. Click **P**aste .... P

Display the Clipboard Task Pane (Ctrl+C, C)

1. Click **Home** tab .... Alt + H
   > Clipboard Group
2. Click **Clipboard** dialog box launcher 🔲 .... F, O

Paste an Item from the Clipboard

1. Display Clipboard task pane.
2. Position insertion point in new location.
3. Click item to paste.
   OR
   Click **Paste All** to paste all selections from the Clipboard to the insertion point location.

Set Clipboard Options

1. Display Clipboard task pane.
2. Click **Options** drop-down arrow.
3. Click desired option:
   - **Show Office Clipboard Automatically** .... A
   - **Show Office Clipboard when Ctrl+C Pressed Twice** .... P
   - **Collect Without Showing Office Clipboard** C
   - **Show Office Clipboard Icon on Taskbar** .... T
   - **Show Status Near Taskbar When Copying** .... S
   ✓ A check mark indicates the option is selected.

Delete Selections from the Clipboard

1. Display Clipboard task pane.
2. Right-click selection to delete.
3. Click **Delete** on shortcut menu .... D
   OR
   Click **Clear All** to delete all selections from the Clipboard.

Use Drag-and-Drop Editing to Copy Text

1. Select text to copy.
2. Move mouse pointer anywhere over selected text.
3. Press and hold left mouse button.
4. Press and hold Ctrl .... Ctrl
5. Drag mouse to position mouse pointer/insertion point at new location.
   ✓ As you drag, the mouse pointer changes to the copy pointer, which is a box with a dotted shadow and a plus sign attached to an arrow 🔲.
6. Release mouse button to copy selection to insertion point location.
7. Release Ctrl.

EXERCISE DIRECTIONS

1. Start Word, if necessary.
2. Open 🔘 **20CAFE**.
3. Save the file as **20CAFE_xx**.
4. Use the following steps to revise the document so it looks like the one in Illustration A.
5. Select the word *Friendly* and copy it to the Clipboard. Do not select the paragraph mark.
   > ✓ It may take a few tries to select the word without the paragraph mark. If necessary, press and hold the Shift key, then use the arrow keys to select each character.
6. Position the insertion point on the last line in the document and paste the selection. Don't worry if the document extends to more than one page.

> ✓ You may want to work in Split Screen view so you can see the text you are copying and the line where you are pasting at the same time.

7. Type a period after the word, and press the Spacebar to insert a blank space.
8. Select the word *Reliable* and copy it to the Clipboard. Again, do not select the paragraph mark.
9. Position the insertion point at the end of the document and paste the selection.
10. Type a period after the word, and press the Spacebar to insert a blank space.

11. Select the word *Fast*. Press and hold [Ctrl] and drag it to the end of the last line. Type a period after the word and press the Spacebar.

12. Select the word *Affordable*. Press and hold [Ctrl] and drag it to the end of the last line. Type a period after the word.

13. Center the text on the last line.

14. Check the spelling and grammar in the document.

15. Display the document in Print Preview and shrink it to fit on one page. It should look similar to the one in the Illustration.

16. Print the document.

17. Close the document, saving all changes.

Illustration A

The MAAC Café
Hours: 7:30 a.m. until 9:30 p.m.

Specializing in:

Light Meals
Healthy Snacks
Smoothies
Fat-free Desserts

Fresh Fruit
Frozen Yogurt
Muffins

Fresh Salad
Bagels
Sandwiches

Friendly

Reliable

Fast

Affordable

Open for breakfast, lunch, and dinner
Menus change often, so check the board daily
Great Food! Reasonable Price!

MAAC café is located on the main concourse overlooking the racquetball courts.

Friendly. Reliable. Fast. Affordable.

ON YOUR OWN

1. Create a new document in Word.

2. Save the file as **OWD20_xx**.

3. Create a letter in which you apply for an officer's position of a group or organization to which you might belong. For example, the group could be a school club. The officer's position could be secretary, treasurer, or president. Remember to use correct formatting for a letter, including line and paragraph spacing.

4. Consider whether you can use any of the information you entered in your resume in the letter. For example, you might want to include information about other clubs to which you belong.

5. Open the document **OWD19_xx**, your resume which you created in the On Your Own section of Exercise 19, or open **20RESUME**.

6. Save the file as **OWD20-2_xx**.

7. Copy at least two items from **OWD20-2_xx** to the **OWD20_xx** document.

   - First, copy an item from **OWD20-2_xx** to the Clipboard. Next position the insertion point in the **OWD20_xx** document. Finally, paste the item from the Clipboard into the **OWD20_xx** document.

8. Complete the letter.

9. Display the document in Print Preview. Make editing or formatting changes as necessary.

10. Check the spelling and the grammar.

11. Print the document.

12. Ask a classmate to review the document and make comments or suggestions.

13. Incorporate the suggestions into the document.

14. Close the document, saving all changes.

Exercise | 21

Skills Covered

- Open a Document as Read-Only
- Open a Document from Windows
- Use Document Properties
- About File Types

Software Skills   You can use Word to open a document as read-only when you do not want to allow changes to the original file. You can use Windows features to open a document and start Word at the same time, and you can use Word to open files created with different word processing programs. Document Properties are details that help you to identify important information about a file, such as the name of the author and the main topic.

Application Skills   Voyager Travel Adventures is organizing a trip to Alaska. The Public Relations Director has a file with some information you need to create a press release, but she doesn't want you editing the file in any way. In this exercise, you will open the file as read-only. You will edit the file to create a press release, and then save it in plain text format so you can deliver it online to clients who may not have Word installed. You will also enter document properties.

TERMS

Compatible file type A file type that Word can open, even though it was created and saved using a different program.

Document properties Categories of information about a document.

File extension A dot followed by three or four characters at the end of a file name, used to indicate the file type.

File icon The icon used to represent a file in a file list.

File type The format in which a file is stored. Usually, the file type corresponds to the program used to create the file.

Keywords Important words found in a document. Keywords can be used to classify a document.

Metadata Data about data, such as file properties.

Read-only A mode of operation in which revisions cannot be saved in the original document.

NOTES

Open a Document as Read-Only

- Opening a document as **read-only** is a safeguard against accidentally making changes.
- You can edit a read-only document, but you cannot save the changes in the original file.
- Word prompts you to use Save As to save the revisions in a new document with a different file name.
- The words *Read-Only* display in the title bar of a document opened as read-only.

Open a Document from Windows

- Windows displays recently-used documents in a list that can be opened from the Start menu.

  ✓ *The list includes files used in any program, not just Word.*

- Click a Word document name in the list to open the document and start Word at the same time.
  - In Windows XP, click My Recent Documents on the Start menu to display the list.
  - In Windows Vista, click Recent Items on the Start menu.
- You can also use Windows navigation tools to locate and open any document.

Document Properties

- With the **Document Properties** feature you can save information that is unique to a particular document.

  ✓ *Document properties may also be called **metadata**.*

- Some properties are updated automatically when you create or modify a document, such as the file name and type, the author, and the file size.

- You can enter more specific properties to help differentiate the file from other, similar, documents.

- There are five categories of document properties that you can view and enter in the document's Properties dialog box.

Summary tab of a document's Properties dialog box

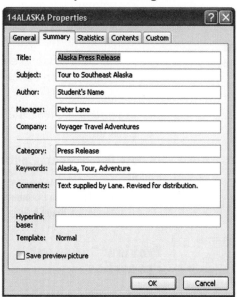

- Three of the more useful categories are:
  - General properties: Include the type of document, its size, its location, when it was created, last accessed, and last modified.
    - *Use General properties to check file storage and access information.*
  - Summary properties: Include a document title, subject, author, **keywords**, and comments.
    - *Use Summary properties to save summary information with a document.*
  - Statistics properties: Include the number of pages, paragraphs, lines, words, characters, and bytes in the document.
    - *Use Statistics properties to create documents of a specific length or word count.*

- You can preview properties in the Open dialog box or the Save As dialog box.

Preview properties in the Open dialog box

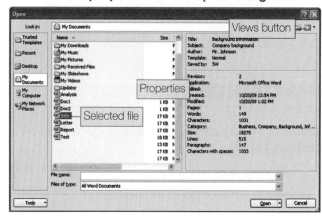

- You can also display properties in the Document Information Panel at the top of the document window.

Document Information Panel

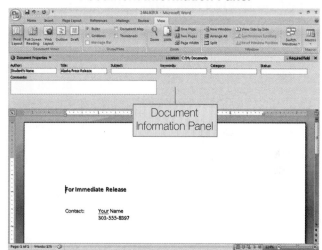

About File Types

- Files are saved in different **file types**, depending on the application used to create, save, and open the file.

- In Windows and Windows applications, file types can be identified by the **file extension** and by the **file icon**.

- Word 2007 can open documents saved in **compatible file types**. For example, Word can open text files, Web page files, XML files, and files created with other versions of Word.

- You can save a compatible file in its original file type or as a Word document file.

- Some common file types include the following:
  - Word 2007 documents ... .docx
  - Word 2007 templates ... .dotx
  - Word 97 - 2003 documents ... .doc
  - Word 97 - 2003 templates ... .dot
  - Text files ... .txt
  - Web pages ... .htm
  - Excel 2007 workbooks ... .xlsx
  - Excel 97- 2003 workbooks ... .xls
  - PowerPoint 2007 files ... .pptx
  - PowerPoint 97 - 2003 files ... .ppt

PROCEDURES

Open a Document as Read-Only (Ctrl+O)

1. Click **Office Button** 🔘 ... Alt+F
2. Click **Open** ... O
3. Click document name ... Tab 7x, ↑, ↓
4. Click **Open** button drop-down arrow ... Tab 3x, ↓
5. Click **Open Read-Only** ... R

To save changes to a read-only document:

1. Click **Save** button on Quick Access Toolbar ... Ctrl+S

   OR
   a. Click **Office Button** 🔘 ... Alt+F
   b. Click **Save** ... S
2. Navigate to desired storage location
3. Click **File name** text box ... Alt+N
4. Type new file name
5. Click **Save** ... Alt+S

Open a Word Document from the Windows Start Menu

In Windows XP:

1. Click **Start** button `start` ... Ctrl+Esc
2. Click **My Recent Documents** ... D
3. Click document name ... ↓, ↵Enter

In Windows Vista:

1. Click **Start** button 🔘 ... Ctrl+Esc
2. Click **Recent Items** ... Tab, R, ↵Enter
3. Click document name ... ↓, ↵Enter

Open a Word Document using Windows Explorer

1. Right-click **Start** button `start` .

   OR

   Right-click **Start** button 🔘 ... Alt+Spacebar
2. Click **Explore** ... X, ↵Enter
3. Use Windows tools to navigate to location where file is stored.
4. Double-click document name.

Use Document Properties

To use Document Information Panel:

1. Click **Office Button** 🔘 ... Alt+F
2. Click **Prepare** ... E
3. Click **Properties** ... P
4. Click desired property box ... Tab
5. Type property information

To use document's Properties dialog box:

1. Click **Office Button** 🔘 ... Alt+F
2. Click **Prepare** ... E
3. Click **Properties** ... P

4. Click **Document Properties** drop-down arrow ℹ Document Properties ▾.
5. Click **Advanced Properties** ... ↓, ↵Enter
6. Click desired tab ... Ctrl+Tab
   - Click **Summary** tab and type summary information.
   - Click **Statistics** tab to see statistical information.
   - Click **General** tab to see file storage and access information.
7. Enter data as desired.
8. Click **OK** ... ↵Enter

To close Document Information Panel:

- Click **Close the Document Information Panel** button ✕.

Preview Document Properties

1. Click **Office Button** 🔘 ... Alt+F
2. Click **Open** ... O

   OR

   Click **Save As** ... A
3. Navigate to location where file is stored.
4. Click document name.
5. Click **Views** button drop-down arrow 🔳 ▾.
6. Click **Properties** ... R

Save a Word Document in a Compatible File Format

1. Open file.
2. Click **Office Button** 🗔 ..... Alt+F
3. Click **Save As** .... A
4. Navigate to desired storage location.
5. Click **File name** text box.... Alt+N
6. Type new file name.
7. Click **Save as type** drop-down arrow .... Alt+T
8. Click desired file type .... ↑, ↓, ↵Enter
9. Click **Save** .... Alt+S

✓ If the File Conversion dialog box displays, click OK.

Open a Compatible File Type (Ctrl+O)

1. Click **Office Button** 🗔 ..... Alt+F
2. Click **Open** .... O

3. Navigate to storage location
4. Click **Files of type** drop-down arrow .... Alt+T
5. Click desired file type .... ↑, ↓, ↵Enter
6. Click file name.
7. Click **Open** .... Alt+O

✓ If the File Conversion dialog box displays, click OK.

Save a Compatible File (Ctrl+S)

1. Open file.
2. Click **Save** button on Quick Access Toolbar .... Ctrl+S

OR

a. Click **Office Button** 🗔 .... Alt+F
b. Click **Save** .... S
3. If prompted, click **Yes** to save the file in its original format .... Y

OR

a. Click **No** to save the file as a Word document .... N
b. Navigate to desired storage location.
c. Click **File name** text box .... Alt+N
d. Type new file name
e. Click **Save** .... Alt+S

Save a Compatible File as a New File in Word Format

1. Open file.
2. Click **Office Button** 🗔 ..... Alt+F
3. Point to **Save As** .... F
4. Click **Word Document** ...... W
5. Navigate to desired storage location.
6. Click **File name** text box.... Alt+N
7. Type new file name.
8. Click **Save** .... Alt+S

EXERCISE DIRECTIONS

Enter Document Properties

1. Open the file 💿 **21ALASKA** and save it as **21ALASKA_xx.**
2. Display the Document Information Panel.
3. Enter the Title property: **Alaska Press Release.**
4. Display the document's Properties dialog box, and check the number of words in the document.
5. Enter the following summary information:

   Subject: **Tour to Southeast Alaska**
   Author: **Your name**
   Manager: **Peter Lane**
   Company: **Voyager Travel Adventures**

   Category: **Press Release**
   Keywords: **Alaska, Tour, Adventure**
   Comments: **Text supplied by Lane. Revised for distribution.**

6. Close the dialog box and close the Document Information Panel.
7. Check the spelling and grammar in the document.
8. Display the document in Print Preview.
9. Print the document.
10. Close the document, saving all changes.

Work with Compatible Files

1. Open **21ALASKA_xx** as read-only, previewing the document properties in the Open dialog box before opening the file.
2. Change the headline to **Tour Southeast Alaska with Voyager Travel.**
3. Save the document in plain text format, with the name **21ALASKA2_xx.**
4. In the File Conversion dialog box, make sure the Insert line breaks checkbox is selected, and then click OK.
5. Close the document.
6. Open the **21ALASKA2_xx** text file in Word. The text file should look similar to the one in the illustration.
7. Close the file, saving all changes.

For Immediate Release

Contact: Your Name
             303-555-8397

Tour Southeast Alaska with Voyager Travel

Denver, CO -- Voyager Travel is offering a 10-day tour of Southeast Alaska. This remarkable part of the state is home to bald eagles, grizzly bears, humpback whales, and orcas, as well as many other species of animals. Join Voyager Travel to experience this exciting area.

Summer in Alaska offers nearly 14 hours of daylight, leaving loads of time for exploration and adventure. Some of the scheduled activities include kayaking, white-water rafting, hiking, and biking. Opportunities for other activities will be available. A registered guide will accompany you on your travels. Some of the destinations include Sitka, Juneau, Skagway, Haines, and Gustavus. Travel from destination to destination may be by ferry, train, floatplane, or automobile. Lodging is at hotels, inns, and bed and breakfasts.

Departure dates are set for July 13 and August 14. The tour is limited to 12 participants, so reserve your space early. The tour is all-inclusive. For complete pricing and other information call 303-555-8397, or visit our website: www.vtadventures.com.

ON YOUR OWN

1. Open OWD20_*xx*, the file you created in the On Your Own section of Exercise 20, or open 21LETTER, as read-only.

2. Use the Properties dialog box to check the number of words in the document.

3. Note the file size, date created, and date last modified.

4. Enter document properties, including Title, Subject, Manager, Company, Category, Keywords, and Comments.

5. Try saving the document.

6. Save the file as OWD21_*xx*.

7. Save the file in plain text format with line breaks as OWD21-2_*xx*.

8. Print the file.

9. Close the document, saving all changes.

Exercise | 22

Skills Covered

- **Preview a Closed Document**
- **Print a Closed Document**

Software Skills Preview a document before opening it or printing it to make sure it is the correct file. Print files without opening them to save time or to print more than one document at once.

Application Skills As a travel agent for Voyager Travel Adventures, you have been asked to find out if any employees are interested in going on the first Alaska tour. In this exercise, you will preview, open, and revise the press release about the tour. Then you will create a memo to employees. Finally, you will print both documents.

TERMS

No new vocabulary in this exercise.

NOTES

Preview a Closed Document

- By default, Word displays a list of files in the Open dialog box.
- You can change the display in the dialog box to show a preview of the document selected in the file list.
- Previewing is useful for making sure a document is the one you want before you open it or print it.
- Most documents are too large to be displayed completely in the dialog box; use the scroll arrows in the preview area to scroll up and down.
- If you don't want to display a preview, you can set the Open dialog box to display large or small file icons, the default file list, file details, such as size, type, and date last saved, or document properties.

Print a Closed Document

- To save time, you can print a document from the Open dialog box without opening it.
- The file prints using the default print settings; the Print dialog box does not display.

Preview a document in the Open dialog box

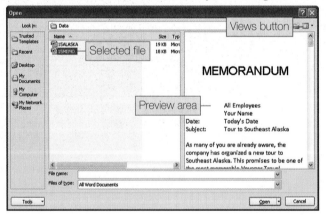

- Print without opening when you are certain the document is ready for printing.
  - ✓ *You can also print a document without opening it from Windows.*
- You can select more than one file at a time for printing in the Open dialog box.
- Selecting multiple files for printing sends them all to the printer, where they will be printed one after the other.
- All selected files must be in the same folder.

PROCEDURES

Preview a Closed Document

1. Click **Office Button** .... Alt+F
2. Click **Open** .... O
3. Navigate to location where file is stored.
4. Click document name.
5. Click **Views** button drop-down arrow ▦ ▾.
6. Click **Pre̲view** V

Change the File List View

1. Click **Office Button** .... Alt+F
2. Click **Open** .... O
3. Click **Views** button drop-down arrow ▦ ▾.

4. Click desired view:
   - ■ Click **Thumbnails** .... T
   - ■ Click **Tile̲s** .... S
   - ■ Click **Icon̲s** .... N
   - ■ Click **L̲ist** L
   - ■ Click **D̲etails** .... D
   - ■ Click **P̲roperties** .... R

   ✓ *Or click the Views button repeatedly to cycle through the Views options.*

Print a Closed File

1. Click **Office Button** .... Alt+F
2. Click **Open** .... O
3. Navigate to location where file is stored.

4. Click file to print.
5. Click **Too̲ls** button .... Alt+L
6. Click **Print** .... P

Print Multiple Closed Files

1. Click **Office Button** .... Alt+F
2. Click **Open** .... O
3. Navigate to location where file is stored.
4. Click first document name.
5. Press and hold Ctrl .... Ctrl
6. Click each additional document name.
7. Click **Too̲ls** button .... Alt+L
8. Click **Print** .... P

EXERCISE DIRECTIONS

1. Start Word, if necessary.
2. In the Open dialog box, preview ▦21ALASKA_*xx*, the document you created in Exercise 21, or preview ⊙22ALASKA.
3. Change the Open dialog box to display Details instead of the preview.
4. Open the document and save it as 22TOUR_*xx*.
5. Make revisions as indicated in Illustration A.
6. Check the spelling and grammar in the document.
7. Close the document, saving all changes.
8. Create a new document and type the memo shown in Illustration B, or open ⊙22MEMO.
9. Save the document as 22MEMO_*xx*, and then close it.
10. Preview the 22MEMO_*xx* document in the Open dialog box.
11. Print both the 22TOUR_*xx* and 22MEMO_*xx* documents without opening them.

Curriculum Connection: Language Arts

Shakespeare

William Shakespeare is considered one of the world's greatest poets and playwrights. He lived and worked in Elizabethan England at the end of the 16th century. He could be romantic, insulting, and very funny. Even though he wrote in English, he used language that seems very different from the English we use today, but if you take a few minutes to read his words carefully, you can understand what he means to say.

Translate Shakespeare

Pick a poem or soliloquy that Shakespeare wrote and translate it into contemporary language you would use today. Use the Internet or the library to locate a poem.

For Immediate Release

Contact: Your Name
             303-555-8397

Voyager Travel Adventures Announces a New Tour to Alaska

Denver, CO -- Voyager Travel is offering a 10-day tour of Southeast Alaska. This remarkable part of the state is home to bald eagles, grizzly bears, humpback whales, and orcas, as well as many other species of animals. Join Voyager Travel to experience this exciting area.

unique and

part of our country

Adventures

Summer in Alaska offers nearly 14 hours of daylight, leaving loads of time for exploration and adventure. Some of the scheduled activities include kayaking, white-water rafting, hiking, and biking. Opportunities for other activities will be available. A registered guide will accompany you on your travels. Some of the destinations include Sitka, Juneau, Skagway, Haines, and Gustavus. Travel from destination to destination may be by ferry, train, floatplane, or automobile. Lodging is at hotels, inns, and bed and breakfasts.

plenty

Departure dates are set for July 13 and August 14. The tour is limited to 12 participants, so reserve your space early. The tour is all-inclusive. For complete pricing and other information call 303-555-8397, or visit our website: www.vtadventures.com.

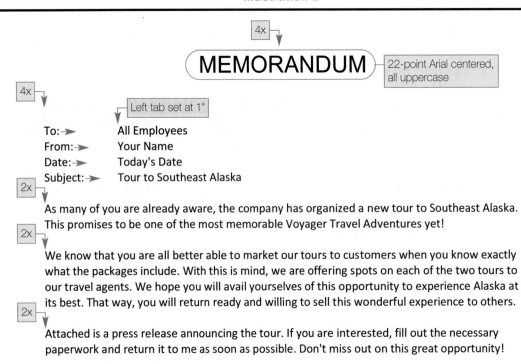

4x

MEMORANDUM

22-point Arial centered, all uppercase

4x

Left tab set at 1"

To:➔   All Employees
From:➔   Your Name
Date:➔   Today's Date
Subject:➔   Tour to Southeast Alaska

2x

As many of you are already aware, the company has organized a new tour to Southeast Alaska. This promises to be one of the most memorable Voyager Travel Adventures yet!

2x

We know that you are all better able to market our tours to customers when you know exactly what the packages include. With this is mind, we are offering spots on each of the two tours to our travel agents. We hope you will avail yourselves of this opportunity to experience Alaska at its best. That way, you will return ready and willing to sell this wonderful experience to others.

2x

Attached is a press release announcing the tour. If you are interested, fill out the necessary paperwork and return it to me as soon as possible. Don't miss out on this great opportunity!

ON YOUR OWN

1. Start Word.
2. Preview some of the documents that you have created for the On Your Own sections of previous exercises, or preview ⊙**22LETTER**, ⊙**22TECH**, and ⊙**22RESUME**
3. Display other views in the Open dialog box instead of the preview.
4. Display the preview again.
5. Print at least two of the documents without opening them.
6. When you are finished, exit Word.

Critical Thinking

Application Skills The Whole Grains Bread franchise manager wants to contact another potential franchisee outside of California. In this exercise, you will open an existing letter, save it with a new name, revise it using the techniques you have learned so far, and add Document Properties. You will then open a document listing factors for franchise success, which you will save in a compatible file format. Finally, you will preview and print both documents.

EXERCISE DIRECTIONS

1. Start Word, if necessary.
2. Open ◎ **23EXPAND** as read-only.
3. Save the file as **23EXPAND_xx**.
4. Insert, delete, and replace text as marked on Illustration A.
5. Enter Document Properties summary information as follows:

   Title: **Letter to Martin Hamilton**
   Subject: **Potential Franchisee**
   Author: **Your Name**
   Manager: **Frank Kaplan**
   Company: **Whole Grains Bread**
   Category: **Letter**
   Keywords: **Franchise, Expansion, Phoenix, Arizona.**
   Comments: **Letter regarding expanding franchises outside California.**

6. Check the spelling and grammar.
7. Save the changes.
8. Close the document.
9. Open ◎ **23SUCCESS** and save the document in Rich Text Format with the file name **23SUCCESS_xx**.

   ✓ *Rich Text Format preserves some of the font formatting that Plain Text format does not preserve. It adds an .rtf file extension to the file name.*

10. Copy and move text as marked on Illustration B.
    a. Copy the word *Five* from the heading above the list and paste it between the words *Franchise* and *Success* in the title, matching the destination formatting.
    b. Move the last sentence of the second paragraph so that it is a new paragraph between the last item in the list and the last paragraph of the document.
11. Close the document, saving all changes.
12. Preview the **23EXPAND_xx** document properties without opening the file.
13. Preview the **23EXPAND_xx** and **23SUCCESS_xx** documents without opening them.

    ✓ *Remember, because the 23SUCCESS_xx document is in rich text format, you will have to selected All Files from the Files of type list to display it in the Open dialog box.*

14. Print both the **23EXPAND_xx** and **23SUCCESS_xx** documents without opening them.
15. Exit Word.

Illustration A

Today's Date

~~CERTIFIED MAIL~~

Ms. Lindsey Perrins
Franchise Owner
WHOLE GRAINS BREAD
456 Main Street
Brentwood, California 94513

Mr. Martin Hamilton
Manager
Osborne Bistro
722 Osborne Street
Phoenix, AZ 85013

Dear ~~Ms. Perrins:~~ — Mr. Hamilton

Subject: Opening A New Franchise

Phoenix, Arizona

Your interest in opening a new franchise in ~~Park City, Utah~~ could not have come at a better time. As you may already know, WHOLE GRAINS BREAD is actively seeking to expand our franchise presence outside of California. As ~~one of our most successful franchisees,~~ we believe you are a prime candidate to pioneer this venture.

a successful bistro manager

document

I have enclosed a ~~memo~~ listing some of the factors we consider vital to the success of a new franchise. Although our expansion plans are in an early stage at the moment, we would like very much to sit down with you to share ideas and information. WHOLE GRAINS BREAD welcomes input from our franchisees. Please call my office at your earliest convenience to set up an appointment. I look forward to hearing from you.

Sincerely,

Frank Kaplan
Franchise Manager
WHOLE GRAINS BREAD
320 Magnolia Avenue
Larkspur, CA 94939

Fk/yo

Enclosure

Copy to: Mr. Anthony Splendoria, CEO

Whole Grains Bread
Franchise Success Factors

Copy and paste

Whole Grains Bread offers fresh breads and pastries to specialty shops up and down the West Coast. In addition, Whole Grains Bread franchises bring a unique dining experience to customers at many locations.

At **Whole Grains Bread**, we believe there are certain standard factors that contribute to the success of any franchise. After careful study, we have found that our most successful operators share some significant values and methods of operation. If a franchisee or manager takes these factors into consideration for day-to-day operations, the success of his or her store is virtually guaranteed.

Five Factors for Success

<u>Cleanliness counts</u>
<u>The customer comes first</u>
<u>Be courteous to all</u>
<u>Treat employees with respect</u>
<u>Listen and respond to compliments, criticism, and complaints</u>

Move sentence to create a new paragraph

At this time, **Whole Grains Bread** is looking to expand outside of the West Coast. We are actively seeking men and women who are willing to incorporate these factors into their daily business lives in order to build and maintain a successful **Whole Grains Bread** franchise. For more information call 415-555-3200.

Exercise | 24

Curriculum Integration

Application Skills   Use the skills you have learned in Lesson 3 to write a review of at least two paragraphs about a book, poem, short story, or play that you have read in your English or Language arts class. (A sample is shown in Illustration A.) Type the title and at the beginning of the document, centered and underlined. Include the author's name on a separate line. Leave space, and then type a brief summary of the plot and your opinion about it. Print the document and then exchange it with a classmate. Handwrite proofreader's marks on your classmate's printed review to indicate suggestions he or she might make. For example, you can mark text that might be made bold, italic, or underlined, or you could indicate where a paragraph might be moved or copied. Retrieve your review from your classmate. Incorporate the suggestions marked on the printed document into your Word file, and then print the finished document.

EXERCISE DIRECTIONS

Start Word, if necessary, and create a new document. Save it as **24REVIEW_xx**.

Select to display elements that might help you while you work, such as the rulers and nonprinting characters, and make sure all the features you want to use are enabled, such as AutoCorrect and Check Spelling as you Type.

Type the title and author at the top of the page. Remember that you can select a font, font size, and font styles, and set line and paragraph spacing.

Leave space, and then type the review, including at least two paragraphs.

Correct spelling and grammatical errors as you type, if necessary, and search the thesaurus to find alternatives to common words, such as *go*, *went*, and *said*.

Save the changes you have made to the document.

Display the document in Print Preview.

If necessary, adjust the vertical alignment, or shrink the document to fit on one page.

Print the document.

Exchange printed documents with a classmate. Read the document carefully, and handwrite proofreader's marks on the document, making suggestions for modifying or improving the review.

Retrieve your own review and incorporate your classmate's suggestions into your Word file.

Correct the spelling and grammar in the document, and save the changes.

Display the document in Print Preview.

If necessary, adjust the vertical alignment, or shrink the document to fit on one page.

Print the document.

Close the document, saving all changes.

Illustration A

Last Days of Summer
By
Steve Kluger

The book **Last Days of Summer** is more than just a baseball story. It is a fun and exciting journey through life with interesting characters. It is funny at times and heartbreaking at other times. I think it will appeal to everyone – not just sports fans.

The book is set during World War II, in Brooklyn, New York. It tells the story of a smart trouble-maker named Joey Margolis, who is in Junior High school. Joey writes letters to Charlie Banks, the third baseman for the New York Giants baseball team, until finally Charlie Banks starts writing back. They strike up a lasting friendship.

Mr. Kluger, the author, uses a unique approach in writing this book. The story is told using the letters written by Joey and Charlie. Other documents are included as well, such as news clippings, letters to and from other people, Joey's report cards, and transcripts of conversations he has was policemen and psychiatrists. At first, this method seems a bit distracting, but Mr. Kluger is such as good storyteller that the reader quickly becomes lost in the plot and the lives of the characters.

I highly recommend **Last Days of Summer**. It has some strong language and mature themes, but it is a deeply moving story of growing up under difficult circumstances.

Lesson | 4

Formatting Basics

Skills Covered

- Apply Font Effects
- Font Color

- Highlight Text
- Format Painter

Software Skills You can enhance text using font effects and colors. You can highlight text to change the color around the text without changing the font color. Highlighting is useful for calling attention to text and for making text stand out on the page. Use the Format Painter to quickly copy formatting from one location to another. The Format Painter saves you time and makes it easy to duplicate formatting throughout a document.

Application Skills You have been asked to design a document advertising the Alaska tour for Adventure Travel, Inc. If the company approves of the document, it will be made available in the office and posted as a Web page on the company Web site. In this exercise, you will create the document using font effects and color. You will also highlight text that you want your manager to approve, and use the Format Painter to copy formatting.

TERMS

Color swatch A block on a color palette that you click to select that color.

Font effects Formatting features used to enhance or emphasize text.

Standard colors Ten primary and secondary colors.

Theme A set of coordinated colors, fonts, and effects.

Theme colors Colors assigned to an element based on the settings of the current theme.

NOTES

Apply Font Effects

- In Word's Font dialog box you can select from a list of **font effects** for enhancing and emphasizing text.
- Three of the effects—Strikethrough, Superscript and Subscript—are also available in the Font group on the Home tab of the Ribbon.

✓ *Hidden is also an option in the Effects area of the Font dialog box. Hidden text is not displayed on-screen or printed unless you select to display it.*

- You can apply font effects to selected text, or select the effects before you type new text.

■ You can apply more than one effect at a time.

The Font dialog box

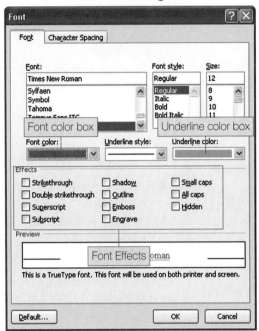

The Font Group

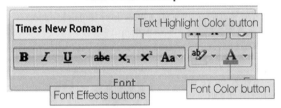

Font Color

■ Use color to enhance text in documents that will be viewed on-screen or printed on a color printer.

■ The most recently selected font color displays on the Font Color button $\boxed{\text{A} \cdot}$.

■ To change font color, you select a **color swatch** from the Font Color palette available in the Font group on the Home tab of the Ribbon, on the Mini Toolbar, or in the Font dialog box.

■ On the palette, you can select from **Theme Colors** and **Standard Colors**. You can also select Automatic, which is the default color.

  ✓ *You learn about themes in Exercise 31.*

■ Rest your mouse pointer on a swatch to see the color name in a ScreenTip, and to preview how the color would affect selected text.

■ You can change the color of an underline independently from the color of the font.

Highlight Text

■ Highlighting calls attention to text by placing a color background on the text.

■ You can highlight text as a decorative or visual effect, but Word's Highlighter feature is commonly used like a highlighter pen on paper to mark text that requires attention.

■ Yellow is the default highlight color, but you can select a different color from the Text Highlight Color palette in the Font group on the Home tab of the Ribbon, or on the Mini Toolbar.

  ✓ *Color highlighting will print in color when printed on a color printer and print in gray when printed on a black and white printer.*

■ The most recently selected highlight color displays on the Text Highlight Color button $\boxed{\text{aby} \cdot}$.

■ You can only apply a highlight to existing text.

Format Painter

■ Use the Format Painter to copy formatting from existing formatted text to existing unformatted text.

■ The Format Painter button is in the Clipboard group on the Home tab of the Ribbon.

Curriculum Connection: Science

Defining Planets

In 2006, an assembly of astronomers refined the definition of what it means to be a planet. As a result, Pluto lost its status as a planet in our solar system and was demoted to the classification of dwarf planet. Not everyone was happy with the change.

What is Pluto?

Research the decision that led to Pluto's reclassification and write your opinion about it. Explain why you either agree or disagree with the change, and back your opinion with facts.

PROCEDURES

Apply Font Effects

1. Select text.

   OR

   Position insertion point where new text will be typed.

2. Click the **Home** tab .... Alt + H

   `Font Group`

3. Click one of the following:
   - **Strikethrough** abc 4
   - **Subscript** x₂ 5
   - **Superscript** x² 6

   OR

   - Click **Font** group dialog box launcher ⬓ .... F, N
   - Click to select checkbox for desired effect(s)
     - **Strikethrough** .... Alt + K
     - **Double strikethrough** .... Alt + L
     - **Superscript** .... Alt + P
     - **Subscript** .... Alt + B
     - **Shadow** .... Alt + W
     - **Outline** .... Alt + O
     - **Emboss** .... Alt + E
     - **Engrave** .... Alt + G
     - **Small caps** .... Alt + M
     - **All caps** .... Alt + A
     - **Hidden** .... Alt + H

   ✓ *Clear check mark to remove effect.*

4. Click **OK** .... ↵Enter

Apply Font Color

1. Select text.

   OR

   Position insertion point where new text will be typed.

2. Click the **Home** tab .... Alt + H

`Font Group`

3. Click **Font Color** button drop-down arrow A⬝ .... F, C

4. Click desired color swatch .... ↑/↓/←/→, ↵Enter

   ✓ *Rest the mouse pointer on a swatch to preview selected text in that color.*

To apply color currently displayed on Font Color button:
   - Click **Font Color** button A⬝.

To use the Font dialog box:

1. Select text.

   OR

   Position insertion point where new text will be typed.

2. Click the **Home** tab .... Alt + H

   `Font Group`

3. Click **Font** group dialog box launcher ⬓ .... F, N

4. Click **Font color** drop-down arrow .... Alt + C

5. Click desired color swatch .... ↑/↓/←/→, ↵Enter

   ✓ *Click Automatic to select default color.*

6. Click **OK** .... ↵Enter

Apply a Highlight

Select and apply a highlight color:

1. Select text.

2. Click the **Home** tab .... Alt + H

   `Font Group`

3. Click **Text Highlight Color** button drop-down arrow ab⬝ I

4. Click desired highlight color swatch .... ↑/↓/←/→, ↵Enter

   ✓ *Rest the mouse pointer on a swatch to preview the highlight in that color.*

OR

1. Click the **Home** tab .... Alt + H

   `Font Group`

2. Click **Text Highlight Color** button drop-down arrow ab⬝ I

3. Click desired highlight color swatch .... ↑/↓/←/→, ↵Enter

   ✓ *Mouse pointer changes to the Highlight Text pointer ⬟.*

4. Drag pointer across text to highlight.

5. Click **Text Highlight Color** button ab⬝ to turn off highlighter .... Esc

Apply the color currently displayed on Text Highlight Color button:

1. Select text.

2. Click the **Home** tab .... Alt + H

   `Font Group`

3. Click **Text Highlight Color** button ab⬝.

   OR

1. Click the **Home** tab .... Alt + H

   `Font Group`

2. Click **Text Highlight Color** button ab⬝.

   ✓ *Mouse pointer changes to the Highlight Text pointer ⬟.*

3. Drag pointer across text to highlight.

4. Click **Text Highlight Color** button ab⬝ to turn off highlighter .... Esc

To remove highlighting:

1. Select highlighted text.

2. Click the **Home** tab .... Alt + H

   `Font Group`

3. Click **Text Highlight Color** button drop-down arrow ab⬝ I

4. Click **No Color** on the color palette .... N

OR

1. Click the **Home** tab........... Alt + H

   Font Group

2. Click **Text Highlight Color** button drop-down arrow [ab🖉▾]........... I

3. Click **No Color** on the color palette........................... N

   ✓ *Mouse pointer changes to the Highlight Text pointer [🖉].*

4. Drag pointer across text to remove highlighting.

5. Click **Text Highlight Color** button [ab🖉▾] to turn off highlighter............................. Esc

Copy Formatting (Ctrl+Shift+C)

Copy formatting once:

1. Select formatted text.

2. Click the **Home** tab........... Alt + H

   Clipboard Group

3. Click **Format Painter** button [🖌]........................... F, P

   ✓ *Mouse pointer changes to the Format Painter pointer [🖌I].*

4. Select text to format.

   ✓ *Click a word to quickly copy the formatting to that word.*

Copy formatting repeatedly:

1. Select formatted text.

2. Click the **Home** tab........... Alt + H

   Clipboard Group

3. Double-click **Format Painter** button [🖌]........................... F, P

   ✓ *Mouse pointer changes to the Format Painter pointer [🖌I].*

4. Select first text to format.

5. Select additional text to format.

6. Repeat step 5 until all text is formatted.

7. Click **Format Painter** button [🖌] to turn it off......... Esc

EXERCISE DIRECTIONS

1. Start Word, if necessary.

2. Open ◉ **25ANNOUNCE**.

3. Save the document as **25ANNOUNCE_xx**.

4. Apply the formatting shown in Illustration A.

   a. Change the font and font size as marked.

   ✓ *If the specified font is not available on your computer, select a different font.*

   b. Set horizontal alignments as marked.

   c. Apply font effects as marked.

   d. Change font color as marked.

   e. Apply highlighting as marked.

   ✓ *Use the Format Painter to copy formatting whenever possible.*

5. Check the spelling and grammar.

6. Display the document in Print Preview. It should look similar to the illustration.

   ✓ *If the document is longer or shorter than the one shown, check to see if you inadvertently formatted the blank lines between paragraphs. In the illustration, all blank lines are formatted with 12-point Calibri.*

7. Save the changes.

8. Print the document.

9. Close the document, saving all changes.

28-point Broadway, centered, standard blue

Voyager Travel Adventures
TRAVEL BEYOND YOUR WILDEST DREAMS

20-point Broadway, centered, standard blue, small caps effect with a standard light green wavy underline

28-point Comic Sans MS, centered, standard blue, outline and all caps effects

EAGLES
AND
WHALES
AND
BEARS

18-point Comic Sans MS, centered, standard light green, shadow and small caps effects

72-point Broadway, centered, standard red, shadow and small caps effects

OH, MY!

14-point Comic Sans MS, justified

Join Voyager Travel Adventures for a guided tour of Southeast Alaska. Spend glorious 14-hour days exploring one of the greatest wilderness areas in the U.S. Enjoy kayaking, rafting, hiking, fishing, and biking through magnificent scenery. Spend relaxing, comfortable evenings in well-equipped lodges and inns. Itinerary includes stops in Sitka, Juneau, Haines, Gustavus, and Skagway.

Bright green highlight

20-point Comic Sans MS, standard red, small caps effect, left tab at 2.5"

DEPARTURE DATES: JULY 13
                     AUGUST 14

For complete itinerary, availability, pricing, and other information call 303-555-8397, or visit our website: www.vtadventures.com.

14-point Comic Sans MS, justified

ON YOUR OWN

1. Create an invitation to an event such as a birthday party, graduation, or meeting.

2. Save the document as OWD25_*xx*.

3. Format the document using the techniques you have learned so far, including fonts, alignment options, and font effects.

4. Change the font color for some text.

5. Try applying underlines using different underline styles and colors.

6. Copy the formatting from one location to another.

7. Preview the document and print it.

8. Ask a classmate to review the document and make comments or suggestions.

9. Incorporate the suggestions into the document.

10. Save your changes, close the document, and exit Word.

Exercise | 26

Skills Covered

- Use Symbols

Software Skills Use symbols to supplement the standard characters available on the keyboard and to add visual interest to documents. For example, you can insert symbols such as hearts and stars into documents as borders or separators.

Application Skills The Marketing Director of Whole Grains Bread has asked you to create a flyer announcing the grand opening of a new cafe. In this exercise, you will create the flyer using the formatting techniques you have learned so far. You will also insert symbols to enhance the flyer.

TERMS

Symbol Shapes, mathematical and scientific notations, currency signs, and other visual elements you can insert in documents by using the Symbol dialog box.

NOTES

Use Symbols

- **Symbols** are characters that cannot be typed from the keyboard, such as hearts, stars, and other shapes, as well as foreign alphabet characters.
- Symbols can be selected, edited, and formatted in a document just like regular text characters.
- Several symbol fonts come with Microsoft Office 2007 and others are available for download on the Internet.
- Many regular character fonts also include some symbol characters.
- You can also insert special characters such as paragraph marks and ellipses.
- You can select from a gallery of common and recently used symbols in the Symbols group on the Insert tab of the Ribbon, or you can select from all available symbols in the Symbol dialog box.
- When you use the Symbol dialog box, you first select a font, and then select the desired symbol.
- There is a list of recently used symbols in the dialog box, as well.

- Some symbols have number codes you can use for identification, and some have shortcut keys you can use to insert the symbol into a document.
- When you insert symbols, the default font formatting is applied to the character. You can change the font size, style, and effects just as you can for regular text characters.

Symbol dialog box

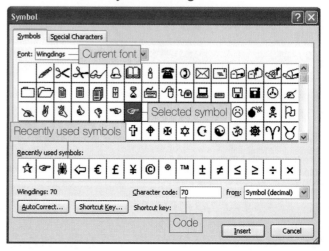

PROCEDURES

Insert a Symbol from the Gallery

1. Position insertion point where you want to insert a symbol.
2. Click **Insert** tab .... `Alt`+`N`

   Symbols Group

3. Click **Symbol** button `Ω` .... `U`
4. Click symbol to insert .... `←`/`→`/`↑`/`↓`, `↵Enter`

Insert a Symbol from the Dialog Box

1. Position insertion point where you want to insert a symbol.
2. Click **Insert** tab .... `Alt`+`N`

   Symbols Group

3. Click **Symbol** button `Ω` .... `U`
4. Click **More Symbols** .... `M`
5. Click **Font** drop-down arrow .... `Alt`+`F`

6. Click symbol font .... `↓`/`↑`, `↵Enter`
7. Click symbol to insert .... `Tab↹` 2x, `←`/`→`/`↑`/`↓`
8. Click **Insert** .... `Alt`+`I`

   ✓ Repeat the steps to insert additional symbols without closing the Symbol dialog box.

9. Click **Close** .... `↵Enter`

EXERCISE DIRECTIONS

1. Start Word, if necessary.
2. Open ⊙ **26GRAND**.
3. Save the document as **26GRAND_xx**.
4. Format the text as marked in Illustration A.

   a. Use a serif font for the entire document. (Times New Roman is used in Illustration A.)

   b. Apply font sizes, colors, and effects as shown.

   ✓ Be sure that the blank lines are also formatted as indicated—12-point Times New Roman.

   c. Apply alignments as shown.

   d. Use the Format Painter to copy formatting whenever possible.

5. Use the Wingdings font to insert symbols as marked in the illustration.

✓ Word might automatically format lines that begin with a symbol followed by a tab as a list. If this happens, click the Automatic Format Options button and click Stop automatically formatting lists, and then try again. You learn about lists in Exercise 28.

✓ Adjust the font size and formatting of symbol characters the same way you adjust the font size and formatting of text characters.

✓ Hint: Use Copy and Paste to copy a symbol from one location to another, or use the Repeat command (Ctrl+Y) to repeat the insertion.

6. Display the document in Print Preview. It should look similar to the illustration.
7. Print the document.
8. Close the document, saving the changes.

20-point, standard blue, centered, all caps effect — GRAND OPENING

☆☆☆☆☆☆☆☆☆☆☆☆☆☆☆☆☆☆☆

36-point, standard blue, centered, engrave and small caps effects — WHOLE GRAINS BREAD

26-point Wingdings symbol #182, standard red, centered

☆☆☆☆☆☆☆☆☆☆☆☆☆☆☆☆☆☆☆

20-point, standard blue, centered, all caps effect — ANNOUNCES

THE GRAND OPENING OF ITS NEWEST CAFÉ

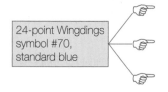

24-point Wingdings symbol #70, standard blue

TASTY TREATS
CONTESTS
AND MORE...

28-point standard blue, engrave and small caps effects

☆☆☆☆☆☆☆☆☆☆☆☆☆☆☆☆☆☆☆

28-point standard blue, centered, engrave and small caps effects —

THURSDAY, DECEMBER 12
2020 MAIN STREET
PARK CITY, UTAH 84060

26-point Wingdings symbol #182, standard red, centered

☆☆☆☆☆☆☆☆☆☆☆☆☆☆☆☆☆☆☆

24-point justified —

Whole Grains Bread features freshly baked breads and pastries as well as soups, salads, and sandwiches. The Park City location is the first Whole Grains Bread shop in Utah.

ON YOUR OWN

1. Open the document 🖮OWD25_*xx*, the document you created in Exercise 25, or open 💿26INVITE.

2. Save the document as **OWD26_*xx***.

3. Use symbols to enhance the document. For example, use symbols as separators between words or paragraphs, or use them to decorate or emphasize the document.

4. Try different symbol fonts.

5. Try changing the font size for a symbol inserted in a document.

6. Try repeating a symbol to create a line across the page.

7. Preview and print the document.

8. Ask a classmate to review the document and offer comments and suggestions.

9. Incorporate the comments and suggestions into the document.

10. Close the document, saving all changes.

Exercise | 27

Skills Covered

- **Indent Text**

Software Skills Use indents in your documents to call attention to a paragraph, to achieve a particular visual effect, or to leave white space along the margins for notes or illustrations.

Application Skills In response to a member survey, the Michigan Avenue Athletic Club is instituting a few new policies and programs. In this exercise, you will use line and paragraph spacing and indents to format a document explaining the new programs. You will also apply font formatting, alignments, and tabs to the document.

TERMS

Indent A temporary left and/or right margin for lines or paragraphs.

NOTES

Indent Text

- There are five types of **indents**:
  - *Left* indents text from the left margin.
  - *Right* indents text from the right margin.
  - *Double* indents text from both the left and right margins.
  - *First line* indents just the first line of a paragraph from the left margin.
  - *Hanging* indents all lines but the first line from the left margin.
- Each paragraph can have different indent settings.
- You can set indents using the Indent options in the Paragraph group on the Page Layout tab of the Ribbon, or in the Paragraph dialog box.
- Use the Increase Indent button 🔢 in the Paragraph group on the Home tab of the Ribbon or on the Mini toolbar to quickly move the current indent .5" to the right.
- Use the Decrease Indent button 🔢 to move the current indent .5" to the left.

- You can use the horizontal ruler to set and adjust indents.
  - You can set a first line indent or a hanging indent using the Tab selector box.
  - You can drag indent markers on the ruler to set or adjust indents.

Indents in a document

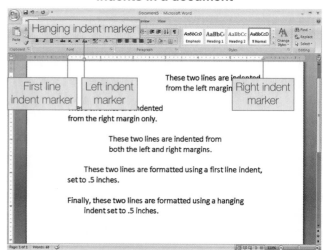

PROCEDURES

Indent Text

To use the Paragraph dialog box:

1. Position insertion point where text will be typed.

   OR

   Position insertion point in paragraph to change.

   OR

   Select paragraph(s) to change.
2. Click the **Home** tab .... Alt + H

   Paragraph Group
3. Click **Paragraph** group dialog box launcher ⬏ .... P, G
4. Click **Indents and Spacing** page tab .... Alt + I
5. Click **Left** text box .... Alt + L

   OR

   Click **Right** text box .... Alt + R
6. Type distance from margin.

   OR

   a. Click **Special** drop-down arrow .... Alt + S
   b. Click **First line** .... ↓, ↵Enter

OR

a. Click **Hanging** .... ↓ 2x, ↵Enter
b. Click **By** text box ...... Alt + Y
c. Type distance to indent or click spin arrows .... ↑/↓
7. Click **OK** .... ↵Enter

Quickly adjust a left indent:

1. Position insertion point where text will be typed.

   OR

   Position insertion point in paragraph to change.

   OR

   Select paragraph(s) to change.
2. Click the **Home** tab .... Alt + H

   Paragraph Group
3. Click **Increase Indent** button 📑 .... A, I

   OR

   Click **Decrease Indent** button 📑 .... A, O

Set Indents using the horizontal ruler:

1. Position insertion point where text will be typed.

   OR

   Position insertion point in paragraph to change.

OR

Select paragraph(s) to change.
2. Click **Tab selector** until desired indent type displays.

   ✓ Only the First-line indent marker and Hanging indent marker are available.
3. Click ruler at location where you want to set indent.

Adjust indents using the horizontal ruler:

1. Position insertion point where text will be typed.

   OR

   Position insertion point in paragraph to change.

   OR

   Select paragraph(s) to change.
2. Do any of the following:
   - Drag **Left indent** marker 🔲
   - Drag **Right indent** marker 🔲
   - Drag **Hanging indent** marker 🔲
   - Drag **First line indent** marker 🔲

EXERCISE DIRECTIONS

1. Start Word, if necessary.
2. Open 💿 **27SURVEY**.
3. Save the document as **27SURVEY_xx**.
4. Follow steps 5 through 9 to achieve the results shown in Illustration A.
5. Apply font formatting as shown.

   ✓ Arial is the only font used in the illustration. Unless otherwise noted, it should be set to 12 points in size.
6. Insert symbols as marked in the illustration.
7. Set alignments and tabs as marked in the illustration.

   ✓ Unless otherwise noted, paragraphs are justified.
8. Set line spacing, paragraph spacing, and indents as shown in the illustration.

   ✓ For a refresher on line and paragraph spacing, refer to Exercise 11.
9. Check spelling and grammar.
10. Display the document in Print Preview. It should look similar to the illustration.
11. Print the document.
12. Close the document, saving all changes.

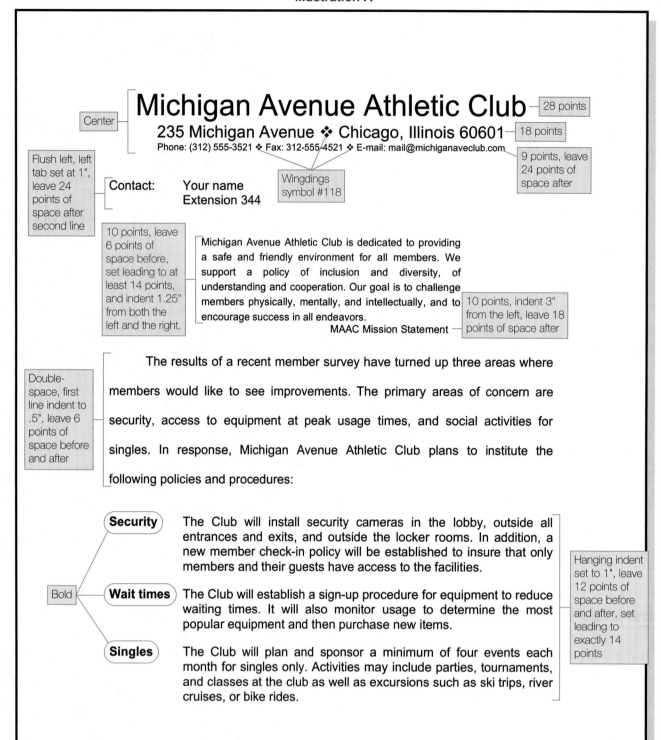

Center

Michigan Avenue Athletic Club
28 points

235 Michigan Avenue ❖ Chicago, Illinois 60601
18 points

Phone: (312) 555-3521 ❖ Fax: 312-555-4521 ❖ E-mail: mail@michiganaveclub.com
9 points, leave 24 points of space after

Flush left, left tab set at 1", leave 24 points of space after second line

Contact: Your name
                   Extension 344

Wingdings symbol #118

10 points, leave 6 points of space before, set leading to at least 14 points, and indent 1.25" from both the left and the right.

Michigan Avenue Athletic Club is dedicated to providing a safe and friendly environment for all members. We support a policy of inclusion and diversity, of understanding and cooperation. Our goal is to challenge members physically, mentally, and intellectually, and to encourage success in all endeavors.

MAAC Mission Statement

10 points, indent 3" from the left, leave 18 points of space after

Double-space, first line indent to .5", leave 6 points of space before and after

The results of a recent member survey have turned up three areas where members would like to see improvements. The primary areas of concern are security, access to equipment at peak usage times, and social activities for singles. In response, Michigan Avenue Athletic Club plans to institute the following policies and procedures:

Security   The Club will install security cameras in the lobby, outside all entrances and exits, and outside the locker rooms. In addition, a new member check-in policy will be established to insure that only members and their guests have access to the facilities.

Bold

Wait times   The Club will establish a sign-up procedure for equipment to reduce waiting times. It will also monitor usage to determine the most popular equipment and then purchase new items.

Hanging indent set to 1", leave 12 points of space before and after, set leading to exactly 14 points

Singles   The Club will plan and sponsor a minimum of four events each month for singles only. Activities may include parties, tournaments, and classes at the club as well as excursions such as ski trips, river cruises, or bike rides.

ON YOUR OWN

1. Think of some documents that could benefit from line spacing, paragraph spacing, and indent formatting. For example, many instructors require reports and papers to be double spaced. First drafts of documents that will be read by others should be double spaced so reviewers can jot notes or make corrections. A resume can be set up neatly using spacing and indent features, as can a reference list.

2. Plan a document that will contain brief (one paragraph each) descriptions of three types of technology used in business.

   a. Start by selecting three items, such as software programs, hardware devices, or the Internet.

   b. If necessary, research the items using a library or the Internet so that you have the information you need to write the descriptions.

3. Create a new document in Word.

4. Save the file as OWD27_*xx*.

5. Type a title or headline at the top of the document and a brief introduction.

6. Type the paragraphs describing each of the three items. Include a definition of each item, and explain its function or purpose. Include information about what tasks the item should be used for. Use proper grammar and punctuation.

7. Format the document using line and paragraph spacing and indents, as well as font formatting, tabs, and alignments.

8. Save the changes and print the document.

9. Ask a classmate to review the document and offer comments and suggestions.

10. Incorporate the suggestions into the document.

11. Save your changes, close the document, and exit Word.

Skills Covered

- Bulleted Lists
- Numbered Lists

- Sort

Software Skills   Lists are an effective way to present items of information. Use a bulleted list when the items do not have to be in any particular order, like a grocery list or a list of objectives. Use a numbered list when the order of the items is important, such as directions or instructions. Use Sort to organize a list into alphabetical or numerical order.

Application Skills   As the Customer Service Manager at the Michigan Avenue Athletic Club, you have recently received a number of complaints about the club's check-in policy. In this exercise, you will edit and format a memo to employees about the proper check-in procedure. You will use a bulleted list and a numbered list, and you will sort the bulleted list into alphabetical order.

TERMS

Bullet   A dot or symbol that marks an important line of information or designates items in a list.

Picture   A graphics image stored in a graphics file format.

Sort   To organize items into a specified order.

NOTES

Bulleted Lists

- Use **bullets** to mark items in a list when the order does not matter.
- To apply the default bullet formatting, click the Bullets button 📋 ▾ in the Paragraph group on the Home tab of the Ribbon or on the Mini toolbar.
- The default bullet symbol is a simple black dot, indented .25" from the left margin. The symbol is followed by a .5" left tab, and the text on subsequent lines is indented to .5".
- You can select a different bullet from the Bullet Library.
- You can create a customized bullet by changing the font and/or paragraph formatting of the bullet, or by selecting a different bullet symbol.
- You can also select a **picture** to use as a bullet.
- Once you customize a bullet, or select a different bullet, that bullet becomes the default until you select a different one.

- The Bullet Library automatically updates to display the bullets you have used recently.
- Word automatically carries bullet formatting forward to new paragraphs in a list.
- To end a bulleted list, press ↵Enter twice.

Bullet Library

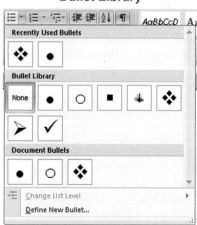

Numbered Lists

- Use numbers to mark items in a list when the order matters, such as for directions or how-to steps.

- Word automatically renumbers a list when you add or delete items.

- To apply the default number formatting, click the Numbering button ⊞ ▾ in the Paragraph group on the Home tab of the Ribbon.

- The default numbering style is an Arabic numeral followed by a period.

- You can customize the number by applying formatting, or by selecting a different numbering style from the Numbering Library.

- Word automatically carries numbering forward to new paragraphs in a list.

- To end a numbered list, press ⏎Enter twice.

- You can restart numbering in the middle of a list.

Numbering Library

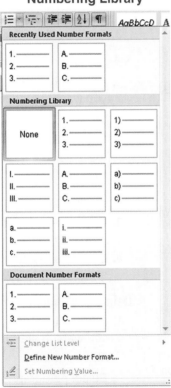

Sort

- Word can automatically **sort** items into alphabetical, numerical, or chronological order.

- A sort can be ascending (A to Z or 0 to 9) or descending (Z to A or 9 to 0).

- The default sort order is alphabetical ascending.

- To sort selected paragraphs, click the Sort button ⧊↓ in the Paragraph group on the Home tab of the Ribbon, and then select options in the Sort Text dialog box.

Sort Text dialog box

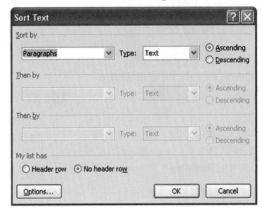

PROCEDURES

Create Bulleted List

Use the default bullet:

1. Position insertion point where you want to start list.

   OR

   Select paragraphs you want in the list.

2. Click the **Home** tab.......... Alt+H

   Paragraph Group

3. Click the **Bullets** button ⊞ ▾.

Select a different bullet style:

1. Position insertion point where you want to start list.

   OR

   Select paragraphs you want in the list.

2. Click the **Home** tab.......... Alt+H

   Paragraph Group

3. Click the **Bullets** button ⊞ ▾ drop-down arrow.......... U

4. Click desired bullet style .... ↑/↓/←/→, ↵Enter

Define a custom bullet:

1. Position insertion point where you want to start list.

   OR

   Select paragraphs you want in the list.

2. Click the **Home** tab.......... Alt+H

   Paragraph Group

3. Click the **Bullets** button ⊞ ▾ drop-down arrow.......... U

4. Click **Define New Bullet** .... D

5. Do one of the following:

   a. Click **Symbol** .... Alt+S

   b. Click symbol to use .... Tab↹, ←/→/↑/↓

   c. Click **OK** .... ↵Enter

   OR

   a. Click **Picture** .... Alt+P

   b. Click picture to use .... Tab↹, ←/→/↑/↓

   c. Click **OK** .... ↵Enter

6. Click the **Alignment** drop-down arrow.......... A+M

7. Click one of the following:.......... ↑/↓, ↵Enter

   ■ **Left** to align the bullet on the left

   ■ **Centered** to center the bullet

   ■ **Right** to align the bullet on the right

8. Click **Font** .... Alt+F

9. Select font formatting as desired.

10. Click **OK** .... ↵Enter

11. Click **OK** .... ↵Enter

Adjust bullet list indents:

1. Right-click a bullet in a list.

2. Click **Adjust List Indents** .... U

3. Click **Bullet position** text box.......... Alt+P

4. Type value to set bullet indent.......... ↑/↓

5. Click **Text indent** text box.......... Alt+T

6. Type value to set text indent (distance between bullet and text).......... ↑/↓

7. Click **Follow number with** drop-down arrow.......... Alt+W

8. Click one of the following:.......... ↑/↓, ↵Enter

   ■ **Tab character** to leave a tab space between the bullet and the text

      ✓ *Tab is the default setting. If desired, click Add tab stop at check box to select it and then type additional tab stop position.*

   ■ **Space** to leave a single space between the bullet and the text

   ■ **Nothing** to leave nothing between the bullet and the text

9. Click **OK** .... ↵Enter

Turn off bullets:

1. Select the bulleted list.

2. Click the **Home** tab.......... Alt+H

   Paragraph Group

3. Click the **Bullets** button ⊞ ▾.

Create Numbered List

Use the default number:

1. Position insertion point where you want to start list.

   OR

   Select paragraphs you want in the list.

2. Click the **Home** tab.......... Alt+H

   Paragraph Group

3. Click the **Numbering** button ⊞ ▾.

Select a different number style:

1. Position insertion point where you want to start list.

   OR

   Select paragraphs you want in the list.

2. Click the **Home** tab.......... Alt+H

   Paragraph Group

3. Click the **Numbering** button ⊞ ▾ drop-down arrow.......... N

4. Click desired number style .... ↑/↓/←/→, ↵Enter

Define a custom number:

1. Position insertion point where you want to start list.

   OR

   Select paragraphs you want in the list.

2. Click the **Home** tab.......... Alt+H

   Paragraph Group

3. Click the **Numbering** button ⊞ ▾ drop-down arrow.......... N

4. Click **Define New Number Format** .... D

5. Click **Number style** drop-down arrow .... Alt+N

6. Click style to use .... ↑/↓, ↵Enter

7. If desired click Number format text box and type text to include in number style .... Alt+O, type text

   ✓ *For example, type Chapter to the left of the number.*

8. Click the **Alignment** drop-down arrow .... A+M

9. Click one of the following: .... ↑/↓, ↵Enter

   ■ **Left** to align the number on the left

   ■ **Centered** to center the number

   ■ **Right** to align the number on the right

10. Click **Font** .... Alt+F

11. Select font formatting as desired.

12. Click **OK** .... ↵Enter

13. Click **OK** .... ↵Enter

Adjust number list indents:

1. Right-click a number in a list.

2. Click **Adjust List Indents** .... U

3. Click **Number position** text box .... Alt+P

4. Type value to set number indent .... ↑/↓

5. Click **Text indent** text box .... Alt+T

6. Type value to set text indent (distance between number and text) .... ↑/↓

7. Click **Follow number with** drop down arrow .... Alt+W

8. Click one of the following: .... ↑/↓, ↵Enter

   ■ **Tab character** to leave a tab space between the number and the text

   ✓ *Tab is the default setting. If desired, click Add tab stop at check box to select it and then type additional tab stop position.*

   ■ **Space** to leave a single space between the number and the text

   ■ **Nothing** to leave nothing between the number and the text

9. Click **OK** .... ↵Enter

Turn off numbering:

1. Select the numbered list.

2. Click the **Home** tab .... Alt+H

   Paragraph Group

3. Click the **Numbering** button ☰▾.

Restart numbering:

1. Right-click a number in a list.

2. Do one of the following:

   ■ Click **Restart at 1** to restart numbering at current location .... R

   ■ Click **Continue numbering** to continue numbering from previous list C

Set a starting value:

1. Right-click a number in a list.

2. Click **Set Numbering Value** V

3. Click **Start new list** option button .... Alt+S

4. Click **Set value to** text box .... Alt+V

5. Type new starting value .... ↑/↓

6. Click **OK** .... ↵Enter

Manually Format Bullets or Numbers

1. Right-click bullet or number in list.

2. Click **Font** .... F

3. Select font formatting options.

4. Click **OK** .... ↵Enter

5. Right-click bullet or number in list.

6. Click **Paragraph** .... P

7. Select paragraph formatting options.

8. Click **OK** .... ↵Enter

Turn Automatic List Formatting On or Off

1. Click **Office Button** 🗔 ..... Alt+F

2. Click **Word Options** I

3. Click **Proofing** .... P

4. Click **AutoCorrect Options** .... Alt+A

5. Click **AutoFormat As You Type** page tab .... Ctrl+Tab⇆

6. Click to select or clear **Automatic bulleted lists** check box .... Tab⇆, Spacebar

7. Click to select or clear **Automatic numbered lists** check box .... Tab⇆, Spacebar

8. Click **OK** .... ↵Enter

9. Click **OK** .... ↵Enter

Sort a List

Use default sort order:

1. Select paragraphs you want to sort.

2. Click the **Home** tab .... Alt+H

   Paragraph Group

3. Click the **Sort** button ⬆↓ ... S, O

4. Click **OK** .... ↵Enter

Customize the sort order:

1. Select paragraphs you want to sort.

2. Click the **Home** tab .... Alt+H

   Paragraph Group

3. Click the **Sort** button ⬆↓ ... S, O

4. Click the **Type** drop-down arrow .... Alt+Y

5. Click one of the following .... ↑/↓, ↵Enter

   ■ **Text**, to sort alphabetically

   ■ **Number**, to sort numerically

   ■ **Date**, to sort chronologically

6. Click one of the following options buttons:

   ■ **Ascending**, to sort in ascending order .... Alt+A

   ■ **Descending**, to sort in descending order .... Alt+D

7. Click **OK** .... ↵Enter

EXERCISE DIRECTIONS

1. Start Word, if necessary.
2. Open ⊙28CHECKIN.
3. Save the document as 28CHECKIN_xx.
4. Edit and format the document as shown in Illustration A.
   a. Set fonts, font sizes, and alignments as shown.
      ✓ *Unless otherwise noted, use 12-point Arial, flush left.*
   b. Set tabs and set paragraph spacing as shown.
   c. Insert symbols as shown.
   d. Use the default bullet style to turn the four guidelines into a bulleted list.
   e. Select the bullet style shown in the illustration.
   f. Use the default number style to turn the four steps for evacuation into a numbered list.
   g. Select a different number style.
   h. Change back to the default number style.
   i. Sort the bulleted list into ascending alphabetical order.
5. Check the spelling and grammar.
6. Display the document in Print Preview. It should look similar to the one in the illustration.
7. Print the document.
8. Close the document, saving all changes.

Illustration A

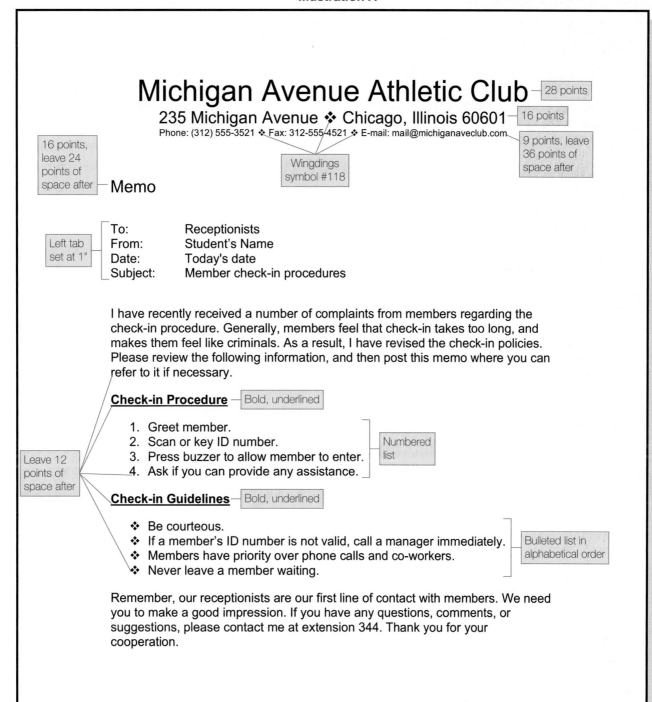

Michigan Avenue Athletic Club

28 points

235 Michigan Avenue ❖ Chicago, Illinois 60601

16 points

Phone: (312) 555-3521 ❖ Fax: 312-555-4521 ❖ E-mail: mail@michiganaveclub.com

9 points, leave 36 points of space after

16 points, leave 24 points of space after

Wingdings symbol #118

Memo

Left tab set at 1"

To: Receptionists
From: Student's Name
Date: Today's date
Subject: Member check-in procedures

I have recently received a number of complaints from members regarding the check-in procedure. Generally, members feel that check-in takes too long, and makes them feel like criminals. As a result, I have revised the check-in policies. Please review the following information, and then post this memo where you can refer to it if necessary.

Check-in Procedure — Bold, underlined

Leave 12 points of space after

1. Greet member.
2. Scan or key ID number.
3. Press buzzer to allow member to enter.
4. Ask if you can provide any assistance.

Numbered list

Check-in Guidelines — Bold, underlined

❖ Be courteous.
❖ If a member's ID number is not valid, call a manager immediately.
❖ Members have priority over phone calls and co-workers.
❖ Never leave a member waiting.

Bulleted list in alphabetical order

Remember, our receptionists are our first line of contact with members. We need you to make a good impression. If you have any questions, comments, or suggestions, please contact me at extension 344. Thank you for your cooperation.

ON YOUR OWN

1. Create a new document in Word.
2. Save the file as **OWD28_*xx***.
3. Type a bulleted list of five things you'd like to accomplish in the next year. These can be goals for school, work, or personal development. Examples might include earning a better grade in math, completing a project on the job, or getting in better shape by exercising and eating right.
4. Sort the list in alphabetical order.
5. Using a different font, type a numbered list that includes at least five steps describing how you expect to accomplish one of the items in the bulleted list.
6. Change the sort order of the bulleted list to descending order.
7. Save the changes and then print the document.
8. Ask a classmate to review the document and make suggestions and comments.
9. Incorporate the suggestions and comments into the document.
10. Save your changes, close the document, and exit Word.

Exercise | 29

Skills Covered

- About Styles
- Apply Styles
- Create a Style

- Edit a Style
- Reapply Direct Formatting
- Clear Formatting

Software Skills   Word provides many ways to apply and remove formatting in documents. Use styles to apply a collection of formatting settings to characters or paragraphs. Styles help ensure continuity in formatting throughout a document. You can select from Word's built-in styles, create new styles, or modify existing styles.

Application Skills   Restoration Architecture has contracted with a training company to provide computer training for employees. You have been asked to prepare a document listing the courses that will be available for the first three months of the year. In this exercise, you will use styles and direct formatting to apply consistent formatting to the document.

TERMS

Direct formatting Individual font or paragraph formatting settings applied directly to text, as opposed to a collection of settings applied with a style.

Style A collection of formatting settings that can be applied to characters or paragraphs.

Style sheet A list of available styles.

NOTES

About Styles

- **Styles** make it easy to apply a collection of formatting settings to characters or paragraphs all at once.
- Word 2007 comes with Quick Style sets, which are groups of coordinated styles designed for formatting common document elements, such as lists, headings, and subheadings.
- Each Quick Style set includes the same styles, but the formatting is different.
- For example, in the Modern style set, the Heading 1 style uses 11 point, bold, all caps while in the Simple style set, the Heading 1 style uses 18 point, small caps.
- The styles in the current Quick Style set display in the Quick Styles Gallery in the Styles group on the Home tab of the Ribbon.

- The default style for new text is called Normal.

Quick Style Gallery

Apply Styles

■ You can apply a style at any time to existing text, or you can select a style before you type new text.

■ To quickly apply a style, click it in the Quick Styles Gallery in the Styles group on the Home tab of the Ribbon.

■ Only one row of styles displays in the Styles group at a time, but you can scroll the gallery, or click the More button ⯆ to display the entire gallery.

■ You can also select a style in the Styles task pane.

■ By default only styles used in the current document display in the task pane, but you can select to display all available styles.

■ You can preview how a style will affect text by resting the mouse pointer on the style in the Quick Styles gallery.

■ You can select a different style set if you want.

✓ *Apply the No Spacing style to quickly remove all default paragraph and line spacing from text.*

Styles group

Create a Style

■ You can create a new Quick Style for formatting your documents.

■ Styles can contain font and/or paragraph formatting.

■ The easiest way to create a style is to format text, select it, and then assign the formatting a style name.

■ Style names should be short and descriptive.

■ The new style is added to the **style sheet** for the current document and displays in the Quick Styles Gallery.

Edit a Style

■ You can modify an existing style.

■ When you modify a style that has already been applied to text in the document, the formatted text automatically changes to the new style.

■ If you modify a style and give it a new name, it becomes a new style; the original style remains unchanged.

Reapply Direct Formatting

■ When you apply **direct formatting** to text in a document, Word automatically adds information about the direct formatting to the name of the current style in the Styles task pane.

■ This makes it easy to reapply direct formatting that you have already used to selected text.

■ This feature is similar to the Format Painter, but instead of scrolling through the document from the formatted text to the text you want to format, you can select the direct formatting in the Styles task pane.

Styles task pane

Clear Formatting

■ You can quickly remove all formatting from selected text.

■ Clearing the formatting from text removes both direct formatting and styles.

■ After you clear the formatting, text is displayed in the default normal style for the current document.

■ You can clear formatting using the Clear Formatting button 🅰 in the Font group on the Home tab of the Ribbon, or in the Quick Styles gallery.

PROCEDURES

Apply a Style

1. Position insertion point in paragraph to format.
2. Click the **Home** tab........... Alt + H

   Styles Group

3. Click style in Quick Styles Gallery.

   ✓ *If necessary, use scroll arrows to scroll the gallery.*

Select from Entire Quick Styles Gallery

1. Position insertion point in paragraph to format.
2. Click the **Home** tab........... Alt + H

   Styles Group

3. Click **More** button 🔽 L
4. Click style to apply .... ←/→/↑/↓, ↵Enter

Apply a Style Using the Task Pane

1. Position insertion point in paragraph to format.
2. Click the **Home** tab.......... Alt + H

   Styles Group

3. Click **Styles** group dialog box launcher 🔲 .... F, Y
4. Click style to apply .... ↑/↓, ↵Enter

Display All Styles in the Task Pane

1. Position insertion point in paragraph to format.
2. Click the **Home** tab.......... Alt + H

   Styles Group

3. Click **Styles** group dialog box launcher 🔲 .... F, Y
4. Click **Options** .... Tab⇆, ↵Enter

5. Click **S**elect styles to show drop-down arrow........... Alt + S
6. Click **All styles** .... ↑/↓, ↵Enter
7. Click **OK** .... ↵Enter

Change the Style Set

1. Click the **Home** tab........... Alt + H

   Styles Group

2. Click **Change Styles** button 🅰🅰 .... G
3. Click **Style Set** .... Y
4. Click name of style set to apply .... ↑/↓, ↵Enter

Create a Style from Formatting

1. Format text or paragraph.
2. Click the **Home** tab.......... Alt + H

   Styles Group

3. Click **More** button 🔽 L
4. Click **Save Selection as a New Quick Style** .... Q
5. Type style name.
6. Click **OK** .... ↵Enter

   OR

1. Format text or paragraph.
2. Click the **Home** tab.......... Alt + H

   Styles Group

3. Click **Styles** group dialog box launcher 🔲 .... F, Y
4. Click **New Style** button 🔳.
5. Type new style name.
6. Click **OK** .... ↵Enter

Modify a Style

1. Change formatting of text.
2. Select modified text.
3. Right-click style to modify in Quick Style Gallery.
4. Click **Update** *stylename* to **M**atch Selection .... A

Delete a Style

1. Click the **Home** tab........... Alt + H

   Styles Group

2. Click **Styles** group dialog box launcher 🔲 .... F, Y
3. Right-click style to delete in task pane.
4. Click **Delete** .... D

   ✓ *If Delete is not available, it means you cannot delete the selected style.*

5. Click **Yes** .... Y

Reapply Direct Formatting

1. Select text to format.
2. Click the **Home** tab.......... Alt + H

   Styles Group

3. Click **Styles** group dialog box launcher 🔲 .... F, Y
4. Click direct formatting to apply .... ↑/↓, ↵Enter

Clear Formatting (Ctrl+Spacebar)

1. Select text.

   OR

   Position insertion point within text.

2. Click **Home** tab................. Alt + H

   Font Group

3. Click **Clear Formatting** button 🔳 .... E

   OR

   Styles Group

   a. Click **More** button 🔽 L
   b. Click **C**lear Formatting.......... C

   OR

   Styles Group

   a. Click **Styles** dialog box launcher 🔲 .... F, Y
   b. Click **Clear All** .. ↑/↓, ↵Enter

EXERCISE DIRECTIONS

1. Start Word, if necessary.
2. Open 29COURSE.
3. Save the document as **29COURSE_xx**.
4. Follow the steps below to apply styles and formatting as marked in Illustration A.
5. Select the Modern Style Set.
6. Apply the Heading 1 style to the company name.
7. Display the Styles task pane and display all styles.
8. Apply the Heading 3 style to the names of the months.
9. Increase the font size of the company name to 26 points, center it, and increase the amount of space after it to 12 points.
10. Create a new style based on the modified Heading 1, named **New Heading 1**.
11. Apply the New Heading 1 style to the text *Training Schedule*.
12. Format the company address line as follows:
    a. Increase the font size to 14 points.
    b. Center the line horizontally.
    c. Apply italics.
13. Reapply the formatting you have just applied to the company address to the names of the three courses.

14. Format the paragraph describing the Word 1 course as follows:
    a. Change the font to 14-point Arial.
    b. Justify the alignment.
    c. Indent the paragraph .5" from both the left and the right.
    d. Leave 0 points of space before and 6 points after the paragraph.
15. Create a style named **Course Description** based on the formatting of the course description.
16. Apply the *Course Description* style to the paragraphs describing the Word 2 and Word 3 courses.
17. Add a new line to the end of the document.
18. Clear all formatting from the new line, then type: **Enrollment forms are available in the HR office or on the company Intranet.**
19. Center the text entered in step 18.
20. Modify the Course Description style to leave 6 points of space before the paragraph.

    ✓ *Notice that when you apply the change, all paragraphs formatted with the style are changed.*

21. Check the spelling, grammar, and formatting in the document.
22. Display the document in Print Preview. It should look similar to the one in Illustration A.
23. Print the document.
24. Close the file, saving all changes.

Curriculum Connection: Mathematics

Math Bases

When we do math, we use a decimal, or base 10 system, which means we use ten digits—0 through 9—to represent all numbers. Through history, other cultures have used different bases, including base 20, used by the Mayans, and base 60, used by the Babylonians.

Explain a Different Base System

Pick a base system other than base 10, and research that system. Then, write a one-page report explaining how it works. Include information about how the system was developed and who used it in the past. Give examples of how you might use it today.

Illustration A

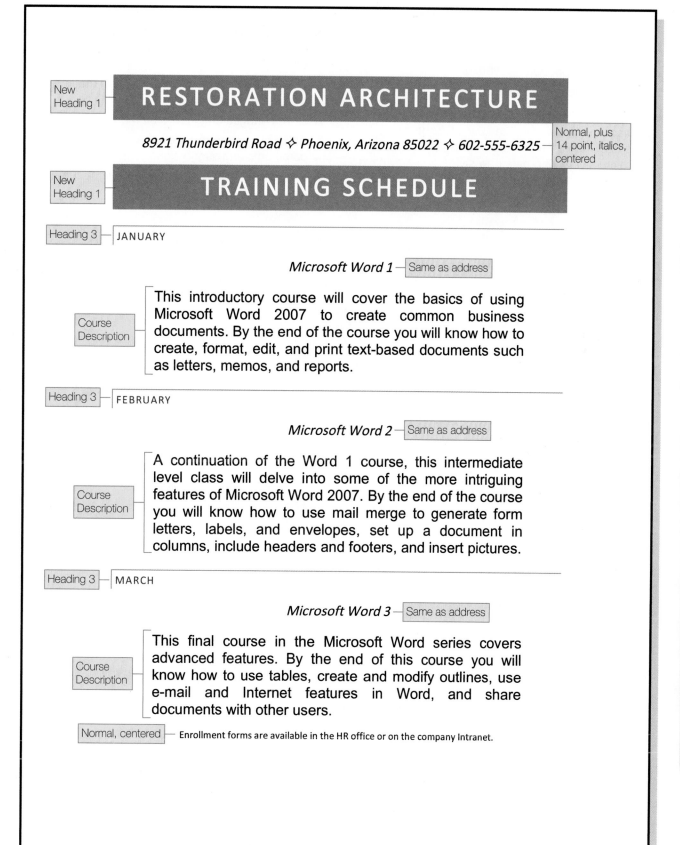

New Heading 1

RESTORATION ARCHITECTURE

8921 Thunderbird Road ✧ Phoenix, Arizona 85022 ✧ 602-555-6325

Normal, plus 14 point, italics, centered

New Heading 1

TRAINING SCHEDULE

Heading 3

JANUARY

Microsoft Word 1 — Same as address

Course Description

This introductory course will cover the basics of using Microsoft Word 2007 to create common business documents. By the end of the course you will know how to create, format, edit, and print text-based documents such as letters, memos, and reports.

Heading 3

FEBRUARY

Microsoft Word 2 — Same as address

Course Description

A continuation of the Word 1 course, this intermediate level class will delve into some of the more intriguing features of Microsoft Word 2007. By the end of the course you will know how to use mail merge to generate form letters, labels, and envelopes, set up a document in columns, include headers and footers, and insert pictures.

Heading 3

MARCH

Microsoft Word 3 — Same as address

Course Description

This final course in the Microsoft Word series covers advanced features. By the end of this course you will know how to use tables, create and modify outlines, use e-mail and Internet features in Word, and share documents with other users.

Normal, centered — Enrollment forms are available in the HR office or on the company Intranet.

ON YOUR OWN

1. Start Word and open OWD28_*xx*, the document you created in the On Your Own section of Exercise 28, or open 29GOALS.

2. Save the document as OWD29_*xx*.

3. Clear all formatting from the document.

4. Select a style set, and then use styles to format the document. You can use existing styles, modify existing styles, or create new styles. You may have to reformat the lists using bullets and numbering.

5. Apply some direct formatting for emphasis, and then reapply the formatting to other text in the document.

6. Check the spelling, grammar, and formatting in the document.

7. Save changes and then print the document.

8. Ask a classmate to review the document and offer comments and suggestions.

9. Incorporate the suggestions into the document.

10. Close the document, saving all changes.

Exercise | 30

Skills Covered

- **About Document Production**
- **Set Margins**
- **Set Page Orientation**
- **Format a One-Page Report**

Software Skills Format a one-page report so that it is attractive and professional. Set margins to meet expected requirements and to improve the document's appearance and readability. For example, leave a wider margin in a report if you expect a reader to make notes or comments; leave a narrower margin to fit more text on a page.

Application Skills The Michigan Avenue Athletic Club has realized that many members are not sure what a personal trainer can offer. In this exercise, you are responsible for formatting a one-page report explaining what a personal trainer is and how to select one. The report will be distributed to all members and will be included in marketing packets given to prospective members.

TERMS

Gutter Space added to the margin to leave room for binding.

Landscape orientation Rotating document text so it displays and prints horizontally across the longer side of a page.

Margins The amount of white space between the text and the edge of the page on all four sides.

Portrait orientation The default position for displaying and printing text horizontally across the shorter side of a page.

Section In Word, a segment of a document defined by a section break. A section may have different page formatting from the rest of the document.

NOTES

About Document Production

- There are three basic steps to producing any business document: planning, creating, and publishing.
- The planning stage requires you to think about such questions as the type of document you want to create, who will receive the document, and whether there are any special publishing requirements.
- For example, you might consider what paper to print on, if color ink should be used, how many copies to print, or whether you will need to print on both sides of a page.
- If the project seems too complex, you may decide to use a desktop publishing package, such as Microsoft Office Publisher, instead of using a word

processing package, such as Microsoft Office Word.

- During the planning stage you should create a schedule that includes milestones, such as how long it will take to gather the information you need, when the first draft will be complete, how long it will take for a review process, and when the final document will be complete.
- The creation stage involves selecting page and document settings, such as margins and page size, and entering and formatting the text and graphics.
- The publishing stage involves outputting the document using either your desktop printer or a commercial printer. In some cases, the document may be published electronically on a Web site.

Set Margins

- **Margins** are measured in inches.
- The Normal default margins in Word 2007 are 1" on the left, right, top, and bottom.

    ✓ *In previous versions of Word, the default margins are 1.25" on the left and right and 1" on the top and bottom.*

- You can select from a list of preset margins using the Margins button's menu in the Page Setup group on the Page Layout tab or the Print Preview tab of the Ribbon.
- Alternatively you can set custom margins.
- If you set custom margins, you can also specify a **gutter** width to leave room for binding multiple pages.
- Margin settings can affect an entire document, or the current **section**.

    ✓ *To set margins for a single paragraph, use indents as described in Exercise 27.*

- On the rulers, areas outside the margins are shaded gray, while areas inside the margins are white.

    ✓ *To see both vertical and horizontal rulers, use Print Layout view.*

- Light gray bars mark the margins on the rulers.
- You can set Word to display margins on the page as nonprinting lines called text boundaries.

Preset margins

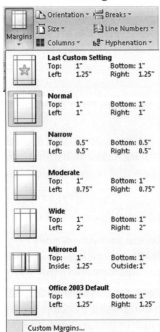

Set Page Orientation

- There are two page orientations:
    - **Portrait**
    - **Landscape**
- Portrait is the default orientation and is used for most documents, including letters, memos, and reports.
- Use landscape orientation to display a document across the wider length of the page. For example, if a document contains a table that is wider than the standard 8.5" page, Word will split it across two pages. When you change to landscape orientation, the table may fit on the 11" page.
- The Page Orientation options are in the Page Setup group on the Page Layout tab or the Print Preview tab of the Ribbon.

Format a One-Page Report

- Traditionally, a one-page report is set up as follows:
    - Left and right margins are 1".
    - The title is positioned 2" from the top of the page.

    ✓ *If you need to fit more text on the page the title may be positioned 1" from the top.*

    - The report title is centered and in either all uppercase or title case.
    - Spacing following the title ranges from 3/4" (54 pts.) to 1" (72 pts.).
    - Text is justified.
    - Lines are double spaced.
    - First-line indents are between .5" and 1".

PROCEDURES

Set Margins Using the Ruler

1. Move the mouse pointer over the margin marker on the ruler.

   ✓ *The mouse pointer changes to the horizontal resize pointer ↔, and the ScreenTip identifies the margin.*

2. Drag the margin marker to a new location.

   ✓ *Press and hold the Alt key while you drag to see the margin width.*

Select Preset Margins

1. Click the **Page Layout** tab .... Alt+P

   Page Setup Group

2. Click the **Margins** button ▢ .... M
3. Click margin preset to apply .... ↑/↓, ↵Enter

In Print Preview:

1. Click **Office Button** ⬚ ..... Alt+F
2. Point to **Print** .... W
3. Click **Print Preview** V

   Page Setup Group

4. Click the **Margins** button ▢ .... Alt+P, M
5. Click margin preset to apply .... ↑/↓, ↵Enter

Set Custom Margins

1. Click the **Page Layout** tab .... Alt+P

   Page Setup Group

2. Click the **Page Setup** group dialog box launcher ▣ .... S, P

   ✓ *If necessary, click the Margins tab Ctrl+Tab.*

OR

a. Click the **Margins** button ▢ .... M
b. Click **Custom Margins** .... A

3. Click **Top** text box .... Alt+T
4. Type top margin width.
5. Click **Bottom** text box ..... Alt+B
6. Type bottom margin width.
7. Click **Left** text box .... Alt+L
8. Type left margin width.
9. Click **Right** text box ..... Alt+R
10. Type right margin width.
11. Click **Gutter** text box ..... Alt+G
12. Type gutter width.
13. Click **Gutter position** drop-down arrow .... Alt+U
14. Select desired gutter location.
15. Click the **Apply to** drop-down arrow .... Alt+Y
16. Select one of the following: .... ↑/↓, ↵Enter

   ■ **This point forward** to create a section starting at the current location

   ■ **Whole document** to apply the margins to the entire document

17. Click **OK** .... ↵Enter

In Print Preview:

1. Click **Office Button** ⬚ ..... Alt+F
2. Point to **Print** .... W
3. Click **Print Preview** V

   Page Setup Group

4. Click the **Page Setup** group dialog box launcher ▣ ...... Alt+P, S, P

   ✓ *If necessary, click the Margins tab Ctrl+Tab.*

OR

a. Click the **Margins** button ▢ .... Alt+P, M
b. Click **Custom Margins** .... A

5. Click **Top** text box .... Alt+T
6. Type top margin width.
7. Click **Bottom** text box ..... Alt+B
8. Type bottom margin width.
9. Click **Left** text box .... Alt+L
10. Type left margin width.
11. Click **Right** text box ..... Alt+R
12. Type right margin width.
13. Click **Gutter** text box ..... Alt+G
14. Type gutter width.
15. Click **Gutter position** drop-down arrow .... Alt+U
16. Select desired gutter location.
17. Click the **Apply to** drop-down arrow .... Alt+Y
18. Select one of the following: .... ↑/↓, ↵Enter

   ■ **This point forward** to create a section starting at the current location

   ■ **Whole document** to apply the margins to the entire document

19. Click **OK** .... ↵Enter

Display Text Boundaries

1. Click **Office Button** ⬚ ..... Alt+F
2. Click **Word Options** I
3. Click **Advanced** .... A
4. Click to select the **Show text boundaries** check box .... Alt+X, Spacebar
5. Click **OK** .... ↵Enter

Hide Text Boundaries

1. Click **Office Button** ⬚ ..... Alt+F
2. Click **Word Options** I
3. Click **Advanced** .... A
4. Click to deselect the **Show text boundaries** check box .... Alt+X, Spacebar
5. Click **OK** .... ↵Enter

Set Page Orientation

1. Click the **Page Layout**
   tab .... Alt + P

   Page Setup Group

2. Click the **Orientation**
   button 🖾 .... O
3. Click one of the
   following: .... ↑/↓, ↵Enter
   - **Portrait**
   - **Landscape**

   OR

1. Click the **Page Layout**
   tab .... Alt + P

   Page Setup Group

2. Click the **Page Setup** group
   dialog box
   launcher 🖾 ...... Alt + P, S, P

   ✓ *If necessary, click the Margins tab*
   Ctrl + Tab↹.

3. Click one of the following:
   - **Portrait** .... Alt + P
   - **Landscape** .... Alt + S

---

4. Click the **Apply to** drop-down
   arrow .... Alt + Y
5. Select one of the
   following: .... ↑/↓, ↵Enter
   - **This point forward** to create a
     section starting at the cur-
     rent location
   - **Whole document** to apply the
     orientation to the entire
     document
6. Click **OK** .... ↵Enter

In Print Preview:

1. Click **Office Button** 🔘 ..... Alt + F
2. Point to **Print** .... W
3. Click **Print Preview** V

   Page Setup Group

4. Click the **Orientation**
   button 🖾 .... Alt + P, O
5. Click one of the
   following: .... ↑/↓, ↵Enter
   - **Portrait**
   - **Landscape**

OR

1. Click **Office Button** 🔘 ..... Alt + F
2. Point to **Print** .... W
3. Click **Print Preview** V

   Page Setup Group

4. Click the **Page Setup** group
   dialog box
   launcher 🖾 ...... Alt + P, S, P

   ✓ *If necessary, click the Margins tab*
   Ctrl + Tab↹.

5. Click one of the following:
   - **Portrait** .... Alt + P
   - **Landscape** .... Alt + S
6. Click the **Apply to** drop-down
   arrow .... Alt + Y
7. Select one of the
   following: .... ↑/↓, ↵Enter
   - **This point forward** to create a
     section starting at the cur-
     rent location
   - **Whole document** to apply the
     orientation to the entire doc-
     ument
8. Click **OK** .... ↵Enter

EXERCISE DIRECTIONS

1. Start Word, if necessary.
2. Open 💿**30TRAINER**.
3. Save the document as **30TRAINER_xx**.
4. Display text boundaries.
5. Change the margins to 1" on all sides of the page.
6. Format the report as shown in Illustration A.
7. Apply the Heading 1 style to the title, then apply
   direct formatting to the title as follows:
   a. All uppercase
   b. Centered
   c. 72 points of space before and 54 points of
      space after

   ✓ *72 points equals 1", plus the 1" top margin leaves a total of*
   2" of space from the top of the page.

8. Format the body text as follows:
   a. Use a 12-point serif font for the body text.
      (Times New Roman is used in the illustration.)
   b. Justify and double-space all body text para-
      graphs.
   c. Indent the first line of each body text paragraph
      by .5".

9. Center the last line of text.
10. Check the spelling and grammar.
11. Change the page orientation to Landscape.
12. Display the document in Print Preview and adjust
    the zoom so you can see the whole page.
13. If the document extends onto a second page,
    change the top margin to .75" and the bottom mar-
    gin to .5".
14. Print the document.
15. Change the page orientation back to Portrait.
16. Change the margins to the Normal preset.
17. Hide the text boundaries. The document should
    look similar to Illustration A.
18. Print the document.
19. Close Print Preview, and then close the document,
    saving all changes.

Illustration A

IS A PERSONAL TRAINER RIGHT FOR YOU?

Almost everyone could benefit from the services of a personal trainer. In addition to designing a personalized workout program, a good trainer provides motivation and encouragement. He or she helps you understand how to fit exercise into your life and teaches you how to make the most out of your exercise time. The lessons you learn from a trainer help insure a safe, effective workout, even when you are exercising on your own.

Working with a trainer should be a satisfying and rewarding experience. There are many different reasons for hiring a personal trainer. Some people want the motivation of a workout partner, others require specialized services for rehabilitation, and still others are interested in achieving weight loss goals. Before hiring a trainer, make sure he or she has experience helping people with goals similar to your own. Ask for references, and then contact at least three. You should also interview the trainer to find out if you are compatible. You should feel comfortable talking and working together, and you should trust the trainer to respect your time and efforts.

Verify that the trainer is certified by a nationally recognized organization such as the American Council on Exercise, the American College of Sports Medicine, or the National Strength and Conditioning Association. Many trainers have degrees in subjects such as sports medicine, physical education, exercise physiology, or anatomy and physiology.

For more information about personal trainers, contact Candace at extension 765.

ON YOUR OWN

1. Create a new document in Word.
2. Save the file as **OWD30_xx**.
3. In the third person, draft a one-page report about yourself. For example, draft a document that you could include in a directory for an organization of which you are a member. Think of the *About the Author* paragraphs found in books and magazines, or the *About the Performers* paragraphs found in a theater program.
4. Double space the report.
5. Use correct document formatting for a one-page report.
6. Use other formatting effects, if appropriate, such as fonts, lists, and symbols.
7. Check the spelling and grammar, then save and print the document.
8. Ask a classmate to review the document and offer comments and suggestions.
9. Incorporate the suggestions into the document.
10. Save your changes and close the document.

Exercise | 31

Skills Covered

- Use Themes
- Use AutoFormat as You Type

Software Skills   Select a theme to apply coordinated sets of colors, fonts, and effects to your document. Select AutoFormat as you type options to automatically apply styles and other common formatting options to a document. Both themes and AutoFormat can save you time and help insure consistent formatting throughout a document.

Application Skills   A personal trainer at Michigan Avenue Athletic Club has given you a report on strength training that she would like to hand out to her clients. In this exercise, you will select a theme and then use AutoFormat to format the report.

TERMS

Effects Visual attributes applied to elements in a document, such as shadows applied to pictures, or borders applied to pages.

Em dash A dash symbol that is approximately the width of the typed letter M.

En dash A dash symbol that is approximately the width of the typed letter N.

Smart quotes Quotation marks that curve left or right toward enclosed text.

Straight quotes Quotation marks that drop straight down instead of curving to the left or right.

Theme A set of coordinated colors, fonts, and effects that can be applied to Office 2007 documents.

NOTES

Use Themes

- Office 2007 comes with built-in **themes** that you can apply to documents.
- Each theme includes a default set of coordinated colors, fonts, and **effects**.
- You can select a theme from the Themes Gallery in the Themes group on the Page Layout tab of the Ribbon.
- To preview how a theme will affect the current document, rest your mouse pointer on it in the gallery.
- After you select a theme, you can modify it by selecting different theme colors, fonts, or effects.
- By using a theme, you can easily create different types of documents that all have a similar look and feel.

Themes Gallery

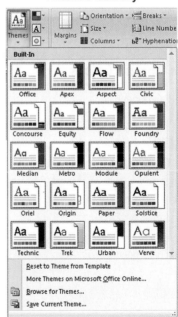

Use AutoFormat As You Type

- You can set Word to automatically apply certain formatting such as styles and lists as you type.

- When AutoFormat As You Type is active, Word automatically replaces typed characters with symbols. For example, it replaces a double hyphen (--) without spaces before and after with an **em dash** (—), a double hyphen with spaces before and after as an **en dash** (–), and **straight quotes** (") with **smart quotes** (").

- You select AutoFormat options on the AutoFormat as You Type tab of the AutoCorrect dialog box.

AutoFormat As You Type options

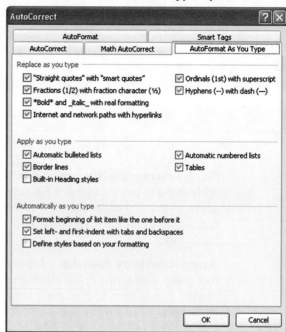

PROCEDURES

Select a Theme

1. Click the **Page Layout** tab .... Alt+P

   Themes Group

2. Click the **Themes** button Aa .... T, H

3. Click theme to apply .... ↑/↓/←/→, ↵Enter

   ✓ To preview a theme, rest the mouse pointer on it in the Themes Gallery.

Change the Theme Colors

1. Click the **Page Layout** tab .... Alt+P

   Themes Group

2. Click the **Theme Colors** button .... T, C

3. Click color scheme to apply .... ↑/↓, ↵Enter

   ✓ To preview a theme color scheme, rest the mouse pointer on it.

Change the Theme Fonts

1. Click the **Page Layout** tab .... Alt+P

   Themes Group

2. Click the **Theme Fonts** button A .... T, F

3. Click font scheme to apply .... ↑/↓, ↵Enter

   ✓ To preview a theme font scheme, rest the mouse pointer on it.

Change the Theme Effects

1. Click the **Page Layout** tab .... Alt+P

   Themes Group

2. Click the **Theme Effects** button .... T, E

3. Click effects scheme to apply .... ↑/↓, ↵Enter

   ✓ To preview a theme effects scheme, rest the mouse pointer on it.

Select AutoFormat as You Type Options

1. Click **Office Button** .... Alt+F

2. Click **Word Options** I

3. Click **Proofing** .... P

4. Click **AutoCorrect Options** .... Alt+A

5. Click **AutoFormat as You Type** tab .... Ctrl+Tab

6. Click to select options you want to use .... Tab, Spacebar

7. Click to clear options you do not want to use .. Tab, Spacebar

   ✓ A check mark in a check box indicates option is selected.

8. Click **OK** .... ↵Enter

9. Click **OK** .... ↵Enter

EXERCISE DIRECTIONS

1. Start Word, if necessary.
2. Open ⊙ 31STRENGTH.
3. Save the document as **31STRENGTH_***xx*.
4. Open the AutoCorrect dialog box and display the AutoFormat as You Type tab.
5. Select all available options in the Replace as you type section.
6. Select the Automatic bulleted lists option in the Apply as you type section.
7. Click OK to close the dialog box, and then click OK to close the Word Options dialog box.
8. Apply the title style to the first line of the document.
9. Apply the Heading 1 style to the second line.
10. Apply the Heading 2 style to the headings *What to Know Before You Start*, *The Workout*, and *Conclusion*.
11. Insert a new line at the end of the document.
12. Type **Strength Training at MAAC** and format it in the Heading 1 style.
13. Start a new line, type an asterisk (*) and then press Tab↹. Word should automatically format the line as a bulleted list.
14. Select the paragraph mark following the tab and change the font to 11-point Calibri to match the rest of the document. Type the following list:

    At Michigan Avenue Athletic Club, we offer strength training equipment for *all* levels and abilities.

    Orientation classes are conducted on the 1st Tuesday of every month—no reservation is required.Other classes may be available.

    Feel free to schedule a complimentary session with one of our personal trainers. They are _all_ certified for strength training and conditioning instruction.

    ✓ *Notice as you type that Word replaces *all* with the bold **all**, the ordinal (1st) with superscript (1st), the double hyphen (--) with a dash (–), and _all_ with the italic all.*

15. Apply the Module Theme to the document. Notice that the fonts and colors change.
16. Change the theme colors to Opulent.
17. Change the theme fonts to Aspect.
18. Check the spelling and grammar in the document.
19. Display the document in Print Preview. It should look similar to Illustration A.
20. Print the document.
21. Close the document, saving all changes.

Title style — # Strength Training

Heading 1 style — ## About Strength Training

Use strength training to increase your metabolism, burn fat, build muscle, and keep your bones and connective tissue strong. Strength training is sometimes called weight training—or weight lifting. It involves using resistance to exercise muscles. The resistance is usually provided by free weights or machines. Machines are generally easier to use, while free weights require a bit more coordination. Most health clubs offer both.

Heading 2 style — ### What to Know Before You Start

A good strength training regimen works all muscle groups 1 or 2 days a week. It is important not to work the same muscle two days in a row. Therefore, you should know which muscles are in each group. If you're a beginner, hire a personal trainer to help you get started. The trainer will help you identify your goals, set the number of repetitions and amount of resistance, and teach you the proper way to use machines or free weights. Using weights or machines incorrectly can result in serious injury.

Heading 2 style — ### The Workout

A key to successful strength training is developing a routine. Always start with a warm up to prevent injury. Move slowly and deliberately. Strength training is not a race. Continue a routine for at least six weeks before increasing the difficulty level. Always stretch between sets and after the workout.

The number of reps and sets you complete depend on your goals as well as your abilities. For example, if you want to lose body fat, you need to use enough weight that you can only complete 10 to 12 reps and 1 to 3 sets, resting no more than 1 minute between sets. For muscle gain you should use enough weight that you can only complete 6 to 8 reps, but you should do at least 3 sets. You should also rest at least three days between sets.

Heading 2 style — ### Conclusion

Strength Training is an excellent way to tone your body. Use it in combination with cardiovascular exercise to maintain a healthy body.

Heading 1 style — ## Strength Training at MAAC

- At Michigan Avenue Athletic Club, we offer strength training equipment for **all** levels and abilities.
  Orientation classes are conducted on the 1st Tuesday of every month—no reservation is required. Other classes may be available.
- Feel free to schedule a complimentary session with one of our personal trainers. They are *all* certified for strength training and conditioning instruction.

ON YOUR OWN

1. Start Word and open 📖OWD30_*xx*, the document you created in the On Your Own section of Exercise 30, or open 💿31MYLIFE.

2. Save the document as OWD31_*xx*.

3. Select all AutoFormat as You Type options.

4. Replace a paragraph in the document using text that will be automatically formatted as you type, such as a list, bold or italics, ordinals, or em dashes.

5. If necessary, edit the document so that it fits on one page.

6. Apply a theme to the document.

7. Change the theme fonts and colors. (You may want to apply different styles so you can see the colors in your document.)

8. Check the spelling and grammar, then save and print the document.

9. Ask a classmate to review the document and offer comments and suggestions.

10. Incorporate the suggestions into the document.

11. Save your changes and close the document.

Critical Thinking

Application Skills You are responsible for preparing a document for Restoration Architecture employees who are participating in the in-house training program. In this exercise, you will format the document using font formatting, symbols, lists, line and paragraph spacing, indents, styles, and margins.

EXERCISE DIRECTIONS

1. Start Word, if necessary.
2. Open ⊙ **32TRAIN**.
3. Save the file as **32TRAIN_xx**.
4. Set the margins to 1" on the top, left and right, and to .75" on the bottom.
5. Apply the Heading 1 style to the title, and change the font size to 18 points.
6. Format the subheading *Introduction* with a 16-point purple, serif font, small caps, and a solid, purple underline. It should have 12 points of space before and after.
7. Create a new Quick Style based on the subheading formatting, named **New Subhead**.
8. Apply the New Subhead style to the headings *Come Prepared,* and *Behavior in Class.*
9. Insert an appropriate Wingding symbol such as #38 at the beginning of each heading.
10. Apply direct formatting to the remaining Normal text as follows:
    a. 14-point serif font, such as Times New Roman
    b. Leading of exactly 17 points
    c. Justified alignment
11. Format the three items in the list under the heading **Introduction** as a numbered list, using letters instead of numbers.
12. Set paragraph spacing to leave 6 points of space before the first item in the list and after the last item in the list.

13. Highlight the first item in the list in bright green.
14. Adjust the indents of the list so the number indent is .5" and the text indent is 1".
15. Create two bulleted lists under the heading *Come Prepared* (refer to the illustration) using an appropriate Wingding symbol as a bullet.
16. Sort the bulleted lists into descending alphabetical order.
17. Set paragraph spacing to leave 6 points of space before the first item in each list and after the last item in each list.
18. Apply the Intense Emphasis style to the text *come prepared* at the end of first sentence under the heading *Come Prepared* and to the text *maintain a professional attitude* in the last paragraph.
19. Check the spelling and grammar.
20. Change the Style Set to Traditional.
21. Apply the Verve Theme to the document.
22. Change the Theme Colors to Concourse.
23. Change the Theme Fonts to Civic.
24. Display the document in Print Preview. It should look similar to the one in the illustration. If necessary use Shrink to Fit to fit it on a single page.
25. Print the document.
26. Close the document, saving all changes.

What to Expect From In-House Training

📖 INTRODUCTION

In-house training courses are offered to insure that employees have the opportunity to stay current in their selected fields, or to provide instruction that the employer requires. In general, you can expect the following from most in-house training courses:

A.   Experienced teachers
B.   Focused content
C.   Hands-on training

📖 COME PREPARED

One of the most important things you can do to insure your success in any in-house training course is to *come prepared*. If there is any homework or outside reading to complete, be sure it is done on time. Also, there are a few basic items you should always bring to class:

☑ Pencil
☑ Pen
☑ Notebook

In addition, there may be items that are specific to the course as well as optional items. For example:

☑ Water bottle
☑ Pencil sharpener
☑ Calculator

📖 BEHAVIOR IN CLASS

Keep in mind that although in-house training classes may feel like a day off, you are still at work. You should *maintain a professional attitude* at all times. The other members of the class are your co-workers, who you will see every day. The information you are learning is designed to enhance your job performance. With that said, you should make every effort to be relaxed, to have fun, and to get as much as possible out of the course. If you pay attention, ask questions, and complete the assignments, you will find that in-house training is a positive, enjoyable experience.

Exercise | 33

Curriculum Integration

Application Skills For your Science class, use the skills you have learned in Lesson 4 to write a one-page report about an inventor. Before writing the report, use your library, books in your classroom, or the Internet to research the inventor. Look for information such as what he or she invented and when. Include information on why the invention was important. Be sure to keep a record of your sources including all books and Web sites, and write or type them on a separate page to include in the report.

For the report, you may want to include background information about the inventor, such as where he or she lived, or went to school. Set up the document using the correct settings for a one-page report. Include a title and your name. Format the report using styles, lists, spacing, and indents. You might want to insert symbols and use font effects for emphasis. Apply a theme to the document. When you are finished, ask a classmate to read the report and make suggestions about how you might improve it. Incorporate your classmate's suggestions. Save the changes and print the finished document.

EXERCISE DIRECTIONS

Start Word, if necessary, and create a new document. Save it as **33INVENT_xx**.

Select to display elements that might help you while you work, such as the rulers, nonprinting characters, and text boundaries, and make sure all the features you want to use are enabled, such as AutoCorrect and AutoFormat as You Type.

Set the margins for a one-page report.

Type the title 2" from the top of the page and type your name under the title.

Leave space, and then type the report. Use proper line spacing and paragraph alignment for a one page report.

Use styles, if appropriate.

Use bulleted or numbered lists, if appropriate. For example, you might want to list all the inventions your inventor created. Remember that you can customize the bullets or numbers. (See Illustration A.)

Correct spelling and grammatical errors as you type, if necessary, and search the thesaurus to find alternatives to common words, such as *go, went,* and *said*.

Try different themes, theme colors, and theme fonts to find a combination that you like.

Display the document in Print Preview.

If necessary, shrink the document to fit on one page. (This may affect the spacing at the top of the document, and between lines.)

Add a second page listing the sources you used while researching the report.

Save the changes you have made to the document.

Ask a classmate to review the document and make suggestions for how you might improve it.

Incorporate the suggestions into your report.

Print the document.

Close the document, saving all changes.

☆Garrett Augustus Morgan☆

By Student's Name

Garrett Augustus Morgan was born in Paris, Kentucky in 1877. He was the son of former slaves. He left school before completing sixth grade, but he always worked on his own to improve his skills at reading and writing. He moved north to Ohio when he was a teenager to find better opportunities for employment. He started a sewing machine repair business in Cleveland.

Morgan was quick to recognize when there was a need for something new. He started a newspaper for the African American community in 1920, called the Cleveland Call. He also invented many items that are still in use today, such as the traffic signal. He was inspired to create the signal after witnessing an accident between a horse-drawn buggy and an automobile. He received a patent for the invention in 1923.

Other Morgan inventions include:

➢ Tonic for straightening hair.

➢ Gas mask.

➢ Safety hood and smoke protector for firefighters.

➢ Zigzag sewing machine attachment.

Morgan died in 1963 at the age of 86 in Cleveland, Ohio. His original traffic signal and gas mask inventions have been refined over the years, but the basic concepts continue to save lives.

Lesson | 5

Word and the World Wide Web

Skills Covered

- ■ **About the World Wide Web**
- ■ **Create a Web Page Document in Word**
- ■ **Use Web Layout View**
- ■ **View a Web Page Document in a Browser**

Software Skills Save Word documents in a Web page format so that you can display them on the World Wide Web or on a company intranet. You can use Word features and tools to edit and format the documents, and then view them in your Web browser.

Application Skills You have been asked to post the in-house training course schedule for Restoration Architecture on the company's intranet. In this exercise, you will open the existing training course document and save it as a Web page. You will work with it in Web Layout View, and then preview it in your browser.

TERMS

Blog A Web log, which is a journal or newsletter that is updated frequently and published online.

HTML Hypertext Markup Language. A file format used for storing Web pages.

Internet A worldwide network of computers.

Internet Service Provider A company that provides access to the Internet for a fee.

MHTML A format used for storing Web pages as single files so they can be easily transmitted over the Internet.

Microsoft Office tags Codes embedded in a Web Page document created with a Microsoft Office program. The codes enable you to edit the document using the original program.

Web browser Software designed for locating and viewing information stored on the Internet. Common browsers include Internet Explorer and Netscape Navigator.

Web page A document stored on the World Wide Web.

Web server A computer connected to the Internet used to store Web page documents.

World Wide Web A system for finding information on the Internet through the use of linked documents.

NOTES

About the World Wide Web

- ■ Anyone with a computer, an **Internet** connection, and communications software can access the Internet and the **World Wide Web**.
- ■ For a fee, **Internet Service Providers (ISP)** provide you with an e-mail account, **Web browser** software, and Internet access.

- ■ Microsoft Office 2007 comes with the Internet Explorer Web browser, although your computer may be set up to use a different browser.
- ■ Some things available via the Internet and the World Wide Web include e-mail communication, product information and support, reference material, shopping, stock quotes, travel arrangements, real estate information, and games.

Create a Web Page Document in Word

■ You can save a new or existing Word document as a **Web page** so it can be stored on a **Web server** and viewed online.

■ When you save a document as a Web page you can choose from three Web page formats:

- Single File Web Page. Saves a Web page and all associated text and graphics in a single file in **MHTML** format. This is the default option.

- Web Page. Saves the document in **HTML** format. Associated graphics files such as bullets, lines, and pictures are stored in a separate folder that is linked to the HTML file.

  ✓ *The folder has the same name as the HTML file, followed by an underscore and the word files, like this: Filename_files. Use caution when moving or renaming the graphics files or the folder they are stored in. If Word cannot identify the files, the page will display without graphics elements.*

- Web Page, Filtered. Saves a file in HTML format without **Microsoft Office tags**. This reduces the file size, but limits some functionality for editing the file.

  ✓ *This option is recommended for advanced users only.*

■ Web page documents are viewed on a computer screen, so it is a good idea to make use of visual elements that will make it appealing, such as colors and bullets.

■ You can also create a **blog** post document in Word that you can publish to your blog account.

  ✓ *You must use a blog account that is compatible with Word 2007.*

Use Web Layout View

■ Web Layout view displays documents in Word as they will look on the Web.

■ Word automatically switches to Web Layout view when you display a Web page document.

■ You can also switch to Web Layout view by clicking the Web Layout button in the Document Views group on the View tab of the Ribbon or from the View buttons on the status bar.

■ Web Layout view lets you edit a document for viewing on-screen, instead of for printing on a page.

■ Features of Web Layout view include:

- Word wrapping to fit the window, not a page.
- Graphics positioned as they would be in a Web browser.
- Backgrounds (if there are any) displayed as they would be in a browser.

View a Web Page Document in a Browser

■ To see how a Web Page Document will look on the Web you can open it in your Web browser.

■ Use Windows to locate and open the document.

PROCEDURES

Save a Document as a Single File Web Page

1. Create a new blank document.
   OR
   Open an existing document.
2. Click **Office Button** .... Alt + F
3. Click **Save As** .... A
4. Click **Save as type** drop-down arrow .... Alt + T
5. Click **Single File Web Page** .... ↓/↑, ↵Enter
6. Select storage location.
   OR
   a. Click **Create New Folder** button.

b. Type new folder name.
c. Click **OK** .... ↵Enter
7. Select **File name** text box .... Alt + N
8. Type **file name**.
9. Click **Save** .... Alt + S

Save a Document in a Different Web Page Format

1. Create a new blank document.
   OR
   Open an existing document.
2. Click **Office Button** .... Alt + F
3. Click **Save As** .... A
4. Click **Save as type** drop-down arrow .... Alt + T

5. Click **Web Page** ...... ↓/↑, ↵Enter
   OR
   Click **Web Page, Filtered** .... ↓/↑, ↵Enter
6. Select storage location.
   OR
   a. Click **Create New Folder** button.
   b. Type new folder name.
   c. Click **OK** .... ↵Enter
7. Select **File name** text box .... Alt + N
8. Type **file name**.
9. Click **Save** .... Alt + S

Create a Blog Post Document

1. Start Word.
2. Click **Office Button** 🖼️ ...... Alt+F
3. Click **New** .... N
4. Click **New blog post** .... →/←
5. Click **Create** .... ↵Enter

✓ *Word will prompt you to register your blog account.*

Change to Web Layout View

■ Display Web page document in Word.

OR

■ Click **Web Layout** button 🖼️ on the Status bar.

OR

1. Click **View** tab .... Alt+W

   Document Views Group

2. Click **Web Layout** button 🖼️ L

Open a Web Page Document in a Web Browser

1. Use Windows to open the folder where the Web page document is stored.
2. Double-click the Web page document file icon.

EXERCISE DIRECTIONS

1. Start Word, if necessary.
2. Open 💿 **34COURSE**.
3. Save the document as a Single File Web page with the name **34COURSE_xx**.
4. Use the following steps to format the document as shown in Illustration A.
5. Apply the Oriel theme to the document.
6. Change the font color of the company name and address to the theme color, Orange, Accent 1.

   ✓ *Use ScreenTips to identify the colors on the Font Color drop-down palette.*

7. Change the font color of the text Training Schedule to the theme color Blue, Accent 2.

8. Format the names of the months as bulleted items, and change the font color to the theme color Red, Accent 3.
9. Change the font color of the course names and descriptions to the theme color Blue-Gray, Text 2.
10. Change the font color of the last line in the document to the theme color, Orange, Accent 1.
11. Check the spelling and grammar in the document. It should look similar to Illustration A.
12. Print the document.
13. Close the file, saving all changes.
14. Open the **34COURSE_xx** Web page document in your Web browser.
15. Close your Web browser.

Illustration A

Restoration Architecture

8921 Thunderbird Road ✧ Phoenix, Arizona 85022 ✧ 602-555-6325

Training Schedule

- **January**

Microsoft Word 1

This introductory course will cover the basics of using Microsoft Word 2007 to create common business documents. By the end of the course you will know how to create, format, edit, and print text-based documents such as letters, memos, and reports.

- **February**

Microsoft Word 2

A continuation of the Word 1 course, this intermediate level class will delve into some of the more intriguing features of Microsoft Word 2007. By the end of the course you will know how to use mail merge to generate form letters, labels, and envelopes, set up a document in columns, include headers and footers, and insert pictures.

- **March**

Microsoft Word 3

This final course in the Microsoft Word series covers advanced features. By the end of this course you will know how to use tables, create and modify outlines, use e-mail and Internet features in Word, and share documents with other users.

Enrollment forms are available in the HR office or on the company Intranet.

ON YOUR OWN

1. Plan a personal Web page. Decide the information you would like to include and how you want the page to look. For example, you should include your first name, what you like to do, and who your favorite musicians and sports teams are. You might include favorite sayings, upcoming events in your life, or fun things your family or friends plan to do. If you have a connection to the Internet, you might browse other pages to get some ideas.

   ✓ *Be careful when including personal information on a Web page or blog. Remember that anyone can access information on the World Wide Web, so be sure not to include your address or phone number.*

2. When you are ready, create a new document in Word.

3. Save the document as a Single File Web page with the name file as **OWD34_xx**.

4. Apply formatting to improve the appearance of your Web page as it will be viewed on-screen. For example, apply a theme, change the font formatting, create lists, and so on.

5. Ask a classmate to view the Web page and to offer comments or suggestions.

6. Incorporate the suggestions into the document.

7. Check the spelling and grammar in the document and then close it, saving all changes.

8. Open the **OWD34_xx** in your Web browser to see how it will look online.

9. Close your Web browser and exit Word.

Exercise | 35

Skills Covered

- Open a Web Page Document in Word
- Apply a Background
- Use Web Page Titles

Software Skills   Open an existing Web page document in Word so you can edit it or format it. Set the Web page title so that people viewing the page in a browser will know what page is currently displayed. Apply a colored or textured background to enhance the page for viewing on a screen.

Application Skills   You have created a Web page document listing training courses for Restoration Architecture. In this exercise, you will open the Web page in Word and change the Web page title. You will also apply a background to the page.

TERMS

Background The color, pattern, or fill displayed on the page behind data in a document.

Fill effect A texture, shading, picture, or pattern used as a background.

Web page title The text that displays in the title bar when a Web page is viewed in a Web browser.

Web site A set of linked Web pages, usually all relating to the same topic.

NOTES

Open a Web Page Document in Word

- Use the Open dialog box to open a Web page document in Word the same way you open a regular Word document.
- The document displays in Web Layout view.
- When you save the document, it remains in its original Web page format.
- By default, if you try to open a Web page document from Windows, the document displays in your Web browser, not in Word.

Use Web Page Titles

- **Web page titles** are displayed in the Web browser title bar.
- By default, Word leaves the Web page title blank.
- You can set or change the page title name from the Save As dialog box.

Apply a Background

- By default, Word documents—including Web pages—have a plain white **background**.
- Add visual interest or create an effect by applying a color, pattern, **fill effect**, or picture to a document background.
- You should coordinate backgrounds for pages in a **Web site** to establish continuity.
- You can apply a background to any Word document, not just a Web page.

PROCEDURES

Open a Web Page Document in Word

1. Click **Office Button** .... Alt + F
2. Click **Open** .... O
3. Navigate to the location where the Web page document is stored.
4. Double-click document name to open it.

    OR

    a. Click document name.
    b. Click **Open** .... Alt + O

Change a Web Page Title

For a new document:

1. Create a new blank document.
2. Click **Office Button** .... Alt + F
3. Click **Save As** .... A
4. Click **Save as type** drop-down arrow .... Alt + T
5. Click **Single File Web Page** .... ↓/↑, ↵Enter

6. Click **Change Title** .... Alt + C
7. Type new Web page title.
8. Click **OK** .... ↵Enter
9. Select storage location

    OR

    a. Click **Create New Folder** button.
    b. Type new folder name.
    c. Click **OK** .... ↵Enter
10. Select **File name** text box .... Alt + N
11. Type **file name**.
12. Click **Save** .... Alt + S

For an existing Web page document:

1. Open Web page document in Word.
2. Click **Office Button** .... Alt + F
3. Click **Save As** .... A
4. Click **Change Title** .... Alt + C
5. Type new Web page title.
6. Click **OK** .... ↵Enter
7. Click **Save** .... Alt + S

Apply a Background

1. Open document to format.
2. Click **Page Layout** tab ..... Alt + P

    Page Background Group

3. Click **Page Color** button .... P, C
4. Click desired color swatch ...... ↑/↓/←/→, ↵Enter

    OR

    a. Click **Fill Effects** .... F
    b. Click desired page tab .... Ctrl + Tab
    c. Select desired effect.
    d. Click **OK** .... ↵Enter

    OR

    ■ Click **No Color** to remove existing background .... N

EXERCISE DIRECTIONS

1. Start Word, if necessary.
2. Open 34COURSE_xx or open 35COURSE.
3. Save the document as a Single File Web page with the name **35COURSE_xx**, and the Web page title **Training Schedule**.
4. Apply the theme color Light Yellow, Background 2 as a background for the Web page.
5. Change the background to the Recycled Paper fill effect.
6. Check the spelling and grammar in the document.
7. Print the document.
8. Close the file, saving all changes.
9. Open the **35COURSE_xx** Web page document in your Web browser. It should look similar to Illustration A, depending on which Web browser you are using, and how it is set up.
10. Close your Web browser.

Illustration A

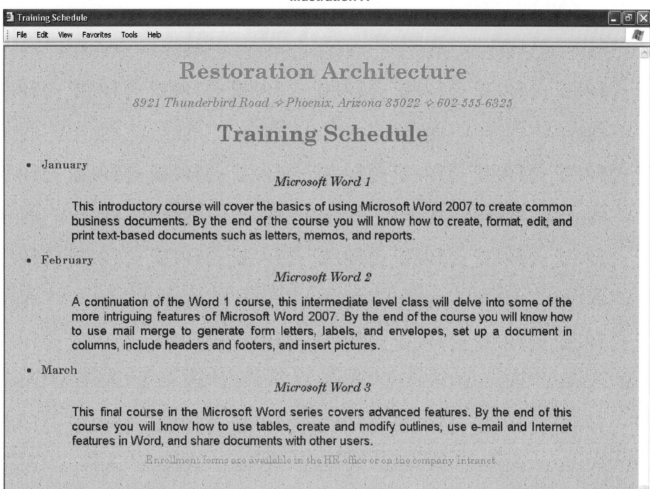

ON YOUR OWN

1. In Word open ⌨OWD34_*xx* or open 💿35WEB.
2. Save the document as a Single File Web page with the name **OWD35_*xx***, and the Web page title **My Web Page**.
3. Apply a background to the Web page.
4. Save the changes, close the document, and open it in your Web browser to see how it looks.
5. Close your browser and open **OWD35_*xx*** in Word again.
6. Try a different background, and view it in your browser.

7. Ask a classmate to view the different backgrounds and help you decide which one enhances the page more.
8. Apply the background you like the best.
9. Check the spelling and grammar in the document and then close it, saving all changes.
10. Open the **OWD35_*xx*** in your Web browser to see how it will look online.
11. Close your Web browser and exit Word.

Skills Covered

■ **Create Hyperlinks**

Software Skills Create a hyperlink to connect related documents to each other, to connect a Word document to a Web site, or to connect one location in a document to another location in the same document. For example, create hyperlinks from a report topic to an Internet site where more information can be found. Hyperlinks let you expand the boundaries among documents and among computers because, in effect, you can link to information stored anywhere on the Internet.

Application Skills In this exercise, you will insert hyperlinks to help readers navigate through the Web page listing training courses for Restoration Architecture. You will also link the Web page to a Word document describing what employees should expect from in-house training and to a Web site that provides more information about Microsoft Office products.

TERMS

Bookmark A nonprinting character that you insert and name so that you can quickly find a particular location in a document.

Hyperlink Text or graphics linked to a destination file or location. Click the link to jump to the destination.

Hyperlink destination The location displayed when the hyperlink is clicked. Sometimes called the target.

Hyperlink source The document where the hyperlink is inserted.

NOTES

Create Hyperlinks

■ **Hyperlinks** can be used to link locations within a single document, to link two documents, or to link a document to a Web page or e-mail address.

   ✓ *You learn more about using e-mail in Exercise 37.*

■ Hyperlinks can be created in any type of Word document.

■ When you format text as a hyperlink, Word automatically applies the Hyperlink style, which by default uses a blue font and a solid underline, but may be different depending on the current theme.

■ Once you click the hyperlink, the font color changes to indicate that the link has been used.

■ A **hyperlink destination** does not have to be in the same file format as the **hyperlink source** document. For example, you can link a Word document file to a Web page file or to an Excel file, and so on.

■ The hyperlink destination can be a file stored on your computer, on your company intranet, or on a Web server as part of a Web site.

■ When you click a hyperlink to a Web page, the document opens in your Web browser program.

■ If the destination Web page is currently open in Word, when you click the hyperlink, the document displays in Word.

■ When you click a hyperlink to an e-mail address, Word starts your e-mail program and displays a new e-mail message. The address and subject are filled in with the hyperlink information.

- You can create a hyperlink within a document for moving to the top of the document, to a specific heading, or to a **bookmark**.

    ✓ *You learn about bookmarks in Exercise 54.*

- By default, in Word documents you must press Ctrl and click the hyperlink in order to go to the hyperlink destination. This helps avoid accidental access.

- If you want, you can change the setting so that you don't have to press Ctrl.

- You can edit and format hyperlink text the same way you edit and format regular text.

- If you change the setting so that you don't have to press Ctrl to follow a hyperlink, you must select the hyperlink before you can edit it or format it.

- You can change a hyperlink destination.
- You can remove a hyperlink completely.

Insert Hyperlink dialog box

PROCEDURES

Insert a Hyperlink within a Document *(Ctrl + K)*

1. Position insertion point where you want to insert hyperlink.

    OR

    Select text to change to a hyperlink.

    ✓ *If existing text is not selected, Word inserts the destination name as the hyperlink text.*

2. Click **Insert** tab .... Alt+N

    Links Group

3. Click **Hyperlink** button 🔗 I

4. Click **Place in this document** in Link to bar .... Alt+A

5. In the **Select a place in this document** list, click hyperlink destination .... Alt+C, ↓/↑

    ✓ *If necessary click the expand symbol (+) to expand the list to show additional headings and/or bookmarks.*

6. Click **OK** .... ↵Enter

Insert a Hyperlink to a Different Document *(Ctrl + K)*

1. Position insertion point where you want to insert hyperlink.

    OR

    Select text to change to a hyperlink.

    ✓ *If existing text is not selected, Word inserts the destination name as the hyperlink text.*

2. Click **Insert** tab .... Alt+N

    Links Group

3. Click **Hyperlink** button 🔗 I

4. Click **Existing File or Web Page** in Link to bar .... Alt+X

5. In the **Address** text box, type the hyperlink destination file name .... Alt+E, type file name

    ✓ *Word automatically completes the file name as you type based on recently used file names; stop typing to accept the entry or keep typing to enter a different name.*

    OR

    a. Click **Current Folder** in the Look in bar to display a list of files stored in the current folder .... Alt+U

    b. Click the file name in the list of files.

OR

a. Click **Browsed Pages** to display a list of recently viewed Web pages.. Alt+B

b. Locate and click file name.

OR

a. Click **Recent Files** to display a list of recently used files .... Alt+C

b. Click the file name in the list of files.

6. If necessary, in the **Text to display** text box, type the text to display as the hyperlink text .... Alt+T, type text

7. Click **OK** .... ↵Enter

Insert a Hyperlink to a Web Page *(Ctrl + K)*

1. Position insertion point where you want to insert hyperlink.

    OR

    Select text to change to a hyperlink.

    ✓ *If existing text is not selected, Word inserts the destination name as the hyperlink text.*

2. Click **Insert** tab .... Alt+N

Links Group

3. Click **Hyperlink** button 🖇️ .... Ⓘ
4. Click **Existing File or Web Page** in Link to bar .... Alt + Ⓧ
5. In the **Address** text box, type the hyperlink destination URL .... Alt + Ⓔ, type URL

   ✓ *Word automatically completes the URL as you type based on recently used URLs; stop typing to accept the entry or keep typing to enter a different URL.*

OR

a. Click **Browsed Pages** to display a list of recently viewed Web pages .... Alt + Ⓑ
b. Locate and click URL or site name in the list of files.
c. Click **OK** .... ↵Enter

6. If necessary, in the **Text to display** text box, type the text to display as the hyperlink text .... Alt + Ⓣ, type text
7. Click **OK** .... ↵Enter

Insert a Hyperlink to an E-Mail Address *(Ctrl + K)*

1. Position insertion point where you want to insert hyperlink.

   OR

   Select text to change to a hyperlink.

   ✓ *If existing text is not selected, Word inserts the destination name as the hyperlink text.*

2. Click **Insert** tab .... Alt + Ⓝ

   Links Group

3. Click **Hyperlink** button 🖇️ .... Ⓘ
4. Click **E-mail Address** in Link to bar .... Alt + Ⓜ
5. In the **E-mail address** text box, type e-mail address .... Alt + Ⓔ, type e-mail address

   ✓ *This is the address that will display in the To: line of the e-mail message header.*

   OR

   Click the address in the **Recently used e-mail addresses** list .... Alt + Ⓒ, Ⓓ/Ⓤ

6. In the **Subject** text box, type the text you want to display in the Subject line of the e-mail message header .... Alt + Ⓤ, type subject
7. Click **OK** .... ↵Enter

Remove a Hyperlink

1. Right-click hyperlink text.
2. Click **Remove Hyperlink** .... Ⓡ

   ✓ *This removes hyperlink, not the text.*

Change a Hyperlink Destination

1. Right-click hyperlink text.
2. Click **Edit Hyperlink** .... Ⓗ
3. Select new destination.
4. Click **OK** .... ↵Enter

Select a Hyperlink

1. Right-click hyperlink text.
2. Click **Select Hyperlink** .... Ⓢ

Set Word to Follow Hyperlink on Click

1. Click **Office Button** 🔘 .... Alt + Ⓕ
2. Click **Word Options** .... Ⓘ
3. Click **Advanced** .... Ⓐ
4. Click to clear the **Use CTRL+Click to follow hyperlink** check box .... Alt + Ⓗ, Spacebar
5. Click **OK** .... ↵Enter

EXERCISE DIRECTIONS

Prepare the Word Document

1. Start Word, if necessary.
2. Open 🖮32TRAIN_*xx* or open 💿36TRAIN.
3. Save the file as **36TRAIN_*xx***.
4. Insert a new line at the top of the document and clear all formatting from it.
5. Type the text **RETURN**.
6. Display the document in Print Preview.
7. If the document extends on to two pages, use the Shrink One Page command to fit it on one page.
8. Close Print Preview.

Prepare the Web Page in Word

1. In Word, open the file 🖮35COURSE_*xx* or open 💿36COURSE.

   ✓ *Remember, this is a Web page document. If you try to open it from Windows, it will open in your browser, not in Word.*

2. Save the file as a single file Web page with the name **36COURSE_*xx***.
3. Edit and format the document using the following steps.

   ✓ *Refer to Illustration A to see the completed document.*

4. Position the insertion point at the end of the heading *Training Schedule* and press Enter.

5. Apply the Normal style to the new blank line.

6. Type **January** and press Enter.

7. Type **February** and press Enter.

8. Type **March** and press Enter twice.

9. Type the following: **Questions?** and press Enter twice.

10. Type **Click here to read about in-house training.** and press Enter twice.

11. Type **Click here to learn more about Microsoft Office 2007**.

12. Insert a hyperlink from the text *January* that you typed in step 6 above to the heading *January*.

13. Insert a hyperlink from the text *February* that you typed in step 7 above to the heading *February*.

14. Insert a hyperlink from the text *March* that you typed in step 8 above to the heading *March*.

15. At the end of each course description paragraph, press Enter and type **Back to Top**.

16. Insert hyperlinks from each occurrence of **Back to Top** to the top of the document.

17. Insert a hyperlink from the text you typed in step 10 above to the **36TRAIN_xx** document.

18. Insert a hyperlink from the text you typed in step 11 above to the URL www.microsoft.com

19. Increase the font size of all hyperlink text to 16 points.

Test Hyperlinks

1. Test the hyperlinks to navigate through the **36COURSE_xx** document.

   ✓ *Use the hyperlinks to go to each month heading, then to return to the top of the document.*

2. Test the hyperlink to go to the **36TRAIN_xx** document.

3. In the **36TRAIN_xx** document, insert a hyperlink from the text *RETURN* back to the **36COURSE_xx** document.

4. Test the hyperlink to return to the **36COURSE_xx** document.

5. Test the hyperlink to go to the Microsoft Web site.

   ✓ *You may be prompted to sign on to your ISP.*

6. Click the Back button on your browser's toolbar to return to the **36COURSE_xx** document.

7. Close all open documents, saving all changes, and disconnect from the Internet, if necessary.

Curriculum Connection: Social Studies

Ancient Olympics

The first recorded winner of an Olympic event was Koroibos, a cook who won a foot race in 776 B.C. Although the games were held every four years, they were quite different from our modern Olympics. For example, there were fewer events, and only free men who spoke Greek were allowed to compete. Still, winners were hailed as heroes, and often became famous.

Ancient Olympics Web Site

Imagine you are a sports writer living in Olympia around 740 B.C. and that you are using a Web site to report on the Olympic Games. Create a Web site that includes a home page and two or three pages devoted to specific events. Write an explanation of each event, and report the results from that day's competition. Link each page to the home page.

Illustration A

Restoration Architecture

8921 Thunderbird Road ❖ Phoenix, Arizona 85022 ❖ 602-555-6325

Training Schedule

January
February
March

Questions?

Click here to read about in-house training.

Click here to learn more about Microsoft Office 2007.

- **January**

Microsoft Word 1

This introductory course will cover the basics of using Microsoft Word 2007 to create common business documents. By the end of the course you will know how to create, format, edit, and print text-based documents such as letters, memos, and reports.

Back to Top

- **February**

Microsoft Word 2

A continuation of the Word 1 course, this intermediate level class will delve into some of the more intriguing features of Microsoft Word 2007. By the end of the course you will know how to use mail merge to generate form letters, labels, and envelopes, set up a document in columns, include headers and footers, and insert pictures.

Back to Top

- **March**

Microsoft Word 3

This final course in the Microsoft Word series covers advanced features. By the end of this course you will know how to use tables, create and modify outlines, use e-mail and Internet features in Word, and share documents with other users.

Back to Top

Enrollment forms are available in the HR office or on the company Intranet.

ON YOUR OWN

1. Think about the documents you have created in the On Your Own sections of previous exercises and identify the ones you might link together into a Web site. For example, you could link the Web page to the list of things you'd like to accomplish, to your resume, or to the announcement of the upcoming event.

2. Open the document ⌨OWD35_*xx*, your personal Web page, or open 💿36WEB.

3. Save the file as OWD36_*xx*.

4. Open the document ⌨OWD20-2_*xx*, your resume, or open 💿36RESUME.

5. Save the file as OWD36-2_*xx*.

6. Create a hyperlink from OWD36_*xx* to OWD36-2_*xx*. You can create new hyperlink text, or use text that is already entered in the document.

7. Create a link back to the Web page from the resume.

8. Open the document ⌨OWD31_*xx*, the one-page biography, or open 💿36MYLIFE.

9. Save the file as OWD36-3_*xx*.

10. Create a hyperlink from OWD36_*xx* to OWD36-3_*xx*. Again, you can create new hyperlink text, or use text that is already entered in the document.

11. Create a link back to the Web page from the biography.

12. If you have access to the Internet, try linking your Web page to a Web site that you like.

13. Test the links.

14. Save the changes to all documents, then close the documents.

Skills Covered

■ **Send a Document as an E-mail Attachment**

Software Skills   You can attach a Word document to an e-mail message, and then send the message using an e-mail software program, such as Outlook or Outlook Express. You can exchange e-mail messages via the Internet or an intranet with anyone who has an e-mail account, including coworkers located down the hall, in a different state, or halfway around the world.

Application Skills   As the assistant to the franchise manager at Whole Grains Food, you have been compiling a list of potential locations for expanding the business outside of California. In this exercise, you will attach the list of potential locations to an e-mail message that you will send to the franchise manager.

TERMS

Attachment A document attached to an e-mail message and sent in its original file format.

E-mail A method of sending information from one computer to another across the Internet or intranet.

E-mail address The string of characters that identifies the name and location of an e-mail user.

Mail service provider A company that maintains and controls e-mail accounts.

Message body The area in an e-mail message where the message body is typed.

Message header The area at the top of the message window where you enter information about where the message is going and what it is about.

NOTES

Send a Document as an E-mail Attachment

■ You can use Word to create an **e-mail** message that automatically inserts the current document as an **attachment**.

■ The original document remains stored on your computer, and a copy is transmitted as the attachment.

■ The attached document is sent in its original format.

■ The message recipient can open the attached Word document on his or her computer in Word, or in another application that is compatible with Word.

■ Before sending the message, you can edit and format it with Word's editing and formatting features, including the spelling and grammar checkers and AutoCorrect.

■ To send e-mail messages you must have the following:
  ● A connection to the Internet or to an intranet.
  ● An account with a **mail service provider**.
  ● An e-mail program such as Outlook or Outlook Express.
  ● The recipient's **e-mail address**.

■ In addition, your e-mail program must be correctly configured with your e-mail account information.

■ When you create an e-mail message in Word, a Message window opens.

- The Message window has two basic parts:
  - The **message header** where you enter the recipient's address in the To: text box, the addresses of other people receiving copies of the message in the Cc: text box, and a title for the message in the Subject text box. Word automatically enters the name of the attached document in an Attachment text box.
    - ✓ *When you create an e-mail message in Word, Word also automatically enters the name of the current document in the Subject text box.*
  - The **message body** where you type and format the message text.
- You send the message using your e-mail program.

- If you are unable to send a message immediately, you can use the File>Save command to save it as a message in your e-mail program.
- If you use the E-mail feature in Word frequently, you can add an E-mail button to the Quick Access Toolbar.

E-mail window

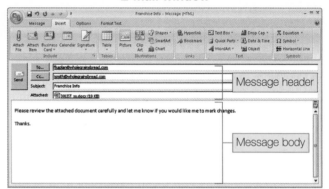

PROCEDURES

Send a Word Document as an E-mail Attachment

1. Open document to send as an attachment.
2. Click **E-Mail** button 📧 on Quick Access Toolbar.

   OR

   a. Click **Office Button** 📧 .... Alt + F
   b. Click **Send** .... D
   c. Click **E-mail** .... E
3. Type recipient's e-mail address in To: box.
4. Press **Tab** .... Tab
5. Type additional recipients' e-mail addresses in Cc: box.
6. Press **Tab** .... Tab

7. Edit Subject text, if necessary.
8. Click in **Message body** Tab 2x
9. Type and format e-mail message text.
10. Click **Send** button 📧Send on Message window toolbar .... Alt + S

    ✓ *Log on to transmit message as necessary.*

Save an E-Mail Message

1. Click **Office Button** 📧 on the Message window toolbar .... Alt + F
2. Click **Save** .... S

   ✓ *The message is stored in your e-mail program.*

Close an E-Mail Message

1. Click **Office Button** 📧 on the Message window toolbar .... Alt + F
2. Click **Close** C
3. If necessary, click **Yes** to save changes .... Y

   OR

   Click **No** to close the Message window without saving the message.

Add E-Mail Button to the Quick Access Toolbar

1. Click the **Customize Quick Access Toolbar** button ▼ .... Alt , ↑ , → , ↵Enter
2. Click **E-mail** .... ↓ , ↵Enter

EXERCISE DIRECTIONS

✓ *This exercise uses a fictitious e-mail address. If you try to send the message, it will be returned as undeliverable. Your instructor may provide you with an actual e-mail address to use.*

1. Start Word, if necessary.
2. Open the document ⊙ **37LIST**.
3. Save the document as **37LIST_xx**.
4. Sort the items in the list alphabetically in ascending order.
5. Apply the default numbered list format to the items.
6. Change paragraph formatting to leave 6 points of space before and after each item in the list.

   ✓ *You may have to deselect the **Don't add space between paragraphs of the same style** check box in the Paragraph dialog box.*

7. Check the spelling and grammar in the document.
8. Print the document, and save it.
9. Select to send the document as an e-mail attachment.

10. In the message header, enter the following information:
    a. Enter the address:

       fkaplan@wholegrainsbread.com

       ✓ *Alternatively, enter a valid e-mail address as allowed by your instructor.*

    b. Skip the Cc box.
    c. Edit the text in the Subject text box to **List of Sites**
11. In the message body, enter the following text:

    Mr. Kaplan,

    As promised, here is the list of potential sites. Let me know what I should do next. Thanks.
12. Format the message text in a 14-point serif font. The message should look similar to the one in Illustration A.
13. With your instructor's permission, if you used a valid e-mail address in step 10a, send the message. Alternatively, save and close the message.

    ✓ *You can check your e-mail program to see the saved message.*

14. Close the **37LIST_xx** document.

Illustration A

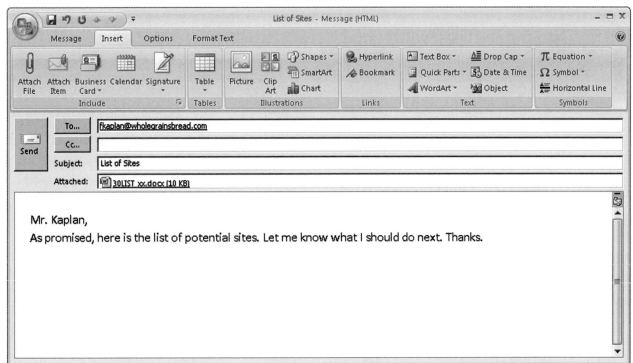

ON YOUR OWN

1. Look up and record e-mail addresses for friends, coworkers, or companies.
2. Create a new document and save it as **OWD37_xx**.
3. Type a letter to someone whose e-mail address you have. For example, type a letter to an instructor requesting a missed homework assignment, or to your employer.
4. Attach the document to an e-mail message and send it.
5. Check your e-mail to see if you received a reply.
6. When you are finished, close all open documents, and exit all open applications.

Exercise | 38

Critical Thinking

Application Skills You have been hired to develop a Web site for Michigan Avenue Athletic Club. In this exercise, you will create and format a Web page document, which you will attach to an e-mail message to the club's manager. You will also insert hyperlinks linking the Web page to a regular Word document.

EXERCISE DIRECTIONS

✓ *This exercise uses a fictitious e-mail address. If you try to send the message, it will be returned as undeliverable. Your instructor may provide you with an actual e-mail address to use.*

1. Start Word, if necessary.
2. Create a new document and save it as a single file Web page with the file name **38WEB_xx**, and the page title **Michigan Avenue Athletic Club Home Page**.
3. Apply the Solstice theme to the document.
4. Apply the Parchment texture as the page background.
5. Type and format the document shown in Illustration A.
6. Check the spelling and grammar in the document.
7. Send the document as an e-mail attachment using the following message header information:
   a. Enter the address: **jstone@michaveclub.com**

   ✓ *Alternatively, enter a valid e-mail address as allowed by your instructor.*

   b. Skip the Cc box.
   c. Edit the text in the Subject text box to **Sample Web Page**.

8. In the message body, enter the following text:
   John,
   What do you think of this Web page design?
9. With your instructor's permission, if you used a valid e-mail address in step 7a, send the message. Alternatively, save and close the message.

   ✓ *You can check your e-mail program to see the saved message.*

10. Open the Word document 💿**38STRENGTH**.
11. Save the file as **38STRENGTH_xx**.
12. Apply the Solstice theme and the Parchment texture to the document.
13. Insert a new blank line at the beginning of the document and clear all formatting from it.
14. On the new line, type **Return to Home Page**.
15. Insert a hyperlink from the text **Return to Home Page** to the **38WEB_xx** document.
16. Insert a new blank line at the end of the **38STRENGTH_xx** document and type: **Click here to request information via e-mail**.

17. Select the text *e-mail* and insert a hyperlink to **mail@michaveclub.com**, with the subject **Strength Training Info**.

18. Test the *Return to Home Page* hyperlink.

19. In the **38WEB_xx** document, insert a hyperlink from the text *Weekly Spotlight* to the **38STRENGTH_xx** document. The page should look similar to the one in the illustration.

20. Test the hyperlink.

21. Close all open documents, saving all changes.

Illustration A

MICHIGAN AVENUE ATHLETIC CLUB

WHERE EVERYONE IS A WINNER

Welcome to the wonderful world of the Michigan Avenue Athletic Club. We're a full-service health and fitness club dedicated to providing a friendly and supportive atmosphere for people of all ages and abilities. We offer a vast array of equipment and classes including aerobics, spinning, yoga, kickboxing, and strength training. We have racquetball and tennis, an indoor pool, spa services, a pro shop, and a café.

Use the links below to learn more about membership, special events, and to access our weekly spotlight on physical fitness.

➢ Membership rates
➢ About the staff
➢ Calendar of events
➢ Weekly spotlight

Curriculum Integration

Application Skills   Use the skills you have learned in Lesson 5 to design a Web page for your English or Language Arts class. Include information about the class, such as the instructor's name, what time the class meets, and current assignments. Format the page using a theme and page background, as well as fonts, colors, and lists. Refer to Illustration A to a see a sample page. If possible, include a hyperlink to the school's Web site. Alternatively, you may want to work in teams for this exercise. Each team member could design a page about one aspect of the class, and then you could link the pages into a Web site.

EXERCISE DIRECTIONS

Start Word, if necessary, and create a new document. Save it as a single file Web page document with the name **39LAPAGE_xx** and an appropriate Web page title.

Select to display elements that might help you while you work, such as the rulers, nonprinting characters, and text boundaries, and make sure all the features you want to use are enabled, such as AutoCorrect and AutoFormat As You Type.

Select a theme, theme colors, and theme fonts, and apply a page background.

Type and format the text you want to include on the page. Use styles as well as direct font and paragraph formatting.

Check the spelling and grammar on the page, and use a thesaurus to replace common or boring words.

Create hyperlinks, if necessary.

Close the document, saving all changes.

Open the Web page in your browser to see how it would look to someone viewing it online.

Ask a classmate to review the page and make suggestions for how you might improve it.

Close your browser and open the page in Word.

Incorporate your classmate's suggestions into the page.

Print the page.

Close the file, saving all changes.

Language Arts

Period B

Mrs. Lamont

About Our Class

Mrs. Lamont's Period B Language Arts class is exciting and fun. We are learning a lot about critical reading and writing. We also work hard on vocabulary. There are 28 students in the class, and we all enjoy studying with Mrs. Lamont.

The Curriculum

- ❖ First Quarter: American Poetry and Poets
- ❖ Second Quarter: Essays and Drama
- ❖ Third Quarter: 20th Century Stories
- ❖ Fourth Quarter: Writing for Real Life

Reading List

- ❖ Robert Frost
- ❖ E. B. White
- ❖ *The Crucible*

Lesson | 6

Working with Tables

Exercise | 40

Skills Covered

- Create a Table
- Enter Data in a Table
- Select in a Table
- Change Table Structure
- Format a Table

Software Skills Create tables to organize data into columns and rows. Any information that needs to be presented in side-by-side columns can be set up in a table. For example, a price list, an invoice, and a resume are all types of documents for which you should use a table. The table format lets you align information side by side and across the page so the information is easy to read.

Application Skills Restoration Architecture is offering the staff training courses. In this exercise, you will create a memo that includes a list of courses being offered. You will set up the course list in a table.

TERMS

Border A line drawn around the edges of an element, such as a table or a table cell. Borders can also be drawn around paragraphs and pages.

Cell The rectangular area at the intersection of a column and a row in a table, into which you enter data or graphics.

Column A vertical series of cells in a table.

Column markers Markers on the horizontal ruler that indicate column dividers.

Column width The width of a column in a table, measured in inches.

Dividers The lines that indicate the edges of cells in a table. Dividers do not print, although they are indicated on-screen by either gridlines or borders.

End of row/cell markers Nonprinting characters used to mark the end of a cell or a row in a table.

Gridlines Nonprinting lines that can be displayed around cells in a table.

Row A horizontal series of cells in a table.

Row height The height of a row in a table, measured in inches.

Table A grid comprised of horizontal rows and vertical columns into which you can enter data.

NOTES

Create a Table

- **Tables** are easier to use than tabbed columns when setting up and organizing data in **columns** and **rows**.
- You can create a table in any Word document; they are frequently used to align data on Web page documents.

- Use the Table button in the Tables group on the Insert tab of the Ribbon to open the Table drop-down menu to access the three basic methods for creating a table:
  - You can drag across the Table menu grid to select the number of columns and rows you want in the table.
  - You can open the Insert Table dialog box to specify the number of columns and rows.

- You can select a table from the Quick Tables gallery.

✓ *You can also draw a table freehand. Drawing a table is covered in Exercise 42.*

Options for creating a table

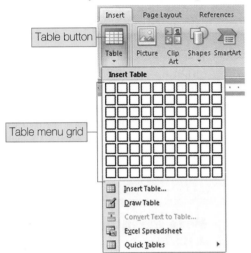

- Whichever method you use, Word creates the table at the insertion point location and adds two Table Tools tabs to the Ribbon: Design and Layout.
- **Column markers** on the horizontal ruler show the location of the right **divider** of each column.
- By default, Word places a 1/2-pt. **border** around all **cells** in a table.
- You can also display three unique nonprinting elements:
  - **End of cell markers**
  - **End of row markers**
  - **Gridlines**

✓ *Gridlines display only if there are no table borders and if you select the View Gridlines button in the Table group on the Layout tab.*

A table with four columns and four rows

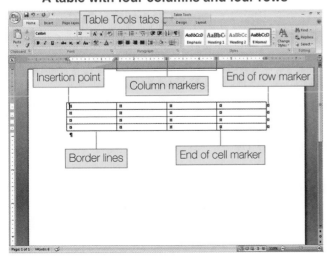

Enter Data in a Table

- You enter data in the cells of a table.
- **Row height** increases automatically to accommodate as much data as you type.
- **Column width** does not change automatically. Text wraps at the right margin of a cell the same way it wraps at the right margin of a page.
- To move from cell to cell you press Tab⇆, or click in another cell with the mouse.

  ✓ *To insert a Tab within a cell, you press Ctrl+Tab⇆.*

- When you press ↵Enter in a cell, Word starts a new paragraph within the cell.
- You can edit and format text within a cell the same way you do outside a table.

Select in a Table

- As with other Word features, you must select table components before you can affect them with commands.
- You select text within a cell using the standard selection commands.
- You can select one or more columns, one or more rows, one or more cells, or the entire table.
- The commands for selecting table components are in the Table group on the Table Tools Layout tab of the Ribbon.
- Selected table components are highlighted.

Change Table Structure

- Change a table's structure by inserting and deleting columns, rows, or cells.
- The commands for inserting and deleting table components are in the Rows & Columns group on the Table Tools Layout tab of the Ribbon.
- You can insert components anywhere in a table.
- You can delete any component.
- Data entered in a deleted column or row is deleted as well.
- If necessary, you can choose which way to shift existing cells when you insert or delete cells.

Format a Table

- You can format text within a table using standard Word formatting techniques. For example, use font formatting, alignments, spacing, indents, and tabs to enhance text in a table.

- You can apply formatting to selected text, or to selected cells, columns, or rows.

- To quickly apply formatting effects to an entire table, you can select a Table Style from the gallery of styles in the Table Styles group on the Table Tools Design tab of the Ribbon.

- As with paragraph and character styles, only one row of styles displays in the Table Styles group at a time, but you can scroll the gallery, or click the More button ▼ to display the entire gallery.

  ✓ For information on working with paragraph and characters styles, refer to Exercise 29.

- Table styles include border lines, shading, color, fonts, and other formatting.

- Rest the mouse pointer on a Table style in the gallery to preview how it will affect the current table, and to see the style name in a ScreenTip.

- When you select a table style, it overrides existing formatting. Therefore, you should apply a style first, and then modify the formatting as needed.

PROCEDURES

Create a Table

To use the Table menu:
1. Position insertion point.
2. Click the **Insert** tab .... Alt + N

   Tables Group

3. Click the **Table** button ▦ .... T
4. Drag the mouse pointer across the Table menu grid to select desired number of columns and rows.
5. Release the mouse button.

To use the Insert Table dialog box:
1. Position insertion point.
2. Click the **Insert** tab .... Alt + N

   Tables Group

3. Click the **Table** button ▦ .... T
4. Click **Insert Table** I
5. Click **Number of columns** box .... Alt + C
6. Type number of columns.
7. Click **Number of rows** box .... Alt + R
8. Type number of rows.
9. Click **OK** .... ↵Enter

To use the Quick Tables gallery:
1. Position insertion point.
2. Click the **Insert** tab .... Alt + N

   Tables Group

3. Click the **Table** button ▦ ...... T
4. Click **Quick Tables** .... T
5. Click desired table in gallery .... ↑/↓, ↵Enter

Show/Hide Nonprinting Table Elements
1. Click the **Home** tab .... Alt + H

   Paragraph Group

2. Click **Show/Hide ¶** button ¶ 8

   ✓ If Show/Hide is already on, clicking it turns it off.

To show/hide gridlines
1. Click anywhere within table.
2. Click **Layout** tab .... Alt + J , L

   Table Group

3. Click **View Gridlines** button ▦ .... T , G.

   ✓ If View Gridlines is already on, clicking it turns it off.

   ✓ Gridlines only display if there is no table border.

Move the Insertion Point in a Table

With the mouse:
- Click mouse pointer where you want to position insertion point.

With the keyboard:
- One cell left .... ◆Shift + Tab↹
- One cell right .... Tab↹
- One cell up .... ↑
- One cell down .... ↓
- First cell in column .... Alt + PgUp
- Last cell in column .... Alt + PgDn
- First cell in row .... Alt + Home
- Last cell in row .... Alt + End

Enter Data in a Table
1. Position insertion point in desired cell.
2. Type data.
3. Repeat until all data is entered.

Select Table Components

1. Position insertion point within table component to select.

   ✓ *For example, click in cell if selecting cell; click anywhere in row if selecting row, etc.*

2. Click **Layout** tab .... Alt+J, L

   Table Group

3. Click **Select** button ![icon] .... K
4. Click one of the following:
   - **Select Cell** button ![icon] L
   - **Select Column** button ![icon] C
   - **Select Row** button ![icon] .... R
   - **Select Table** button ![icon] .... T

To select a cell with the mouse:

1. Position mouse pointer in lower left corner of cell to display selection pointer ![icon].
2. Click.

To select a column with the mouse:

1. Position mouse pointer above column to display selection pointer ![icon].
2. Click.

To select a row with the mouse:

1. Position mouse pointer to left of row to display selection pointer ![icon].
2. Click.

To select adjacent components:

1. Select first component.
2. Press and hold **Shift** .... ↑Shift
3. Click in last component to select.

   ✓ *This method enables you to select adjacent columns, adjacent rows, or adjacent cells.*

To select nonadjacent components:

1. Select first component.
2. Press and hold **Ctrl** .... Ctrl
3. Select next component to select.
4. Repeat step 3 to select additional components.

   ✓ *This method enables you to select nonadjacent columns, rows, or cells.*

Insert Table Component

1. Position insertion point within table.

   ✓ *To insert more than one of the same component, select as many as you want to insert. For example, to insert two columns, select two columns.*

2. Click **Layout** tab .... Alt+J, L

   Rows & Columns Group

3. Click one of the following:
   - **Insert Above** button ![icon] to insert row above current row .... A
   - **Insert Below** button ![icon] to insert row below current row .... E
   - **Insert Left** button ![icon] to insert column to left of current column L
   - **Insert Right** button ![icon] to insert column to right of current column .... R

Delete Table Component

1. Position insertion point within table.

   ✓ *To delete more than one of the same component, select as many as you want to delete. For example, to delete two columns, select two columns.*

2. Click **Layout** tab .... Alt+J, L

   Rows & Columns Group

3. Click **Delete** button ![icon] .... D
4. Click one of the following:
   - **Delete Cells** button ![icon] .... D

     ✓ *Select option for shifting existing cells to fill in deleted cell area, then click OK.*

   - **Delete Columns** button ![icon] C
   - **Delete Rows** button ![icon] .... R
   - **Delete Table** button ![icon] .... T

Apply a Table Style

1. Position insertion point in table to format.
2. Click **Design** tab .... Alt+J, T

   Table Styles Group

3. Click style in Table Styles Gallery.

   ✓ *If necessary, use scroll arrows to scroll the gallery.*

   OR

   a. Click **More** button ![icon] .... S
   b. Click style to apply ..... ←/→/↑/↓, ↵Enter

Format Text in a Table

1. Select text or cell(s) to format.
2. Apply formatting as with regular document text.

EXERCISE DIRECTIONS

1. Start Word, if necessary.
2. Open the document ⊙40SCHEDULE and save it as 40SCHEDULE_xx.
3. Replace the text *Your Name* with your own name and *Today's Date* with the actual date.
4. Position the insertion point on the last blank line at the end of the document.
5. Insert a table with three columns and four rows.
6. Enter the following data:

Course Name	Location	Time
Word for Beginners	Conference Room A	8:30 – 11:45
Advanced Excel	Conference Room B	8:30 – 11:45
Introduction to the Internet	Media Lab	1:30 – 3:30

   ✓ To enter an en dash between the times, simply type a space, a hyphen, and a space. By default, AutoFormat automatically replaces the hyphen and spaces with an en dash after the second number is typed.

7. Select the last two rows in the table.
8. Insert two new rows above the selected rows.
9. Enter following data in the new rows:

Advanced Word	Conference Room A	8:30 – 11:45
Excel for Beginners	Conference Room B	1:30 – 3:30

10. Insert a new column to the left of the *Time* column.
11. Enter the following data in the new column:

    Days
    Tuesday, Thursday
    Monday, Wednesday
    Tuesday, Wednesday
    Monday, Thursday
    Friday

12. Delete the row for the *Word for Beginners* course.
13. Apply the Colorful Grid - Accent 1 table style to the table.

   ✓ The Colorful Grid - Accent 1 style may be on the last row in the gallery, or the next to last row. Rest the mouse pointer on a style to display its name in a ScreenTip.

14. Apply italics to the column headings. That is, to the text in the first row of each column.

   ✓ Select the text, then apply the formatting.

15. Check the spelling and grammar in the document.
16. Preview the document. It should look similar to the one in Illustration A.
17. Save the changes and print the document.
18. Close the document, saving all changes.

Illustration A

MEMO

To:	All Employees
From:	Student's Name
Date:	Today's Date
Subject:	Training Schedule

Here is the schedule of courses being offered next week. If you haven't signed up yet, please see me immediately.

Course Name	Location	Days	Time
Advanced Word	Conference Room A	Monday, Wednesday	8:30 – 11:45
Excel for Beginners	Conference Room B	Tuesday, Wednesday	1:30 – 3:30
Advanced Excel	Conference Room B	Monday, Thursday	8:30 – 11:45
Introduction to the Internet	Media Lab	Friday	1:30 – 3:30

ON YOUR OWN

1. Think of documents that would benefit from table formatting. Some examples include a weekly schedule, meeting agenda, travel itinerary, sales report, telephone/address list, and roster.
2. Create a new document in Word.
3. Save the file as **OWD40_xx**.
4. Use a table to set up the document as a telephone list. The list could include friends, family members, or members of a club or organization to which you belong.
5. Use at least three columns—one for the first name, one for the last name, and one for the telephone number. You may use more columns if you want to include mailing addresses, e-mail addresses, cell phone numbers, or other information.
6. Include at least eight names in the list.
7. Apply a Table style to the table. If you are not satisfied with the results, try a different style.
8. Check the spelling and grammar in the document, then print it.
9. Ask a classmate to review the document and offer comments or suggestions.
10. Incorporate the suggestions into the document.
11. Close the document, saving all changes.

Exercise | 41

Skills Covered

- **Set Alignments within Table Cells**
- **Set Cell Margins**
- **Align a Table on a Page**
- **Column Width and Row Height**

Software Skills   Use alignment options and tabs to make tables easy to read. Numbers are usually aligned flush right in a cell, while text can be flush left, centered, justified, or rotated to appear vertical. You can vertically align data with the top, center, or bottom of a cell as well. Decimal tabs are especially useful in tables for aligning dollar values. Other ways to improve the appearance of a table include aligning the table horizontally on the page and adjusting column width and row height.

Application Skills   Michigan Avenue Athletic Club is planning a major renovation. In preparation, it has surveyed members to find whether they want more tennis courts, more racquetball courts, more equipment rooms, or a lap pool. In this exercise, you will create a memo to the general manager that includes the results of the survey. You will use alignment options to set up the data in the table. You will also set row heights and column widths, and you will align the table horizontally on the page.

TERMS

No new vocabulary in this exercise.

NOTES

Set Alignments within Table Cells

- You can set horizontal and vertical alignment within a cell.
- There are nine possible alignments available in the Alignment group on the Table Tools Layout tab of the Ribbon:
  - Align Top Left
  - Align Top Center
  - Align Top Right
  - Align Center Left
  - Align Center
  - Align Center Right
  - Align Bottom Left
  - Align Bottom Center
  - Align Bottom Right

- In a table, numbers are usually right aligned, and text is either left aligned or centered.
- All tab stops can be used within a table cell, but the most useful is the decimal tab stop.
- Decimal tab stops automatically align numbers such as dollar values within a cell or a column.

Text aligned in a table

Align Top Left	Align Top Center	Align Top Right
Align Center Left	Align Center	Align Center Right
Align Bottom Left	Align Bottom Center	Align Bottom Right
		$2,500.00
		$25,000.32
		$325,000.23
		$325.02

Set Cell Margins

- By default, the top and bottom margins in a cell are set to 0" and the left and right margins are set to .08".
- You can use the Table Options dialog box to set margins within a cell.

Align Table on the Page

- You can left align, right align, or center a table on the page.
- The options for aligning a table on the page are found in the Table Properties dialog box, which you can open from the Table group on the Table Tools Layout tab of the Ribbon.

Table Properties dialog box

Column Width and Row Height

- By default, Word creates columns of equal column width, sized so the table extends from the left margin to the right margin.
- Rows are sized according to the line spacing on the line where the table is inserted.
- By default, row height automatically increases to accommodate lines of text typed in a cell.
- You can drag column dividers to increase or decrease column width.

  ✓ *Press and hold the Alt key as you drag to see the column width measurements displayed on the ruler.*

- In Print Layout view, you can drag row dividers to increase or decrease row height.
- You can set precise measurements for columns, rows, cells, and entire tables in the Cell Size group on the Table Tools Layout tab of the Ribbon, or in the Table Properties dialog box.
- You can select to automatically distribute the height of the rows equally among the total height of selected rows.
- You can also automatically distribute the width of the columns equally across the total width of selected columns.
- Finally, you can automatically adjust the column width and row height to fit the contents of each cell, or to fit the width of the current window.

PROCEDURES

Set Alignment in a Table Cell

1. Position insertion point in cell.
   OR
   Select cell(s).
2. Click **Layout** tab .... Alt+J, L

   Alignment Group

3. Click one of the following alignment options:
   - **Align Top Left** ⊟ .... T, L
   - **Align Top Center** ⊟ .... T, C
   - **Align Top Right** ⊟ .... T, R
   - **Align Center Left** ⊟ .... C, L
   - **Align Center** ⊟ .... C, C
   - **Align Center Right** ⊟ ...... C, R
   - **Align Bottom Left** ⊟ .... B, L
   - **Align Bottom Center** ⊟ .. B, C
   - **Align Bottom Right** ⊟ .... B, R

   ✓ *You can also use the horizontal alignment buttons in the Font group on the Home tab to align text horizontally in a cell. If you justify text in a cell, be sure you have at least three lines of text.*

Set Tabs in a Table Cell

1. Position insertion point in cell.
2. Click Tab selector until desired tab type displays.
3. Click horizontal ruler at location where you want to set tab stop.

   ✓ *For more information on tabs, refer to Exercise 13.*

To advance insertion point one tab stop within a cell:

- Press .... Ctrl + Tab

Set Margins in a Table Cell

1. Position insertion point in cell.
   OR
   Select cell(s).
2. Click **Layout** tab .... Alt + J, L

   Alignment Group

3. Click **Cell Margins** button .... N
4. Click **Top** text box .... Alt + T
5. Type top margin value.
6. Click **Left** text box .... Alt + L
7. Type left margin value.
8. Click **Bottom** text box .... Alt + B
9. Type bottom margin value.
10. Click **Right** text box ...... Alt + R
11. Type right margin value.
12. Click **OK** .... ↵Enter

Align Table Horizontally on Page

1. Position insertion point anywhere in table.
2. Click **Layout** tab .... Alt + J, L

   Table Group

3. Click **Properties** button .... O
4. Click **Table** tab, if necessary .... Alt + T
5. Click one of the following alignment options:
   - **Left** .... Alt + L
   - **Center** .... Alt + C
   - **Right** .... Alt + H
6. Click **OK** .... ↵Enter

Change Column Width

1. Position mouse pointer on column divider.

   ✓ *Pointer changes to a double-vertical line with arrows pointing left and right* ✛.

2. Click and drag divider left or right.

   ✓ *Press* Alt *at the same time that you drag the divider to see the width displayed on the horizontal ruler.*

   OR

1. Click in column to resize.
2. Click **Layout** tab .... Alt + J, L

   Cell Size Group

3. Click the **Table Column Width** box 3.08" .... W
4. Type column width.
5. Press ↵Enter .... ↵Enter

Change Row Height

1. Change to Print Layout view, if necessary.
2. Position mouse pointer on row divider.

   ✓ *Pointer changes to a double-horizontal line with arrows pointing up and down* ↕.

3. Click and drag divider up or down.

   ✓ *Press* Alt *at the same time that you drag the divider to see the height displayed on the vertical ruler.*

   OR

1. Click in row to resize.
2. Click **Layout** tab .... Alt + J, L

   Cell Size Group

3. Click the **Table Row Height** box 0.21" .... H
4. Type row height.
5. Press **Enter** .... ↵Enter

Distribute Rows Evenly

1. Select rows to resize.
2. Click **Layout** tab .... Alt + J, L

   Cell Size Group

3. Click the **Distribute Rows** button .... U, R

Distribute Columns Evenly

1. Select columns to resize.
2. Click **Layout** tab .... Alt + J, L

   Cell Size Group

3. Click the **Distribute Columns** button .... U, C

Automatically Adjust Row Height and Column Width

1. Position insertion point in table.
2. Click **Layout** tab .... Alt + J, L

   Cell Size Group

3. Click the **AutoFit** button .... F
4. Click one of the following:
   - **AutoFit Contents** C
   - **AutoFit Window** .... W
   - **Fixed Column Width** ...... N
   OR
1. Position mouse pointer on row divider.

   ✓ *Pointer changes to a double-horizontal line with arrows pointing up and down* ↕.

2. Double-click.
   OR
1. Position mouse pointer on column divider.

   ✓ *Pointer changes to a double-vertical line with arrows pointing left and right* ↕.

2. Double-click.

EXERCISE DIRECTIONS

1. Start Word, if necessary.
2. Create a new document.
3. Save the file as **41DATA_xx**.
4. Use the following steps to create the document shown in Illustration A.
5. Type the memo text, using 12-point Calibri, single line spacing, and no spacing before or after paragraphs.
6. Create a table with five columns and five rows and enter the data as shown.

    ✓ *You can enter the data before setting alignments in step 7, or after.*

7. Set alignment as follows:
    a. Column 1: align center.
    b. Columns 2, 3, and 4: align bottom right.
    c. Column 5: align bottom left.
    d. Row 1: align top center.
    e. Use a decimal tab to align the prices in the fifth column, approximately .5" from the right edge of the column.

    ✓ *Notice that the numbers align automatically as soon as you set the tab.*

8. Make the text in the first column and the first row 14 points and bold.
9. Set column widths as follows:
    - Column 1: 1.5"
    - Column 2: .75"
    - Column 3: .75"
    - Column 4: .75"
    - Column 5: 1.5"
10. Set all rows to be 0.5" high.
11. Center the entire table horizontally on the page.
12. Check the spelling and grammar.
13. Display the document in Print Preview. It should look similar to the one in Illustration A.

    ✓ *If necessary, adjust the column widths so your document looks like the illustration.*

14. Print the document.
15. Close the document, saving all changes.

Illustration A

MEMO

To: Ray Peterson
From: Student's Name
Date: Today's Date
Subject: Member Survey

Here are the results of the member survey. I have also included information about the potential costs associated with each item. We can use this data to help decide where we want to focus our efforts during the renovation.

	Want	**Do not Care**	**Do not Want**	**Potential Cost**
Tennis court	19	10	5	$50,000.00
Racquetball court	25	15	7	$50,000.00
Equipment room	45	22	2	$75,000.00
Lap pool	8	5	12	$115,000.00

ON YOUR OWN

1. Plan and conduct a survey in class. You might survey your classmates about a current issue such as school dress codes or how much they are willing to pay for lunch or you might just ask classmates to name their favorite color, favorite food, or favorite animal.

2. When you have completed the survey and have the results handy, create a new document in Word.

3. Save the file as OWD41_*xx*.

4. Type a title for the document.

5. Create a table in the document so you can enter the results of the survey. Use as many as columns and rows as necessary.

6. Apply a table style if you want, or manually format the text in the table.

7. Set column width and row height as necessary.

8. Align the data so it looks good and is easy to read. Remember, numbers are usually aligned right and text is usually aligned left.

9. Center the table on the page.

10. Type a brief summary or conclusion paragraph based on the data.

11. Check the spelling and grammar in the document.

12. Save the changes and print the document.

13. Ask a classmate to review the document and offer comments and suggestions.

14. Incorporate the suggestions in the document.

15. Close the document, saving all changes.

Exercise | 42

Skills Covered

- Draw a Table
- Move and Resize Tables
- Merge and Split Cells
- Rotate Text
- Wrap Text

Software Skills   Word's Draw Table tool gives you great flexibility to organize tables the way you want them, not necessarily in rigid columns and rows. You can layout the table cells exactly as you want them in order to organize text and data. You can then move and resize the table, if necessary, merge and split cells, and rotate the text to achieve the exact effect you need.

Application Skills   The Exercise Director at Michigan Avenue Athletic Club has asked you to design a flyer announcing a series of new classes. In this exercise, you will open and format a document describing the classes. You will then create a table listing the schedule of classes, and integrate it into the flyer.

TERMS

Header row   A row across the top of a table in which heading information is entered.

Merge   Combine multiple adjacent cells together to create one large cell.

Sizing handle   A nonprinting icon that displays outside the lower-right corner of a table that you use to resize the table.

Split   Divide one cell into multiple cells, either vertically to create columns or horizontally to create rows.

Table anchor   A nonprinting icon that displays outside the upper-left corner of a table, that you use to move or select a table.

NOTES

Draw a Table

- Word's Draw Table feature lets you create tables with uneven or irregular columns and rows.
- Access Draw Table from the Tables group on the Insert tab of the Ribbon, or in the Draw Borders group on the Table Tools Design tab.
- When you draw a table, the mouse pointer looks and functions like a pencil ✎.
- You drag the pointer to draw lines vertically or horizontally to create cell dividers.

- Word creates straight lines at 90 degree angles to existing cell dividers, even if you do not drag in a straight line.
- You can draw a diagonal line across a cell as a visual element or border, not to split the cell diagonally.
- New cells can be drawn anywhere. Rows and columns do not have to extend across the entire table.
- You can use the Draw Table command to create a new table, or to customize an existing table.
- You must use Print Layout view to draw a table.

Move and Resize Tables

- You can drag the **table anchor** to move the table anywhere on the page.
- You can drag the table's **sizing handle** to change the table size.
- The anchor and sizing handle only display when the mouse pointer is resting on the table, the insertion point is within the table.

Table anchor and sizing handle

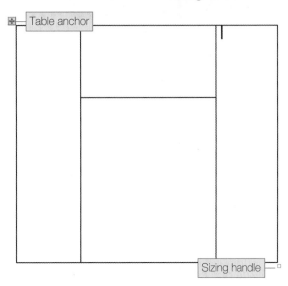

Merge and Split Cells

- You can **merge** horizontally adjacent cells or vertically adjacent cells using commands in the Merge group on the Table Tools Layout tab of the Ribbon.
- You can use the Eraser tool in the Draw Borders group on the Table Tools Design tab on the Ribbon to erase dividers between cells, thus merging the cells.
- If you erase a divider on the outer edge of the table, you simply erase the border line, not the divider itself.
- Merging is useful for creating a **header row** across a table.
- **Split** a cell to insert dividers to create additional columns or rows. You can split a cell using the Split Cells command in the Merge group on the Table Tools Layout tab of the Ribbon, or using the Draw Table tool in the Draw Borders group on the Table Tools Design tab.

Rotate Text

- Rotate text direction within a cell so text runs from left to right, from top to bottom, or from bottom to top.

Rotate text in a table

| Text direction is vertical bottom to top. | Text direction is the default left to right. | Text direction is vertical top to bottom. |

Wrap Text

- By default, tables are inserted on a blank line above or below existing text.
- You can set Word to wrap text around the table.
- Wrapping text around a table integrates the table object into the text so text appears above, below, and on either side of the table.

PROCEDURES

Draw a New Table

1. Position insertion point.
2. Click the **Insert** tab .... Alt + N

   Tables Group
3. Click the **Table** button ⊞ ...... T
4. Click **Draw Table** .... D

   ✓ *The mouse pointer changes to resemble a pencil ✎.*
5. Click where you want to position upper-left corner of the table.
6. Drag diagonally down and to the right.
7. Release mouse button where you want to position lower-right corner of the table.

   ✓ *This draws one cell.*
8. Click and drag mouse pointer to draw horizontal dividers and vertical dividers.

   ✓ *As you drag, Word displays a dotted line where the divider will be. Once you drag far enough, Word completes the line when you release the mouse button.*
9. Press **Esc** to turn off Draw Table .... Esc

   OR

   Click **Draw Table** button ✎ in Draw Borders group on Table Tools Design tab on the Ribbon.

Use Draw Table to Modify an Existing Table

1. Position insertion point within table.
2. Click **Design** tab .... Alt + J, T

   Draw Borders Group
3. Click the **Draw Table** button ✎ .... D

   ✓ *The mouse pointer changes to resemble a pencil ✎.*
4. Click and drag to draw horizontal or vertical dividers.

5. Press **Esc** to turn off Draw Table .... Esc

   OR

   Click **Draw Table** button ✎.

Move a Table

1. Rest mouse pointer on table so anchor displays.
2. Click and drag table anchor to new location.

   ✓ *A dotted outline moves with the mouse pointer to show new location.*
3. Release mouse button to drop table in new location.

Resize a Table

1. Rest mouse pointer on table so sizing handle displays.
2. Click and drag sizing handle to increase or decrease table size.

   ✓ *A dotted outline moves with the mouse pointer to show new size.*
3. Release mouse button to resize table.

Merge Cells

1. Select cells to merge.
2. Click **Layout** tab .... Alt + J, L

   Merge Group
3. Click **Merge Cells** button ▦ .... M

Merge Cells Using the Eraser

1. Position insertion point within table
2. Click **Design** tab .... Alt + J, T

   Draw Borders Group
3. Click the **Eraser** button ✎ .... E

   ✓ *The mouse pointer changes to resemble an eraser ✎.*
4. Click divider to erase.

5. Repeat step 4 to erase additional dividers.
6. Press **Esc** to turn off Eraser .... Esc

   OR

   Click **Eraser** button ✎.

Split a Cell

1. Select cell to split.
2. Click **Layout** tab .... Alt + J, L

   Merge Group
3. Click **Split Cells** button ▦ ...... P
4. Click **Number of columns** to create box .... Alt + C
5. Type number of columns.
6. Click **Number of rows** to create box .... Alt + R
7. Type number of rows.
8. Click **OK** .... ↵Enter

Rotate Text

1. Click in cell to format.

   OR

   Select components to format.
2. Click **Layout** tab .... Alt + J, L

   Alignment Group
3. Click **Text Direction** button ▦ .... G
4. Click button repeatedly to toggle through the three available directions.

Wrap Text Around a Table

1. Position insertion point anywhere in table
2. Click **Layout** tab .... Alt + J, L

   Table Group
3. Click **Properties** button ▦ ...... O
4. Click **Table** tab, if necessary .... Alt + T
5. Click **Around** .... Alt + A
6. Click **OK** .... ↵Enter

EXERCISE DIRECTIONS

Draw the Table

1. Start Word, if necessary.
2. Open ◉**42WORKOUT**.
3. Save the file as **42WORKOUT_xx**.
4. Starting on the first line of the document, use the Draw Table tool to draw a cell approximately 4" wide and 4" high.

   ✓ *Use the rulers as guides to measure the height and width of cells as you draw, but don't worry if the table components are not sized exactly.*

5. Create three columns by drawing vertical lines through the cell. Try to size the columns as follows (it is okay if the sizes are not exact):
   - Column 1: 1" wide
   - Columns 2 and 3: 1.5" wide
6. Leave the first column intact, and create five rows across the second and third columns as follows (again, it is okay of the sizes are not exact):
   - Row 1: .5" high
   - Rows 2, 3, and 4: 1" high
   - Row 5: .5" high
7. Merge the cells in the top row of the right two columns, and then merge the corresponding cells in the bottom row. (Refer to Illustration A to see the desired result.)
8. Leaving the top and bottom rows intact, use the Split Cells tool to create two rows within each of the cells in the third column. (Refer to Illustration A to see the desired result.)

Enter and Format Text

1. Enter the text in the table as shown in Illustration A, using the following formatting and alignments to achieve the desired result:
   a. Column 1 (program name): 28-pt. serif, rotated so it runs from top to bottom centered horizontally and vertically.
   b. Row 1 (table title): 28-pt. serif, bold, centered horizontally and vertically.
   c. Dates: 16-pt. serif, aligned left, and centered vertically.
   d. Exercise types: 16-pt. serif, aligned left, and aligned with the cell bottom vertically.
   e. Bottom row: 10-pt. serif, centered horizontally and vertically.

   ✓ *Adjust the column widths as necessary.*

2. Format the text that is not in the table in a 14-point sans serif font. (Comic Sans MS is used in the illustration.)
3. Apply bold to the title.
4. Center the first three paragraphs of text.
5. Underline the first 4 words of the fourth paragraph.
6. Leave 30 points of space after the third paragraph, and 6 points of space after all other paragraphs in the document.
7. Set text to wrap around the table.
8. Position the table about 3" from the top of the page and about 1" from the right side of the page.
9. Resize the table to decrease its height to about 3.5".
10. Check the spelling and grammar in the document.
11. Display the document in Print Preview. It should look similar to the one in the illustration.
12. Print the document.
13. Close the document, saving all changes.

Curriculum Connection: Social Studies

Political Vocabulary

What's the difference between a dark horse and a lame duck? Sometimes it seems as if the American political system is based on words in a foreign language. If you are going to participate in the system, it is important to understand the language.

Glossary of Political Terms

Set up a table as a glossary of political terms. Use the Internet and other resources to locate the terms. The table only needs two columns—one for the term and one for the definition—but you can add as many rows as you need for all of the terms you define. Arrange the terms in alphabetical order.

Illustration A

Work Out with David
A series of introductory exercise classes with
Personal Trainer David Fairmont

Work Out with David is a series of three classes designed to introduce members to some of the exercise opportunities here at Michigan Avenue Athletic Club.

Each hour-long session focuses on two complementary types of exercise. The first 15 minutes will be spent learning about the exercises, including the equipment that may be involved. The rest of the class includes

Work Out with David	Schedule	
	January 8	Step Aerobics
		Pilates
	January 15	Spinning
		Yoga
	January 22	Kickboxing
		Free Weights
	Space is limited. Please sign up as soon as possible	

a warm up, active participation and a cool down.

David Fairmont is our newest personal trainer. He holds a master's degree in health management from the University of Vermont in Burlington, Vermont, and he is certified in cardiovascular exercise and strength training.

Work Out with David is geared toward those with limited exercise class experience, but all members are welcome to join. There is no fee for participation, but class size is limited. Please see Katie at the front desk to enroll.

ON YOUR OWN

1. Create a new document in Word.
2. Save the file as **OWD42_*xx*.**
3. Type a personal business letter to an employer or to your parents explaining why you need a raise. Write at least two paragraphs about why you deserve the raise and what you plan to do with the additional funds. Include information about how you spend the money you receive now.
4. To illustrate your point, draw a table in the letter and list items that you have purchased in the past two weeks. For example, include CDs, books, meals, movie tickets, and other expenses. The table should have at least three columns—for the date, the item, and the cost. List at least four items.
5. Merge a row across the top of the table and type in a title.
6. Try rotating text in some of the cells.
7. Use different alignments in the table cells.
8. Set the text in the letter to wrap around the table.
9. Try moving and resizing the table to improve the appearance of the letter.
10. When you are satisfied with the appearance of the table and the letter, check the spelling and grammar and print the document.
11. Ask a classmate to review the document and offer comments and suggestions.
12. Incorporate the suggestions into the document.
13. Close the document, saving all changes.

Skills Covered

- **Calculations in a Table**
- **Number Formats**
- **Sort Rows**
- **Cell Borders and Shading**

Software Skills Perform basic calculations in tables to total values in a column or row. If the values change, you can update the result without redoing the math. At the same time, you can format the calculation results with one of Word's built-in number formats. Sorting rows helps you keep your tables in order, while cell borders and shading let you dress up your tables to make them look good as well as to highlight important information.

Application Skills A Whole Grains Bread franchise is offering a special gift basket for Earth Day. In this exercise, you will create a document to advertise the gift basket. You will use a table to organize the information and to calculate costs. You will format the table using cell borders and shading.

TERMS

Field A placeholder used to insert information that changes, such as the date, the time, a page number, or the results of a calculation.

Formula A mathematical equation.

Function A built-in **formula** for performing calculations, such as addition, in a table.

Line style The appearance of a line.

Line weight The thickness of a line.

Shading A color or pattern used to fill the background of a cell.

Spreadsheet A document created with an application, such as Microsoft Office Excel 2007, used for setting up mathematical calculations.

NOTES

Calculations in a Table

- Use Word's Formula command to access basic **spreadsheet functions** so you can perform calculations on data entered in tables.

- The Formula command is in the Data group on the Table Tools Layout tab.

- By default, Word assumes you want to add the values entered in the column above the current cell or in the row beside the current cell.

- Word enters the calculation result in a **field**, so it can be updated if the values in the table change.

- You must update the total each time one of the values used in the formula is changed. The total does not update automatically.

- For anything other than basic calculations, use an Excel worksheet, not a Word table.

The Formula dialog box

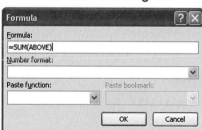

Number Formats

- When you set up a calculation in a table, you can select a number format in the Formula dialog box to apply to the calculation result.
- Number formats include dollar signs, commas, percent signs, and decimal points.

Sort Rows

- Sort rows in a table using the Sort dialog box, the same way you sort lists or paragraphs.

  ✓ *See Exercise 28.*

- For tables, the Sort command is available in the Data group on the Table Tools Layout tab of the Ribbon.
- Rows can be sorted according to the data in any column.
- For example, in a table of names and addresses, rows can be sorted alphabetically by name or by city, or numerically by Postal Code.
- Word rearranges the rows in the table but does not rearrange the columns.
- You can even sort by up to three columns. For example, you can sort alphabetically by name and then numerically by Postal Code.
- By default, Word identifies the type of data in the selected column as either Text, Number, or Date.
- The default sort order is ascending, but you can select descending if you want.
- You can specify whether or not the table includes a header row that you do not want to include in the sort.
- You cannot sort rows containing merged cells.

Cell Borders and Shading

- By default, Word applies a 1/2-pt. black solid line border around all table cells.
- You can select to display or hide border lines along one or more sides of a cell.
- You can also modify the **line style**, **line weight**, and color of borders.
- When you select a line style, weight, or color, the Draw Table tool becomes active so you can draw new cells or dividers using the selected options.
- Alternatively, you can format existing cells, by selecting the border options, and then selecting the borders you want to format.
- You can apply background color or **shading** to a cell.
- Selected border and shading formatting remain in effect until new formatting is selected.
- Table style formatting takes precedence over direct border and shading formatting. Apply Table styles first, then modify the styles if necessary using the direct formatting.

  ✓ *When table borders are removed, you can see table cells on-screen by displaying gridlines. Refer to Exercise 40 for information on showing and hiding gridlines.*

- Line style, line weight, and line color options are available in the Draw Borders group of the Table Tools Design tab on the Ribbon.
- Borders and Shading options are available in the Table Styles group on the Design tab.

PROCEDURES

Total Values in a Column or Row

1. Click in cell where you want the total to display.
2. Click **Layout** tab .... Alt +J, L

   Data Group

3. Click **Formula** button 𝑓ₓ ... U, L

   ✓ *By default, Word enters the formula for totaling the values in the cells in the column above or the row to the left.*

4. Click **Number format** drop-down arrow .... Alt +N
5. Click desired format .... ↓/↑, ↵Enter
6. Click **OK** .... ↵Enter

Update the Total

1. Select the field in the cell where the total is displayed.
2. Press **F9** F9

   OR

1. Right-click selection.
2. Click **Update Field** .... U

Sort Rows

1. Select the column by which you want to sort.
2. Click **Layout** tab .... Alt +J, L

   Data Group

3. Click **Sort** button ⟱ .... S, O

   ✓ *Word displays the Sort dialog box with the options for sorting by the current column in ascending order selected.*

4. Click one of the following, if necessary:
   - **A**scending .... Alt+A
   - **D**escending .... Alt+D
5. Click one of the following option buttons:
   - Header **r**ow .... Alt+R
   - No header ro**w** .... Alt+W

   ✓ *If you select Header row, Word does not include the first row in the sort.*

6. Click **OK** .... ↵Enter

Sort by Multiple Columns

1. Select the column by which you want to sort.
2. Click **Layout** tab .... Alt+J, L

   Data Group

3. Click **Sort** button ▲↓ .... S, O

   ✓ *Word displays the Sort dialog box with the options for sorting by the current column in ascending order selected.*

4. Click one of the following, if necessary:
   - **A**scending .... Alt+A
   - **D**escending .... Alt+D
5. Click **Then by** drop-down arrow .... Alt+T
6. Click second column to sort by .... ↓/↑, ↵Enter
7. Click one of the following, if necessary:
   - As**c**ending .... Alt+C
   - Desce**n**ding .... Alt+N
8. Click **Then by** drop-down arrow .... Alt+B
9. Click third column to sort by .... ↓/↑, ↵Enter
10. Click one of the following, if necessary:
    - Ascend**i**ng .... Alt+I
    - Descendin**g** .... Alt+G
11. Click one of the following option buttons:
    - Header **r**ow .... Alt+R
    - No header ro**w** .... Alt+W

   ✓ *If you select Header row, Word does not include the first row in the sort.*

12. Click **OK** .... ↵Enter

Select Line Style

1. Click anywhere within table.
2. Click **Design** tab .... Alt+J, T

   Draw Borders Group

3. Click **Line Style** button
   [─────── ▼] L
4. Click line style to apply .... ↓/↑, ↵Enter

   ✓ *Click No Border to remove border lines.*

5. Draw new cell.

   OR

   Click existing border to modify formatting.

   OR

   Apply borders to existing cells.

Select Line Weight

1. Click anywhere within table.
2. Click **Design** tab .... Alt+J, T

   Draw Borders Group

3. Click **Line Weight** button
   [½ pt ─── ▼] .... W
4. Click line weight to apply .... ↓/↑, ↵Enter
5. Draw new cell.

   OR

   Click existing border to modify formatting.

   OR

   Apply borders to existing cells.

Select Line Color

1. Click anywhere within table.
2. Click **Design** tab .... Alt+J, T

   Draw Borders Group

3. Click **Pen Color** button 🖊 C
4. Click color to apply .... ↓/↑,/←/→, ↵Enter

5. Draw new cell.

   OR

   Apply borders to existing cells as described in next procedure.

Apply Cell Borders

1. Select cell(s) to format.
2. Select line style, line weight, and line color, as desired.
3. Click **Design** tab .... Alt+J, T

   Table Styles Group

4. Click **Borders** button ▦ .... B
5. Click border style to apply:
   - **Bottom Border** .... B
   - **Top Border** .... P
   - **Left Border** L
   - **Right Border** .... R
   - **No Border** .... N
   - **All Borders** .... A
   - **Out**s**ide Borders** .... S
   - **Inside Borders** I
   - **Inside Horizontal Border** .... H
   - **Inside Vertical Border** V
   - **Diagonal Down Border** .... W
   - **Diagonal Up Border** .... U

   ✓ *Border styles are toggles—click on to display border; click off to hide border.*

Select Cell Shading

1. Select cell(s) to format.
2. Click **Design** tab .... Alt+J, T

   Table Styles Group

3. Click **Shading** button 🎨 .... H
4. Click color to apply .... ↓/↑,/←/→, ↵Enter

   OR

   Click **No Color** to remove shading .... N

EXERCISE DIRECTIONS

Create a Table

1. Start Word, if necessary.
2. Open 43BASKET.
3. Save the file as **43BASKET_xx**.
4. Move the insertion point to the last blank line at the end of the document.
5. Use either the Draw Table tool or the Insert Table command to create a table with two columns and five rows.
6. Enter the data shown in Illustration A.
7. Align all dollar values in Column 2 with a decimal tab set at approximately 4" on the Horizontal ruler.
8. Preview the document. It should look similar to the one in Illustration A.

Perform Calculations in a Table

1. Sort all rows except the header row into descending order based on the values in the Column 2.

   ✓ *Remember not to sort the header row.*

2. Insert a new row at the end of the table.
3. In the first cell in the new row, type **Total**.
4. In the last cell of the new row, insert a formula to calculate the total cost, apply the currency number format with two decimal places.
5. Insert a row above the total.
6. In Column 1, type **1 bottle all natural white grape juice**.
7. In Column 2 type **$6.59**.
8. Update the calculation result.

Format a Table

1. Apply the Table Grid 8 Table style to the table.

   ✓ *The style should be in the middle of the fourth row in the Table Styles gallery.*

2. Apply a dark blue, 1 1/2 pt. double-line border around all of the cells in the bottom row.

   ✓ *If you have trouble seeing the change on-screen, try zooming in to a higher magnification.*

3. Remove the printing border lines between columns in the bottom row.

   ✓ *Do not merge the cells.*

4. Apply a 15% gray shading to all of the cells in the bottom row.

   ✓ *Gray shades display in the left column of the Shading color palette. Use ScreenTips to display the shading %.*

5. Resize the table so it is approximately 4" wide by 3 1/2" high.
6. Set Column 1 to be approximately 2.5" wide and Column 2 to be approximately 1.5" wide.
7. Align the text in the top and bottom rows with the bottom left.
8. Center the text in rows 2, 3, 4, 5, and 6 horizontally and vertically.
9. Center the table horizontally on the page.
10. Check the spelling and grammar.
11. Preview the document. It should look similar to the one in Illustration B.
12. Print the document.
13. Close the document, saving all changes.

Curriculum Connection: Language Arts

Prefixes

A prefix is a letter or syllable that you add to the beginning of a word to change the word's meaning. Most prefixes used to be words on their own in Greek or Latin, and they have their own meaning. For example, the prefix *pre* means before, and the prefix *sub* means under. If you understand the meaning of a prefix, you can usually figure out the meaning of a word that has that prefix.

Using Common Prefixes

Create a three-column table listing common prefixes in the first column, the meaning of the prefix in the second column and at least one example of a word that uses the prefix in the third column. Add as many different prefixes as you can to the table.

Illustration A

Whole Grains Bread
Earth Day Gift Basket
Specially Priced at $49.99

Celebrate Earth Day by sending someone you love a beautiful gift basket filled with all natural treats. The basket includes all of the items listed below, as well as an Earth Day surprise. The basket is beautifully arranged and wrapped using recycled materials. Local delivery is included in the special price.

Basket includes:	Regularly priced:
1 tin granola	$10.99
5 organic pears	$5.99
1 dozen specialty muffins	$15.99
2 8-ounce all natural fruit preserves	$12.99

Illustration B

Whole Grains Bread
Earth Day Gift Basket
Specially Priced at $49.99

Celebrate Earth Day by sending someone you love a beautiful gift basket filled with all natural treats. The basket includes all of the items listed below, as well as an Earth Day surprise. The basket is beautifully arranged and wrapped using recycled materials. Local delivery is included in the special price.

Basket includes:	Regularly priced:
1 dozen specialty muffins	$15.99
2 8-ounce all natural fruit preserves	$12.99
1 tin granola	$10.99
5 organic pears	$5.99
1 bottle all natural white grape juice	$6.59
Total	$ 52.55

ON YOUR OWN

1. Open the document **OWD42_xx**, the letter asking for a raise that you wrote in the On Your Own section of Exercise 42, or open ⊙**43RAISE**.

2. Save the file as **OWD43_xx**.

3. Sort the rows in the table into descending numerical order, according to the amount of the expenses.

   ✓ *You cannot sort rows that contain merged cells. If you have a merged header row, select all rows but the header row, and then sort the rows.*

4. Add a row to the bottom of the table.

5. In column 2, label the row **Total**.

6. Calculate the total amount of expenses in the table. Make sure the result displays in dollar format.

7. Change one or more of the values in the table.

8. Update the calculation.

9. Format the table using cell borders and shading. For example, use borders and shading to highlight the cell in which the total is displayed. You may want to start with a Table style and then modify the style formatting.

10. Check the spelling and grammar, then print the document.

11. Ask a classmate to review the document and offer comments and suggestions.

12. Incorporate the suggestions into the document.

13. Close the document, saving all changes.

Exercise | 44

Critical Thinking

Application Skills Voyager Travel Adventures has been collecting demographic information about clients who participate in adventure travel vacations. In this exercise, you will create a memo to the vice president of marketing listing some of the interesting demographics in table form

EXERCISE DIRECTIONS

Table 1

1. Start Word, if necessary.
2. Open ⊙ 44DEMO.
3. Save the document as 44DEMO_xx.
4. In the memo heading, replace the sample text *Your Name* and *Today's Date* with the appropriate information.
5. Between the first two paragraphs of the memo, insert a table with three columns and eight rows.
6. Set all columns to be 1" wide and all rows to be .25" high.
7. Enter the following data:

Age	0 – 18	3%
	19 – 25	17%
	26 – 35	20%
	36 – 45	30%
	46 – 55	20%
	55 +	10%
Gender	Male	54%
	Female	46%

8. Align the data in Columns 1 and 2 with the top left.
9. Align the data in Column 3 with the top right.
10. Insert a new row at the top of the table.
11. Merge the cells in the new row.
12. In the new row, type the table title: **CLIENT DEMOGRAPHICS**.
13. Center the table title horizontally.
14. Insert another blank row above the row labeled **Gender**.
15. Apply the Light Shading table style to the table.
16. Apply a single line black 3/4-pt. outside border to the entire table.
17. Save the changes to the document.

Table 2

1. Between the second and third paragraphs of the memo, insert a table with two columns and five rows.
2. Enter the following data:

River Rafting	77
Backpacking	25
Kayaking	84
Biking	43
Skiing	21

3. Align the data in Column 1 with the bottom left and Column 2 with the bottom right.
4. Sort the rows in ascending alphabetical order by the data in column 1.
5. Delete the label and data for *Skiing*, leaving a blank row at the bottom of the table.
6. In the blank cell at the bottom of column 1, type **Total** and right align it.
7. In the blank cell at the bottom of column 2, insert a formula to calculate the total number of respondents.
8. Insert a new column at the left side of the table.
9. Set the new column to be 1" wide, column 2 to be 1.5" wide and column 3 to be .5" wide.
10. Set all rows to be .25" high.
11. Merge the cells in the first column.
12. Using 14-pt. bold, type **Favorite Activity per Respondent** in column 1.

13. Rotate the text in column 1 so it reads from the bottom of the table to the top, and center the text horizontally and vertically.

14. Apply a 1-pt. Blue border around the inside and outside of all cells in the table.

15. Apply a 5% gray shading to column 1.

16. Apply a 15% gray shading to rows 1, 3, and 5.

17. Center the table on the page.

18. Change the number of respondents who prefer kayaking to **95**.

19. Update the result of the calculation.

20. Check the spelling and grammar in the document.

21. Display the document in Print Preview. It should look similar to the illustration.

22. Print the document.

23. Close the document, saving all changes.

Illustration A

MEMO

To:	Dan Euell, V.P. Marketing
From:	Student's Name
Date:	Today's Date
Subject:	Client Demographics

I thought you might like a preview of the client demographic data we have been collecting. I find the age breakdowns quite interesting. Based on what we know of spending patterns, we might want to consider targeting some tours to families with teenagers.

CLIENT DEMOGRAPHICS		
Age	0 – 18	**3%**
	19 – 25	**17%**
	26 – 35	**20%**
	36 – 45	**30%**
	46 – 55	**20%**
	55 +	**10%**
Gender	Male	**54%**
	Female	**46%**

Also of note: based on the data you see in the table below, our clients would most like to experience tours that involve water.

Favorite Activity per Respondent	Backpacking	25
	Biking	43
	Kayaking	95
	River Rafting	77
	Total	240

We should have the complete report by the end of next week. We'll meet then to go over the results.

Exercise | 45

Curriculum Integration

Application Skills   As you have learned in Lesson 6, a table is ideal for presenting information such as survey or lab results in columns in rows. For your social studies class, prepare questions for a survey about your classmates. The survey might concern a topic such as where students were born, whether they have always lived in your town, how many siblings they have, whether they have pets, or any topic you and your instructor agree on. You might work alone or in a team. Once you have the questions ready, ask at least ten students to respond. You can then record the results in a table in a Word document, including at least one formula. Also include a title and a paragraph or two explaining the survey and the results. Format the table using a table style or direct border and shading formatting. Refer to Illustration A to see a sample.

EXERCISE DIRECTIONS

Prepare and conduct your survey.

Start Word, if necessary, and create a new document. Save it as **45SURVEY_xx**.

Select to display elements that might help you while you work, such as the rulers, nonprinting characters, and text boundaries, and make sure all the features you want to use are enabled, such as AutoCorrect and AutoFormat as You Type.

Type and format a title, and an introductory paragraph.

Create the table, using the appropriate number of columns and rows, and enter the table data.

Adjust the structure of the table as necessary. For example, you may need to add or delete columns, rows, or cells, or resize components.

Format the table using alignments, styles, borders, and shading. Select a theme, theme colors, and theme fonts, and apply a page background.

Type a closing paragraph, and then integrate the table with the plain text. For example, you might want to wrap the text around the table, and position the table on the page.

Check the spelling and grammar on the page, and use a thesaurus to replace common or boring words.

Ask a classmate to review the document and make suggestions for how you might improve it.

Incorporate your classmate's suggestions into the document.

Print the document.

Close the file, saving all changes.

Social Studies
Student's Name
Today's Date

Birthplace Survey

I chose to survey classmates about where they were born. I thought this would be interesting because it would show how many people were born nearby, and how many were born far away. From this information we might learn whether families are moving to our town from other places. The table below illustrates the survey results.

Birthplace Survey Results	
Born in this state	16
Born in a different state	5
Born in a different country	3
Not sure	1
Total	**25**

I included 25 students in my survey. The question I asked was "In what state were you born?" As you can see in the table above, the majority of students were born in this state. I think the survey accurately reflects the birthplace locations of the respondents. However, it could be incorrect if students lied, or answered incorrectly. I think a good follow-up survey might be to ask those who were born somewhere else where they were born.

Lesson | 7

Creating Documents with Merge

Exercise | 46

Skills Covered

- **Mail Merge Basics**
- **Use Mail Merge**
- **Create a New Address List**
- **Use Merge Fields**

Software Skills Use Mail Merge to customize mass mailings. For example, with Mail Merge you can store a document with standard text, such as a form letter, and then insert personalized names and addresses on each copy that you generate or print. You can also use Mail Merge to generate envelopes, labels, e-mail messages, and directories, such as a telephone list.

Application Skills A letter inviting Michigan Avenue Athletic Club members to join a volleyball team becomes a simple task using the Mail Merge feature. The form letter will be personalized with each person's name and address. In this exercise, you will create the letter document and the data source address list, and you will merge them to generate the letters.

TERMS

Address list A simple data source file stored in Access file format, which includes the information needed for an address list, such as first name, last name, street, city, state, and so on.

Data source The document containing the variable data that will be inserted during the merge.

Field One item of variable data, such as a first name, a last name, or a ZIP Code.

Mail Merge A process that inserts variable information into a standardized document to produce a personalized or customized document.

Main document The document containing the standardized text that will be printed on all documents.

Merge block A set of merge fields stored as one unit. For example, the Address block contains all of the name and address information.

Merge document The customized document resulting from a merge.

Merge field A placeholder in the main document that marks where and what will be inserted from the data source document.

Microsoft Office Access database A file created with the Access program, used for storing information.

Outlook contact list The names, addresses, and other information stored as contacts for use in the Microsoft Office Outlook personal information manager program.

Record A collection of variable data about one person or thing. In a form letter merge, for example, each record contains variable data for each person receiving the letter: first name, last name, address, city, state, and ZIP Code.

NOTES

Mail Merge Basics

■ **Use Mail Merge** to create mass mailings, envelopes, e-mail messages, or labels.

■ To ccreate a mail merge, you must have two files:

● A **main document**, which contains information that won't change, as well as **merge fields** and **merge blocks**, which act as placeholders for variable information. For example, you might have a form letter that has merge fields where the address and greeting should be.

A main document

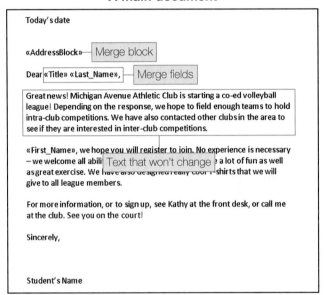

● A **data source** file, which contains variable information such as names and addresses. Word lets you use many types of data source files for a merge, including an **address list**, an **Outlook contact list**, or a **Microsoft Office Access database**.

■ During the merge, Word generates a series of **merge documents** in which the variable information from the data source replaces the merge fields entered in the main document.

■ You can print the merge documents or save them in a file for future use.

■ You can use the Mail Merge task pane or the commands on the Mailings tab of the Ribbon to access Mail Merge features.

A merge document

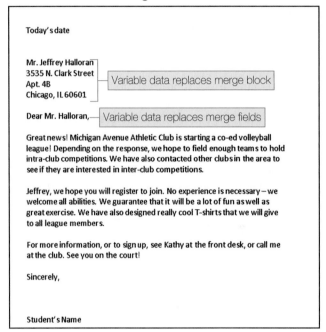

Use Mail Merge

■ There are six steps involved in completing a merge:

● The first step is to select the type of main document you want to create:

Letters	used for letters or other regular Word documents such as reports, flyers, or memos.
E-mail messages	used to create messages to send via e-mail.
Envelopes	used to create personalized envelopes.
Labels	used to create personalized labels.
Directory	used for lists such as rosters, catalogs or telephone lists.

● The second step is to select a starting document. You may select to start from the current document, an existing document, or a new document based on a template.

● The third step is to select recipients. In this step, you locate or create the data source file, and then select the individual recipients to include in the merge.

- If you select to create a new list, Word prompts you through the steps for creating the data source file by entering the variable data for each recipient.
- The fourth step is to create the main document. In this step, you type and format the data you want included in each merge document, and you insert the merge fields or merge blocks where Word will insert the variable data.

    ✓ *If the text is already typed in the document, you simply insert the merge fields and merge blocks in step 4.*

- The fifth step is to preview the merge documents. In this step, you have the opportunity to see the merge documents before you print them. This lets you check for spelling, punctuation, and grammatical errors and make corrections.
- The final step is to complete the merge. You have the option of printing the merge documents, or saving them in a new file for later use.
- You may use the commands on the Mailings tab of the Ribbon to conduct a merge.
- Alternatively, the Mail Merge Wizard prompts you through the step-by-step process of conducting a merge.
- You may also use a combination of the two methods.

Create a New Address List

- An address list is a simple data source file used to store all of the variable information required to complete a mail merge.
- The data is stored in a table format, with each column containing one **field** of information and each row containing the **record** for one recipient.

Address list of recipients

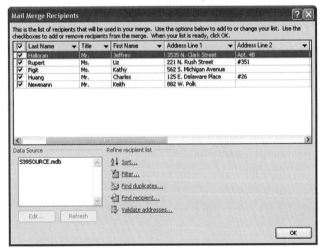

- You enter the data in a table that has already been set up to include the necessary fields.
- You save the file the same way you save any Office file—by giving it a name and selecting a storage location.
- By default, Word stores the file in the My Data Sources folder, which is a subfolder of My Documents. You can store the file in any location you choose.

    ✓ *If you are using Windows Vista, Word stores the file in Data Sources in Documents.*

- If a field in the data source is blank, the information is left out of the merge document for that record.

Use Merge Fields

- Word has a preset list of merge fields that correspond to variable information typically used in a mail merge, such as First Name, Last Name, and ZIP Code.
- It also creates merge blocks for certain common sets of fields, such as a complete Address, so that you can insert one merge block instead of inserting numerous merge fields.
- You insert the merge fields or blocks in the main document at the location where you want the corresponding variable data to print.
- You must type all spaces and punctuation between merge fields. Merge blocks, however, include standard punctuation and spacing, such as a comma between the city and state in an address.
- By default, when you insert a merge field, you see the field name enclosed in merge field characters (<< >>). The field may be shaded, depending on your system's field code option settings.

    ✓ *To locate the field code option settings click the Office Button, click Word Options, and then click Advanced. The field code options are under Show document content.*

- You may insert merge fields more than once in a document. For example, you can insert a name merge field in multiple locations in order to personalize a letter.

PROCEDURES

Create a Form Letter Merge Using a New Address List Data Source File using Commands on the Ribbon

To select the document type and create an address list:

1. Open a new blank document.

   OR

   Open an existing letter document.

2. Click the **Mailings** tab .... Alt + M

   Start Mail Merge Group

3. Click the **Start Mail Merge** button .... S

4. Click **Letters** L

5. Click the **Select Recipients** button .... Alt + M, R

6. Click **Type New List** .... N

   ✓ The Address list table displays.

7. In the **Title** field, type the title of the first recipient.

8. Press **Tab** to move to the next field .... Tab⇥

   ✓ Press Shift+Tab to move to previous field.

9. Type the recipient's first name.

10. Press **Tab** .... Tab⇥

11. Continue typing variable data until record is complete.

    ✓ You may leave blank any fields for which information is not available or necessary.

12. Click **New Entry** .... Alt + N

    ✓ Word adds a new, blank row to the list.

13. Repeat steps 7–12 until you have entered the information for all recipients.

    ✓ You can go back to edit data in any record. Simply click in the field you want to change.

14. Click **OK** .... ↵Enter

    ✓ Word displays the Save Address List dialog box.

15. Type file name.

16. If necessary, select storage location.

17. Click **Save** .... Alt + S

18. Continue with steps for setting up the form letter.

To set up the form letter:

1. Select a document type and create a new data source as described in previous steps, if you have not already done so.

2. In the main document, begin typing the letter, including all text and formatting as you want it to appear on each merge document. For example, type the date and move the insertion point down four lines.

3. Position the insertion point at the location where you want to insert a field.

4. Click the **Mailings** tab ..... Alt + M

   Write & Insert Fields Group

5. Do one of the following:

   a. Click the **Address block** button .... A

   ✓ Word displays the Insert Address Block dialog box.

   b. Select desired options for formatting address.

   c. Click **OK** .... ↵Enter

   OR

   a. Click the **Greeting Line** button .... G

   ✓ Word displays the Insert Greeting Line dialog box.

   b. Select desired options for formatting greeting line.

   c. Click **OK** .... ↵Enter

   OR

   a. Click **Insert Merge Field** button I

   b. Click field to insert .... ↓/↑, ↵Enter

6. Continue typing and formatting letter, repeating steps to insert merge fields or merge blocks at desired location(s).

7. Save the document.

To preview merge documents:

1. Click the **Mailings** tab ..... Alt + M

   Preview Results Group

2. Click the **Preview Results** button .... P

3. Click the **Next record** button .... Alt + M, X

   OR

   Click the **First record** button .... Alt + M, Q

   OR

   Click the **Previous record** button .... Alt + M, M

   OR

   Click the **Last record** button .... Alt + M, V

To complete the merge:

1. Click the **Mailings** tab ..... Alt + M

   Finish Group

2. Click the **Finish & Merge** button .... F

3. Do one of the following:

   a. Click **Print Documents** ...... P

   ✓ Word displays the Merge to Printer dialog box.

   b. Specify records to print.

   c. Click **OK** .... ↵Enter

   ✓ Word displays the Print dialog box.

   d. Select print options.

   e. Click **OK** .... ↵Enter

   OR

   a. Click **Edit Individual Documents** .... E

   ✓ Word displays the Merge to New Document dialog box.

   b. Specify records to include in new document.

   c. Click **OK** .... ↵Enter

   ✓ You can make changes to individual letters, and/or save the entire merge document to print later.

Create a Form Letter Merge Using a New Address List Data Source File using the Mail Merge Wizard

To select the document type and create an address list:

1. Open a new blank document.

   OR

   Open an existing letter document.

2. Click the **Mailings** tab ...... `Alt`+`M`

   Start Mail Merge Group

3. Click the **Start Mail Merge** button 🖹 .... `S`

4. Click **Step by Step Mail Merge Wizard** .... `W`

   ✓ *The Mail Merge Wizard opens in the Mail Merge task pane.*

5. Click to select the **Letters** option button.

6. Click **Next: Starting document**.

7. Click the **Use the current document** option button.

8. Click **Next: Select recipients**.

9. Click the **Type a new list** option button.

10. Click **Create**.

    ✓ *The Address list table displays.*

11. In the **Title** field, type the title of the first recipient.

12. Press **Tab** to move to the next field .... `Tab⇆`

    ✓ *Press Shift+Tab to move to previous field.*

13. Type the recipient's first name.

14. Press **Tab** .... `Tab⇆`

15. Continue typing variable data until record is complete.

    ✓ *You may leave blank any fields for which information is not available or necessary.*

16. Click **New Entry** .... `Alt`+`N`

    ✓ *Word adds a new, blank row to the list.*

17. Repeat steps 11–16 until you have entered the information for all recipients.

    ✓ *You can go back to edit data in any record. Simply click in the field you want to change.*

18. Click **OK** .... `↵Enter`

    ✓ *Word displays the Save Address List dialog box.*

19. Type file name.

20. If necessary, select storage location.

21. Click **Save** .... `Alt`+`S`

22. Click **Next: Write your letter**.

To set up the form letter:

1. In the main document, begin typing the letter, including all text and formatting as you want it to appear on each merge document. For example, type the date and move the insertion point down four lines.

2. Position the insertion point at the location where you want to insert a field.

3. In the task pane, do one of the following:

   a. Click a merge block name.

   b. In the displayed dialog box, select options for formatting block.

   c. Click **OK** .... `↵Enter`

   OR

   a. Click **More items**.

   b. Click field to insert ...... `↓`/`↑`

   c. Click **Insert** .... `Alt`+`I`

   d. Repeat steps b and c to insert additional fields.

   e. Click **Cancel** .... `Esc`

4. Continue typing and formatting letter, repeating steps to insert merge fields or merge blocks at desired location(s).

5. Save the document.

6. Click **Next: Preview your letters** in the Mail Merge task pane.

   ✓ *Word displays the first merge document.*

To preview merge documents:

1. Click the **Next recipient** button `>>` in the Mail Merge task pane.

   OR

   Click the **Previous recipient** button `<<` in the Mail Merge task pane.

2. Click **Next: Complete the Merge** in the Mail Merge task pane.

Complete the merge:

- Do one of the following:

   a. Click **Print**.

   ✓ *Word displays the Merge to Printer dialog box.*

   b. Specify records to print.

   c. Click **OK** .... `↵Enter`

   ✓ *Word displays the Print dialog box.*

   d. Select print options.

   e. Click **OK** .... `↵Enter`

   OR

   a. Click **Edit individual letters**.

   ✓ *Word displays the Merge to New Document dialog box.*

   b. Specify records to include in new document.

   c. Click **OK** .... `↵Enter`

   ✓ *You can make changes to individual letters, and/or save the entire merge document to print later.*

EXERCISE DIRECTIONS

1. Start Word, if necessary.
2. Create a new blank document.
3. Save the file as **46FORM_xx**.
4. Create a form letter, using the current document.
5. Create a new address list to use as a data source document.
6. Enter the recipients from Illustration A below into the data source file.
7. Save the data source file as **46SOURCE_xx**.
8. Type the document shown in Illustration B, inserting the merge fields and merge blocks as marked.

   a. Set address options to exclude the company address and only include the country if it is not the United States.

   b. Insert the Greeting line merge block, using the recipient's first name only.

   c. Remember, merge blocks include punctuation and spacing, but merge fields do not.

9. Check the spelling and grammar in the document.
10. Preview the merged documents.
11. Complete the merge by generating a new document containing all of the individual records.
12. Save the file as **46LETTERS_xx**.
13. Print the file.
14. Close all open documents, saving all changes.

Illustration A

Title	First Name	Last Name	Address Line 1	Address Line 2	City	State	ZIP Code
Mr.	Jeffrey	Halloran	3535 N. Clark Street	Apt. 4B	Chicago	IL	60601
Ms.	Liz	Rupert	221 N. Rush Street	#351	Chicago	IL	60601
Ms.	Kathy	Figit	562 S. Michigan Avenue		Chicago	IL	60601
Mr.	Charles	Huang	125 E. Delaware Place	#26	Chicago	IL	60601
Mr.	Keith	Newmann	882 W. Polk		Chicago	IL	60601

Illustration B

Today's date

«AddressBlock»

«GreetingLine»

Great news! Michigan Avenue Athletic Club is starting a co-ed volleyball league! Depending on the response, we hope to field enough teams to hold intra-club competitions. We have also contacted other clubs in the area to see if they are interested in inter-club competitions.

«First_Name», we hope you will register to join. No experience is necessary – we welcome all abilities. We guarantee that it will be a lot of fun as well as great exercise. We have also designed really cool T-shirts that we will give to all league members.

For more information, or to sign up, see Kathy at the front desk, or call me at the club. See you on the court!

Sincerely,

Student's Name

ON YOUR OWN

1. Think of ways Mail Merge would be useful to you. For example, are you involved in any clubs or organizations that send out mass mailings? Do you send out "Holiday Letters" every year? Are you responsible for regular reports that contain variable data, such as sales reports or forecasts?

2. Use Mail Merge to create a form letter.

3. Save the main document as **OWD46-1_xx**.

4. Create an address list data source file that includes at least five records.

5. Save the data source file as **OWD46-2_xx**.

6. Type the letter, inserting merge fields and merge blocks as necessary.

7. Check the spelling and grammar in the document.

8. Merge the documents into a new file.

9. Save the merge document file as **OWD46-3_xx**.

10. Print the letters.

11. Close all open documents, saving all changes.

Skills Covered

- Merge with an Existing Address List
- Edit an Address List
- Customize Merge Fields
- Merge Envelopes and Labels

Software Skills   If you have an existing data source document, you can merge it with any main document to create new merge documents. This saves you from retyping repetitive data. For example, using an existing Address List data source makes it easy to create envelopes and labels to accompany a form letter merge that you created previously. You can edit the data source to add or remove records, or to customize merge fields to include specialized information not included in the default Address List data source file.

Application Skills   To mail out the form letters for Michigan Avenue Athletic Club, you need to print envelopes. In this exercise, you will create an envelope main document and merge it with the same address list file you used in Exercise 46. You will then edit the address list and customize the merge fields. Finally, you will use the address list to print labels to use on the packages containing the T-shirts promised to every person who joins the league.

TERMS

No new vocabulary in this exercise.

NOTES

Merge with an Existing Address List

- Once you create and save an address list data source file, you can use it with different main documents.
- To use an existing data source, you simply select it in the Select Data Source dialog box, which you access from the Select Recipients button in the Start Mail Merge group on the Mailings tab of the Ribbon, or in step 3 of the Mail Merge Wizard.
- You can use existing data source files created with other applications, including Microsoft Office Access.
  - ✓ *If you select a data source created with Access, you must specify which table or query to use, and the merge fields inserted in the Word document must match the fields used in the Access file.*
- Using an existing data source saves you the time and trouble of retyping existing data.

Edit an Address List

- You can easily edit an existing address list.
- You can change information that is already entered.
- You can add or delete information, including entire records.

Customize Merge Fields

- Customize merge fields to change field names, delete unused fields, or add fields specific to your needs. For example, you might want to add a field for entering a job title.
- You can also move fields up or down in the field list.

Merge Envelopes and Labels

- To create envelopes using Mail Merge, select Envelopes as the main document type.
- To create labels using Mail Merge, select Labels as the main document type.
- When you create an envelopes main document, Word prompts you to select envelope options so that the main document is laid out just like the actual paper envelopes on which you will print.
- Likewise, when you create a labels main document, you must select label options so that the label layout on-screen is the same as the actual labels.

- When you select the size and format of the envelopes or labels, Word changes the layout of the current document to match. Any existing data in the document is deleted.
- The label main document is set up using a table, so the Table Tools Ribbon tabs become available.
- To merge with envelopes or labels, you can create a new data source file as covered in Exercise 46, or use an existing data source file.
- You can merge the envelopes or labels to a printer or to a new document to save, edit, or use at a later time.

PROCEDURES

Generate Envelopes or Labels with an Existing Address List Data Source File Using Commands on the Ribbon

To select the document type:

1. Open a new blank document.
2. Click the **Mailings** tab..... Alt+M

   Start Mail Merge Group

3. Click the **Start Mail Merge** button 🗒 ....S
4. Click **Envelopes** to generate envelopes................................V

   ✓ *The Envelope Options dialog box displays*

   OR

   Click **Labels** to generate labels ....A

   ✓ *The Label Options dialog box displays*

5. Do one of the following:
   a. For envelope options, click **Envelope size** drop-down arrow...................Alt+S
   b. Click desired size...............↑/↓, ↵Enter
   c. Click **OK**.......................↵Enter

   OR

   a. For label options, select options.

      ✓ *For more information on label options, refer to Exercise 14.*

   b. Click **OK**.......................↵Enter

   ✓ *Word changes the layout of the current document. If a warning displays, click OK to continue or Cancel to cancel the change.*

To select an existing data source:

1. Open main document.
2. Click the **Mailings** tab..... Alt+M

   Start Mail Merge Group

3. Click the **Select Recipients** button 🗒 ....R
4. Click **Use existing list**............E

   ✓ *The Select Data Source dialog box displays.*

5. Locate and select the data source file.
6. Click **Open**....................Alt+O

To arrange envelopes:

1. In the main document, type and format any text you want to display on all envelopes, such as a return address in the upper-left corner.

2. Position the insertion point at the location where you want the recipient's address to display.

   ✓ *By default, Word creates a text box on the envelope document where the address should print. Position the insertion point in the text box.*

3. Click the **Mailings** tab..... Alt+M

   Write & Insert Fields Group

4. Do one of the following:
   a. Click the **Address block** button 🗒 ....A

      ✓ *Word displays the Insert Address Block dialog box.*

   b. Select desired options for formatting address.
   c. Click **OK**.......................↵Enter

   OR

   a. Click **Insert Merge Field** button 🗒 I
   b. Click field to insert............↓/↑, ↵Enter

5. Repeat step 4 to insert additional blocks and fields, as necessary.
6. Insert and format additional text and/or punctuation as necessary.
7. Save the document, if desired.

   ✓ *If you are only going to generate the envelopes once, you do not have to save the document.*

To arrange labels:

1. In the first label, position the insertion point at the location where you want the recipient's address to display.

   ✓ *You may want to view gridlines to see the borders between labels. Click the Table Tools Layout tab and then click the View Gridlines button in the Table group. Refer to Exercise 40 for more information.*

2. Click the **Mailings** tab ..... Alt + M

   Write & Insert Fields Group

3. Do one of the following:

   a. Click the **Address block** button 🖹 .... Ⓐ

   ✓ *Word displays the Insert Address Block dialog box.*

   b. Select desired options for formatting address.

   c. Click **OK** .... ↵Enter

   OR

   a. Click **Insert Merge Field** button 🖺 .... Ⓘ

   b. Click field to insert .... ↓/↑, ↵Enter

4. Repeat step 3 to insert additional blocks and fields on the first label, as necessary.

5. Insert and format additional text and/or punctuation on the first label, as necessary.

6. Click the **Update Labels** button 🗐 .... Alt + M + B

   ✓ *Word copies the layout from the first label to all other labels, and also inserts a Next Record field on each label.*

7. Save the document, if necessary.

   ✓ *If you are only going to generate the labels once, you do not have to save the document.*

To preview merge documents:

1. Click the **Mailings** tab ..... Alt + M

   Preview Results Group

2. Click the **Preview Results** button 🔍 .... Ⓟ

3. Click the **Next record** button ▶ .... Alt + M, Ⓧ

   OR

   Click the **First record** button ◀◀ .... Alt + M, Ⓠ

   OR

   Click the **Previous record** button ◀ .... Alt + M, Ⓜ

   OR

   Click the **Last record** button ▶▶ .... Alt + M, Ⓥ

To complete the merge:

1. Click the **Mailings** tab ..... Alt + M

   Finish Group

2. Click the **Finish & Merge** button 🗎 .... Ⓕ

3. Do one of the following:

   a. Click **Print Documents** .... Ⓟ

   ✓ *Word displays the Merge to Printer dialog box.*

   b. Specify records to print.

   c. Click **OK** .... ↵Enter

   ✓ *Word displays the Print dialog box.*

   d. Select print options.

   e. Click **OK** .... ↵Enter

   OR

   a. Click **Edit Individual Documents** .... Ⓔ

   ✓ *Word displays the Merge to New Document dialog box.*

   b. Specify records to include in new document.

   c. Click **OK** .... ↵Enter

   ✓ *You can make changes to individual envelopes or labels, and/or save the entire merge document to print later.*

Generate Envelopes or Labels with an Existing Address List Data Source File Using the Mail Merge Wizard

To select the document type and a data source file:

1. Open a new blank document.

2. Click the **Mailings** tab ..... Alt + M

   Start Mail Merge Group

3. Click the **Start Mail Merge** button 🖹 .... Ⓢ

4. Click **Step by Step Mail Merge Wizard** .... Ⓦ

   ✓ *The Mail Merge Wizard opens in the Mail Merge task pane.*

5. Click to select the **Envelopes** option button.

   OR

   Click to select the **Labels** option button.

6. Click **Next: Starting document**.

7. Under Change document layout, click **Envelope options** or **Label options**.

   ✓ *A dialog box for selecting envelope or label options displays.*

8. Do one of the following:

   a. For envelope options, click **Envelope size** drop-down arrow .... Alt + S

   b. Click desired size .... ↑/↓, ↵Enter

   c. Click **OK** .... ↵Enter

   OR

   a. For label options, select options.

   ✓ *For more information on label options, refer to Exercise 14.*

   b. Click **OK** .... ↵Enter

   ✓ *Word changes the layout of the current document. If a warning displays, click OK to continue or Cancel to cancel the change.*

9. Click **Next: Select recipients**.

10. Click the **Use an existing list** option button.

11. Click **Browse**.

   ✓ *The Select Data Source dialog box displays.*

12. Locate and select the data source file.

13. Click **Open** .... `Alt`+`O`

   ✓ *Word displays the Mail Merge Recipients dialog box.*

14. Click **OK** .... `↵Enter`

15. Click **Next: Arrange your envelope/labels**.

To arrange envelopes:

1. In the main document, type and format any text you want to display on all envelopes, such as a return address in the upper-left corner.

2. Position the insertion point at the location where you want the recipient's address to display.

   ✓ *By default, Word creates a text box on the envelope document where the address should print. Position the insertion point in the text box.*

3. In the task pane, do one of the following:

   a. Click **Address Block**.

   ✓ *Word displays the Insert Address Block dialog box.*

   b. Select desired options for formatting address.

   c. Click **OK** .... `↵Enter`

   OR

   a. Click **More items**.

   b. Click field to insert ...... `↓`/`↑`

   c. Click **Insert** .... `Alt`+`I`

   d. Repeat steps b and c to insert additional fields.

   e. Click **Cancel** .... `Esc`

4. Repeat step 3 to insert additional blocks and fields, as necessary.

5. Insert and format additional text and/or punctuation as necessary.

6. Save the document, if desired.

   ✓ *If you are only going to generate the envelopes once, you do not have to save the document.*

7. Click **Next: Preview your envelopes** in the Mail Merge task pane.

To arrange labels:

1. In the first label, position the insertion point at the location where you want the recipient's address to display.

   ✓ *You may want to view gridlines to see the borders between labels. Click the Table Tools Layout tab and then click the View Gridlines button in the Table group. Refer to Exercise 40 for more information.*

2. In the task pane, do one of the following:

   a. Click **Address block**.

   ✓ *Word displays the Insert Address Block dialog box.*

   b. Select desired options for formatting address.

   c. Click **OK** .... `↵Enter`

   OR

   a. Click **Insert Merge Field**.

   b. Click field to insert ...... `↓`/`↑`

3. Repeat step 2 to insert additional blocks and fields on the first label, as necessary.

   c. Click Insert .... `Alt`+`I`

   d. Repeat steps b and c to insert additional fields.

   e. Click Cancel .... `Esc`

4. Insert and format additional text and/or punctuation on the first label, as necessary.

5. Click **Update all labels** to copy the layout from the first label to all other labels.

   ✓ *Word copies the layout from the first label to all other labels, and also inserts a Next Record field on each label.*

6. Save the document, if necessary.

   ✓ *If you are only going to generate the labels once, you do not have to save the document.*

7. Click **Next: Preview your labels**.

To preview merge documents:

1. Click the **Next recipient** button `>>` in the Mail Merge task pane.

   OR

   Click the **Previous recipient** button `<<` in the Mail Merge task pane.

2. Click **Next: Complete the merge** in the Mail Merge task pane.

Complete the merge:

■ Do one of the following:

   a. Click **Print**.

   ✓ *Word displays the Merge to Printer dialog box.*

   b. Specify records to print.

   c. Click **OK** .... `↵Enter`

   ✓ *Word displays the Print dialog box.*

   d. Select print options.

   e. Click **OK** .... `↵Enter`

   OR

   a. Click **Edit individual envelopes/labels**.

   ✓ *Word displays the Merge to New Document dialog box.*

   b. Specify records to include in new document.

   c. Click **OK** .... `↵Enter`

   ✓ *You can make changes to individual envelopes or labels, and/or save the entire merge document to print later.*

Edit an Existing Address List

1. Open main document.
2. Click the **Mailings** tab ..... `Alt`+`M`

   `Start Mail Merge Group`

3. Click the **Edit Recipient list** button `🖉` .... `D`

   OR

   In Step 3 or Step 5 of Mail Merge Wizard, in task pane, click **Edit recipient list**.

   ✓ *Word displays the Mail Merge Recipients dialog box.*

4. In the Data Source list, click to select the data source file.
5. Click **Edit** .... `Alt`+`E`

   ✓ *Word displays the Edit Data Source dialog box.*

6. Do any of the following:

To add an entry:

a. Click **New Entry** .... `Alt`+`N`
b. Enter variable information as covered in Exercise 46.

To delete an entry:

a. Click to select a record.
b. Click **Delete Entry** .... `Alt`+`D`
c. Click **Yes** .... `Y`

To edit an entry:

a. Click to select field to edit.
b. Edit fields as necessary.

7. Click **OK** .... `↵Enter`
8. Click **Yes** .... `Y`
9. Click **OK** .... `↵Enter`

Customize Merge Fields

1. Open main document.
2. Click the **Mailings** tab ..... `Alt`+`M`

   `Start Mail Merge Group`

3. Click the **Edit Recipient list** button `🖉` .... `D`

   OR

   In Step 3 or Step 5 of Mail Merge Wizard, in task pane, click **Edit recipient list**.

   ✓ *Word displays the Mail Merge Recipients dialog box.*

4. In the Data Source list, click to select the data source file.
5. Click **Edit** .... `Alt`+`E`

   ✓ *Word displays the Edit Data Source dialog box.*

6. Click **Customize Columns** .... `Alt`+`Z`

   ✓ *If a dialog box displays prompting you to save, click Yes to continue. Word displays the Customize Address List dialog box.*

7. Do any of the following:

To add a field:

a. Click **Add** .... `Alt`+`A`
b. Type field name.
c. Click **OK** .... `↵Enter`

To delete a field:

a. Click field to delete .... `↓`/`↑`
b. Click **Delete** .... `Alt`+`D`
c. Click **Yes** .... `Alt`+`Y`

To rename a field:

a. Click field to rename .... `↓`/`↑`
b. Click **Rename** .... `Alt`+`R`
c. Type new name.
d. Click **OK** .... `↵Enter`

To change the order of fields in the field list:

a. Click field to move ...... `↓`/`↑`
b. Click **Move Up** to move the field up one line in list ..... `Alt`+`U`

   OR

   ■ Click **Move Down** to move field down one line in list ..... `Alt`+`N`

8. Click **OK** .... `↵Enter`
9. Click **OK** .... `↵Enter`
10. Click **Yes** .... `Y`
11. Click **OK** .... `↵Enter`

Curriculum Connection: Language Arts

Persuasive Writing

Persuasive writing is designed to convince the reader that the point of view or course of action recommended by the writer is valid. For example, you can write a persuasive essay to advance your opinion, or to win someone over to your side of a debate. You can write a persuasive letter to prompt someone into responding favorably to your request.

Writing for Charity

Write a persuasive letter asking for donations for a charity that you support. Be sure to use proper persuasive writing techniques to convince the reader that the cause is worthy of support. You might ask for money, or you might ask for resources, such as clothing for a homeless shelter, or canned goods for a food bank. Set up the letter for a mail merge, creating a data source of names and addresses of friends and family members to whom you can send the letter.

EXERCISE DIRECTIONS

Create Envelopes

1. Start Word, if necessary.
2. Create a new blank document.
3. Save the document as **47MAIN_xx**.
4. Use Mail Merge to create an envelope main document.
5. Select the envelope size 10.
6. Select to use an existing address list file as a data source document.
7. Locate and open **46SOURCE_xx** or **47SOURCE_xx**.
8. Set up the envelope main document as shown in Illustration A.
   a. Type the return address.
   b. Insert the Address merge block.
9. Check the spelling and grammar in the document.
10. Preview the merged documents and make corrections if necessary.
11. Complete the merge by generating a file containing all of the individual envelopes.
12. Save the file as **47ENV_xx**.
13. If requested by your instructor, print the merge documents.

   ✓ *If you do not have actual envelopes, you can print the merge documents on regular paper.*

14. Close all open files, saving all changes.

Create Labels

1. Create a new blank document.
2. Save the file as **47MAINLAB_xx**.
3. Use Mail Merge to create a Labels main document.
4. For Label options, select to use U.S. Avery Letter 5159 labels.

   ✓ *If you are planning to print on actual labels, select the actual label manufacturer and label number.*

5. Select to use an existing address list file as a data source document.
6. Locate and open **46SOURCE_xx** or **47SOURCE_xx**.
7. Customize the merge fields as follows:
   a. Delete the Company Name field.
   b. Delete the Work Phone field.
   c. Add a T-Shirt Size field.
   d. If necessary, move the new field down after the E-mail Address field.
   e. Add a Membership Type field.
   f. If necessary, move the new field down after the T-shirt Size field.
8. Add a new entry to the address list using the following information:

   Ms. Janine Flaherty
   391 S. Wabash Avenue
   Chicago, IL 60601
   T-Shirt Size: M
   Membership Type: Full

9. Fill in the new fields for all existing records using the information in the following table:

	T-Shirt Size	Membership Type
Jeffrey Halloran	XL	Full
Liz Rupert	S	Student
Kathy Figit	L	Junior
Charles Huang	M	Full
Keith Newmann	XL	Full

10. Close all open dialog boxes.
11. Set up the labels main document as shown in Illustration B.
   a. Insert the individual merge fields as shown.
   b. Type text, punctuation, and spacing as shown. (You may have to set line spacing to Single and paragraph spacing to 0 pts. before and after.)
   c. Once you set up the first label, use Update Labels to automatically set up the other labels.
12. Check the spelling and grammar in the document.
13. Preview the merged documents.
14. Complete the merge by generating a file containing all of the individual labels.
15. Save the file as **47LABELS_xx**.
16. Close all open files, saving all changes.

Illustration A

Michigan Avenue Athletic Club
235 Michigan Avenue
Chicago, IL 60601

«AddressBlock»

Illustration B

«Title» «First_Name» «Last_Name»
«Membership_Type» Member
«Address_Line_1»
«Address_Line_2»
«City», «State» «ZIP_Code»

Enclosed T-shirt size: «TShirt_Size»

ON YOUR OWN

1. Create a new document in Word.
2. Save it as OWD47-1_xx.
3. Use Mail Merge to create envelopes, using OWD46-2_xx as the data source.

   ✓ If OWD46-2_xx is not available, make a copy of 47DATA and save it as OWD47-2_xx.

4. Add at least one new record to the data source.
5. Delete at least one field.
6. Add at least one field.
7. Fill in all missing information for the existing records.
8. Set up the envelopes with a return address and a delivery address.
9. Merge the envelopes to a new document.
10. Save the merge document as OWD47-3_xx.
11. Close all open documents, saving all changes.

Exercise | 48

Skills Covered

- Sort Recipients in an Address List
- Select Specific Recipients
- Create a Directory with Mail Merge

Software Skills You can use Mail Merge to create a directory, such as a telephone directory, an address list, or a customer directory. Mail Merge makes it easy to select records in your data source file so you can include only specific recipients in a merge. You can also sort the data source file so that the merge documents are generated in alphabetical or numerical order.

Application Skills Michigan Avenue Athletic Club has asked you to create a directory of its personal trainers to give out to members. You have an existing address list file that lists all trainers and exercise instructors. In this exercise, you will use the existing address list data source file, from which you will select the records you need. You will also sort the list before generating the directory.

TERMS

Column heading The label displayed at the top of a column.

Directory A single document listing data source file entries.

NOTES

Sort Recipients in an Address List

- You can quickly change the order of records in an address list based on the data entered in any column in the list.
- Simply click any **column heading** in the Mail Merge Recipients dialog box to sort the records into ascending order.
- Click the column heading again to sort the records into descending order.

Select Specific Recipients

- By default, all recipients in an address list are selected to be included in a merge.
- You can select the specific recipients you want to include. For example, you might want to send letters only to the people who live in a specific town.
- To indicate that a recipient is selected, Word displays a check in the check box at the left end of the recipient's row in the Mail Merge Recipients dialog box.

- You click the check box to clear the check, or click the empty box to select the recipient again.

An Address List with only some recipients selected

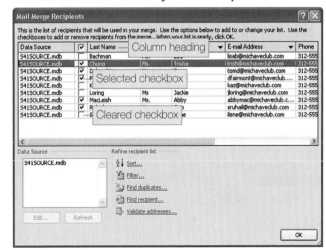

Create a Directory with Mail Merge

- Use Mail Merge to create a **directory**, such as a catalog, an inventory list, or a membership address list.
- When you merge to a directory, Word creates a single document that includes the variable data for all selected recipients.
- You arrange the layout for the first entry in the directory; Mail Merge uses that layout for all entries.
- You may type text, spacing, and punctuation, and you can include formatting. For example, you might want to include labels such as *Name:*, *Home Phone:*, *and E-Mail:*.

PROCEDURES

Generate a Directory with an Existing Address List Data Source File Using Commands on the Ribbon

To select the document type:
1. Open a new blank document.
2. Click the **Mailings** tab ..... Alt+M

   Start Mail Merge Group

3. Click the **Start Mail Merge** button 📄 ..... S
4. Click **Directory** ..... D

To select an existing data source:
1. Open main document.
2. Click the **Mailings** tab ..... Alt+M

   Start Mail Merge Group

3. Click the **Select Recipients** button 📇 ..... R
4. Click **Use existing list** ..... E

   ✓ *The Select Data Source dialog box displays.*

5. Locate and select the data source file.
6. Click **Open** ..... Alt+O

To arrange the directory:
1. In the main document, position the insertion point at the location where you want the first entry in the directory to display.
2. Click the **Mailings** tab ..... Alt+M

   Write & Insert Fields Group

3. Insert merge fields and merge blocks as necessary to set up the first entry.
4. Type any additional text, spacing, or punctuation that you want in the first entry.

   ✓ *Typed data will be repeated as part of each entry in the directory.*

5. Save the document.

To preview merge documents:
1. Click the **Mailings** tab ..... Alt+M

   Preview Results Group

2. Click the **Preview Results** button 🔍 ..... P
3. Click the **Next record** button ▶ ..... Alt+M, X

   OR

   Click the **First record** button ◀◀ ..... Alt+M, Q

   OR

   Click the **Previous record** button ◀ ..... Alt+M, M

   OR

   Click the **Last record** button ▶▶ ..... Alt+M, V

To complete the merge:
1. Click the **Mailings** tab ..... Alt+M

   Finish Group

2. Click the **Finish & Merge** button 📄 ..... F

3. Click **Edit Individual Documents** ..... E

   ✓ *Word displays the Merge to New Document dialog box.*

4. Specify records to include in new document.
5. Click **OK** ..... ↵Enter

   ✓ *You can make changes to individual entries, and/or save the entire merge document to print later.*

Generate a Directory with an Existing Address List Data Source File Using the Mail Merge Wizard

To select the document type and a data source file:
1. Open a new blank document.
2. Click the **Mailings** tab ..... Alt+M

   Start Mail Merge Group

3. Click the **Start Mail Merge** button 📄 ..... S
4. Click **Step by Step Mail Merge Wizard** ..... W

   ✓ *The Mail Merge Wizard opens in the Mail Merge task pane.*

5. Click to select the **Directory** option button.
6. Click **Next: Starting document**.
7. Click the **Use the current document** option button.
8. Click **Next: Select recipients**.

9. Click the **Use an existing list** option button.
10. Click **Browse**
    ✓ *The Select Data Source dialog box displays.*
11. Locate and select the data source file.
12. Click **Open** .... Alt + O
    ✓ *Word displays the Mail Merge Recipients dialog box.*
13. Click **OK** .... ↵Enter
14. Click **Next: Arrange your directory**.

To arrange the directory:

1. In the main document, position the insertion point at the location where you want the first entry in the directory to display.
2. Insert merge fields and merge blocks as necessary to set up the first entry.
3. Type any additional text, spacing, or punctuation that you want in the first entry.
    ✓ *Typed data will be repeated as part of each entry in the directory.*
4. Save the document.
5. Click **Next: Preview your directory** in the Mail Merge task pane.

To preview merge documents:

1. Click the **Next recipient** button >> in the Mail Merge task pane.
    OR
    Click the **Previous recipient** button << in the Mail Merge task pane.
2. Click **Next: Complete the merge** in the Mail Merge task pane.

Complete the merge:

1. Click **To New Document**.
    ✓ *Word displays the Merge to New Document dialog box.*
2. Specify records to merge.
3. Click **OK** .... ↵Enter

Sort Recipients in an Address List

1. Open main document.
2. Click the **Mailings** tab ..... Alt + M
    Start Mail Merge Group
3. Click the **Edit Recipient list** button .... D
    OR
    In Step 3 or Step 5 of Mail Merge Wizard, in task pane, click **Edit recipient list**.
    ✓ *Word displays the Mail Merge Recipients dialog box.*
4. Click **column heading** by which you want to sort.
    ✓ *To reverse sort order, click column heading again.*
5. Click **OK** .... ↵Enter
    ✓ *Records will be merged in current sort order.*

Select Specific Recipients

1. Open main document.
2. Click the **Mailings** tab ..... Alt + M
    Start Mail Merge Group
3. Click the **Edit Recipient list** button .... D
    OR
    In Step 3 or Step 5 of Mail Merge Wizard, in task pane, click **Edit recipient list**.
    ✓ *Word displays the Mail Merge Recipients dialog box.*
4. Do one of the following:
    ■ Click to clear check box to right of data source file name to deselect recipient.
    ■ Click to select check box to right of data source file name to select recipient.
    ■ Click to deselect check box to right of Data Source column heading to deselect all recipients.
    ■ Click to select check box to right of Data Source column heading to select all recipients.
5. Click **OK** .... ↵Enter

EXERCISE DIRECTIONS

1. Make a copy of the address list file ⊙**48SOURCE**, and name the copy **48SOURCE_xx**.

   ✓ *To copy the file, right-click the file name and select Copy. Right-click the destination folder and select Paste. Right-click the copied file name and select Rename. Type the new file name and press Enter.*

2. Start Word, if necessary.

3. Create a new blank document.

4. Save the document as **48MAIN_xx**.

5. Use Mail Merge to create a directory main document.

6. Select to use an existing address list file as a data source document.

7. Locate and open **48SOURCE_xx**.

8. Sort the records by Position.

9. Deselect all records for exercise instructors.

10. Sort the list in ascending order by Last Name.

11. Verify that all of the records for personal trainers are selected.

12. Close the Mail Merge Recipients dialog box.

13. Set up the directory main document as shown in Illustration A.

    a. Set line spacing to Single and leave no space after paragraphs.

    b. Type the labels using a 14-point serif font such as Times New Roman, in bold.

    c. Leave a 1.5" tab space after each label, and then insert the merge field.

    d. If necessary, format the merge field to match the labels.

    e. Enter two blank lines at the end of the document.

14. Complete the merge by generating a new directory document.

15. Save the directory document in a new file, named **48DIRECTORY_xx**.

16. Edit the file as shown in Illustration B.

    a. Insert five new lines at the beginning of the document.

    b. Centered on line 1, type **Michigan Avenue Athletic Club**. in a 26-point serif font.

    c. Centered on line 2, type the address as shown in a 12-point serif font.

    d. Leave line 3 blank.

    e. Centered on line 4, type **Directory of Personal Trainers** in a 20-point serif font.

    f. Leave remaining line blank.

17. Check the spelling and grammar in the document.

18. Display the document in Print Preview. It should look similar to the one shown in Illustration B.

19. Print the directory.

20. Close all open files, saving all changes.

Illustration A

> **Name:** → «First_Name»«Last_Name»¶
> **Phone:** → «Phone»¶
> **E-Mail:** → «Email_Address»¶
> **Specialty:** → «Specialty»¶
> ¶
> ¶

Illustration B

Michigan Avenue Athletic Club

235 Michigan Avenue, Chicago, Illinois 60601

Directory of Personal Trainers

Name:	Trisha Chung
Phone:	312-555-3523
E-Mail:	trish@michaveclub.com
Specialty:	Strength Training

Name:	Tom Dybreski
Phone:	312-555-3524
E-Mail:	tomd@michaveclub.com
Specialty:	Cardio Health

Name:	David Fairmont
Phone:	312-555-3525
E-Mail:	dfairmont@michaveclub.com
Specialty:	All

Name:	Abby MacLeish
Phone:	312-555-3528
E-Mail:	abbymac@michaveclub.com
Specialty:	Rehabilitation

Name:	Sam Ruhail
Phone:	312-555-3529
E-Mail:	sruhail@michaveclub.com
Specialty:	Weight Loss

ON YOUR OWN

1. Create a new document in Word.
2. Save it as **OWD48-1_xx**.
3. Use Mail Merge to create a directory main document, using ⌨**OWD47-2_xx** as the data source.

   ✓ If ⌨**OWD47-2** is not available, make a copy of ⊙**48DATA** and save it as **OWD48-2_xx**.

4. Select to include only certain entries.
5. Sort the list.
6. Insert merge fields and blocks to create a directory in the main document.
7. Merge the main document to a new document.
8. Save the merge document as **OWD48-3_xx**.
9. Edit the directory document to include a title.
10. Check the spelling and grammar.
11. Print the directory.
12. Close all open documents, saving all changes.

Exercise | 49

Skills Covered

■ **Filter Recipients**   ■ **Merge to an E-mail Message**

Software Skills You can use Mail Merge to generate mass e-mailings in much the same way you can generate form letters. You type the message text you want each recipient to read, and insert merge fields to customize or personalize the message. Word automatically uses your e-mail program to send the messages. Filter the recipient list to quickly select the records you want to use.

Application Skills You must notify all Michigan Avenue Athletic Club exercise instructors that there is an important meeting tomorrow. In this exercise, you will use Mail Merge to create an e-mail message about the meeting, and you will filter an existing data source file to select only exercise instructors as recipients.

TERMS

Criteria Specific data used to match a record or entry in a data source file or list.

Filter To display records based on whether or not they match specified criteria.

MAPI A Microsoft standard that allows messaging programs to work together.

NOTES

Filter Recipients

■ You can **filter** the records in an Address List in order to display records that match specific **criteria**.

■ The records that match the criteria are displayed, while those that don't match are hidden.

■ Only the displayed records are used in the merge.

Merge to an E-mail Message

■ Use Mail Merge to set up and complete a merge using e-mail messages as the main document.

■ You type the message text, and then insert merge fields as desired.

■ You must be sure your data source includes a field for an e-mail address; the information entered in the e-mail address field will be inserted as the recipient's address in the message header.

■ You select options for merging to e-mail in the Merge to E-mail dialog box. For example, you may enter the text that will be displayed in the Subject field of the message header, and select the format to use for the message—either HTML, plain text, or as an attachment.

**Filter recipients in the Mail
Merge Recipients dialog box**

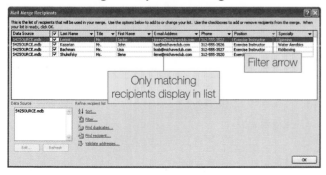

- When you merge to e-mail, Word does not create a merge document as it does when you merge letters, envelopes, or labels. Instead, the messages are created and sent to your e-mail program's Outbox.
- To successfully complete a merge to e-mail, you must have a **MAPI**-compatible e-mail program, such as Microsoft Office Outlook, installed and set up for use with Microsoft Office Word.

Merge to E-Mail dialog box

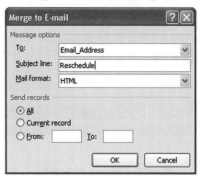

PROCEDURES

Merge to E-Mail with an Existing Address List Data Source File Using Commands on the Ribbon

To select the document type:
1. Open a new blank document.
2. Click the **Mailings** tab .....(Alt)+(M)

   Start Mail Merge Group

3. Click the **Start Mail Merge** button 📄 ....(S)
4. Click **E-Mail Messages**..............(E)

   ✓ *Word changes to Web Layout View.*

To select an existing data source:
1. Open main document.
2. Click the **Mailings** tab .....(Alt)+(M)

   Start Mail Merge Group

3. Click the **Select Recipients** button 📄 ....(R)
4. Click **Use Existing List**..............(E)

   ✓ *The Select Data Source dialog box displays.*

5. Locate and select the data source file.
6. Click **Open** ....(Alt)+(O)

To arrange the messages:
1. In the main document, type the message text as you want it to appear on each e-mail message.
2. Click the **Mailings** tab .....(Alt)+(M)

   Write & Insert Fields Group

3. Insert merge fields and merge blocks as necessary to personalize the message.
4. Type any additional text, spacing, or punctuation that you want in the message.
5. Save the document, if necessary.

To preview merge documents:
1. Click the **Mailings** tab .....(Alt)+(M)

   Preview Results Group

2. Click the **Preview Results** button 🔍 ....(P)
3. Click the **Next record** button ▶ ....(Alt)+(M), (X)

   OR

   Click the **First record** button ◀◀ ....(Alt)+(M), (Q)

   OR

   Click the **Previous record** button ◀ ....(Alt)+(M), (M)

   OR

   Click the **Last record** button ▶▶ ....(Alt)+(M), (V)

To complete the merge:
1. Click the **Mailings** tab .....(Alt)+(M)

   Finish Group

2. Click the **Finish & Merge** button 📄 ....(F)
3. Click **Send E-Mail Messages** ....(S)

   ✓ *Word displays the Merge to E-mail dialog box.*

4. Click **To** drop-down arrow ....(Alt)+(O)
5. Select field that specifies recipient's e-mail address.................(↑)/(↓), (↵Enter)
6. Click **Subject line** box ....(Alt)+(S)
7. Type text you want displayed in message header subject line.
8. Click **Mail format** drop-down arrow ....(Alt)+(M)
9. Select desired format.
10. Select other options as necessary.
11. Click **OK** ....(↵Enter)

    ✓ *Messages are sent to your Outbox. If necessary, start your e-mail program, sign on to the Internet, and send the messages.*

Merge to E-Mail with an Existing Address List Data Source File Using the Mail Merge Wizard

To select the document type and a data source file:

1. Open a new blank document.
2. Click the **Mailings** tab ...... Alt + M

   Start Mail Merge Group

3. Click the **Start Mail Merge** button 🗋 .... S
4. Click **Step by Step Mail Merge Wizard** .... W

   ✓ *The Mail Merge Wizard opens in the Mail Merge task pane.*

5. Click to select the **E-mail messages** option button.
6. Click **Next: Starting document**.
7. Click the **Use the current document** option button.
8. Click **Next: Select recipients**.
9. Click the **Use an existing list** option button.
10. Click **Browse**

    ✓ *The Select Data Source dialog box displays.*

11. Locate and select the data source file.
12. Click **Open** .... Alt + O

    ✓ *Word displays the Mail Merge Recipients dialog box.*

13. Click **OK** .... ←Enter
14. Click **Next: Write your e-mail message**.

To arrange the messages:

1. In the main document, type the message text as you want it to appear on each e-mail message.
2. Insert merge fields and merge blocks as necessary to personalize the message.
3. Type any additional text, spacing, or punctuation that you want in the message.
4. Save the document, if necessary.
5. Click **Next: Preview your e-mail messages** in the Mail Merge task pane.

To preview merge documents:

1. Click the **Next recipient** button >> in the Mail Merge task pane.

   OR

   Click the **Previous recipient** button << in the Mail Merge task pane.

2. Click **Next: Complete the merge** in the Mail Merge task pane.

Complete the merge:

1. Click **Electronic Mail**

   ✓ *Word displays the Merge to E-mail dialog box.*

2. Click **To** drop-down arrow .... Alt + O
3. Select field that specifies recipient's e-mail address. .... ↑/↓, ←Enter
4. Click **Subject line** box ...... Alt + S
5. Type text you want displayed in message header subject line.
6. Click **Mail format** drop-down arrow .... Alt + M
7. Select desired format.
8. Select other options as necessary.
9. Click **OK** .... ←Enter

   ✓ *Messages are sent to your Outbox. If necessary, start your e-mail program, sign on to the Internet, and send the messages.*

Filter Recipients

1. Open main document.
2. Click the **Mailings** tab ..... Alt + M

   Start Mail Merge Group

3. Click the **Edit Recipient list** button 🗒 .... D

   OR

   In Step 3 or Step 5 of Mail Merge Wizard, in task pane, click **Edit recipient list**.

   ✓ *Word displays the Mail Merge Recipients dialog box.*

4. Click **filter arrow** on column heading by which you want to filter.

   ✓ *Word displays a list of data.*

5. Select data to filter by.

   ✓ *Word displays only those entries that match the selected data in the list of recipients*

   OR

   Select one of the following:

   ■ **(All)** to display all entries.

   ✓ *Use this option to remove an existing filter.*

   ■ **(Blanks)** to display entries in which the current field is blank.

   ■ **(Nonblanks)** to display entries in which the current field is not blank.

   ✓ *The filter arrow on the column heading changes to blue so you know which column is used for the filter.*

6. Click **OK** .... ←Enter

EXERCISE DIRECTIONS

✓ *This exercise uses fictitious e-mail addresses. If you try to send the message, they will be returned as undeliverable. Your instructor may ask you to edit the e-mail addresses in the data source file to actual addresses so that you can send the messages.*

1. Make a copy of the data source file ⊙ 49SOURCE, and name the copy **49SOURCE_xx.**

    ✓ *To copy the file, right-click the file name and select Copy. Right-click the destination folder and select Paste. Right-click the copied file name and select Rename. Type the new file name and press ↵Enter).*

2. Start Word, if necessary.
3. Create a new blank document.
4. Save the document as **49MAIN_xx.**
5. Use Mail Merge to create an e-mail message main document.
6. Select to use an existing data source file.
7. Locate and open **49SOURCE_xx.**
8. Filter the recipient list to display only exercise instructors.
    a. Display the Mail Merge Recipients dialog box.
    b. Click the filter arrow on the Position column heading.
    c. Click Exercise Instructor.

9. Close the Mail Merge Recipients dialog box.
10. Set up the e-mail message main document as shown in Illustration A, using a 14-point sans serif font, such as Arial, single line space, and no spacing after paragraphs.
11. Check the spelling and grammar in the document.
12. Preview the messages.
13. Complete the merge to e-mail, using the following options:
    a. In the Merge to E-mail dialog box, leave Email_Address as the option in the To box.
    b. Type **Instructor Info Session** in the Subject line box.
    c. Leave HTML as the option in the Mail format box.
    d. Select to send All records.
    e. Click OK.
14. Launch your e-mail program and check to see if the messages are in the Outbox.
15. If your instructor asked you to use actual e-mail addresses, send the messages.
16. Close all open files, disconnect if necessary, and save all changes.

Illustration A

«First_Name»,

Please note that the information session for exercise instructors has been rescheduled to 3:30 p.m. tomorrow (Wednesday) in Aerobics Studio 1. See you there.

Curriculum Connection: Science

Everyday Chemicals

Do you know the chemical name for aspirin? How about table salt? Many everyday items can be defined by their chemical names, including vinegar, caffeine, nail polish remover, and vitamin C.

A Directory of Common Chemicals

Use merge to create a directory of common chemicals. Include the everyday name, the chemical name, and the chemical formula. You may want to include additional information such as whether the chemical is toxic or not, and some common uses. Use the Internet and other resources to locate the information.

ON YOUR OWN

1. Create a new document in Word.
2. Save it as **OWD49-1_xx**.
3. Use Mail Merge to create e-mail messages using OWD47-2_xx (the data source document you first used in Exercise 47) as the data source.

   ✓ *If* **OWD47-2_xx** *is not available, create a copy of* **49DATA** *to use, renaming the copy as* **OWD49-2_xx**.

4. If necessary, edit the list to fill in the e-mail address information for all records.

5. Filter the list to only the records you want to include in the merge.
6. Type the e-mail message, inserting merge fields as necessary.
7. Check the spelling and grammar.
8. Complete the merge and send the e-mail messages.
9. Close all open documents, saving all changes.

Exercise | 50

Critical Thinking

Application Skills Voyager Travel Adventures wants you to create participant directories for three upcoming tours so the leaders know the experience level of each person in the group. In addition, you need to send out letters to all participants confirming tour selections. In this exercise, you will use Mail Merge to create the letters and the directories. You will create a new data source file that you can use for all merges. The file will need to be customized to include fields specific to your needs. It will also need to be filtered and sorted to complete each merge.

EXERCISE DIRECTIONS

Create Form Letters

1. Start Word, if necessary.
2. Create a new blank document.
3. Save the file as **50TOURS_xx**.
4. Use Mail Merge to create a form letter main document, using the current document.
5. Create a new data source file to use as an address list.

6. Customize the address list as follows:
   a. Rename the Company Name field to **Level**.
   b. Add a field named **Tour**.
   c. Delete the Work Phone field.
   d. Delete the Home Phone field.
   e. Delete the E-Mail Address field.
   f. Move the Level and the Tour fields down to the bottom of the list.
7. Enter the recipient information from the following table into the data source file:

Mr.	Gary	Doone	10 Quail Drive	Largo	FL	33771	Beginner	Alaska
Ms.	Elizabeth	Dubin	1001 Starkey Road	Northborough	MA	01532	Beginner	Alaska
Ms.	Janice	Loring	17 Cherlyn Drive	Westford	MA	01886	Advanced	Kenya
Mr.	Antonio	DiBuono	2 Parkview Circle	Chelmsford	MA	01824	Intermediate	Costa Rica
Ms.	Katharine	Peterson	27 Concord Road	Bethesda	MD	20814	Intermediate	Alaska
Ms.	Marianne	Flagg	314 Green Street	Washington	DC	20015	Advanced	Costa Rica
Mr.	Howard	Jefferson	41 Marvel Court	Marlboro	MA	01752	Intermediate	Alaska
Mr.	Julian	Lovett	4526 Amherst Lane	Sudbury	MA	01776	Advanced	Kenya
Ms.	Christine	Bottecelli	49 Weatherly Place	Etna	NH	03750	Intermediate	Kenya
Ms.	Rose	Mekalian	6409 33rd Street N.W.	Auburn	ME	04210	Beginner	Costa Rica
Mr.	Dana	Teng	7 Ranch Road	San Francisco	CA	94121	Intermediate	Kenya
Mr.	Luis	Martinez	98 Sudbury Street	Northborough	MA	01532	Beginner	Costa Rica

8. Save the data source file as **50NAMES_xx**.

9. Sort the data source file alphabetically in ascending order by Level.

10. Select to use all recipients in the merge, then close the Mail Merge Recipients dialog box.

11. Set up the form letter main document as shown in Illustration A, inserting the merge fields as marked.

   a. Use 12-point Calibri.

   b. Set the line spacing to Single, and the spacing before and after paragraphs to 0 pts.

   c. Set the margins to 1-inch on the top and bottom, and 1.25-inches on the left and right.

12. Check the spelling and grammar in the document.

13. Preview the merged documents and make corrections to the main document as necessary.

14. Complete the merge by generating a new file containing all merged records.

15. Save the file as **50CONFIRM_xx**.

16. With your instructor's permission, print the file.

17. Close all open documents, saving all changes.

Create a Directory

1. Create a new blank document.

2. Save the file as **50ENROLLED_xx**.

3. Use Mail Merge to create a directory main document, using the current document.

4. Use the **50NAMES_xx** address list as the data source file.

5. Sort the list alphabetically by last name.

6. Filter the list to display only the people signed up for the Alaska tour.

7. Set up the directory as shown in Illustration B, using a 12-point serif font.

8. Preview the directory and make corrections to the main document as necessary.

9. Generate the directory and save it in a new file named **50ALASKA_xx**.

10. Add the title **Alaska Tour Participant List** in a 24-point serif font, centered at the top of the directory.

11. Check the spelling and grammar in the document.

12. Print the document.

13. Close the document, saving all changes.

   ✓ *The 50ENROLLED_xx main document should still be open.*

14. Edit the Recipient list to change the filter from Alaska to Costa Rica.

   ✓ *First, display all records, and then filter the list to Costa Rica only.*

15. Preview the directory.

16. Generate the directory and save it in a new file named **50COSTARICA_xx**.

17. Add the title **Cost Rica Tour Participant List** in a 24-point serif font, centered at the top of the directory.

18. Check the spelling and grammar in the document.

19. Print the document.

20. Close the document, saving all changes.

21. Repeat steps 14–20 to create a directory for the Kenya tour, naming the directory merge document **50KENYA_xx**.

22. When you are finished, close all open documents, saving all changes.

Today's Date

«AddressBlock»

«GreetingLine»

This letter confirms that you have registered for our «Tour» tour. This tour is one of our most popular, and we know you will have a wonderful time.

On your registration form you specified that your level of experience is «Level». If this is not accurate, please let us know as soon as possible. Your tour guide customizes some parts of the tour based on each participant's experience.

We will send you more information two weeks prior to your departure date, including a participant list, a packing list and a detailed itinerary. In the meantime, if you have any questions, please feel free to call.

Thank you for choosing Voyager.

Sincerely,

Your Name

```
¶
¶
¶
«Title»· «First_Name»· «Last_Name»¶
«City», ·«State»¶
Level:→ «Level»¶
¶
¶
¶
¶
```

Exercise | 51

Curriculum Integration

Application Skills Have you ever considered studying science after high school? Do you know what types of science majors most colleges and universities offer? For your science class, use Mail Merge to generate form letters to science departments at colleges and universities that you might want to attend. In the letter, identify yourself and your grade level, and ask about the admissions requirements and types of majors offered at the school. Use the Internet or your school guidance office to locate the addresses for at least five schools and the names of the heads of specific science departments. For example, you might include the Chemistry, Biology, Physics, or Environmental Science department heads. If you cannot locate the names of the department heads, you can send the letter to the department itself, using a Dear Sir or Madam greeting line. Create a new data source file that includes the variable information you will need to customize the form letters. Set up the form letter main document using merge blocks and fields, and write the letter using proper letter formatting. Refer to Illustration A to see a sample. With your instructor's permission, print the letters and corresponding envelopes, and mail the letters.

EXERCISE DIRECTIONS

Locate the information you need for your data source file.

Start Word, if necessary, and create a new document. Save it as **51SCIENCE_xx**.

Select to display elements that might help you while you work, such as the rulers, nonprinting characters, and text boundaries, and make sure all the features you want to use are enabled, such as AutoCorrect and AutoFormat As You Type.

Use Mail Merge to make the current document a form letter main document.

Select to use a new data source.

Enter the data source information, customizing the fields as necessary.

When the data source is complete, save the file as **51DATA_xx**.

Type the form letter, inserting merge blocks and fields as necessary to customize the letters. Use proper letter formatting.

Check the spelling and grammar in the letter, and use a thesaurus to replace common or boring words.

Ask a classmate to review the document and make suggestions for how you might improve it.

Incorporate your classmate's suggestions into the document, and save it.

Generate the merge documents by printing, or by saving them in a new document, named **51LETTERS_xx**.

Close all files, saving all changes.

Use the **51DATA_***xx* data source file to generate envelopes that you can use to mail the letters. Save the main document as **51SCIENV_***xx*. Print the letters, or save them in a new document named **51ENV_***xx*.

Close all files, saving all changes.

Illustration A

Today's Date

«Department»«AddressBlock»

«GreetingLine»

I am currently a junior in high school, and I am interested in the «Department» at the «Company_Name». I would like more information about your admission requirements, as well as different types of majors and programs that you offer.

I appreciate that you are taking the time to read this letter. You can reach me at the address or e-mail below.

Thank you very much. I look forward to hearing from you.

Sincerely,

Student's Name
Address
City, State Postal Code
E-mail address

Lesson | 8

Creating and Editing Long Documents

Skills Covered

- **Create an Outline**
- **Edit an Outline**
- **Collapse and Expand Outlines**
- **Number an Outline**

Software Skills Create an outline to organize ideas for any document that covers more than one topic, such as an article, a report, a presentation, or a speech. For example, you might create an outline to list the chapters or headings in a report or to arrange main subjects for a presentation. The outline serves as a map you can follow as you complete the entire document.

Application Skills The Michigan Avenue Athletic Club wants to publish a document describing some of the benefits of regular exercise. In this exercise, you will create an outline for that document.

TERMS

Collapse To hide subtopics in an outline.

Demote To move down one level in an outline.

Expand To show subtopics in an outline.

Outline A document that lists levels of topics.

Promote To move up one level in an outline.

NOTES

Create an Outline

- Use Outline view to create and edit **outlines**.
- When you switch to Outline view, the Outlining tab becomes available on the Ribbon. Use the tools in the Outline Tools Group to create, edit, and manage your outline.

Outline Tools Group

- Outline topics are set up in levels, which are sometimes called headings: Level 1 is a main heading, Level 2 is a subheading, Level 3 is a sub-subheading, and so on up to 9 heading levels.

- Word automatically applies different styles to different levels in an outline.
- By default the formatting displays in the document, but you can toggle it off if you want.
- By default all heading text displays in the document, but if you have multiple lines in each heading, you can select to show only the first line.
- Headings in an outline are preceded by one of three outline symbols:
  - Levels that have sublevels under them are preceded by a gray circle with a plus sign in it ⊕.
  - Levels that do not have sublevels are preceded by a gray circle with a minus sign in it ⊖.
  - Regular document text—called Body Text in an Outline—is preceded by a small gray circle ●.

- In Outline view, the document displays the way it will print. If you use Print Preview or Print Layout view, the display is not the way the outline prints.

An outline in Word 2007

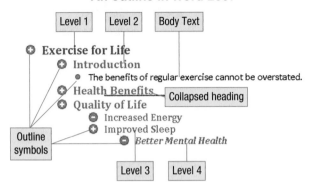

Edit an Outline

- You can edit an outline using the same techniques you use to edit regular document text. For example, you can insert and delete text at any location.

- To reorganize an outline, you can **promote** or **demote** heading levels. For example, you can demote a Level 1 paragraph to a Level 2 paragraph.

- You can also move headings and subheadings up or down the outline to reorganize the outline.

Collapse and Expand Outlines

- When you want to work with only some heading levels at a time, you can **collapse** the outline.
- Collapsing an outline hides lower-level headings.
- A gray line displays under a collapsed heading to indicate there are subheadings that are not displayed.
- To see hidden or collapsed levels, you can **expand** the outline.

Number an Outline

- Traditional outlines are numbered using a multilevel list numbering style.
- Different number and letter styles are used for each outline level.
- You can select a multilevel numbering style using the Multilevel List button in the Paragraph Group on the Home tab of the Ribbon.

PROCEDURES

Create an Outline

1. Click the **Outline** button on the status bar.

   OR

   a. Click **View** tab .... Alt+W

   Document Views Group

   b. Click **Outline** .... U

2. Type Level 1 text.
3. Press **Enter** .... Enter

   ✓ Heading level is carried forward to the new paragraph.

4. Type next Level 1 text.

   OR

   a. Click the **Demote** button .... Tab
   b. Type Level 2 text.

5. Press **Enter** .... Enter
6. Type next Level 2 text.

   OR

   - Click the **Demote** button to type Level 3 text .... Tab

   OR

   - Click the **Promote** button to type Level 1 text .... Shift+Tab

7. Press **Enter** .... Enter
8. Continue until outline is complete.

To type body text: (Ctrl+Shift+N)

1. Position insertion point where you want to type body text.
2. Click the **Outlining** tab ..... Alt+U

   Outline Tools Group

3. Click **Demote to Body Text** button .... B
4. Type text.

Edit an Outline

To select headings:

- Click outline symbol preceding the heading or or .

  ✓ The heading and all subheadings are selected.

To change a heading level:

1. Position insertion point anywhere on heading line.

   OR

   Select heading.

2. Drag **outline symbol** or or left or right to new level.

   OR

   Click **Promote** button to promote heading one level .... Shift+Tab

OR

Click **Demote** button ⬇ to demote heading one level .... Tab↹

OR

a. Click the **Outlining** tab .... Alt+U

Outline Tools Group

b. Click **Outline Level** drop-down arrow `Body text ▾` .... O

c. Click desired level .... ↓/↑, ↵Enter

To promote to Heading 1:

1. Position insertion point anywhere on heading line.

   OR

   Select heading.

2. Click the **Outlining** tab .... Alt+U

   Outline Tools Group

3. Click **Promote to Heading 1** button ⬆⬆ .... R

To move a heading:

1. Position insertion point anywhere on heading line.

   OR

   Select heading.

2. Drag **outline symbol** ⊕ or ⊖ or ● up or down to a new location.

   OR

   Click **Move Up** button ⬆ .... Alt+U, U

   OR

   Click **Move Down** button ⬇ .... Alt+U, D

To collapse or expand outline:

- ■ Double-click **outline symbol** ⊕ or ⊖ or ● preceding heading.

   OR

1. Position insertion point anywhere on heading line.

   OR

   Select heading.

2. Click **Expand** button ➕ .... Alt+U, E

   OR

   Click **Collapse** button ➖ .... Alt+U, L

   OR

1. Position insertion point anywhere on heading line.

   OR

   Select heading.

2. Click the **Outlining** tab .... Alt+U

   Outline Tools Group

3. Click **Show Level** drop- down arrow `Show Level: All Levels ▾` V

4. Click desired level .... ↓/↑, ↵Enter

Hide Outline Formatting

1. Click the **Outlining** tab .... Alt+U

   Outline Tools Group

2. Click to deselect the **Show Text Formatting** check box .... T

   ✓ *Click to select the check box to display the formatting.*

Show Only First Line of Heading

1. Click the **Outlining** tab .... Alt+U

   Outline Tools Group

2. Click to select the **Show First Line Only** check box .... F

   ✓ *Click to deselect the check box to display all lines in the heading.*

Apply a Numbering Style

1. Position the insertion point where the outline will begin.

   OR

   Select headings to number.

2. Click the **Home** tab .... Alt+H

   Paragraph Group

3. Click the **Multilevel List** button ⸬▾ .... M

4. Click style to apply .... ↓/↑/←/→, ↵Enter

Close Outline View

1. Click the **Outlining** tab .... Alt+U

   Outline Tools Group

2. Click the **Close Outline View** button ✖ C

EXERCISE DIRECTIONS

1. Start Word, if necessary.
2. Create a new document and save it as **52EXERCISE_xx**.
3. Change to Outline view.
4. Select the Numbering style used in Illustration A.
5. Type the outline shown in Illustration A.
   - Press Tab or click Demote to demote a level.
   - Press Shift+Tab, or click Promote to promote a level.
   - Press Ctrl+Shift+N or click Demote to Body Text to type regular text.
6. Collapse the outline to show only levels 1 and 2.
7. Display all levels.
8. Move the heading *Instruction* and its subheadings down so it is the second subheading under *Getting Started*.

   ✓ *Notice that Word renumbers the outline automatically.*

9. Promote the subheading *Better Mental Health* to level 3, and move it up so it is the third subheading under the heading *Health Benefits*.
10. Promote the subheading *Tips* to level 3.
11. Check the spelling in the document.
12. Print the document.
13. Close the document, saving all changes.

Illustration A

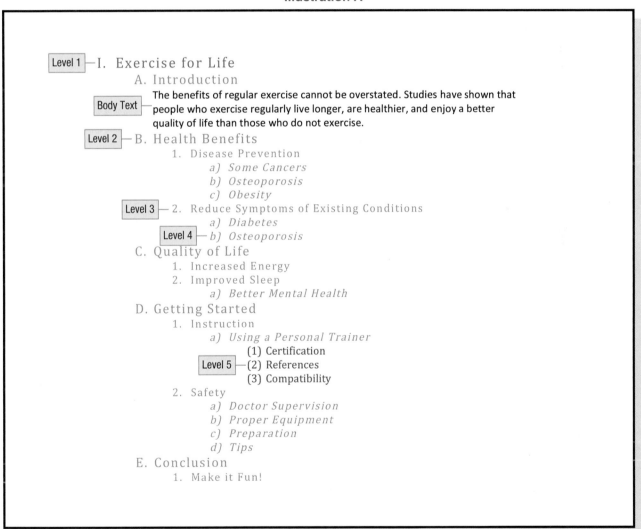

Level 1 — I. Exercise for Life
  A. Introduction
Body Text — The benefits of regular exercise cannot be overstated. Studies have shown that people who exercise regularly live longer, are healthier, and enjoy a better quality of life than those who do not exercise.
Level 2 — B. Health Benefits
    1. Disease Prevention
        a) Some Cancers
        b) Osteoporosis
        c) Obesity
Level 3 — 2. Reduce Symptoms of Existing Conditions
        a) Diabetes
Level 4 — b) Osteoporosis
  C. Quality of Life
    1. Increased Energy
    2. Improved Sleep
        a) Better Mental Health
  D. Getting Started
    1. Instruction
        a) Using a Personal Trainer
            (1) Certification
Level 5 — (2) References
            (3) Compatibility
    2. Safety
        a) Doctor Supervision
        b) Proper Equipment
        c) Preparation
        d) Tips
  E. Conclusion
    1. Make it Fun!

ON YOUR OWN

1. Begin planning a research report on a topic of your choice.

    ■ Start by selecting a topic. You may want to base the report on something you are learning in a class at school, or you may want to research something new. Think of three to five possible topics, and then ask your instructor to approve one of them.

2. Conduct some preliminary research that will help you organize the report. You may use books, magazine articles, or the Internet to locate useful information.

    ✓ *Remember to record all sources for use in a bibliography, source list, or for footnote references.*

3. Create a new document in Word.

4. Save the file as **OWD52_xx**.

5. Using the preliminary research, create an outline for the report. The outline will help you organize the topics you plan to include. Try to list at least four headings in the outline, along with the necessary subheadings.

6. Number the outline.

7. Examine the outline and make sure all headings are at the correct level. Change the levels if necessary.

8. Try rearranging the headings to see if you can improve the organization.

9. Check the spelling in the outline, save changes, and print it.

10. Ask a classmate to review the outline and offer comments and suggestions.

11. Incorporate the suggestions into the outline.

12. Close the document, saving all changes.

Exercise | 53

Skills Covered

- Set Margins for Multiple Page Documents
- Insert Page Breaks
- Insert Section Breaks
- Insert Headers and Footers
- Insert Page Numbers
- View the Word Count

Software Skills Make a long document easier to read and work in by inserting page breaks and section breaks, page numbers, and headers and footers and by adjusting margins to accommodate binding. Page breaks let you control where a new page should start, avoiding page layout problems such as headings at the bottom of a page. Section breaks let you apply different page formatting to different areas of your document. Headers and footers let you print information on the top or bottom of every page.

Application Skills In this exercise, you will work with a version of the exercise report you outlined in Exercise 52. You will set margins, insert page breaks and section breaks, apply formatting, and insert headers and footers. When the report is complete, you will print it.

TERMS

Binding Securing pages using stitching, staples, wire, plastic, tape, or glue.

Facing pages A left and a right page set to open opposite each other. Also called mirrored pages or a two-page spread.

Footer Text or graphics printed at the bottom of all pages in a document.

Gutter Space added to a margin to leave room for binding.

Hard page break A nonprinting character that tells Word to start a new page, even if the current page is not filled with text.

Header Text or graphics printed at the top of all pages in a document.

Inside margins Margins along the side of the page where binding is placed. Usually, the left side of right pages and the right side of left pages.

Mirror margins Margins set on facing pages so that the inside margin on both pages are the same and the outside margin on both pages are the same.

Outside margins Margins along the side of the page opposite the binding. Usually, the left side of left pages and the right side of right pages.

Section Part of a document that can be formatted independently from other sections.

Section break A nonprinting character that tells Word to start a new section within a document.

Soft page break The place where Word automatically starts a new page when the current page is filled with text.

Word count The number of words in a document or selection.

NOTES

Set Margins for Multiple Page Documents

- Adjust the **gutter** width of a document to leave room for binding multiple pages.

- You can position the gutter on either side of a page or across the top, depending on where you plan to place the **binding**.

- Use **mirror margins** to set up **facing pages** when you plan to bind double-sided documents.

- With mirror margins, you set **inside margins** for the side of the page along the binding and **outside margins** for the side away from the binding.

- Word 2007 comes with a default Mirrored Margins option that sets the top, bottom, and outside margins to 1" and the inside margin to 1.25".

  ✓ *For more information about setting margins, refer to Exercise 30.*

Insert Page Breaks

- A standard 8.5" by 11" sheet of paper with 1" top and bottom margins has 9" of vertical space for entering text.

  ✓ *The number of lines depends on the font size and spacing settings.*

- Word inserts a **soft page break** to start a new page when the current page is full.

- Soft page breaks adjust automatically if text is inserted or deleted, so a break always occurs when the current page is full.

- Insert a **hard page break** to start a new page before the current page is full. For example, insert a hard page break before a heading that falls at the bottom of a page; the break forces the heading to the top of the next page.

- Breaks move like characters when you insert and delete text. Therefore, you should insert hard page breaks after all editing is complete to avoid having a break occur at an awkward position on the page.

- In Draft view, a soft page break is marked by a dotted line across the page.

- By default, in Print Layout view page breaks are indicated by a space between the bottom of one page and the top of the next page; if you have nonprinting characters displayed, the space where you insert a hard page break is marked by a dotted line with the words *Page Break* centered in it.

- You can hide the space between pages in Print Layout view. If you do, page breaks are marked by a solid black line.

- In Draft view, a hard page break is marked by a dotted line with the words *Page Break* centered in it.

Insert Section Breaks

- A default Word document contains one **section**.

- You can divide a document into multiple sections to apply different formatting to each section. For example, you can set different margins, headers, or footers for each section.

- There are four types of **section breaks**:

  - Next page: inserts a section break and a page break so that the new section will start on the next page.

  - Continuous: inserts a section break so that the new section will start at the insertion point.

  - Even page: inserts a section break and page breaks so the new section will start on the next even-numbered page.

  - Odd page: inserts a section break and page breaks so the new section will start on the next odd-numbered page.

- In Draft view, section breaks display as solid double lines across the width of the page with the words *Section Break* in the middle, followed by the type of break in parentheses.

- In Print Layout view section breaks display only if nonprinting characters display.

Insert Headers and Footers

- Insert a **header** and/or **footer** to print repetitive information such as page numbers, dates, author, or subject on every page of a document.

- By default, headers print .5" from the top of the page; footers print .5" from the bottom of the page.

- Word 2007 comes with a selection of built-in headers available in the Header gallery and footers in the Footer gallery.

- Use the Header & Footer group on the Insert tab of the Ribbon to access the Header and Footer galleries.

- The built-in headers and footers include placeholders—called content controls, or fields—for text. Some also include graphics elements and formatting, and some include fields for data such as the year or the date.

  ✓ *Built-in headers and footers are building blocks, or preformatted objects. For more information on building blocks, refer to Exercise 66. For more information on content controls and fields, refer to Exercise 84.*

- You click a placeholder in the header or footer to type the text you want to display.

  ✓ *Some placeholders have drop-down lists of options; when you click the placeholder, the drop-down arrow displays.*

- When you insert a header/footer, Word displays the header/footer area in Header and Footer view.

- In Header and Footer view, the Header & Footer Tools Design tab becomes available on the Ribbon.

- To edit an existing header or footer, you must change to Header and Footer view.

- By default, a header/footer is linked to the header/footer in the previous section so that they display the same information. You can toggle off the link so that you can enter a different header/footer in each section in a document.

- You can set up a different header/footer on the first page. This is useful for omitting the header/footer on the first page.

- You can set up different headers on odd and even pages.

- Headers and footers do not display in Draft view; use Print Preview or Print Layout view to see them on the screen.

Insert Page Numbers

- Word 2007 comes with galleries of page numbers you can insert into your documents.

- You can insert page numbers in the header, footer, or margins of the page, or at the current insertion point location.

- You can apply formatting to change the number style, include chapter numbers, or restart numbering in a new section.

- Restarting page numbering is useful when your document has a title page that you do not want numbered.

View the Word Count

- Word keeps track of statistics for the current document, such as the **word count**.

- By default the word count displays in the Words area on the status bar.

- If you select part of the document, the status bar displays the word count of the selection and the total word count.

- You can open the Word Count dialog box to view additional statistics such as the number of lines, paragraphs, and characters.

Status bar displays the word count

Header and Footer view

PROCEDURES

Set a Gutter

1. Click the **Page Layout** tab .... `Alt`+`P`

   Page Setup Group

2. Click the Page Setup group **dialog box launcher** 🔲 .... `S`, `P`

   ✓ *If necessary, click the Margins tab* `Ctrl`+`Tab⇄`.

   OR

   a. Click the **Margins** button 🔲 .... `M`
   b. Click **Custom Margins** .... `A`

3. Click **Gutter** text box ...... `Alt`+`G`
4. Type gutter width.
5. Click **Gutter position** drop-down arrow .... `Alt`+`U`
6. Select desired gutter location.
7. Click the **Apply to** drop-down arrow .... `Alt`+`Y`
8. Select one of the following: .... `↓`/`↑`, `↵Enter`

   ■ **This point forward** to create a section starting at the current location.

   ■ **Whole document** to apply the gutter to the entire document.

   ■ **This section** to apply the gutter to the current section.

   ✓ *This section is only available if the document is divided into sections.*

9. Click **OK** .... `↵Enter`

Set Mirror Margins

To use the default mirrored margins:

1. Click the **Page Layout** tab .... `Alt`+`P`

   Page Setup Group

2. Click the **Margins** button 🔲 .... `M`
3. Click **Mirrored** .... `↓`/`↑`, `↵Enter`

To use customized mirrored margins:

1. Click the **Page Layout** tab .... `Alt`+`P`

   Page Setup Group

2. Click the Page Setup group **dialog box launcher** 🔲 .... `S`, `P`

   ✓ *If necessary, click the Margins tab* `Ctrl`+`Tab⇄`.

   OR

   a. Click the **Margins** button 🔲 .... `M`
   b. Click **Custom Margins** .... `A`

3. Click **Multiple pages** drop-down arrow .... `Alt`+`M`
4. Click **Mirror margins** .... `↓`/`↑`, `↵Enter`
5. Click **Top** text box .... `Alt`+`T`
6. Type top margin width.
7. Click **Bottom** text box ..... `Alt`+`B`
8. Type bottom margin width.
9. Click **Inside** text box ...... `Alt`+`N`
10. Type inside margin width.
11. Click **Outside** text box ..... `Alt`+`O`
12. Type outside margin width.
13. Click the **Apply to** drop-down arrow .... `Alt`+`Y`
14. Select one of the following: .... `↓`/`↑`, `↵Enter`

    ■ **This point forward** to create a section starting at the current location.

    ■ **Whole document** to apply the gutter to the entire document.

    ■ **This section** to apply the gutter to the current section.

    ✓ *This section is only available if the document is divided into sections.*

15. Click **OK** .... `↵Enter`

Insert a Hard Page Break (Ctrl+Enter)

1. Click the **Page Layout** tab .... `Alt`+`P`

   Page Setup Group

2. Click the **Breaks** button 🔳 .... `B`
3. Click **Page** .... `P`

   OR

1. Click the **Insert** tab .... `Alt`+`N`

   Pages Group

2. Click the **Page Break** button 🔳 .... `B`

Delete a Hard Page Break

1. Position insertion point on hard page break.
2. Press **Delete** .... `Del`

Insert a Section Break

1. Click the **Page Layout** tab .... `Alt`+`P`

   Page Setup Group

2. Click the **Breaks** button 🔳 .... `B`
3. Click one of the following:

   ■ **Next page** .... `Alt`+`N`
   ■ **Continuous** .... `Alt`+`O`
   ■ **Even page** .... `Alt`+`E`
   ■ **Odd page** .... `Alt`+`D`

Delete a Section Break

1. Position insertion point on break.
2. Press **Delete** .... `Del`

Create Headers/Footers

To insert the same header on every page:

1. Click the **Insert** tab .... Alt + N

   Header & Footer Group

2. Click the **Header** button 🖻 ..... H
3. Click the header you want to insert .... ↓/↑, ↵Enter
4. In the document, click the placeholder and type the text you want in the header.

   ✓ *If a drop-down arrow displays when you click a placeholder, click it to select data to insert.*

   ✓ *You may apply formatting to the text, including fonts, font effects, alignment, tabs, and spacing.*

5. Repeat step 4 for additional placeholders.
6. Click **Close Header and Footer** button ☒ .... Alt + J, H, C

To insert the same footer on every page:

1. Click the **Insert** tab .... Alt + N

   Header & Footer Group

2. Click the **Footer** button 🖻 ..... O
3. Click the footer you want to insert .... ↓/↑, ↵Enter
4. In the document, click the placeholder and type the text you want in the footer.

   ✓ *If a drop-down arrow displays when you click a placeholder, click it to select data to insert.*

   ✓ *You may apply formatting to the text, including fonts, font effects, alignment, tabs, and spacing.*

5. Repeat step 4 for additional placeholders.
6. Click **Close Header and Footer** button ☒ .... Alt + J, H, C

To edit a header:

1. Double-click header to change to Header and Footer view.

   OR

   a. Click the **Insert** tab ... Alt + N

      Header & Footer Group

   b. Click the **Header** button 🖻 .... H
   c. Click **Edit Header** .... E

2. Make changes to header.
3. Click **Close Header and Footer** button ☒ .... Alt + J, H, C

To edit a footer:

1. Double-click header to change to Header and Footer view.

   OR

   a. Click the **Insert** tab ... Alt + N

      Header & Footer Group

   b. Click the **Footer** button 🖻 .... O
   c. Click **Edit Footer** .... E

2. Make changes to footer.
3. Click **Close Header and Footer** button ☒ .... Alt + J, H, C

To switch between header and footer:

1. Double-click header to change to Header and Footer view.

   OR

   a. Click the **Insert** tab ... Alt + N

      Header & Footer Group

   b. Click the **Header** button 🖻 .... H
   c. Click **Edit Header** .... E

      Navigation Group

2. Click **Go to Footer** button 🖻 to display footer area .... Alt + J, H, G
3. Click **Go to Header** button 🖻 to display header area .... Alt + J, H, E

To set up a different first page header/footer:

1. Double-click header to change to Header and Footer view.

   OR

   a. Click the **Insert** tab .... Alt + N

      Header & Footer Group

   b. Click the **Header** button 🖻 .... H
   c. Click **Edit Header** .... E

      Options Group

2. Click to select **Different First Page** check box .... Alt + J, H, A

   ✓ *Click to deselect check box to revert to a single header/footer.*

3. In First Page Header area in document type first page header text.

   ✓ *Leave blank to suppress header on first page.*

   OR

      Header & Footer Group

   a. Click the **Header** button 🖻 ..... Alt + J, H, H
   b. Click the header you want to insert .... ↓/↑, ↵Enter
   c. Click **placeholder(s)** and type text.

      Navigation Group

4. Click **Next Section** button 🖻 .... Alt + J, H, X
5. In Header area type text to display in header on all pages except first page.

   OR

      Header & Footer Group

   a. Click the **Header** button 🖻 ..... Alt + J, H, H
   b. Click the header you want to insert .... ↓/↑, ↵Enter
   c. Click **placeholder(s)** and type text.

Navigation Group

6. Click **Go to Footer** button ▥ to display footer area .... `Alt`+`J`, `H`, `G`

7. In Footer area, type text to display in footer on all pages except first page.

OR

Header & Footer Group

a. Click the **Footer** button 📄 ...... `Alt`+`J`, `H`, `O`

b. Click the footer you want to insert .... `↓`/`↑`, `↵Enter`

c. Click **placeholder(s)** and type text.

Navigation Group

8. Click **Previous Section** button ▦ .... `Alt`+`J`, `H`, `R`

9. In First Page Footer area in document type first page footer text.

✓ *Leave blank to suppress footer on first page.*

OR

Header & Footer Group

a. Click the **Footer** button 📄 ...... `Alt`+`J`, `H`, `O`

b. Click the footer you want to insert .... `↓`/`↑`, `↵Enter`

c. Click **placeholder(s)** and type text.

10. Click **Close Header and Footer** button ✕ .... `Alt`+`J`, `H`, `C`

To use different header/footer in a section:

1. Create sections.
2. Insert header/footer.
3. Display header/footer in next section.

Navigation Group

4. Click **Link to Previous** button ▦ to toggle it off .... `Alt`+`J`, `H`, `K`

5. Edit header/footer as desired.

To set up different odd and even headers/footers:

1. Double-click header to change to Header and Footer view.

OR

a. Click the **Insert** tab .... `Alt`+`N`

Header & Footer Group

b. Click the **Header** button 📄 .... `H`

c. Click **Edit Header** .... `E`

Options Group

2. Click to select **Different Odd & Even Pages** check box .... `Alt`+`J`, `H`, `V`

✓ *Click to deselect check box to revert to a single header/footer.*

3. In Even Page Header area in document, type even page header text.

✓ *If Odd Page Header displays first, click Next Section ▦ or Previous Section ▦ button.*

OR

Header & Footer Group

a. Click the **Header** button 📄 ...... `Alt`+`J`, `H`, `H`

b. Click the header you want to insert .... `↓`/`↑`, `↵Enter`

c. Click **placeholder(s)** and type text.

Navigation Group

4. Click **Next Section** button ▦ .... `Alt`+`J`, `H`, `X`

5. In Odd Page Header area type odd page header text.

OR

Header & Footer Group

a. Click the **Header** button 📄 ...... `Alt`+`J`, `H`, `H`

b. Click the header you want to insert .... `↓`/`↑`, `↵Enter`

c. Click **placeholder(s)** and type text.

Navigation Group

6. Click **Go to Footer** button ▥ .... `Alt`+`J`, `H`, `G`

7. In Odd Page Footer area, type odd page footer text.

OR

Header & Footer Group

a. Click the **Footer** button 📄 ...... `Alt`+`J`, `H`, `O`

b. Click the footer you want to insert .... `↓`/`↑`, `↵Enter`

c. Click **placeholder(s)** and type text.

Navigation Group

8. Click **Previous Section** button ▦ .... `Alt`+`J`, `H`, `R`

9. In Even Page Footer area type even page footer text.

OR

Header & Footer Group

a. Click the **Footer** button 📄 ...... `Alt`+`J`, `H`, `O`

b. Click the footer you want to insert .... `↓`/`↑`, `↵Enter`

c. Click **placeholder(s)** and type text.

10. Click **Close Header and Footer** button ✕ .... `Alt`+`J`, `H`, `C`

Remove All Headers

1. Click the **Insert** tab .... `Alt`+`N`

Header & Footer Group

2. Click the **Header** button 📄 .... `H`

3. Click **Remove Header** .... `R`

Remove All Footers

1. Click the **Insert** tab .... `Alt`+`N`

Header & Footer Group

2. Click the **Footer** button 📄 .... `O`

3. Click **Remove Footer** .... `R`

Insert Page Numbers

1. Click the **Insert** tab .... `Alt`+`N`

   Header & Footer Group

2. Click the **Page Number** button 🔢 .... `N`, `U`

3. Click one of the following locations:
   - **Top of Page** .... `T`
   - **Bottom of Page** .... `B`
   - **Page Margins** .... `P`
   - **Current Position** .... `C`

4. Click page number style to insert .... `↓`/`↑`, `↵Enter`

To insert page numbers in a header/footer placeholder:

1. Double-click header to change to Header and Footer view.

   OR

   a. Click the **Insert** tab ... `Alt`+`N`

      Header & Footer Group

   b. Click the **Header** button 📄 .... `H`
   c. Click **Edit Header** .... `E`

   ✓ If placeholder is in footer, click Go to Footer button.

2. Click placeholder.

   Header & Footer Group

3. Click the **Page Number** button 🔢 .... `N`, `U`

4. Click one of the following locations:
   - **Top of Page** .... `T`
   - **Bottom of Page** .... `B`
   - **Page Margins** .... `P`
   - **Current Position** .... `C`

5. Click page number style to insert .... `↓`/`↑`, `↵Enter`

6. Click **Close Header and Footer** button ❎ .... `Alt`+`J`, `H`, `C`

Change Page Number Formatting

1. Click the **Insert** tab .... `Alt`+`N`

   Header & Footer Group

2. Click the **Page Number** button 🔢 .... `N`, `U`

3. Click **Format Page Numbers** .... `F`

4. Click the **Number format** drop-down arrow .... `Alt`+`F`

5. Click desired format .... `↓`, `↵Enter`

6. Click **OK** .... `↵Enter`

Remove All Page Numbers

1. Click the **Insert** tab .... `Alt`+`N`

   Header & Footer Group

2. Click the **Page Number** button 🔢 .... `N`, `U`

3. Click **Remove Page Numbers** .... `Alt`+`J`, `H`, `R`

View Word Count

- Look at **Words** area on status bar

To display Word Count dialog box:

- Click **Words** area on status bar.

   OR

1. Click **Review** tab .... `Alt`+`R`

   Proofing Group

2. Click **Word Count** button 🔢 .... `W`

   ✓ Click Close or press `Esc` to close dialog box when done.

EXERCISE DIRECTIONS

Apply Formatting

1. Start Word, if necessary.
2. Open ⊙ **53HEALTH**.
3. Save the file as **53HEALTH_xx**.
4. Apply direct formatting as follows: (refer to Illustration A to see the finished result):
   a. Format the title *Exercise for Life* in 26-point Arial, centered, with 12 points of space after.
   b. Format the following four lines in 14-point Arial, centered.
5. Replace the text *Student's Name* with your own name.
6. Apply the Heading 1 style to the following headings: *Introduction, The Impact on Your Health, Getting Started*, and *Conclusion*.
7. Apply the Heading 4 style to the following subheadings: *Disease Control, Weight Control, Mental Health, Doctor Supervision*, and *Safety*

   ✓ *To make the Header 4 style available, you must display All Styles in the Styles task pane. Click the Styles group dialog box launcher, click Options in the task pane, select to show All Styles, and then click OK.*

8. Format the five tips at the end of the text under the subheading **Safety** as a bullet list, as shown in the illustration.
9. Apply the Normal style to all remaining paragraphs, and justify them.

Insert Breaks, Headers, and Page Numbers

1. Position the insertion point at the end of the last paragraph in the introduction and insert a hard page break.
2. Position the insertion point at the beginning of the heading *Getting Started* and insert a next page section break.
3. Position the insertion point anywhere within the first section of the document (pages 1 and 2)
4. Change the margins for the first section to 1.25 inches on the left and right, and leave a gutter of .25" along the left edge of the page.

5. In section 1, insert the Blank (Three Columns) header on page one, as follows:
   a. Click on page 1.
   b. Insert the header.
   c. Click to select the Different First Page check box.
   d. Click the Next Section button to go to the header area on page 2.
   e. Click the placeholder on the left and type **Michigan Avenue Athletic Club**.
   f. Click the placeholder in the center and delete it.
   g. Click the placeholder on the right and type today's date.

   ✓ *You can also insert the date using the Date and Time button on the Ribbon. Refer to Exercise 12 for more information.*

6. Edit the header in section 2 as follows:
   a. Click the Next Section button to go to the Section 2 header area on page 3.
   b. Toggle off the Link to Previous button.
   c. Delete the text **Michigan Avenue Athletic Club** and in its place type **Exercise for Life.**
7. Insert the Plain Number 2 page number at the bottom of the first page.
8. Insert the Plain Number 2 page number at the bottom of the other pages.

   ✓ *Because you have the document set for a different first page, you must insert the page numbers on the first page and then on the other pages.*

9. Close Header and Footer view.
10. Check the spelling and grammar in the document.
11. Check the word count.
12. Display the document in Print Preview. It should look similar to the illustration (3 pages).
13. Print the document.
14. Close the document, saving all changes.

Illustration A

Exercise for Life

Prepared for
Michigan Avenue Athletic Club
by
Student's Name

Introduction

The benefits of regular exercise cannot be overstated. Studies have shown that people who exercise regularly live longer, are healthier, and enjoy a better quality of life than those who do not exercise. It is now generally accepted knowledge that even moderate physical activity performed regularly improves the health and well-being of all individuals.

Despite this knowledge, studies show that more than 60% of American adults are not regularly active and that an astonishing 25% of adults are not active at all. Therefore, the government recommends that schools and communities provide education to promote exercise to people of all ages.

This report has been prepared for Michigan Avenue Athletic Club in order to help spread the word on the importance of physical activity for the health of our members. It is meant as an introduction only. For more information about the health benefits of exercise, or about a particular type of exercise program, please contact any member of our staff. He or she will be happy to help you find the information you need.

1

Michigan Avenue Athletic Club   Today's Date

The Impact on Your Health

It is believed that lack of physical activity and poor diet taken together are the second largest underlying cause of death in the United States. Studies show that even the most inactive people can gain significant health benefits if they accumulate 30 minutes or more of physical activity per day. Some of the known benefits of exercise include disease prevention and control, weight control, and improved mental health.

Exercise can also have an impact on your lifestyle as well. Getting out to exercise may improve your social life by giving you an opportunity to meet new people. It may open up opportunities for your career as well. For example, it is commonly believed that a lot of business is conducted on the golf course or tennis court!

Disease Control

Daily physical activity can help prevent heart disease and stroke by strengthening the heart muscle, lowering blood pressure, raising the levels of good cholesterol and lowering bad cholesterol, improving blood flow, and increasing the heart's working capacity.

By reducing body fat, physical activity helps prevent obesity and may help to prevent and control noninsulin-dependent diabetes.

By increasing muscle strength and endurance and improving flexibility and posture, regular exercise helps to prevent back pain. Regular weight-bearing exercise promotes bone formation and may prevent many forms of bone loss associated with aging.

Weight Control

Research shows that regular physical activity, combined with healthy eating habits, is the most efficient and healthful way to control your weight. Regular physical activity uses excess calories that otherwise would be stored as fat. It also builds and preserves muscle mass and improves the body's ability to use calories.

Mental Health

Studies on the psychological effects of exercise have found that regular physical activity can improve your mood and the way you feel about yourself. Researchers also have found that exercise is likely to reduce depression and anxiety and help you to better manage stress.

2

Illustration A - continued

Exercise for Life   Today's Date

Getting Started

Put some thought and planning into your new exercise routine. You want to set a course that you will be able to maintain. One of the primary problems with exercise programs is that people quit after a short time. Things to consider include what activities you want to do, where you want to do them, and how often you want to participate. It is probably a good idea to find a program or class when you are just starting out. A program will provide you with instruction and supervision. Check out local gyms, universities, or hospitals. You may have community resources as well, such as recreation department or civic center. You may want to join a health club or hire a personal trainer.

Doctor Supervision

Anyone just beginning an exercise regimen should consult a doctor. If you see a doctor regularly he or she may be able to give you a go-ahead on the phone. If not, you should have a complete physical check up.

Safety

Frequently, safety is simply a matter of common sense. You should dress appropriately for the activity, environment, and the weather, including safety equipment and appropriate footwear. If you are using any equipment, make sure it is in proper condition, is appropriate for the activity, and that you know how to use it.

The following are some things you can do to make sure you are exercising safely:

- Start slowly.
- Use safety equipment, such as helmets, knee and elbow pads, and eye protection, to keep you from getting hurt.
- Drink plenty of water.
- Stop if you feel pain.
- Allow your body time to cool down.

Conclusion

Anyone can exercise. Take a walk. Ride a bike. Join a team. Whatever you decide, make physical activity a part of your everyday life. You will see the benefits almost immediately, as you lose weight, lower your blood pressure, and feel better overall.

3

ON YOUR OWN

1. Continue working on the report you started in the On Your Own section of Exercise 52.

2. Use sources such as the Internet or library to research your topic, remembering to record the source information.

3. Start Word and open ⌨OWD52_*xx*, the outline you created in Exercise 52.

4. Save the document as OWD53_*xx*.

5. Change to Print Layout view and start writing the first draft of your report.

6. Keep track of the word count. Your instructor may ask for a minimum or maximum number of words.

7. Use proper formatting for the report. For example, your instructor may want you to double-space the body text paragraphs and use a first line indent.

8. Set appropriate margins. If you plan to bind the report using staples or a clip folder, leave room for the binding.

9. Create headers and footers for the document. Include your name and the date in the header, and center the page numbers in the footer.

10. Insert page breaks if necessary so that headings or paragraphs start at the top of a page instead of at the bottom of one.

11. Insert section breaks as necessary. For example, you may want to have a different header or footer in section 2.

12. When you have completed the first draft, ask a classmate to review it and offer comments and suggestions.

13. Incorporate the comments and suggestions into the document.

14. Check the spelling and grammar in the document.

15. Print the document.

16. Close the document, saving all changes.

Exercise | 54

Skills Covered

■ **Footnotes and Endnotes**

■ **Find and Replace**

■ **Insert Bookmarks**

■ **Select Browse Object**

Software Skills Include footnotes or endnotes in documents to provide information about the source of quoted material, or to supplement the main text. Use the Find, Bookmark, and Browse Object features to locate specific parts of a document, including text, graphics, paragraph marks, etc. Use Find and Replace when you want to automatically replace existing text or formatting with something different.

Application Skills You have been working to complete a report on exercise for Michigan Avenue Athletic Club. In this exercise, you will edit a version of the document using Find and Replace. You will also insert footnotes, endnotes, and bookmarks into the document, browse through the document, and modify the formatting.

TERMS

Bookmark A nonprinting character that you insert and name so that you can quickly find a particular location in a document.

Browse Object A specified element that Word locates and displays when you scroll through a document.

Endnote An explanation or reference to additional material that prints at the end of a document.

Footnote An explanation or reference to additional material that prints at the bottom of a page.

Note reference mark A number or character inserted in the document to refer to footnote or endnote text.

Note text The text of the footnote or endnote citation.

NOTES

Footnotes and Endnotes

■ **Footnotes** or **endnotes** are required in documents that include quoted material, such as research papers.

■ Standard footnotes and endnotes include the following information:

- The author of the quoted material (first name first) followed by a comma.
- The title of the book (in italics), article (in quotation marks), or Web page (in quotation marks) followed by a comma.
- The name of the publication if it is a magazine or journal (in italics).

- The publication volume, number, and/or date (date in parentheses) followed by a colon.
- The page number(s) where the material is located, followed by a period.
- If the source is a Web page, the citation should also include the URL address, enclosed in angle brackets <> and the date you accessed the information.

  ✓ *There are other styles used for footnotes and endnotes. For example, some use periods between parts instead of commas. If you are unsure which style to use, ask your instructor for more information.*

- Footnotes or endnotes can also provide explanations or supplement text. For example, an asterisk footnote might provide information about where to purchase a product mentioned in the text.
- The commands for inserting footnotes and endnotes are in the Footnotes Group on the References tab of the Ribbon.
- When you insert a footnote, Word first inserts a **note reference mark** in the text, then a separator line following the last line of text on the page, and finally the note number corresponding to the note mark below the separator line. You then type and format the **note text** in the note area below the separator line.

Footnotes at the bottom of a page

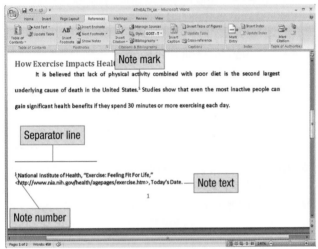

- Endnotes include the same parts as footnotes but are printed on the last page of a document.
- Notes can also be displayed in a ScreenTip by resting the mouse pointer on the note mark.
- Word uses arabic numerals for footnote marks; if endnotes are used in the same document, the endnote marks are roman numerals.
- You can select a different number format or a symbol for the note mark.
- By default, numbering is consecutive from the beginning of the document. You can set Word to restart numbering on each page or each section. You can also change the starting number if you want.
- Word automatically updates numbering if you add or delete footnotes or endnotes, or rearrange the document text.

- Footnotes and endnotes are not displayed in Draft view; to see them, use Print Preview or Print Layout view.
- It is easiest to insert footnotes or endnotes in Print Layout view.

Find and Replace

- Use the options in the Find and Replace dialog box to find and/or replace specific text, nonprinting characters, symbols, formatting, graphics, objects, and other items in a document.
- There are three tabs in the Find and Replace dialog box: Find, Replace, and Go To.
- Use the options on the Find tab to scroll one by one through each occurrence of the Find text, or you can find and replace all occurrences at once.
- You can also highlight all occurrences of the Find text.
- Use the Replace tab to find and then replace items.
- Replace is useful for correcting errors that occur several times in a document, such as a misspelled name.
- In addition to text, you can find and replace formatting, symbols, and special characters such as paragraph marks.
- You can also refine the find procedure by specifying criteria, such as matching whole words only or case.
- Use the Go To tab to move the insertion point to a particular part of the document, such as a bookmark, page, heading, or footnote.
- The Find and Replace commands are in the Editing Group of the Home tab on the Ribbon.

Replace tab of the Find and Replace dialog box

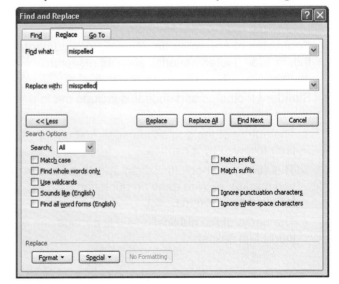

Insert Bookmarks

■ Use a **bookmark** to mark a specific location in a document, such as where you stopped working or where you need to insert information.

■ You can use many bookmarks in one document.

■ Use descriptive bookmark names to make it easier to find the bookmark location that you want.

✓ *You cannot include spaces in a bookmark name.*

■ Use the Go To feature to go directly to a bookmark.

Select Browse Object

■ Use **browse object** to scroll to specific points in a document.

■ There are twelve browse objects from which to choose; rest the mouse pointer on an object to see its name across the top of the object pallet.

● When you choose the Go To browse object, you must specify the object to go to.

● When you choose the Find browse object, you must enter text to Find and/or Replace.

PROCEDURES

Footnotes and Endnotes

To insert a footnote in Print Layout view:

1. Position insertion point after text to footnote.

✓ *If there is a punctuation mark, position it after the punctuation mark.*

2. Click the **References** tab .... Alt+S

   Footnotes Group

3. Click the **Insert Footnote** button AB¹ .... F

4. Type note text.

To insert an endnote in Print Layout view:

1. Position insertion point after text to endnote.

✓ *If there is a punctuation mark, position it after the punctuation mark.*

2. Click the **References** tab .... Alt+S

   Footnotes Group

3. Click the **Insert Endnote** button .... E

4. Type note text.

To display Note Text in ScreenTip:

■ Rest mouse pointer on note reference mark.

To move the insertion point to the next or previous note reference mark:

1. Click the **References** tab .... Alt+S

   Footnotes Group

2. Click the **Next Footnote** button drop-down arrow AB̄ .... O

3. Click one of the following:

   ■ **Next Footnote** .... N
   ■ **Previous Footnote** .... P
   ■ **Next Endnote** X
   ■ **Previous Endnote** V

To display the note area:

1. Click the **References** tab .... Alt+S

   Footnotes Group

2. Click the **Show Notes** button .... H

   ✓ *If there are both footnotes and endnotes in the document, Word displays the View Footnotes dialog box. Click the option button for the area you want to view and then click OK.*

Edit a Footnote or Endnote

1. Double-click note reference mark in text.

   ✓ *The insertion point moves to the note text.*

2. Edit note text.

Delete a Footnote or Endnote

1. Position insertion point to the right of note reference mark in text.

2. Press **Backspace** .... ←Backspace

   ✓ *Mark is selected.*

3. Press **Backspace** .... ←Backspace

   ✓ *Note is deleted.*

Customize the Footnote or Endnote Marks

1. Click the **References** tab .... Alt+S

   Footnotes Group

2. Click the Footnotes Group **dialog box launcher** .... Q

3. Click the **Footnotes** option button .... Alt+F

OR

To change endnotes,
click the **Endnotes** option
button .... Alt + E

4. Click the drop-down
arrow .... Tab⇆ + ↓

5. Click desired
location .... ↓/↑, ⏎Enter

6. Click **Number format** drop-down
arrow .... Alt + N

7. Click desired
format .... ↓/↑, ⏎Enter

OR

a. Click in **Custom Mark** text
box .... Alt + U

b. Type character to use as
mark.

OR

a. Click **Symbol** .... Alt + Y

b. Select
font .... Alt + F, ↓/↑, ⏎Enter

c. Click symbol to
use .... ↓/↑/←/→, ⏎Enter

d. Click **OK** .... ⏎Enter

8. Click **Apply Changes to** drop-down
arrow .... Alt + P

9. Click area to which you
want to apply the
change .... ↓/↑, ⏎Enter

10. Click **Insert** to insert a mark at
current location .... Alt + I

OR

Click **Apply** to apply the
changes without inserting
a mark .... Alt + A

To change the mark starting value:

1. Click the **References**
tab .... Alt + S

Footnotes Group

2. Click the **Footnotes** Group
dialog box launcher ⌐ .... Q

3. Click the **Footnotes** option
button .... Alt + F

OR

To change endnotes, click the
Endnotes option button .... Alt + E

---

4. Click the **Start at** box ...... Alt + S

5. Type starting value or click
increment arrows to set value.

6. Click the **Numbering** drop-down
arrow .... Alt + M

7. Click desired numbering
option .... ↓/↑, ⏎Enter

8. Click **Insert** to insert a mark at
current location .... Alt + I

OR

Click **Apply** to apply the
changes without inserting a
mark .... Alt + A

Find Text (Ctrl+F)

1. Position the insertion point
at the beginning of the
document .... Ctrl + Home

✓ You may start searching at any
point in the document, or you may
search selected text. However, to
be sure to search the entire document, start at the top.

2. Click the **Home** tab .... Alt + H

Editing Group

3. Click the **Find**
button 🔍 .... F, D, F

4. In the Find what box, type text
to find.

5. Click **Find Next** .... Alt + F

✓ Word highlights first occurrence of
text in document. You can click in
the document to edit or format the
text, while leaving the Find and
Replace dialog box open.

6. Repeat step 5 until finished.

✓ Click Cancel at any time to close
the dialog box.

7. Click **OK** .... ⏎Enter

8. Click **Cancel** .... Esc

To find and select all matches at once:

1. Position the insertion point
at the beginning of the
document .... Ctrl + Home

✓ You may start searching at any
point in the document, or you may
search selected text. However, to
be sure to search the entire document, start at the top.

2. Click the **Home** tab .... Alt + H

Editing Group

3. Click the **Find**
button 🔍 .... F, D, F

4. In the Find what box, type text
to find.

5. Click **Find in** .... Alt + I

6. Click **Main Document** .... M

✓ Other locations may be available.
For example, if you have text
selected, you may search the
selected text only.

7. Click **Close** .... Esc

To find and highlight all matches at once:

1. Position the insertion point
at the beginning of the
document .... Ctrl + Home

✓ You may start searching at any
point in the document, or you may
search selected text. However, to
be sure to search the entire document, start at the top.

2. Click the **Home** tab .... Alt + H

Editing Group

3. Click the **Find**
button 🔍 .... F, D, F

4. In the Find what box, type text
to find.

5. Click **Reading Highlight** .... Alt + R

6. Click **Highlight All** .... H

✓ Click **Clear Highlighting** to
remove highlighting.

7. Click **Close** .... Esc

Find and Replace Text (Ctrl+H)

1. Position the insertion point at the beginning of the document.................. Ctrl + Home

   ✓ You may start searching at any point in the document, or you may search selected text. However, to be sure to search the entire document, start at the top.

2. Click the **Home** tab.......... Alt + H

   Editing Group

3. Click the **Replace** button 🔲.... R

4. In the Find what box, type text to find.

5. Click the **Replace with** box.................................. Alt + I

6. Type replacement text.

   ✓ To replace with nothing, leave the Replace with text box blank.

7. Click **Find Next**.......... Alt + F

   ✓ Word highlights first occurrence of text in document.

8. Click **Replace** to replace single occurrence...................... Alt + R

9. Repeat steps 7 and 8 until finished.

   ✓ Click Cancel at any time to close the dialog box.

   OR

   Click **Replace All** to find and replace all occurrences................. Alt + A

10. Click **OK**...................... ↵Enter

11. Click **Close**.................. Esc

To select Find and/or Replace criteria:

1. Position the insertion point at the beginning of the document................. Ctrl + Home

   ✓ You may start searching at any point in the document, or you may search selected text. However, to be sure to search the entire document, start at the top.

2. Click the **Home** tab.......... Alt + H

   Editing Group

3. Click the **Find** button 🔭.............. F, D, F

   OR

   Click the **Replace** button 🔲.... R

4. In the Find what box, type text to find.

5. If necessary, click the **Replace with** box and type replacement text.............. Alt + I, type text

6. Click **More**.................. Alt + M

   ✓ Click Less to hide the criteria and options.

7. Click to select or deselect desired options:

   ■ **Match case** to find only words in same case as text to find.................. Alt + H

   ■ **Find whole words only** to find text as a whole word, not as part of a longer word.................. Alt + Y

   ■ **Use wildcards** to find text specified with wildcard characters.................. Alt + U

   ■ **Sounds like** to find homonyms.................. Alt + K

   ■ **Find all word forms** to find all grammatical forms of text.................. Alt + W

   ■ **Match prefix** to find words with the same prefix.................. Alt + X

   ■ **Match suffix** to find words with the same suffix.................. Alt + T

   ■ **Ignore punctuation characters** to find matching text even if it contains punctuation.................. Alt + S

   ■ **Ignore white-space characters** to find text even if it contains white space.................. Alt + W

8. Complete find and/or replace procedure.

Enter a Special Character to Find or Replace (Ctrl+H)

1. Position the insertion point at the beginning of the document.................. Ctrl + Home

   ✓ You may start searching at any point in the document, or you may search selected text. However, to be sure to search the entire document, start at the top.

2. Click the **Home** tab.......... Alt + H

   Editing Group

3. Click the **Replace** button 🔲.... R

4. Click the **Find what** box... Alt + N

   OR

   Click the **Replace with** box.................................. Alt + I

5. Click **More**.................. Alt + M

6. Click **Special**.................. Alt + E

7. Click special character.............. ↑/↓, ↵Enter

8. Complete find and/or replace procedure.

Select Formatting to Find or Replace (Ctrl+H)

1. Position the insertion point at the beginning of the document............`Ctrl`+`Home`

   ✓ You may start searching at any point in the document, or you may search selected text. However, to be sure to search the entire document, start at the top.

2. Click the **Home** tab..........`Alt`+`H`

   `Editing Group`

3. Click the **Replace** button ...`R`
4. Click the **Find what** box....`Alt`+`N`

   OR

   Click the **Replace with** box..........`Alt`+`I`

5. Click **More**..........`Alt`+`M`
6. Click **Format**..........`Alt`+`O`
7. Click type of formatting to find/replace:

   ■ **Font**..........`F`
   ■ **Paragraph**..........`P`
   ■ **Tabs**..........`T`
   ■ **Language**..........`L`
   ■ **Frame**..........`M`
   ■ **Style**..........`S`
   ■ **Highlight**..........`H`

8. Select specific formatting to find/replace.
9. Click **OK**..........`↵Enter`
10. Complete find and/or replace procedure.

Insert a Bookmark

1. Position the insertion point where you want the bookmark.
2. Click the **Insert** tab..........`Alt`+`N`

   `Links Group`

3. Click the **Bookmark** button ....`K`
4. Click the **Bookmark name** text box..........`Alt`+`B`
5. Type bookmark name.
6. Click **Add**..........`Alt`+`A`

Go To a Bookmark

1. Click the **Insert** tab..........`Alt`+`N`

   `Links Group`

2. Click the **Bookmark** button ....`K`
3. Click name of bookmark to go to..........`↑`/`↓`
4. Click **Go To**..........`Alt`+`G`
5. Click **Close**..........`Esc`

   OR

1. Click the **Home** tab..........`Alt`+`H`

   `Editing Group`

2. Click the **Find** button drop-down arrow..........`F`, `D`
3. Click the **Go To** button ....`G`
4. Click the **Go to what** list..`Alt`+`O`
5. Click **Bookmark**..........`↑`/`↓`

   ✓ Select any object in the Go to what list to browse directly to that object.

6. Click **Enter bookmark name**..........`Alt`+`E`
7. Type bookmark name.

   OR

   Select bookmark name from drop-down list.....`↑`/`↓`, `↵Enter`

8. Click **Go To**..........`Alt`+`T`
9. Click **Close**..........`Esc`

Browse by Object (Alt+Ctrl+Home)

1. Click the **Select Browse Object** button .
2. Click the desired browse object..........`↑`/`↓`/`←`/`→`, `↵Enter`

   ✓ If you select Find or Go To, the appropriate dialog box is displayed.

3. Click the **Previous** button to scroll up to the previous browse object.

   ✓ The ScreenTip for the Previous button includes the name of the current browse object.

   OR

   Click the **Next** button to scroll down to the next browse object.

   ✓ The ScreenTip for the Next button includes the name of the current browse object.

EXERCISE DIRECTIONS

Use Find and Replace

1. Start Word, if necessary.
2. Open ⊙ **54HEALTH**.

    ✓ *This is a version of the report used in Exercise 53.*

3. Save the file as **54HEALTH_xx**.
4. Edit the Header to display the current date in place of the text *Today's Date* on page 2.
5. Edit the fifth line of the document to replace the text *Student's Name* with your name.
6. Use the Replace command with the Match Case option selected to locate the first occurrence of *MAAC* and to replace it with the full name **Michigan Avenue Athletic Club**.
7. Replace all remaining occurrences of the text *MAAC* in the entire document (including header) with **Michigan Avenue Athletic Club**.

    ✓ *Make sure the Search option is set to All.*

8. Use the Find command to highlight all occurrences of the club name—*Michigan Avenue Athletic Club*—in the main document.
9. Close the Find dialog box and format the selected text with italics.

Insert Footnotes, Endnotes, and Bookmarks

1. Position the insertion point at the end of the third sentence in the first paragraph of the introduction—to the right of the final punctuation. (See Illustration A.)
2. Insert a footnote as follows:

    National Center for Chronic Disease Prevention and Health Promotion, "Physical Activity and Health: A Report of the Surgeon General," *Executive Summary* **(11/17/99): page 12.**

3. At the end of the first sentence under the heading *How Exercise Impacts Health*, insert the following footnote:

    National Institute of Health, "Exercise: Feeling Fit For Life," <http://www.nia.nih.gov/health/agepages/exercise.htm>, Today's Date.

4. At the end of the third paragraph under the heading **How Exercise Impacts Health** insert the following endnote:

    For more information, write to the President's Council on Physical Fitness and Sports, Room 738-H Humphrey Building, 200 Independence Avenue, SW, Washington, DC 20201-0004.

5. Move the insertion point to the beginning of the document and then open the Find dialog box.
6. Clear all selected options, and then locate the first occurrence of the word *stress*.
7. Insert a bookmark at the found location, named **Stress**.

Browse by Object

1. Move the insertion point back to the beginning of the document.
2. Use Browse by Object to go to the first footnote.
3. Use Browse by Object to go to the second footnote.
4. Use Browse by Object to go to the Stress bookmark.

    ✓ *Select the Go To object.*

5. Close the Go To dialog box.
6. Check the spelling and grammar in the document and correct or ignore errors as necessary.
7. Display the document in Print Preview. It should look similar to the one in Illustration A.
8. Close Print Preview.
9. Print the document.
10. Close the document, saving all changes.

Exercise for Life

Prepared for

Michigan Avenue Athletic Club

by

Student's Name

Introduction

The benefits of regular exercise cannot be overstated. It is now generally accepted knowledge that even moderate physical activity performed regularly improves the health and well-being of all individuals. Despite this knowledge, studies show that more than 60% of American adults are not regularly active and that an astonishing 25% of adults are not active at all.[1] Therefore, the government recommends that schools and communities provide education to promote exercise to people of all ages.

This report has been prepared for *Michigan Avenue Athletic Club* in order to help spread the word on the importance of physical activity. It is meant as an introduction only. For more information please contact any staff member.

How Exercise Impacts Health

It is believed that lack of physical activity combined with poor diet is the second largest underlying cause of death in the United States.[2] Studies show that even the most inactive people can gain significant health benefits if they spend 30 minutes or more exercising each day.

---

[1] National Center for Chronic Disease Prevention and Health Promotion, "Physical Activity and Health: A Report of the Surgeon General," Executive Summary (11/17/99): page 12.
[2] National Institute of Health, "Exercise: Feeling Fit For Life,"
<http://www.nia.nih.gov/health/agepages/exercise.htm>, Today's Date.

1

Illustration A - continued

Michigan Avenue Athletic Club   Today's Date

Daily physical activity can help prevent heart disease and stroke by strengthening the heart muscle, lowering blood pressure, raising the levels of good cholesterol, lowering bad cholesterol, improving blood flow, and increasing the heart's working capacity.

By increasing muscle strength and endurance and improving flexibility and posture, regular exercise helps to prevent back pain. Regular weight-bearing exercise promotes bone formation and may prevent many forms of bone loss associated with aging.[i]

Regular physical activity, combined with healthy eating habits, is considered the most efficient and healthful way to control weight. Regular exercise uses excess calories that otherwise would be stored as fat. By reducing body fat, physical activity helps prevent obesity and may help to prevent and control noninsulin-dependent diabetes. It also builds and preserves muscle mass, and improves the body's ability to use calories.

Studies on the psychological effects of exercise have found that regular physical activity can improve your mood and the way you feel about yourself. Researchers also have found that exercise is likely to reduce depression and anxiety and help you to better manage stress.

Conclusion

Anyone can exercise. Take a walk. Ride a bike. Join a team. You will see the benefits almost immediately, as you lose weight, lower your blood pressure, and feel better overall. Exercise can also have an impact on your lifestyle. Getting out to exercise may improve your social life by giving you an opportunity to meet new people. It may open up opportunities for your career as well. For example, it is commonly believed that a lot of business is conducted on the gold course or tennis court! Whatever you decide, make physical activity a part of your everyday life.

---

[i] For more information, write to the President's Council on Physical Fitness and Sports, Room 738-H Humphrey Building, 200 Independence Avenue, SW, Washington, DC 20201-0004.

2

ON YOUR OWN

1. Continue working on your research report by adding citations and marking text that needs additional work.
2. Open the document 🖮 OWD53_*xx* that you used in the On Your Own section of Exercise 53.
3. Save the document as OWD54_*xx*.
4. Use Find to locate text that requires citations.
5. Insert footnotes or endnotes as necessary.
6. Use Browse to check your footnotes or endnotes.
7. If necessary, use Find and Replace to locate and replace specific text, such as an abbreviation or acronym.
8. Insert bookmarks to mark text that needs additional work. For example, you may want to mark a fact for which you need to check a citation, or a paragraph that you think needs to be rewritten.
9. Make edits as necessary, and save your changes.
10. Ask a classmate to review the document and make comments or suggestions.
11. Incorporate the suggestions into the paper.
12. Print the document.
13. Close the document, saving all changes.

Exercise | 55

Skills Covered

- **Use Full Screen Reading View**
- **Use Document Map**
- **Use Thumbnails**
- **Preview Multiple Pages**

- **Copy or Move Text from One Page to Another**
- **Print Specific Pages**

Software Skills Full Screen Reading view makes it easier to read a document on-screen. Preview multiple pages to see how an entire multipage document will look when it is printed. For example, when you preview more than one page at a time, you can see headers and footers on every page and determine whether the text flow from one page to the next looks professional. The Document Map helps you quickly locate sections of a long document without spending time scrolling through pages. Printing specific pages or selected text is an option that can save paper and time if you find that you only need hard copies of parts of a document.

Application Skills Michigan Avenue Athletic Club has expanded the report on exercise. In this exercise, you will preview, proofread, and edit the document. You will use the Document Map to navigate through the document to find headings and paragraphs. You will move text from one page to another. You will preview multiple pages to determine whether page breaks are in the correct locations. Finally, you will print selected pages of the document.

TERMS

Document Map A vertical pane that opens on the left side of the document window to show the major headings and sections in a document; click a topic in the pane to go to it.

Thumbnails Small pictures.

NOTES

Use Full Screen Reading View

- Use Full Screen Reading view to read documents on-screen.
- When you switch to Full Screen Reading view, the document text is formatted to display by the screen—not by the page.
- Buttons at the top of the screen provide access to tools and options you might need while working in Full Screen Reading view.

- By default, two pages display on screen at once, but you can select to display only one page.
- You can also select to display pages as they will print.
- You can increase or decrease the size of the text on the screen without changing the actual size of the font in the document.
- Some visual elements—such as tables and pictures—may not display properly in Full Screen Reading view.

- By default, you cannot enter, edit, or format text in Full Screen Reading view, but you can select an option to allow typing so you can make changes while you read.

Full Screen Reading view

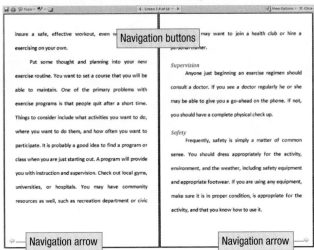

- You toggle the Document Map on and off by selecting the Document Map check box in the Show/Hide Group on the View tab of the Ribbon.

Document Map

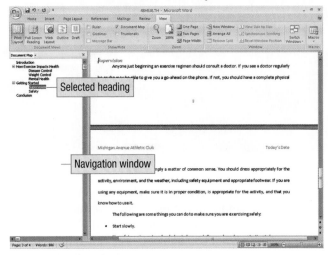

Use Document Map

- **Document Map** is useful for navigating through long documents.
- Word displays the Document Map in the Navigation window, which is a pane on the left side of the document window.
- The Document Map shows headings and major topics in an outline format.

  ✓ *Outlines are covered in Exercise 52.*

- If there are no headings or major topics, the Document Map is empty.
- You can expand and collapse the Document Map as you would an outline to show the headings you need.
- To move the insertion point to a heading, click it in the Document Map.

Use Thumbnails

- **Thumbnails** are also useful for navigating in a longer document.
- Word displays thumbnails in the Navigation window on the left side of the screen.
- Each thumbnail represents one document page.

  ✓ *In Full Screen Reading view, each thumbnail represents one screen.*

- Click a thumbnail to go to that page.
- You toggle Thumbnails on and off by selecting the Thumbnails check box in the Show/Hide Group on the View tab of the Ribbon.

Thumbnails

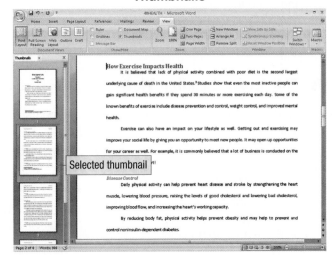

Preview Multiple Pages

- You can preview multiple pages in either Print Layout view or Print Preview.
- Preview multiple pages to get an overall view of the document, not to edit or format text.

  ✓ *You can edit in Print Preview, but it is difficult if the pages are small.*

- You can select the number of pages you want to display using the tools in the Zoom group on the View tab of the Ribbon in Print Layout view, or on the Print Preview tab.
- The more pages that display, the smaller the pages appear on the screen, so the harder it is to read the text.

  ✓ *For more on using Print Preview, refer to Exercise 9.*

Copy or Move Text from One Page to Another

- Use standard copy and move techniques to copy or move text from one page in a document to another page.

  ✓ *Moving text is covered in Exercise 9; Copying text is covered in Exercise 20.*

- Use Cut and Paste to move text.
- Use Copy and Paste to copy text.
- If you can see both locations on the screen at the same time, you can drag and drop selections. Otherwise, you can use the Clipboard.
- Copying and/or moving text may affect hard breaks already inserted in a document.

Print Specific Pages

- Select Print options to print a specific page, several pages, selected text, or the current page.
- In the Print dialog box, you can specify consecutive pages or nonconsecutive pages. You can also specify pages to print by page number.

PROCEDURES

Use Full Screen Reading View

To display Full Screen Reading view:

- Click the **Full Screen Reading** button on the status bar:

  OR

1. Click **View** tab .... Alt + W

   Document Views Group

2. Click the **Full Screen Reading** button .... F

To close Full Screen Reading view:

- Click the **Close** button ☒ in the upper-right corner of the screen .... Esc

To display one page:

1. Display Full Screen Reading View.
2. Click **View Options** button in the upper right of the screen.
3. Click **Show One Page** .... H

To display two pages:

1. Display Full Screen Reading View.
2. Click **View Options** button in the upper right of the screen.
3. Click **Show Two Pages** .... W

To display pages as they will print:

1. Display Full Screen Reading View.
2. Click **View Options** button in the upper right of the screen.
3. Click **Show Printed Page** .... P

   ✓ *Repeat steps 1-3 to return to displaying screens.*

To increase text size:

1. Display Full Screen Reading View.
2. Click **View Options** button in the upper right of the screen.
3. Click **Increase Text Size** I

To decrease text size:

1. Display Full Screen Reading View.
2. Click **View Options** button in the upper right of the screen.
3. Click **Decrease Text Size** .... D

To allow typing and formatting:

1. Display Full Screen Reading View.
2. Click **View Options** button in the upper right of the screen.
3. Click **Allow Typing** .... Y

Navigate in Full Screen Reading View

To display next screen:

- Click **Next Screen** navigation button ▶ at top of screen .... Ctrl + PgDn
- Click **Next Screen** arrow ➡ in lower right of page .... Ctrl + PgDn

To display previous screen:

- Click **Previous Screen** navigation button ◀ at top of screen......................Ctrl)+(PgUp)
- Click **Previous Screen** arrow ← in lower left of page.............................Ctrl)+(PgUp)

To jump to a screen:

1. Type number of screen to go to.
2. Press **Enter**.......................(↵Enter)

   OR

1. Click **Navigation** drop-down arrow Screen 3 of 9 ▾.
2. Click one of the following:
   - **Go Back**......(B), (→), (↓), (↵Enter)

   ✓ *If more than one screen has been displayed, a submenu may display. Click screen on submenu, or use arrow keys to select screen on submenu and press (↵Enter).*

   - **Go Forward**......(F), (→), (↓), (↵Enter)

   ✓ *If more than one screen has been displayed, a submenu may display. Click screen on submenu, or use arrow keys to select screen on submenu and press (↵Enter).*

   - **Go to Farthest Read Screen**......(A)
   - **Go to First Screen**......(O)
   - **Go to Last Screen**......(L)

To jump to a heading:

1. Click **Navigation** drop-down arrow Screen 3 of 9 ▾.
2. Click heading.

Use Document Map

To display Document Map:

1. Click **View** tab...............(Alt)+(W)

   Show/Hide Group

2. Click to select **Document Map** check box.......................(V), (M)

   ✓ *If Thumbnails are displayed, click Switch Navigation Window drop-down arrow and click Document Map.*

To display Document Map in Full Screen Reading view:

1. Display Full Screen Reading view.
2. Click **Navigation** drop-down arrow Screen 3 of 9 ▾.
3. Click **Document Map**......(D)

To hide Document Map:

- Click **Close** button ✕ in Navigation window.

   OR

1. Click **View** tab.........(Alt)+(W)

   Show/Hide Group

2. Click to deselect **Document Map** check box.....................(V), (M)

To jump to a heading:

- Click heading in Document Map.

To expand/collapse a heading:

- Click **Expand** ⊞ or **Collapse** ⊟ next to heading in Document Map.

   OR

1. Click heading in Document Map.
2. Right-click blank area in Navigation window.
3. Click one of the following:
   - **Expand**......(E)
   - **Collapse**......(C)

To select levels to display:

1. Right-click blank area in Navigation window.
2. Click heading level to display.................*level number*

Use Thumbnails

To display Thumbnails:

1. Click **View** tab.................(Alt)+(W)

   Show/Hide Group

2. Click to select **Thumbnails** check box.................(H)

   ✓ *If Document Map is displayed, click Switch Navigation Window drop-down arrow and click Thumbnails.*

To display Thumbnails in Full Screen Reading view:

1. Display Full Screen Reading view.
2. Click **Navigation** drop-down arrow Screen 3 of 9 ▾.
3. Click **Thumbnails**......(H)

To hide Thumbnails:

- Click **Close** button ✕ in Navigation window.

   OR

1. Click **View** tab.........(Alt)+(W)

   Show/Hide Group

2. Click to deselect **Thumbnails** check box.......................(H)

To jump to a page:

- Click thumbnail in Navigation window.

Preview Multiple Pages

In Print Layout View:

1. Click the **View** tab...........(Alt)+(W)

   Zoom Group

2. Click **Two Pages** button ⊡ to display two pages.................(2)

   OR

   a. Click **Zoom** button 🔍......(Q)
   b. Click **Many Pages**......(Alt)+(M)
   c. Drag across number of rows and pages to display.
   d. Click **OK**.................(↵Enter)

In Print Preview:

1. Click **Office Button** 🔘......(Alt)+(F)
2. Point to **Print**.......................(W)
3. Click **Print Preview**.................(V)

   Zoom Group

4. Click **Two Pages** button ⊡ to display two pages...(Alt)+(P), (2)

   OR

   a. Click **Zoom** button 🔍.........(Alt)+(P), (Q)
   b. Click **Many Pages**.........(Alt)+(M)
   c. Drag across number of rows and pages to display.
   d. Click **OK**.................(↵Enter)

Change Back to One Page Preview

In Print Layout View:
1. Click the **View** tab .... Alt + W

   > **Zoom Group**

2. Click **One Page** button 🔳 1

In Print Preview:
1. Click **Office Button** 🔳 ..... Alt + F
2. Point to **Print** .... W
3. Click **Print Preview** V

   > **Zoom Group**

4. Click **One Page**
   button 🔳 .... Alt + P , 1

Use Copy and Paste to Copy Text from One Page to Another *(Ctrl+C, Ctrl+V)*

1. Select text to copy.
2. Click **Home** tab .... Alt + H

   > **Clipboard Group**

3. Click **Copy** button 📋 C

   OR

   a. Right-click selection.
   b. Click **Copy** C

4. Display other page and position insertion point in new location.
5. Click **Paste**
   button 📋 .... Alt + H , V , P

   OR

   a. Right-click insertion point location.
   b. Click **Paste** .... P

Use Drag-and-Drop Editing to Copy Text

1. Display multiple pages.
2. Select text to copy.
3. Move mouse pointer anywhere over selected text.
4. Press and hold Ctrl .... Ctrl
5. Drag mouse to position mouse pointer/insertion point at new location.

   > ✓ As you drag, the mouse pointer changes to the copy pointer, which is a box with a dotted shadow and a plus sign attached to an arrow 🔳 .

6. Release mouse button to copy selection to insertion point location.
7. Release Ctrl .

Move Text from One Page to Another

1. Select text to move.
2. Press F2 .... F2
3. Display other page and position insertion point at new location.
4. Press ↵Enter .... ↵Enter

Use Cut and Paste to Move Text *(Ctrl+X, Cltr+V)*

1. Select text to move.
2. Click **Home** tab .... Alt + H

   > **Clipboard Group**

3. Click **Cut** button ✂ X

   OR

   a. Right-click selection.
   b. Click **Cut** .... T

4. Display other page and position insertion point in new location.

Use Drag-and-Drop Editing to Move Text

1. Display multiple pages on screen.
2. Select text to move.

   > ✓ If necessary, in Print Preview, toggle off the Magnifier check box in Zoom group.

3. Move mouse pointer anywhere over selected text.
4. Click and drag selection to new location.

   > ✓ As you drag, the mouse pointer changes to the move pointer, which is a box with a dotted shadow attached to an arrow 🔳 .

5. Release mouse button to move selection to insertion point location.

Print Specific Pages *(Cltr+P)*

To print a single page:
1. Click **Office Button** 🔳 ..... Alt + F
2. Click **Print** .... P
3. Click **Pages** .... Alt + G
4. Type page number.
5. Click **OK** .... ↵Enter

To print consecutive pages:
1. Click **Office Button** 🔳 ..... Alt + F
2. Click **Print** .... P
3. Click **Pages** .... Alt + G
4. Type first page number, hyphen, last page number.

   > ✓ For example: to print pages 3 through 5, type: 3-5.

5. Click **OK** .... ↵Enter

To print nonconsecutive pages:
1. Click **Office Button** ⬚ ...... Alt + F
2. Click **Print** .... P
3. Click **Pages** .... Alt + G
4. Type each page number separated by commas.

   ✓ *For example: to print pages 3, 5 and 7, type: 3,5,7.*

5. Click **OK** .... ↵Enter

   ✓ *You can combine consecutive and nonconsecutive pages. For example, 2-5, 7,10.*

To print current page:
1. Click **Office Button** ⬚ ...... Alt + F
2. Click **Print** .... P
3. Click **Current Page** .... Alt + E
4. Click **OK** .... ↵Enter

To print selected text:
1. Select text to print.
2. Click **Office Button** ⬚ ...... Alt + F
3. Click **Print** .... P
4. Click **Selection** .... Alt + S
5. Click **OK** .... ↵Enter

EXERCISE DIRECTIONS

Use Full Screen Reading View
1. Start Word, if necessary.
2. Open 💿 **55HEALTH**.

   ✓ *This is a version of the report used in Exercise 54.*

3. Save the file as **55HEALTH_xx**.
4. Change the text *Student's Name* on line 5 to your own name, and edit the header on page 2 to display the actual date instead of the text Today's Date.
5. Change to Full Screen Reading view.
6. Display one page instead of two. (If one is displayed, display two.)
7. Go to screen 3.
8. Display pages as they will print.
9. Go to the last page.
10. Display two pages.
11. Switch back to displaying screens.
12. Increase the size of the text.
13. Go to the first page.
14. Close Full Screen Reading view.

Use Document Map and Thumbnails
1. Display the Document Map.
2. Using the Document Map, go to the heading *Introduction* and change the formatting to leave 12 points of space after.
3. Repeat step 2 for each heading and subheading in the document.
4. Go to the heading *Disease Control*.
5. Select the heading and the three paragraphs under it and print the selection.
6. Display Thumbnails.
7. Display page 1.
8. Display page 5.
9. Close the Navigation window.
10. Display all pages of the document on-screen at the same time.
11. Zoom in on the bottom of page 4.
12. Insert a hard page break to move the heading *Conclusion* to the top of page 5.
13. Display two pages at the same time, then page up to display pages 3 and 4.
14. Select the first paragraph under the heading *Getting Started* on page 3 and move it so it becomes the second paragraph under the heading *Supervision* on page 4. The screen should look similar to Illustration A.
15. Print pages 3 and 5.
16. Close the document, saving all changes.

Illustration A

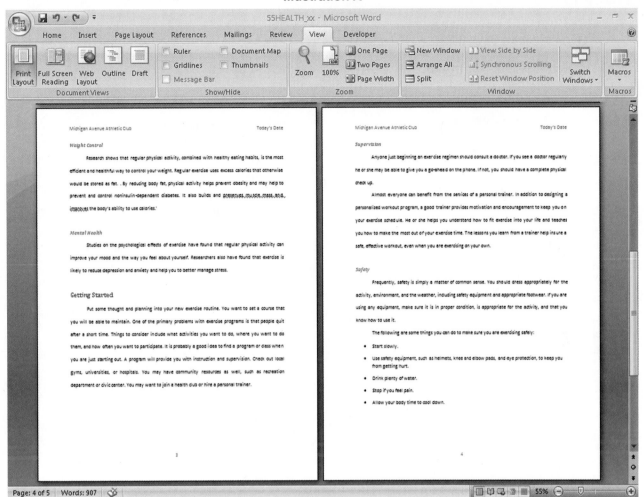

ON YOUR OWN

1. Continue working on your research report using the skills you learned in this exercise to edit and improve the document.
2. Open the document ⌨OWD54_*xx* that you used in the On Your Own section of Exercise 54.
3. Save the document as **OWD55_*xx***.
4. Change to Full Screen Reading view and proofread the document. If necessary, enable typing and make edits and improvements.
5. Use the Document Map or Thumbnails to navigate through the document.
6. When you have completed proofreading the document, close Full Screen Reading view.
7. Preview multiple pages of the document at one time.
8. If necessary, move or copy text from one page in the document to another to improve the flow of the report. (You can always use Undo to revert back, if necessary.)
9. Preview all pages at once.
10. If necessary, adjust page and section breaks.
11. Print one page of the document and ask a classmate to read it and offer comments and suggestions.
12. If there is a particular part of the document that you feel needs work, select it, print it, and ask another classmate to read it and offer comments and suggestions.
13. Use the feedback you get from your classmates to make changes and corrections to improve the report.
14. Close the document, saving all changes.

- **Insert Comments**
- **Track Changes**
- **Customize Revision Marks**

- **Compare and Combine Documents**
- **Accept/Reject Changes**

Software Skills   Insert comments in a document when you want to include a private note to the author, another reader, or to yourself, in much the same way you might attach a slip of paper to a hard copy print out. Track changes made to a document to monitor when and how edits are made. Tracking changes lets you consider revisions before incorporating them into a document. If you agree with the change, you can accept it, but if you disagree with the change, you can reject it. You can track changes made by one person, or by many people, which is useful when you are collaborating on a document with others. When you compare and merge documents, differences between the two are marked as revisions.

Application Skills   The Director of Training at Restoration Architecture has asked you to revise a document listing in-house training courses. In this exercise, you will use the Track Changes feature while you edit the document and insert comments. You will then review the document to accept or reject the changes. Finally, you will compare the document to an earlier version, then print it.

TERMS

Balloon An area in which comment text or revisions are displayed.

Comment A hidden note attached to a document for reference.

Comment mark Color-coded brackets that mark the location of a comment in a document.

Ink annotations Comments, notes, and other marks added to a document using a tablet PC or other type of pen device.

Inline Within the document text.

Reviewing pane A window where revisions and comments can be entered and displayed.

Revision marks Formatting applied to text in a document to identify where insertions, deletions, and formatting changes have been made.

NOTES

Insert Comments

- Insert **comments** to annotate text, communicate with readers, or to attach reminders or questions to a document.

- When you insert a comment, Word inserts **comment marks** around the word to the left of the current insertion point location, or around selected text.

- You can select to display comments **inline** or in **balloons**.

  - If you select inline, you type the comment text in the **Reviewing pane**.

  - If you select balloons, you type the comment text in a balloon, which is connected to the comment mark with a dotted line.

  ✓ *In Draft view, you must use the Reviewing pane.*

- Comment marks and comment balloons are color coded by reviewer.

- In addition, the reviewer's initials display with the comment, either inline or in the comment balloon, and each comment by a reviewer is numbered sequentially.

- You can select whether or not you want to display comments on the screen.

- Comments can be printed with a document.

- The command for inserting a comment is in the Comments group on the Review tab of the Ribbon.

- You can use options in the Tracking group on the Review tab to control the way comments display.

Comment in a balloon

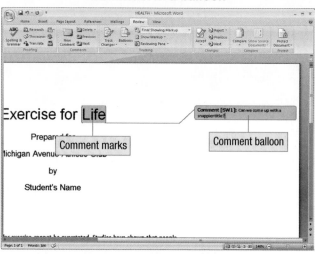

Comment in Reviewing pane

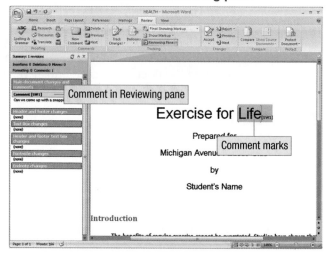

Track Changes

- Turn on Word's Track Changes feature to apply **revision marks** to all insertions, deletions, and formatting changes in a document.

- When Track Changes is active, the Track Changes button in the Tracking group on the Review tab of the Ribbon is highlighted.

- The way that revisions are marked on-screen depends on whether you are using the Reviewing pane or balloons, and on the selected Display for Review option:

  - Final Showing Markup (default). This option displays inserted text in color with an underline, and all formatting changes are applied. Deleted text is either displayed in a balloon or it is marked inline using a colored strikethrough effect.

  - Final. This option displays the document as it would look if all of the revisions that had been entered were incorporated in the document.

  - Original Showing Markup. This option displays deleted text in color with a strikethrough effect. Inserted text and formatting are either displayed in revision balloon or marked inline using a colored underline.

  - Original. This option displays the document as it would look if no revisions had been made.

- Like comments, revisions are color coded by reviewer.

- By default, Word also inserts a vertical line to the left of any changed line to indicate where revisions occur in the document.

- You can view descriptions of all revisions in the Reviewing pane.

- You can select which changes you want displayed on-screen. For example, you can display insertions and deletions, but not formatting.

- You can even set Word to show only the changes made by one reviewer at a time.

  ✓ *Word 2007 also supports the use of **ink annotations**.*

- The commands for tracking changes are in the Tracking group on the Review tab of the Ribbon.

Tracked changes in balloons

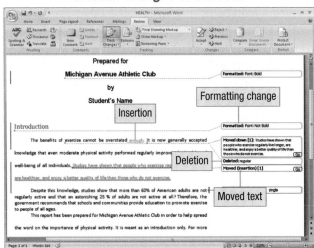

Tracked changes in Reviewing pane

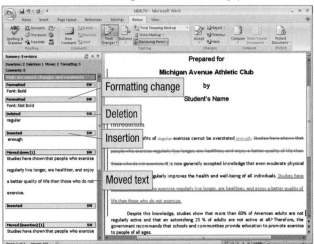

Customize Revision Marks

- You can customize revision marks in the Track Changes Options dialog box as follows:
  - You can select the color you want to use.
  - You can select the formatting used to indicate changes. For example, you can mark formatting changes with a double-underline, or insertions with color only instead of color and an underline.
  - You can customize the location of the vertical bar used to mark lines that have been changed.
  - You can also customize the way balloons are displayed in a document.

Compare and Combine Documents

- You can compare two documents to mark the differences between them.
- To compare documents, you select the original document and the revised document.
- Word uses revision marks to indicate the differences between the two.
- You can display the revision marks in the original document, the revised document, or in a new document.
- By default, the initials of the person who edited the revised document are used to mark the revisions, but you can use different initials or text if you want.
- Comparing documents is useful if you have more than one version of a document and need to see what changes have been made, or if someone has edited a document without using the track changes features.
- Use the Combine feature to combine revisions made by more than one reviewer into a single document.

- The commands for comparing and combining documents are in the Compare group on the Review tab of the Ribbon.

Compare Documents dialog box

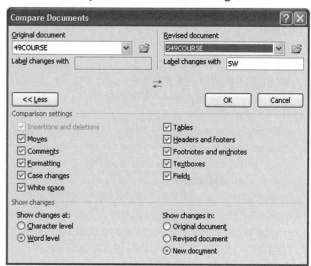

Accept/Reject Changes

- Revision marks remain stored as part of a document until the changes are either accepted or rejected.
- To incorporate edits into a document file, accept the changes.
- To cancel the edits and erase them from the file, reject the changes.
- You can also delete comments.
- The commands for accepting and rejecting changes are in the Changes group on the Review tab of the Ribbon.

PROCEDURES

Display Reviewing Pane

1. Click **Review** tab .... Alt+R

   Tracking Group

2. Click **Reviewing Pane** button 🔲 drop-down arrow .... T, P
3. Click one of the following:
   - **Reviewing Pane Vertical** to display the pane vertically on the left side of the window V
   - **Reviewing Pane Horizontal** to display the pane horizontally at the bottom of the window .... H

   ✓ *Repeat steps to hide reviewing pane.*

Select Balloon Options

1. Click **Review** tab .... Alt+R

   Tracking Group

2. Click **Balloons** button 🔲 drop-down arrow .... T, B
3. Click one of the following:
   - **Show Revisions in Balloons** to display all comments and revisions in balloons .... B
   - **Show All Revisions Inline** to display all comments and revisions in Reviewing pane I
   - **Show Only Comments and Formatting in Balloons** to display comments and formatting revisions in balloons, and insertions and deletions in the Reviewing pane C

   ✓ *A check mark next to option indicates it is already selected.*

Insert a Comment

1. Position insertion point where you want to insert comment.
   OR
   Select text to comment on.
2. Click **Review** tab .... Alt+R

---

3. Click **New Comment** button 🔲 C

   ✓ *Depending on balloon options, insertion point displays in either Reviewing pane or comment balloon.*

4. Type comment text.

Edit a Comment

1. Click in comment text.
   OR
   a. Right-click text within comment marks.
   b. Click **Edit Comment** .... E
2. Edit comment text.

Browse through Comments

1. Display Reviewing pane.
2. Scroll up and down in Reviewing pane.
   OR
1. Click **Review** tab .... Alt+R

   Comments Group

2. Do one of the following:
   - Click **Next** Comment button 🔲 .... N
   - Click **Previous** Comment button 🔲 V

Delete a Comment

1. Right-click text within comment marks.
2. Click **Delete Comment** .... M
   OR
1. Click text within comment marks.
2. Click **Review** tab .... Alt+R

   Comments Group

3. Click **Delete Comment** button 🔲 .... D, D

Delete all Comments

1. Click text within comment marks.
2. Click **Review** tab .... Alt+R

   Comments Group

3. Click **Delete Comment** button 🔲 drop-down arrow .... D
4. Click **Delete All Comments in Document** .... O

Turn On Track Changes (Ctrl+Shift+E)

1. Click **Review** tab .... Alt+R

   Tracking Group

2. Click **Track Changes** button 🔲 .... G, G

   ✓ *Repeat steps to turn feature off.*

Select Display for Review

1. Click **Review** tab .... Alt+R

   Tracking Group

2. Click **Display for Review** 🔲 drop-down arrow .... T, D
3. Click one of the following: .... ↓/↑, ↵Enter
   - **Final Showing Markup**
   - **Final**
   - **Original Showing Markup**
   - **Original**

Select Marks to Display

1. Click **Review** tab .... Alt+R

   Tracking Group

2. Click **Show Markup** 🔲 drop-down arrow .... T, M
3. Click option to show/hide:
   - **Comments** C
   - **Ink** .... K
   - **Insertions and Deletions** I
   - **Formatting** .... F
   - **Markup Area Highlight** .... H

   ✓ *A checkmark indicates option is displayed. Click to hide it.*

Select Reviewers Marks to Display

1. Click **Review** tab .... `Alt`+`R`

   Tracking Group

2. Click **Show Markup** 📄 drop-down arrow .... `T`, `M`
3. Click **Reviewers** .... `R`
4. Click **All Reviewers** .... `A`

   OR

   Click name of reviewer to display.

   ✓ *Repeat to select additional reviewers.*

   ✓ *A checkmark indicates reviewer's marks are displayed.*

Compare Documents

1. Click **Review** tab .... `Alt`+`R`

   Compare Group

2. Click **Compare** button 🔳 .... `M`
3. Click **Compare** .... `C`
4. Click **Original document** drop-down arrow .... `Alt`+`O`
5. Click document name .... `↓`/`↑`, `↵Enter`

   ✓ *If document is not in list, click Browse for Original button to locate and select document.*

6. Click **Revised document** drop-down arrow .... `Alt`+`R`
7. Click document name .... `↓`/`↑`, `↵Enter`

   ✓ *If document is not in list, click Browse for Revised button to locate and select document.*

8. Click **Label changes with** box .... `Alt`+`B`
9. Type text to use to label changes, if necessary.
10. Click **More** .... `Alt`+`M`
11. Under Comparison settings, click to select or clear options to display.

---

12. Under Show changes at, click one of the following:
    - **Character level** to mark revisions character .... `Alt`+`C`
    - **Word level** to mark revisions by word .... `Alt`+`W`
13. Under Show changes in, click one of the following:
    - **Original document** ...... `Alt`+`T`
    - **Revised document** .... `Alt`+`I`
    - **New document** .... `Alt`+`U`
14. Click **OK** .... `↵Enter`

Combine Documents

1. Click **Review** tab .... `Alt`+`R`

   Compare Group

2. Click **Compare** button 🔳 .... `M`
3. Click **Combine** .... `M`
4. Click **Original document** drop-down arrow .... `Alt`+`O`
5. Click document name .... `↓`/`↑`, `↵Enter`

   ✓ *If document is not in list, click Browse for Original button to locate and select document.*

6. Click **Label unmarked changes with** box .... `Alt`+`E`
7. Type text to use to label changes, if necessary.
8. Click **Revised document** drop-down arrow .... `Alt`+`R`
9. Click document name .... `↓`/`↑`, `↵Enter`

   ✓ *If document is not in list, click Browse for Revised button to locate and select document.*

10. Click **Label unmarked changes with** box .... `Alt`+`B`
11. Type text to use to label changes, if necessary.
12. Click **More** .... `Alt`+`M`
13. Under Comparison settings, click to select or clear options to display.

---

14. Under Show changes at, click one of the following:
    - **Character level** to mark revisions character .... `Alt`+`C`
    - **Word level** to mark revisions by word .... `Alt`+`W`
15. Under Show changes in, click one of the following:
    - **Original document** ...... `Alt`+`T`
    - **Revised document** .... `Alt`+`I`
    - **New document** .... `Alt`+`U`
16. Click **OK** .... `↵Enter`

Print Comments and Revisions

1. Click **Office Button** 🔲 ...... `Alt`+`F`
2. Click **Print** .... `P`
3. Click **Print what** drop-down arrow .... `Alt`+`W`
4. Click one of the following .... `↓`/`↑`, `↵Enter`
   - **Document showing markup** to print comment and revision balloons with the document.
   - **List of markup** to print a list of comments and revisions separate from the document.
5. Click **OK** .... `↵Enter`

Customize Revision Marks

1. Click **Review** tab .... `Alt`+`R`

   Tracking Group

2. Click **Track Changes** button 📝 drop-down arrow .... `G`
3. Click **Change Tracking Options** .... `O`
4. Select options as necessary.
5. Click **OK** .... `↵Enter`

Accept/Reject Changes One by One

1. Right-click revision in document, balloon, or Reviewing pane.
2. Click **Accept revision** .... `E`

OR

Click **Reject** *revision* .... R

✓ *The type of revision displays in the command in place of the text* **revision**.

OR

1. Position insertion point at beginning of document .... Ctrl + Home
2. Click **Review** tab .... Alt + R

Changes Group

3. Click **Next** change button ⟫ .... H
4. Do one of the following:
   - Click **Accept Change** button ✎ to accept the change and move to the next change .... Alt + R, A, M

- Click **Reject Change** button ⟳ to reject the change and move to the next change .... Alt + R, J, M
- Click **Next Change** button ⟫ to leave the change and move to the next change .... Alt + R, H
- Click **Previous Change** button ⟪ to leave the change and move to the previous change .... Alt + R, F

5. Repeat steps 3–4 for all changes in the document.

Accept All Changes

1. Position insertion point at beginning of document .... Ctrl + Home
2. Click **Review** tab .... Alt + R

Changes Group

3. Click **Accept Change** button ✎ drop-down arrow .... A
4. Click **Accept All Changes in Document** .... D

Reject All Changes

1. Position insertion point at beginning of document .... Ctrl + Home
2. Click **Review** tab .... Alt + R

Changes Group

3. Click **Reject Change** button ⟳ drop-down arrow .... J
4. Click **Reject All Changes in Document** .... D

EXERCISE DIRECTIONS

Track Changes

1. Start Word, if necessary.
2. Open ⊙ **56COURSE**.

   ✓ *This is a version of the course list document you worked with earlier in this book.*

3. Save the file as **56COURSE_xx**.
4. Position the insertion point at the end of line two, after the phone number, and insert a comment.
5. Type the comment text: **Should we add the Web site URL?**
6. Turn on the Track Changes feature.
7. Set markup options to display comments, insertions, deletions, and formatting changes, only.
8. Customize the marks to set the Changed lines color to blue, to track formatting changes, and to mark formatting changes with a double-underline.

   ✓ *Note that revision marks display based on the settings in effect on the computer where a document is opened. Customizations are not saved with a document.*

9. Make the insertions, deletions, and formatting changes shown in Illustration A.
10. Set the Display for Review to Final.
11. Set the Display for Review to Original Showing Markup.
12. Set the Display for Review to Final Showing Markup.

13. Print the document with the comments and changes.
14. Save the document.

Accept/Reject Changes

1. Save the document as **56REVISED_xx**.
2. Delete the comment.
3. Accept the insertion of the word *Spring*.
4. Accept the changes to the names of the months.
5. Reject all formatting changes.
6. Accept all editing changes to the last sentence in the document.
7. Turn off the Track Changes feature.
8. Save the document and close it.

Compare Documents

1. Compare the original **56COURSE_xx** document to the revised **56REVISED_xx** document, showing the changes in a new document.

   ✓ *If Word displays a dialog box informing you that it will consider tracked changes to have been accepted, click Yes to continue.*

2. Accept all changes in the document.
3. Delete all comments.
4. Check the spelling and grammar in the document.
5. Print the document.
6. Save the document as **56FINAL_xx**.
7. Close the document, saving all changes.

Restoration Architecture

8921 Thunderbird Road ✧ Phoenix, Arizona 85022 ✧ 602-555-6325

Training Schedule

Spring — ∧

~~January~~ e

April — ∧

Microsoft Word 1 — Underline

This introductory course will cover the basics of using Microsoft Word 2007 to create common business documents. By the end of the course you will know how to create, format, edit, and print text-based documents such as letters, memos, and reports.

~~February~~ e

May — ∧

Microsoft Word 2 — Underline

A continuation of the Word 1 course, this intermediate level class will delve into some of the more intriguing features of Microsoft Word 2007. By the end of the course you will know how to use mail merge to generate form letters, labels, and envelopes, set up a document in columns, include headers and footers, and insert pictures.

~~March~~ e

June — ∧

Microsoft Word 3 — Underline

This final course in the Microsoft Word series covers advanced features. By the end of this course you will know how to use tables, create and modify outlines, use e-mail and Internet features in Word, and share documents with other users.

~~Enrollment~~ forms are available in the HR office or on the company Intranet.

Pick up enrollment — ∧

, or call ext. 98 — ∧

ON YOUR OWN

1. In this exercise, complete your research paper by conducting a peer review and making final changes.

2. Open ⌨OWD55_*xx*, the research paper you have been working on.

3. Save the document as OWD56_*xx*.

4. Turn on the Track Changes feature.

5. Proofread the document. Insert comments as necessary. For example, remind yourself to check your citations or your facts.

6. Make corrections and improvements as necessary.

7. Save the changes.

8. Swap research paper files with a classmate. While your classmate enters comments and revision suggestions in your paper, you make comments and revision suggestions in his or hers.

9. When you are both ready, swap back. Review your classmate's comments and suggestions and accept or reject them as necessary.

10. Review the comments and suggestions you made yourself and accept or reject them as necessary.

11. Proofread the entire document again.

12. Check the spelling and grammar.

13. When you are satisfied with the report, print it.

14. Close the document, saving all changes.

Skills Covered

- Insert a Cross-reference
- Insert a Caption
- Create an Index
- Modify an Index

Software Skills Sometimes it may be difficult for readers to locate the specific information they need in long or complex documents. To quickly refer a reader from one location to another related location, you can create a cross-reference. To help readers identify illustrations such as tables or figures, you can insert captions. To help readers find the page containing specific information, you can create an index in which topics and subtopics are listed; Word automatically fills in the correct page number.

Application Skills A local flower shop has hired you to prepare a report about roses to publish in its monthly newsletter. The report is almost complete, but would benefit from features that will help readers find the information they need. In this exercise, you will create cross-references in the report and insert captions. You will also generate an index to help readers locate specific topics in the document quickly and easily.

TERMS

Caption A text label that identifies an illustration such as a figure, table, or picture.

Cross-reference Text that refers a reader to a different location in a document.

Cross-reference text The information entered in a document to introduce a cross-reference.

Cross-reference type The type of object which is being referred to, such as a bookmark or heading.

Field code The instructions inserted in a field that tell Word what results to display.

Field results The information displayed in a field.

Index An alphabetical list of topics and/or subtopics in a document along with the page numbers where they appear.

Tab leaders Characters inserted to the left of text aligned with a tab stop, such as page numbers in an index.

NOTES

Insert a Cross-reference

- A **cross-reference** is text that directs a reader to another location in the same document for more information. For example, "*For more information, see page 22*" is a cross-reference.

- You can create cross-references to existing headings, footnotes, bookmarks, captions, numbered paragraphs, tables, and figures, as well as to endnotes and equations.

- When you create a cross-reference with Word, you enter the **cross-reference text**, and then select the **cross-reference type**.

- After you select the reference type, you select whether you want Word to reference the item by page number, text, or paragraph. This is the information Word will automatically insert in the document.

- Word enters the reference as a field, so it can be updated if necessary. This means that if you reference a heading and then move the heading to another location in the document, you can update the cross-reference to reflect the change.

- By default Word inserts a cross-reference as a hyperlink. Ctrl+click the cross-reference to jump to the specified destination.

- You can change the setting if you do not want the cross-reference inserted as a hyperlink.

  ✓ *See Exercise 36 for more information on hyperlinks.*

- If the cross-reference **field code** is displayed in your document instead of the **field results**, you must deselect the Show field codes instead of their values check box in the Advanced group in the Word Options dialog box.

The Cross-reference dialog box

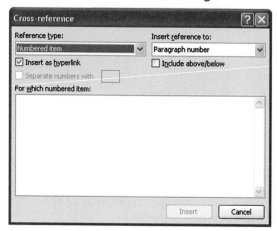

Insert a Caption

- Insert a **caption** to label an item.
- Each caption includes a text label and a number field.
- By default, Word comes with labels for tables, figures, and equations.
- You can create new labels for other items or to use different label text. For example, you might want to label a figure as Illustration.
- By default, Word uses Arabic numbers and positions the captions below the item. You can customize the number format, and select to position the caption above the item.
- Word automatically updates the numbers for each caption entered; however, if you delete or move a caption, you must manually update the remaining captions.

- You can insert a caption manually or set Word to automatically insert captions.

The Caption dialog box

Create an Index

- An **index** lists topics and subtopics contained in a document, along with the page numbers where they appear.
- Word automatically generates an alphabetical index based on index entries you mark in the document text.
- Word comes with a selection of index formats.
- Other index layout options include the number of columns in the index and whether subtopics should be run in on the same line or if each subtopic should be indented. The default setting is for two columns and indented subtopics.
- You can also choose to right-align page numbers and to precede page numbers with **tab leaders**.

Index dialog box

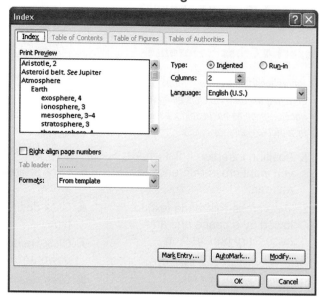

- You can index a single character, a word, a phrase, or a topic that spans multiple pages.

- You can mark all occurrences of the same text, or mark a single occurrence. Keep in mind that Word only marks all occurrences of *exactly* the same text. That means that the formatting, capitalization, tense, etc. must be exactly the same.

- Index entries can cross-reference a different index entry. For example, *Cats, see Pets* is a cross-referenced index entry.

- If you index many subtopics, you can use a multi-level index. For example, *Pets* may be the main index topic, with *Cats, Dogs*, and *Goldfish* as subtopics.

- To mark entries for an index, you select an item you want marked for inclusion in the index, then open the Mark Index Entry dialog box and type the entry text as you want it displayed in the index.

- You can type the entry text using any formatting; it does not have to match the selected text in the document. However, if you are marking all items, only the items that appear exactly as the *selected text* will be marked. It doesn't matter what you type in the Main entry text box.

- If the selected item is exactly as you want it to appear in the index, you do not have to retype the entry text.

- If the entry is for a subtopic, you type the main entry topic under which the subtopic should be listed, then the subentry text as you want it displayed.

- Word automatically inserts an Index Entry field in the document following the selected item.

  ✓ *If hidden text is displayed, you see the Index Entry fields in the document. This makes the document appear longer than it will be when printed. To see the document as it will print, hide hidden text or change to Print Preview.*

Mark Index Entry dialog box

Modify an Index

- You can edit existing index entries by editing the text in the Index Entry field.

- If you add, delete, or move indexed items in the document, you must update the index so that Word changes the page numbers.

PROCEDURES

Insert a Cross-Reference

✓ *Before inserting a cross-reference, make sure that the item which is being referenced—such as the heading, bookmark, or footnote—already exists.*

1. Position insertion point where you want cross-reference to appear.

2. Type cross-reference text, followed by a space and any necessary punctuation.

   ✓ *For example, type the text: For more information see.*

3. Click **References tab** .... Alt+S

Captions Group

4. Click **Cross-reference** button .... R, F

   ✓ *You can also click the Cross-reference button in the Links group on the Insert tab.*

5. Click **Reference type:** drop-down arrow .... Alt+T

6. Click desired reference type .... ↑/↓, ↵Enter

7. Click **Insert reference to:** drop-down arrow .... Alt+R

8. Click desired reference option .... ↑/↓, ↵Enter

9. Select specific item in **For which** list .... Alt+W, ↑/↓

   ✓ *If you do not want cross-reference inserted as a hyperlink, deselect the **Insert as hyperlink** check box.*

10. Click **Insert** .... Alt+I

11. Click **Close** .... Esc

Update a Cross-reference

1. Select cross reference to update.

2. Press **F9** F9

   OR

   a. Right-click cross-reference to update.

   b. Click **Update Field** .... U

Insert a Caption Manually

1. Select item to caption.
2. Click **References tab** .... Alt + S

   Captions Group

3. Click **Insert Caption** button ▣ .... P
4. Click **Label** drop-down arrow .... Alt + L
5. Select desired label.
   OR
   a. Click **New Label** .... Alt + N
   b. Type label name.
   c. Click **OK** .... ↵Enter
6. Click **Position** .... Alt + P
7. Select either **Below selected item** (default) or **Above selected item**.
8. To customize number format, click **Numbering** .... Alt + U
9. Click **Format** drop-down arrow .... F
10. Click format to use.
11. Click **OK** .... ↵Enter
12. Click **OK**.

Insert a Caption Automatically

1. Click **References tab** .... Alt + S

   Captions Group

2. Click **Insert Caption** button ▣ .... P
3. Click **AutoCaption** .... Alt + A
4. In **Add caption when inserting** list, click check box(es) for item(s) you want to label .... ↑/↓, Spacebar
5. Click **Use label** .... Alt + L
6. Click desired label.
   OR
   a. Click **New Label** .... Alt + N
   b. Type label name.
   c. Click **OK** .... ↵Enter
7. Click **Position** .... Alt + P
8. Click desired position.

9. To customize number format, click **Numbering** .... Alt + U
10. Click **Format** drop-down arrow .... F
11. Click format to use.
12. Click **OK** .... ↵Enter
13. Click **OK** .... ↵Enter

Create an Index

Mark index entries:

1. Click **References tab** .... Alt + S

   Index Group

2. Click **Mark Entry** button ▣ .... N
3. In document, select text to mark.

   ✓ *Mark Entry dialog box remains open while you select text to mark. If necessary, move Mark Entry dialog box out of the way.*

4. Click **Main entry** text box.
5. Type main index entry text.
6. Click **Subentry** text box .... Alt + S
7. Type subentry text if necessary.
8. Do one of the following:
   ■ Click **Mark** to mark selected occurrence only .... Alt + M
   OR
   ■ Click **Mark All** to mark all occurrences of selected text in document .... Alt + A
9. Repeat steps 3-8 until all entries are marked.
10. Click **Close** .... ↵Enter

Mark a cross-referenced entry:

1. Click **References tab** .... Alt + S

   Index Group

2. Click **Mark Entry** button ▣ .... N
3. In document, select text to mark.

   ✓ *Mark Entry dialog box remains open while you select text to mark. If necessary, move Mark Entry dialog box out of the way.*

4. Click **Main entry** text box.
5. Type main index entry text.
6. Click **Cross-reference** option button .... Alt + C
7. In Cross-reference text box, following the word *See*, type referenced main entry.
8. Click **Mark** .... Alt + M
9. Repeat steps 3–8 until all entries are marked.
10. Click **Close** .... ↵Enter

Generate index:

1. Position insertion point in document where you want index displayed.
2. Click **References tab** .... Alt + S

   Index Group

3. Click **Insert Index** button ⊞ X
4. Click **Formats** drop-down arrow .... Alt + T
5. Click desired format .... ↑/↓, ↵Enter
6. Select any other desired options.
7. Click **OK** .... ↵Enter

Update index:

1. Click **References tab** .... Alt + S

   Index Group

2. Click **Update Index** button ▣ .... D
   OR
   a. Click in index.
   b. Press **F9** F9
   OR
   a. Right-click index.
   b. Click **Update Field** .... U

EXERCISE DIRECTIONS

1. Start Word, if necessary.
2. Open the document ⊙57ROSES.
3. Save the document as **57ROSES_xx**.
4. Replace the text *Student's Name* in the header with your own name.
5. Replace the text *Today's Date* in the header with the current date.

Insert Captions

1. Select the first table in the document.
2. Insert a caption to label the table. Use the label text **Table**, the default numbering scheme, and position the caption above the table.
3. Insert a page break before the caption.
4. Select the second table in the document.
5. Insert a caption to label the table, using the same options that you used to create the first caption.
6. Insert a page break before the caption.

Insert Cross-references

1. Position the insertion point at the end of the first paragraph under the heading *History*.

   ✓ *You may want to use the Document Map to navigate through the document.*

2. Type the following cross-reference text: **(For information on types of roses, refer to the section.)** Be sure to leave a space between the last word and the period.
3. Position the insertion point to the left of the period you just typed, and insert a hyperlinked cross-reference to the heading *Types of Roses*.
4. Scroll down to the heading *Types of Roses* on page 2 (or use the cross-reference hyperlink you inserted in step 3).
5. At the end of the paragraph under the heading Types of Roses, type the following cross-reference text: **For a description of common types of roses, refer to**
6. Position the insertion point to the right of the space after the word to, and insert a hyperlinked cross-reference to the entire caption for Table 1.
7. Position the insertion point after the cross-reference field, type a space followed by the text **on page**.
8. Position the insertion point to the left of the period and then insert a hyperlinked cross-reference to the page number on which Table 1 is located.

9. Ctrl+click the page number to go to the table.
10. In the document, move the insertion point to the end of the sentence under the heading Grafted Roses and type the following cross-reference text **For information about the grading system, refer to**
11. Position the insertion point to the right of the space after the word to, and insert a hyperlinked cross-reference to the entire caption for Table 2.
12. Position the insertion point after the cross-reference field, type a space followed by the text **on page**.
13. Position the insertion point to the left of the period and then insert a hyperlinked cross-reference to the page number on which Table 2 is located.
14. Close the Cross-reference dialog box and then check the spelling and grammar in the document.
15. Display the document in Print Preview. Page 3 should look similar to Illustration A.

    ✓ *If you have the Field shading option set to Always in the Advanced group of the Word Options dialog box, the table number and cross-reference text will be shaded with gray.*

Create an Index

1. Close Print Preview and then press Ctrl+Home to move the insertion point to the beginning of the document.
2. Mark entries for an index as follows:

   ✓ *You might want to use the Find command to locate the specified text.*

   a. Select the text *roses* in the first sentence of the introduction, open the Mark Index Entry dialog box and mark all entries of the text *roses*.
   b. Select the text *symbol*, and mark all entries.
   c. Mark all entries of the text *cultivation*, *types*, *varieties*, and *hybrids*.
   d. Select the text *ornamental decorations* in the first sentence under the heading *The Rose in Use*. Edit the text in the Main entry box to usage, and then type **ornamental decoration** in the Subentry box. Mark the entry.
   e. Select the text *confetti*, and again, edit the Main entry text to usage, and then type the text **confetti** in the Subentry box. Mark the entry.
   f. Continue entering the following as subentries for the Main entry usage: **Egyptian mummies, perfume, medicine,** and **currency.**

g. Select the text *white rose* under the heading The *Rose as Symbol*. Type **York** as the Subentry text. Select the Cross-reference option button, and type **Symbol** after the word *See* in the Cross-reference box, then mark the entry.

h. Select the text *red rose*. Type **Lancaster** as the Subentry text. Select the Cross-reference option button and type **Symbol** after the word *See* in the Cross-reference box, then mark the entry.

i. Mark the phrase *Wars of the Roses*.

j. Mark the phrase *American Nursery Standards*.

k. Mark all occurrences of the following words: *diseases*, *quality*, and *insects*. If necessary, edit the main entry text so there are no initial capital letters.

l. Mark the first occurrence of the word *pests* and add a cross-reference to insects.

3. When you have finished marking the necessary entries, close the Mark Index Entry dialog box.

4. Press Ctrl+End to move the insertion point to the end of the document.

5. Insert a page break.

6. At the top of the new page, type **Index**, and format it with the Heading 1 style.

7. Press Enter to move the insertion point to a blank line.

8. Generate the index as follows:

   a. Select the Classic style.

   b. Right align page numbers.

   c. Use a dotted tab leader.

   d. Use two columns.

   e. Indent the subtopics.

9. When the index is inserted in the document, save the changes.

10. Preview the document.

11. Close Print Preview and mark all occurrences of the text *rose water* as a main index entry.

12. Update the index to reflect the change.

13. Preview the index page. It should look similar to Illustration B.

14. Close the document, saving all changes.

Student's Name   Today's Date

Table 1

Species Roses	These are uncultivated varieties. They are Usually hardy and disease resistant. They come in a wide variety of types and colors.
Old European Garden Roses	These are the oldest group of cultivated roses. They are hybrid groups common in European gardens prior to the 18th century. They usually have a strong fragrance and can withstand cold winters, but are susceptible to heat, drought, and disease.
Hardy Repeat-Blooming Old Roses	These plants are similar to the Old European Garden Roses but they will bloom more than once each season.
Modern Roses	These include the varieties developed after the 18th century.
Miniature Roses	Small plants that are extremely useful for small gardens and container planting.
Shrub Roses	Plants that are noted for their rounded shape, winter hardiness and disease resistance. Shrub roses tend to be free-flowering, which means they provide blooms all season long, and are suitable for using as hedges and in border gardens.

Judging Rose Quality

The quality of rose plants varies depending on the vendor. Ask for references before purchasing to make sure that other customers have been satisfied with the plants. You can order plants by mail or on-line, but unless you are completely certain that you are dealing with a reputable vendor, you may prefer purchasing plants locally, so you can see them before you buy, and so that you can return them if necessary.

Grafted Roses

Grafted roses are rated based on an American Nursery Standards grading system. For information about the grading system, refer to Table 2 on page 4.

3

Illustration B

Student's Name   Today's Date

Index

A

American Nursery Standards 4

C

cultivation 1

D

diseases 5

H

hybrids 1

I

insects 5

P

pests .... 5, *See* insects

Q

quality 4, 5

R

red rose
   Lancaster .... *See* Symbol

rose water 1, 2
roses 1, 2, 4, 5

S

symbol 1, 2

T

types 1, 3, 4

U

usage
   confetti 1
   currency 2
   Egyptian mummies 1
   medicine 2
   ornamental decorations 1
   perfume 2

V

varieties 1, 4

W

Wars of the Roses 2
white rose
   York .... *See* Symbol

5

ON YOUR OWN

1. Start Word and open 📼OWD56_xx, the research report you have been working on.

2. Save the document as **OWD57_xx**.

3. If you have not already done so, create one or two tables to illustrate the text, and then insert captions for the tables.

4. Insert cross-references in the document. Try using different cross-reference types. For example, select a heading for one cross-reference and a footnote or table for another.

5. Create an index for the document. Mark main entries and subentries.

6. Insert the index on a new page at the end of the document. Try different formatting options, such as the fancy format with dotted tab leaders.

7. Preview the document and insert page breaks as necessary.

8. Update the index and the cross-references if necessary.

9. Print the document. Ask a classmate to review the document and offer comments or suggestions.

10. Incorporate the comments and suggestions into the document.

11. Close the document, saving all changes, and exit Word.

Curriculum Connection: Language Arts

Song Lyrics as Poetry

Have you ever listened to a song and thought it seemed just like a poem set to music? Many songwriters are talented poets as well as musicians. Rap lyrics in particular make use of many techniques found in poetry, like figurative language, rhythm, rhyme, and alliteration.

Write a Rap

Write a rap that uses poetic language and conventions such as metaphors, similes, and rhythmic meter. The rap might rhyme or not, but it should evoke emotion and make a point.

Exercise | 58

Skills Covered

- ■ **Create a Table of Contents**
- ■ **Create a Table of Figures**
- ■ **Create a Bibliography**

- ■ **Manage Sources**
- ■ **Create a Table of Authorities**
- ■ **Update a Table**

Software Skills Professional documents and reports use tables to present lists to help readers locate and understand information. A table of contents helps readers locate information they need in a long document by listing headings and the page numbers where each heading starts. Likewise, a table of figures lists the page numbers where tables are located. A table of authorities is used specifically in a legal document to list references such as cases, statutes, and rules. A bibliography lists sources of information used to develop and create the document. Use Word to automatically generate a table of contents, table of figures, table of authorities, or bibliography. If the page numbers or information change, you can update the table.

Application Skills You have just about completed the Roses document for Liberty Blooms. The final touch is to add a table of contents and table of figures to help readers locate the information they need, and then to create a bibliography. In this exercise, you will generate the table of figures. You will check that all topics you want included in the table of contents are formatted with heading styles. Then, you will generate the table of contents. You will insert citations for a bibliography and then generate the bibliography. Finally, you will make some editing changes to the report, and update the tables to reflect the changes.

TERMS

Bibliography A list of sources of information used to develop and create a document.

Bibliography citation style The style used to organize and format source information in a bibliography. Some common styles include Chicago and MLA.

Citation A reference to a source of information. In legal documents, it is a reference to previous court decisions or authoritative writings.

Passim A word used in citations of cases, articles, or books in a legal document to indicate that the reference is found in many places within the work.

Table of authorities A list of citations in a legal document, usually accompanied by the page numbers where the references occur.

Table of contents A list of topics and subtopics in a document, usually accompanied by the page numbers where the topics begin and placed before the main body of the document.

Table of figures A list of figures in a document, usually accompanied by the page numbers where the figures are located.

NOTES

Create a Table of Contents

- Word generates a **table of contents** based on paragraphs formatted with the built-in heading styles.
- You can select from a list of built-in preformatted styles, or you can create a customized table using the options in the Table of Contents dialog box.
- If you create a customized table of contents, you can use as many levels as you want, depending on how many levels of headings are used in the document.
- You do not have to include all heading levels in the table of contents. For example, you may have paragraphs formatted with up to four heading levels, but select to include only two heading levels in the table of contents.
- Paragraphs formatted with the same level of heading style will be listed at the same level in the table of contents.
- Word comes with a selection of table of contents formats which you can preview in the Table of Contents dialog box.
- You can also select whether to include page numbers and whether to right-align them.
- If you right-align page numbers, you can select a tab leader.
- By default, Word formats the headings in a table of contents as hyperlinks. Ctrl+click the heading in the table to jump to the destination.
- If you don't want to use hyperlinks in your table of contents, deselect the Use hyperlinks instead of page numbers check box in the Table of Contents dialog box.

Table of Contents dialog box

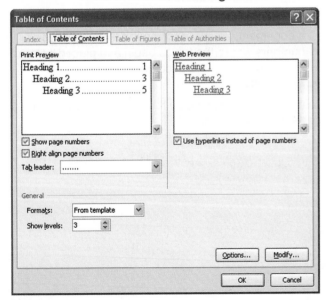

Create a Table of Figures

- A **table of figures** includes a list of the captions used to identify items in a document.
- To create the table, specify the captions you want to include.
- Word sorts the captions by number and displays them in the table of figures.

  ✓ *For information on inserting captions, refer to Exercise 57.*

Table of Figures dialog box

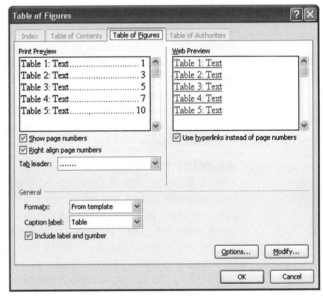

Create a Bibliography

- Create a **bibliography** to list the sources you use to find information included in a document or report.
- Word creates a bibliography by compiling a list of all **citations** you insert in the document.
- You insert a citation at the location where you include information you obtained from the source.
- For each citation, you enter source information in bibliography fields such as the type of source, the author, the publisher, and the publication date.

- The bibliography fields depend on the type of source. For example, a Web site source type includes fields for URL and date accessed. An article in a periodical source type includes fields for article title, periodical title, and pages.

  ✓ *You can select to display all bibliography fields, if you want.*

Create Source dialog box

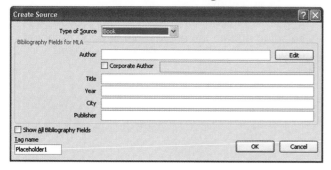

- The citation displays inline at the insertion point location; the format depends on the selected **bibliography citation style**.

- For example, in MLA style, the author's last name displays in parentheses.

- Alternatively, you can insert a citation placeholder which displays as a question mark in the document, reminding you to fill in the source information at a later time.

- You can also quickly insert a citation using information already entered for a source.

- After entering the citations, you can automatically generate a bibliography that lists all of the source information entered in the citations.

- The bibliography is formatted in the selected bibliography citation style.

- If you add or edit sources, you can update the bibliography.

Manage Sources

- Bibliography source information is stored in the Source Manager.

- The Source Manager displays a list of sources in the current document and a master list of all sources you have entered for all documents.

- You can use the Source Manager to edit and delete sources, to fill in information for a placeholder source, and to add a source from the master list to the current document.

- You can also preview sources in the current bibliography citation style.

Source Manager

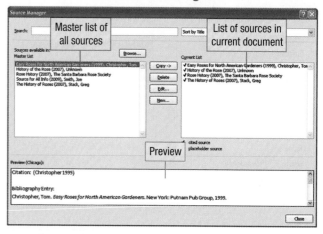

Create a Table of Authorities

- Create a **table of authorities** to list citations in a legal document, along with the page numbers where the references are located.

- If a citation appears on five or more pages, you may select to substitute the word **passim** for the page numbers.

- Word comes with built-in categories of common citations, such as cases, statutes, regulations, and rules. You can create new categories if you want.

- Use the Mark Citation dialog box to mark each citation in the document with a table of authorities field code.

  ✓ *This process is similar to marking items for an index. For information on creating an index, refer to Exercise 57.*

- You can mark each occurrence manually, or automatically mark all occurrences.

- You can also specify a short version of a citation to mark automatically along with the long version.

  ✓ *As with index entries, you see the field codes in the document if you have hidden text displayed. To see the document as it will print, hide hidden text or change to Print Preview.*

- Word can automatically search through a document to find citations, or you can scroll through manually. To find citations, Word searches for the text ***v***.

- When all items are marked, use the Table of Authorities dialog box to select options and generate the table.

■ Word sorts the citations by category.

Table of Authorities dialog box

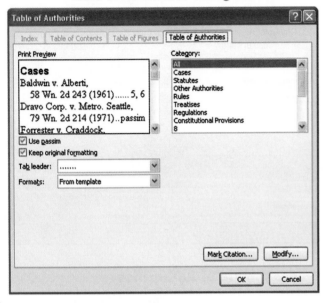

Update a Table

■ If the page numbers where items in a table are located change, you can automatically update the table.

■ Likewise, you can update heading text in a table of contents, caption text in a table of figures, citation text in a table of authorities, or source information in a bibliography.

■ In a table of contents or table of figures, you can select to update the entire table or page numbers only.

PROCEDURES

Insert a Built-in Table of Contents

1. Apply heading styles to all paragraphs you want in table of contents.
2. Position insertion point where you want table of contents to display.
3. Click **References tab** .... Alt + S

   Table of Contents Group

4. Click **Table of Contents button** .... T
5. Click a table of contents in the gallery of built-in styles .... ↓/↑, ↵Enter

Create a Table of Contents

1. Apply heading styles to all paragraphs you want in table of contents.
2. Position insertion point where you want table of contents to display.

3. Click **References tab** .... Alt + S

   Table of Contents Group

4. Click **Table of Contents button** .... T
5. Click **Insert Table of Contents** I
6. Click **Formats**: list box ..... Alt + T
7. Select desired format .... ↑/↓, ↵Enter
8. Click **Show levels** box ...... Alt + L
9. Enter number of heading levels to include.
10. Select or deselect **Show page numbers** .... Alt + S
11. Select or deselect **Right align page numbers** .... Alt + R

    ✓ If you select to right-align page numbers, select a tab leader option from **Tab leader** drop-down list.

12. Select or deselect **Use hyperlinks instead of page numbers** .... Alt + H
13. Click **OK**.

Update a Table of Contents

1. Position insertion point anywhere in table.
2. Click **References tab** .... Alt + S

   Table of Contents Group

3. Click **Update Table button** .... U
4. Click **Update page numbers only** .... Alt + P

   OR

   Click **Update entire table** .... Alt + E
5. Click **OK** .... ↵Enter

   OR

1. Position insertion point anywhere in table.
2. Press **F9**.

   OR

   a. Right-click anywhere in table.
   b. Click **Update Field** .... U
3. Click **Update page numbers only** .... Alt + P

   OR

   Click **Update entire table** .... Alt + E
4. Click **OK** .... ↵Enter

Create a Table of Figures

1. Insert captions as desired.

    ✓ *Refer to Exercise 57 for information on inserting captions.*

2. Position insertion point where you want table to display.
3. Click **References tab** .... Alt + S

    Captions Group

4. Click **Insert Table of Figures** button 🔲 .... G
5. Click **Forma̲ts**: list box .... Alt + T
6. Select desired format .... ↑/↓, ↵Enter
7. Click **Caption l̲abel** list box .... Alt + L
8. Select label to include .... ↑/↓, ↵Enter
9. Select or deselect **Include label and n̲umber** .... Alt + N
10. Select or deselect **S̲how page numbers** .... Alt + S
11. Select or deselect **R̲ight align page numbers** .... Alt + R

    ✓ *If you select to right-align page numbers, select a tab leader option from **Tab leader** drop-down list.*

12. Select or deselect **Use h̲yperlinks instead of page numbers** .... Alt + H
13. Click **OK**.

Update a Table of Figures

1. Position insertion point anywhere in table.
2. Click **References tab** .... Alt + S

    Captions Group

3. Click **Update Table** button 🔳 V
4. Click **Update page numbers only** .... Alt + P

    OR

    Click **Update e̲ntire table** .... Alt + E
5. Click **OK** .... ↵Enter

OR

1. Position insertion point anywhere in table.
2. Press **F9**.

    OR

    a. Right-click anywhere in table.
    b. Click **Update Field** .... U
3. Click **Update page numbers only** .... Alt + P

    OR

    Click **Update e̲ntire table** .... Alt + E
4. Click **OK** .... ↵Enter

Create a Bibliography

Select a citation style:

1. Click **References tab** .... Alt + S

    Citations & Bibliography Group

2. Click **Style** button drop-down arrow 🔽 Style: MLA .... L, ↓
3. Click desired style .... ↑/↓, ↵Enter

Insert a citation by adding a new source

1. Position insertion point after the text you want to cite.
2. Click **References tab** .... Alt + S

    Citations & Bibliography Group

3. Click **Insert Citation** button 🔲 C
4. Click **Add New S̲ource** .... S

    ✓ *To insert a placeholder, click Add New P̲laceholder. Edit the source to fill in the citation information.*

5. Click **Type of S̲ource** drop-down arrow .... Alt + S
6. Select source type .... ↑/↓, ↵Enter
7. Press Tab to move insertion point to first field.
8. Type information.
9. Press Tab to move insert point to next field.

10. Repeat steps 8 and 9 to fill in fields as necessary.

    ✓ *Click to select Show A̲ll Bibliography Fields check box to display all available fields.*

11. Click **OK**.

Insert a citation using an existing source:

1. Position insertion point after the text you want to cite.
2. Click **References tab** .... Alt + S

    Citations & Bibliography Group

3. Click **Insert Citation** button 🔲 C
4. Click source to insert .... ↑/↓, ↵Enter

Generate a bibliography:

1. Insert citations as necessary.
2. Position insertion point where you want bibliography to display.
3. Click **References tab** .... Alt + S

    Citations & Bibliography Group

4. Click **Bibliography** button 🔲 .... B
5. Click a bibliography in the gallery of built-in styles .... ↓/↑, ↵Enter

    OR

    Click **Insert B̲ibliography** .... B

Update a Bibliography

1. Position insertion point anywhere in table.
2. Press **F9**.

    OR

    a. Right-click anywhere in table.
    b. Click **Update Field** .... U

Manage Sources

Edit a source:
1. Click **References tab** .... Alt + S

   Citations & Bibliography Group
2. Click **Manage Sources** button 🗂 .... M
3. Click source to edit .... ↑/↓

   ✓ *To change to Current list, press* Alt + U.
4. Click **Edit** .... Alt + E
5. Edit information as necessary.
6. Click **OK** .... ↵Enter
7. Click **Yes** to update source .... Y

Delete a source:
1. Click **References tab** .... Alt + S

   Citations & Bibliography Group
2. Click **Manage Source** button 🗂 .... M
3. Click source to delete .... ↑/↓

   ✓ *To change to Current list, press* Alt + U
4. Click **Delete** .... Alt + D

Find a source in the Master List:
1. Click **References tab** .... Alt + S

   Citations & Bibliography Group
2. Click **Manage Source** button 🗂 .... M
3. Click in **Search** text box .... Alt + S
4. Type the title or author of the source.

Copy a source from the Master List to the Current List or vice versa:
1. Click **References tab** .... Alt + S

   Citations & Bibliography Group
2. Click **Manage Source** button 🗂 .... M
3. Click source to copy .... ↑/↓

   ✓ *To change to Current list, press* Alt + U.
4. Click **Copy** .... Alt + C

Sort sources:
1. Click **References tab** .... Alt + S

   Citations & Bibliography Group
2. Click **Manage Source** button 🗂 .... M
3. Click **Sort by** list box .... Alt + S, Tab↹, ↓
4. Select sort type .... ↑/↓

Create a new source:
1. Click **References tab** .... Alt + S

   Citations & Bibliography Group
2. Click **Manage Source** button 🗂 .... M
3. Click **New** .... Alt + N
4. Click **Type of Source** drop-down arrow .... Alt + S
5. Select source type .... ↑/↓, ↵Enter
6. Press Tab↹ to move insertion point to first field.
7. Type information.
8. Press Tab↹ to move insert point to next field.
9. Repeat steps 7 and 8 to fill in fields as necessary.

   ✓ *Click to select Show All Bibliography Fields check box to display all available fields.*
10. Click **OK**.

Create a Table of Authorities

Mark entries:
1. Click **References tab** .... Alt + S

   Table of Authorities Group
2. Click **Mark Citation** button 🖹 I
3. In document, select text to mark.

   ✓ *Mark Citation dialog box remains open while you select text to mark. If necessary, move dialog box out of the way.*
4. Click **Category** drop-down arrow .... Alt + C
5. Selected desired category .... ↑/↓, ↵Enter
6. Click **Short citation** box .... Alt + S
7. Type short version of citation, if necessary.
8. If necessary, edit or format text in **Selected text** box. .... Alt + T, edit text
9. Do one of the following:
   - Click **Mark** to mark selected occurrence only .... Alt + M

   OR
   - Click **Mark All** to mark all occurrences of selected text in document .... Alt + A
10. Repeat steps 3-9 until all entries are marked.

    ✓ *To search for the next citation in the document, click the **Next Citation** button.*
11. Click **Close** .... ↵Enter

Generate table:

1. Position insertion point in document where you want table displayed.
2. Click **References tab** .... Alt+S

> Table of Authorities Group

3. Click **Insert Table of Authorities** button .... R, T
4. Click **Category** list .... Alt+G
5. Click category to include .... ↑/↓

> ✓ Click All to include all citations.

6. Click **Formats** drop-down arrow .... Alt+T
7. Click desired format .... ↑/↓, ↵Enter
8. Select or deselect **Use passim** .... Alt+P
9. Select or deselect **Keep original formatting** .... Alt+R
10. Click **Tab leader** drop-down arrow .... Alt+B
11. Click desired tab leader .... ↑/↓, ↵Enter
12. Click **OK**.

Update a Table of Authorities

1. Position insertion point anywhere in table.
2. Click **References tab** .... Alt+S

> Table of Authorities Group

3. Click **Update Table** button .... R, U

OR

1. Position insertion point anywhere in table.
2. Press **F9**.

OR

a. Right-click anywhere in table.
b. Click **Update Field** .... U

EXERCISE DIRECTIONS

1. Start Word, if necessary.
2. Open the document ⊙**58ROSES**, a version of the report you used in the previous exercise.
3. Save it as **58ROSES_xx**.
4. Replace the text *Student's Name* in the header with your own name.
5. Replace the text *Today's Date* in the header with the current date.

Generate a Table of Figures

1. Display page 5 and position the insertion point at the end of the last paragraph of text in the document.
2. Press Enter to insert a blank line after the document text but before the page break.

> ✓ Display paragraph marks, if necessary, so you can see the page break. However, be aware that displayed hidden text affects the position of text in the document.

3. Using the Heading 1 style, type **Table of Figures**.
4. Press Enter to move the insertion point to a new blank line.
5. Generate a table of figures using the following options:
   a. Distinctive format.
   b. Caption label: **Table**.
   c. Include label and number.
   d. Show page numbers.
   e. Right align page numbers.

f. Use a dot tab leader.
g. Do not use hyperlinks.
6. Save the changes.

Generate a Table of Contents

1. Press Ctrl+Home to move the insertion point to the beginning of the document.
2. Scroll through the document to verify that all headings are formatted with heading styles.
3. Press Ctrl+Home again to move the insertion point to the beginning of the document.
4. Insert two blank lines after the title.
5. Clear all formatting from the new blank lines.
6. On the first blank line type **Table of Contents** in 20-point Arial, centered.
7. Position the insertion point on the second blank line.
8. Create a table of contents using the following options:
   a. Distinctive format.
   b. 3 heading levels.
   c. Right-aligned page numbers.
   d. Dot tab leader.
   e. Use page numbers, not hyperlinks.
9. Preview the first page of the document. It should look similar to Illustration A.
10. Close Print Preview.
11. Change the heading *Diseases and Insects* from Heading 2 to Heading 1.

Add Sources

1. Select the MLA bibliography citation style.
2. Position the insertion point after the first sentence under the heading History and insert a new bibliography citation.
3. Add a new source and enter the following source information:
   a. Type of source: **Web site**
   b. Author: **The Santa Barbara Rose Society**. Click to select the Corporate Author check box.
   c. Name of Web Page: **Rose History**
   d. Year: **2007**
   e. Year Accessed: **2008**
   f. Month Accessed: **May**
   g. Day Accessed: **15**
   h. URL: **http://www.sbrose.org/rosehistory.htm**
4. Click OK to add the source to the document.
5. Position the insertion point after the fourth sentence under the heading *History* and insert a new bibliography citation.
6. Add a new source and enter the following source information:
   a. Type of source: **Web site**
   b. Author: **Greg Stack**
   c. Name of Web Page: **The History of Roses**
   d. Year: **2007**
   e. Year Accessed: **2008**
   f. Month Accessed: **May**
   g. Day Accessed: **15**
   h. URL: **http://www.urbanext.uiuc.edu/roses/history.html**
7. Click OK to add the source to the document.
8. Position the insertion point after the first paragraph under the heading *The Rose in Use*, and insert a citation referencing the Stack source.
9. Position the insertion point after the second paragraph under the heading *The Rose in Use*, and insert a citation referencing the Santa Barbara Rose Society source.
10. Position the insertion point after the paragraph under the heading *The Rose as Symbol* and insert a new bibliography citation.
11. Add a new source and enter the following source information:
    a. Type of source: **Web site**
    b. Author: **Unknown**
    c. Name of Web Page: **History of the Rose**
    d. Year: **2007**
    e. Year Accessed: **2008**
    f. Month Accessed: **May**
    g. Day Accessed: **15**
    h. URL: **http://www.herbs2000.com/flowers/r_history.htm**
12. Position the insertion point after the paragraph under the heading *Types of Roses* and insert a new bibliography citation.
13. Add a new source and enter the following source information:
    a. Type of source: **Book**
    b. Author: **Tom Christopher**
    c. Title: **Easy Roses for North American Gardens**
    d. Year: **1999**
    e. City: **New York**
    f. Publisher: **Putnam Pub Group**
14. Position the insertion point after the paragraph under the heading *Grafted Roses*, and insert a citation referencing the Stack source.
15. Position the insertion point after the first paragraph under the heading *Diseases and Insects*, and insert a citation referencing the Christopher source.
16. Save the changes to the document.

Generate the Bibliography

1. Press Ctrl+End to move the insertion point to the end of the document and insert a page break.
2. Using the Heading 1 style, type **Bibliography** and then press Enter to insert a blank line.
3. Insert a bibliography.
4. Change the Bibliography citation style to Chicago. Note that the bibliography updates automatically. It should look similar to Illustration B.

Complete the Document

1. Preview all pages of the document. Notice that the hard page breaks are not necessarily in the correct positions.
2. Delete the hard page breaks and any extra blank lines before table 1, table 2, and then preview the document again.
3. Insert a hard page break before the heading *Judging Rose Quality*, and before the Table of Figures.
4. Update the page numbers and headings in the table of contents.
5. Update the page numbers in the table of figures.
6. Update the page numbers in the index.
7. Check the spelling and grammar in the document.
8. Print the document.
9. Close the document, saving all changes.

Illustration A

Student's Name   Today's Date

ROSES

Table of Contents

Throughout history, roses have been considered a symbol of love and beauty. Did you know they have also been a symbol of war and death? In the following pages you will learn the story of the rose as well how to select and care for these beautiful flowers.

History

Fossil evidence shows that there were roses on earth more than 35 million years ago (The Santa Barbara Rose Society 2007). Roses are believed to have grown wild throughout most of the world. The earliest roses were all red, or shades of red. In fact, the genus name, *Rosa*, means red in Latin. The first cultivation probably began 5,000 years ago in China (Stack 2007). Human beings have been captivated by the flower ever since. They have worked hard to nurture and develop these wondrous blooms so that now there are hundreds of types, varieties, and hybrids. (For information on types of roses, refer to the section Types of Roses.)

1

Student's Name   Today's Date

Bibliography

Christopher, Tom. *Easy Roses for North American Gardeners*. New York: Putnam Pub Group, 1999.
Stack, Greg. *The History of Roses*. 2007. http://www.urbanext.uiuc.edu/roses/history.html (accessed May 15, 2008).
The Santa Barbara Rose Society. *Rose Hstory*. 2007. http://www.sbrose.org/rosehistory.htm (accessed May 15, 2008).
Unknown. *History of the Rose*. 2007. http://www.herbs2000.com/flowers/r_history.htm (accessed May 15, 2008).

8

ON YOUR OWN

1. Start Word and open 🖮OWD57_*xx*, the research report you have been working on.
2. Save the document as **OWD58_*xx***.
3. Complete the research project.
4. Finish adding and editing content as necessary.
5. Insert source citations as necessary.
6. Create a table of figures, if appropriate.
7. Create a table of authorities, if appropriate.
8. Create a table of contents.
9. Create a bibliography.
10. Preview the document.
11. Adjust page breaks as necessary.
12. Update all tables.
13. Check the spelling and grammar.
14. Ask a classmate to review the report and make comments and suggestions.
15. Incorporate the comments and suggestions.
16. Adjust page formatting and update tables as necessary.
17. Print the report.
18. Close the document, saving all changes, and exit Word.

Curriculum Connection: Social Studies

Real Life Pirates

Pirates are more than just legends and movie characters. Since ancient times, real pirates have haunted the world's oceans, terrorizing legitimate sailors, stealing cargo, and capturing people to hold for ransom or sell into slavery. Some famous pirates include Blackbeard, Henry Morgan, and William Jackson. There were even female pirates like Anne Bonney and Mary Reade.

Pirate Report

Write a report about a pirate, or a group of pirates. Use the Internet to research your subject, and include information such as where the pirate came from, and where he or she sailed. You should be able to find information about the pirate ship, pirate flag, and weapons of choice. Don't forget to include footnotes or endnotes, if necessary, and to add a page of works cited or a bibliography.

Exercise | 59

Critical Thinking

Application Skills You have been working on a report about eye care for the elderly for StyleEyes. Your supervisor has decided the store should develop a directory that describes the different services it offers and that your report on eye care for seniors should be included. She has an outline of the directory and has asked you to organize the project.

In this exercise, you will modify and format a multi-page document about eye care for seniors. You will use the find and replace feature, create bookmarks, headers and footers, and captions. You will insert section and page breaks, control text flow as necessary, and insert cross-references. You will also create a table of figures, an index, a table of contents, and a bibliography.

EXERCISE DIRECTIONS

Insert Comments, Track Changes, and Use Find and Replace

1. Start Word, if necessary.
2. Open the **59SENIORS** document and save it as **59SENIORS_*xx*.**
3. Use Find to locate the first occurrence of the text *the elderly.*
4. Insert the following comment: **I think this term is outdated. We should use Seniors or Senior Citizens instead.**
5. Turn on the Track Changes feature.
6. Find and replace all occurrences of the text *the elderly* with the text **seniors**. Use the match case option.
7. Find and replace all occurrences of the text *the Elderly* with the text **Seniors**. Use the match case option.

Edit and Format the Document

1. In the **59SENIORS_*xx*** document, change to Full Screen Reading view.
2. Go to screen 3.
3. Go to screen 1.

4. Close Full Screen Reading view.
5. Display Thumbnails.
6. Display the Document Map.
7. Go to the heading *Nutrition.*
8. Insert a bookmark named *Nutrition.*
9. Go to the heading *Eye Site and Medication.*
10. Under the heading *Eye Site and Medication*, move the paragraph beginning with the text *The U.S. Department of Agriculture* and the list that follows it to the end of the section *Nutrition.*
11. Go to the section *Common Eye Ailments.*
12. Close the Document Map.
13. Save the changes to the document.
14. Save a copy of the document with the name **59SENIORSR_*xx*.**
15. In the **59SENIORSR_*xx*** document, accept all changes, and then turn off the Track Changes feature.
16. Delete the comment.
17. Delete the bookmark.

Insert Captions and Cross-References

1. Insert the caption Table 1 for the first table in the document, using the default settings.

2. Insert the caption Table 2 for the second table in the document, using the default settings.

3. In the second column of Table 1, insert hyperlinked cross-references to the page numbers where the reader can find the corresponding heading.

4. At the end of the text in the sections on *Presbyopia*, *Cataracts*, and *Macular Degeneration* insert the cross-reference text **For a list of symptoms, refer to**, and insert a cross-reference to Table 2. Insert the same cross-reference before the last sentence in the section on *Glaucoma*.

Create a Bibliography

1. Select the MLA style of bibliography citations.

2. Position the insertion point after the first sentence under the heading *Common Eye Ailments*, and insert the following bibliography citation:

   a. Type of Source: **Web site**

   b. Author: **American Academy of Ophthalmology**

   c. Select the Corporate Author checkbox

   d. Name of Web Page: **EyeSmart**

   e. Year: **2007**

   f. Year Accessed: **2008**

   g. Month: **May**

   h. Day: **20**

   i. URL: **http://www.geteyesmart.org/**

3. Position the insertion point after the last sentence under the heading *Common Eye Ailments*, and insert the following bibliography citation:

   a. Type of Source: **Web site**

   b. Author: **Family Vision Care Center**

   c. Select the Corporate Author checkbox

   d. Name of Web Page: **Senior Eye Care**

   e. Year: **2007**

   f. Year Accessed: **2008**

   g. Month Accessed: **May**

   h. Day Accessed: **20**

   i. URL: **http://www.saratogasight.com/Seniors.htm**

4. Position the insertion point after the first sentence under the heading *Cataracts*, and insert the following bibliography citation:

   a. Type of Source: **Web site**

   b. Author: **Burcham Eyecare Center**

   c. Select the Corporate Author checkbox

   d. Name of Web Page: **Helpful Eye Health Information**

   e. Year: **2007**

   f. Year Accessed: **2008**

   g. Month Accessed: **May**

   h. Day Accessed: **20**

   i. URL: **http://www.denver-eye.com/ eye-health.htm#Cataracts**

5. Position the insertion point at the end of the text under the heading *Glaucoma*, and insert the following bibliography citation:

   a. Type of Source: **Document from Web site**

   b. Author: **University of Illinois Eye & Ear Infirmary**

   c. Select the Corporate Author checkbox

   d. Name of Web Page: **Glaucoma causes Optic Nerve Cupping (atrophy) and Vision Loss**

   e. Name of Web site: **The Eye Digest**

   f. Year: **2007**

   g. Month: **June**

   h. Day: **16**

   i. Year Accessed: **2008**

   j. Month Accessed: **May**

   k. Day Accessed: **20**

   l. URL: **http://www.agingeye.net/glaucoma/ glaucoma information.php**

6. Position the insertion point after the first sentence under the heading *Eye Sight and Medication*, and insert the following bibliography citation:

   a. Type of Source: **Web site**

   b. Author: **Transitions Optical, Inc.**

   c. Select the Corporate Author checkbox

   d. Name of Web Page: **Medications**

   e. Year: **2007**

   f. Year Accessed: **2008**

   g. Month Accessed: **May**

   h. Day Accessed: **20**

   i. URL: **http://www.eyeglassguide.com/visiting/ Medications.aspx**

7. Position the insertion point at the end of the second sentence under the heading *Lifestyle Choices*, and insert the following bibliography citation:

   a. Type of Source: **Document from Web site**

   b. Author: **George L. Schmidt, O.D.**

   c. Name of Web Page: **Preventing Eye Disease and Blindness**

   d. Name of Web site: **The Eye Site**

   e. Year Accessed: **2008**

   f. Month Accessed: **May**

   g. Day Accessed: **20**

   h. URL: **http://www.i-care.net/eyereport.html**

8. Position the insertion point at the end of the first paragraph under the heading *Nutrition* and insert the University of Illinois bibliography citation.

9. Insert a page break at the end of the document.

10. At the top of the last page, type the heading **Bibliography**, using the Heading 1 style, centered.

11. Below the new heading, insert the bibliography.

Create an Index, Table of Figures, and a Table of Contents

1. Insert a page break after the heading *Conclusion* and before the bibliography.

2. At the top of the new page, type the heading **Table of Figures** using the Heading 1 style, centered.

3. On a new line below the heading, insert a table of figures, using the Classic format, with page numbers right-aligned, using dot tab leaders.

4. Leave a blank line and then type the heading **Index** using the Heading 1 style, centered.

5. Mark items to create an index for the document. Use your judgment as to which words to include. Include at least ten words. Include at least two cross-references. Include at least three subentries.

6. When all items are marked, move the insertion point to a blank line below the heading, Index, and create the index. Use the Classic format, with page numbers right-aligned, using dot tab leaders, indented in two columns.

7. Display the index in Print Preview.

8. Insert a blank line before the heading *Overview* near the beginning of the document, and clear all formatting from it.

9. Generate a table of contents in the Classic format, with page numbers right-aligned, using dot tab leaders, with no hyperlinks.

10. Insert a next page section break between the table of contents and the heading *Overview*.

11. Set the margins in the first section of the document to be 1.5" on the left and right.

Complete the Document

1. Insert a header on all but the first page that has your name flush left and the company name (**StyleEyes, Inc.**) flush right.

   ✓ *Adjust the right tab stop if necessary.*

2. Insert a footer on all pages that has today's date flush left and the page number in the format of *Page X of N* flush right.

   ✓ *Adjust the tab stops if necessary.*

3. Preview all pages of the document and check the overall layout and formatting.

4. Insert a page break before Table 2.

5. Update the page numbers in cross-references, the table of contents, the table of figures, and the index.

6. Check the spelling and grammar in the document.

7. Display the document in Print Preview again. With two pages displayed at a time, it should look similar to the following illustrations.

8. If necessary, make adjustments and corrections.

9. Print the document.

10. Close the document, saving all changes.

Illustration A, Pages 1 and 2

Eye Care for Seniors
How Aging Affects the Health of Our Eyes
Prepared by
StyleEyes, Inc.

Today's Date

Student's Name   StyleEyes, Inc.

Overview

As people age their bodies change in many ways. One feature that may be overlooked is the effects of aging on eyesight. And yet, good vision may have a positive impact on a senior's ability to enjoy life to its fullest, while poor vision can lead to an inability to function in society which in turn may lead to depression and lost quality of life.

This report takes a look at some of the unique eye care challenges facing seniors, as well as actions they and their caregivers can take to insure proper eye health.

Common Eye Ailments

According to the American Academy of Ophthalmology, most Americans begin experiencing some form of vision loss starting at age forty (American Academy of Ophthalmology). Many seniors are afraid to admit that they are experiencing vision problems, because they think it will be seen as a sign that they cannot continue lively independently. However, most of the common eye ailments can be prevented, cured, or treated successfully. The most common eye ailments affecting seniors are listed in Table 1. (Family Vision Care Center)

Table 1

Common Eye Ailments	
Ailment	For more information, refer to page:
Presbyopia	2
Cataracts	3
Glaucoma	3
Macular degeneration	3

Presbyopia

Presbyopia is the gradual decline in the ability to focus on close objects, or to see small print. It is the result of a normal process of aging in which the lens of the eye becomes thicker, which causes it to lose its ability to properly focus light. This condition can easily be corrected by proper eyeglasses. For a list of symptoms, refer to Table 2.

Today's Date

Illustration B, Pages 3 and 4

Student's Name   StyleEyes, Inc.

Cataracts

The leading cause of reversible blindness in the United States is cataracts. (Burcham Eyecare Center) Cataracts cloud the eye's normally clear, transparent lens, resulting in blurred vision. This is one of the most common and most treatable eye conditions among seniors. Vision can usually be restored by eye surgery, usually done on an outpatient basis. For a list of symptoms, refer to Table 2.

Glaucoma

Glaucoma is caused by a progressive increase of pressure within the eye. It can lead to irreversible damage to the optic nerve, which is responsible for carrying images to the brain. In the early stages it may have no symptoms, but it can be diagnosed during an eye exam. When caught early, vision loss can be prevented. For a list of symptoms, refer to Table 2. Anyone can get glaucoma, but those at higher risk include (University of Illinois Eye and & Ear Infirmary):

- African-Americans over the age of forty.
- Anyone over the age of sixty.
- People with a family history of glaucoma.

Macular Degeneration

Macular degeneration occurs when the macula, or central point of focus on the retina, is damaged. This may occur naturally with aging, as the macula becomes thin. It reduces the ability of the eye to see fine detail, and may eventually lead to blindness. It affects as many as 15 million people over the age of fifty. There is no proven treatment, but many people believe that nutrition may play a role. For a list of symptoms, refer to Table 2.

Today's Date

Student's Name   StyleEyes, Inc.

Table 2

Some Symptoms of Common Eye Ailments	
Symptom	Ailment
Straining to read newsprint	Presbyopia
Confusing similar numerals	Presbyopia
Difficulty focusing on price tags	Presbyopia
Blurry vision	Cataracts
Loss of night vision	Cataracts
Cloudiness on the eye lens	Cataracts
Difficulty judging distances	Cataracts
Seeing halos	Cataracts
Reduced ability to see fine detail	Macular degeneration
General loss of vision	Glaucoma

Maintaining Eye Health

In addition to annual eye exams, many people consider that eye health, like general body health, can be affected by lifestyle choices and diet. As such, seniors can take steps to maintain their vision.

Nutrition

It is generally accepted that food choices can help reduce the risk for chronic diseases such as heart disease, cancers, diabetes, stroke, and osteoporosis. However, few people stop to consider that diet and nutrition can also play a role in reducing eye ailments and vision problems. (University of Illinois Eye and & Ear Infirmary)

The U.S Department of Agriculture states that the basic checklist for insuring proper nutrition is the same for all people, no matter what their age:

- Eat a variety of foods.
- Choose a diet high in grain products, vegetables, and fruits.
- Choose a diet low in fat, saturated fat, and cholesterol.
- Choose a diet moderate in sugars.
- Choose a diet moderate in salt and sodium.
- Drink alcohol only in moderation.
- Drink plenty of water.

Today's Date

Illustration C, Pages 5 and 6

Page 5:

Student's Name   StyleEyes, Inc.

Lifestyle Choices

    The single most important step anyone can take to improve health is to stop smoking. Smoking increases your risk of developing macular degeneration by up to 600%, and more than doubles your risk for cataracts. (George L. Schmidt) Other factors that impact eye health include physical fitness, family and social networks, intellectual activity, and economics

Eye Sight and Medication

    Both prescription and over the counter medications can affect vision (Transitions Optical, Inc.). Some side effects of medications may be only temporary, but others can cause long-term changes in your eyes. Combining medications can also cause visual side effects, so seniors must be sure doctors know what drugs they are already taking before prescribing new drugs. Also, it is important to let optometrists know about any medications. Medications affect each person differently, but some common side effects include:

- Blurry vision
- Poor night vision
- Dry eyes
- Double vision
- Increased pupil dilation
- Sensitivity to light
- Excessive tearing

Conclusion

    Maintaining eye health and proper vision is important for seniors because as people age, nervous system response time slows. Proper vision helps insure seniors will function correctly in situations where response time matters, such as while driving, biking, or even walking on city streets. They will also enjoy life more.

Today's Date   Page 5 of 7

Page 6:

Student's Name   StyleEyes, Inc.

Table of Figures

Index

Today's Date   Page 6 of 7

Illustration D, Page 7

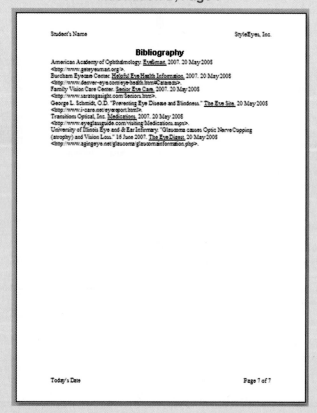

Student's Name   StyleEyes, Inc.

Bibliography

American Academy of Ophthalmology. *EyeSmart.* 2007. 20 May 2008 <http://www.geteyesmart.org/>.

Burcham Eyecare Center. *Helpful Eye Health Information.* 2007. 20 May 2008 <http://www.denver-eye.com/eye-health.html#Cataracts>.

Family Vision Care Center. *Senior Eye Care.* 2007. 20 May 2008 <http://www.saratogasight.com/Seniors.htm>.

George L. Schmidt, O.D. "Preventing Eye Disease and Blindness." *The Eye Site.* 20 May 2008 <http://www.i-care.net/eyereport.html>.

Transitions Optical, Inc. *Medications.* 2007. 20 May 2008 <http://www.eyeglassguide.com/vision/Medications.aspx>.

University of Illinois Eye and & Ear Infirmary. "Glaucoma causes Optic Nerve Cupping (atrophy) and Vision Loss." 16 June 2007. *The Eye Digest.* 20 May 2008 <http://www.agingeye.net/glaucoma/glaucomainformation.php>.

Today's Date   Page 7 of 7

Curriculum Integration

Application Skills   A thesis is an unproven statement set forward in an argument. Of course, if you present a thesis, you should provide supporting evidence that you are right in order to make the point and win the argument. For your language arts class, develop a thesis about a book you are reading or a topic you are studying. Write a multi-page report presenting and defending your thesis. Once you select your thesis you might want to conduct research in your school library or on the Internet. Take notes and keep track of your sources. When you understand the argument you want to make, and the supporting facts you will use, use the tools you have learned in Lesson 8 to create the report. Use Outlining to develop the structure of the report, keep track of the word count, and use the different tools available to view and preview the document, and to edit and improve it. Based on how your instructor wants you to include citations, insert footnotes and endnotes or use section breaks to create a separate works cited page. Insert headers and footers and create a title page, like the one shown in Illustration A. Have a classmate read the report and use comments and revision marks to make suggestions on how you can improve it. You can then accept or reject the changes.

EXERCISE DIRECTIONS

Select a thesis and conduct research that will help you support your argument.

Start Word, if necessary, and create a new document. Save it as **60THESIS_xx**.

Select to display elements that might help you while you work, such as the rulers, nonprinting characters, and text boundaries, and make sure all the features you want to use are enabled, such as AutoCorrect and AutoFormat as You Type.

Change to Outline view and create an outline for your thesis.

Change to Print Layout view and add the body text to fill out the report, applying formatting as you work.

Complete a first draft and proofread it for organization as well as for errors. Make edits and improvements.

Ask a classmate to review the report and use Track Changes and Comments to suggest improvements.

Read the document again, accepting and rejecting the changes and addressing the comments.

When the second draft is complete, proofread it again and make edits and improvements.

Insert footnotes and endnotes, or insert citations and create a bibliography.

Create a title page.

Insert headers and footers.

Before finalizing the report, proofread it again, and ask a classmate to proofread it as well. Check the layout to determine if you should insert hard page breaks.

Check the spelling and grammar.

Print the report.

Close the document, saving all changes.

Illustration A, first and last pages

How Historical Events Influence Character Behavior in Ernest Hemingway's *The Sun Also Rises*

By

Student's Name

Today's Date

Language Arts

8 Period

Student's Name   Today's Date

Works Cited

Macnaughton, W.R. "Maisie's Grace Under Pressure: Some Thoughts on James and Hemingway." *Contemporary Literary Criticism*

Pope, Nakia S. *The Saloon Must Go and I Will Take It With Me: American Prohibition, Nationalism, and Expatriation in "The Sun Also Rises"*, 15 May 2005. <etext.lib.virginia.edu/railton/onam311/onam711/popst2.html>.

Schmalbach, John Newman and John. *United States History: Preparing for the Advanced Placement Examination*. New York: Amsco Publications, 1985.

Spilka, Mark. "The Death of Love in "The Sun Also Rises"." *Contemporary Literary Criticism* 254-255.

Unknown. *Lady Ashley - Distressed Diva or Dynamite Dame?* 17 May 2005. 30 May 2005 <http://cfb.vg/essay.html>.

---. "Themes, Motifs, and Symbols of" The Sun Also Rises". 15 May 2005. 30 May 2005 <http://www.sparknotes.com>.

Wyatt, David M. "Hemingway's Uncanny Beginnings." *Contemporary Literary Criticism*

- Many documents can be **published** using the computer, printer, and software that you already have at home, work, or school.

- If you have complex publishing requirements such as color matching or binding, you may be able to design the document on your own equipment, but you may need to use a **commercial printer** to produce the final product.

- A third alternative for publishing a document is to create a file, then print it or e-mail it to a copy shop for reproduction.

Create Newsletter Columns

- By default, a Word document has one column, the width of the page from the left margin to the right margin.

- Use Word's Columns feature to divide a document into more than one **newsletter-style column**.

  ✓ *Use tables to create side-by-side columns; use the Columns feature to create newsletter-style columns; use tabs to align data along a single line in a document.*

- You can apply column formatting to an entire document or to the current section.

- By dividing a document into sections using section breaks, you can combine different numbers of columns within a single document.

- Multiple columns are not displayed in Draft view. Switch to Print Layout view or Print Preview to see the column formatting in a document.

- You can apply column formatting to existing text or you can set column formatting before typing new text.

Set Column Width

- By default, Word creates columns of equal width, but you can change the width of any column.

- Click the Columns button ▦ to select from Word's five preset column width arrangements or to open the Columns dialog box.

- In the Columns dialog box, you can select a preset column width, set precise columns widths, or adjust the amount of space in the **gutter** between columns.

- You can also drag the column margins to adjust column widths and gutter spacing.

Columns dialog box

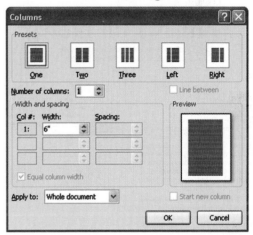

Insert Column Breaks

- By default, text flows to the top of the next column when the current column is filled.

- Use a column break to force text to flow to the top of the next column before the current column is filled.

- Column breaks are useful for moving headings or headlines to the top of a column.

Newsletter columns

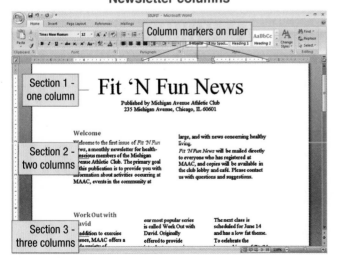

Balance Columns

- If there is not enough text to fill the last column in a document, the columns will appear uneven.
- You can balance the amount of text in multiple columns on a page by inserting a continuous section break at the end of the last column on the page.

About Layout and Design

- The way you set up a page affects the way the reader sees and interprets the textual information.
- Effective **page layout** uses the basic principles of design, including **contrast**, **balance**, and **consistency** to highlight the text and capture the reader's attention.
- In addition to newsletter columns, you can use features such as tables, borders, font formatting, lists, alignment, pictures, and spacing to create interesting and informative documents.

Unbalanced columns

Fit 'N Fun News
Published by Michigan Avenue Athletic Club
235 Michigan Avenue, Chicago, IL 60601

Welcome

Welcome to the first issue of *Fit 'N Fun News*, a monthly newsletter for health-conscious members of the Michigan Avenue Athletic Club. The primary goal of this publication is to provide you with information about activities occurring at MAAC, events in the community at large, and with news concerning healthy living.

Fit 'N Fun News will be mailed directly to everyone who has registered at MAAC, and copies will be available in the club lobby and café. Please contact us with questions and suggestions. We will do our best to address your comments in future issues.

Work Out with David

In addition to exercise classes, MAAC offers a wide variety of specialized instruction to help you maintain a healthy lifestyle. One of our most popular series is called Work Out with David. Originally offered to provide introductory exercise classes, the program has been expanded to cover all facets of healthy living.

The next class is scheduled for June 14 and has a low fat theme. Topics include Low fat vs. No fat, how to read nutrition labels, and low fat dining out.

To celebrate the inaugural issue of *Fit 'N Fun News*, we are offering our readers early registration. Bring this issue to the front desk before May 30 to guarantee your place. Call 312-555-3521 for more information.

Balanced columns

Fit 'N Fun News
Published by Michigan Avenue Athletic Club
235 Michigan Avenue, Chicago, IL 60601

Welcome

Welcome to the first issue of *Fit 'N Fun News*, a monthly newsletter for health-conscious members of the Michigan Avenue Athletic Club. The primary goal of this publication is to provide you with information about activities occurring at MAAC, events in the community at large, and with news concerning healthy living.

Fit 'N Fun News will be mailed directly to everyone who has registered at MAAC, and copies will be available in the club lobby and café. Please contact us with questions and suggestions. We will do our best to address your comments in future issues.

Work Out with David

In addition to exercise classes, MAAC offers a wide variety of specialized instruction to help you maintain a healthy lifestyle. One of our most popular series is called Work Out with David. Originally offered to provide introductory exercise classes, the program has been expanded to cover all facets of healthy living.

The next class is scheduled for June 14 and has a low fat theme. Topics include Low fat vs. No fat, how to read nutrition labels, and low fat dining out.

To celebrate the inaugural issue of *Fit 'N Fun News*, we are offering our readers early registration. Call 312-555-3521 for more information.

PROCEDURES

Create Columns of Equal Width

To select preset column widths:

1. Click the **Page Layout** tab .... Alt + P

    Page Setup Group

2. Click the **Columns** button .... J

3. Click the number of columns to create .... ↓/↑, ↵Enter

To set precise column widths:

1. Click the **Page Layout** tab .... Alt + P

    Page Setup Group

2. Click the **Columns** button .... J

3. Click **More Columns** C

4. Click **Number of columns** box .... Alt + N

5. Type the number of columns to create.

    OR

    Click the increment arrows to enter the number of columns.

6. If necessary, click to select the **Equal column width** checkbox .... Alt + E

7. Click in Column 1 **Width** box .... Alt + I

8. Type column width in inches.

    ✓ You may click the increment arrows to enter the width.

9. Click in Column 1 **Spacing** box .... Alt + S

10. Type gutter width in inches

    ✓ You may click the increment arrows to enter the width.

11. Click **OK** .... ↵Enter

Create Columns of Unequal Width

1. Click the **Page Layout** tab .... Alt + P

    Page Setup Group

2. Click the **Columns** button .... J

3. Click **More Columns** C

4. Click **Number of columns** box .... Alt + N

5. Type the number of columns to create.

    OR

    Click the increment arrows to enter the number of columns.

6. For column 1, do the following:

    a. Click in Column 1 **Width** box .... Alt + I

    b. Type column width in inches.

        ✓ You may click the increment arrows to enter the width.

    c. Click in Column 1 **Spacing** box .... Alt + S

    d. Type gutter width in inches

        ✓ You may click the increment arrows to enter the width.

7. Click to deselect the **Equal column width** check box ...... Alt + E

8. Repeat step 6 to set column and gutter widths for additional columns.

9. Click **OK** .... ↵Enter

Adjust Column Widths and Gutter Spacing with the Mouse

1. Create columns.

2. Position mouse pointer on column margin marker in ruler.

    ✓ When positioned correctly, the mouse pointer changes to a horizontal resize pointer ↔ and the ScreenTip displays either Left Margin or Right Margin.

3. Drag left or right.

    ✓ Press and hold Alt while you drag to see the current width of all columns and gutters.

Return to One Column Formatting

1. Click the **Page Layout** tab .... Alt + P

    Page Setup Group

2. Click the **Columns** button .... J

3. Click **One** .... ↵Enter

Insert Column Break

1. Position insertion point where you want the break.

2. Click the **Page Layout** tab .... Alt + P

    Page Setup Group

3. Click the **Breaks** button .... B

4. Click **Column** C

Balance Columns

1. Position insertion point at end of last column.

2. Click the **Page Layout** tab .... Alt + P

    Page Setup Group

3. Click the **Breaks** button .... B

4. Click **Continuous** .... O

EXERCISE DIRECTIONS

Apply Formatting

1. Start Word, if necessary.
2. Open ◉61FIT.
3. Save the file as **61FIT_xx**.
4. Format the document as follows:
   a. Center the title and increase the font size to 48 points.
   b. Center the company name and address (lines 2 and 3).
   c. Leave 12 points of space after the address (line 3).
   d. Format the three headlines (*Welcome*, *Work Out with David*, and *Recipe Showcase*) using the Heading 1 style.
   e. Format the three occurrences of *Fit 'N Fun News* in the body of the newsletter in italic.
   f. Create a bulleted list out of the three topics listed in the *Work Out with David* article.
   g. Insert 3 points of space before and 3 points of space after all body text paragraphs in the first two articles (excluding the items in the bulleted list).
   h. Format the recipe title and serving information (*Ginger Chicken and Corn* and *Yield: Six Servings*) with the Heading 2 style.
   i. Insert a right tab stop on that line to align the serving information at the 5" mark on the horizontal ruler.
   j. Apply the Heading 3 style to the text *Ingredients* and *Directions*.

   ✓ *To locate the Heading 3 style, display the Styles task pane, and set options to show All Styles.*

   k. Format the directions as a numbered list.

Create Columns

1. Format the entire document into three columns of equal width.
2. Preview the document.
3. Return to one column formatting.
4. Position the insertion point at the beginning of the heading *Welcome* and insert a continuous section break to create two sections in the document.
5. Format the second section (from the headline *Welcome* to the end of the document) into two columns of equal width.
6. Preview the document.
7. Insert another continuous section break before the headline *Recipe Showcase* to create three sections in the document.
8. Insert another continuous section break before the heading *Ingredients* to create four sections in the document.
9. Apply one-column formatting to the third section (the section containing the headline *Recipe Showcase*).
10. Format the fourth section (from the heading *Ingredients* to the end of the document) using the Left Preset arrangement.
11. Decrease the gutter spacing between the columns in the fourth section to .25".
12. Preview the document. It should look similar to the one in Illustration A.
13. Check the spelling and grammar in the document.
14. Print the document.
15. Close the document, saving all changes.

Illustration A

Fit 'N Fun News

Published by Michigan Avenue Athletic Club
235 Michigan Avenue, Chicago, IL 60601

Welcome

Welcome to the first issue of *Fit 'N Fun News*, a monthly newsletter for health-conscious members of the Michigan Avenue Athletic Club. The primary goal of this publication is to provide you with information about activities occurring at MAAC, events in the community at large, and with news concerning healthy living.

Fit 'N Fun News will be mailed directly to everyone who has registered at MAAC, and copies will be available in the club lobby and café. Please contact us with questions and suggestions. We will do our best to address your comments in future issues.

Work Out with David

In addition to exercise classes, MAAC offers a wide variety of specialized instruction to help you maintain a healthy lifestyle. One of our most popular series is called Work Out with David. Originally offered to provide introductory exercise classes, the program has been expanded to cover all facets of healthy living.

The next class is scheduled for June 14 and has a low fat theme. Topics include:

- Low fat vs. No fat
- How to read nutrition labels
- Low fat Dining Out

To celebrate the inaugural issue of *Fit 'N Fun News*, we are offering our readers early registration. Bring this issue to the front desk before May 30 to guarantee your place. Call 312-555-3521 for more information.

Recipe Showcase

Ginger Chicken and Corn

Yield: Six Servings

Ingredients

3 ears of corn on the cob
12 chicken wings
1" piece of ginger root
6 tblsp. lemon juice
4 tsp sunflower oil
1 tblsp. sugar

Directions

1. Peel and grate gingerroot into a bowl.
2. Mix in lemon juice, sunflower oil and sugar.
3. Clean corn and cut each horizontally into 6 pieces.
4. Add corn and chicken to ginger mixture and toss to coat evenly.
5. Thread corn and chicken on to skewers.
6. Cook under broiler or on grill, basting frequently, until corn is golden brown and tender and chicken is cooked through, about 20 minutes.

ON YOUR OWN

1. Research the types of technologies available for desktop publishing. For example, look up information about different software programs, the types of printers that might be appropriate, and other equipment that might be useful.
2. Start Word and create a new document.
3. Save the document as **OWD61_xx**.
4. Create a newsletter.
5. Set up the newsletter so it has a one-column title at the top.
6. Divide the rest of the document into either two or three columns.
7. Write two or three articles for the newsletter, including one that explains what you have learned about desktop publishing technology. The others might include information about your classes, job, movies or television shows you enjoy, or a trip you have taken recently.
8. Try adjusting the widths of the columns.
9. Try changing the number of columns.
10. Insert column breaks as necessary.
11. Balance the columns if necessary.
12. Check the spelling and grammar in the document.
13. Ask a classmate to review the document and make comments or suggestions.
14. Incorporate the suggestions into the document.
15. Print the document.
16. Close the document, saving all changes.

Skills Covered

- Use Dropped Capitals
- Enhance a Document with Borders and Shading

Software Skills   Dropped capital letters, borders, and shading can call attention to a single word, a line, a paragraph, or an entire page. They make a document visually appealing and interesting to the reader, so the reader will be more likely to take the time to read and remember the text.

Application Skills   Voyager Travel Adventures has asked you to create a one-page flyer for its customers. You'll use newsletter-style columns for the flyer, and you will enhance the document with dropped capitals, borders, and shading.

TERMS

3D   A perspective added to a border or object to give the appearance of three dimensions.

Border   A line placed on one or more sides of a paragraph(s), page, or text box.

Dropped capital   An enlarged capital letter that drops below the first line of body text in the paragraph.

Opacity   A measurement of the transparency of a color.

Shading   A color or pattern applied to a paragraph(s), page, or text box.

Shadow   An effect designed to give the appearance of a shadow behind a border or object.

NOTES

Use Dropped Capitals

- A **dropped capital** letter, called *drop cap,* is used to call attention to an opening paragraph.
- Word 2007 comes with two preset drop cap formats that drop the character three lines.
  - The Dropped format places the drop cap within the paragraph text.
  - The In margin format places the drop cap in the margin to the left of the paragraph.
- You can select options in the Drop Cap dialog box to change the font of the drop cap, the number of lines that the character drops, and the distance the drop character is placed from the paragraph text.
- Selecting a font that is different and more decorative than the paragraph font can enhance the drop cap effect.

- In Draft view, drop caps will not appear exactly as they will in a printed document. Use Print Layout view or Print Preview to display the drop cap correctly.
- Options for applying and formatting drop caps are in the Text group on the Insert tab of the Ribbon.

Drop Cap dialog box

Enhance a Document with Borders and Shading

- You can apply **borders** and/or **shading** to paragraphs or pages.
- Paragraph borders can be placed around a single paragraph or selected paragraphs.
- Page borders can be placed around all pages in a document, or pages in a specified section.
- Basic border and shading options are similar to those for tables, including line style, line width (weight), and line color.

   ✓ *Refer to Exercise 43 for information on table borders and shading.*

- Additional border options include **3D** or **Shadow** effects.
- In addition to using basic border options, Word has a built-in list of artwork designed for page borders. Art borders are useful for stationery, invitations, and other informal, decorative documents.
- When you select shading, you can select a solid color, or you can select a pattern style and color.
- The pattern styles include built-in geometric patterns as well as percentages of **opacity**.
   - The higher the percentage, the more opaque the color, with 100% being solid.
   - The lower the percentage, the more transparent the color, with 0% being no color.
- You apply paragraph and page borders and shading using the options in the Borders and Shading dialog box which you access from the Page Background group on the Page Layout tab of the Ribbon.
   - Use the Borders tab to apply borders to paragraphs

Borders and Shading dialog box: Borders tab

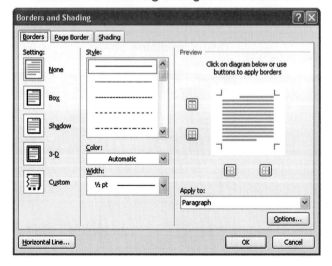

- Use the Page Border tab to apply borders to pages.

Borders and Shading dialog box: Page Border tab

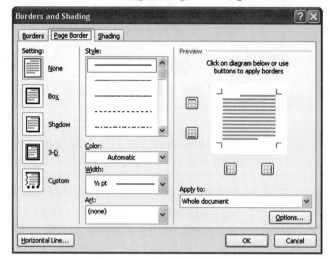

- Use the Shading tab to apply shading to paragraphs.

Borders and Shading dialog box: Shading tab

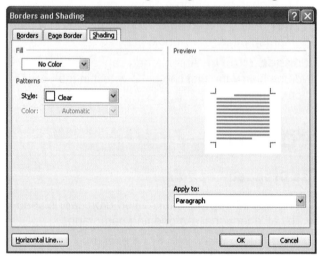

PROCEDURES

Create a Default Dropped Capital

1. Position insertion point in the paragraph.
2. Click the **Insert** tab .... Alt+N

   Text Group

3. Click the **Drop Cap** button 📰 .... R, C
4. Click an option on the drop-down menu .... ↓/↑, ↵Enter
   - **None**, to remove an existing drop cap.
   - **Dropped**, to drop the cap within the paragraph.
   - **In margin**, to drop the cap to the left of the paragraph.

Select Drop Cap Options

1. Position insertion point in the paragraph.
2. Click the **Insert** tab .... Alt+N

   Text Group

3. Click the **Drop Cap** button 📰 .... R, C
4. Click **Drop Cap Options** .... D
5. Click a drop cap position:
   - **None** .... N
   - **Dropped** .... D
   - **In margin** .... M
6. Click the **Font** drop-down arrow .... Alt+F
7. Click desired font .... ↓/↑, ↵Enter
8. Click the **Lines to drop** box .... Alt+L
9. Type number of lines to drop.

   OR

   Click increment arrows to enter number of lines to drop.

10. Click **Distance from text** box .... Alt+X
11. Enter distance from text in inches.

    OR

    Click increment arrows to enter distance from text.
12. Click **OK** .... ↵Enter

Apply Paragraph Borders

1. Position insertion point in the paragraph.

   OR

   Select paragraphs.
2. Click the **Page Layout** tab .... Alt+P

   Page Background Group

3. Click the **Page Border** button ▢ .... P, B
4. Click the **Borders** tab .... Ctrl+Tab↹, Ctrl+Tab↹
5. Click a Setting option:
   - **Box** .... Alt+X
   - **Shadow** .... Alt+A
   - **3-D** .... Alt+D
   - **Custom** .... Alt+U

   ✓ Click *None* to remove existing border.

6. Click desired line **Style** .... Alt+Y, ↓/↑
7. Click desired line **Color** .... Alt+C, ↓/↑/←/→, ↵Enter
8. Click desired line **Width** ...... Alt+W, ↓/↑, ↵Enter
9. For a custom border, in the Preview area click a paragraph side to add or remove border, or click a button:
   - ▦ to apply/remove top border.
   - ▦ to apply/remove bottom border.
   - ▦ to apply/remove left border.
   - ▦ to apply/remove right border.

   ✓ To adjust the spacing between the text and the border, click the Options button, enter spacing values, and then click OK.

10. Click **OK** .... ↵Enter

Apply Page Borders

1. Position insertion point on page.
2. Click the **Page Layout** tab .... Alt+P

   Page Background Group

3. Click the **Page Border** button ▢ .... P, B
4. Click the **Page Border** tab .... Alt+P
5. Click a Setting option:
   - **Box** .... Alt+X
   - **Shadow** .... Alt+A
   - **3-D** .... Alt+D
   - **Custom** .... Alt+U

   ✓ Click *None* to remove existing border.

6. Click desired line **Style** .... Alt+Y, ↓/↑
7. Click desired line **Color** .... Alt+C, ↓/↑/←/→, ↵Enter
8. Click desired line **Width** ...... Alt+W, ↓/↑, ↵Enter

   OR

   Select desired **Art** ...... Alt+R, ↓/↑, ↵Enter

   ✓ If art borders are not installed on your system, Word prompts you to install them.

9. Click **Apply to** drop-down arrow .... Alt+L
10. Click section to format .... ↓/↑, ↵Enter

11. For a custom border, in the Preview area click a paragraph side to add or remove border, or click a button:

- ⬛ 🔲 to apply/remove top border.
- ⬛ 🔲 to apply/remove bottom border.
- ⬛ 🔲 to apply/remove left border.
- ⬛ 🔲 to apply/remove right border.

✓ *To adjust the spacing between the text and the border, click the Options button, enter spacing values, and then click OK.*

12. Click **OK** .... ⏎Enter

Apply Shading

1. Position insertion point on page.

2. Click the **Page Layout** tab .... Alt+P

   Page Background Group

3. Click the **Page Border** button 🔲 .... P, B

4. Click the **Shading** tab ...... Alt+S

5. Click the **Fill** drop-down arrow .... Tab↹+↓

6. Click desired fill color .... ↓/↑/←/→, ⏎Enter

7. If desired, select pattern options as follows:

   a. Click **Style** drop-down arrow .... Alt+Y

   b. Click an opacity percentage or pattern .... ↓/↑, ⏎Enter

   c. Click **Color** drop-down arrow .... Alt+C

   d. Click pattern color ...... ↓/↑/←/→, ⏎Enter

8. Click **OK** .... ⏎Enter

EXERCISE DIRECTIONS

Apply Text, and Paragraph Formatting

1. Start Word, if necessary.
2. Open 💿 **62VOYAGER**.
3. Save the file as **62VOYAGER_xx**.
4. Apply a 36-point sans serif font such as Arial (which is used in the illustration) to lines 1 and 2.
5. Increase the font size on line 3 (the address) to 16 points and set 6 points of space after.
6. Increase the font size on line 4 (the volume name and date) to 14 points and set 12 points of space after.
7. On line 4, set a right tab stop flush with the right page margin (6" on the horizontal ruler). This will right-align the date, *Spring/Summer*, while keeping the text *Traveler's Newsletter* flush left.
8. Apply the Heading 1 style to the headlines: *Eco-Travel Symposium*, *Expanded Hours*, *New Agent*, and *Safety Booklet Available*.
9. Modify the formatting of the headline *Eco-Travel Symposium* to set only 12 points of space before.
10. Set 6 points of space before and after all body text paragraphs. Do not leave space before and after the three items in the list in the article about the Safety Booklet.
11. Insert a continuous section break before the headline *Eco-Travel Symposium*.
12. Format section 2 into three newsletter-style columns of equal width.

Apply Drop Caps, Borders, and Shading

1. Apply the default Dropped drop cap formatting to the first character under the headlines *Eco-Travel Symposium*, *New Agent*, and *Safety Booklet Available*.
2. Select the headline *Expanded Hours*, and the paragraph following it, and apply a 1 1/2-point solid line shadow border and a 12.5% gray shading.
3. Apply bullet list formatting to the questions listed as being answered in the booklet (if necessary, change the paragraph formatting so there is no space before or after the bulleted items), setting the bullet indent to 0 and the text indent to .25".
4. Select the bulleted list and apply a 1 1/2-point solid line outside border.
5. Select line 4 and apply the border shown in Illustration A along the top of the line, only.

   a. Open the Borders and Shading dialog box.

   b. Click the Borders tab.

   c. Select the line style (unequal double-line with the thinner line on the bottom).

   d. Select the line weight (3 points).

   e. Click to select the top border and to deselect the left, right, and bottom borders in the Preview area.

6. Add the border shown in Illustration A along the bottom of line 4.

   a. Open the Borders and Shading dialog box.

   b. Click the Borders tab.

   c. Select the line style (unequal double-line with the thinner line on the top).

   d. Select the line weight (3 points).

   e. Click to select the bottom border in the Preview area.

7. Apply a 10% gray shading to line 4, as shown in Illustration A.

8. Apply the Globes page border (select the border from the Art drop-down list) to the entire document, setting the line width to 24 points.

9. Check the spelling and grammar.

10. Display the document in Print Preview. It should look similar to the one in Illustration A.

11. Print the document.

12. Close the document, saving all changes.

Illustration A

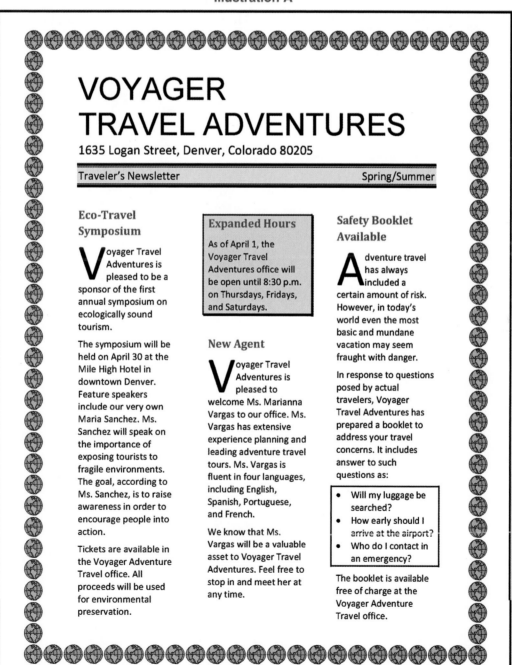

ON YOUR OWN

1. Open OWD61_xx, the newsletter document you created in the On Your Own section of Exercise 61, or open 62NEWS.

2. Save the file as OWD62_xx.

3. Apply dropped capitals to the first paragraph of each article.

4. Use borders to call attention to paragraphs. Try different effects, including different line styles, shadows, and 3-D. You might want to insert a border between the single column section and the multicolumn section, or after the last paragraph in each article.

5. Apply a page border.

6. If necessary, adjust paragraph spacing and column breaks and balance columns to improve the appearance of the newsletter.

7. Check the spelling and grammar in the document.

8. Preview the document.

9. Print the document.

10. Ask a classmate to review the document and offer comments and suggestions about the layout and design.

11. Incorporate the suggestions into the document.

12. Close the document, saving all changes.

Exercise | 63

Skills Covered

- **Set Paper Size**
- **Adjust Character Spacing**
- **Control Text Flow**
- **Insert a Blank Page**

Software Skills You can improve the appearance of a document and make the content easier to read by adjusting the amount of space around and between text and by controlling the way text flows from the bottom of one page to the top of the next. Specifically, you can set character spacing to make words easier to read, control text line and page breaks, and set a paper size. You can also insert a blank page anywhere in a document, or select a preformatted cover page design from a gallery to insert at the beginning of your document.

Application Skills Liberty Blooms, the flower shop, has asked you to prepare a handout brochure about selecting roses. They plan to print the handout on custom-sized paper. In this exercise, you will select a paper size, adjust character spacing, select options to control the text flow, and insert a cover page.

TERMS

Baseline The bottom of a line of text.

Content control A feature of Word 2007 that acts as a placeholder for information.

Cover page The first page of a document that usually displays such information as the document title and subtitle, the author's name, and the date.

Kerning Spacing between pairs of characters.

Orphan line The first line of a paragraph printed alone at the bottom of a page.

Page size The dimensions of a finished document page.

Paper size The dimensions of the sheet of paper on which a document is printed. Also called *sheet size*.

Widow line The last line of a paragraph printed alone at the top of a page.

NOTES

Set Paper Size

- The default **paper size** in Word 2007 is Letter, which is 8.5 inches by 11 inches.

- You can select from a list of different sizes such as Legal, which is 8.5 inches by 14 inches, Half Letter, which is 5.5 inches by 8.5 inches, 8 x 10, 5 x 7, or 4 x 6.

- You can also set your own custom size using the options on the Paper tab of the Page Setup dialog box.

  - ✓ *Note that although the term* **page size** *is often used interchangeably with the term paper size, they are not exactly the same. Page size is the dimensions of a finished document page, while paper size is the dimensions of the sheet of paper on which the document is printed.*

Paper tab of the Page Setup dialog box

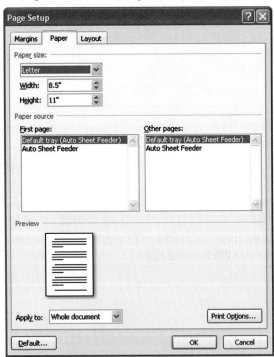

Adjust Character Spacing

- Use character spacing to improve the readability of the text, as well as to control the amount of text that fits on a line or on a page.

- In Word, the amount of space between characters is determined by the current font set.

- When certain characters that are wider than other characters in a font set are next to each other, they may appear to run together.

- Set the **kerning** to automatically adjust the space between selected characters, when the characters are larger than a particular point size.

- You can also adjust spacing between characters by changing the scale, the spacing, or the position.

  - Set the scale to stretch or compress selected text based on a percentage. For example, set the character spacing scale above 100% to stretch the text, or below 100% to compress the text.

  - Set the spacing to expand or condense the spacing between all selected characters by a specific number of points.

  - Set the position to raise or lower characters relative to the text **baseline** by a specific number of points.

Character Spacing tab of the Font dialog box

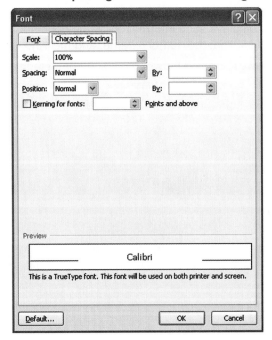

Control Text Flow

- Use text flow options to control the way Word breaks paragraphs and lines at the end of a page. For example, you can control whether or not a heading stays on the same page as the paragraph that follows it.

- The following text flow options are available on the Line and Page Breaks tab of the Paragraph dialog box:

  - **Widow/Orphan** control. Select this option to prevent either the first or last line of a paragraph from printing on a different page.

  - Keep with next. Select this option to prevent a page break between the current paragraph and the following paragraph.

  - Keep lines together. Select this option to prevent a page break within a paragraph.

  - Page break before. Select this option to force a page break before the current paragraph.

- You can also use shortcut keys or the Break dialog box to manually insert a hard line break.

- A hard line break forces Word to wrap text before reaching the right margin.

  ✓ *To see hard line breaks on-screen, display nonprinting characters.*

Line and Page Breaks tab of the Paragraph dialog box

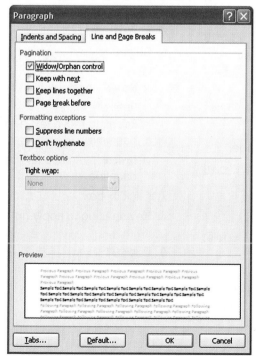

Insert a Blank Page

- You can insert a blank page anywhere in a document by selecting Blank Page in the Pages group on the Insert tab of the Ribbon.

- When you insert a blank page, Word inserts hard page breaks before and after the new page.

- You can insert a **cover page** by selecting Cover Page in the Pages group on the Insert tab of the Ribbon.

- Word includes a gallery of preformatted cover pages that include page layout and design features as well as placeholders—called **content controls**—for standard text, such as the document title and the author's name.

- You replace the sample text by typing new text, or by selecting data from the content control's drop-down list.

  ✓ *For more information on placeholders and content controls, refer to Exercise 66.*

PROCEDURES

Set Paper Size

1. Click **Page Layout** tab ...... Alt+P

   Page Setup Group

2. Click **Size** button 🗔 .... S, Z
3. Click desired size in gallery .... ↑/↓, ↵Enter

   OR

   a. Click **More Paper Sizes** .... A
   b. Click Paper size drop-down arrow .... Alt+R
   c. Click desired size .... ↑/↓, ↵Enter

   ✓ *To insert a continuous section break and format only the section following the insertion point location, click the Apply to drop-down arrow and click This point forward.*

   d. Click **OK** .... ↵Enter

Set a Custom Paper Size

1. Click **Page Layout** tab .... Alt+P

   Page Setup Group

2. Click **Size** button 🗔 .... S, Z
3. Click **More Paper Sizes** .... A
4. Click **Width** box .... Alt+W
5. Enter paper width.
6. Click **Height** box .... Alt+E
7. Enter paper height.

   ✓ *To insert a continuous section break and format only the section following the insertion point location, click the Apply to drop-down arrow and click This point forward.*

8. Click **OK** .... ↵Enter

Adjust Character Spacing

Set automatic kerning:

1. Select text to format.
2. Click the **Home** tab .... Alt+H

   Font Group

3. Click the **Font** group dialog box launcher 🗔 .... F, N
4. Click the **Character Spacing** tab .... Alt+R
5. Click to select **Kerning for fonts:** check box .... Alt+K
6. Click in **Points and above** box .... Alt+O
7. Key font size above which you wish to kern (in points).
8. Click **OK** .... ↵Enter

Set scale:

1. Select text to format.
2. Click the **Home** tab .... Alt+H

   Font Group

3. Click the **Font** group dialog box launcher 🗔 .... F, N
4. Click the **Character Spacing** tab .... Alt+R
5. Click the **Scale** drop-down arrow .... Alt+C
6. Select desired percentage .... ↑/↓, ↵Enter

   OR

   Enter custom percentage.

7. Click **OK** .... ↵Enter

Set spacing

1. Select text to format.
2. Click the **Home** tab .... Alt+H

   Font Group

3. Click the **Font** group dialog box launcher 🗔 .... F, N

4. Click the **Character Spacing** tab .... Alt+R
5. Click the **Spacing** drop-down arrow .... Alt+S
6. Select desired option: .... ↑/↓, ↵Enter
   - **Normal**, to use default spacing.
   - **Expanded**, to increase spacing.
   - **Condensed**, to decrease spacing.
7. Click **By** box .... Alt+B
8. Key spacing to apply (in points).
9. Click **OK** .... ↵Enter

Set position

1. Select text to format.
2. Click the **Home** tab .... Alt+H

   Font Group

3. Click the **Font** group dialog box launcher 🗔 .... F, N
4. Click the **Character Spacing** tab .... Alt+R
5. Click the **Position** drop-down arrow .... Alt+P
6. Select desired option .... ↑/↓, ↵Enter
   - **Normal**, to use default position.
   - **Raised**, to move text above baseline.
   - **Lowered**, to move text below baseline.
7. Click **By** box .... Alt+Y
8. Key spacing to apply (in points).
9. Click **OK** .... ↵Enter

Control Text Flow

1. Click the **Home** tab.............(Alt)+(H)

   Paragraph Group

2. Click the **Paragraph** group dialog box launcher [⌐] ....(P), (G)
3. Click the **Line and Page Breaks** tab ....(Alt)+(P)
4. Select or deselect desired option(s):
   - **Widow/Orphan control**...(Alt)+(W)
   - **Keep with next**............(Alt)+(X)
   - **Keep lines together**......(Alt)+(K)
   - **Page break before**........(Alt)+(B)
5. Click **OK** ....(↵Enter)

Insert a Blank Page

1. Position insertion point where you want to insert blank page.
2. Click the **Insert** tab ....(Alt)+(N)

   Pages Group

3. Click the **Blank Page** button [▯] ....(N), (P)

Insert a Cover Page

1. Position insertion point anywhere in document.
2. Click the **Insert** tab ....(Alt)+(N)

   Pages Group

3. Click the **Cover Page** button [▤] ....(V)
4. Click desired cover page in gallery ....(↑)/(↓)/(←)/(→)
5. Click text to replace.
6. Key new text.

EXERCISE DIRECTIONS

1. Start Word, if necessary.
2. Open the document ⊚**63HANDOUT**.
3. Save the document as **63HANDOUT**_xx_.
4. Set the paper size to 6.5 inches wide by 6.5 inches high.
5. Select the title heading and expand the character spacing by 1 point.
6. Scale the text in both bulleted lists to 90% of their original spacing.
7. Scroll down and position the insertion point in the orphan line of text at the bottom of page 2.
8. Select to use Widow/Orphan control. The line should move to the top of page 3.
9. Scroll down and select the second paragraph under the heading _Judging Rose Quality_.
10. Select the Keep lines together option. The entire paragraph should move to the top of page 4.
11. Scroll down and position the insertion point in the heading at the bottom of page 4.
12. Select the Keep with next option. The heading should move to the top of page 5.
13. Justify all body text paragraphs except the bulleted lists.
14. Insert the Tiles cover page.
15. On the cover page, click the Type the Company Name placeholder and type **Liberty Blooms**.
16. Select the text in the Title placeholder and type **Selecting Roses**.
17. Click the Subtitle placeholder and type **A Buyer's Guide**.
18. Click the Author placeholder and type your name.
19. Click the Year placeholder and type the current year. If necessary, decrease the font size of the year to 26 points.
20. Click the Address placeholder and type **345 Chestnut Street, Philadelphia, PA**.
21. Check the spelling and grammar in the document.
22. Display the cover page in Print Preview. It should look similar to Illustration A.
23. Close print preview and print the document.
24. Close the document, saving all changes.

LIBERTY BLOOMS FLOWER SHOP

Selecting Roses

A Buyer's Guide

Student's Name

2008

345 CHESTNUT STREET, PHILADELPHIA, PA

ON YOUR OWN

1. Start Word and create a new document.
2. Save the document as **OWD63_xx**.
3. Create a handout with at least three pages to give out at a meeting of a club, team, or organization.
4. Select a paper size and set margins as necessary.
5. Type the information you want to distribute. You might include articles about different subjects, or write about one subject.
6. Insert a cover page and replace the sample text by typing new text.
7. Preview the document and use character spacing and text flow options to adjust the spacing and position of text and paragraphs.
8. Preview the document again.
9. Print the document. Ask a classmate to review the document and offer comments or suggestions.
10. Incorporate the comments and suggestions into the document.
11. Close the document, saving all changes, and exit Word.

Exercise | 64

Skills Covered

- **Reveal Style Formatting**
- **Keep Track of Formatting**

- **Mark Formatting Inconsistencies**

Software Skills Consistent formatting insures that your documents look professional and are easy to read. Microsoft Office Word 2007 includes tools that help you monitor and track inconsistent formatting. You can use the Style Inspector to reveal details about paragraph and character formatting, and you can track and mark formatting inconsistencies as you work. Once you identify inconsistencies, you can use tools such as styles, themes, and direct formatting to correct them.

Application Skills You are preparing a document for the Liberty Blooms flower shop that lists classes the shop is offering in the coming months. However, the document does not appear to be formatted consistently. In this exercise, you will turn on the check formatting and mark formatting features, and you will reveal style formatting in order to identify and correct formatting inconsistencies.

TERMS

There is no new vocabulary in this exercise.

NOTES

Reveal Style Formatting

- Use Word's Style Inspector and Reveal Formatting task panes to display specific information about formatting applied to the current text.
- The Style Inspector displays the name of the current paragraph style and/or character style, as well as any direct formatting that has been manually applied.

  ✓ *For information on applying, creating, and modifying styles, refer to Exercise 29.*

Style Inspector task pane

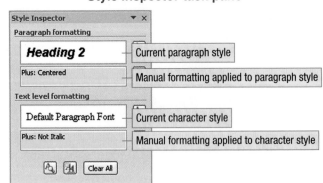

■ In the Reveal Formatting task pane, you can view specific details about font formatting, paragraph formatting, and page setup.

Reveal Formatting task pane

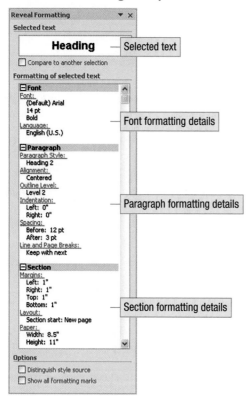

Keep Track of Formatting

■ As you learned in Exercise 29, Word 2007 keeps track of direct formatting that you apply manually.

■ You can turn the feature off by selecting it on the Advanced tab of the Word Options dialog box.

■ You can also customize the feature in the Style Pane Options dialog box to keep track of paragraph level formatting, font formatting, and/or bullet and numbering formatting.

Mark Formatting Inconsistencies

■ You can set Word to check formatting while you work in much the same way that it checks spelling and grammar.

■ If Word identifies a formatting inconsistency, it marks it with a wavy blue underline.

■ For example, if you apply direct formatting instead of a style, Word would identify the formatting as inconsistent.

■ You can ignore the blue lines and keep typing, or you can use a shortcut menu to correct the formatting error.

■ The automatic format checker is off by default; you must turn it on to use it.

✓ *You must have Keep Track of Formatting enabled in order to check formatting while you type.*

Mark formatting Inconsistencies

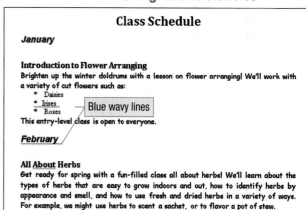

PROCEDURES

Reveal Formatting in the Style Inspector

1. Position insertion point in formatted text.
   OR
   Select formatted text.
2. Click the **Home** tab .... Alt + H
   > **Styles Group**
3. Click Styles group **dialog box launcher** 🔲 .... F, Y
4. Click **Style Inspector** button 🔲 .... Tab⁺ *5x*, ↵Enter
   ✓ *You can move the insertion point with the Style Inspector open in order to reveal formatting for different text.*

Reveal Formatting in the Reveal Formatting Task Pane

1. Position insertion point in text.
   OR
   Select formatted text.
2. Display Style Inspector.
3. Click **Reveal Formatting** button 🔲.

Turn Keep Track of Formatting Off or On

1. Click the **Office Button** 🔲 .... Alt + F
2. Click **Word Options** I
3. Click **Advanced** .... A
4. Click to select or deselect the **Keep track of formatting** check box .... Alt + E, E, Spacebar
   ✓ *A check mark in the check box indicates the option is selected.*
5. Click **OK** .... ↵Enter

Select Type of Formatting to Track

1. Turn on Keep Track of Formatting.
2. Click the **Home** tab .... Alt + H
   > **Styles Group**
3. Click Styles group **dialog box launcher** 🔲 .... F, Y
4. Click **Options** ..... Tab⁺ *7x*, ↵Enter
5. Click to select/deselect formatting to show as styles:
   ▪ **Paragraph level formatting** .... Alt + P
   ▪ **Font formatting** .... Alt + O
   ▪ **Bullet and numbering formatting** .... Alt + B
   ✓ *If the Select formatting to show as styles options are not available, the Keep Track of Formatting feature is off.*
6. Click **OK** .... ↵Enter

Turn on Automatic Format Checking

1. Click the **Office Button** 🔲 .... Alt + F
2. Click **Word Options** I
3. Click **Advanced** .... A
4. Click to select the **Keep track of formatting** check box .... Alt + E, E, Spacebar
   ✓ *A check mark in the check box indicates the option is selected.*
5. Click to select the **Mark formatting inconsistencies** check box .... Alt + F, Spacebar
   ✓ *A check mark in the check box indicates the option is selected.*
6. Click **OK** .... ↵Enter

Check Formatting as You Type

1. Right-click formatting inconsistency marked with blue, wavy underline.
2. Click desired correct formatting option on shortcut menu.
   OR
   Click **Ignore Once** to hide this occurrence I
   OR
   Click **Ignore Rule** to hide all occurrences .... U

EXERCISE DIRECTIONS

1. Start Word, if necessary.
2. Open the document ◉**64CLASSES**.
3. Save it as **64CLASSES_xx**.
4. Set Word to keep track of formatting and to mark formatting inconsistencies.
5. Notice that Word identifies a formatting inconsistency in the bulleted list, and marks it with a wavy blue underline.
6. Click on the underlined word—*Irises*—and then display the Style Inspector. Note that there are no styles applied to the text.
7. Keeping the Style Inspector open, click on the first bulleted item—*Daisies*. Note in the Style Inspector that it is formatted with the List Paragraph style.
8. Click on the third bulleted item—*Roses*. Note that it, too, is formatted with the List Paragraph style.
9. Delete the asterisk character and the following tab preceding the text Irises in the second bulleted item.
10. Use the Format Painter to copy the formatting from the first bulleted item to the second bulleted item—*Irises*. Note that now all three items have consistent formatting, and the blue wavy underline no longer displays.
11. Select the text *February* and format it in 14-pt., bold, italic, Arial.
12. Copy the formatting to the text *March*. Note that both words are now marked with blue wavy underlines.
13. Display the Reveal Formatting task pane, and then close the Style Inspector.
14. Examine the formatting for the text *March*.
15. Click in the text *February* in the document, and then examine its formatting in the Reveal Formatting task pane.
16. Right-click the text *February* in the document and click Replace direct formatting with style Heading 2 on the shortcut menu.
17. Right-click the text *March* in the document and click Replace direct formatting with style Heading 2 on the shortcut menu.
18. Examine the formatting in the Reveal Formatting task pane again. All three month headings should now be the same.
19. Check the spelling and grammar in the document.
20. Preview the document. It should look similar to Illustration A.
21. Print the document.
22. Set Word to track formatting, but deselect all options under Select formatting to show as styles in the Style Pane Options dialog box.
23. Turn off the Mark formatting inconsistencies feature.
24. Close the document, saving all changes.

Liberty Blooms

345 Chestnut Street, Philadelphia, PA 19106

Class Schedule

January

Introduction to Flower Arranging
Brighten up the winter doldrums with a lesson on flower arranging! We'll work with a variety of cut flowers such as:
* Daisies
* Irises
* Roses

This entry-level class is open to everyone.

February

All About Herbs
Get ready for spring with a fun-filled class all about herbs! We'll learn about the types of herbs that are easy to grow indoors and out, how to identify herbs by appearance and smell, and how to use fresh and dried herbs in a variety of ways. For example, we might use herbs to scent a sachet, or to flavor a pot of stew.

March

Perennial Garden Design
A successful perennial garden enhances blooms all season long, year after year. This seminar will cover the basics of planning a perennial garden. Learn how to determine the amount of space you need, how to lay out the garden, and how to select the right types of plants. Time permitting, we will discuss soil composition and planting techniques.

Space is limited for all classes and seminars. For more information or to register, call 215-555-2837 or visit our Web site www.libertyblooms.net.

ON YOUR OWN

1. Start Word and open OWD63_*xx*, the document you created in the On Your Own section of Exercise 63, or open 64NEWS.

2. Save the document as OWD64_*xx*.

3. Set Word to track formatting and to mark formatting inconsistencies.

4. If Word identifies formatting inconsistencies, use the Style Inspector or the Reveal Formatting task pane to review the formatting to determine the problems.

5. Correct the problems so that the formatting is consistent throughout the document.

   ✓ *If Word does not identify any inconsistencies, you might try to apply direct formatting in place of headings to see if Word marks the inconsistency.*

6. Check the spelling and grammar in the document.

7. Save changes and then print the document.

8. Ask a classmate to review the document and offer comments and suggestions.

9. Incorporate the suggestions into the document.

10. Set Word to track formatting but not to mark formatting inconsistencies.

11. Close the document, saving all changes.

Skills Covered

- Templates
- Set a Default Theme

- Restore a Template Theme

Software Skills Templates help you create consistent documents efficiently—and time after time. Most templates have a default theme which includes page setup and formatting settings to insure that new documents will be uniform. In many cases they include standard text and graphics as well. You can set a default theme for documents and templates, and you can restore a template theme to its original settings.

Application Skills The Michigan Avenue Athletic Club has asked Restoration Architecture to consult on its remodeling plan. Marilyn Stewart, a design consultant at Restoration Architecture, is planning a trip to discuss the work with the club's general manager. As an administrative assistant at Restoration Architecture, you are responsible for coordinating the travel arrangements. In this exercise, you will save a memo document as a template and then use it to create a memo to the client, detailing the itinerary. You will then use one of Word's built-in Fax Cover templates to create a fax cover sheet that you could use when transmitting the memo. You will also set a default template theme, and restore the theme to its original settings.

TERMS

Normal.dotx The default template used to create new, blank documents in Word 2007.

Template A sample or model document on which new documents are based. Templates include formatting settings, text, and graphics used to create the new documents.

NOTES

Templates

- All new Word documents are based on a **template**.
- Templates include formatting settings based on the default theme and style set, as well as page settings such as margins.
- For example, by default, the Normal template used for creating new blank documents uses the Office Theme and the Word 2007 Style Set.

  ✓ *For more information on style sets, refer to Exercise 29. For more information on themes, refer to Exercise 31.*

- Some templates include boilerplate text and graphics that are part of new documents.
- All new documents based on the same template will have the same default formatting settings and will display any boilerplate text and graphics entered in the template file.
- Some templates include editing directions or content controls that prompt you for the information you need to complete the document. You replace sample text, fill in missing information, and customize the document using standard editing and formatting commands.

- Word comes with built-in templates for creating common documents, such as memos, letters, Web pages, and resumes.
- You can create your own templates.
- You can select and preview templates in the New Document dialog box.
- Items in the left pane let you select from different categories of existing templates:
  - *Blank and recent* includes templates for blank documents and templates that you have used recently.
  - *Installed Templates* includes all templates installed on your computer.
  - *My templates* includes templates that you have created or customized and stored in the Templates folder.
  - ✓ *This includes templates created with previous versions of Microsoft Office Word.*
  - *New from existing* lets you create a new document based on an existing document or template, no matter where the file is stored.
- You can also preview and download templates from the Microsoft Office Online Web site.
- The templates available online are organized into categories, such as letters, memos, and reports. You select a category to view the available templates.
- Templates usually come in a variety of themes. Each theme includes different formatting, so you can select a theme that best suits your purpose.
- In addition, you can coordinate your documents by theme. For example, you can select a letter template and a resume template in the same theme.

- Template files have a .dotx extension. The default template for creating a blank document is called Normal, so it is named **Normal.dotx**.

Templates in New Document dialog box

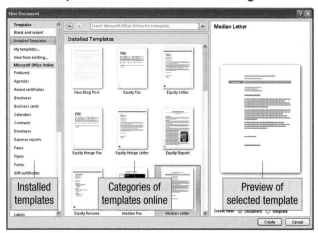

Installed templates

Categories of templates online

Preview of selected template

Set a Default Theme

- You can select a different theme and style set for a template, and set them as the default.
- If you change the default, new documents based on the template are created using the new default theme and style set.
- Take care when modifying the theme and style set associated with the Normal template, as the changes will affect all new, blank documents.

Restore a Template Theme

- If you modify the theme associated with a template, you can restore it by resetting the original template theme.
- Likewise, you can reset the style set associated with a template.
- If you change the default theme associated with a template, you can select the original settings, and then set them as the default.

PROCEDURES

Create a Document Using a Template

To use installed templates:
1. Click **Office Button** ...... Alt+F
2. Click **New** .... N

   ✓ *If desired template is listed in the Recently Used Templates list, click it and skip to step 5.*

3. In left pane, click **Installed Templates**.
4. In middle pane, click desired template.

   ✓ *A preview displays in the preview pane on the right.*

5. Click **Create** .... ↵Enter
6. Replace directions and prompts with text.
7. Edit and format document as desired.
8. Name and save document.

To use My templates:
1. Click **Office Button** ...... Alt+F
2. Click **New** .... N
3. In left pane, click **My templates**.
4. Click desired template.

   ✓ *If a preview is available, it displays in the preview pane on the right.*

5. Click **OK** .... ↵Enter
6. Replace directions and prompts with text.
7. Edit and format document as desired.
8. Name and save document.

To use New from existing:
1. Click **Office Button** ...... Alt+F
2. Click **New** .... N
3. In left pane, click **New from existing.**
4. If necessary, click common storage location in the Places bar, or click the **Save in** drop-down arrow and select storage location .... Alt+I

   ✓ *If you are using Windows Vista, click Browse Folders and then use Windows Vista tools to navigate to desired storage location.*

5. Click desired template or document file.
6. Click **Create New** .... ↵Enter
7. Replace directions and prompts with text.
8. Edit and format document as desired.
9. Name and save document.

Access Templates Online

1. Establish a connection to the Internet.
2. Click **Office Button** ...... Alt+F
3. Click **New** .... N

   ✓ *If desired template is listed in the Recently Used Templates list, click it and skip to step 6.*

4. In left pane, under Microsoft Office Online, click category of template.
5. Click desired template.
6. Click **Download.**

   ✓ *If necessary, read the license agreement and click Accept button.*

7. Follow prompts to complete download.

Save a Word Document as a Template

1. Create document to save as template.

   ✓ *Include all formatting and text you want included in new documents based on the template.*

2. Click **Office Button** ...... Alt+F
2. Point to **Save As** .... F
3. Click **Word Template** .... T
4. If necessary, click common storage location in the Navigation bar, or click the **Save in** drop-down arrow and select storage location .... Alt+I

   ✓ *If you are using Windows Vista, click Browse Folders and then use Windows Vista tools to navigate to desired storage location.*

   OR

   a. Click **Create New Folder** button.
   b. Type new folder name.
   c. Click **OK** .... ↵Enter
5. Select **File name** text box .... Alt+N
6. Type **file name**
7. Click **Save** .... Alt+S

Set a Default Theme and Style Set

1. Create a new document.

   ✓ *Use the template for which you want to change the theme and style set.*

2. Click the **Page Layout** tab .... Alt+P

Themes Group

3. Click the **Themes**
   button [A] .... [T], [H]
4. Click theme to
   apply .... [↑]/[↓]/[←]/[→], [↵Enter]

   ✓ *For more information on working
   with themes, refer to Exercise 31.*

5. Click the **Home** tab .... [Alt]+[H]

Styles Group

6. Click **Change Styles**
   button [A] .... [G]
7. Click **Style Set** .... [Y]
8. Click name of style set to
   apply .... [↑]/[↓], [↵Enter]

   ✓ *For more information on working
   with styles, refer to Exercise 29.*

9. Click **Change Styles**
   button [A] .... [Alt]+[H], [G]
10. Click **Set as Default** .... [S]

Restore a Template Theme

1. Click the **Page Layout**
   tab .... [Alt]+[P]

Themes Group

2. Click the **Themes**
   button [A] .... [T], [H]
3. Click **Reset to Theme from
   Template** .... [R]

Restore a Style Set

1. Click the **Home** tab .... [Alt]+[H]

Styles Group

2. Click **Change Styles**
   button [A] .... [G]
3. Click **Style Set** .... [Y]
4. Click **Reset to Quick Styles from
   Template** .... [R]

Restore the Default Normal Template Theme and Style Set

1. Create a new blank document.
2. Click the **Page Layout**
   tab .... [Alt]+[P]

Themes Group

3. Click the **Themes**
   button [A] .... [T], [H]
4. Click
   Office .... [↑]/[↓]/[←]/[→], [↵Enter]
5. Click the **Themes**
   button [A] .... [Alt]+[P], [T], [H]
6. Click **Reset to Theme from
   Template** .... [R]
7. Click the **Home** tab .... [Alt]+[H]

Styles Group

8. Click **Change Styles**
   button [A] .... [G]
9. Click **Style Set** .... [Y]
10. Click **Word 2007** .... [↑]/[↓], [↵Enter]
11. Click **Change Styles**
    button [A] .... [Alt]+[H], [G]
12. Click **Style Set** .... [Y]
13. Click **Reset to Quick Styles from
    Template** .... [R]
14. Click **Change Styles**
    button [A] .... [Alt]+[H], [G]
15. Click **Set as Default** .... [S]

EXERCISE DIRECTIONS

Save a Document as a Template

1. Start Word, if necessary.
2. Open the document ⊙**65MEMO**.
3. Change the theme to Oriel.
4. Change the style set to Traditional.
5. Set the theme and style set as the default.
6. Save the document as a template with the name
   65TEMPLATE_xx.
7. Close the template document.

Create a New Document from an Existing Template

1. Create a new document based on the
   65TEMPLATE_xx template.
   a. Click Office Button and then click New.
   b. Click New from existing.
   c. Locate and select the **65TEMPLATE_xx** template
      file.
   d. Click Create New.
2. Save the document as **65MEMO_xx**.

3. Replace the sample text with the following information as shown in Illustration A:
   - To: **Ray Peterson**
   - From: **Your Name**
   - CC: **Marilyn Stewart**
   - Date: **Today's date**
   - Subject: **Travel Plans.**
4. Replace the sample sentence of body text with the paragraphs shown in Illustration A.
5. Check the spelling and grammar in the document.
6. Display the document in Print Preview. It should look similar to the one in Illustration A.
7. Print the document.
8. Close the document, saving all changes.

Create a New Document from an Installed Template

1. Create a new document based on the Urban Fax template.
2. Save the file as **65FAX_***xx.*
3. Replace the sample text and content controls using the following information:
   - Sender name: **Your name**
   - Sender company name: **Restoration Architecture**
   - Sender company address: **8921 Thunderbird Road, Phoenix, Arizona 85022**
   - Sender company fax: **602-555-6425**
   - Sender company phone: **602-555-6325**
   - Recipient name: **Ray Peterson**
   - Recipient company name: **Michigan Avenue Athletic Club**
   - Recipient company fax: **312-555-4521**
   - Recipient company phone: **312-555-3521**
   - Number of pages: **2, including cover**
   - RE: **Travel Plans**

4. Delete the prompts for the Web address and the CC:.
5. Type the comments shown in Illustration B.
6. Type an **X** in the Please review check box.
7. Check the spelling and grammar in the document.
8. Display the document in Print Preview. It should look similar to the one in Illustration B.
9. Print the document.
10. Close the document, saving all changes.
11. Create a new blank document.
12. Change the theme to Office.
13. Change the style set to Office 2007.
14. Set the theme and style set as the default.
15. Close the document without saving any changes.

MEMO

To: Ray Peterson
From: Student's Name
Cc: Marilyn Stewart
Date: Today's Date
Subject: Travel Plans

I have finalized the travel plans for Ms. Stewart's visit to the Michigan Avenue Athletic Club next week. She will be arriving at O'Hare Airport at approximately 8:40 a.m. I have arranged for a car service to pick her up and take her directly to the club. Assuming the flight is on schedule, she should be there in time for the 11:00 a.m. meeting.

Ms. Stewart is scheduled to depart from O'Hare at 4:15 p.m. The same car service will pick her up at the club at 2:15 p.m. to insure that she is on time for departure.

Please notify me as soon as possible if there are any problems or conflicts with these arrangements. In addition, please send me an agenda as well as any other information about activities that you have scheduled for Ms. Stewart. She likes to be prepared.

Thank you for your assistance.

Restoration Architecture
8921 Thunderbird Road, Phoenix, Arizona 85022
Phone: 602-555-6325 ❖ Fax: 602-555-6425

Fax

RESTORATION ARCHITECTURE
8921 Thunderbird Road, Phoenix, Arizona85022
602-555-6325

Today's Date

TO: Ray Peterson	**FROM: Student's Name**
MICHIGAN AVENUE ATHLETIC CLUB	PAGES: 2, including cover
FAX: 312-555-4521	FAX: 602-555-6425
PHONE: 312-555-3521	PHONE: 602-555-6325

RE: Travel Plans

COMMENTS:

Mr. Peterson—Here's a memo with some information about Ms. Stewart's visit.

Thanks,

Student's Name

☐ Urgent

☒ Please review

☐ Please comment

☐ For your records

ON YOUR OWN

1. Word includes templates for a wide variety of documents, including publications such as manuals and brochures. In this exercise, think of a task for which you could create an instruction manual. The task might be school or class related, or it might be extracurricular. For example, you might create a manual about how to fill out a course registration form, how to throw a shot put, prepare a science fair exhibit, or use a self-serve gas pump.

2. Once you select a task, gather all of the information you need. Decide how many chapters or sections you will need, what the titles will be, and map out the precise steps the reader will have to follow to complete the task.

3. When you are ready, start Word and use the Manual template to create a new document.

   ✓ *If you cannot locate the Manual template, use the file ⊙ 65MANUAL provided with this book. In the New Document dialog box, click New from existing, locate and select 65MANUAL, and then click Create New.*

4. Save the document as **OWD65_xx**.

5. Scroll through the document to see the components of the manual. Note that the Manual template creates a complex document that includes a table of contents, an index, and a lot of sample text and instructions. As you work, you can delete the sections, text, and graphics you don't need, and retain those that you want to use.

6. Replace the sample text, headings, and graphics with your own information. Simply type your text, and insert graphics or symbols to illustrate the document.

7. Save your document frequently so that you do not accidentally lose information.

8. When you have entered all of the text and graphics and have deleted the sample information that you don't need, check the spelling and grammar in the document.

9. Print the document.

10. Ask a classmate to review the manual and offer suggestions and comments on both the content and the design.

11. Incorporate the suggestions into the document.

12. Close the documents, saving all changes.

Skills Covered

- Insert a File in a Document
- Use Building Blocks

Software Skills   Insert a file into another file to save time retyping existing text. When you insert a file, the entire contents of the file become part of the current document, while the original file remains unchanged. Use building blocks to design and save common parts of a document so you can insert them in any document as any time.

Application Skills   As an administrative assistant at Michigan Avenue Athletic Club, you want to show that you are resourceful. In this exercise, you will design a letterhead that you will save as a Header building block. You can then insert it in a press release you will write announcing the club renovation. You also need to include the company's mission statement in the press release. Since you already have a document containing the mission statement, you can simply insert it directly into the press release.

TERMS

Building block A feature of Microsoft Office 2007 that lets you insert reusable pieces of content such as headers, footers, or tables created from saved text and graphics.

Quick Parts A feature of Microsoft Office 2007 that lets you organize and manage building blocks.

NOTES

Insert a File in a Document

- You can insert one file into another file to incorporate the first file's contents into the second file.
- The entire contents are saved as part of the second file.
- The first file remains unchanged.
- Inserting a file is different from copying and pasting, because you do not have to open the file to insert it and the entire file contents are inserted— no selecting is necessary.

  ✓ *To mark where a file is inserted into an existing document, turn on the Track Changes feature before the insertion.*

- The command for inserting a file is available on the Object menu in the Text group on the Insert tab of the Ribbon.

Use Building Blocks

- **Building blocks** are a feature of Microsoft Office 2007 designed to make it easy to save content so you can insert it into any document at any time.
- For example, you can use building blocks to insert headers and footers, text boxes, page numbers, cover pages, and tables.
- Word 2007 comes with built-in building blocks, and you can create your own customized building blocks.
- Building blocks display in galleries throughout Word 2007. For example, the Header building blocks display when you click the Header button on the Insert tab of the Ribbon, and the Text Box building blocks display when you click the Text Box button.

- Click a building block in a gallery to insert it in a document.

  ✓ *You may have to adjust formatting in the building block content after inserting it in a document.*

- If the content you want to store is not intended for a specific part of a document—such as a header or footer—you can store it in the **Quick Parts** gallery.

- You enter a name and select properties for your building block in the Create New Building Block dialog box.

- You can also select from a complete list of all available building blocks in the Building Blocks Organizer, which is available from the Quick Parts menu in the Text group on the Insert tab of the Ribbon.

Building Blocks Organizer

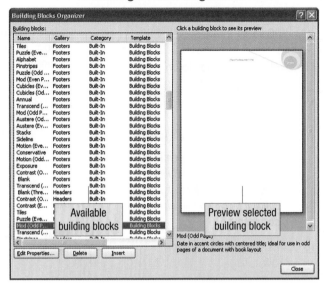

Create New Building Block dialog box

PROCEDURES

Insert a File

1. Position the insertion point where you want file inserted.
2. Click the **Insert** tab .... Alt + N

   Text Group

3. Click the **Object** button [icon] drop-down arrow .... J
4. Click **Text from File** .... F
5. Locate and select file to insert.
6. Click **Insert** .... Alt + S

Use Building Blocks

To insert a building block:

1. Display gallery in which building block is stored.
2. Click building block to insert.

To create a custom building block:

1. Select content to save as building block.
2. Click the **Insert** tab .... Alt + N

   Text Group

3. Click the **Quick Parts** button [icon] .... Q

4. Click **Save Collection to Quick Part Gallery** .... S

   ✓ *The Create New Building Block dialog box displays.*

5. Click the **Name** box, if necessary .... Alt + N
6. Type building block name.
7. Click **Gallery** drop-down arrow .... Alt + G
8. Select gallery where you want to store building block .... ↓/↑, ↵Enter

   ✓ *If desired, click Category drop-down arrow and select category, or create a new category.*

9. Click **Description** text box .... `Alt`+`D`

10. Type description of building block.

11. Click **Save in** drop-down arrow .... `Alt`+`S`

12. Click template in which to store building block .... `↓`/`↑`, `↵Enter`

   ✓ *A template must be open to display in the list. Select Building Block if you want the custom building block to be available in all documents.*

13. Click **Options** drop-down arrow .... `Alt`+`O`

14. Click one of following options .... `↓`/`↑`, `↵Enter`

   ■ **Insert content only**, to insert the content as saved at the insertion point location.

   ■ **Insert content in its own paragraph**, to insert the content with a paragraph mark before and after.

   ■ **Insert content in its own page**, to insert the content with a page break before and after.

15. Click **OK** .... `↵Enter`

To display Building Blocks Organizer:

1. Click the **Insert** tab .... `Alt`+`N`

   Text Group

2. Click the **Quick Parts** button .... `Q`

3. Click **Building Blocks Organizer** .... `B`

   OR

1. Display a building blocks gallery.

2. Right-click any building block.

3. Click **Organize and Delete** .... `O`

To delete a building block:

1. Display Building Blocks Organizer.

2. Click **Building blocks** list .... `Alt`+`B`

3. Click building block to delete .... `↓`/`↑`

4. Click **Delete** .... `Alt`+`D`

5. Click **Yes** .... `Alt`+`Y`

6. Click **Close** .... `Esc`

EXERCISE DIRECTIONS

Create a Building Block

1. Start Word, and create a new document.

2. Design the letterhead shown in Illustration A.

   a. Type the company name in a 28-point bold serif font (Garamond is used in the illustration), small caps, flush right.

   b. Type the address in the same font in 16-point bold, also flush right, using Wingdings symbol #118 as a separator. Do not use small caps.

   c. Type the phone, fax, and Web site information in the same font in 11 points, using the same symbol as a separator.

   d. Select all paragraphs and apply a gray pattern style fill of 12.5%.

3. Save the letterhead as a building block with the name Letterhead, in the Quick Parts gallery.

   a. Press Ctrl+A to select everything in the document.

   b. Click the Quick Parts button on the Insert tab and click Save Collection to Quick Parts Gallery.

   c. Type the name **Letterhead**.

   d. Use the default Gallery, Save in, and Options settings.

   e. Type the description **Letterhead for Michigan Avenue Athletic Club**.

   f. Click OK.

4. Close the document without saving any changes.

Illustration A

MICHIGAN AVENUE ATHLETIC CLUB

325 Michigan Avenue❖Chicago, Illinois 60601

Phone: (312)555-3521❖Fax: (312)555-4521❖www.michaveclub.com

Insert a File and a Building Block to Create a Document

1. Open ⊙66RENOVATE.
2. Save the file as 66RENOVATE_*xx*.
3. Position the insertion point at the beginning of the document, and then insert the Letterhead building block from the Quick Parts gallery.
4. If necessary, set line spacing in the letterhead to Single, and set the space after to 0 points.
5. Move the insertion point to the end of the document and insert the file ⊙66MISSION.
5. Check the spelling and grammar in the document.
6. Display the document in Print Preview. It should look similar to the one in Illustration B.
7. Print the document.
8. Close the file, saving all changes.

Illustration B

MICHIGAN AVENUE ATHLETIC CLUB

325 Michigan Avenue❖Chicago, Illinois 60601
Phone: (312)555-3521❖Fax: (312)555-4521❖www.michaveclub.com

For Immediate Release

Contact: Ray Peterson
                (312) 555-3521
                ray@michaveclub.com

Michigan Avenue Athletic Club Begins Renovation

Chicago, Illinois–The Michigan Avenue Athletic Club (MAAC) has recently announced plans for a wholesale renovation of the club's building at 235 Michigan Avenue. The renovation will increase the amount of space available for all club activities and modernize the facility.

MAAC has hired the renowned Phoenix, Arizona-based Restoration Architecture to supervise the renovation. Restoration Architecture specializes in remodeling, redesign, and restoration of existing properties.

"We want to retain as much of the original flavor of the building as possible, while bringing the club into the 21st century," said Ray Peterson, MAAC's general manager. "We believe this renovation fits our mission as a health club community for all."

The Michigan Avenue Athletic Club is committed to excellence. MAAC encourages employees and members to strive for the highest goals, meet all challenges with spirit and enthusiasm, and work hard to achieve personal and professional harmony.

At MAAC, individuality is respected and diversity is valued. Under the guidance of General Manager Ray Peterson and Exercise Director Charudutta Saroj, MAAC provides an environment where people feel comfortable, safe, and free to pursue their physical fitness goals.

ON YOUR OWN

1. Start Word and create a new document.
2. Design a letterhead for yourself.
3. Save the letterhead as a building block in the Quick Parts gallery, with a descriptive name, such as **MYLETTERHEAD**.
4. Close the document without saving the changes.
5. Create a new document and save it as **OWD66-1_xx**.
6. Type a brief biography of no more than two paragraphs that would be appropriate for inclusion in a publication such as a yearbook, a team or club roster, or a theater program biography.
7. Check the spelling and grammar in the document.
8. Close the document, saving all changes.
9. Create another new document and save it as **OWD66-2_xx**.
10. Insert your letterhead at the top of the document.
11. Type a letter to the yearbook editor, a club president, or whoever is responsible for printing the collection of biographies. Somewhere in the body of the letter, insert the **OWD66-1_xx** document.
12. Check the spelling and grammar in the document.
13. Display the document in Print Preview.
14. Print the document.
15. Ask a classmate to review the document and offer comments and suggestions.
16. Incorporate the suggestions into the document.
17. Close the document, saving all changes.

Skills Covered

- **Record a Macro**
- **Run a Macro**

Software Skills Macros let you simplify tasks that ordinarily require many keystrokes or commands, such as creating a header or footer, or changing line spacing and indents for a paragraph. Once you record a macro, you can run it at any time to repeat the recorded actions. You can use macros for tasks as simple as opening and printing a document, or for more complicated tasks such as creating a new document, inserting a table, entering text, and applying an AutoFormat.

Application Skills As an administrative assistant at Michigan Avenue Athletic Club you frequently have to format reports by changing the margins to 1.25" on all sides and by inserting a standard header and footer. In this exercise, you will create macros for setting the margins and creating a header and footer. You will then use the macros to format a one-page report.

TERMS

Macro A series of commands and keystrokes that you record and save together. You can run the macro to replay the series.

Shortcut key A combination of keys (including Alt, Ctrl, and/or Shift, and a regular keyboard key) that you assign to run a macro.

NOTES

Record a Macro

- Record a **macro** to automate tasks or actions that you perform frequently.
- A single macro can store an unlimited number of keystrokes or mouse actions.
- Macros can save time and help eliminate errors.
- By default, new macros are stored in the Normal template, so they are available for use in all new documents created with the Normal template.
- As soon as you start recording, everything you input into your computer is stored in the macro.
- You can record mouse actions that select commands on the Ribbon or in dialog boxes; however, you cannot record mouse actions that select text or position the insertion point.

- Note that you cannot include building blocks in a macro.
- You can assign a **shortcut key** that combines Alt, Ctrl, and/or Shift and a regular keyboard key to a macro when you record it. You can then use the shortcut key to play the macro back at any time.

  ✓ *You can also create a Quick Access Toolbar button to assign to the macro.*

- If a macro doesn't work the way you want, you can delete it and record it again.

Run a Macro

- Once you have recorded a macro, you can run it at any time.
- When you run a macro, Word executes the recorded commands and actions in the current document.

- Use the key combination you assigned when you recorded the macro to run the macro.
- To perform the macro on part of a document, be sure to select the part first.

PROCEDURES

Record a Macro

1. Position the insertion point where you want it to be when you start recording the macro.
2. Click the **View** tab .... Alt + W

   Macros Group

3. Click the **Macros** group button ▦ .... M
4. Click **Record Macro** .... R
5. Click **Macro name** box, if necessary .... Alt + M
6. Type a macro name.
7. Click **Description** box .... Alt + D
8. Type a description of the macro.
9. Click **Keyboard** .... Alt + K
10. Press a shortcut key combination.

    ✓ *Word displays a message indicating whether the combination is unassigned or already assigned to a Word command. If you use a combination that is already assigned, the original purpose of the combination is replaced. For example, if you assign the combination Ctrl+S, you will no longer be able to use that combination to save a file.*

11. Click **Assign** .... ↵Enter
12. Click **Close** .... Esc
13. Perform actions to record.

To stop recording a macro:

1. Click the **View** tab .... Alt + W

   Macros Group

2. Click the **Macros** group button ▦ .... M
3. Click **Stop Recording** .... R

   OR

   Click the **Stop Recording** button ▦ on the Status bar.

To pause recording:

1. Click the **View** tab .... Alt + W

   Macros Group

2. Click the **Macros** group button ▦ .... M
3. Click **Pause Recording** .... P

To resume recording:

1. Click the **View** tab .... Alt + W

   Macros Group

2. Click the **Macros** group button ▦ .... M
3. Click **Resume Recorder** .... R, R, ↵Enter

Run a Macro

- Press assigned key combination.

  OR

1. Click the **View** tab .... Alt + W

   Macros Group

2. Click the **Macros** group button ▦ .... M
3. Click **View Macros** V
4. Click the name of macro to run.
5. Click **Run** .... Alt + R

Delete a Macro

1. Click the **View** tab .... Alt + W

   Macros Group

2. Click the **Macros** group button ▦ .... M
3. Click **View Macros** V
4. Click the name of macro to delete.
5. Click **Delete** .... Alt + D
6. Click **Yes** .... Alt + Y
7. Click **Close** .... Esc

EXERCISE DIRECTIONS

1. Start Word, if necessary, and create a new blank document.
2. Select to record a new macro as follows:
   a. Name the macro **Margins**.
   b. Enter the description: **Sets all margins to 1.25"**.
   c. Assign the macro to the key combination Alt+M.
   d. Click Assign and then Close to begin recording the macro keystrokes.
   e. Set all page margins to 1.25".
   f. Stop recording the macro.
3. Select to record a second macro as follows:
   a. Name the macro **MAAC_Header**.
   b. Include the description: **Creates a header and footer in MAAC documents**.
   c. Assign the macro to the key combination Alt+H.
   d. Click Assign and then Close to begin recording the macro keystrokes using Illustration A as a guide.
   e. Click the Insert tab and then click Header. Click Edit Header.
   f. Type the company name (**Michigan Avenue Athletic Club**) flush left on line 1, press Enter and then type today's date flush left on line 2.
   g. Click the Go to Footer button and type your name flush left.
   h. Close Header/Footer view.
   i. Stop recording the macro.
4. Close the blank document without saving any changes.
5. Open ⊙ **67TRAINER**.
6. Save the file as **67TRAINER_xx**.
7. Run the MAAC_Header macro.
8. Run the Margins macro.
9. Preview the document. It should look similar to the one in Illustration A.
10. Check the spelling and grammar in the document.
11. Print the document.
12. Delete the MAAC_Header macro and then delete the Margins macro.
13. Close the document, saving all changes.

Michigan Avenue Athletic Club
Today's Date

IS A PERSONAL TRAINER RIGHT FOR YOU?

Almost everyone could benefit from the services of a personal trainer. In addition to designing a personalized workout program, a good trainer provides motivation and encouragement. He or she helps you understand how to fit exercise into your life and teaches you how to make the most out of your exercise time. The lessons you learn from a trainer help insure a safe, effective workout, even when you are exercising on your own.

Working with a trainer should be a satisfying and rewarding experience. There are many different reasons for hiring a personal trainer. Some people want the motivation of a workout partner, others require specialized services for rehabilitation, and still others are interested in achieving weight loss goals. Before hiring a trainer, make sure he or she has experience helping people with goals similar to your own. Ask for references, and then contact at least three. You should also interview the trainer to find out if you are compatible. You should feel comfortable talking and working together, and you should trust the trainer to respect your time and efforts.

Verify that the trainer is certified by a nationally recognized organization such as the American Council on Exercise, the American College of Sports Medicine, or the National Strength and Conditioning Association. Many trainers have degrees in subjects such as sports medicine, physical education, exercise physiology, or anatomy and physiology.

For more information about personal trainers, contact Candace at extension 765.

Student's Name

ON YOUR OWN

1. Start Word and open OWD66-1_*xx*, the brief biography you created in the On Your Own section of Exercise 66, or open 67BIO.

2. Save the document as OWD67-1_*xx*, and then close it.

3. Create a new blank document.

4. Create a new macro named **Insertbio** and assign it to a shortcut key combination, such as Shift+ B.

5. Record the keystrokes for inserting the OWD67-1_*xx* file into the open document.

6. After you stop recording the macro, close the current document without saving the changes.

7. Create a new blank document and save it as OWD67-2_*xx*.

8. Type a document in which you can include your biography. You might type a letter to someone other than the person you wrote to in Exercise 66, or you might type part of a program or yearbook page.

9. At the appropriate location, use the Insertbio macro to insert the OWD67-1_*xx* file into the OWD67-2_*xx* document.

   ✓ *If you want to work in groups, each classmate could insert his or her bio file into the same document, thereby creating a complete document such as a program or yearbook.*

10. Check the spelling and grammar in the document.

11. Preview the document.

12. Print the document.

13. Ask a classmate to review the document and offer comments or suggestions.

14. Incorporate the suggestions into the document.

15. Delete the Insertbio macro.

16. Close the document, saving all changes.

Critical Thinking

Application Skills Enrollment in the in-house training courses at Restoration Architecture has been low. Caroline Gagas, the Director of Training, has asked you to design a one-page flyer advertising the benefits of in-house training. She has supplied you with a file containing the information she wants included in the flyer. In this exercise, you will use a template to create a memo to Ms. Gagas. You will then create the flyer by creating and inserting a building block and then inserting a file. To make the document appealing you will use desktop publishing features, such as newsletter columns and graphics.

EXERCISE DIRECTIONS

Record a Macro

1. Start Word, if necessary.
2. Create a new document.
3. Record a macro, as follows:
   a. Name the new macro **Columns**.
   b. Type the description: **Inserts a section break and divides the new section into two columns**.
   c. Assign the key combination Alt+C.
   d. Record the steps for inserting a continuous section break and formatting the new section into two columns of equal width, then stop recording.
4. Close the current document without saving it.

Create and Use a Template

1. Open the file ⊙**68MEMO**.
2. Save it as a template with the name **68TEMPLATE_xx**, and then close it.
3. Create a new document based on the **68TEMPLATE_xx** file.
4. Save the new file as **68MEMO_xx**.

5. Delete the sample text and fill in the memo using the following information:
   - To: **Ms. Caroline Gagas**
   - From: **Your Name**
   - CC:
   - Date: **Today's Date**
   - Subject: **Training Flyer**
6. Replace the sample body text sentence with the paragraphs shown in Illustration A.

Create a Building Block

1. Apply a black, 3-point triple-line border along the bottom of the title line as shown in Illustration A.
2. Select the title and save it as a building block in the Quick Parts gallery with the name **RA Title**.
3. Check the spelling and grammar in the document.
4. Display the document in Print Preview. It should look similar to the one in Illustration A.
5. Print the document.
6. Close the document, saving all changes.

Create a Document Using Macros and Building Blocks

1. Create a new blank document.
2. Save the document as **68FLYER_xx**.
3. Insert the file ○**68INFO**.
4. Move the insertion point to the beginning of the document.
5. Run the Columns macro.
6. Move the insertion point to the beginning of the document again.
7. Insert the RA Title building block.

Complete the Document

1. Center the title line horizontally.
2. Apply the Heading 1 style to the three main headlines (refer to Illustration B).
3. Apply the Subtitle style to the three course titles in the article *Stay in Tune with the Times*, and change the paragraph spacing to leave 6 points before each title.

4. Create a bulleted list from the three items in the first article beginning with the word *Increase*.
5. Format the first letter in each of the three main articles as a dropped capital.
6. Insert a column break above *Stay in Tune with the Times*.
7. Insert a continuous section break at the beginning of the last sentence in the document.
8. Format the new third section in one column.
9. Center the text in the last sentence, and set paragraph spacing to leave 24 points before.
10. Check the spelling and grammar in the document.
11. Display the document in Print Preview.
12. Print the document.
13. Delete the Columns macro.
14. Close the document, saving all changes.

RESTORATION ARCHITECTURE

To:	Ms. Caroline Gagas
From:	Student's Name
Cc:	
Date:	Today's Date
Re:	Training Flyer

In order to effectively market the in-house training courses to employees, I have decided to create a flyer using many exciting graphics elements. Once we catch their attention, I believe we will be able to convince a significant number of employees to enroll in the upcoming training session.

With that in mind, I have attached a copy of the proposed flyer to this memo. Notice the use of columns, borders, shading, and graphics elements. These features are designed to draw the reader's eyes to specific paragraphs. In addition, I can easily keep the document up to date in case of changes such as different course offerings or different locations.

Please let me know what you think. With your approval I can have the flyer ready for distribution by the end of the day.

Attachments

Restoration Architecture
8921 Thunderbird Road, Phoenix, Arizona 85022
Phone: 602-555-6325 ❖ Fax: 602-555-6425

Curriculum Integration

Application Skills   For your science class, use the skills you have learned in Lesson 9 to create a newsletter about a lab experiment, science fair project, or class assignment you have conducted recently. Design the newsletter to include a title, headlines, body text, columns, sections, and graphics. The newsletter may be a single page, or multiple pages. Refer to Illustration A to see a sample of a single page document. You can work alone or in teams to complete this assignment. If you work in teams, you can insert files created by each team member into the newsletter document so that you don't have to retype the text. When you are finished, print the newsletter and distribute it to your classmates.

EXERCISE DIRECTIONS

Start Word, if necessary, and create a new document. Save it as **69SCIENCE_xx**.

Select to display elements that might help you while you work, such as the rulers, nonprinting characters, and text boundaries, and make sure all the features you want to use are enabled, such as AutoCorrect and AutoFormat as You Type.

Select a theme, style set, and colors for the document.

Set the paper size.

Type and format the text you want to include in the newsletter. Insert section breaks so you can apply different page layout settings. For example, you probably want the newsletter title in one column, but the articles in two or three columns.

Use dropped capitals and borders and shading to enhance the appearance of the document

Check the spelling and grammar in the letter, and use a thesaurus to replace common or boring words.

Ask a classmate to review the document and make suggestions for how you might improve it.

Incorporate your classmate's suggestions into the document, and save it.

Print the newsletter.

Close all files, saving all changes.

SPLAT—A SCIENCE EXPERIMENT

Published by Mrs. Smith's Third Period Science Class   Spring

The Hypothesis

We believe that the yolks of uncooked, unbroken eggs dropped from different heights will have different diameters of splatter. Particularly, we believe that the higher the drop point, the larger the diameter of yolk splatter will be.

The Experiment

1. Drop egg 1-1 from height 1.
2. Measure diameter of yolk splatter.
3. Drop egg 1-2 from height 1.
4. Measure diameter of yolk splatter.
5. Repeat for eggs 1-3, 1-4, and 1-5.
6. Drop egg 2-1 from height 2.
7. Repeat with eggs 2-2, 2-3, 2-4, and 2-5.
8. Drop egg 3-1 from height 3.
9. Repeat with eggs 3-2, 3-3, 3-4, and 3-5.

Equipment List

- Eggs
- Ladder
- Measuring tape
- Sponge
- Water

The Results

Our hypothesis was incorrect. There was very little difference in the diameter of yolk splatter despite the different heights. We believe this is due to gravity.

We also believe that if the drop heights were significantly different there might be a difference in the yolk splatter diameters. For example, an egg dropped from one mile up would have a greater diameter yolk splatter than an egg dropped from one meter.

Lesson | 10

Graphics

Skills Covered

- **About Graphics Objects**
- **Insert Shapes**
- **Select Objects**

- **Resize Drawing Objects**
- **Set Text Wrap Options**
- **Move an Object**

Software Skills   Use graphics objects such as shapes to illustrate and enhance text documents. You can insert, size, and position the shapes on the page, and set text wrap options to integrate them with the text, making the document easier to read and more interesting for the reader.

Application Skills   In this exercise, you will enhance a newsletter for Liberty Blooms by inserting shapes.

TERMS

Anchor An element in a document, such as the margin or the page itself, relative to which you can position an object.

AutoShapes Pre-drawn shapes that come with Word 2007.

Drawing canvas A drawing object that defines an area in a document in which you can insert other drawing objects.

Drawing object A shape or line created in Word and saved as part of the Word document.

Floating object An object that is positioned independently from the document text

Object A graphic, picture, chart, shape, text box or other element that can be inserted into a document.

Picture object A graphics object created using a different application and then inserted into a Word document.

Sizing handles Rectangular boxes around the edges of a selected object that you use to resize the object.

Text box A rectangular drawing object in which text or graphics images can be inserted and positioned anywhere on a page.

NOTES

About Graphics Objects

- You can insert two types of graphics **objects** into a Word document: **drawing objects** and **pictures**.
- Common types of drawing objects include shapes and **text boxes**.

  ✓ Text boxes are covered in Exercise 71.

- Common types of pictures include photographs and clip art.

  ✓ Clip art is covered in Exercise 73.

Insert Shapes

- In Word 2007 you can insert closed shapes, such as ovals and rectangles, lines, such as curves and arrows, or **AutoShapes**, such as hearts, stars, and lightning bolts.
- When you click the Shapes button 🔲 in the Illustrations group on the Insert tab of the Ribbon, Word displays a gallery of shapes organized into palettes.

  ✓ Rest the mouse pointer on a shape in the gallery to display a ScreenTip describing the shape.

- Click a shape in the gallery to select it, and then click, or click and drag, in the document to insert the shape.
- By default, Word inserts shapes as **floating objects** so they can be positioned anywhere on a page.
- You can insert a single shape, or insert multiple shapes to create a larger drawing.
- Use Print Layout view to insert drawing objects.
- You can select to use a **Drawing canvas**, if you want.

Select a shape to insert in a document

Select Objects

- You must select an object in order to change it.
- **Sizing handles** display around a selected object.
- When a shape is selected in a document, the Drawing Tools Format tab displays on the Ribbon.

  ✓ *You learn more about formatting objects in Exercises 72, 74, and 75.*

- To select a single object you click it. You can also select more than one object at a time; changes will affect all selected objects.

Resize Drawing Objects

- You can resize an object evenly so the height and width remain proportional, or you can resize objects unevenly, distorting the image.
- Drag the sizing handles to resize an object, or enter a precise size using the Shape Height and Shape Width boxes in the Size group on the Format tab of the Ribbon.

Set Text Wrap Options

- You can change an object's wrapping style to affect the way the object is integrated into the document text.
- Select from seven wrapping options:
  - In Line with Text: Object is positioned on a line with text characters.
  - Square: Text is wrapped on all four sides of the object's bounding box.
  - Tight: Text is wrapped to the contours of the image.
  - Behind Text: Text continues in lines over the object, obscuring the object.
  - In Front of Text: Text continues in lines behind the object, which may obscure the text.
  - Top and Bottom: Text is displayed above and below object but not on left or right sides.
  - Through: Text runs through the object.
- You can set advanced text wrapping options on the Text Wrapping tab of the Advanced Layout dialog box.

Text Wrapping tab of the Advanced Layout dialog box

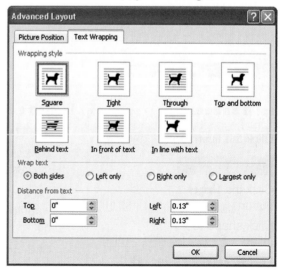

Move an Object

- The easiest way to move an object is to drag it to a new location.

- You can also select a built-in position from the Position gallery, including in line with the text, or left, right, or centered relative to the top, bottom, or center of the page.

- To position an object precisely, use the options on the Picture Position tab of the Advanced Layout dialog box.

- On the Picture Position tab, you can select from four horizontal alignment options and three vertical alignment options. Each option has its own set of parameters:

- For horizontal alignment, select:

  - *Alignment* to align the object left, right, or centered relative to the selected **anchor** (margin, page, column, or character).

  - *Book layout* to align the object on the inside or outside of the anchor (margin or page).

  - *Absolute position* to specify the precise distance (in inches or points) that you want to leave between the left edge of the object and the anchor (margin, page, column, or character).

  - *Relative position* to specify the distance that you want to leave between the left edge of the object and the anchor (margin or page) as a percentage.

- For vertical alignment, select:

  - *Alignment* to align the object on the top, bottom, inside, outside, or centered relative to the anchor (margin, page, or line).

- *Absolute position* to specify the precise distance (in inches or points) that you want to leave between the top edge of the object and the anchor (margin, page, paragraph, or line).

- *Relative position* to specify the distance that you want to leave between the top edge of the object and the anchor (margin or page) as a percentage.

- Note that when nonprinting characters are displayed, an anchor icon indicates the location of an object's anchor.

- By default, the object moves with the anchor if you insert or delete text, graphics, or white space in the document.

- You can set Word so the object stays in place even if the surrounding content moves, and you can lock the anchor to keep the object in its same position relative to the page, even if it moves to a different page.

Picture Position tab of the Advanced Layout dialog box

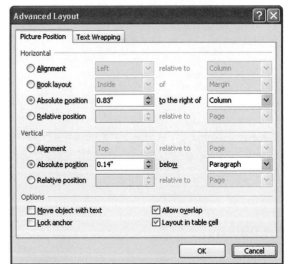

PROCEDURES

Insert a Shape

1. Click the **Insert** tab .... Alt+N

   Illustrations Group

2. Click the **Shapes** button .... S, H

3. Click shape to insert .... ↓/↑/←/→, ↵Enter

4. Follow steps for selected shape type, as described in the following procedures.

To insert a closed shape:

1. Select desired shape.

   ✓ Mouse pointer changes to crosshair +.

2. Click in document where you want to insert shape.

   OR

   Click and drag to draw shape.

   ✓ Press and hold Shift while dragging to draw perfect square or circle.

To insert a straight line or arrow:

1. Select desired shape.

   ✓ Mouse pointer changes to crosshair +.

2. Click in document where you want line or arrow to begin.

3. Drag to point where you want line or arrow to end.

4. Release mouse button.

To insert a curved line:

1. Select desired shape.

   ✓ *Mouse pointer changes to crosshair* ⊞ .

2. Click in document where you want line to begin.

3. Click at point where you want line to curve.

4. Repeat step 3 at each point where you want line to curve.

5. Double-click to end line.

To insert a freeform line:

1. Select desired shape.

2. Click in document where you want line to begin.

   ✓ *Mouse pointer changes to a pencil icon* 🖉 .

3. Drag to draw freehand as if you were using a pencil.

   OR

   Release mouse button and click to draw straight lines.

4. Double-click to end line.

To insert a scribble line:

1. Select desired shape.

2. Click in document where you want line to begin.

   ✓ *Mouse pointer changes to a pencil icon* 🖉 .

3. Drag to draw freehand as if you were using a pencil.

4. Release mouse button to end line.

Insert a Drawing Canvas

1. Click the **Insert** tab .... Alt + N

   Illustrations Group

2. Click the **Shapes** button 🔲 .... S , H

3. Click **New Drawing Canvas** .... N

Select an Object

- Click object to select.

  OR

- Click object's anchor icon.

Select Multiple Objects

1. Click first object to select.

2. Press and hold **Shift** .... ⬆Shift

3. Click next object to select.

4. Repeat until desired objects are selected.

5. Release **Shift** .... ⬆Shift

   OR

   a. Click **Home** tab .... Alt + H

      Editing Group

   b. Click **Select** button 🔲 .... S , L

   c. Click **Select Objects** .... O

   d. Click and drag to draw a box around all objects to select.

Resize an Object Using the Mouse

1. Click object to select it.

2. Drag a corner sizing handle to resize both height and width.

   ✓ *Press and hold Shift while dragging a corner hander to resize proportionally.*

   OR

   Drag a side sizing handle to resize height or width only.

Resize an Object Precisely

1. Click object to select it.

2. Click the **Drawing Tools Format** tab .... Alt , J , D

   Size Group

3. Click **Shape Height** box 🔲 1.51" ⬍ .... H

4. Type height in inches .... *type height*, ↵Enter

   OR

   Click increment arrows to enter height.

5. Click **Shape Width** box 🔲 1.43" ⬍ .... Alt , J , D , W

6. Type width in inches .... *type height*, ↵Enter

   OR

   Click increment arrows to enter width.

Set Text Wrap Options

1. Click object to select it.

2. Click the **Drawing Tools Format** tab .... Alt , J , D

   Arrange Group

3. Click **Text Wrapping** button 🔲 .... T , W

4. Click desired option:

   - **In Line With Text** I
   - **Square** .... S
   - **Tight** .... T
   - **Behind Text** .... D
   - **In Front of Text** .... N
   - **Top and Bottom** .... O
   - **Through** .... H

Set Advanced Text Wrap Options

1. Click object to select it.
2. Click the **Drawing Tools Format** tab .... `Alt`, `J`, `D`

3. Click **Text Wrapping** button ▣ .... `T`, `W`
4. Click **More Layout Options** .... `L`:
5. Click **Text Wrapping** tab .... `Ctrl`+`Tab⇄`
6. Select desired text wrapping style:
   - ■ **Square** .... `Alt`+`Q`
   - ■ **Tight** .... `Alt`+`T`
   - ■ **Through** .... `Alt`+`H`
   - ■ **Top and bottom** .... `Alt`+`O`
   - ■ **Behind text** .... `Alt`+`B`
   - ■ **In front of text** .... `Alt`+`F`
   - ■ **In line with text** .... `Alt`+`I`
7. For Square, Through, and Tight styles, select desired text wrapping options:
   - ■ **Both sides** .... `Alt`+`S`
   - ■ **Left only** .... `Alt`+`L`
   - ■ **Right only** .... `Alt`+`R`
   - ■ **Largest only** .... `Alt`+`A`
8. For Square, Through, Top and bottom, and Tight styles, set distance from text, as follows:
   a. Click **Top** .... `Alt`+`P`
   b. Type distance to leave between text and top of object.
   c. Click **Bottom** .... `Alt`+`M`
   d. Type distance to leave between text and bottom of object.
   e. Click **Left** .... `Alt`+`E`
   f. Type distance to leave between text and left of object.

   g. Click **Right** .... `Alt`+`G`
   h. Type distance to leave between text and right of object.

   ✓ *Not all distance options will be available for all styles.*

9. Click **OK** .... `↵Enter`

Move an Object

1. Select object.
2. Position the mouse pointer over object until pointer changes to a four-headed arrow ✛.
3. Drag object to new location.
4. Release mouse button.

To move horizontally or vertically only:

1. Select object.
2. Position the mouse pointer over object until pointer changes to a four-headed arrow ✛.
3. Press and hold **Shift** .... `⇧Shift`
4. Drag object to new location.
5. Release mouse button.

To move in small increments:

1. Select object.
2. Press an arrow key:
   - ■ **Up arrow** to move up 1 pixel .... `↑`
   - ■ **Down arrow** to move down 1 pixel .... `↓`
   - ■ **Left arrow** to move left 1 pixel .... `←`
   - ■ **Right arrow** to move right 1 pixel .... `→`
3. Repeat step 2 until object is positioned as desired.

Position a Shape

1. Click shape to select it.
2. Click the **Drawing Tools Format** tab .... `Alt`, `J`, `D`

3. Click **Position** button ▣ .... `P`, `O`
4. Click position to apply .... `↓`/`←`/`→`/`↑`, `↵Enter`

Position a Shape Precisely

1. Click shape to select it.
2. Click the **Drawing Tools Format** tab .... `Alt`, `J`, `D`

3. Click **Position** button ▣ .... `P`, `O`
4. Click **More Layout Options** .... `L`
5. Click **Picture Position** tab .... `Ctrl`+`Tab⇄`
6. Do one of the following to set horizontal position:
   a. Click **Alignment** drop-down arrow .... `Alt`+`A`, `Tab⇄`, `↓`
   b. Click desired alignment .... `↓`/`↑`, `↵Enter`
   c. Click **relative to** drop-down arrow .... `Alt`+`R`
   d. Click desired anchor .... `↓`/`↑`, `↵Enter`

   OR

   a. Click **Book layout** drop-down arrow .... `Alt`+`B`, `Tab⇄`, `↓`
   b. Click desired position .... `↓`/`↑`, `↵Enter`
   c. Click **of** drop-down arrow .... `Alt`+`F`
   d. Click desired anchor .... `↓`/`↑`, `↵Enter`

OR

a. Click **Absolute position** drop-down arrow ...Alt+P, Tab, ↓/↑

b. Type amount of space to leave.

c. Click **to the right of** drop-down arrow ....Alt+T

d. Click desired anchor ....↓/↑, ↵Enter

OR

a. Click **Relative position** drop-down arrow ...Alt+R, Tab, ↓/↑

b. Type percentage to leave.

c. Click **relative to** drop-down arrow ....Alt+E

d. Click desired anchor ....↓/↑, ↵Enter

7. Do one of the following to set vertical position:

a. Click **Alignment** drop-down arrow ....Alt+G, Tab, ↓

b. Click desired alignment ....↓/↑, ↵Enter

c. Click **relative to** drop-down arrow ....Alt+E

d. Click desired anchor ....↓/↑, ↵Enter

OR

a. Click **Absolute position** drop-down arrow ...Alt+S, Tab, ↓/↑

b. Type amount of space to leave.

c. Click **below** drop-down arrow ....Alt+W

d. Click desired anchor ....↓/↑, ↵Enter

OR

a. Click **Relative position** drop-down arrow ...Alt+I, Tab, ↓/↑

b. Type percentage to leave.

c. Click **relative to** drop-down arrow ....Alt+O

d. Click desired anchor ....↓/↑, ↵Enter

8. Select check box options as necessary:

■ **Move object with text** ....Alt+M
■ **Lock anchor** ....Alt+L
■ **Allow overlap** ....Alt+V
■ **Layout in table cell** ....Alt+C

9. Click **OK** ....↵Enter

Delete an Object

1. Click the object to select it.

2. Press **Del** ....Del

EXERCISE DIRECTIONS

1. Start Word, if necessary.

2. Open 🔘 **70BLOOMS**.

3. Save the file as **70BLOOMS_xx**.

4. Insert a Sun shape from the Basic Shapes palette, sized to 1" by 1".

5. Position the shape in the top-left corner of the document.

6. Set the text wrapping to Tight.

7. Insert a Heart shape from the Basic Shapes palette, sized to 1.25" by 1.5".

8. Position the shape centered horizontally and vertically on the page.

9. Set the text wrapping to Tight.

10. Preview the document. It should look similar to Illustration A.

11. Check the spelling and grammar in the document.

12. Print the document.

13. Close the file, saving all changes.

Liberty Blooms News

Published by the Liberty Blooms Flower Shop
345 Chestnut Street, Philadelphia, PA 19106

Welcome

Welcome to the first issue of *Liberty Blooms News,* a monthly newsletter for people who visit the Liberty Blooms Flower Shop. The primary goal of this publication is to provide you with news about activities and events that you might find of interest. In addition, we intend to publish class schedules, gardening tips, and general information about related topics.

Liberty Blooms News will be mailed directly to everyone who has registered at our Chestnut Street store. Please contact us with questions and suggestions. We will do our best to address your comments in future issues.

Classes and Seminars

If you are a frequent visitor to Liberty Blooms, you know there is always something going on at 345 Chestnut Street. From flower arranging to cooking with herbs, we try to fill the calendar with interesting and informative activities that the whole family will enjoy.

The following events are scheduled for the coming months. Some events require registration, so please call ahead for more information.

Edible Gardens	May 13
Flower Arranging	May 21
Water Gardens	June 3
Potpourri Designs	June 11

Recipe Showcase

Chicken with Tomatoes and Herbs   *Yield: Four Servings*

Ingredients

8 boneless chicken pieces
1 tablespoon olive oil
10 ½ oz. tomatoes, drained
¾ cup chicken stock
2 teaspoons mixed herbs, chopped
1 ½ oz. black olives, chopped
1 teaspoon sugar
Fresh basil to garnish

Directions

1. Heat oil in large skillet.
2. Add chicken pieces and cook until browned on all sides.
3. Add the tomatoes, stock and mixed herbs and simmer for 30 minutes or until chicken is cooked through.
4. Add the olives and sugar and simmer for an additional 5 minutes.
5. Garnish with fresh basil and serve with rice or pasta.

ON YOUR OWN

1. Open OWD62_*xx*, the newsletter document you used in the On Your Own section of Exercise 62, or open 70NEWS.

2. Save the file as **OWD70_*xx***.

3. Insert at least one shape in the newsletter title.

4. Insert at least two shapes in the body of the newsletter.

5. Format, size, and position the shapes for the best effect.

6. Try different text wrapping options.

7. Check spelling and grammar in the document.

8. Preview the document.

9. If necessary, adjust paragraph and font formatting as well as column breaks so that the document fits on a single page and looks good.

10. Print the document.

11. Ask a classmate to review the document and offer comments and suggestions, particularly about the layout and design.

12. Incorporate the suggestions into the document.

13. Close the document, saving all changes.

Exercise | 71

Skills Covered

- Insert a Text Box
- Link Text Boxes
- Align Drawing Objects
- Copy Objects

Software Skills   Insert a text box in a document so you can position and format text independently from the rest of the document. You can link the text boxes so that the text flows from one to another. Align objects to improve the appearance of the document. Copy objects to save time and to insure consistency between similar objects in a document.

Application Skills   Blue Sky Dairy, a dairy farm in Wisconsin, is sponsoring an essay writing contest for local students. In this exercise, you will open an existing flyer advertising the contest and edit it. You will use text boxes and shapes to make the flyer interesting.

TERMS

Link   Establish a connection between text boxes so that text that does not fit within the borders of the first text box flows into the next, linked text box.

Text box   A rectangular drawing object in which text or graphics images can be inserted and positioned anywhere on a page.

NOTES

Insert a Text Box

- Insert a **text box** to position several blocks of text on a page or to change the direction of the text.
- The command for inserting a text box is in the Text group on the Insert tab of the Ribbon.
- You can create a text box by selecting one from the Text Box gallery and then typing text into the text box.
- Alternatively, you can draw your own blank text box, draw a text box around existing text, or add a text box to an existing shape.
- You can format text within a text box using the same commands as you would to format regular text.
- You can change the direction in which text displays within the text box to one of three settings:
  - Horizontal left to right
  - Vertical top to bottom
  - Vertical bottom to top

- You can size and position a text box using commands similar to those for sizing and positioning shapes.

Text box gallery

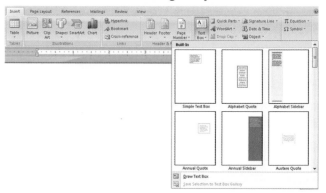

Link Text Boxes

- You can **link** text boxes in a document so that text that does not fit within the first text box automatically flows into the next linked text box.
- To link one text box with another, select the first text box, click the Create Link button in the Text group on the Format tab of the Ribbon, then click the next text box.
- The second text box must not contain text when you establish the link.
- A series of linked text boxes is called a text box chain.
- Text flows through the chain in the order in which you link the text boxes, not in the order in which the text boxes appear in the document, or in the order in which the text boxes were created.
- Use the Break Link button to break the link and move all text into the first text box.

Align Drawing Objects

- You can align an object horizontally or vertically relative to the page or to the margins.
- You can also align selected objects relative to each other.
- You can display gridlines to help you align objects if you want.

Copy Objects

- Duplicate an object by using the standard Copy and Paste commands.
- For example, you can use the Copy and Paste buttons on the Home tab of the Ribbon, or you can use the commands on a shortcut menu.
- Duplicating is useful for creating an exact copy of an object, which you can then edit or format.
- When you duplicate a floating object, you cannot control where Word will insert the new copy; drag the copy to move it to its new location.

PROCEDURES

Insert a Text Box

To select a text box from the gallery:

1. Click the **Insert** tab .... Alt+N

   Text Group

2. Click the **Text Box** button A X
3. Click text box style .... ↓/↑/←/→, ↵Enter
4. Type text to replace sample text in text box.

To draw a text box:

1. Click the **Insert** tab .... Alt+N

   Text Group

2. Click the **Text Box** button A X
3. Click **Draw Text Box** .... D

   ✓ *Mouse pointer changes to crosshair* +.

4. Position the mouse pointer where you want to position the upper-left corner of the text box.

5. Click and drag diagonally to draw the text box.
6. Release the mouse button.
7. Type text.

To draw a text box in a document that already contains at least one text box:

1. Select an existing text box.
2. Click the **Text Box Tools Format** tab .... Alt, J, X

   Text Group

3. Click the **Draw Text Box** button A X

   ✓ *Mouse pointer changes to crosshair* +.

4. Position the mouse pointer where you want to position the upper-left corner of the text box.
5. Click and drag diagonally to draw the text box.
6. Release the mouse button.
7. Type text.

To draw a text box around existing text:

1. Select paragraph(s).
2. Click the **Insert** tab .... Alt+N

   Text Group

3. Click the **Text Box** button A X
4. Click **Draw Text Box** .... D

To add a text box to a shape:

1. Right-click shape.
2. Click **Add Text** X
3. Type text.

   OR

1. Click shape to select it.
2. Click the **Drawing Tools Format** tab .... Alt, J, D

   Insert Shapes Group

3. Click **Edit Text** button A X
4. Type text.

Change the Direction of Text in a Text Box

1. Click object to select it.
2. Click the **Text Box Tools Format** tab .... Alt, J, X

   Text Group

3. Click **Text Direction** button ⬛ .... G

   ✓ *Click Text Direction button again to cycle through available text directions.*

Resize a Text Box Precisely

1. Click object to select it.
2. Click the **Text Box Tools Format** tab .... Alt, J, X

   Size Group

3. Click **Shape Height** box ⬛ 1.51" ⬛ .... H
4. Type height in inches .... *type height*, ↵Enter

   OR

   Click increment arrows to enter height.
5. Click **Shape Width** box ⬛ 1.43" ⬛ .... Alt, J, X, W
6. Type width in inches .... *type width*, ↵Enter

   OR

   Click increment arrows to enter width.

Set Text Wrap Options for a Text Box

1. Click object to select it.
2. Click the **Text Box Tools Format** tab .... Alt, J, X

   Arrange Group

3. Click **Text Wrapping** button ⬛ .... T, W
4. Click desired option:
   - **In Line with Text** I
   - **Square** .... S
   - **Tight** .... T
   - **Behind Text** .... D
   - **In Front of Text** .... N
   - **Top and Bottom** .... O
   - **Through** .... H

Set Advanced Text Wrap Options for a Text Box

1. Click object to select it.
2. Click the **Text Box Tools Format** tab .... Alt, J, X

   Arrange Group

3. Click **Text Wrapping** button ⬛ .... T, W
4. Click **More Layout Options** .... L:
5. Click **Text Wrapping** tab .... Ctrl+Tab
6. Select desired text wrapping style:
   - **Square** .... Alt+Q
   - **Tight** .... Alt+T
   - **Through** .... Alt+H
   - **Top and bottom** .... Alt+O
   - **Behind text** .... Alt+B
   - **In front of Text** .... Alt+F
   - **In line with text** .... Alt+I

7. For Square, Through, and Tight styles, select desired text wrapping options:
   - **Both sides** .... Alt+S
   - **Left only** .... Alt+L
   - **Right only** .... Alt+R
   - **Largest only** .... Alt+A
8. For Square, Through, Top and bottom, and Tight styles, set distance from text, as follows:
   a. Click **Top** .... Alt+P
   b. Type distance to leave between text and top of object.
   c. Click **Bottom** .... Alt+M
   d. Type distance to leave between text and bottom of object.
   e. Click **Left** .... Alt+E
   f. Type distance to leave between text and left of object.
   g. Click **Right** .... Alt+G
   h. Type distance to leave between text and right of object.

   ✓ *Not all distance options will be available for all styles.*

9. Click **OK** .... ↵Enter

Position a Text Box

1. Click text box to select it.
2. Click the **Text Box Tools Format** tab .... Alt, J, X

   Arrange Group

3. Click **Position** button ⬛ .... P
4. Click position to apply .... ↓/←/→/↑, ↵Enter

Position a Text Box Precisely

1. Click text box to select it.
2. Click the **Text Box Tools Format** tab .... (Alt), (J), (X)

   Arrange Group

3. Click **Position** button 📷 .... (P)
4. Click **More Layout Options** .... (L)
5. Click **Picture Position** tab .... (Ctrl)+(Tab⇆)
6. Do one of the following to set horizontal position:
   a. Click **Alignment** drop-down arrow .... (Alt)+(A), (Tab⇆), (↓)
   b. Click desired alignment .... (↓)/(↑), (↵Enter)
   c. Click **relative to** drop-down arrow .... (Alt)+(R)
   d. Click desired anchor .... (↓)/(↑), (↵Enter)

   OR

   a. Click **Book layout** drop-down arrow .... (Alt)+(B), (Tab⇆), (↓)
   b. Click desired position .... (↓)/(↑), (↵Enter)
   c. Click **of** drop-down arrow .... (Alt)+(F)
   d. Click desired anchor .... (↓)/(↑), (↵Enter)

   OR

   a. Click **Absolute position** drop-down arrow ... (Alt)+(P), (Tab⇆), (↓)/(↑)
   b. Type amount of space to leave.
   c. Click **to the right of** drop-down arrow .... (Alt)+(T)
   d. Click desired anchor .... (↓)/(↑), (↵Enter)

OR

a. Click **Relative position** drop-down arrow .... (Alt)+(R), (Tab⇆), (↓)/(↑)
b. Type percentage to leave.
c. Click **relative to** drop-down arrow .... (Alt)+(E)
d. Click desired anchor .... (↓)/(↑), (↵Enter)

7. Do one of the following to set vertical position:
   a. Click **Alignment** drop-down arrow .... (Alt)+(G), (Tab⇆), (↓)
   b. Click desired alignment .... (↓)/(↑), (↵Enter)
   c. Click **relative to** drop-down arrow .... (Alt)+(E)
   d. Click desired anchor .... (↓)/(↑), (↵Enter)

   OR

   a. Click **Absolute position** drop-down arrow ... (Alt)+(S), (Tab⇆), (↓)/(↑)
   b. Type amount of space to leave.
   c. Click **below** drop-down arrow .... (Alt)+(W)
   d. Click desired anchor .... (↓)/(↑), (↵Enter)

   OR

   a. Click **Relative position** drop-down arrow .... (Alt)+(I), (Tab⇆), (↓)/(↑)
   b. Type percentage to leave.
   c. Click **relative to** drop-down arrow .... (Alt)+(O)
   d. Click desired anchor .... (↓)/(↑), (↵Enter)

8. Select check box options as necessary:
   - **Move object with text** .... (Alt)+(M)
   - **Lock anchor** .... (Alt)+(L)
   - **Allow overlap** .... (Alt)+(V)
   - **Layout in table cell** .... (Alt)+(C)
9. Click **OK** .... (↵Enter)

Link Text Boxes

1. Insert text boxes.
2. Select first text box.
3. Click the **Text Box Tools Format** tab .... (Alt), (J), (X)

   Text Group

4. Click the **Create Link** button 🔗 .... (C)

   ✓ *The mouse pointer changes to display a pouring pitcher when it is over a text box 🫗 or an upright pitcher when it over anything other than a text box 🫙.*

5. Click the next text box.
6. Repeat steps 3-5 to link additional text boxes.

Break a Text Box Link

1. Select a linked text box.
2. Click the **Text Box Tools Format** tab .... (Alt), (J), (X)

   Text Group

3. Click the **Break Link** button 🔗 .... (B)

Align an Object on the Page

1. Click object to select it.
2. For a shape, click the **Drawing Tools Format** tab .... (Alt), (J), (D)

   OR

   For a text box, click the **Text Box Tools Format** tab .... (Alt), (J), (X)

   OR

   For a picture, click the **Picture Tools Format** tab .... (Alt), (J), (P)

   OR

   For a WordArt object, click the **WordArt Tools Format** tab .... (Alt), (J), (W)

3. Click **Align** button ▣ ▾ ...... Ⓐ, Ⓐ
4. Click alignment option:
   - ■ Align **L**eft .... Ⓛ
   - ■ Align **C**enter .... Ⓒ
   - ■ Align **R**ight .... Ⓡ
   - ■ Align **T**op .... Ⓣ
   - ■ Align **M**iddle .... Ⓜ
   - ■ Align **B**ottom .... Ⓑ

To select to align to the page or the margin:

1. Click object to select it.
2. For a shape, click the **Drawing Tools Format** tab .... Ⓐⁱᵗ, Ⓙ, Ⓓ
   OR
   For a text box, click the **Text Box Tools Format** tab .... Ⓐⁱᵗ, Ⓙ, Ⓧ
   OR
   For a picture, click the **Picture Tools Format** tab .... Ⓐⁱᵗ, Ⓙ, Ⓟ
   OR
   For a WordArt object, click the **WordArt Tools Format** tab .... Ⓐⁱᵗ, Ⓙ, Ⓦ

3. Click **Align** button ▣ ▾ ...... Ⓐ, Ⓐ
4. Click one of the following:
   - ■ Align to **P**age to align object with the page .... Ⓟ
   - ■ Align to **M**argin to align object with the margins .... Ⓐ

Align an Object with another Object

1. Select objects to align.
   - ✓ *You may select different types of objects, such as shapes and text boxes.*
2. Click the **Drawing Tools Format** tab .... Ⓐⁱᵗ, Ⓙ, Ⓓ
   OR
   Click the **Text Box Tools Format** tab .... Ⓐⁱᵗ, Ⓙ, Ⓧ
   OR
   Click the **Picture Tools Format** tab .... Ⓐⁱᵗ, Ⓙ, Ⓟ
   OR
   For a WordArt object, click the **WordArt Tools Format** tab .... Ⓐⁱᵗ, Ⓙ, Ⓦ

3. Click **Align** button ▣ ▾ ..... Ⓐ, Ⓐ
4. Click **Align** **S**elected **O**bjects .... Ⓞ
5. Click **Align** button
   ▣ ▾ .... Ⓐⁱᵗ, Ⓙ, Ⓓ, Ⓐ, Ⓐ
   OR
   Click **Align** button
   ▣ ▾ .... Ⓐⁱᵗ, Ⓙ, Ⓧ, Ⓐ, Ⓐ
6. Click alignment option:
   - ■ Align **L**eft .... Ⓛ
   - ■ Align **C**enter .... Ⓒ
   - ■ Align **R**ight .... Ⓡ
   - ■ Align **T**op .... Ⓣ
   - ■ Align **M**iddle .... Ⓜ
   - ■ Align **B**ottom .... Ⓑ

Display or Hide Gridlines

1. Click object to select it.
2. For a shape, click the **Drawing Tools Format** tab .... Ⓐⁱᵗ, Ⓙ, Ⓓ
   OR
   For a text box, click the **Text Box Tools Format** tab .... Ⓐⁱᵗ, Ⓙ, Ⓧ

3. Click **Align** button ▣ ▾ ..... Ⓐ, Ⓐ
4. Click **View Gridlines** .... Ⓢ

Copy an Object

1. Right-click object to copy.
2. Click **Copy** .... Ⓒ
3. Right-click blank area of document.
4. Click **Paste** .... Ⓟ, ↵Enter
5. Position copy as necessary.
   OR
1. Select object to copy.
2. Click the **Home** tab .... Ⓐⁱᵗ+Ⓗ

3. Click **Copy** button ▣ .... Ⓒ
4. Position insertion point.
   OR
   Deselect selected object.
5. Click the **Home** tab .... Ⓐⁱᵗ+Ⓗ

6. Click **Paste** button ▣ .... Ⓥ, Ⓟ

EXERCISE DIRECTIONS

Insert Shapes

1. Start Word, if necessary.
2. Open ⊙71ESSAY.
3. Save the file as 71ESSAY_*xx*.
4. Insert the Explosion 1 shape from the Stars and Banners palette.
5. Resize the shape to 2.25" high by 2.75" wide.
6. Align the shape left horizontally relative to the margin.
7. Position the shape vertically .5" below the page.
8. Copy the object and align the copy on the right horizontally, relative to the margin.
9. Select both shapes and align the tops to each other.
10. Set the text wrapping to Behind text.
11. Save the document.

Insert Text Boxes

1. Position the insertion point on the 10th line in the document, the topic *Break Away from the Herd*.

   ✓ *This positions the object's anchor.*

2. Insert a blank text box approximately .75" high and 1.75" wide.
3. Position the text box horizontally aligned on the left, relative to the margin, and vertically aligned .5" below the line where the anchor is located. (Lock the anchor so it does not move.)

   ✓ *If necessary, display hidden characters to see the anchor.*

4. Set the text wrapping for the text box to Top and Bottom.
5. Copy the text box, and position the copy centered horizontally relative to the margin and vertically aligned .5" below the line.
6. Copy the text box again, and position the third copy horizontally aligned on the right, relative to the margin, with the right margin, and vertically aligned .5" below the line.

7. Centered in first text box—on the left—type the following lines of text, in 16-point Arial, centered:

   Junior Division
   Grades 1 - 4
   Middle Division
   Grades 5 - 9
   Senior Division
   Grades 10 – 12

   ✓ *Some of the text will not display within the boundaries of the text box.*

8. Link the text box on the left to the text box in the center, and then link the text box in the center to the text box on the right.
9. Save the changes.

Insert a Shape with Added Text

1. Insert the 5-point Star AutoShape from the Stars and Banners palette.
2. Resize it to 2.75" high by 3" wide.
3. Center the shape horizontally relative to the page, and position it vertically 4.5" below the margin.
4. Set the text wrapping to Top and bottom.
5. Add the following text to the shape, using 14-point Arial in bold and centered: **Winners will be announced June 1!**

   ✓ *The text should wrap within the shape.*

6. Save the document.
7. Check the spelling and grammar.
8. Display the document in Print Preview. It should look similar to Illustration A.
9. Print the document.
10. Close the file, saving all changes.

BLUE SKY DAIRY CO.

Proudly Announces
Its First Ever

ESSAY CONTEST

Topic:

BREAK AWAY FROM THE HERD

Junior Division Grades 1-4	Middle Division Grades 5 – 9	Senior Division Grades 10-12

Winners
will be
announced
June 1!

The Grand Prize winner will receive a $2,500 scholarship and a personal computer. Other prizes include gift certificates, computer equipment, travel vouchers, and more. For more information call: 608-555-2697, or consult the dairy's Web site: www.blueskydairy.net.

ON YOUR OWN

1. Open OWD70_*xx*, the newsletter document you used in the On Your Own section of Exercise 70, or open 71NEWS.

2. Save the file as OWD71_*xx*.

3. Insert a text box and type in a headline, quotation, or other important information you want to stand out in the document. Alternatively, insert a text box around existing text.

4. If you want, try using more than one text box and linking them.

5. Position and align the text box(es) for the best visual effect.

6. Copy a shape and position the copy somewhere else in the document.

7. Check spelling and grammar in the document.

8. Preview the document.

9. Adjust column breaks, balance columns, and otherwise edit or reformat the document as necessary.

10. Print the document.

11. Ask a classmate to review the document and make comments and suggestions, paying particular attention to layout and design.

12. Incorporate the suggestions as necessary.

13. Close the document, saving all changes.

Skills Covered

- Apply Quick Styles to Objects
- Format the Shape Outline
- Format the Shape Fill
- Apply Shadows and 3-D Effects

Software Skills Use color and special effects with drawing objects to create professional-looking graphics and pictures. You can change the color and style of the lines used to draw both closed shapes and lines, and you can enhance closed shapes by filling them with color or patterns. Shadows behind an object give a document the appearance of depth, while 3-D effects give depth to the object itself.

Application Skills In this exercise, you will modify the graphics objects that you used in the flyer announcing the essay contest for Blue Sky Dairy. You will change the line color, style, and fill color of one shape, apply shadows to the text boxes, and apply a 3-D effect to the star.

TERMS

3-D effect An effect applied to objects to make them look as if they are three dimensional.

Fill Color or patterns used to fill a closed shape.

Line style The width and appearance of a line used to draw an object.

Outline The line or border around a shape, text box, or other graphics object.

Shadow An effect applied to objects to make it look as if the object is casting a shadow.

NOTES

Apply Quick Styles to Objects

- When a shape is selected in a document, the Drawing Tools Format tab displays on the Ribbon.

- Likewise, when a text box is selected, the Text Box Tools Format tab displays on the Ribbon.

Drawing Tools Format tab

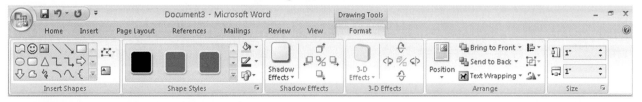

Text Box Tools Format tab

- Select a quick style from the Styles gallery to quickly apply a coordinated set of formatting options to the selected object.
- Alternatively, using the tools on these Format tabs let you apply formatting such as **outlines** and **fills**, **shadows**, and **3-D effects**.

  ✓ *You can also use these tools for formatting WordArt objects and pictures. You learn more about pictures in Exercise 73. You learn more about WordArt in Exercise 76.*

Format the Shape Outline

- By default, drawing objects have a solid single line border on all sides.
- You can format the shape **outline** by changing the **line style** and/or color.
- The outline options are similar to those used for tables and paragraphs. For example, you can select a 3 pt., turquoise dashed border.

Format the Shape Fill

- You can apply a shape **fill** to fill an object with color, texture, a gradient, or a pattern.
- Fill color options are similar to those available for table cells and paragraphs. For example, you can fill an object with a color or gray shading.
- Remember that color and textures are best used in documents designed to be viewed on-screen, such as Web pages, or documents that will be printed on a color printer.

Apply Shadows and 3-D Effects

- **Shadows** and **3-D effects** can be applied to any drawing object.
- You can select from a gallery of built-in effects, or you can customize the effects.
- For example, you can customize a shadow effect by changing the shadow color and/or by adjusting the position of the shadow.
- You can customize the 3-D effect by changing the color, lighting, depth, direction, angle, and/or surface of the object.

PROCEDURES

Apply a Quick Style to a Shape

1. Click shape to select it.
2. Click the **Drawing Tools Format** tab .... (Alt), (J), (D)

   Shape Styles Group

3. Click style to apply.

   ✓ *If necessary, use scroll arrows to scroll the gallery.*

   OR

   a. Click **More** button (▼) .... (K)
   b. Click style to apply..... (←)/(→)/(↑)/(↓), (↵Enter)

Apply a Quick Style to a Text Box

1. Click text box to select it.
2. Click the **Text Box Tools Format** tab .... (Alt), (J), (X)

   Text Box Styles Group

3. Click style in Text Box Styles Gallery.

   ✓ *If necessary, use scroll arrows to scroll the gallery.*

   OR

   a. Click **More** button (▼) .... (K)
   b. Click style to apply..... (←)/(→)/(↑)/(↓), (↵Enter)

Apply a Fill

1. Click object to select it.
2. For a shape, click the **Drawing Tools Format** tab .... (Alt), (J), (D)

   OR

   For a text box, click the **Text Box Tools Format** tab .... (Alt), (J), (X)

   OR

   For a WordArt object, click the **WordArt Tools Format** tab .... (Alt), (J), (W)

   Shape/Text Box/WordArt Styles Group

3. Click **Shape Fill** button (🎨▾) drop-down arrow .... (S), (F)

   ✓ *To quickly apply color displayed on button, click button instead of drop-down arrow.*

4. Click color to
apply............ ←/→/↑/↓, ↵Enter

OR

Click one of the following:

- ■ **No Fill** to remove current fill....................................... N
- ■ **More Fill Colors** to select a custom color..................... M
- ■ **Picture** to select options for a picture fill....................... P
- ■ **Gradient** to select a gradient fill...................................... G
- ■ **Texture** to select a texture fill...................................... T
- ■ **Pattern** to select options for a pattern fill....................... A

Format the Outline

1. Click object to select it.
2. For a shape, click the **Drawing Tools Format** tab.......... Alt, J, D

   OR

   For a text box, click the **Text Box Tools Format** tab.......... Alt, J, X

   OR

   For a WordArt object, click the **WordArt Tools Format** tab .... Alt, J, W

   <u>Shape/Text Box/WordArt Styles Group</u>

3. Click **Shape Outline** button 🖉 ▾ drop-down arrow .... S, O

   ✓ To quickly apply color displayed on button, click button instead of drop-down arrow.

4. Click color to
apply............ ←/→/↑/↓, ↵Enter

   OR

   Click one of the following:

- ■ **No Outline** to remove current outline........................... N
- ■ **More Outline Colors** to select a custom color..................... M
- ■ **Weight** to select a line weight..................................... W

- ■ **Dashes** to select a dash style...................................... S
- ■ **Arrows** to select an arrow style...................................... R

   ✓ Arrows is only available if you select an arrow or line shape

- ■ **Pattern** to select options for a pattern fill....................... A

Apply Shadows

To turn shadow effect off or on:

1. Click object to select it.
2. For a shape, click the **Drawing Tools Format** tab.......... Alt, J, D

   OR

   For a text box, click the **Text Box Tools Format** tab.......... Alt, J, X

   OR

   For a WordArt object, click the **WordArt Tools Format** tab .... Alt, J, W

   <u>Shadow Effects Group</u>

3. Click **Shadow On/Off** button 🔲 .... O

To apply a shadow effect:

1. Click object to select it.
2. For a shape, click the **Drawing Tools Format** tab.......... Alt, J, D

   OR

   For a text box, click the **Text Box Tools Format** tab.......... Alt, J, X

   OR

   For a WordArt object, click the **WordArt Tools Format** tab .... Alt, J, W

   <u>Shadow Effects Group</u>

3. Click **Shadow Effects** button 🔲 V
4. Click effect to
apply............ ←/→/↑/↓, ↵Enter

   ✓ Click Shadow Color to select a color and/or transparency for the shadow.

To increase or decrease the width of a shadow:

1. Click object to select it.
2. For a shape, click the **Drawing Tools Format** tab.......... Alt, J, D

   OR

   For a text box, click the **Text Box Tools Format** tab.......... Alt, J, X

   OR

   For a WordArt object, click the **WordArt Tools Format** tab .... Alt, J, W

   <u>Shadow Effects Group</u>

3. Click one of the following:
- ■ **Nudge shadow up** 🔲 1
- ■ **Nudge shadow left** 🔲 2
- ■ **Nudge shadow right** 🔲 3
- ■ **Nudge shadow down** 🔲 4

Apply 3-D Effects

To turn 3-D effects off or on for shapes:

1. Click shape to select it.
2. Click the **Drawing Tools Format** tab .... Alt, J, D

   <u>3-D Effects Group</u>

3. Click the **3-D On/Off** button 🔲 .... O

To turn 3-D effects off or on for text boxes or WordArt:

1. Click text box to select it.
2. Click the **Text Box Tools Format** tab .... Alt, J, X

   OR

   For a WordArt object, click the **WordArt Tools Format** tab .... Alt, J, W

   <u>3-D Effects Group</u>

3. Click the **3-D Effects** group button 🔲 .... Z, 3
4. Click the **3-D On/Off** button 🔲 .... O

To adjust position of 3-D effect for a shape:

1. Click shape to select it.
2. Click the **Drawing Tools Format** tab .... Alt, J, D

3-D Effects Group

3. Click one of the following:
   - **Tilt Up** 🔄 5
   - **Tilt Right** ◁▷ 7
   - **Tilt Left** ◁▷ 6
   - **Tilt Down** 🔄 8

To adjust position of 3-D effect for a text box or WordArt:

1. Click text box to select it.
2. Click the **Text Box Tools Format** tab .... Alt, J, X

   OR

   For a WordArt object, click the **WordArt Tools Format** tab .... Alt, J, W

3-D Effects Group

3. Click the **3-D Effects** group button 🔲 .... Z, 3
4. Click one of the following:
   - **Tilt Up** 🔄 5
   - **Tilt Right** ◁▷ 7
   - **Tilt Left** ◁▷ 6
   - **Tilt Down** 🔄 8

To apply a 3-D effect to a shape:

1. Click shape to select it.
2. Click the **Drawing Tools Format** tab .... Alt, J, D

3-D Effects Group

3. Click the **3-D Effects** button 🔲 .... U
4. Click effect to apply .... ←/→/↑/↓, ↵Enter

To apply a 3-D effect to a text box or WordArt:

1. Click text box to select it.
2. Click the **Text Box Tools Format** tab .... Alt, J, X

   OR

   For a WordArt object, click the **WordArt Tools Format** tab .... Alt, J, W

3-D Effects Group

3. Click the **3-D Effects** group button 🔲 .... Z, 3
4. Click the **3-D Effects** button 🔲 .... U
5. Click effect to apply .... ←/→/↑/↓, ↵Enter

EXERCISE DIRECTIONS

1. Start Word, if necessary.
2. Open 🖮71ESSAY_*xx* or open 💿72ESSAY.
3. Save the document as **72ESSAY_*xx***.
4. Select the explosion shape in the upper-left corner.
5. Apply the Linear Up Gradient – Accent 1 quick style to the shape.
6. Change the outline weight to 3 pts.
7. Select the explosion shape in the upper-right corner.
8. Apply the Linear Up Gradient – Accent 2 quick style to the shape.
9. Change the outline weight to 3 pts.
10. Select all three text boxes.

    ✓ *Select the first box, press and hold Shift, then select the other two boxes.*

11. Apply the Drop Shadow style 4 effect to the selected text boxes.
12. Change the shadow color to the theme color, Blue, Accent 1.
13. Select the Star shape.
14. Change the fill color to the theme color Orange, Accent 6, Lighter 60%.
15. Apply the 3-D Style 2.
16. Customize the 3-D effect by clicking the Tilt Right button three times and the Tilt Up button twice.
17. Preview the document. It should look similar to the one in Illustration A.
18. Print the document.
19. Close the document, saving all changes.

BLUE SKY DAIRY CO.

Proudly Announces
Its First Ever

ESSAY CONTEST

Topic:

BREAK AWAY FROM THE HERD

| Junior Division Grades 1-4 | Middle Division Grades 5 – 9 | Senior Division Grades 10-12 |

Winners will be announced June 1!

The Grand Prize winner will receive a $2,500 scholarship and a personal computer. Other prizes include gift certificates, computer equipment, travel vouchers, and more. For more information call: 608-555-2697, or consult the dairy's Web site: www.blueskydairy.net.

ON YOUR OWN

1. Start Word, and create a new blank document.
2. Save the document as **OWD72_xx**.
3. Type an announcement for an event such as a birthday, graduation, performance, or meeting.
4. Insert graphics objects such as shapes and text boxes.
5. Format the objects using line colors, styles, fills, and effects.
6. Resize and position the objects as necessary.
7. Set text wrapping options.
8. When you achieve the look you want, print the document.
9. Ask a classmate to review the document and offer comments and suggestions.
10. Incorporate the suggestions into the document as necessary,
11. Close the document, saving all changes, and exit Word.

Curriculum Connection: Language Arts

Personification

Personification is a writing technique in which human qualities are assigned to an object or animal. Carl Sandburg used personification in the poem *Fog* when he wrote, "The fog comes in on little cat feet."

Use Personification

Create an advertising flyer using personification. You might advertise the opening of a furniture store and use personification to describe a chair as having arms that hug. Or, advertise an apartment for rent, and use personification to describe the rooms, neighborhood, or building. Enhance the flyer by using graphics features such as shapes and text boxes, as well as desktop publishing features such as dropped capitals and borders.

Exercise | 73

Skills Covered

- Insert Clip Art
- Format Clip Art
- Adjust Brightness, Contrast, and Color
- Compress a Picture
- Use the Clip Organizer

Software Skills   Insert clip art into documents to illustrate and enhance your text. You can format clip art pictures using many of the same options you use for shapes and text boxes. You can also adjust the brightness and contrast of pictures, and compress them so they take up less storage space.

Application Skills   Voyager Travel Adventures has asked you to embellish an existing newsletter using graphics. In this exercise, you insert clip art pictures into the newsletter.

TERMS

Brightness   The amount of white or black added to a color. Sometimes called *tint*.

Clip art   Files such as pictures, sounds, and videos that you can insert into an Office document.

Clip collection   A folder used to store clip files.

Compress   To reduce the size of something, such as a file.

Contrast   The difference between the color values of different parts of an image.

NOTES

Insert Clip Art

- You can insert **clip art** into your Office documents.
- Clip art files include pictures, sounds, and videos created in different programs—but fully supported and editable in Word.
- You can use the Clip Art task pane to locate and insert clip art by searching for files based on a keyword.
- In the task pane, you select the locations where you want to search and the type of clips you want to find.
- Word displays thumbnail-sized previews of each matching clip in the task pane so you can select the one you want to insert.
- Small Icons on the thumbnails indicate if the clip file is stored on a removable disc or online, or if it is an animation.

Clip Art task pane

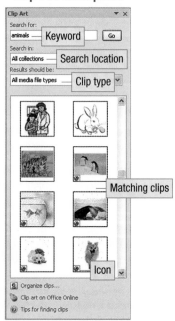

■ You can also insert a picture from a file, which is useful when you know where a particular clip art file is stored.

■ The commands for inserting Clip Art and pictures are in the Illustrations group on the Insert tab of the Ribbon.

Format Clip Art

■ When you select a clip art object, commands for editing and formatting clip art become available on the Picture Tools Format tab of the Ribbon.

■ Many of the commands are similar to those you use for editing and formatting shapes and text boxes. For example, you can resize, move, set text wrapping options, position, and align clip art objects.

  ✓ *For information on deleting, moving, or resizing an object with a mouse, refer to Exercise 70. For information on aligning and copying objects, refer to Exercise 71.*

■ You can select Picture Styles or Picture Effects to apply a collection of formatting settings all at once.

Adjust Brightness, Contrast, and Color

■ You can use the buttons in the Adjust group on the Picture Tools Format tab of the Ribbon to change the **brightness** and **contrast** of colors.

■ You can also adjust the transparency of one color in a picture, or recolor all colors.

■ If you are not happy with the changes, you can reset the picture to its original formatting.

Compress a Picture

■ Picture files may be large, and therefore take up a lot of disk space, or take a long time to transmit.

■ You can **compress** a picture to make its file size smaller.

■ Compressing reduces the color format of the image which makes the color take up fewer bits per pixel.

■ You can select options to control the final resolution of the compressed picture. For example, if you plan to print the picture, you can select a higher resolu-

tion than if you plan to display the picture on-screen, or send the picture by e-mail.

■ You can compress the selected picture or all pictures in the document.

Use the Clip Organizer

■ To make it easy to find the clips you want, Word sorts the files into **clip collections** and stores them in the Microsoft Clip Organizer.

■ By default, the Clip Organizer includes the following clip collections:

  ● *My Collections*, which includes clips that you have stored on your system and sorted into folders such as *Favorites*. It may also include a Windows folder containing clips that come with Windows, other Windows programs, or clips that you had installed before you installed Microsoft Office 2007.

  ● *Office Collections*, which includes the clips that come with the Microsoft Office 2007 suite of programs that are sorted into folders such as *People, Animals, Emotions,* and *Food.*

  ● *Web Collections*, which automatically uses an open Internet link to access clips stored on Microsoft Office Clip Art and Media online Web site.

■ You can use the Clip Organizer to browse through clip collections, create new collections, add clips from other locations, and copy or move clips from one collection to another.

Microsoft Clip Organizer

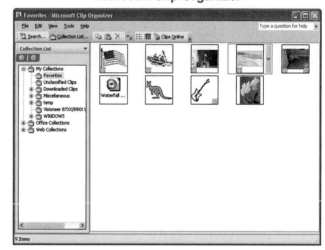

Picture Tools Format tab

PROCEDURES

Insert Clip Art

1. Click **Insert** tab..............Alt+N

   Illustrations Group

2. Click **Clip Art** button 🔲 .... F

   ✓ *The Clip Art task pane displays.*

3. Click in **Search for** text box.

4. Type keyword(s).

   ✓ *If necessary, delete existing text, first.*

5. Click **Search in**: drop-down arrow.

6. Click to select and deselect collection folders as necessary, using the follows methods:
   - Click **plus sign** to expand list......................→
   - Click **check box** to select folder............↑/↓, Spacebar

7. Click outside expanded list to close list......................Tab↹

8. Click **Results should be:** drop-down arrow.........Tab↹, Spacebar

9. Click **plus sign** to expand list......................↓, →

10. Click to select or deselect clip type(s) as necessary............↑/↓, Spacebar

11. Click **Go** button Go ......↵Enter

    ✓ *Word displays clips that match your criteria.*

12. Click clip to insert.

Insert Picture from File

1. Click **Insert** tab..............Alt+N

   Illustrations Group

2. Click **Picture** button 🖼 ....P

   ✓ *The Insert Picture dialog box displays.*

3. Navigate to location where picture file is stored.

4. Click picture to insert.

5. Click **Insert** ....Alt+S

Adjust Brightness

1. Click picture to select it.

2. Click the **Picture Tools Format** tab ....Alt, J, P

   Adjust Group

3. Click the **Brightness** button ☀ ....B

4. Click desired brightness............↓/↑, ↵Enter

Adjust Contrast

1. Click picture to select it.

2. Click the **Picture Tools Format** tab ....Alt, J, P

   Adjust Group

3. Click the **Contrast** button ◑ ....N

4. Click desired contrast..............↓/↑, ↵Enter

Recolor a Picture

1. Click picture to select it.

2. Click the **Picture Tools Format** tab ....Alt, J, P

   Adjust Group

3. Click the **Recolor** button 🖼 ....E

4. Click desired color effect............↓/↑/←/→, ↵Enter

Set the Transparency of One Color

1. Click picture to select it.

2. Click the **Picture Tools Format** tab ....Alt, J, P

   Adjust Group

3. Click the **Recolor** button 🖼 ....E

4. Click **Set Transparent Color**......................S

   ✓ *The mouse pointer changes to display the pickup color tool ✐ .*

5. In the picture, click the color you want to make transparent.

Reset a Picture

1. Click picture to select it.

2. Click the **Picture Tools Format** tab ....Alt, J, P

   Adjust Group

3. Click the **Reset Picture** button 🖼 ....Q

Compress Pictures

To compress all pictures in the document:

1. Click any picture to select it.

2. Click the **Picture Tools Format** tab ....Alt, J, P

   Adjust Group

3. Click the **Compress Pictures** button 🖼 ....M

4. Click **OK** ....↵Enter

To compress only the selected picture:

1. Click picture to select it.

2. Click the **Picture Tools Format** tab ....Alt, J, P

   Adjust Group

3. Click the **Compress Pictures** button 🖼 ....M

4. Click to select **Apply to selected pictures only check box** ....Alt+A

5. Click **OK** ....↵Enter

To select compression options:

1. Click picture to select it.

2. Click the **Picture Tools Format** tab ....Alt, J, P

   Adjust Group

3. Click the **Compress Pictures** button 🖼 ....M

4. Click **Options** ....Alt+O

5. Select or deselect compression options:
   - **Automatically perform basic compression on save** .... `Alt`+`A`
   - **Delete cropped areas of pictures** .... `Alt`+`D`
6. Select desired target output resolution:
   - **Print (220 ppi)** .... `Alt`+`P`
   - **Screen (150 ppi)** .... `Alt`+`S`
   - **E-mail (96 ppi)** .... `Alt`+`E`
7. Click **OK** .... `↵Enter`

Apply a Picture Style

1. Click picture to select it.
2. Click the **Picture Tools Format** tab .... `Alt`, `J`, `P`

   Picture Styles Group

3. Click style in Picture Styles Gallery.

   ✓ *If necessary, use scroll arrows to scroll the gallery.*

   OR

   a. Click **More** button `▼` .... `K`
   b. Click style to apply ..... `←`/`→`/`↑`/`↓`, `↵Enter`

Format the Picture Border

1. Click picture to select it.
2. Click the **Picture Tools Format** tab .... `Alt`, `J`, `P`

   Picture Styles Group

3. Click **Picture Border** button `☑▾` drop-down arrow .... `S`, `O`

   ✓ *To quickly apply color displayed on button, click button instead of drop-down arrow.*

4. Click color to apply .... `←`/`→`/`↑`/`↓`, `↵Enter`

   OR

   Click one of the following:
   - **No Outline** to remove current outline .... `N`
   - **More Outline Colors** to select a custom color .... `M`
   - **Weight** to select a line weight .... `W`
   - **Dashes** to select a dash style .... `S`

Apply Picture Effects

1. Click picture to select it.
2. Click the **Picture Tools Format** tab .... `Alt`, `J`, `P`

   Picture Styles Group

3. Click the **Picture Effects** button `◻` .... `F`
4. Click desired category of effect .... `↓`/`↑`, `→`
5. Click desired effect .... `↓`/`↑`/`←`/`→`, `↵Enter`

Resize a Picture Precisely

1. Click picture to select it.
2. Click the **Picture Tools Format** tab .... `Alt`, `J`, `P`

   Size Group

3. Click **Shape Height** box `1.51"` .... `H`
4. Type height in inches .... *type height*, `↵Enter`

   OR

   Click increment arrows to enter height.
5. Click **Shape Width** box `1.43"` .... `Alt`, `J`, `P`, `W`
6. Type width in inches .... *type width*, `↵Enter`

   OR

   Click increment arrows to enter width.

Position a Picture

1. Click picture to select it.
2. Click the **Picture Tools Format** tab .... `Alt`, `J`, `P`

   Arrange Group

3. Click **Position** button `▦` .... `P`, `O`
4. Click position to apply .... `↓`/`←`/`→`/`↑`, `↵Enter`

Position a Picture Precisely

1. Click shape to select it.
2. Click the **Picture Tools Format** tab .... `Alt`, `J`, `P`

   Arrange Group

3. Click **Position** button `▦` .... `P`, `O`
4. Click **More Layout Options** .... `L`
5. Click **Picture Position** tab .... `Ctrl`+`Tab↹`
6. Do one of the following to set horizontal position:
   a. Click **Alignment** drop-down arrow .... `Alt`+`A`, `Tab↹`, `↓`
   b. Click desired alignment .... `↓`/`↑`, `↵Enter`
   c. Click **relative to** drop-down arrow .... `Alt`+`R`
   d. Click desired anchor .... `↓`/`↑`, `↵Enter`

   OR

   a. Click **Book layout** drop-down arrow .... `Alt`+`B`, `Tab↹`, `↓`
   b. Click desired position .... `↓`/`↑`, `↵Enter`
   c. Click **of** drop-down arrow .... `Alt`+`F`
   d. Click desired anchor .... `↓`/`↑`, `↵Enter`

OR

a. Click **Absolute position** drop-down arrow ...... `Alt`+`P`, `Tab⇆`, `↓`/`↑`

b. Type amount of space to leave.

c. Click **to the right of** drop-down arrow .... `Alt`+`T`

d. Click desired anchor .... `↓`/`↑`, `↵Enter`

OR

a. Click **Relative position** drop-down arrow ... `Alt`+`R`, `Tab⇆`, `↓`/`↑`

b. Type percentage to leave.

c. Click **relative to** drop-down arrow .... `Alt`+`E`

d. Click desired anchor .... `↓`/`↑`, `↵Enter`

7. Do one of the following to set vertical position:

a. Click **Alignment** drop-down arrow .... `Alt`+`G`, `Tab⇆`, `↓`

b. Click desired alignment .... `↓`/`↑`, `↵Enter`

c. Click **relative to** drop-down arrow .... `Alt`+`E`

d. Click desired anchor .... `↓`/`↑`, `↵Enter`

OR

a. Click **Absolute position** drop-down arrow ... `Alt`+`S`, `Tab⇆`, `↓`/`↑`

b. Type amount of space to leave.

c. Click **below** drop-down arrow .... `Alt`+`W`

d. Click desired anchor .... `↓`/`↑`, `↵Enter`

OR

a. Click **Relative position** drop-down arrow ... `Alt`+`I`, `Tab⇆`, `↓`/`↑`

b. Type percentage to leave.

c. Click **relative to** drop-down arrow .... `Alt`+`O`

d. Click desired anchor .... `↓`/`↑`, `↵Enter`

---

8. Select check box options as necessary:
   - **Move object with text** .... `Alt`+`M`
   - **Lock anchor** .... `Alt`+`L`
   - **Allow overlap** .... `Alt`+`V`
   - **Layout in table cell** ...... `Alt`+`C`

9. Click **OK** .... `↵Enter`

Set Text Wrap Options for a Picture

1. Click picture to select it.
2. Click the **Picture Tools Format** tab .... `Alt`, `J`, `P`

   Arrange Group

3. Click **Text Wrapping** button 🖾 .... `T`, `W`
4. Click desired option:
   - **In Line with Text** .... `I`
   - **Square** .... `S`
   - **Tight** .... `T`
   - **Behind Text** .... `D`
   - **In Front of Text** .... `N`
   - **Top and Bottom** .... `O`
   - **Through** .... `H`

Set Advanced Text Wrap Options for a Picture

1. Click object to select it.
2. Click the **Picture Tools Format** tab .... `Alt`, `J`, `P`

   Arrange Group

3. Click **Text Wrapping** button 🖾 .... `T`, `W`
4. Click **More Layout Options** ... `L`
5. Click **Text Wrapping** tab .... `Ctrl`+`Tab⇆`

---

6. Select desired text wrapping style:
   - **Square** .... `Alt`+`Q`
   - **Tight** .... `Alt`+`T`
   - **Through** .... `Alt`+`H`
   - **Top and bottom** .... `Alt`+`O`
   - **Behind text** .... `Alt`+`B`
   - **In front of text** .... `Alt`+`F`
   - **In line with text** .... `Alt`+`I`

7. For Square, Through, and Tight styles, select desired text wrapping options:
   - **Both sides** .... `Alt`+`S`
   - **Left only** .... `Alt`+`L`
   - **Right only** .... `Alt`+`R`
   - **Largest only** .... `Alt`+`A`

8. For Square, Through, Top and bottom, and Tight styles, set distance from text, as follows:

   a. Click **Top** .... `Alt`+`P`

   b. Type distance to leave between text and top of object.

   c. Click **Bottom** .... `Alt`+`M`

   d. Type distance to leave between text and bottom of object.

   e. Click **Left** .... `Alt`+`E`

   f. Type distance to leave between text and left of object.

   g. Click **Right** .... `Alt`+`G`

   h. Type distance to leave between text and right of object.

   ✓ *Not all distance options will be available for all styles.*

9. Click **OK** .... `↵Enter`

Use the Clip Organizer

To display Clip Organizer:
1. Click **Insert** tab.............. Alt + N

   Illustrations Group
2. Click **Clip Art** button ▦.......... F

   ✓ The Clip Art task pane displays.
3. Click **Organize clips** ▣.

   ✓ The Microsoft Clip Organizer window opens, with the Favorites collection displayed.
4. Click folder in Collection List to view its contents.

   ✓ If necessary, click **plus sign** next to a folder to expand list.

To insert a clip:
1. Display Clip Organizer.
2. Open collection containing clip.
3. Drag clip from Organizer to desired location in document.

   OR
   a. Click clip.
   b. Click clip's drop–down arrow.
   c. Click **Copy**................ C
   d. Right-click location in document where you want to insert clip.

      ✓ Move organizer out of the way or minimize it if necessary.
   e. Click **Paste**........... P, ↵Enter

To copy a clip to a different collection:
1. Display Clip Organizer.
2. Open collection containing clip.
3. Click clip.
4. Click clip's drop-down arrow.
5. Click **Copy to Collection**......... Y

   ✓ The Copy to Collection dialog box opens.
6. Select collection to copy to.

   OR
   a. Click **New** to create a new collection............. Alt + N
   b. Type new collection name.
   c. Click **OK**............. ↵Enter
7. Click **OK**.

To move a clip to a different collection:
1. Display Clip Organizer.
2. Open collection containing clip.
3. Click clip.
4. Click clip's drop-down arrow.
5. Click **Move to Collection**........ M

   ✓ The Move to Collection dialog box opens. Not that the Move to Collection options may not be available for all clips.
6. Select collection to move to.

   OR
   a. Click **New** to create a new collection............. Alt + N
   b. Type new collection name.
   c. Click **OK**.
7. Click **OK**.............. ↵Enter

To add a clip to the Clip Organizer:
1. Display Clip Organizer.
2. Open collection containing clip.
3. Click **File**........... Alt + F
4. Point to **Add Clips to Organizer**. A
5. Do one of the following:

   To have Word automatically locate and add clips stored on your system:
   a. Click **Automatically**......... M
   b. Click **OK** to begin....... ↵Enter

   OR

   To manually select clips to add:
   a. Click **On My Own**......... O
   b. Locate and select desired clip file(s).
   c. Click **Add**......... Alt + A

   OR

   To upload a clip from a scanner device or camera device attached to your system:
   a. Click **From Scanner or Camera**........... S
   b. Follow steps for your scanner or camera.

To delete a clip from the current folder:
1. Display Clip Organizer.
2. Open collection containing clip.
3. Click clip.
4. Click clip's drop-down arrow.
5. Click **Delete from "Collection Name"**............ F

To delete a clip from the Clip Organizer:
1. Display Clip Organizer.
2. Open collection containing clip.
3. Click clip.
4. Click clip's drop-down arrow.
5. Click **Delete from Clip Organizer**............ D
6. Click **OK**............ ↵Enter

EXERCISE DIRECTIONS

1. Start Word, if necessary.
2. Open 🔘 **73VOYAGER**.
3. Save the file as **73VOYAGER_xx**.
4. Position the insertion point at the beginning of the first line in the document.
5. Use the Clip Art task pane to search for clips with the keyword **Passport**.
6. Insert the clip shown in Illustration A.

   ✓ *If you cannot locate the same clip, select a different clip, or insert the picture file* 🔘 **73PASSPORT** *supplied with this book.*

7. Resize the picture to approximately 1" high (the width should adjust automatically).
8. Change the text wrapping setting for the picture to Square.
9. Position the picture as shown in Illustration A—to the left of the newsletter title.
10. Reduce the contrast to -20%.
11. Close the clip art task pane.
12. Position the insertion point at the beginning of the headline *Safety Booklet Available*, and then insert a continuous section break.
13. Change the formatting for the new section from three columns to two columns.
14. Use the Clip Art task pane to search for clips with the keyword **Question**.
15. Insert the clip shown in the illustration and then close the task pane.

    ✓ *If you cannot locate the same clip, select a different clip, or insert the picture file* 🔘 **73QUESTION** *supplied with this book.*

16. Set the text wrapping to Square.
17. Align the picture right horizontally relative to the margin, and 6" below the margin vertically, as shown in Illustration A.
18. Increase the brightness of the picture to 20%.
19. Compress all of the pictures in the document, using the default settings.
20. Check the spelling and grammar in the document.
21. Display the document in Print Preview. It should look similar to the one in Illustration A.
22. Print the document.
23. Close the file, saving all changes.

Illustration A

VOYAGER TRAVEL ADVENTURES

1635 Logan Street, Denver, Colorado 80205

Traveler's Newsletter   Spring/Summer

Eco-Travel Symposium

Voyager Travel Adventures is pleased to be a sponsor of the first annual symposium on ecologically sound tourism.

The symposium will be held on April 30 at the Mile High Hotel in downtown Denver. Feature speakers include our very own Maria Sanchez. Ms. Sanchez will speak on the importance of exposing tourists to fragile environments. Tickets are available in the Voyager Adventure Travel office. All proceeds will be used for environmental preservation.

New Agent

Voyager Travel Adventures is pleased to welcome Ms. Marianna Vargas to our office. Ms. Vargas has extensive experience planning and leading adventure travel tours. Ms. Vargas is fluent in four languages, including English, Spanish, Portuguese, and French.

Ms. Vargas will report directly to our President, Maria Sanchez (see chart below). Feel free to stop in and meet her at any time.

Safety Booklet Available

In response to questions posed by actual travelers, Voyager Travel Adventures has prepared a booklet to address your travel concerns. It includes answer to such questions as:

- Will my luggage be searched?
- How early should I arrive at the airport?
- Who do I contact in an emergency?

The booklet is available free of charge at the Voyager Adventure Travel office.

ON YOUR OWN

1. Enhance the newsletter you have been working on by inserting and formatting clip art.

2. Start Word and open ⌨OWD71_*xx*, the newsletter you last worked on in Exercise 71, or open 💿73NEWS.

3. Save the document as OWD73_*xx*.

4. Delete some of the drawing objects and insert clip art images instead.

5. Size and position the clip art to enhance the document.

6. Use formatting to improve the appearance of the clip art.

7. Select text wrapping that integrates the graphics effectively with the document text.

8. Preview the document.

9. Adjust breaks and formatting as necessary.

10. Check the spelling and grammar in the document.

11. Preview the document again.

12. Print the document.

13. Ask a classmate to review the report, offering comments and suggestions.

14. Incorporate the suggestions into the document.

15. Close the document, saving all changes.

Skills Covered

- **Adjust Objects**
- **Rotate and Flip Objects**
- **Crop a Picture**

Software Skills You can manipulate objects to make sure they are positioned the way you want in a document. You can rotate objects around an axis and flip them horizontally or vertically. Many drawing objects have adjustment handles, which you can use to alter the most prominent feature of the object. For example, you can change the mouth on a smiley face from a smile to a frown.

Application Skills You've been hired to design a logo for Long Shot, Inc., a company that manufacturers golf products. The company president wants the logo suitable for use on everything from the letterhead and business cards to golf shirts and umbrellas. In this exercise, you will use text and two graphics objects—one AutoShape and one clip art picture—to create the logo. You will resize, adjust, and rotate the AutoShape and you will resize, crop, and flip the clip art picture.

TERMS

Adjustment handle A small yellow diamond used to alter the most prominent feature of an AutoShape. The mouse pointer is an arrowhead when resting on an adjustment handle.

Crop Trim or hide one or more edges of a picture.

Flip Reverse the position of an object.

Outcrop Use the cropping tool to add a margin around an object.

Rotate Shift the position of an object in a circular motion around its axis, or center point.

Rotation handle A small, green circle used to drag an object around in a circle. The mouse pointer looks like a circular arrow when resting on a rotation handle.

NOTES

Adjust Objects

- Some—but not all—AutoShapes have one or more **adjustment handles** that look like a small yellow diamond.
- You can drag the adjustment handle, to alter the most prominent feature of the shape.
- For example, you can drag an adjustment handle on a block arrow AutoShape to change the width of the arrow body, or the length of the arrowhead.

- When the mouse pointer touches an adjustment handle, it looks like an arrowhead ⬚.

Some shapes have adjustment handles and/or rotation handles

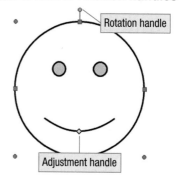

Rotate and Flip Objects

- You can **rotate** an object to the left or right around its center point, or axis.
- If a selected object has a green **rotation handle**, you can drag the handle to freely rotate the object in either direction.

  ✓ *Hold down the Shift key while you drag to rotate in 15 degree increments.*

- When the mouse pointer touches the rotation handle, it looks like a circular arrow ⟳.
- Alternatively, use commands in the Arrange group to rotate the object left or right by 90 degrees.
- You can also use the Size dialog box or Size tab on the Format AutoShape dialog box to set a precise rotation amount for the selected object, relative to its original position.

  - For example, enter 90 to rotate the object 90 degrees—or 1/4 turn—to the right; enter 270 to rotate the object 270 degrees—or 3/4 turn.
  - Enter negative values to rotate the object to the left. For example, -90 rotates the object to the same position as 270.

- **Flip** an object to reverse it, or create a mirror image.
- You can flip an object horizontally or vertically.
- You cannot rotate or flip a text box.

Crop a Picture

- **Crop** a picture to remove or trim one or more of the edges.
- You can crop from the left, right, top, and/or bottom.
- Cropping hides the edges, but does not permanently delete them.
- You can reset a cropped picture to its original appearance.
- If you want to add a margin around a picture, you can **outcrop** it.

PROCEDURES

Adjust an Object

1. Click object to select it.
2. Position the mouse pointer over yellow adjustment handle.

   ✓ *When pointer is positioned correctly, it resembles the outline of an arrowhead* ▷.

3. Drag handle as necessary to change the shape of the object.
4. Release mouse button when object is adjusted as desired.

Rotate an Object by Dragging

1. Click object to select it.
2. Position the mouse pointer over green rotation handle.

   ✓ *When pointer is positioned correctly, it resembles a circular arrow* ⟳.

3. Drag handle clockwise or counterclockwise.
4. Release mouse button when object is positioned as desired.

Rotate or Flip an Object

1. Click object to select it.
2. Click the **Drawing Tools Format** tab .... Alt, J, D

   OR

   Click the **Picture Tools Format** tab .... Alt, J, P

   OR

   Click the **WordArt Tools Format** tab .... Alt, J, W

   Arrange Group

3. Click **Rotate** button 🔄 .... A, Y
4. Click desired option:
   - **Rotate Right 90** .... R
   - **Rotate Left 90** L
   - **Flip Vertical** V
   - **Flip Horizontal** .... H

Rotate an Object Precisely

1. Click object to select it.
2. Click the **Drawing Tools Format** tab .... Alt, J, D

   OR

   Click the **Picture Tools Format** tab .... Alt, J, P

   OR

   Click the **WordArt Tools Format** tab .... Alt, J, W

   Arrange Group

3. Click **Rotate** button 🔄 .... A, Y
4. Click **More Rotation Options** ...... M
5. Click the **Rotation** increment box .... Alt+T
6. Enter rotation amount.

   ✓ *Enter a positive value to rotate to the right; enter a negative value to rotate to the left.*

7. Click **OK** .... ↵Enter

Reset an Object

1. Click object to select it.
2. Click the **Drawing Tools Format** tab .... Alt, J, D
   OR
   Click the **Picture Tools Format** tab .... Alt, J, P
   OR
   Click the **WordArt Tools Format** tab .... Alt, J, W

3. Click **Rotate** button .... A, Y
4. Click **More Rotation Options** ...... M
5. Click **Reset** .... Alt + S
6. Click **OK** .... ↵Enter

Crop a Picture

1. Click picture to select it.
2. Click the **Picture Tools Format** tab .... Alt, J, P

3. Click the **Crop** button C
   ✓ *Crop handles display on side and corners of picture.*
4. Drag a crop handle in to crop picture.
   OR
   Drag a crop out to outcrop picture.
5. Click the **Crop** button to turn the feature off C

EXERCISE DIRECTIONS

1. Start Word, if necessary.
2. Create a new document and save it as *74LOGO_xx*.
3. Insert three blank lines.
4. Using a sans serif font in a large font size in dark blue (Arial Rounded MT in 72 pts. is used in the illustration), type **LSI**.
5. Insert the 8-Point Star AutoShape from the Stars and Banners palette.
6. Resize the star so it is .75" high and .75" wide.
7. Drag the adjustment handle toward the center of the star to make the points thinner (refer to the illustration).
8. Rotate the star 25 degrees to the right.
9. Position the star above the *I* in *LSI* as shown in the illustration.

   ✓ *The absolute position shown in the illustration is 1.07" to the right of the column and -.01" below the paragraph.*

10. Apply the Center Gradient – Accent 1 style to the shape.
11. Open the Clip Art task pane and search for pictures related to golf.
12. Locate the picture of the golf ball and club head shown in the illustration.

    ✓ *If you cannot locate the picture as shown, insert the file* **74GOLF** *supplied with this book.*

13. Insert the clip into the *74LOGO_xx* document.
14. Flip the picture horizontally.
15. Resize the picture so it is 1.5" high (the width will adjust automatically).
16. Crop the picture about .5" from the left side only, just far enough to remove the tee and ball (refer to the illustration).
17. Recolor the picture using the Accent Color 1 Light variation.
18. Adjust the brightness of the picture to +20%.
19. Set the text wrapping for the picture to Behind text.
20. Position the picture so the bottom half of the *S* in *LSI* is sitting in the flat part of the club head.

    ✓ *The absolute position shown is .26" to the right of the column and .3" below the paragraph.*

21. Preview the document. It should look similar to the one in Illustration A.
22. Make any adjustments necessary to the size and position of the objects.
23. Print the document.
24. Close the document, saving all changes.

Illustration A

ON YOUR OWN

1. Start Word and create a new document.
2. Save the document as **OWD74_*xx*.**
3. Use graphics objects and text to design a logo for yourself, a club, or organization.
4. Adjust, rotate, and flip the objects as necessary.
5. Resize and position the objects as necessary.
6. Preview the document and then print it.
7. Ask a classmate to review the document and offer suggestions and comments.
8. Incorporate the suggestions and comments into the logo as necessary.
9. Close the document, saving all changes, and exit Word.

Exercise | 75

Skills Covered

- Group and Ungroup Objects
- Layer Objects with Other Objects or Text

Software Skills   Integrate drawing objects with text to illustrate and enhance documents. Objects can be layered with each other and with text to create different effects. For example, you can design a letterhead with text layered on top of a logo created from drawing objects. You can group objects together to create one complete picture, and ungroup objects to edit them individually.

Application Skills   In this exercise, create a version of the logo for Long Shot, Inc. that does not include a picture by layering a text box and a shape and then grouping them together. You will then copy the entire logo into a memo document.

TERMS

Group   Select multiple objects and combine them into a single object.

Layer   Position objects and/or text so they overlap on the page.

Regroup   Group objects that have been separated again.

Ungroup   Separate a grouped object into individual objects.

NOTES

Group and Ungroup Objects

- **Group** objects together to create a single unified object.
- Sizing handles are displayed around the entire grouped object, not around the individual objects.
- The entire group has a single rotation handle.
- All changes are made to the entire group.
- You can group shapes with other shapes, text boxes with other text boxes, or text boxes with shapes.
- You cannot include a picture object in a group.
- You must **ungroup** the objects in order to edit them individually.

- After you ungroup objects that have been grouped, you can use the **Regroup** command to group them again without having to select them all again.

Group multiple objects into a single unit

423

Layer Objects with Other Objects or Text

- **Layer** drawing objects with other objects or with document text to control the order in which text and objects overlap in a document.

- Elements layered in front of other elements appear to be on the top; elements layered behind—or in back of—other elements appear to be on the bottom.

- All text is always in the same layer. However, you can layer objects in front of or behind the text layer.
  - Layering an object in front of text is the same as setting the text wrapping for the object to the In front of text setting.
  - Layering an object behind text is the same as setting the text wrapping for the object to the Behind text setting.

- Objects in layers can be rearranged layer by layer using the Bring Forward command to move an object forward one layer at a time or the Send Backward command to move an object backward one layer at a time.

- The Send to Back command lets you move the selected object in back of all other objects.

- The Bring to Front command lets you bring an object in front of all other objects.

- Use the Send Behind Text or Bring in Front of Text commands to layer objects that combine text and graphics, such as text boxes and AutoShapes that have added text.

PROCEDURES

Group Objects

1. Click first object to select.
2. Press and hold **Shift**.
3. Click next object to select.
4. Repeat step 3 to select additional objects.
5. Release **Shift**.
6. For shapes, click the **Drawing Tools Format** tab .... Alt, J, D

   OR

   For text boxes, click the **Text Box Tools Format** tab .... Alt, J, X

   OR

   For WordArt, click the **WordArt Tools Format** tab .... Alt, J, W

   ✓ If you select a combination of objects, all Format tabs become available.

   Arrange Group

7. Click **Group** button ⊞▾ ..... A, G
8. Click **Group** .... G

Ungroup Objects

1. Click to select grouped objects.
2. For shapes, click the **Drawing Tools Format** tab .... Alt, J, D

   OR

   For text boxes, click the **Text Box Tools Format** tab .... Alt, J, X

   OR

   For WordArt, click the **WordArt Tools Format** tab .... Alt, J, W

   ✓ If you select a combination of objects, all Format tabs become available.

   Arrange Group

3. Click **Group** button ⊞▾ ..... A, G
4. Click **Ungroup** .... U

Layer Objects with Other Objects or Text

To move an object forward:

1. Click object to select it.
2. For a shape, click the **Drawing Tools Format** tab .... Alt, J, D

   OR

   For a text box, click the **Text Box Tools Format** tab .... Alt, J, X

   OR

   For a picture, click the **Picture Tools Format** tab .... Alt, J, P

   OR

   For WordArt, click the **WordArt Tools Format** tab .... Alt, J, W

   Arrange Group

3. Click **Bring to Front** button drop-down arrow ▣ .... A, F
4. Click one of the following:
   - **Bring to Front** .... R
   - **Bring Forward** .... F
   - **Bring in Front of Text** .... T

   ✓ To quickly move the selected object to the front layer, click the **Bring to Front** button ▣.

To move an object back:

1. Click object to select it.
2. For a shape, click the **Drawing Tools Format** tab........ Alt, J, D

   OR

   For a text box, click the **Text Box Tools Format** tab........ Alt, J, X

OR

For a picture, click the **Picture Tools Format** tab........ Alt, J, P

OR

For WordArt, click the **WordArt Tools Format** tab........ Alt, J, W

3. Click **Send to Back** button drop-down arrow 📚 .... A, E
4. Click one of the following:
   - **Send to Back** .... K
   - **Send Backward** .... B
   - **Send Behind Text** .... H

   ✓ *To quickly move the selected object to the back layer, click the **Send to Back** button* 📚.

EXERCISE DIRECTIONS

1. Start Word, if necessary.
2. Open 💿 **75LOGO**.
3. Save the document as **75LOGO_xx**. The document contains a text box and two shapes that you will use to create the logo.
4. Select the text box and set it to have no outline and no fill.
5. Select the star shape and position it above the *I* in *LSI* by setting the absolute position to 1.44" to the right of the column and 0" below the paragraph.
6. Select the banner shape and send it back behind the text.
7. Set the position for the banner shape behind the text box, as shown in Illustration A.

   ✓ *In the illustration, the absolute position is .91" to the right of the page and .42" below the paragraph.*

8. Select the banner and the text box and group them together.

   ✓ *If you have trouble selecting objects, use the Select Objects tool in the Editing group on the Home tab of the Ribbon: Click the Home tab, click the Select button, then click Select Objects.*

9. Send the group—the banner shape and the text box—behind the star shape.
10. Select the group and then select the star shape, and group them together.
11. Position the object in the top center relative to the margins. The page should look similar to Illustration A.
12. Select the grouped object and copy it to the Clipboard.
13. Open 💿 **75MEMO**.
14. Save the file as **75MEMO_xx**.
15. Paste the logo object into the document.
16. Position the object in the bottom center of the page, relative to the margins.
17. Preview the memo document. It should look similar to the one in Illustration B.
18. If necessary, make adjustments to the position of the logo.
19. Print the document.
20. Close all open documents, saving all changes.

Illustration A

Long Shot, Inc.

234 Simsbury Drive ⚑ Ithaca, NY 14850

Telephone: 607-555-9191 ⚑ **Fax: 607-555-9292** ⚑ **E-mail: mail@longshot.net**

MEMO

To: Harold Cantor
From: Your Name
Date: Today's date
Subject: Travel Plans

I have finalized my travel plans and will be arriving on flight 6234 at 9:55 a.m. on Friday the 13th. Assuming the traffic is light, I should reach your office by 11:00 a.m.

I look forward to meeting you on the 13th. Please contact me if you have any questions. Also, if you are able to arrange a tee time for Friday afternoon, I will be happy to bring along my golf gear.

ON YOUR OWN

1. Start Word if necessary.
2. Open the file 📟OWD72_*xx*, the document you worked with in the On Your Own section of Exercise 72, or open ⊙75ANNOUNCE.
3. Save the file as OWD75_*xx*.
4. Modify the document by layering objects and text. For example, overlap existing objects, or insert new objects in front of or behind existing objects.
5. Make use of line styles, colors, fills and effects to achieve the look you want. Group objects to apply formatting to all of them.

6. If necessary, rotate, flip, and adjust objects so they look good on the page.
7. When you are satisfied with the document, print it.
8. Ask a classmate to review the document and make comments and suggestions.
9. Incorporate the comments and suggestions as necessary.
10. Close the document, saving all changes, and exit Word.

Skills Covered

- **Create WordArt**
- **WordArt Text**
- **WordArt Shapes and Formatting**

Software Skills   Use WordArt to transform text into artwork for letterheads, logos, brochures, and other documents. WordArt lets you create special effects using any text that you type. You can stretch characters, rotate them, reverse direction, and even arrange the text in shapes such as circles, waves, or arcs.

Application Skills   Liberty Blooms is opening a new store. In this exercise, you will design a flyer announcing the grand opening.

TERMS

WordArt A feature of Word used to transform text into a drawing object.

NOTES

Create WordArt

- **WordArt** is a Word feature that you use to transform text into a drawing object.
- By default, WordArt objects are inserted in-line with text, but you can change the text wrapping to make them float.
- The WordArt Gallery includes a selection of styles you can quickly apply to any text.
- You can customize WordArt objects to achieve the specific results you want.

WordArt Gallery

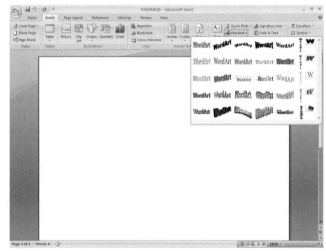

WordArt Text

- You enter WordArt text when you create the WordArt object.
- The placeholder text is: *Your Text Here,* which is replaced by any text you type.
- You can select text already typed in the document to use as the WordArt text.
- You can edit the text displayed in a WordArt object at any time.
- You can change the font, font size, and font style used for WordArt text.

Enter WordArt text

WordArt Shapes and Formatting

- The WordArt styles in the WordArt Gallery include shape and formatting characteristics.
- When you select a WordArt object, the WordArt Tools Format tab displays on the Ribbon, so you can edit and format the object.
- You can quickly apply a set of formatting characteristics to the WordArt object by selecting a style from the WordArt Styles gallery.
- Alternatively, you can manually format the WordArt object.
- Many of the formatting commands are similar to those used to format other objects, such as shapes and text boxes.
- For example, you can set text wrapping, resize, position, and align the WordArt object, or change the outline or fill. You can also rotate and adjust a WordArt object, or apply shadows and 3-D effects.

   ✓ *Refer to Exercise 71 for information on aligning objects. Refer to Exercise 72 for information on applying fills, outlines, shadows and 3-D effects. Refer to Exercise 74 for information on adjusting, rotating, and flipping objects. Refer to Exercise 75 for information on grouping and layering.*

- Some formatting commands are unique to WordArt. For example, you can change the shape of a WordArt object by selecting a different shape from the WordArt Shape palette.
- You can also format the text in the WordArt object using buttons in the Text group on the Format tab.
   - You can make all characters the same height.
   - You can align WordArt text vertically.
   - You can align WordArt text horizontally.
   - You can adjust the spacing between characters in a WordArt object.

PROCEDURES

Create WordArt

1. Click the **Insert** tab .... Alt + N

   Text Group

2. Click the **WordArt** button drop-down arrow ▣ WordArt ▾ .... W
3. Click desired WordArt style .... ↑/↓/←/→, ↵Enter
4. Type WordArt text.
5. Click **OK**.

WordArt Text

To edit WordArt text:

1. Click object to select it.
2. Click the **WordArt Tools Format** tab .... Alt, J, W

   Text Group

3. Click **Edit Text** button ▣ .... E
4. Type new text.
5. Click **OK**.

To format WordArt text:

1. Click object to select it.
2. Click the **WordArt Tools Format** tab .... Alt, J, W

   Text Group

3. Click **Edit Text** button ▣ .... E
4. Click **Font** drop-down arrow .... Alt + F
5. Click desired font .... ↑/↓, ↵Enter

6. Click **Size** drop-down
   arrow .... Alt + S
7. Click desired
   size .... ↑/↓, ↵Enter
8. Click Font style buttons as
   necessary:
   ■ **Bold** B .... Alt + B
   ■ **Italic** I .... Alt + I
9. Click **OK**.

Apply a WordArt style

1. Click object to select it.
2. Click the **WordArt Tools Format**
   tab .... Alt, J, W

   WordArt Styles Group

3. Click style to apply.

   ✓ *If necessary, use scroll arrows to
   scroll the gallery.*

   OR
   a. Click **More** button ≡ .... D
   b. Click style to
      apply ..... ←/→/↑/↓, ↵Enter

Change WordArt shape

1. Click object to select it.
2. Click the **WordArt Tools Format**
   tab .... Alt, J, W

   WordArt Styles Group

3. Click **Change WordArt Shape**
   button A▾ I
4. Click shape to
   apply .... ←/→/↑/↓, ↵Enter

Set Even Character Height

1. Click object to select it.
2. Click the **WordArt Tools Format**
   tab .... Alt, J, W

   Text Group

3. Click **Even Height**
   button Aa .... A, H

   ✓ *Repeat to return text to normal
   height.*

Align WordArt Text Vertically

1. Click object to select it.
2. Click the **WordArt Tools Format**
   tab .... Alt, J, W

   Text Group

3. Click **WordArt Vertical Text**
   button ᵇᵇ .... A, V

   ✓ *Repeat to return text to horizontal
   alignment.*

Adjust Character Spacing

1. Click object to select it.
2. Click the **WordArt Tools Format**
   tab .... Alt, J, W

   Text Group

3. Click **Spacing** button AV .... A, S
4. Click one of the following
   options:
   ■ **Very Tight** I
   ■ **Tight** .... T
   ■ **Normal** .... N
   ■ **Loose** L
   ■ **Very Loose** V
   ■ **Kern Character Pairs** .... K

Align WordArt Text Horizontally

1. Click object to select it.
2. Click the **WordArt Tools Format**
   tab .... Alt, J, W

   Text Group

3. Click **Align Text**
   button ☰▾ .... A, L
4. Click one of the following
   options:
   ■ **Left Align** L
   ■ **Center** C
   ■ **Right Align** .... R
   ■ **Word Justify** .... W
   ■ **Letter Justify** .... T
   ■ **Stretch Justify** .... S

Resize WordArt Precisely

1. Click object to select it.
2. Click the **WordArt Tools Format**
   tab .... Alt, J, W

   Size Group

3. Click **Shape Height**
   box 1.51" .... H
4. Type height in
   inches .... *type height*, ↵Enter
   OR
   Click increment arrows to
   enter height.
5. Click **Shape Width** box
   1.43" .... Alt, J, W, W
6. Type width in
   inches .... *type width*, ↵Enter
   OR
   Click increment arrows to
   enter width.

Position WordArt

1. Click object to select it.
2. Click the **WordArt Tools Format**
   tab .... Alt, J, W

   Arrange Group

3. Click **Position** button ▦ .... P, O
4. Click position to
   apply .... ↓/←/→/↑, ↵Enter

Position WordArt Precisely

1. Click object to select it.
2. Click the **WordArt Tools Format**
   tab .... Alt, J, W

   Arrange Group

3. Click **Position** button ▦ .... P, O
4. Click **More Layout Options** L
5. Click **Picture Position**
   tab .... Ctrl + Tab↹

6. Do one of the following to set horizontal position:

  a. Click **Alignment** drop-down arrow .... `Alt`+`A`, `Tab⇆`, `↓`

  b. Click desired alignment .... `↓`/`↑`, `↵Enter`

  c. Click **relative to** drop-down arrow .... `Alt`+`R`

  d. Click desired anchor .... `↓`/`↑`, `↵Enter`

OR

  a. Click **Book layout** drop-down arrow .... `Alt`+`B`, `Tab⇆`, `↓`

  b. Click desired position .... `↓`/`↑`, `↵Enter`

  c. Click **of** drop-down arrow .... `Alt`+`F`

  d. Click desired anchor .... `↓`/`↑`, `↵Enter`

OR

  a. Click **Absolute position** drop-down arrow .... `Alt`+`P`, `Tab⇆`, `↓`/`↑`

  b. Type amount of space to leave.

  c. Click **to the right of** drop-down arrow .... `Alt`+`T`

  d. Click desired anchor .... `↓`/`↑`, `↵Enter`

OR

  a. Click **Relative position** drop-down arrow .... `Alt`+`R`, `Tab⇆`, `↓`/`↑`

  b. Type percentage to leave.

  c. Click **relative to** drop-down arrow .... `Alt`+`E`

  d. Click desired anchor .... `↓`/`↑`, `↵Enter`

7. Do one of the following to set vertical position:

  a. Click **Alignment** drop-down arrow .... `Alt`+`G`, `Tab⇆`, `↓`

  b. Click desired alignment .... `↓`/`↑`, `↵Enter`

  c. Click **relative to** drop-down arrow .... `Alt`+`E`

  d. Click desired anchor .... `↓`/`↑`, `↵Enter`

OR

  a. Click **Absolute position** drop-down arrow .... `Alt`+`S`, `Tab⇆`, `↓`/`↑`

  b. Type amount of space to leave.

  c. Click **below** drop-down arrow .... `Alt`+`W`

  d. Click desired anchor .... `↓`/`↑`, `↵Enter`

OR

  a. Click **Relative position** drop-down arrow .... `Alt`+`I`, `Tab⇆`, `↓`/`↑`

  b. Type percentage to leave.

  c. Click **relative to** drop-down arrow .... `Alt`+`O`

  d. Click desired anchor .... `↓`/`↑`, `↵Enter`

8. Select check box options as necessary:

  ■ **Move object with text** `Alt`+`M`

  ■ **Lock anchor** .... `Alt`+`L`

  ■ **Allow overlap** .... `Alt`+`V`

  ■ **Layout in table cell** .... `Alt`+`C`

9. Click **OK** .... `↵Enter`

Set Text Wrap Options for WordArt

1. Click object to select it.

2. Click the **WordArt Tools Format** tab .... `Alt`, `J`, `W`

  Arrange Group

3. Click **Text Wrapping** button ⊠ .... `T`, `W`

4. Click desired option:

  ■ **In Line With Text** .... `I`

  ■ **Square** .... `S`

  ■ **Tight** .... `T`

  ■ **Behind Text** .... `D`

  ■ **In Front of Text** .... `N`

  ■ **Top and Bottom** .... `O`

  ■ **Through** .... `H`

Set Advanced Text Wrap Options for WordArt

1. Click object to select it.

2. Click the **WordArt Tools Format** tab .... `Alt`, `J`, `W`

  Arrange Group

3. Click **Text Wrapping** button ⊠ .... `T`, `W`

4. Click **More Layout Options** .... `L`:

5. Click **Text Wrapping** tab .... `Ctrl`+`Tab⇆`

6. Select desired text wrapping style:

  ■ **Square** .... `Alt`+`Q`

  ■ **Tight** .... `Alt`+`T`

  ■ **Through** .... `Alt`+`H`

  ■ **Top and bottom** .... `Alt`+`O`

  ■ **Behind text** .... `Alt`+`B`

  ■ **In front of text** .... `Alt`+`F`

  ■ **In line with text** .... `Alt`+`I`

7. For Square, Through, and Tight styles, select desired text wrapping options:

  ■ **Both sides** .... `Alt`+`S`

  ■ **Left only** .... `Alt`+`L`

  ■ **Right only** .... `Alt`+`R`

  ■ **Largest only** .... `Alt`+`A`

8. For Square, Through, Top and bottom, and Tight styles, set distance from text, as follows:

  a. Click **Top** .... `Alt`+`P`

  b. Type distance to leave between text and top of object.

  c. Click **Bottom** .... `Alt`+`M`

  d. Type distance to leave between text and bottom of object.

  e. Click **Left** .... `Alt`+`E`

  f. Type distance to leave between text and left of object.

  g. Click **Right** .... `Alt`+`G`

  h. Type distance to leave between text and right of object.

  ✓ *Not all distance options will be available for all styles.*

9. Click **OK** .... `↵Enter`

EXERCISE DIRECTIONS

1. Start Word, if necessary.
2. Create a new document.
3. Save the document as **76GRAND_xx**.
4. Using a 36-point script or handwriting font, such as Freestyle Script, type the following five lines of text:

   Announces
   The
   Grand Opening
   of a
   New Store

5. Center the five lines of text horizontally, and change the spacing to leave only 6 pts. of space after each line.
6. Make sure there is no text selected in the document and then select to insert a WordArt object.
7. Select the style in the fourth row of the second column (refer to Illustration A).
8. Using a 40-point sans serif font, such as Tahoma, enter the WordArt text: **Liberty Blooms**, and then click OK to create the object.
9. Set Text Wrapping to Top and Bottom.
10. Resize the WordArt object to approximately 1" high and 5.5" wide.
11. Set the character spacing to Very Tight.
12. Center align the object horizontally, relative to the margins.
13. Position the object vertically .5" below the margin.
14. Set paragraph formatting to leave 54 pts. of space before the first line of text *Announces*.
15. Create another WordArt object using the arc style that is in the first row of the third column.
16. Using a 28-point serif font, such as Times New Roman, type the following address and URL information on three separate lines, and then click OK to insert the object into the document:

    345 Chestnut Street
    Philadelphia, PA
    http://www.libertyblooms.net

17. Change the text wrapping to Top and Bottom.
18. Change the WordArt object shape to Button (Curve).
    a. Select the object.
    b. Click the Change WordArt Shape button on the WordArt Styles group.
    c. Click the Button (Curve) shape.

    ✓ *Use ScreenTips to identify the names of the shapes.*

19. Set the size of the WordArt object to approximately 2.5" by 3.25".
20. Position the object in the bottom center of the page.
21. Insert the Explosion 1 AutoShape from the Stars and Banners palette.
22. Resize the shape to approximately 1.75" by 1.75", and position it in the upper-left corner of the page.
23. Apply the Liner Up Gradient – Accent 6 style to the shape, and set the text wrapping to Behind Text.
24. Search for clip art images of roses.
25. Locate the image shown in Illustration A and insert it into the document.

    ✓ *If you cannot locate the image, use the* ⊙ *76ROSE file provided with this book.*

26. Set the text wrap for the picture to Behind text.
27. Align the picture on the left horizontally, relative to the margins, and 4" below the margin vertically.
28. Create a copy of the picture, or insert a second copy.
29. Flip the copy horizontally.
30. Align the copy on the right horizontally, relative to the margins, and 4" below the margin vertically.
31. Apply an art page border of flowers around the page.
32. Preview the document. It should look similar to Illustration A.
33. If necessary, make adjustments to the size and position of all objects in the document.
34. Print the document.
35. Close the document, saving all changes.

ON YOUR OWN

1. Start Word and create a new document.
2. Save the document as **OWD76_xx**.
3. Use WordArt to create a logo for a business, club, or organization to which you belong.
4. Try different WordArt Shapes.
5. Try different formatting such as Even Height, Character Spacing, or Vertical Text.
6. Try applying effects such as 3-D or Shadows to the WordArt object.
7. See how rotating or adjusting the WordArt object affects its appearance.
8. When you are satisfied with the result, print the document.
9. Ask a classmate to review the document and offer comments and suggestions.
10. Incorporate the comments and suggestions into the document as necessary.
11. Close the document, saving all changes, and exit Word.

Curriculum Connection: Language Arts

Famous Quotations

What is it about a quotation that makes it memorable? From John F. Kennedy's entire inaugural address, why do people remember the single line: "...ask not what your county can do for you—ask what you can do for your country?" Famous quotes have a way of meaning something to many different people, and of providing a common understanding.

Analyze a Quotation

Prepare a document about a famous quotation. Select the quote, and insert it in a text box at the top of a document page. Include quotation marks, and the name of the speaker. Make the text box narrower than the page margins so the quote appears indented from both sides. Below the quote, write a paragraph explaining why the quote is famous, and what it means to you. Embellish the page with graphics objects, such as pictures and shapes. Apply formatting to enhance the position of objects and to integrate the objects with the text so the document is pleasant to look at and easy to read.

Skills Covered

- ■ **Watermarks**

Software Skills   Place a watermark on almost any document to make an impression on readers, convey an idea, or provide a consistent theme. For example, a watermark on corporate stationery can create a corporate identity. Watermarks can be fun or serious, barely noticeable or strikingly bold. You can save a watermark as part of a template and use it on new documents.

Application Skills   Long Shot, Inc. is growing by leaps and bounds. To fill job vacancies, it is hosting an open house and career fair. In this exercise, you will create a notice announcing the event. You use a picture to create a watermark on the document.

TERMS

Watermark A pale or semi-transparent graphic object positioned behind text in a document.

NOTES

Watermarks

- ■ Insert text or graphics objects as a **watermark** to provide a background image for text-based documents.
- ■ In Word 2007, you can select a watermark from the Watermark gallery in the Page Background group on the Page Layout tab.
- ■ You can also create a custom watermark using the options in the Printed Watermark dialog box.
- ■ A watermark may be a graphics object, such as clip art, a text box, WordArt, or a shape.
- ■ You can also create a watermark from text.
- ■ To achieve a watermark effect, the inserted object should be centered horizontally and vertically on the page, and its color should be adjusted to make it appear faded, or washed out.

- ■ Watermarks are usually inserted into the document header so that they automatically appear on every page, and so that they are not affected by changes made to the document content.
- ■ To view or edit the watermark, use Print Preview, Full Screen Reading View, or display headers and footers.
- ■ When you use the Printed Watermark dialog box, Word 2007 automatically sizes, formats, and positions the object.
- ■ If you manually create a watermark, you must size, position, and format it manually.
- ■ Watermarks are a nice feature to add to a template because every document based on the template will display the same watermark.

PROCEDURES

Insert a Built-In Watermark

1. Click the **Page Layout** tab .... Alt + P

   Page Background Group

2. Click the **Watermark** button [icon] .... P , W

3. Click built-in watermark to insert .... ↑ / ↓ / ← / →

Automatically Create a Watermark from a Picture File

1. Click the **Page Layout** tab .... Alt + P

   Page Background Group

2. Click the **Watermark** button [icon] .... P , W

3. Click **Custom Watermark** .... W

4. Click **Picture watermark** option button I

5. Click **Select Picture** .... Alt + P

6. Locate and select desired picture file.

7. Click **Insert** .... ↵Enter

8. Click **Scale** drop-down arrow .... Alt + L

9. Select size as a percentage of the original picture size .... ↑ / ↓ , ↵Enter

   ✓ Select Auto (the default) to have Word automatically size the object to fit on the page.

10. Click to select **Washout** check box .... Alt + W

    ✓ A check mark indicates the option is already selected.

11. Click **OK** .... ↵Enter

Automatically Create a Watermark from Text

1. Click the **Page Layout** tab .... Alt + P

   Page Background Group

2. Click the **Watermark** button [icon] .... P , W

3. Click **Custom Watermark** .... W

4. Click **Text watermark** option button X

5. Click **Text** drop-down arrow .... Alt + T

6. Select built-in text option .... ↑ / ↓ , ↵Enter

   OR

   a. Type desired text.
   b. Press **Enter** .... ↵Enter

7. Click **Font** drop-down arrow .... Alt + F

8. Select font .... ↑ / ↓ , ↵Enter

9. Click **Size** drop-down arrow .... Alt + S

10. Select font size .... ↑ / ↓ , ↵Enter

11. Click **Color** drop-down arrow .... Alt + C

12. Select color .... ↑ / ↓ / → / ← , ↵Enter

13. Click one of the following layout options:

    ■ **Diagonal** .... Alt + D
    ■ **Horizontal** .... Alt + H

14. Click **OK**.

Remove an Automatic Watermark

1. Click the **Page Layout** tab .... Alt + P

   Page Background Group

2. Click the **Watermark** button [icon] .... P , W

3. Click **Remove Watermark** .... R

Manually Create a Watermark from a Picture

1. Click the **Insert** tab .... Alt + N

   Header & Footer Group

2. Click the **Header** button [icon] ..... H

3. Click **Edit Header** .... E

4. Click **Insert** tab .... Alt + N

   Illustrations Group

5. Click **Picture** button [icon] .... P

   ✓ The Insert Picture dialog box displays.

6. Navigate to location where picture file is stored.

7. Click picture to insert.

8. Click **Insert** .... S

9. Position and size picture as desired.

10. Click the **Picture Tools Format** tab .... Alt , J , P

    Adjust Group

11. Click the **Recolor** button [icon] ..... E

12. Under Color Modes, click **Washout** .... ↓ , ← , ← , ↵Enter

13. Click the **Picture Tools Format** tab .... Alt , J , P

    Arrange Group

14. Click **Text Wrapping** button [icon] .... T , W

15. Click **Behind Text** .... D

16. Click Header and Footer Tools **Design** tab .... Alt , J , H

    Close Group

17. Click **Close Header and Footer** button [icon] C

Manually Create a Watermark from a Graphics Object

1. Click the **Insert** tab .... Alt + N

   Header & Footer Group

2. Click the **Header** button 🖺 .... H
3. Click **Edit Header** .... E
4. Click **Insert** tab .... Alt + N

   Illustrations Group

5. Insert desired object.

   ✓ *For example, insert a shape, a text box, or WordArt.*

6. Format object fill and outline using light colors or gray shading.
7. Size and position object, as desired.
8. Layer object behind text.
9. Click **Header and Footer Tools Design** tab .... Alt , J , H

   Close Group

10. Click **Close Header and Footer** button ⊠ C

Remove a Manual Watermark

1. Click the **Insert** tab .... Alt + N

   Header & Footer Group

2. Click the **Header** button 🖺 .... H
3. Click **Edit Header** .... E
4. Click to select watermark object.
5. Press **Delete** .... Del
6. Click **Header and Footer Tools Design** tab .... Alt , J , H

   Close Group

7. Click **Close Header and Footer** button ⊠ C

EXERCISE DIRECTIONS

1. Start Word, if necessary.
2. Open ⊙**77JOBFAIR.**
3. Save the file as **JOBFAIR_xx**.
4. Create a printed watermark using the picture file ⊙**77SOAR** supplied with this book.

   ✓ *Alternatively, select a picture of an eagle or other soaring bird from the Clip Organizer.*

5. Select to edit the header and then select the picture object.
6. Rotate the object approximately 70 degrees.
7. Resize the picture so the width is 10" (the height should adjust automatically).
8. Close the header and footer.
9. Check the spelling and grammar in the document.
10. Preview the document. It should look similar to the one in Illustration A.
11. Print the document.
12. Close the document, saving all changes.

SOAR

to new heights
with

Long Shot, Incorporated

Please Come to Our
Open House and Career Fair

Saturday April 15th and Sunday April 16th
10:00 a.m. – 3:00 p.m.
234 Simsbury Drive
Ithaca, NY 14850

Learn about
career opportunities in

Manufacturing
Design
Marketing

For more information call 607-555-0909.

ON YOUR OWN

1. Start Word and open the document ⌨OWD66-2_*xx*, the document you used in the On Your Own section of Exercise 66, or open the template ◉77LETTER.

2. Delete the letter text, leaving only the letterhead at the top of the document, and then save the document as a document template with the name OWD77-1_*xx*.

3. Locate a clip art picture or create your own object to use as a watermark on the template.

4. Insert and format the watermark.

5. Make sure the watermark is correctly sized and positioned on the page.

6. Check the spelling and grammar in the document.

7. Preview the template with the watermark.

8. Print the template.

9. Ask a classmate to review the document and offer comments and suggestions.

10. Incorporate the comments and suggestions into the document.

11. Save the changes and close the template.

12. Create a new document based on the OWD77-1_*xx* template, and save it as OWD77-2_*xx*.

13. In the new document, write a personal business letter to someone. For example, write to a club advisor, a coach, a teacher, an employer, or a relative.

14. Use proper formatting and page layout settings.

15. Check the spelling and grammar in the letter.

16. Print the document.

17. Close the document, saving all changes, and exit Word.

Exercise | 78

Critical Thinking

Application Skills   You've been asked to design an invitation to a luncheon honoring the judges of Blue Sky Dairy's Name that Flavor contest. The invitation will integrate a text box, an AutoShape, WordArt, and a watermark created from a clip art picture to create an effective, eye-catching document.

EXERCISE DIRECTIONS

1. Start Word, if necessary.
2. Create a new document and save it as **78INVITE_xx.**

Create a Text Box

1. In a 16-point script font, type the following lines of text (Brush Script MT is used in Illustration A):

   You are cordially invited
   To attend a luncheon
   In honor of
   The Name that Flavor Judges
   Friday, October 19
   12:30 in the afternoon
   Blue Sky Dairy Bar
   Highway 73
   Cambridge, WI 53523
   RSVP (608) 555-2697

2. Insert a text box around the text.
3. Set text wrap for the text box to Behind Text.
4. Center the text box horizontally and vertically, relative to the margins.
5. Remove the fill and the outline from the text box.

Create WordArt

1. Create a WordArt object as follows:
   a. Select the style in the first row of the third column.
   b. Use a sans serif font in 40 points (Arial Black is used in the illustration).
   c. For the WordArt text, type **Blue Sky Dairy.**
2. Set text wrapping to Top and Bottom.
3. Size the WordArt object to approximately 2" high by 7" wide.
4. Center the object horizontally between the margins and align it vertically 1" below the margin.
5. Set the line color to Dark Blue and the fill color to Pale Blue.
6. Create a second WordArt object as follows:
   a. Select the style in the second row of the fourth column.
   b. Use a serif font in 28 points (Garamond is used in Illustration A).
   c. Type **Contest Judges** as the WordArt text.
7. Set the text wrapping for the object to Square.
8. Size the new WordArt object to approximately .75" high by 4.5" wide.
9. Change the line color of the WordArt object to Pale Blue.
10. Change the shadow color of the WordArt object to Dark Blue.
11. Center the object horizontally between the margins and position it vertically 2" below the margin.

Insert an AutoShape

1. Insert the Down Ribbon AutoShape from the Stars and Banners palette.

2. Size it to 2.25" high by 5.75" wide.

3. Center the shape horizontally between the margins and position it vertically 6.5" below the top margin.

4. In a 20-point serif font, centered and in bold, add the following text to the AutoShape: **Honorees**.

5. Leave 6 points of space, and then type the following in a 14-point serif font, centered (use the Wingdings symbol 171 as the separator):

   Alex Gogan ★ Oliver Tesini
   Marie Chang ★ Patty McKay
   Mikel Arroyo ★ Jonathan Zabriskie
   Chris Lewis ★ Sharon Zide
   Jackie Neuwirth ★ Larry Vieth
   Deb Bastion ★ Bob Sanchez

   ✓ *Do not leave extra space between the lines. Also, the word wrap should break each line after the second name. Only insert paragraph marks if necessary.*

6. Fill the AutoShape with Pale Blue.

Create a Watermark

1. Create a Watermark using the ⊙78COW picture file supplied with this book. Or, select an appropriate clip.

2. Check the spelling and grammar in the document.

3. Preview the document. It should look similar to the one in Illustration A.

4. Print the document.

5. Close the document, saving all changes.

Blue Sky Dairy
Contest Judges

You are cordially invited
To attend a luncheon
In honor of
The Name that Flavor Judges
Friday, October 19
12:30 in the afternoon
Blue Sky Dairy Bar
Highway 73
Cambridge, WI 53523
RSVP (608) 555-2697

Honorees

Alex Gogan ★ Oliver Tesini
Marie Chang ★ Patty McKay
Mikel Arroyo ★ Jonathan Zabriskie
Chris Lewis ★ Sharon Zide
Jackie Neuwirth ★ Larry Vieth
Deb Bastion ★ Bob Sanchez

Curriculum Integration

Application Skills For your mathematics class, use the skills you have learned in Lesson 10 to design and create a poster illustrating a concept you have learned about this year. For example, you might illustrate geometric shapes, or curves, or you might use graphics objects to create a picture about a mathematician. Include shapes and text boxes in the poster, and clip art, if appropriate. Apply formatting to enhance the poster. Refer to Illustration A to see a sample of a poster. When you are finished, print the poster and distribute it to your classmates.

EXERCISE DIRECTIONS

Start Word, if necessary, and create a new document. Save it as **79MATH_xx**.

Select to display elements that might help you while you work, such as the rulers, nonprinting characters, and gridlines.

Select a theme, style set, and colors for the document. You may want to use a page background, as well.

Set the paper size, and set margins.

Insert the objects and pictures you want to include on the poster, sizing and positioning them as appropriate.

Use text boxes to add text labels to objects, and remember to set text wrapping and layering. Group objects, if necessary, so they stay together when you move them.

Check the spelling and grammar in the poster.

Ask a classmate to review the document and make suggestions for how you might improve it.

Incorporate your classmate's suggestions into the document, and save it.

Print the poster.

Close all files, saving all changes.

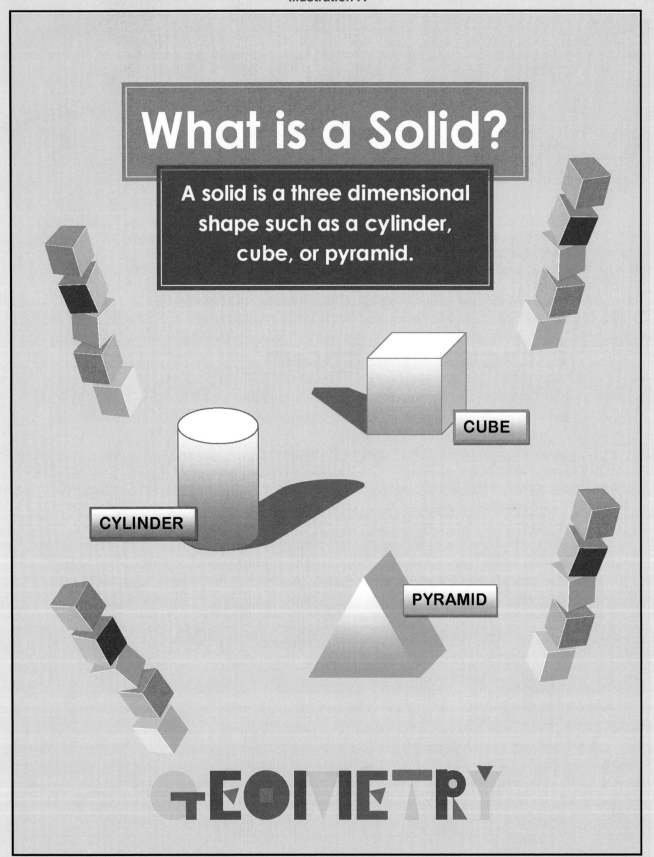

What is a Solid?

A solid is a three dimensional shape such as a cylinder, cube, or pyramid.

CUBE

CYLINDER

PYRAMID

GEOMETRY

Lesson | 11

Securing Documents

Skills Covered

- **Protect a Document**
- **Set Protection Exceptions**

- **Apply Password Protection**

Software Skills   With Word, you can protect documents that you do not want others to change. You can set password protection to limit unauthorized access to a document, and you can set different levels of access to allow others to read but not edit or format a document, or to require the track changes feature to mark all edits.

Application Skills   The Manager of Corporate Communications at Long Shot, Inc. wants her staff to collaborate on a new version of the company's mission statement. As the team leader for this project, she has asked you to create the first new version of the mission statement, which other members can then revise. In this exercise, you will first create a one-page report drafting the new mission statement. You will protect the document so that all changes are tracked with revision marks.

TERMS

Digital signature   An electronic, encryption-based, secure stamp of authentication on a macro or document.

Encryption   Scrambling so as to be indecipherable.

Password   A string of characters used to authenticate the identity of a user, and to limit unauthorized access.

Workgroup   A group of individuals who work together on the same projects, usually connected via a network.

NOTES

Protect a Document

- You can restrict others from editing or formatting a document, or parts of a document.

- To protect a document from formatting changes, you limit the ability of others to modify selected styles and apply direct formatting.

- To protect a document from editing changes, you may select from four options:
  - Tracked Changes. Use this option to automatically display changes to a document with revision marks.

    ✓ *Tracking changes is covered in Exercise 56.*

  - Comments. Use this option to allow **workgroup** members to enter comments without being able to edit document text.

    ✓ *Using comments is covered in Exercise 56.*

  - Filling in Forms. Use this option to allow changes in form fields only.

    ✓ *Forms and form fields are covered in Exercise 84.*

  - No changes (Read only). Use this option when you do not want to allow any changes at all.

- The options for protecting a document are found in the Restrict Formatting and Editing task pane, which you can access using the Protect Document button on the Review tab of the Ribbon.

- When you open a protected document, the Restrict Formatting and Editing task pane displays information about the changes you may or may not make to the document.
- You can remove the protection to enable unlimited editing.

Restrict Formatting and Editing task pane

Set Protection Exceptions

- By default, an entire document is protected from changes made by all users.
- If you set formatting, read only, or comments protection, you may specify exceptions by allowing some people or groups access to all or parts of the document.
- To add a person to the exceptions list, you must know his or her e-mail address or Microsoft Windows user account name.
- After assigning an exception, you can select the specific part or parts of the document that a person or group may access, or you may allow access to the entire document.

Apply Password Protection

- To ensure that users cannot remove or change document protection, you can assign **password** protection. Only someone who enters the assigned password can change the document protection settings.
- While using the Save As command to save a file, you may open the General Options dialog box to assign a password to limit unauthorized users from opening the file.
- You may also add **encryption** using the General Options dialog box.
- Encryption increases the security of the document, because only authenticated owners of the document can remove the protection.

    ✓ *Authenticity is based on use of a valid **digital signature**. Digital signatures are covered in Exercise 83.*

- Take care when assigning passwords. If you forget the password, you will not be able to access the document.

General Options dialog box

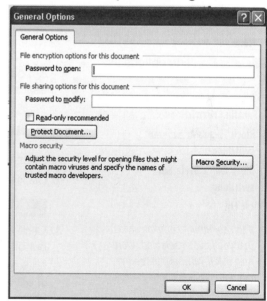

PROCEDURES

Protect a Document from Formatting Changes

1. Open the document to protect.
2. Click the **Review** tab...... `Alt`+`R`

   `Protect Group`

3. Click the **Protect Document** button 📄..................... `P`, `R`
4. Click **Limit formatting to a selection of styles** check box......... `Spacebar`
5. Click the **Settings** link.
6. Deselect the check boxes beside the styles which you want to restrict........ `↓`, `Spacebar`

   ✓ *Selected styles may be modified.*

   OR

   Click one of the following:
   - **All**..................... `Alt`+`L`
   - **Recommended Minimum**................. `Alt`+`R`
   - **None**..................... `Alt`+`N`

7. Select Formatting options as desired:
   - **Allow AutoFormat to override formatting restrictions**........ `Alt`+`A`
   - **Block Theme or Scheme switching**................. `Alt`+`W`
   - **Block Quick Style Set switching**................. `Alt`+`K`

8. Click **OK**..................... `↵Enter`

   ✓ *If the document contains styles that you have deselected, Word may ask if you want to remove them from the document. Click Yes to remove the formatting or click No to preserve the existing formatting.*

9. Click **Yes, Start Enforcing Protection**.
10. Click **OK**..................... `↵Enter`

    OR

    Set password protection as described at right.

Protect a Document from Editing Changes

1. Open the document to protect.
2. Click the **Review** tab...... `Alt`+`R`

   `Protect Group`

3. Click the **Protect Document** button 📄..................... `P`, `R`
4. Click **Allow only this type of editing in the document** check box.............. `↓`, `↓`, `Spacebar`
5. Click **Editing restrictions** drop-down arrow................. `Tab`, `↓`
6. Select restriction to apply:.................. `↓`/`↑`, `↵Enter`
   - **Tracked changes**
   - **Comments**
   - **Filling in Forms**
   - **No changes (Read only)**
7. Click **Yes, Start Enforcing Protection**.
8. Click **OK**..................... `↵Enter`

   OR

   Set password protection as described at right.

Set Protection Exceptions

1. Open the document to protect.
2. Click the **Review** tab...... `Alt`+`R`

   `Protect Group`

3. Click the **Protect Document** button 📄..................... `P`, `R`
4. Click to select **Allow only this type of editing in the document** check box.............. `↓`, `↓`, `Spacebar`
5. Click **Editing restrictions** drop-down arrow................. `Tab`, `↓`
6. Click **No changes (Read only)**............ `↓`, `↓`, `↓`, `↵Enter`
7. If necessary, select parts of the document which may be edited.

   ✓ *Use standard selection techniques to select paragraphs, pages, or sections in the document.*

8. Click the check box beside each individual or group who may edit the selected sections.

   OR
   a. Click **More users** link.
   b. Type user account names or e-mail addresses, separated by semicolons.
   c. Click **OK**..................... `↵Enter`
9. Click **Yes, Start Enforcing Protection**.
10. Click **OK**..................... `↵Enter`

    OR

    Set password protection as described below.

Add Password Protection

1. Open the document to protect.
2. Click the **Review** tab...... `Alt`+`R`

   `Protect Group`

3. Click the **Protect Document** button 📄..................... `P`, `R`
4. Select desired type of protection.
5. Click **Yes, Start Enforcing Protection**.
6. Click **Enter new password** text box..................... `Alt`+`E`
7. Type password.
8. Click **Reenter password to confirm** text box..................... `Alt`+`P`
9. Type password.
10. Click **OK**..................... `↵Enter`

Edit a Protected Document

1. Open the document to edit.
2. In the Restrict Formatting and Editing task pane, click **Find Next Region I Can Edit**.

   OR

   Click **Show All Regions I Can Edit**.
3. Edit document as usual.

Remove Document Protection

1. Open the document to protect.
2. Click the **Review** tab .... `Alt`+`R`

   Protect Group

3. Click the **Protect Document** button 🔒 .... `P`, `R`
4. Click **Stop Protection**.

   ✓ *If password protection has been applied, Word will prompt you to enter the correct password and then click OK.*

5. Deselect protection options as necessary.
6. Close the Restrict Formatting and Editing task pane.

Require a Password to Open a File

1. Open the document to protect.
2. Click the **Office Button** 📋 .... `Alt`+`F`
3. Click **Save As** .... `A`
4. Click **Tools** drop-down arrow .... `Alt`+`L`, `↓`
5. Click **General Options** .... `G`
6. Click **Password to open** text box .... `Alt`+`O`
7. Type password.
8. Click **OK** .... `↵Enter`
9. Click **Reenter password to confirm** text box .... `Alt`+`P`
10. Type password.
11. Click **OK** .... `↵Enter`
12. Select options and save file as usual.

Require a Password to Modify a File

1. Open the document to protect.
2. Click the **Office Button** 📋 .... `Alt`+`F`
3. Click **Save As** .... `A`
4. Click **Tools** drop-down arrow .... `Alt`+`L`, `↓`
5. Click **General Options** .... `G`
6. Click **Password to modify** text box .... `Alt`+`M`
7. Type password.
8. Click **OK** .... `↵Enter`
9. Click **Reenter password to confirm** text box .... `Alt`+`P`
10. Type password.
11. Click **OK** .... `↵Enter`
12. Select options and save file as usual.

Add Encryption Protection for Opening a File

1. Open the document to protect.
2. Click the **Office Button** 📋 .... `Alt`+`F`
3. Click **Prepare** .... `E`
4. Click **Encrypt Document** .... `E`
5. Click **Password** text box .... `Alt`+`R`
6. Type password.
7. Click **OK** .... `↵Enter`
8. Click **Reenter password** text box .... `Alt`+`R`
9. Type password.
10. Click **OK** .... `↵Enter`

EXERCISE DIRECTIONS

1. Start Word, if necessary.
2. Open the file 💿 **80MISSION**.
3. Save the document as **80MISSION_***xx*.
4. Set editing restrictions so that all changes will be displayed with revision marks.
5. Do not enter a password.
6. Make the following edits to the document (refer to Illustration A to see the end results):

   a. On a new line at the beginning of the document insert the title **Long Shot, Inc. Mission Statement** in the Heading 1 style.

   b. On a new line, type the text **Customer Satisfaction** using the Heading 2 style.

   c. Edit the first paragraph to read: **Long Shot, Inc. is committed to providing quality service to all of our clients at every level of our organization. Our ultimate goal is to hear our clients say, "Thank you. That is just what we wanted."**

   d. On a new line, type the text **Employee Well-Being** using the Heading 2 style.

   e. Edit the second paragraph to read: **Second only to customer satisfaction is the happiness and well-being of our employees. The employees at Long Shot, Inc. are encouraged to set personal and professional goals. We respect all employees as individuals and believe that fostering a strong community within the workplace strengthens our position in the marketplace.**

   ✓ *You can leave the last sentence of the second paragraph in the document to use in the new conclusion, as described in Step g, below.*

   f. On a new line, type the text **Conclusion** using the Heading 2 style.

   g. On a new line, in the Normal style, type the following: **At Long Shot, Inc. we vow to maintain the highest standards, pursue the extraordinary, and guarantee customer satisfaction. We are confident that our commitment to quality will make us leaders in our industry.**

7. Check the spelling and grammar in the document.

8. Save the changes.

9. Save the document as **80REV01_xx**.

10. Remove document protection.

11. Accept all changes to the document.

12. Check the spelling and grammar in the document.

13. Preview the document. It should look similar to the one in Illustration A.

14. Protect the document from all changes by everyone, and apply the password **LSIxx02**.

15. Save the document and close it.

16. Open the document.

17. Try to delete the first line.

   ✓ *You will not be able to edit the document.*

18. Remove document protection. When prompted, type the password **LSIxx02**.

19. Delete the first line.

20. Close the document, saving all changes, and exit Word.

Illustration A

Long Shot, Inc. Mission Statement

Customer Satisfaction
Long Shot, Inc. is committed to providing quality service to all of our clients at every level of our organization. Our ultimate goal is to hear our clients say, "Thank you. That is just what we wanted."

Employee Well-Being
Second only to customer satisfaction is the happiness and well-being of our employees. The employees at Long Shot, Inc. are encouraged to set personal and professional goals. We respect all employees as individuals and believe that fostering a strong community within the workplace strengthens our position in the marketplace.

Conclusion
At Long Shot, Inc. we vow to maintain the highest standards, pursue the extraordinary, and guarantee customer satisfaction. We are confident that our commitment to quality will make us leaders in our industry.

ON YOUR OWN

1. Start Word and create a new document.

2. Save the document as **OWD80_xx**.

3. Type three or four paragraphs describing a group, club, class, or organization to which you belong.

4. Check the spelling and save the changes.

5. Protect the document so that only comments may be entered.

6. Exchange files with a classmate.

7. Read your classmate's document and insert at least two comments.

8. Change the protection to allow tracked changes.

9. Exchange files with another classmate.

10. Make editing and formatting changes to the document.

11. Save the document.

12. Return the file to the original author. You should now have your original document back.

13. Remove all protection from the document.

14. Review the comments and changes.

15. Accept or reject the changes, and respond to the comments as necessary.

16. Close the document, saving all changes, and exit Word.

Exercise | 81

Skills Covered

■ **Use the Document Inspector**   ■ **Use the Compatibility Checker**

Software Skills   Use the Document Inspector to remove personal or confidential information from your Word documents. Use the Compatibility Checker to identify features that might not be compatible with earlier versions of Microsoft Office Word.

Application Skills   You want all managers at Long Shot, Inc. to have the opportunity to read and comment on the company's new mission statement. In this exercise, you will use the Document Inspector to locate and remove any personal or confidential information that might be part of the document. Also, because you know some managers are using previous versions of Word, you will use the Compatibility Checker to identify and modify any incompatible features.

TERMS

There are no new terms for this exercise.

NOTES

Use the Document Inspector

■ Run the Document Inspector to remove personal or confidential information from your Word documents.

■ When you start the Document Inspector, you can select to check for the following types of information:
  ● comments, revisions, versions, and annotations
  ● document properties and personal information
  ● custom XML data
  ● headers, footers, and watermarks
  ● text formatted as Hidden

■ After inspecting the document, Document Inspector displays a list of found items.

■ You have the option of leaving the found items in the document, or removing them.

Select information to find using the Document Inspector

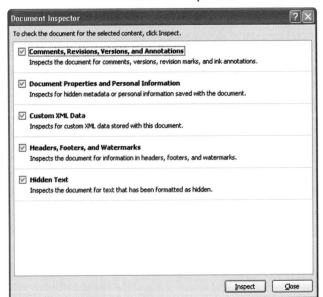

- You can reinspect the document to verify that all items have been removed.
- It is a good idea to save a copy of the document before removing information with the Document Inspector, because you may not be able to undo the action.

Select whether to remove information

Use the Compatibility Checker

- The Compatibility Checker checks a document created with Word 2007 to identify features that might not be supported by earlier versions of Word.
- By default, the Compatibility Checker runs automatically when you use the Save As command to save a document in Word 97-2003 format.

- You can run the Compatibility Checker at any time to check the document, by opening the Office menu and then selecting the Run Compatibility Checker command from the Prepare submenu.
- After checking the document, Word 2007 displays a summary list of incompatible features.
- The summary list includes the number of times the feature is used, and explains the action Word 2007 will take to resolve the incompatibility issue when the document is saved in Word 97-2003 format.
- For example, if the Word 2007 document contains a content control, such as a date in a header, it will convert the control to text when the file is saved in Word 97-2003 format.
- The changes are only made in the documents saved in Word 97-2003 format; the original Word 2007 documents remain unchanged.
- Alternatively, you can edit the document to remove the incompatible features manually, or to replace them with features that are compatible with previous versions of Word.

Compatibility Checker summary list

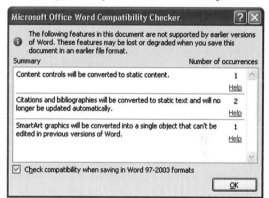

PROCEDURES

Use the Document Inspector

1. Open the document to inspect.
2. Click the **Office Button** .... Alt + F
3. Point to **Prepare** .... E
4. Click **Inspect Document** I

   ✓ If necessary, click Yes in the dialog box that displays to save document and continue.

5. Click to select or deselect desired items ...... ↓/↑, Spacebar
   - **Comments, Revisions, Versions, and Annotations**
   - **Document Properties and Personal Information**
   - **Custom XML Data**
   - **Headers, Footers, and Watermarks**
   - **Hidden Text**

   ✓ Word checks for the selected items; a check mark indicates an item is selected.

6. Click **Inspect** I
7. For first set of found items, do one of the following:
   - Click **Remove All** .... Tab↹, ↵Enter
   - Take no action.
8. Repeat step 7 for each set of found items.
9. Click **Close** .... Alt + C

   OR

   a. Click **Reinspect** .... Alt + R
   b. Repeat steps 7-9.

Use the Compatibility Checker

1. Open the document to check.
2. Click the **Office Button** ⬚ .... Alt + F
3. Point to **Pr_e_pare** .... E
4. Click **R_u_n _C_ompatibility Checker** .. C
5. Review found items.
6. Click **OK** .... ↵Enter

To Toggle the Automatic Check Compatibility When Saving in Word 97-2003 Format Feature Off or On:

1. Open the document to inspect.
2. Click the **Office Button** ⬚ .... Alt + F
3. Point to **Pr_e_pare** .... E
4. Click **R_u_n _C_ompatibility Checker** C

5. Click to select or deselect **Check compatibility when saving in Word 97-2003 formats** check box .... H

   ✓ *A check mark indicates the option is on.*

6. Click **OK** .... ↵Enter

EXERCISE DIRECTIONS

1. Start Word, if necessary.
2. Open the file ⊙81MISSION.
3. Save the document as **81MISSION_*xx***.
4. Start the Document Inspector.
5. Select to look for all possible information, and then inspect the document.
6. Select to remove all comments, revisions, versions, and annotations.
7. Select to remove all document properties and personal information.
8. Do not remove all headers, footers, and watermarks.
9. Reinspect the document to make sure the data you selected to remove has been removed, and then close the Document Inspector.
10. Save the changes to the **81MISSION_*xx*** document.
11. Run the Compatibility Checker, review the incompatible features, and then close the Compatibility Checker.

12. Delete the SmartArt graphic object below the text by clicking it and pressing Delete.

    ✓ *You learn about SmartArt graphics in Exercise 89.*

13. Save the document in Word 97-2003 format, with the file name **81MISSIONa_*xx***
14. When the Compatibility Checker displays, click Continue to convert the incompatible features to compatible features.

    ✓ *The document will display in Compatibility Mode.*

15. Display the **81MISSIONa_*xx*** document in Print Preview. It should look similar to Illustration A.
16. Print the document.
17. Protect the document from all changes, but do not apply a password.
18. Close the document, saving all changes, and exit Word.

Illustration A

Long Shot, Inc. Mission Statement

Customer Satisfaction

Long Shot, Inc. is committed to providing quality service to all of our clients at every level of our organization. Our ultimate goal is to hear our clients say, "Thank you. That is just what we wanted."

Employee Well-Being

Second only to customer satisfaction is the happiness and well-being of our employees. The employees at Long Shot, Inc. are encouraged to set personal and professional goals. We respect all employees as individuals and believe that fostering a strong community within the workplace strengthens our position in the marketplace.

Conclusion

At Long Shot, Inc. we vow to maintain the highest standards, pursue the extraordinary, and guarantee customer satisfaction. We are confident that our commitment to quality will make us leaders in our industry.

August 31, 2009

ON YOUR OWN

1. Start Word.
2. Open the document 🖮OWD80_*xx*, the document you worked with in the On Your Own section of Exercise 80, or open 💿81INSPECT.
3. Save the document as **OWD81-1_*xx***.
4. Insert document properties such as a title, author, and subject, or other properties that may not already be entered in the document.
5. Insert a header and footer. Select one from the gallery that includes content controls for inserting text or the date.
6. Insert a watermark.
7. Run the Document Inspector, saving the document as prompted.
8. Remove all properties, but keep the header, footer, and watermark.
9. Save the document in Word 97-2003 format, with the name **OWD81-2_*xx***.
10. In the Compatibility Checker dialog box, review the changes that Word will make, and then click Continue to save the document.
11. Print the document.
12. Close the document, saving all changes, and exit Word.

Curriculum Connection: Language Arts

Copyright Protection

A copyright is protection given by the government to authors, artists, and other creators and owners of intellectual property.

Research Copyrights

Using the Internet, research copyright and intellectual property laws. Pay particular attention to how these laws apply to schools and students. Remember to keep track of the sources you use to find information. When you have completed your research, write a report explaining what you have learned. Include a bibliography or Sources Cited list. To protect your own work from would-be plagiarists, apply document protection to the completed document.

Skills Covered

- Mark a Document as Final

Software Skills   Mark a document as final to indicate to others that they are viewing a completed or final version of a document, and to prevent others from making unauthorized or inadvertent changes to the document.

Application Skills   Now that everyone has seen, read, and approved of the new mission statement for Long Shot, Inc., you will mark the document as final.

TERMS

There are no new terms for this exercise.

NOTES

Mark a Document as Final

- You can select the Mark as Final command from the Prepare menu when you plan to share a completed document with others.

- The Mark as Final command changes the status of the document to Final, and sets the document to open in Read-only mode.

- Typing, editing commands, and track changes commands are not available in a document marked as final, so that no changes can be made to the document.

- A document marked as Final has a Mark as Final icon in the Status bar.

- You can remove the Mark as Final status from the document at any time.

- Alternatively, you can save a copy of the document so you can edit it.

- The Mark as Final command is not compatible with previous versions of Word, so when you open a Word 2007 document in a previous version it can be edited.

Mark as Final icon in Status bar

Page: 2 of 2 | Words: 130 | | | 110% | | | |

Icon

PROCEDURES

Mark a Document as Final

1. Open the document.
2. Click the **Office Button** .... Alt + F
3. Point to **Prepare** .... E

4. Click **Mark as Final** .... F
5. Click **OK** .... ↵Enter
6. If a second confirmation dialog box displays, click **OK** .... ↵Enter

Remove the Mark a Document as Final Status

1. Open the document.
2. Click the **Office Button** .... Alt + F
3. Point to **Prepare** .... E
4. Click **Mark as Final** .... F

EXERCISE DIRECTIONS

1. Start Word, if necessary.
2. Open the file ⊙ **82MISSION**.
3. Save the document as **82MISSION_*xx***.
4. Mark the document as final.
5. Try to edit the document.

6. Display the document in Print Preview. It should look similar to Illustration A.
7. Print the document.
8. Close the document, saving all changes.

Illustration A

Long Shot, Inc. Mission Statement

Customer Satisfaction

Long Shot, Inc. is committed to providing quality service to all of our clients at every level of our organization. Our ultimate goal is to hear our clients say, "Thank you. That is just what we wanted."

Employee Well-Being

Second only to customer satisfaction is the happiness and well-being of our employees. The employees at Long Shot, Inc. are encouraged to set personal and professional goals. We respect all employees as individuals and believe that fostering a strong community within the workplace strengthens our position in the marketplace.

Conclusion

At Long Shot, Inc. we vow to maintain the highest standards, pursue the extraordinary, and guarantee customer satisfaction. We are confident that our commitment to quality will make us leaders in our industry.

August 31, 2009

ON YOUR OWN

1. Start Word.

2. Open ⌨OWD81-1_*xx*, the document you worked with in the On Your Own section of Exercise 81, or open ⊙82FINAL.

3. Save the document as OWD82_*xx*.

4. If there is text or a watermark indicating that the document is a draft, remove it, or edit it to say Final, and then save the changes.

   ✓ *You may use the Document Inspector to remove watermarks.*

5. Mark the document as final.

6. Print the document.

7. Close the document, saving all changes, and exit Word.

Skills Covered

- **About Digital Signatures**
- **Use a Visible Digital Signature**
- **Use an Invisible Digital Signature**
- **Verify a Digital Signature**

Software Skills Use a visible or invisible digital signature to verify the authenticity of a document. Once you add a digital signature, the document is automatically marked as final, and cannot be edited.

Application Skills Unauthorized versions of the Long Shot, Inc. mission statement have been circulating through the corporate offices. In this exercise, you will add an invisible digital signature to the authorized mission statement document. You will then save a copy of the mission statement document and add a visible digital signature line which you will sign.

TERMS

Digital certificate An attachment for a file, macro, project, or e-mail message that vouches for its authenticity, provides secure encryption, or supplies a verifiable signature.

Invisible digital signature A digital signature that is attached to a document, but does not display in the document.

Signature line A graphics object inserted in a document on which a person can insert, type, or handwrite a digital signature.

Visible digital signature A digital signature that displays on a signature line in a document.

NOTES

About Digital Signatures

- A digital signature can be used like a written signature to verity the authenticity of information.
- A digital signature indicates the following:
  - The signer is who he or she claims to be.
  - The content has not changed since the digital signature was applied.
  - The signer read and approved the document.
- A digital signature is created using a **digital certificate**, which can be obtained from an authorized vendor, or from the internal security administrator responsible for your computer system.
- Windows usually creates a personal digital certificate—called a digital ID—for each user account.

- If you attempt to add a digital signature to a document, but you do not have a digital certificate, Word will display the Get a Digital ID dialog box, from which you can create your own personal digital certificate.
- A personal digital certificate is only authorized on the computer on which it is created.
- Once a digital signature is added, the document becomes read-only, and the Signatures icon displays in the Status bar.
- With Word 2007, you can either apply a **visible digital signature** or an **invisible digital signature** to a document.

Use a Visible Digital Signature

- A visible signature is similar to a standard signature line on a contract or other type of agreement.
- When you add a visible signature, Word inserts a **signature line** into the document.
- You can use the options in the Signature Setup dialog box to add information about the signer, such as a name and a title, as well as instructions for the signer on how to add a digital signature.
- To sign the document, the signer opens the Sign dialog box in which he or she may type a signature or insert a digital image of the signature.

  ✓ *If the signer has Tablet PC, he or she may use the Inking feature to sign the document.*

Signature Setup dialog box

Sign dialog box

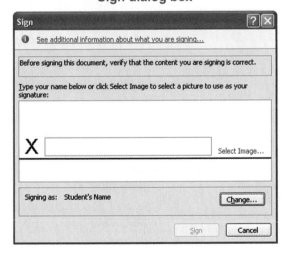

Use an Invisible Digital Signature

- An invisible digital signature is attached to the document, but does not display as an actual signature in the document.
- You can verify that the document has been signed by viewing the document's digital signature(s) in the Signatures task pane.

Verify a Digital Signature

- An authorized digital signature is listed as having a valid digital certificate.
- If the certificate is not valid, it is listed as Invalid.
- If the status of a certificate cannot be verified, the signature is listed as having certificate issues.
- Some factors that might cause an invalid certificate or certificate issues include:
  - The content of the document has been changed since the signature was applied.
  - The digital signature has a time limit, which has expired.
  - The certificate associated with the signature is unauthorized.
- You can manually change a certificate from invalid to valid in the Signature Details dialog box, by adding it to a list of trusted certificates.

Signatures listed in the Signatures task pane

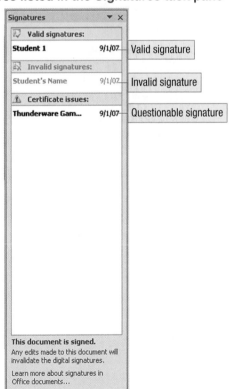

PROCEDURES

Insert a Signature Line for a Visible Digital Signature

1. Position the insertion point where you want the signature to display.
2. Click the **Insert** tab .... `Alt`+`N`

   Text Group

3. Click the **Signature Line** button 📝 .... `G`, `↵Enter`
4. If a confirmation dialog box displays, click **OK**.
5. If desired, do the following:
   a. Click the **Suggested signer** text box .... `Alt`+`S`
   b. Type the signer's name.
   c. Click the **Suggested signer's title** text box .... `Alt`+`T`
   d. Type the signer's title.
   e. Click the **Suggested signer's e-mail address** text box .... `Alt`+`E`
   f. Type the signer's e-mail address.
   g. Click the **Instructions to the signer** text box .... `Alt`+`I`
   h. Type instructions.
   i. Click to select or deselect the **Allow the signer to add comments in the Sign dialog** check box .... `Alt`+`C`
   j. Click to select or deselect the **Show the sign date in signature line** check box .... `Alt`+`D`
6. Click **OK** .... `↵Enter`

Attach a Visible Digital Signature

1. Open the document.
2. Double-click the signature line.
   OR
   a. Right-click the signature line.
   b. Click **Sign** .... `S`
3. Click **OK**.

   ✓ *At this point, if you do not already have a digital ID, Word may prompt you to get one. See the steps Create a Digital ID for more information.*

4. Do one of the following:
   a. Click in the **Type your name below** text box .... `Alt`+`T`
   b. Type your signature.
   OR
   a. Click **Select Image.**
   b. Locate and select digital signature image.
   c. Click **Select** .... `Alt`+`S`
   OR
   a. Click **Change** .... `Alt`+`H`
   b. Select digital certificate .... `↑`/`↓`
   c. Click **OK** .... `↵Enter`
5. Click **Sign** .... `Alt`+`S`
6. Click **OK** .... `↵Enter`

Attach an Invisible Digital Signature

1. Position the insertion point where you want the signature to display.
2. Click the **Office Button** 📄 .... `Alt`+`F`
3. Point to **Prepare** .... `E`

4. Click **Add a Digital Signature** ...... `S`
5. If a confirmation dialog box displays, click **OK**.
6. Click the **Purpose for signing this document** text box .... `Alt`+`P`
7. Type the reason why you are attaching the digital signature.

   ✓ *Steps 6 and 7 are optional.*

8. Click **Sign** .... `Alt`+`S`
   OR
   a. Click **Change** .... `Alt`+`H`
   b. Click the digital certificate to use .... `↑`/`↓`
   c. Click **OK** .... `↵Enter`
   d. Click **Sign** .... `Alt`+`S`
9. Click **OK** .... `↵Enter`

Create a Digital ID

1. Position the insertion point where you want the signature to display.
2. Click the **Office Button** 📄 .... `Alt`+`F`
3. Point to **Prepare** .... `E`
4. Click **Add a Digital Signature** .... `S`

   ✓ *If you do not have a digital certificate, the Create a Digital ID dialog box displays.*

5. Type your name in the Name box.
6. Type your e-mail address in the E-mail address box.
7. Type your company or organization name in the Organization box.
8. Type your geographic location in the Locate box.
9. Click **Create** .... `↵Enter`

View Digital Signatures Attached to a Document

- Click **Signatures** icon 🔏 on Status bar.

  OR

  a. Click the **Office Button** 🔲 .... Alt + F
  b. Point to P**r**epare .... E
  c. Click Vie**w** Signatures .... W

View/Change Status of Digital Signature

1. Click **Signatures** icon 🔏 on Status bar.

   OR

   a. Click the **Office Button** 🔲 .... Alt + F
   b. Point to P**r**epare .... E
   c. Click Vie**w** Signature .... W
2. Click a signature's drop-down arrow.
3. Click **Signature Details** .... G
4. Click **Click here to trust this user's identity** to make signature valid.

View Digital Certificate Associated with a Digital Signature

1. Click **Signatures** icon 🔏 on Status bar.

   OR

   a. Click the **Office Button** 🔲 .... Alt + F
   b. Point to P**r**epare .... E
   c. Click Vie**w** Signature .... W
2. Click a signature's drop-down arrow.
3. Click **Signature Details** .... G
4. Click **V**iew V
5. Click **OK** .... ↵Enter
6. Click **Close** .... Esc

Remove a Digital Signature

1. Right-click the visible digital signature line.

   OR

   a. Open the document.
   b. Click the **Office Button** 🔲 .... Alt + F
   c. Point to P**r**epare .... E
   d. Click Vie**w** Signature .... W
   e. Click the signature's drop-down arrow.
2. Click **Remove Sig**n**ature** .... N
3. Click **Yes** .... Y
4. If a confirmation dialog box displays, click **OK** .... ↵Enter

EXERCISE DIRECTIONS

1. Start Word, if necessary.
2. Open the file 🔘**83MISSION**.
3. Save the document as **83MISSION_xx**.
4. Select to attach an invisible digital signature to the document.
5. In the Purpose for signing this document text box, type **Verify the authentic mission statement**.
6. Use the default digital certificate to sign the document.

   ✓ If necessary, create a digital ID.

7. Save a copy of the **83MISSION_xx** document as **83MISSIONa_xx**.
8. Check the details of the invalid signature, and then remove it from the document.
9. Press Ctrl + End to move the insertion point to the end of the document.
10. Insert a visible signature line using your own name and the title **Marketing Manager**. Leave the e-mail address information blank, and use the default instructions.
11. Sign the document by typing your name.
12. If the signature is marked as invalid, display the signature details and select to trust the user's identity.
13. Close the Signatures task pane.
14. Display the document in Print Preview. It should look similar to Illustration A.

    ✓ Your complete name may not fit within the signature line object.

15. Print the document.
16. Close the document and exit Word.

Long Shot, Inc. Mission Statement

Customer Satisfaction

Long Shot, Inc. is committed to providing quality service to all of our clients at every level of our organization. Our ultimate goal is to hear our clients say, "Thank you. That is just what we wanted."

Employee Well-Being

Second only to customer satisfaction is the happiness and well-being of our employees. The employees at Long Shot, Inc. are encouraged to set personal and professional goals. We respect all employees as individuals and believe that fostering a strong community within the workplace strengthens our position in the marketplace.

Conclusion

At Long Shot, Inc. we vow to maintain the highest standards, pursue the extraordinary, and guarantee customer satisfaction. We are confident that our commitment to quality will make us leaders in our industry.

9/1/09

X Name
_____
Name
Marketing Manager

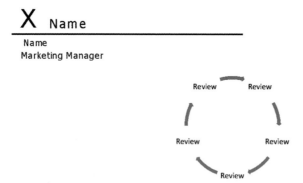

August 31, 2009

ON YOUR OWN

1. Start Word.
2. Open ⌨OWD82_*xx*, the document you worked with in the On Your Own section of Exercise 82, or open 💿83SIGN.
3. Save the document as **OWD83-1_*xx***.
4. Remove the final status from the document.
5. Add an invisible digital signature to the document.
6. Save a copy of the **OWD83-1_*xx*** document as **OWD83-2_*xx***.
7. Remove the invalid signature from the document.

8. Insert a signature line at the bottom of the document. Set it up for a classmate's signature, and have the classmate set his or her document up for your signature.
9. Save the changes and close the document.
10. Exchange documents with the classmate.
11. Sign the document.
12. Print the document.
13. Close the document and exit Word.

Exercise | 84

Skills Covered

- **Create a Form**
- **Insert Content Controls and Form Fields**
- **Set Content Control and Form Field Properties**
- **Fill Out a Form**
- **About Legal Documents**

Software Skills Use forms to collect information such as names and addresses for product registrations, data for surveys, or products and pricing for invoices or purchase orders. With Word, you can create forms that can be printed and filled out manually. You can also store forms on a computer so they can be filled out on-screen.

Application Skills As the Manager of in-house training at Long Shot, Inc., you have decided to survey the employees to find out what types of training classes they are interested in. In this exercise, you will create a form that employees can fill out indicating their class preferences, time preferences, whether they have ever taken an in-house training class, and, if so, whether they were satisfied with the class. You will print the form, and, finally, you will test the form by filling it out on the computer.

TERMS

Form A document used to collect and organize information.

Form field A field inserted in a form document, where users can enter variable information.

NOTES

Create a Form

- In Word, you can create a form by combining content controls and instructional text in a template file.

  ✓ *For information on using templates, refer to Exercise 65.*

- You can also use **form fields**.
- To use the form, you create a document based on the template.
- Forms are protected so that users can enter data in the content controls or form fields, but cannot change any other parts of the document.
- You can protect the entire form, or you can protect individual content controls.

  ✓ *If you only protect the content controls, users may be able to edit the other content in the form document.*

- You can print the document and fill out the form on paper, or you can fill out the form on your computer and store it on a disk.
- If you plan to print the form, you should use form fields instead of content controls, because content controls are designed to be used on-screen in Word.
- You can save a new Word document as a form, or you can save an existing Word document as a form.
- In some ways, Word forms are similar to mail merge documents. They contain standard text and graphics that appear the same on every document, and they contain content controls and/or form fields where users can enter variable data.

Insert Content Controls and Form Fields

- Use the buttons in the Controls group on the Developer tab of the Ribbon to insert content controls or form fields.

- The Developer tab does not display by default; you must set options to make it available.

- Content controls, which are suitable for forms that you intend to fill out on-screen, include:
  - Rich Text
  - Text
  - Drop-Down List
  - Combo Box

- Form Fields, which are suitable for forms that you intend to print to fill out on paper, or fill out on-screen, include:
  - Text Form Field
  - Check Box Form Field
  - Drop Down Form Field

- Instructional text automatically displays in each content control that you insert.

- For example, if you insert a Text control, it displays: Click here to enter text. If you enter a Drop-Down List control, it displays: Choose an item.

- Form fields do not include instructional text.

- When inserting content controls and form fields, give some consideration to the form layout. You may want to use a table or tab stops to be sure items are aligned to look good on the page and so that it will be easy for users to fill out the form.

- Also, it is important to keep in mind that when a user fills out a form on-screen, Word moves the insertion point based on the order in which fields and controls are inserted in the document.

- To ensure a logical order for users filling out the form, you should give some thought to the order in which you insert the form fields and controls.

- You can use both content controls and form fields in the same form document.

Set Content Control and Form Field Properties

- By default, Word inserts content controls and form fields using basic settings. For example, text form fields are set to allow users to enter an unlimited number of text characters.

- You can customize the content control and form field options in the item's Properties dialog box.

- For example, you can set text form field options to limit users to entering valid dates, or no more than ten characters, and you can assign a style to text entered in a plain text content control.

- You can also change the instructional text that displays in a content control.

- You must set properties for drop-down form fields or content controls in order to enter the drop-down list items.

Fill Out a Form

- To fill out a form manually, simply print it.

- To fill out a form on-screen, create a new document based on the form template, enter data in the form fields, then save the document.

- You can leave form fields blank.

About Legal Documents

- Legal documents are used to insure the legal rights of people, groups, or organizations.

- Legal documents may be as simple as a handwritten note that is signed by all concerned parties and witnessed by a third party.

- Alternatively, legal documents may be long, complex, and written using legal terms and language.

- Many legal documents are forms that combine text and blank spaces or form fields where you may enter customized information.

- Other legal documents are reports, case studies, or opinions that include references to legal authorities.

  ✓ *Creating a table of authorities is covered in Exercise 58.*

- Some common legal forms include the following:
  - Bill of Sale
  - Last Will and Testament
  - Rental Agreement
  - General Release
  - Living Will

- The laws governing legal documents vary from state to state.

- You may be able to find legal document forms on the Internet.

PROCEDURES

Display the Developer Tab on the Ribbon

1. Click the **Office Button** ... Alt+F
2. Click **Word Options** ... I
3. Click **Popular**, if necessary ... P, P
4. Click to select **Show Developer tab in the Ribbon** checkbox ... Alt+D

   ✓ *A checkmark in the checkbox indicates the option is selected.*

5. Click **OK** ... ↵Enter

Create a Form Template

1. Create a new Word document.
   OR
   Open an existing document.
2. Click the **Office Button** ... Alt+F
3. Point to **Save As** ... F
4. Click **Word Template** ... T
5. Type template file name.
6. Select location where you want form template stored.
7. Click **Save** ... ↵Enter
8. In the document, type standard text that will display on all forms.
9. If necessary, delete variable text that you do not want to display on forms.
10. Insert content controls and form fields as necessary.

    ✓ *Refer to Insert Content Controls and Form Fields procedures for step-by-step instructions on inserting form fields.*

11. Click **Developer** tab ... Alt+L

    Protect Group

12. Click **Protect Document** button ... P, R
13. Click to select **Allow only this type of editing in the document** check box ... ↓, ↓, Spacebar
14. Click **Editing restrictions** drop-down arrow ... Tab↹, ↓
15. Click **Filling in forms** ... ↓, ↓, ↵Enter
16. Click **Yes, Start Enforcing Protection**.
17. Click **OK** ... ↵Enter
    OR
    Set password protection, as desired.

    ✓ *For information on protecting documents and setting exceptions, refer to Exercise 80.*

18. Close the template file ... Alt+F, C

Open Form Template for Editing

1. Open form template document.
2. Click **Developer** tab ... Alt+L

   Protect Group

3. Click **Protect Document** button ... P, R
4. Click **Stop Protection**.

Insert Content Controls

1. Open form template for editing.
2. Click **Developer** tab ... Alt+L

   Controls Group

3. Click **Design Mode** button ... D+M
4. Position insertion point where you want to insert content control.
5. Click **Developer** tab ... Alt+L

   Controls Group

6. Click button for content control to insert:
   - **Rich Text** Aa ... Q
   - **Text** Aa ... E
   - **Picture** ... I
   - **Combo Box** ... C, O
   - **Drop-Down List** ... O
   - **Date Picker** ... K
   - **Building Block Gallery** ... B
7. Repeat steps 4 – 6 to insert additional content controls.

   ✓ *You may combine content controls and form fields in the same form.*

8. Click **Developer** tab ... Alt+L

   Controls Group

9. Click **Design Mode** button ... D+M
10. Protect, save, and close form template document.

Remove Content Control

1. Right-click content control.
2. Click **Remove Content Control** ... E

Insert Form Fields

1. Open form template for editing.
2. Position insertion point where you want to insert form field.
3. Click **Developer** tab ... Alt+L

   Controls Group

4. Click **Legacy Tools** button ... N
5. Click form field to insert:
   - **Text Form Field** abl ... E
   - **Check Box Form Field** ☑ ... H
   - **Drop-Down Form Field** ... C

6. Repeat steps to insert additional form fields.

   ✓ You may combine content controls and form fields in the same form.

   ✓ To toggle form field shading off or on, click the **Form Field Shading** button 🅰 in the Legacy Tools gallery.

7. Protect, save, and close form template document.

Set Content Control Properties

1. Click content control.
2. Click **Developer** tab .... Alt+L

   Controls Group

3. Click **Properties** button 🖼 L
4. Select options as desired.
5. Click **OK** .... ↵Enter

Set Form Field Properties

Text form fields:

1. Click text form field.
2. Click **Developer** tab .... Alt+L

   Controls Group

3. Click **Properties** button 🖼 L
4. Select options as follows:
   - Select type of text allowed from **Type** drop-down list ...... Alt+P, ↓/↑, ↵Enter
   - Enter default text to display in **Default text** text box .... Alt+E
   - Enter number of characters allowed in **Maximum length** text box .... Alt+M
   - Select format from **Text format** drop-down list ..... Alt+F

   ✓ Name of format box changes depending on the type of text selected from **Type** drop-down list.

5. Click **OK** .... ↵Enter

Check box form fields:

1. Click check box form field.
2. Click **Developer** tab .... Alt+L

   Controls Group

3. Click **Properties** button 🖼 L
4. Set size options as follows:
   - Select **Auto** option button to set size according to current font size .... Alt+A
   - Select **Exactly** option button to type specific size ...... Alt+E, type size in points
5. Set default value options as follows:
   - Select **Not checked** to display check box not checked by default .... Alt+K
   - Select **Checked** to display check box checked by default .... Alt+D
6. Click **OK** .... ↵Enter

Drop-down form fields:

1. Click drop down form field.
2. Click **Developer** tab .... Alt+L

   Controls Group

3. Click **Properties** button 🖼 L
4. Click **Drop-down item**: text box .... Alt+D
5. Type first option you want displayed in drop-down list.
6. Click **Add** .... Alt+A
7. Repeat steps 4-6 until all drop-down options are entered.
8. Click **OK** .... ↵Enter

Fill Out a Form On-Screen

1. Start Word.
2. Create a new document based on the form template.

   ✓ For information on using templates, refer to Exercise 65.

3. To enter data, use the action appropriate for the different types of form fields or content controls as follows:
   - Click content control and type text.
   - Click content control drop-down arrow and select option.
   - Type text in text form field.
   - Click check box form field to select or deselect check box .... Spacebar
   - Click drop-down form field arrow, then click desired option .... Alt+↓, ↑/↓, ↵Enter
4. Press **Tab** or click to move to next form field .... Tab⇆

   ✓ You do not have to enter data in every field.

5. Save and name document.

EXERCISE DIRECTIONS

Design the Form Template

1. Start Word, if necessary.
2. Open ⊙84LSI.
3. Save the document as a template with the name **84LSI_xx**.

   ✓ Ask your instructor where to store the new template file.

4. Draw a table in the document as shown in Illustration A. Keep gridlines displayed, but do not use any borders.

   ✓ Cell measurements are approximate.

   ✓ For a refresher on drawing tables, see Exercise 41.

5. Using a 16-point serif font, type the text in the table shown in Illustration A.
6. Center the words *Yes, No,* and *Maybe* in their cells.
7. Check the spelling and grammar in the document.
8. Preview the document. It should look similar to Illustration A.

   ✓ Gridlines are displayed in the illustration so you can see the size of columns and rows; they will not display in Print Preview.

9. Print the document.

Insert Content Controls and Form Fields

1. In row 1, column 2, insert a Text content control using default properties.
2. In row 2, column 2, insert another Text content control, using default properties.
3. In row 3, column 2, insert a Date Picker content control, using the default properties.
4. In rows 5 and 6, insert check box form fields with the default properties under the text *Yes* and *No* in columns 2 and 3.

   ✓ Position the insertion point at the end of the text and press Enter to position the insertion point centered on the next line in the cell.

5. In row 7, column 2, insert a Text content control, using the default properties.
6. In row 8, insert check box form fields under the text *Yes, No,* and *Maybe* in columns 2, 3, and 4.
7. In row 9, insert a Drop-Down List content control.

8. Customize the properties to enter the following three drop-down list items: **Corporate Headquarters, Local Office, Off-site Training Center**.

   a. Select the content control and click Properties.
   b. Click Add.
   c. Type the first list item.
   d. Click OK.
   e. Click Add.
   f. Type the second list item.
   g. Click OK.
   h. Click Add.
   i. Type the third list item.
   j. Click OK.
   k. Click OK.

9. In row 10, column 2, insert a Text content control.
10. Form protect the template.
11. Preview the document. It should look similar to the one in Illustration B.
12. Close the template document, saving all changes.

Fill Out the Form

1. Create a new document based on the **84LSI_xx** form template.
2. Save the document as **84SURVEY_xx**.
3. Fill out the form as follows:

   a. Enter your name in the first Text content control.
   b. Enter **Marketing** in the second Text content control.
   c. Select the current date from the Date Picker content control.
   d. Select *Yes* for whether or not you have attended in-house training classes.
   e. Select *No* for whether or not you were satisfied.
   f. For the reason why you were not satisfied, type that you thought the course was not challenging enough.
   g. Select *Maybe* for whether or not you are interested in future classes.
   h. Select *Off-site Training Center* as the location you would prefer.
   i. Enter any comments you would like in the final text content control.

4. Print the document.
5. Close the document, saving all changes.

Illustration A

Long Shot, Inc.

234 Simsbury Drive ⚑ Ithaca, NY 14850

Telephone: 607-555-9191 ⚑ Fax: 607-555-9292 ⚑ E-mail: mail@longshot.net

Name:	
Department:	
Date:	

Have you attended in-house training classes in the past?	Yes	No
If so, were you satisfied with the class?	Yes	No
If you were not satisfied, why not?		

Are you interested in attending in-house training classes in the future?	Yes	No	Maybe
Where would you like training classes held?			

Comments:	

Long Shot, Inc.

234 Simsbury Drive ⚑ Ithaca, NY 14850
Telephone: 607-555-9191 ⚑ Fax: 607-555-9292 ⚑ E-mail: mail@longshot.net

Name: Click here to enter text.

Department: Click here to enter text.

Date: Click here to enter a date.

Have you attended in-house training classes in the past? Yes ☐ No ☐

If so, were you satisfied with the class? Yes ☐ No ☐

If you were not satisfied, why not? Click here to enter text.

Are you interested in attending in-house training classes in the future? Yes ☐ No ☐ Maybe ☐

Where would you like training classes held? Choose an item.

Comments: Click here to enter text.

ON YOUR OWN

1. Plan a form that could be used as a legal document for a club or organization to which you belong. For example, a field trip permission slip is a legal form. If the organization rents or loans equipment, you might create a rental form. Decide the content controls and/or form fields you would need on the form, as well as the standard text. Plan the layout and design of the form.

2. Start Word and create a new document.

3. Save the document as a template with the name OWD84-1_*xx*.

4. Enter all of the standard text you want on your form. Use a table if it helps you line up the information neatly on the page.

5. Insert the content controls and form fields you will need on your form. Remember to enter them in the order in which you want users to fill them out.

6. Check the spelling and grammar in the document.

7. Form protect the document.

8. Print the document.

9. Ask a classmate to review the document and offer comments and suggestions.

10. Incorporate the comments and suggestions into the form template.

11. Save the template and close it.

12. Create a new document based on the OWD84-1_*xx* template.

13. Save the document as OWD84-2_*xx*.

14. Fill out the form on the screen, or print it and fill it out manually.

15. Save the form, close it, and exit Word.

Curriculum Connection: Science

Classification

In science, classification is an important part of studying and understanding similar items. The process is called Taxonomy, which means the science of identifying and naming species and organisms, and organizing them into groups.

Design a Classification Form

Plan a form that you can use to record the information you need to classify objects. For example, you might create a form to use for classifying rocks, or species of animals, or planets. Think about the standard text you want on the form, as well as the types of content controls or form fields you will need for recording variable information. Create a document template and enter the data, using a table to help you align the information on the page. Remember to protect the template. Create a new document based on the template and use it to classify information for a science lab.

Exercise | 85

Critical Thinking

Application Skills In this exercise you will create a registration form that Blue Sky Dairy employees can use to offer their services as contest judges. You will test the registration form by filling it out on-screen, and you will attach a digital signature to the completed form.

EXERCISE DIRECTIONS

1. Create a new blank document and save it as a template with the name **85FORM_xx**.
2. Type and format the document shown in Illustration A, using a table to arrange the content.
3. Insert content controls and form fields as follows:
   - First Name: Text content control with default properties.
   - Last Name: Text content control with default properties.
   - Department: Drop-Down List content control with options for **Administration, Field, Manufacturing, Marketing, Personnel, Quality Control, Sales, Other.**
   - Phone Extension: Text content control with default properties.
   - Email Address: Text content control with default properties.
   - Contest for which you would like to be a judge: Drop Down List content control with options for **Art, Contest Ideas, Essay, Games, Name that Flavor.**
   - Yes: Check box form field.
   - No: Check box form field.
   - Comments: Text field with default properties.

4. Check the spelling and grammar.
5. Form protect the document.
6. Preview the document. It should look similar to Illustration A.

   ✓ *If there are border lines in your document, remove them.*

7. Print the form.
8. Close the document, saving all changes.
9. Create a new document based on the **85FORM_xx** template.
10. Save the document as **85FORMa_xx**.
11. Fill out the form.
12. Print the document and then save it.
13. Attach your digital signature to the form.
14. Close the document and exit Word.

Blue Sky Dairy Co.
Contest Judge Registration Form

First Name: Click here to enter text.

Last Name: Click here to enter text.

Department: Choose an item.

Phone Extension: Click here to enter text.

Email Address: Click here to enter text.

Contest for which you would like to be a judge: Choose an item.

Have you ever been a Blue Sky Dairy judge before?   Yes   No
                                                          ☐   ☐

Comments: Click here to enter text.

Curriculum Integration

Application Skills For your social studies class, use the skills you have learned in Lesson 11 to design and create a form that you can use to survey classmates about an issue that you have been studying, or a topic that has been in the news. For example, you might survey classmates about who they would endorse in an upcoming election, or you might ask them their opinion about underage drinking or smoking. When you are finished, ask your classmates to fill out the form on-screen or in print. You can use the results of the survey to create a chart or table, or to write a newspaper article. Refer to Illustration A to see a sample of a survey form.

EXERCISE DIRECTIONS

Pick a topic that you want to use for your survey. The topic should relate to the subject you are studying in school, or to current events.

Plan a form that can be used to collect responses to your survey. Consider the type of content controls and forms you will need, the standard text, and how you want to design the form so that it is easy to fill out. Also, think about whether you want the responses to be anonymous.

Start Word, if necessary, and create a new document. Save it as a Word template with the name 86SURVEY_xx.

Select to display elements that might help you while you work, such as the rulers, nonprinting characters, and gridlines.

Enter all of the standard text you want on your form. You can insert graphics as well, such as a clip art picture, or shapes. Use a table if it helps you line up the information neatly on the page. Alternatively, you might want to use text boxes.

Insert the content controls and form fields you will need on your form. Remember to enter them in the order in which you want users to fill them out.

Check the spelling and grammar in the document.

Form protect the document.

Print the document.

Ask a classmate to review the document and offer comments and suggestions.

Incorporate the comments and suggestions into the form template.

Save the template and close it.

Ask your classmates to fill out the form on-screen, or printed.

Collect the results and analyze them. Create a chart, graph, or table illustrating the results, or write an article explaining them.

Social Studies

Please take the time to complete this survey. The results are strictly confidential.

Age: Click here to enter text.

Gender: Male Female
☐ ☐

Date: Click here to enter a date.

Political Affiliation: Republican Democrat Other
☐ ☐ Click here to enter text.

Do you support term limits? Yes No I Don't Know
☐ ☐ ☐

Do you support reinstating the draft? Yes No I Don't Know
☐ ☐ ☐

Comments: Click here to enter text.

Lesson | 12

Integration

Skills Covered

- ■ Microsoft Office 2007
- ■ Run Multiple Programs at the Same Time
- ■ Arrange Multiple Program Windows
- ■ Switch among Open Programs
- ■ Copy and Move Data from One Office Document to Another

Software Skills   If you use Microsoft Office 2007, you may find it necessary to work with more than one application at a time. For example, you might want to create a report detailing your department's decreased costs by combining a Word document with an Excel spreadsheet. Or, you might want to illustrate a Word letter using an Excel chart. You can open multiple applications at the same time and easily switch among them. You can also arrange the open applications on the screen so you can quickly find the information you need.

Application Skills   The owners of Blue Sky Dairy are thinking about starting a home delivery service. You have been asked to coordinate a feasibility study, and the owners have sent you information prepared in Word, Excel, and PowerPoint. In this exercise, you will start Word and open a memo document. You will then start the other Office programs, open the other program files, arrange the windows on-screen, and switch among the open windows. You will also copy data from an Excel worksheet into a Word document.

TERMS

Active window   The window in which you are currently working.

Cascade   Arrange open windows on-screen so they overlap, with the active window displayed on top.

Database   An organized collection of records, such as client records, a personal address book, or product inventory.

Destination file   The file where the data is pasted.

Group button   A taskbar button that represents all open windows for one application.

Personal information manager (PIM)   A program that keeps track of such items as addresses and phone numbers, appointments and meetings, and things to do.

Presentation graphics   A program used to create presentations, such as slide shows.

Software suite   A group of software applications sold as a single unit. Usually, the applications have common features that make it easy to integrate and share data among documents.

Source file   The file that contains the data to be copied.

Spreadsheet   A program used to organize data in columns and rows. Spreadsheets are often used for performing calculations, such as financial or budget analysis.

Tile   Arrange open windows on-screen so they do not overlap.

NOTES

Microsoft Office 2007

- Microsoft Office 2007 is a new version of the popular Microsoft Office 2003 **software suite**.
- Microsoft Office 2007 programs are fully compatible with files created with previous versions.
- Different editions of the suite are available to suit the needs of different people and businesses.
- Most editions include the following core Microsoft Office System programs:
  - Word, a word processing program.
  - Excel, a spreadsheet program.
  - PowerPoint, a presentation graphics program.
  - Outlook, a personal information manager and communications program.
- Some editions may include the following additional programs:
  - Access, a database application.
  - Publisher, a desktop publishing program.
  - OneNote, a note-taking and management program.
  - InfoPath, an information gathering and management program.
- Microsoft Office 2007 can run with either the Microsoft Windows XP or the Microsoft Windows Vista operating system.

Run Multiple Programs at the Same Time

- You can open multiple program windows at the same time. This is useful for comparing the data in different files, as well as for exchanging data between files.
- Use Windows to start an Office program.
  - You can select the program you want to start from the Microsoft Office folder accessed from the Windows All Programs menu.
  - If the program has been used recently, or pinned to the Windows Start menu, you can select it directly from the Windows Start menu.
  - You can double-click a program shortcut icon on the desktop, if available.

Arrange Multiple Program Windows

- Each open window is represented by a button on the Windows taskbar.
- If there is not room on the taskbar to display buttons for each open window, Windows displays a **group button**.
  - ✓ *The taskbar may not be visible on-screen if Windows is set to hide the taskbar, or to display windows on top of the taskbar. To see the taskbar, move the mouse pointer to the edge of the screen where it usually displays, or press* Ctrl + Esc.
- You can **tile** windows if you want to see all of them at the same time. Tiled windows do not overlap.
  - ✓ *You can tile windows horizontally or vertically.*

Tiled windows

- The more windows you have open, the smaller they display when tiled.
  - If necessary in smaller windows, the program may hide common screen elements such as the Office Button, Quick Access Toolbar, and Ribbon and display only a program icon on the left end of the title bar.
  - You can click the program icon to display a shortcut menu of commands including Maximize, Minimize, and Close.

- You can **cascade** windows if you want to see the active window in its entirety, with the title bars of all open windows displayed behind it.

Cascading windows

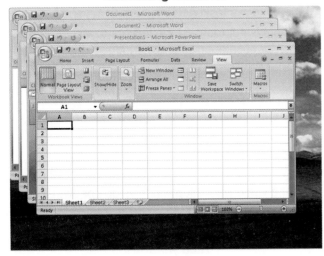

Switch among Open Windows

- Only one window can be active—or current—at a time.
- The **active window** displays on top of other open windows. Its title bar is darker than the title bars of other open windows, and its taskbar button appears pressed in.
- You can switch among open windows to make a different window active.

Copy and Move Data from One Office Document to Another

- Use the Windows Clipboard or drag-and-drop editing to copy or move data from one Office document to another.
- The **source file** contains the original data and the **destination file** is where the data is pasted.
- Data pasted into a destination file becomes part of the destination file. There is no link to the source file.
- Word may automatically format pasted data. For example, Excel data pasted into a Word document is displayed as a table, and a PowerPoint slide pasted into a Word document is formatted as a picture.
- You edit pasted data using standard commands for the destination application.

PROCEDURES

Start an Office Program

1. Click **Start** button
   start / 🪟 .... Ctrl + Esc
2. Click **All Programs** .... P, ↵Enter
   ✓ If you are using Windows Vista, the keystrokes to open the All Programs menu are ↑, ↵Enter.
3. Point to the Microsoft Office folder icon .... ↓, →
4. Click the name of the Office program .... ↓, ↵Enter

OR

1. Click **Start** button
   start / 🪟 .... Ctrl + Esc

2. Click the name of the Office program in the list of recently used programs .... ↓, ↵Enter

OR

- Double-click a program shortcut icon on the desktop:
  - Word shortcut icon 📄 to start Word.
  - Excel shortcut icon 📊 to start Excel.
  - PowerPoint shortcut icon 📑 to start PowerPoint.
  - Access shortcut icon 🔑 to start Access.
  - Outlook shortcut icon 📧 to start Outlook.

Exit an Office Program

- Click **Program Close** button ☒ at the right end of the program's title bar.
  ✓ If you are using Windows Vista, the Program Close button may look different.

OR

1. Click **Office Button** 🔘 ..... Alt + F
2. Click **Exit** _program name_ X
3. Click **Yes** .... Y to save open documents.

OR

Click **No** .... N
to exit without saving.

Arrange Program Windows

1. Right-click on blank area of Windows taskbar.
2. Select desired option:
   - **Cascade Windows** ..... (S), (←Enter)
   - **Tile Windows Horizontally** .... (H)
     - ✓ *In Windows Vista, select Show Windows Stacked.*
   - **Tile Windows Vertically** .... (E)
     - ✓ *In Windows Vista, select Show Windows Side by Side.*
     - ✓ *Maximize active window to display active window only.*

Switch between Open Windows

- Click taskbar button of desired window.

   OR
- Click in desired window.

   OR
1. Click group taskbar button.
2. Click name of window.

   OR
1. Press and hold **Alt** .... (Alt)
2. Press **Tab** to cycle through open windows .... (Tab⇆)
3. Release both keys when desired window is selected.

Copy Data from One Office Document to Another
(Ctrl+C, Ctrl+V)

Use the Clipboard:
1. Start programs.
2. Open source file.
3. Open destination file.
4. Select data to copy in source file.
5. Click **Home** tab .... (Alt)+(H)

Clipboard Group

6. Click **Copy** button 🗐 .... (C)

   OR
   a. Right-click selection.
   b. Click **Copy** .... (C)
7. Make destination file active.
8. Position insertion point in new location.
9. Click **Home** tab .... (Alt)+(H)

Clipboard Group

10. Click **Paste** button 🗐 .... (V), (P)

    OR
    a. Right-click insertion point location.
    b. Click **Paste** .... (P), (←Enter)

Use drag-and-drop editing:
1. Start programs.
2. Open source file.
3. Open destination file.
4. Right-click on blank area of Windows taskbar.
5. Select **Tile Windows Vertically** .... (E)
   - ✓ *In Windows Vista, select Show Windows Side by Side.*
6. Select data to copy in source document.
7. Scroll in destination document to display desired new location.
8. Move pointer to edge of selection.
9. Press and hold down **Ctrl** .... (Ctrl)
10. Drag selected data to correct position in destination file.
    - ✓ *A gray vertical bar indicates location where selection will be dropped.*
11. Release mouse button.
12. Release **Ctrl**.

Move Data from One Office Document to Another
(Ctrl+X, Ctrl+V)

Use the Clipboard:
1. Start programs.
2. Open source file.
3. Open destination file.
4. Select data to move in source file.
5. Click **Home** tab .... (Alt)+(H)

Clipboard Group

6. Click **Cut** button ✂ .... (X)

   OR
   a. Right-click selection.
   b. Click **Cut** .... (T)
7. Make destination file active.
8. Position insertion point in new location.
9. Click **Home** tab .... (Alt)+(H)

Clipboard Group

10. Click **Paste** button 🗐 .... (V), (P)

    OR
    a. Right-click insertion point location.
    b. Click **Paste** .... (P), (←Enter)

Use drag-and-drop editing:
1. Start programs.
2. Open source file.
3. Open destination file.
4. Right-click on blank area of Windows taskbar.
5. Select **Tile Windows Vertically** ... (E)
   - ✓ *In Windows Vista, select Show Windows Side by Side.*
6. Select data to move in source document.
7. Scroll in destination document to display desired new location.
8. Move pointer to edge of selection.
9. Drag selected data to correct position in destination file.
   - ✓ *A gray vertical bar indicates location where selection will be dropped.*
10. Release mouse button.

EXERCISE DIRECTIONS

✓ *This exercise assumes you know how to locate and select data in an Excel worksheet. If you do not, ask your instructor for more information.*

Start and Arrange Multiple Program Windows

1. Start Word, if necessary, and open the document ⊙ **87MEMO.** Save the file as **87MEMO_xx.**
2. Start Excel and open the workbook ⊙ **87DATA.** You do not have to save the workbook file.
3. Start PowerPoint and open the presentation ⊙ **87PRES.** You do not have to save the presentation file.
4. Tile the windows vertically on-screen. They should look similar to Illustration A, although the order may vary.
5. Make the file **87MEMO_xx** active.
6. Tile the windows horizontally.
7. Make the file **87DATA** active.
8. Cascade the windows.
9. Make the file **87PRES** active.
10. Maximize the PowerPoint window.
11. Exit PowerPoint without saving any changes.

Copy Data from one Program to Another

1. Make the file **87MEMO_xx** active.
2. Replace the text *Your Name* with your own name.
3. Replace the text *Today's date* with the current date.
4. Position the insertion point on the last line at the end of the document.
5. Make the **87DATA** file active, and maximize the window.
6. Select cells A4 through B9.
    a. Click the cell in the fourth row of the first column (it contains the text *Initial Investment*).
    b. Press and hold Shift.
    c. Click the cell in the ninth row of the second column (it contains the value *$243,500.00*).
7. Copy the selected range of cells to the last line of the **87MEMO_xx** document.
    a. Click the Copy button on the Home tab of the Ribbon.
    b. Switch to the **87MEMO_xx** document.
    c. Make sure the insertion point is on the last line.
    d. Click the Paste button on the Home tab of the Ribbon.
8. Apply the Table 3D effects 2 style to the table.

    ✓ *For a refresher on formatting tables, refer to Exercise 40.*

9. Center the table horizontally on the page.
10. Check the spelling and grammar in the document.
11. Preview the **87MEMO_xx** document. It should look similar to Illustration B.
12. Print the document.
13. Close the **87DATA** workbook file and exit Excel, without saving any changes.
14. Close the **87MEMO_xx**, saving all changes, and exit Word.

Illustration A

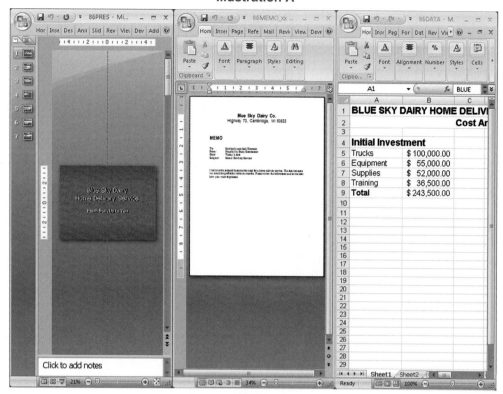

Illustration B

Blue Sky Dairy Co.
Highway 73, Cambridge, WI 53523

MEMO

To:	Kimberly and Jack Thomson
From:	Student's Name
Date:	Today's date
Subject:	Home Delivery Service

I believe the research bears out the need for a home delivery service. The data indicates we could be profitable within six months. Please review the information and let me know how you want to proceed.

Initial Investment	
Trucks	$ 100,000.00
Equipment	$ 55,000.00
Supplies	$ 52,000.00
Training	$ 36,500.00
Total	$ 243,500.00

ON YOUR OWN

1. Start Word and create a new document.
2. Save the document as **OWD87-1_xx.**
3. Type a letter addressed to your friends and/or family telling them that you have made up a list of books and/or CDs that you would like to receive as birthday or holiday gifts.
4. Start Excel and create a new worksheet, or open the workbook ◉**87GIFTS.**
5. Save the file as **OWD87-2_xx.**

   ✓ *The steps for saving an Excel file are the same as those for saving a Word file.*

6. Create a worksheet listing the names and prices of CDs and/or books you would like to receive.

7. Select the Excel worksheet data and copy it to the Word document.
8. Format the data in the Word document to improve its appearance and make it easier to read.
9. Check the spelling and grammar in the document.
10. Print the document.
11. Ask a classmate to review the document and make comments or suggestions.
12. Incorporate the comments and suggestions into the document.
13. Close all files and programs, saving all changes.

Exercise | 88

Skills Covered

- ■ Link Files
- ■ Edit a Linked Object
- ■ Update Links

Software Skills   Link files when you have existing data in one file that you want to use in one or more other files. Whenever the original data is changed, the link ensures that it will be updated in all other files. Linking lets you maintain data in a single file location, yet use it in other files as well.

Application Skills   As the new Training Director at Long Shot, Inc., you have been asked to submit the department's expenses for the first quarter to the Director of Human Resources. However, you only have preliminary data available. In this exercise, you will link the preliminary data stored in an Excel worksheet into a Word memo. You will then change the data to reflect actual expenses, and update the link to update the data in the Word document.

TERMS

Link   To insert an object in a destination file. When the source file is edited, the linked object in the destination file is updated to reflect the change.

NOTES

Link Files

- ■ **Link** data to create a dynamic connection between two files. Linking enables you to keep files that include the same data up to date, without having to edit the data in every file.
- ■ The source file contains the original data and the destination file contains the linked object.
- ■ Source data can be linked to many destination files. For example, data in an Excel worksheet can be linked to multiple Word documents and to a PowerPoint slide.
- ■ When you edit the source file, the linked object in the destination file(s) is changed as well.
- ■ Use the Paste Special command with the Paste Link option enabled to link files.
- ■ In the Paste Special dialog box you can also select how you want to format the selected object. The choices depend on the source program.

- ■ A description of the selected format displays in the Result area of the dialog box.

Paste Special dialog box

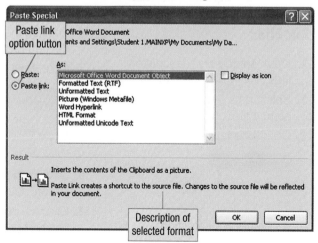

Edit a Linked Object

- To make sure that the original data is always up-to-date, you use the source program to edit a linked object.
- For example, if you have a linked Excel object in a Word memo you must use Excel to edit the object in the memo.
- When you double-click a linked object, the source program and file open so you can access the appropriate commands.
- Changes made to the original source file are reflected in the linked object when the link is updated.
- Although you cannot edit a linked object using the destination program, linked objects can be formatted, moved, and resized using many techniques you learned for working with graphics objects.

  ✓ *See Lesson 10 for information about working with graphics objects.*

Update Links

- By default, links update automatically.
- When both the source and destination files are open, the linked object must be selected for the update to occur.
- When only the source file is open, the linked object is updated when you open the destination file.
- If there are many links in a file, automatic updating can slow down your system.
- You can turn off automatic updates and manually update links.

- When you open a document that contains linked objects, Word prompts you to update the document with data from the linked files.
- If Word cannot locate the source file (for example, if it has been deleted, renamed, or moved) it will display a warning message telling you that it cannot update the link. You can use the Links dialog box to break the link or to change the location of the source file.
- Breaking the link leaves the object in the destination document without a link to a source document or program.
- Changing the source file in the Links dialog box links the object to a different source file.
- You can lock a link to prevent it from being updated.
- You can set Word options so that no links in any Word document will be updated.

Links dialog box

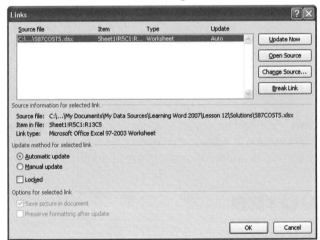

PROCEDURES

Link Files

1. Open source and destination files.
2. Select data to be linked in source file.
3. Click **Home** tab .... Alt+H

   Clipboard Group

4. Click **Copy** button 🗐 C
   OR
   a. Right-click selection.
   b. Click **Copy** C
5. Make destination file active.

6. Position insertion point in the desired location.
7. Click **Home** tab .... Alt+H

   Clipboard Group

8. Click **Paste** button drop-down arrow 🗐 V
9. Click **Paste Special** .... S
10. Click **Paste link** option button .... Alt+L
11. Click **As** box, if necessary .... Alt+A
12. Click format to use .... ↓/↑
13. Click **OK** .... ↵Enter

Edit a Linked Object

1. Open file containing linked object.
2. Double-click linked object.

   ✓ *Source program and file open.*

3. Edit source file.
4. Close source program and file, saving all changes.

Turn Off Automatic Updating

1. Open the document.
2. Click the **Office Button** ▣ .... Alt+F
3. Click P**r**epare .... E
4. Click Edit **L**inks to Files L

   ✓ If there are multiple links in the
   file, click the specific link in the
   Source file list.

5. Click **M**anual update option button .... Alt+M
6. Click **OK** .... ↵Enter

Update a Link Manually (Ctrl+Shift+F7)

1. Open the document.
2. Click the **Office Button** ▣ .... Alt+F
3. Click P**r**epare .... E
4. Click Edit **L**inks to Files L

   ✓ If there are multiple links in the
   file, click the specific link in the
   Source file list.

5. Click **U**pdate Now .... Alt+U
6. Click **OK** .... ↵Enter
   OR
1. Open the document.
2. Right-click object.
3. Click Up**d**ate Link .... D

Turn On Automatic Updating

1. Open the document.
2. Click the **Office Button** ▣ .... Alt+F
3. Click P**r**epare .... E
4. Click Edit **L**inks to Files L

   ✓ If there are multiple links in the
   file, click the specific link in the
   Source file list.

5. Click **A**utomatic update option button .... Alt+A
6. Click **OK** .... ↵Enter

Lock a Link *(Ctrl+F11)*

1. Open the document.
2. Click the **Office Button** ▣ .... Alt+F
3. Click P**r**epare .... E
4. Click Edit **L**inks to Files L

   ✓ If there are multiple links in the
   file, click the specific link in the
   Source file list.

5. Click to select **Loc**k**ed** check box .... Alt+K
6. Click **OK** .... ↵Enter

Unlock a Link *(Ctrl+Shift+F11)*

1. Open the document.
2. Click the **Office Button** ▣ .... Alt+F
3. Click P**r**epare .... E
4. Click Edit **L**inks to Files L

   ✓ If there are multiple links in the
   file, click the specific link in the
   Source file list.

5. Click to deselect **Loc**k**ed** check box .... Alt+K
6. Click **OK** .... ↵Enter

Prevent All Links in All Documents from Updating:

1. Open the document.
2. Click the **Office Button** ▣ .... Alt+F
3. Click Word Opt**i**ons I
4. Click **A**dvanced .... A
5. Under General, click to deselect **Update automatic links at open** check box ...... Alt+U, U, U, Spacebar

   ✓ Select the check box to allow links
   to update.

6. Click **OK** .... ↵Enter

Break a Link *(Ctrl+Shift+F9)*

1. Open the document.
2. Click the **Office Button** ▣ .... Alt+F
3. Click P**r**epare .... E
4. Click Edit **L**inks to Files L

   ✓ If there are multiple links in the
   file, click the specific link in the
   Source file list.

5. Click **B**reak Link .... Alt+B
6. Click **OK** .... ↵Enter

Change a Link's Source

1. Open the document.
2. Click the **Office Button** ▣ .... Alt+F
3. Click P**r**epare .... E
4. Click Edit **L**inks to Files L

   ✓ If there are multiple links in the
   file, click the specific link in the
   Source file list.

5. Click Cha**n**ge Source .... Alt+N
6. Locate and select new source file.
7. Click **O**pen .... Alt+O
8. Click **OK** .... ↵Enter

EXERCISE DIRECTIONS

✓ *The steps in this exercise assume you know how to select and enter data in an Excel worksheet. If necessary, ask your instructor for more information.*

Link Data from Excel to Word

1. Start Word, if necessary.
2. Create the document shown in Illustration A, or open ⊙88MEMO.
3. Save the document as **88MEMO_xx**.
4. Replace the sample text *Your Name* with your own name.
5. Replace the sample text *Today's date* with the current date.
6. Position the insertion point on the blank line at the end of the document.
7. Start Excel and open the workbook file ⊙88COSTS.
8. Save the file as **88COSTS_xx**.

   ✓ *Use the File, Save As command just as you would in Word.*

9. Link the Excel workbook data onto the last line of the **88MEMO_xx** document:
   a. Select cells A5:E13 in the **88COSTS_xx** worksheet.

      ✓ *Click cell A5, press and hold Shift, and then click cell E13.*

   b. Copy the selected range to the Clipboard.
   c. Switch to the **88MEMO_xx** document.
   d. Make sure the insertion point is on the last line of the document.
   e. Click the Paste button drop-down arrow and then click Paste Special.
   f. Select Microsoft Office Excel Worksheet Object as the format type.
   g. Select the Paste link option button.
   h. Click OK.
10. Center the object in the memo horizontally on the page.

    ✓ *Click the object to select it, then click the Center button in the Paragraph group on the Home tab of the Ribbon.*

11. Save the changes to the Word document.

Edit the Data and Update the Link

1. Double-click the object in the Word document.

   ✓ *Excel displays the 88COSTS_xx workbook.*

2. Press Esc to cancel the selection marquee.
3. In cell C9—*February Facility rentals* (the empty cell)—type **1,500** and then press Enter.

   ✓ *Excel is set to automatically format the data as currency.*

4. Close the workbook, saving the changes, and exit Excel.
5. Switch to the **88MEMO_xx** document.
6. Manually update the link:
   a. Right-click the object.
   b. Click Update Link.

   OR

   a. Click the Office Button.
   b. Click Prepare.
   c. Click Edit Links to Files.
   d. Click Update Now.
   e. Click OK.
7. Double-click the Excel object in the Word memo.

   ✓ *Excel starts and opens the 88COSTS_xx workbook.*

8. Click cell D12—*March Miscellaneous* expenses—and type **150** to edit the entry. Press Enter to enter the data in the cell.
9. Close the workbook, saving the changes, and exit Excel.
10. Manually update the link in Word.
11. Preview the **88MEMO_xx** document. It should look similar to Illustration B.
12. Print the document.
13. Close the document, saving all changes, and exit Word.

Illustration A

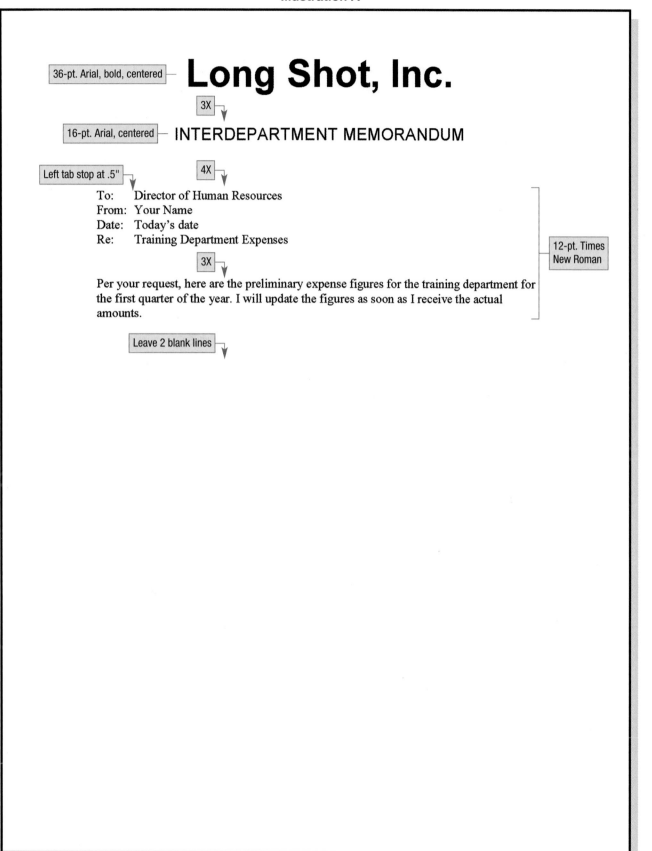

36-pt. Arial, bold, centered — # Long Shot, Inc.

3X

16-pt. Arial, centered — INTERDEPARTMENT MEMORANDUM

Left tab stop at .5"   4X

To: Director of Human Resources
From: Your Name
Date: Today's date
Re: Training Department Expenses

12-pt. Times
New Roman

3X

Per your request, here are the preliminary expense figures for the training department for
the first quarter of the year. I will update the figures as soon as I receive the actual
amounts.

Leave 2 blank lines

Long Shot, Inc.

INTERDEPARTMENT MEMORANDUM

To: Director of Human Resources
From: Student's Name
Date: Today's date
Re: Training Department Expenses

Per your request, here are the preliminary expense figures for the training department for the first quarter of the year. I will update the figures as soon as I receive the actual amounts.

	January	February	March	Total
Salaries	$135,000.00	$135,000.00	$135,000.00	$405,000.00
Overtime	$30,000.00	$32,000.00	$29,000.00	$91,000.00
Entertainment	$1,500.00	$1,750.00	$1,200.00	$4,450.00
Facility rentals	$2,000.00	$1,500.00	$1,500.00	$5,000.00
Books	$500.00	$250.00	$500.00	$1,250.00
Supplies	$250.00	$150.00	$375.00	$775.00
Miscellaneous	$200.00	$175.00	$150.00	$525.00
Total	$169,450.00	$170,825.00	$167,725.00	$508,000.00

ON YOUR OWN

1. Start Word and open 🖮OWD87-1_*xx*, the letter you created in the On Your Own section of Exercise 87, or open 💿88REQUEST.

2. Save the document as OWD88-1_*xx*.

3. Delete the table from the document.

4. Start Excel and open 🖮OWD87-2_*xx*, the workbook containing the list of books or CDs you created in the On Your Own section of Exercise 87, or open 💿88GIFTS.

5. Save the workbook as OWD88-2_*xx*.

6. Link the worksheet data to the Word document.

7. Change some of the data in the Excel worksheet.

8. Make sure the data updates in the Word document. Manually update the link, if necessary.

9. Close the Excel workbook, saving all changes, and exit Excel.

10. Close the Word document, saving all changes, and exit Word.

■ **Embed Objects**   ■ **Edit Embedded Objects**

Software Skills   Embed data when you do not want a link between the source data and the embedded object. You can edit embedded data without the changes affecting the source. This is useful for illustrating changes that might occur, or for submitting information that might vary depending on the recipient, such as a proposal bid, or a contract.

Application Skills   As the new Training Director at Long Shot, Inc., you are planning a weekend training retreat for upper-level management. The Director of Human Resources has asked you to submit a preliminary budget for the event. In this exercise, you will embed an existing budget in a Word memo. You will then edit and format the object using Excel.

TERMS

Embed To insert an object in a file. The embedded object is not linked to a source file, but it is linked to the source application. You edit the object using the source application, but changes do not affect the source file data.

NOTES

Embed Objects

■ **Embed** an object to insert it into a destination file.

■ There is no link between the original data in the source file and the embedded object; however, you can use all of the source program's commands to edit, format, and manipulate the embedded object.

■ Use the Paste Special command to create an embedded object from existing data.

■ Use the Object button in the Text group on the Insert tab of the Ribbon to create a new embedded object.

■ Embedding an object uses more disk space than linking an object, because the same data is stored in more than one file.

Edit Embedded Objects

■ Edit and format embedded objects using the source program.

■ When you edit embedded objects in Word, the source application commands display in the Word window.

■ Changes you make to the embedded object do not affect the original file.

Edit an embedded Excel Worksheet object in Word

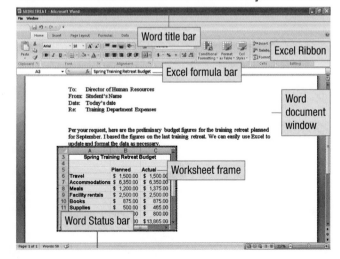

PROCEDURES

Embed Selected Data

1. Open source file.
2. Select data to be copied.
3. Click **Home** tab .... Alt+H

   Clipboard Group

4. Click **Copy** button C

   OR

   a. Right-click selection.
   b. Click **Copy** C
5. Make destination file active.
6. Position insertion point in the desired location.
7. Click **Home** tab .... Alt+H

   Clipboard Group

8. Click **Paste** button drop-down arrow V
9. Click **Paste Special** .... S
10. Click **As** box, if necessary .... Alt+A
11. Click format to use .... ↓/↑
12. Click **Paste** option button .... Alt+P
13. Click **OK** .... ↵Enter

Embed a New Object

1. Open destination file.
2. Position insertion point.
3. Click **Insert** tab .... Alt+N

   Text Group

4. Click the **Object** button .... J, J
5. Click **Create New** tab .... Alt+C
6. Click **Object type** list box .... Alt+O
7. Select object type. .... ↓/↑
8. Click **OK**. .... ↵Enter

   ✓ *Selected application opens.*

9. Enter, edit, and format data to create object.
10. Click outside of object to close source application and display object in destination file.

Embed Entire File

1. Open destination file.
2. Position insertion point.
3. Click **Insert** tab .... Alt+N

   Text Group

4. Click the **Object** button .... J, J
5. Click **Create from File** tab .... Alt+F
6. Click **Browse** .... Alt+B
7. Locate and select file.
8. Click **Insert** .... Alt+S
9. Click **OK** .... ↵Enter

Edit Embedded Object

1. Open file containing embedded object.
2. Double-click embedded object.

   ✓ *Source application commands display within destination application.*

3. Edit embedded data using source application commands.
4. Click outside embedded object to close source application.

EXERCISE DIRECTIONS

Embed an Excel Object in a Word Document

1. Start Word, if necessary.
2. Create the document shown in Illustration A, or open ⊙89RETREAT.
3. Save the document as **89RETREAT_xx**.
4. Replace the sample text *Your Name* with your name.
5. Replace the sample text *Today's date* with the current date.
6. Position the insertion point on the blank line at the end of the document.
7. Start Excel and open the workbook file ⊙89BUDGET.
8. Save the file as **89BUDGET_xx**.

9. Embed the cells A3:C13 as an Excel Worksheet Object on the last line of the Word document.

   a. Select cells A3 through C13.

   ✓ *Click cell A3, press and hold Shift, and then click cell C13.*

   b. Copy the selection to the Clipboard.
   c. Position the insertion point at the end of the Word document.
   d. Choose the Paste Special command.
   e. Select the Microsoft Office Excel Worksheet Object as the format type.
   f. Select the Paste option button.
   g. Click OK.
10. Close the **89BUDGET_xx** file and exit Excel.

Edit and Format the Embedded Object

1. Double-click the Excel object in the Word document.

   ✓ *Excel commands become available in Word.*

2. Edit the worksheet title from *Spring Training Retreat Budget* to **Fall Training Retreat Budget**.

   a. Click cell A3 in the embedded object.

   b. Type **Fall Training Retreat Budget** and press Enter, or click in the Formula bar, replace the text *Spring* with the text **Fall**, and then press Enter.

3. Delete all of the data from the Actual column.

   a. Select cells C5:C13.

   b. Press Delete.

4. Apply the 20% - Accent 1 cell style to cell A3.

   a. Select cell A3.

   b. Click the Cell Styles button drop-down arrow in the Styles group on the Home tab of the Ribbon.

   c. Click the 20% - Accent 1 style in the gallery.

5. Apply the 60% - Accent 1 cell style to cells A5:A13.

   a. Select cells A5:A13.

   b. Click the Cell Styles button drop-down arrow in the Styles group on the Home tab of the Ribbon.

   c. Click the 60% - Accent 1 style in the gallery.

6. Increase the font size of the data in cells A3:C13 to 12 points.

   a. Select cells A3:C13.

   b. Click the Font Size drop-down arrow in the Font group on the Home tab of the Ribbon.

   c. Click 12.

7. If necessary, adjust the widths of columns A and B so all data is visible.

   ■ Drag borders between columns, or double-click borders between columns on worksheet frame.

8. Click outside the embedded object to close Excel.

9. Center the embedded object horizontally on the page.

   ■ Click the object to select it, and then click the Center button on the Home tab of the Ribbon.

10. Check the spelling and grammar in the document.

11. Save the document and preview it. It should look similar to the one in Illustration B.

12. Print the document.

13. Start Excel and open the worksheet **89BUDGET_***xx*. Notice that the changes you made to the object in Word did not affect the original worksheet.

14. Close the worksheet and exit Excel.

15. Close the **89RETREAT_***xx* document, saving all changes.

Illustration A

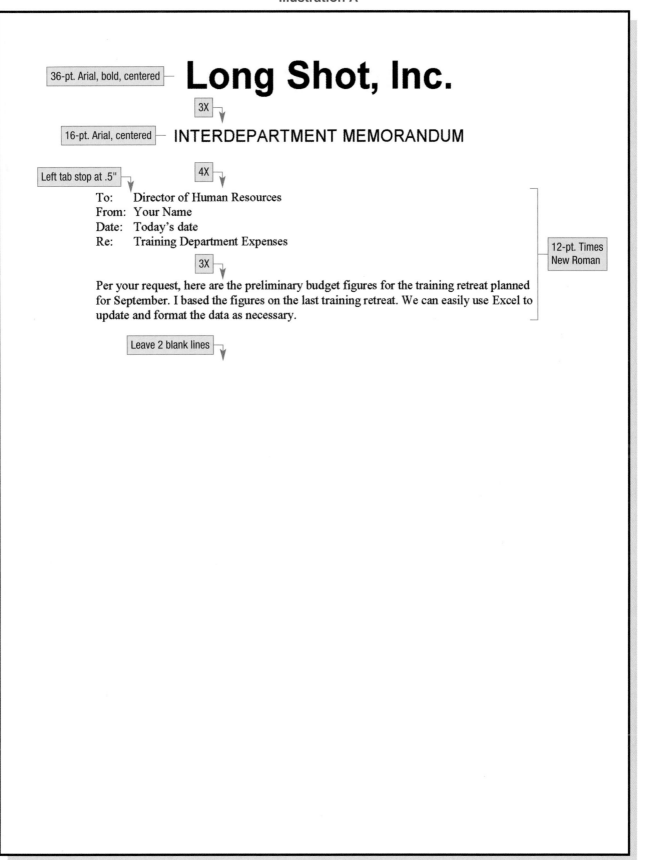

36-pt. Arial, bold, centered

Long Shot, Inc.

3X

16-pt. Arial, centered

INTERDEPARTMENT MEMORANDUM

Left tab stop at .5"

4X

To: Director of Human Resources
From: Your Name
Date: Today's date
Re: Training Department Expenses

12-pt. Times New Roman

3X

Per your request, here are the preliminary budget figures for the training retreat planned for September. I based the figures on the last training retreat. We can easily use Excel to update and format the data as necessary.

Leave 2 blank lines

Long Shot, Inc.

INTERDEPARTMENT MEMORANDUM

To: Director of Human Resources
From: Student's Name
Date: Today's date
Re: Training Department Expenses

Per your request, here are the preliminary budget figures for the training retreat planned for September. I based the figures on the last training retreat. We can easily use Excel to update and format the data as necessary.

Fall Training Retreat Budget

	Planned
Travel	$ 1,500.00
Accommodations	$ 6,350.00
Meals	$ 1,200.00
Facility rentals	$ 2,500.00
Books	$ 875.00
Supplies	$ 500.00
Miscellaneous	$ 1,000.00
Total	$ 13,925.00

ON YOUR OWN

1. Start Word and open OWD88-1, the letter you modified in the On Your Own section of Exercise 88, or open 89REQUEST.

   ✓ *If Word prompts you to update links, click No.*

2. Save the document as **OWD89-1_*xx***.

3. Delete the linked object from the document.

4. Start Excel and open OWD88-2, the worksheet containing the list of books or CDs you created in the On Your Own section of Exercise 88, or open 89GIFTS.

5. Save the file as **OWD89-2_*xx***.

6. Embed the worksheet data into the Word document.

7. Close the Excel worksheet and exit Excel.

8. Use Excel to edit the data in the embedded object in the Word document.

9. Apply formatting to the embedded object.

10. If you want, check to see that the original data has not changed in Excel.

11. Print the Word document.

12. Close the Word document, saving all changes, and exit Word.

- Insert SmartArt
- Insert a Chart

- Enter Chart Data
- Modify a Chart

Software Skills Charts are an effective way to illustrate numeric data and trends. For example, you can use charts to plot sales over time, compare projected income to actual income, or to show a breakdown in revenue sources. You can use Word's SmartArt tool to create diagrams and organization chart objects in any Word document. You can also use the Chart tool to create other types of graphs and charts. You can enter new data to create the chart, or you can copy data from an existing source, such as a table or an Excel worksheet.

Application Skills As the person in charge of researching the feasibility of the home delivery service for Blue Sky Dairy, you have recently completed two surveys of people in your target areas. The first asked a group of 100 people how likely they were to use a dairy home delivery service. The second asked groups in each of four target areas whether they would be more likely to use a dairy home delivery service for milk, ice cream, eggs, or butter. In this exercise, you will create charts detailing this information and include them in a memo to the company owner. You will also include an organization chart for the project.

TERMS

Cell The rectangular area at the intersection of a column and row where you enter data in a worksheet.

Chart object A chart embedded in a Word document.

Chart title The name of the chart.

Data axis The scale used to measure the data in the chart. The Y axis shows the vertical scale, and the X axis shows the horizontal scale.

Data label Text that identifies the units plotted on the chart, such as months or dollar values.

Data range A range of cells in which you may enter data.

Data series A range of values plotted in a chart.

Diagram A chart or graph usually used to illustrate a concept or describe the relationship of parts to a whole.

Legend The key that identifies what each color or symbol in the chart represents.

Organization chart A chart that depicts hierarchical relationships, such as a family tree or corporate management.

NOTES

Insert SmartArt

■ Word 2007 comes with a set of SmartArt graphics objects that you can insert to create **diagrams** and charts in a document.

■ SmartArt is organized into the following categories, and each category contains a selection of object types::

  ● List
  ● Process
  ● Cycle
  ● Hierarchy
  ● Relationship
  ● Matrix
  ● Pyramid

■ Use SmartArt graphics to illustrate information, concepts, and ideas such as the relationship between employees in an **organization chart**, or the steps in a procedure.

■ To insert SmartArt, click the SmartArt button in the Illustrations group on the Insert tab of the Ribbon.

■ You then select a category and a specific object to insert in the Choose a SmartArt Graphic dialog box.

■ To add text to the diagram, you can type in the text pane that displays when you create the object, or directly in the SmartArt object.

■ To format the object, use the commands on the SmartArt Tools Format tab on the Ribbon.

■ Many of the formatting commands are the same as those for formatting pictures, shapes, and text boxes. For example, you can resize the diagram, apply styles, set text wrapping, and position the object on the page.

■ You can also change design elements of the diagram using the SmartArt Tools Design tab on the Ribbon.

Choose a SmartArt Graphic dialog box

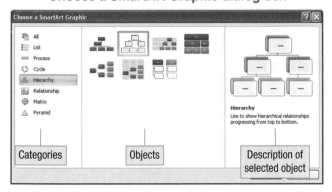

Insert a Chart

■ Word comes with a Chart tool that lets you use Microsoft Office Excel charting features to embed **chart objects** in Word documents.

■ To create the chart, you click the Chart button in the Illustrations group on the Insert tab of the Ribbon to open the Insert Chart dialog box.

■ In the Insert Chart dialog box, you choose from a wide selection of chart types and subtypes, which you can use to plot your data.

Insert Chart dialog box

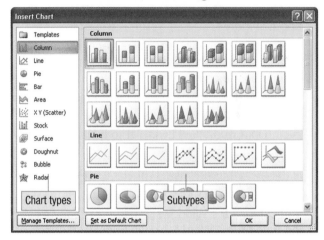

■ Some of the chart types available include the following:

  ● *Column* Compares values across categories in vertical columns.
  ● *Line* Displays trends over time or categories.
  ● *Pie* Displays the contributions of each value to a total value. Often used to show percentages of a whole.
  ● *Bar* Compares values across categories in horizontal bars.
  ● *Area* Displays trends over time or categories by showing the contribution of each value to the whole.
  ● *XY (Scatter)* Compares pairs of values.

■ Additional chart types include Stock, Surface, Doughnut, Bubble, and Radar.

Enter Chart Data

- When you select to insert a chart, Word creates the chart object in the document, and then displays an Excel worksheet where you enter the chart data.
- When you insert a chart with Word, Excel opens with sample data entered in a **data range** in the worksheet.
- The data is organized for the type of chart you selected.
- For example, if you select to create a Column chart, the top row in the worksheet displays sample **data labels** for three columns: *Series1, Series2,* and *Series3*.
- The left column displays sample **data series** labels for four rows: *Category1, Category2, Category3,* and *Category4*.
- To create your own chart, you replace the sample data in the worksheet **cells**. Excel automatically generates the chart.
- You can resize the data range by dragging its lower right corner, if necessary.
- Typing in a worksheet is similar to typing in a Word table.

    ✓ *For more information on entering data in tables, see Exercise 40.*

- You can use the Windows Clipboard to copy existing data from a Word table, an Excel worksheet, or an Access table into a chart's Excel worksheet.

Modify a Chart

- Charts are linked to the data you enter in the Excel worksheet, so when you edit the worksheet, the chart changes, too.
- To open the Excel worksheet to edit a chart, click the Edit Data button in the Data group on the Chart Tools Design tab of the Ribbon.
- You can change the chart type by selecting a different type in the Change Chart Type dialog box.
- You can resize and position a chart object the same way you do other graphics objects in a Word document.

    ✓ *For more information on working with graphics objects, see Lesson 10.*

- You can apply a chart layout, which controls the way chart elements are positioned in the chart.
- You can also apply a chart style to quickly format the chart elements with color and effects.
- Alternatively, you can select to display and format different elements of the chart, including the **chart titles**, the **data axis** names, the **legend**, gridlines, and the data labels.

PROCEDURES

Insert SmartArt

1. Click **Insert** tab .... `Alt`+`N`

    Illustrations Group

2. Click **SmartArt** button 🖼 .... `M`

    ✓ *The Choose a SmartArt Graphic dialog box displays.*

3. Click a category in the left pane .... `↓`/`↑`
4. Click an object in the center pane .... `Tab⇄`, `↓`/`↑`/`←`/`→`
5. Click **OK** .... `←Enter`
6. Type text and apply formatting as necessary.

Format SmartArt

To apply a fill:

1. Click object to select it.
2. Click the **SmartArt Tools Format** tab .... `Alt`+`J`, `O`

    Shape Styles Group

3. Click **Shape Fill** button 🎨▾ drop-down arrow .... `S`, `F`

    ✓ *To quickly apply color displayed on button, click button instead of drop-down arrow.*

4. Click color to apply .... `←`/`→`/`↑`/`↓`, `←Enter`
    OR
    Click one of the following:
    - **No Fill** to remove current fill .... `N`
    - **More Fill Colors** to select a custom color .... `M`
    - **Picture** to select options for a picture fill .... `P`
    - **Gradient** to select a gradient fill .... `G`
    - **Texture** to select a texture fill .... `T`

To apply an outline:

1. Click object to select it.
2. Click the **SmartArt Tools Format** tab .... Alt+J, O

Shape Styles Group

3. Click **Shape Outline** button ☑▾ drop-down arrow .... S, O

   ✓ *To quickly apply color displayed on button, click button instead of drop-down arrow.*

4. Click color to apply .... ←/→/↑/↓, ↵Enter

   OR

   Click one of the following:

   - **No Outline** to remove current outline .... N
   - **More Outline Colors** to select a custom color .... M
   - **Weight** to select a line weight .... W
   - **Dashes** to select a dash style .... S
   - **Arrows** to select an arrow style .... R

To apply a style:

1. Click object to select it.
2. Click the **SmartArt Tools Format** tab .... Alt+J, O

Shape Styles Group

3. Click style in Shape Styles Gallery.

   ✓ *If necessary, use scroll arrows to scroll the gallery.*

   OR

   a. Click **More** button ▼ .... S, S
   b. Click style to apply ..... ←/→/↑/↓, ↵Enter

To apply effects:

1. Click object to select it.
2. Click the **SmartArt Tools Format** tab .... Alt+J, O

Shape Styles Group

3. Click the **Shape Effects** button ▢ .... S, E
4. Click desired category of effect .... ↓/↑
5. Click desired effect .... ↓/↑/←/→, ↵Enter

To resize the object precisely:

1. Click object to select it.
2. Click the **SmartArt Tools Format** tab .... Alt+J, O
3. Click the **Size Group** button ▣ .... Z, Z

Size Group

4. Click **Shape Height** box ▯ 1.51" ▢ .... H
5. Type height in inches .... *type height*, ↵Enter

   OR

   Click increment arrows to enter height.
6. Click **Shape Width** box ▯ 1.43" ▢ .... Alt+J, O, Z, Z, W
7. Type width in inches .... *type width*, ↵Enter

   OR

   Click increment arrows to enter width.

To position the object:

1. Click object to select it.
2. Click the **SmartArt Tools Format** tab .... Alt+J, O
3. Click the **Arrange Group** button ▣ .... Z, A

Arrange Group

4. Click **Position** button ▣ ... P, O
5. Click position to apply .... ↓/←/→/↑, ↵Enter

To align the object:

1. Click object to select it.
2. Click the **SmartArt Tools Format** tab .... Alt+J, O
3. Click the **Arrange Group** button ▣ .... Z, A

Arrange Group

4. Click **Align** button ▣▾ ..... A, A
5. Click alignment option:
   - **Align Left** L
   - **Align Center** C
   - **Align Right** .... R
   - **Align Top** .... T
   - **Align Middle** .... M
   - **Align Bottom** .... B

To select to align to the page or the margin:

1. Click object to select it.
2. Click the **SmartArt Tools Format** tab .... Alt+J, O
3. Click the **Arrange Group** button ▣ .... Z, A

Arrange Group

4. Click **Align** button ▣▾ ..... A, A
5. Click one of the following:
   - **Align to Page** to align object with the page .... P
   - **Align to Margin** to align object with the margins .... A

To set text wrapping:

1. Click object to select it.
2. Click the **SmartArt Tools Format** tab .... Alt+J, O
3. Click the **Arrange Group** button ▣ .... A, A

Arrange Group

4. Click **Text Wrapping** button ▣ .... T, W

5. Click desired option:
   - **I**n Line With Text .... Ⓘ
   - **S**quare .... Ⓢ
   - **T**ight .... Ⓣ
   - Behin**d** Text .... Ⓓ
   - I**n** Front of Text .... Ⓝ
   - T**o**p and Bottom .... Ⓞ
   - Th**r**ough .... Ⓗ

To delete an object:

1. Click object to select it.
2. Press **Delete** .... Ⓓⓔⓛ

Create a Chart

1. Position insertion point in document.
2. Click **Insert** tab .... Ⓐⓛⓣ+Ⓝ

   Illustrations Group

3. Click the **Chart** button 📊 .... Ⓒ
4. Click chart type .... Ⓓ/Ⓤ
5. Click chart
   subtype .... Ⓣⓐⓑ, Ⓓ/Ⓤ/Ⓛ/Ⓡ
6. Click **OK** .... ↵Enter

   ✓ Chart is created with sample data entered in worksheet.

To enter data in worksheet:

1. Click in worksheet cell.
2. Type new data.
3. Press **Tab** to move to cell to right .... Ⓣⓐⓑ

   ✓ Use the arrow keys to move to other cells in the datasheet.

4. Type new data.
5. Repeat steps 3 and 4 until data is entered.

To change size of chart data range:

- Drag lower-right corner of current range to new position.

To edit data in worksheet:

1. Select chart object.
2. Click **Chart Tools Design** tab .... Ⓐⓛⓣ+Ⓙ, Ⓒ

   Data Group

3. Click the **Edit Data** button 📊 .... Ⓓ
4. Click in worksheet cell.
5. Type new data.
6. Press **Tab** to move to cell to right .... Ⓣⓐⓑ

   ✓ Use the arrow keys to move to other cells in the datasheet.

7. Type new data.
8. Repeat steps 6 and 7 until data is edited.

Copy Data into a Chart's Worksheet

1. Select table or worksheet data to copy in source file.
2. Click **Home** tab .... Ⓐⓛⓣ+Ⓗ

   Clipboard Group

3. Click **Copy** button 📋 .... Ⓒ
   OR
   a. Right-click selection.
   b. Click **Copy** .... Ⓒ
4. Open Word document and select chart object.
5. Click **Chart Tools Design** tab .... Ⓐⓛⓣ+Ⓙ, Ⓒ

   Data Group

6. Click the **Edit Data** button 📊 .... Ⓓ
7. Click cell in datasheet where inserted data should start.
8. Click **Home** tab .... Ⓐⓛⓣ+Ⓗ

   Clipboard Group

9. Click **Paste** button 📋 ...... Ⓥ, Ⓟ
   OR
   a. Right-click insertion point location.
   b. Click **Paste** .... Ⓟ, ↵Enter

Change Chart Type

1. Open Word document and select chart object.
2. Click **Chart Tools Design** tab .... Ⓐⓛⓣ+Ⓙ, Ⓒ

   Type Group

3. Click the **Change Chart Type** button 📊 .... Ⓒ
4. Click chart type .... Ⓓ/Ⓤ
5. Click chart
   subtype .... Ⓣⓐⓑ, Ⓓ/Ⓤ/Ⓛ/Ⓡ
6. Click **OK** .... ↵Enter

Switch the Display of Rows and Columns

1. Open Word document and select chart object.
2. Click **Chart Tools Design** tab .... Ⓐⓛⓣ+Ⓙ, Ⓒ

   Data Group

3. Click the **Switch Row/Column** button 📊 .... Ⓦ

Apply Chart Layout

1. Open Word document and select chart object.
2. Click **Chart Tools Design** tab .... Ⓐⓛⓣ+Ⓙ, Ⓒ

   Chart Layouts Group

3. Click the **Chart Layouts More** button ▾ .... Ⓛ
4. Click layout to
   apply .... Ⓓ/Ⓤ/Ⓛ/Ⓡ, ↵Enter

Apply Chart Style

1. Open Word document and select chart object.
2. Click **Chart Tools Design** tab .... Alt + J , C

   Chart Styles Group

3. Click the **Chart Styles More** button ⮟ .... S
4. Click style to apply .... ↓ / ↑ / ← / → , ↵Enter

Display Chart Elements

To display chart title:

1. Open Word document and select chart object.
2. Click **Chart Tools Layout** tab .... Alt + J , A

   Labels Group

3. Click the **Chart Title** button .... T
4. Click chart title option to apply .... ↓ / ↑ , ↵Enter

   ✓ *Click More Title Options to display additional options for positioning and formatting titles.*

To display axis titles:

1. Open Word document and select chart object.
2. Click **Chart Tools Layout** tab .... Alt + J , A

   Labels Group

3. Click the **Axis Title** button I
4. Click one of the following:
   - **Primary Horizontal Axis Title** .... H
   - **Primary Vertical Axis Title** V
5. Click axis position to option .... ↓ / ↑ , ↵Enter

   ✓ *Click More Axis Title Options to display additional options for positioning and formatting titles.*

To display legend:

1. Open Word document and select chart object.
2. Click **Chart Tools Layout** tab .... Alt + J , A

   Labels Group

3. Click the **Legend** button L
4. Click legend option to apply .... ↓ / ↑ , ↵Enter

   ✓ *Click More Legend Options to display additional options for positioning and formatting legend.*

To display data labels:

1. Open Word document and select chart object.
2. Click **Chart Tools Layout** tab .... Alt + J , A

   Labels Group

3. Click the **Data Labels** button .... B
4. Click data label option to apply .... ↓ / ↑ , ↵Enter

   ✓ *Click More Data Label Options to display additional options for positioning and formatting data labels.*

To display data table:

1. Open Word document and select chart object.
2. Click **Chart Tools Layout** tab .... Alt + J , A

   Labels Group

3. Click the **Data Table** button .... D
4. Click data table option to apply .... ↓ / ↑ , ↵Enter

   ✓ *Click More Data Table Options to display additional options for positioning and formatting data table.*

To display axis:

1. Open Word document and select chart object.
2. Click **Chart Tools Layout** tab .... Alt + J , A

   Axes Group

3. Click the **Axes** button .... A
4. Click one of the following:
   - **Primary Horizontal Axis** .... H
   - **Primary Vertical Axis** V
5. Click axis option to apply .... ↓ / ↑ , ↵Enter

   ✓ *Click More Axis Options to display additional options for positioning and formatting axis.*

To display gridlines:

1. Open Word document and select chart object.
2. Click **Chart Tools Layout** tab .... Alt + J , A

   Axes Group

3. Click the **Gridlines** button .... G
4. Click one of the following:
   - **Primary Horizontal Gridlines** .... H
   - **Primary Vertical Gridlines** V
5. Click gridline option to apply .... ↓ / ↑ , ↵Enter

   ✓ *Click More Gridline Options to display additional options for positioning and formatting axis.*

Edit Text Labels

1. Open Word document and select chart object.
2. Click element to edit.
3. Type new text.

Format Chart

To apply a fill:

1. Click chart to select it.
2. Click the **Chart Tools Format**
   tab .... Alt+J, O

   Shape Styles Group

3. Click **Shape Fill** button [⬧ ▾] drop-
   down arrow .... S, F

   ✓ *To quickly apply color displayed on*
   button, click button instead of
   drop-down arrow.

4. Click color to
   apply .... ←/→/↑/↓, ↵Enter
   OR
   Click one of the following:
   - **No Fill** to remove current
     fill .... N
   - **More Fill Colors** to select a
     custom color .... M
   - **Picture** to select options for a
     picture fill .... P
   - **Gradient** to select a gradient
     fill .... G
   - **Texture** to select a texture
     fill .... T

To apply an outline:

1. Click chart to select it.
2. Click the **Chart Tools Format**
   tab .... Alt+J, O

   Shape Styles Group

3. Click **Shape Outline** button [✎ ▾]
   drop-down arrow .... S, O

   ✓ *To quickly apply color displayed on*
   button, click button instead of
   drop-down arrow.

4. Click color to
   apply .... ←/→/↑/↓, ↵Enter
   OR
   Click one of the following:
   - **No Outline** to remove current
     outline .... N
   - **More Outline Colors** to select a
     custom color .... M
   - **Weight** to select a line
     weight .... W
   - **Dashes** to select a dash
     style .... S
   - **Arrows** to select an arrow
     style .... R

To apply a style:

1. Click chart to select it.
2. Click the **Chart Tools Format**
   tab .... Alt+J, O

   Shape Styles Group

3. Click style in Shape Styles
   Gallery.

   ✓ *If necessary, use scroll arrows to*
   scroll the gallery.

   OR
   a. Click **More**
      button [▾] .... S, S
   b. Click style to
      apply ..... ←/→/↑/↓, ↵Enter

To apply effects:

1. Click chart to select it.
2. Click the **Chart Tools Format**
   tab .... Alt+J, O

   Shape Styles Group

3. Click the **Shape Effects**
   button [◻] .... S, E
4. Click desired category of
   effect .... ↓/↑
5. Click desired
   effect .... ↓/↑/←/→, ↵Enter

To resize the chart precisely:

1. Click chart to select it.
2. Click the **Chart Tools Format**
   tab .... Alt+J, O
3. Click the **Size Group**
   button [⬚] .... Z, Z

   Size Group

4. Click **Shape Height**
   box [⬚ 1.51" ▾] .... H
5. Type height in
   inches .... *type height*, ↵Enter
   OR
   Click increment arrows to
   enter height.
6. Click **Shape Width** box
   [⬚ 1.43" ▾] .... Alt+J, O, Z,
                                Z, W
7. Type width in
   inches .... *type width*, ↵Enter
   OR
   Click increment arrows to
   enter width.

To position the chart:

1. Click chart to select it.
2. Click the **Chart Tools Format**
   tab .... Alt+J, O
3. Click the **Arrange Group**
   button [⬚] .... Z, A

   Arrange Group

4. Click **Position** button [⬚] .. P, O
5. Click position to
   apply .... ↓/←/→/↑, ↵Enter

To align the chart:

1. Click chart to select it.
2. Click the **Chart Tools Format**
   tab .... Alt+J, O
3. Click the **Arrange Group**
   button [⬚] .... Z, A

   Arrange Group

4. Click **Align** button [⬚ ▾] ..... A, A

5. Click alignment option:
   - **Align Left**..........................⬜ L
   - **Align Center**.......................⬜ C
   - **Align Right**.........................⬜ R
   - **Align Top**...........................⬜ T
   - **Align Middle**.......................⬜ M
   - **Align Bottom**......................⬜ B

To select to align to the page or the margin:

1. Click chart to select it.
2. Click the **Chart Tools Format** tab...............................Alt+J, O
3. Click the **Arrange Group** button 🔲..........................Z, A

   Arrange Group

4. Click **Align** button 📊.......A, A
5. Click one of the following:
   - **Align to Page** to align object with the page.................P
   - **Align to Margin** to align object with the margins............A

To set text wrapping:

1. Click chart to select it.
2. Click the **Chart Tools Format** tab................Alt+J, O
3. Click the **Arrange Group** button 🔲.................A, A

   Arrange Group

4. Click **Text Wrapping** button ❌................T, W
5. Click desired option:
   - **In Line With Text**............I
   - **Square**......................S
   - **Tight**.......................T
   - **Behind Text**.................D
   - **In Front of Text**............N
   - **Top and Bottom**.............O
   - **Through**.....................H

To delete a chart:

1. Click chart to select it.
2. Press **Delete**..................Del

Format Chart Elements

1. Right-click element in chart.
2. Select **Format** *element name* from shortcut menu.
3. Select desired formatting options.
4. Click **OK**....................↵Enter

EXERCISE DIRECTIONS

Create Chart 1

1. Start Word, if necessary.
2. Create the document shown in Illustration A, or open 🔘**90CHARTS**.
3. Save the document as **90CHARTS_*xx***.
4. Position the insertion point on the blank line at the end of the document.
5. Insert a Clustered Column chart object.
6. Replace the sample data in the worksheet with the following:

	No	Maybe	Yes	Don't Know
Responses	10	38	49	3

7. Delete the sample data not replaced by new data in rows 2 and 3 as follows:
   a. Click the row number in the worksheet frame.
   b. Press Delete.
8. Resize the data range to include only the cells that contain data (A1:E2).

   ✓ *Drag the lower-right corner of the data range up to the lower right corner of cell E2.*

9. Minimize the worksheet.

10. Change the chart type to Pie in 3-D.
11. Switch the display of rows and columns to change the data series.
12. Edit the title to **Likely to Purchase Home Delivery** and change the font size to 12 points.
13. Hide the chart legend.
14. Display data labels and format them to display category names and percentages, with leader lines.
    a. Right-click a data label.
    b. Click Format Data Labels.
    c. Select the check boxes for Category Name, Percentage, and Show Leader Lines.
    d. Deselect all other check boxes.
    e. Click OK.
15. Display the worksheet and change the number of responses for *Maybe* to **36** and the number for *Yes* to **51**. Notice the changes in the chart.
16. Resize the chart object to 3.5" wide by 2.06" high.
17. Drag the data labels to position them so they can be seen clearly.
18. Set the text wrapping for the chart to square, and center it horizontally relative to the margins.

Create Chart 2

1. Insert a new blank line at the end of the document.
2. Insert a Clustered Column chart.
3. In Excel, open the workbook file 🔘 **90SURVEY**.
4. Copy the data in cells A4:E8 to the Clipboard.

   ✓ *Click cell A4, press and hold Shift, then click cell E8. Click the Copy button.*

5. Switch to the chart's worksheet in Excel.
6. Position the insertion point in the upper-left cell of the worksheet.
7. Paste the data from the Clipboard into the worksheet.
8. Minimize the worksheet.
9. Resize the chart to about 3.75" wide by 2.5" high.
10. Overlay the title **Product Preference by Area** on the chart, using a 12-point font.
11. Set text wrapping for the chart to square, and center it horizontally relative to the margins.
12. Preview the document. It should look similar to Illustration B.

    ✓ *If necessary, adjust the vertical position of the chart objects.*

13. Exit Excel.

Create Chart 3

1. Move the insertion point to the end of the document and insert a page break.
2. On the new page, type the following using a 22-point serif font, centered:

   Home Delivery Service
   Organization Chart

3. Leave two blank lines and then insert a SmartArt Organization Chart graphic as follows:
   a. Click the SmartArt button in the Illustrations group on the Insert tab.
   b. Select the Hierarchy group.
   c. Select the Organization Chart object.
   d. Click OK.
4. Fill in the default shapes as follows:
   - Top: **Director of Services**
   - Third row left: **Driver Manager**
   - Third row middle: **Inventory Manager**
   - Third row right: **Customer Service Manager**
5. Delete the shape on the second row.
6. Add a shape as follows:
   a. Right-click the Driver Manager shape.
   b. Point to Add Shape.
   c. Click Add Shape Below.
   d. Type the text: **Two Drivers**.
7. Add another shape as follows:
   a. Right-click the Customer Service Manager shape.
   b. Point to Add Shape.
   c. Click Add Shape Below.
   d. Type the text: **Two Customer Service Representatives**.
8. Apply the Intense Effect SmartArt style.
9. Insert a plain page number centered on the bottom of both pages in the document.
10. Check the grammar and spelling in the document.
11. Preview the document. Page 2 should look similar to Illustration C.
12. Print both pages of the document.
13. Close the document, saving all changes, and exit Word.

Illustration A

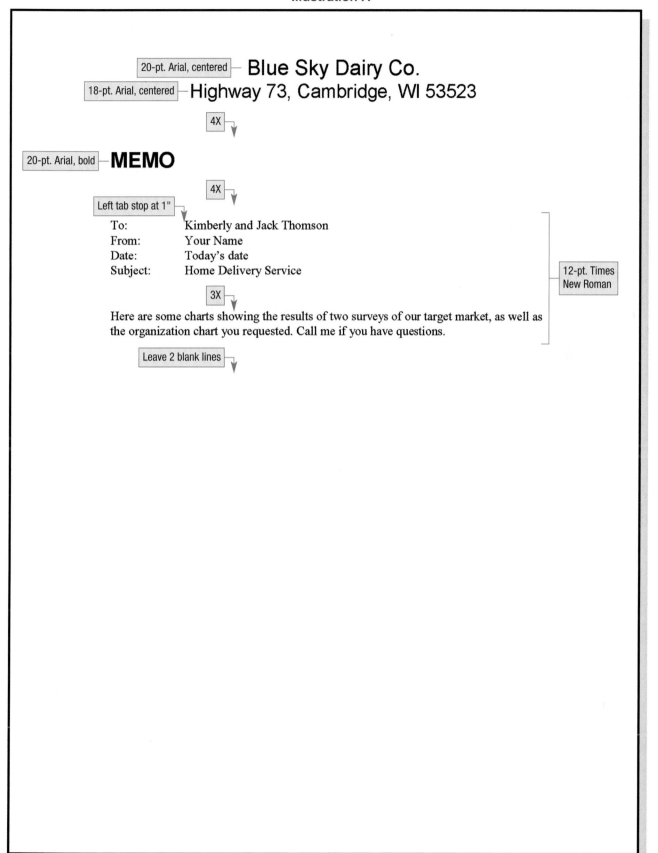

20-pt. Arial, centered — **Blue Sky Dairy Co.**

18-pt. Arial, centered — **Highway 73, Cambridge, WI 53523**

4X

20-pt. Arial, bold — **MEMO**

4X

Left tab stop at 1"

To: Kimberly and Jack Thomson
From: Your Name
Date: Today's date
Subject: Home Delivery Service

3X

Here are some charts showing the results of two surveys of our target market, as well as the organization chart you requested. Call me if you have questions.

12-pt. Times New Roman

Leave 2 blank lines

Blue Sky Dairy Co.
Highway 73, Cambridge, WI 53523

MEMO

To: Kimberly and Jack Thomson
From: Your Name
Date: Today's date
Subject: Home Delivery Service

Here are some charts showing the results of two surveys of our target market, as well as the organization chart you requested. Call me if you have questions.

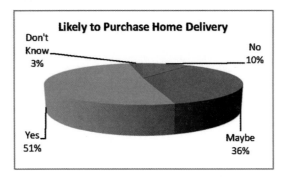

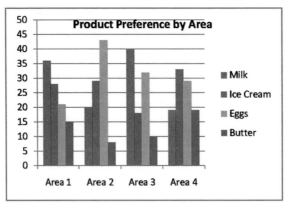

Illustration C

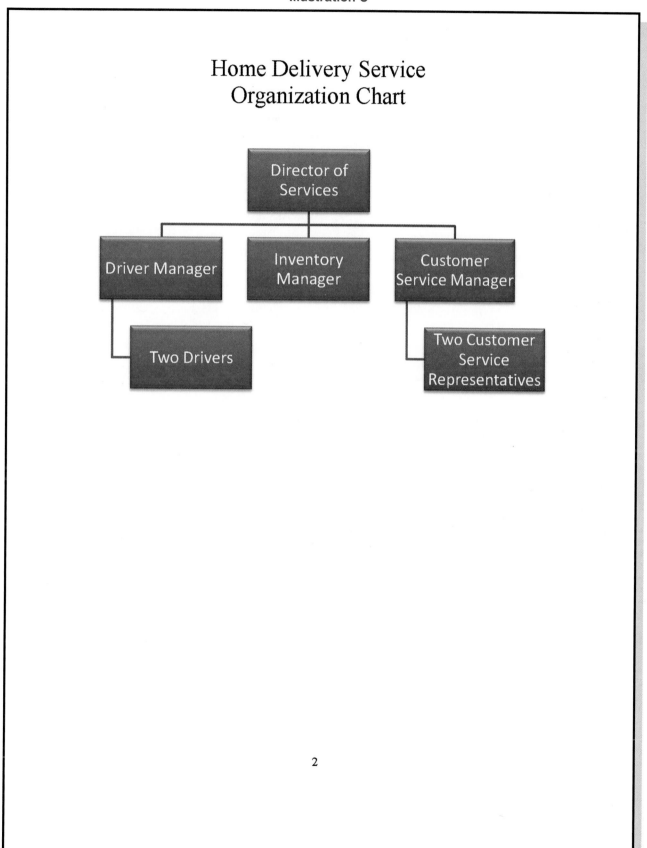

Home Delivery Service
Organization Chart

2

ON YOUR OWN

1. Start Word and create a new document.

2. Save the document as **OWD90_xx**.

3. Type a letter, memo, or note to a friend or relative explaining that you are planning an event. The event might be a party, a graduation, a fundraiser, or anything you want. You can even use the same event you used in earlier On Your Own exercises.

4. Explain that you have surveyed people involved with planning or attending the event and that the results indicate when the event should be held. For example, some people might want the event in the morning, some in the afternoon, and some at night. Alternatively, explain that the survey indicates the type of event people want, such as a bowling party, a barbeque, or a dance.

5. Insert a chart in the memo to illustrate the results of your survey.

6. Enter the data in the datasheet; add a title and any necessary labels.

7. Select the chart type that best illustrates your data. For example, use a pie chart to show percentages of a whole, or a line chart to show values over time.

8. Save the document.

9. Preview it. If necessary, change the formatting of the chart.

10. Print the document.

11. Ask a classmate to review the document and make comments or suggestions.

12. Incorporate the comments and suggestions into the document.

13. Close the document, saving all changes.

Curriculum Connection: Mathematics

Trends

A trend is a measurable change in a set of data over a period of time. You can use a chart or graph to create a visual representation of a trend. One axis—usually the X—shows the time period, while the other axis—usually the Y—shows the changes in the data. A line graph is useful if the change is small, while a bar graph is better for depicting larger changes.

Plot a Trend

Select a set of data that you think will change over the course of a week. For example, you might select the daily rainfall, the daily high temperature, the number of students who are absent each day, or even how many students bring lunch to school. Create a document and write a paragraph explaining the trend you are following, and what you expect to happen. Then, track the trend by recording the data for each day of the week. At the end of the week, create a graph in your document that shows the trend over time. Write a new paragraph explaining the trend.

Skills Covered

- ■ Convert a Table to Text
- ■ Convert Text to a Table

Software Skills You can quickly use Word commands to convert existing text into a table or an existing table into document text. These features can be particularly helpful for exchanging data with Excel, because you can make Excel data more readable by converting it to text, and make Word data easier to copy to a worksheet by converting it to a table.

Application Skills You have been working with the President of the Horticultural Shop Owners Association to select a location for a national meeting. You have information about different cities stored in an Excel worksheet. In this exercise, you will copy the Excel data to a Word document, and convert it to paragraph text. You will also convert a list of association members who have volunteered to help into a table.

TERMS

Separator character A character such as a comma or a tab used to delineate the location where text should be divided into columns and/or rows.

NOTES

Convert a Table to Text

- ■ Convert an entire table or selected table rows into regular document text.

  ✓ *For information about working with Tables, refer to the exercises in Lesson 6.*

- ■ Word inserts the specified separator character into the text at the end of each column.

- ■ Word starts a new paragraph at the end of each row.

- ■ If document text is set to wrap around a table, when you convert the table to text Word inserts the text in a text box.

  ✓ *For information about working with text boxes, refer to Exercise 71.*

Convert Table to Text dialog box

513

Convert Text to a Table

- You can easily convert existing document text into a table format.

- Word automatically divides text into columns based on the location of a specified **separator character** such as a comma or tab.

- Word starts a new row at each paragraph mark.

- When you convert the text into a table, you can specify a column width or an AutoFit behavior.

- For example, you can AutoFit the table to its contents, which adjusts the column width to accommodate the widest content, or you can AutoFit the table to the window, which adjusts the column width to fit within the current window size.

Convert Text to Table dialog box

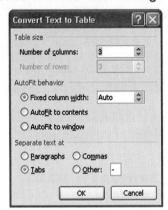

PROCEDURES

Convert a Table to Text

1. Select table to convert.
   OR
   Select rows to convert.
2. Click **Table Tools Layout** tab .... Alt + J , L

   > **Data Group**

3. Click **Convert To Text** button ⬚ V
4. Click separator character to insert:
   - **Paragraph marks** .... Alt + P
   - **Tabs** .... Alt + T
   - **Commas** .... Alt + M
   - **Other** .... Alt + O ,
     type character
5. Click **OK** .... ↵Enter

Convert Text to a Table

1. If necessary, insert separator characters in text where you want new columns to begin.
2. Select text to convert.
3. Click **Insert** tab .... Alt + N

   > **Tables Group**

4. Click the **Table** button ⬚ .... T
5. Click **Convert Text to Table** V
6. If necessary, enter the number of columns to create .... Alt + C , *type number*

7. Select AutoFit behavior:
   - **Fixed column width** .... Alt + W
   - **AutoFit to contents** .... Alt + F
   - **AutoFit to window** .... Alt + D
8. Select separator character used in selected text:
   - **Paragraphs** .... Alt + P
   - **Tabs** .... Alt + T
   - **Commas** .... Alt + M
   - **Other** .... Alt + O ,
     type character
9. Click **OK** .... ↵Enter

EXERCISE DIRECTIONS

1. Start Word, if necessary.
2. Open the Word document ⊙ **91MEMO**.
3. Save the document as **91MEMO_xx**.
4. Replace the sample text *Your Name* with your own name, and the sample text *Today's date* with the current date.
5. Open the Excel workbook ⊙ **91DATA**.

6. Select the data in cells B3:B13 and copy it to the Clipboard.
7. Close the Excel workbook and exit Excel.
8. Make the **91MEMO_xx** document active, and position the insertion point on the second blank line after the first paragraph in the body of the memo.
9. Paste the data from the Clipboard into the document. It is pasted as a table.

10. Select the table, and convert it to text, using paragraph marks as the separator.
11. Select the list of volunteers at the end of the document.
12. Convert the text to a table, selecting to AutoFit the table to the contents, and separating the text at the commas.
13. Apply the Table Contemporary table style to the table.
14. Remove the bold from the first row in the table.
15. Center the table horizontally on the page.
16. Check the spelling and grammar in the document.
17. Preview the document. It should look similar to Illustration A.
18. Print the document.
19. Close the document, saving all changes.

Illustration A

Horticultural Shop Owners Association
452 Cathedral Street ⊛ Baltimore, MD 21201

MEMORANDUM

Date: Today's date
To: Ms. Knowlton
From: Student's Name
Subject: Regional Meetings

Following is a list of potential sites for the national meeting. Let me know if you have a preference.

Cleveland, Ohio
Rock and Roll Hall of Fame
No trip to Cleveland would be complete without paying a visit to the Rock Hall! See exhibits and maybe catch a concert!

Philadelphia, Pennsylvania
Independence Hall
A World Heritage Site where both the Declaration of Independence and the U.S. Constitution were created.

Phoenix, Arizona
The Desert Botanical Garden
Combines desert plants with desert wildlife that can both be seen from short trails that are well marked.

Here is the contact information for the association members who have volunteered to help plan the national meeting:

Alyssa Jenkins	Volunteer	410-555-5678	Mid West
Stephen Knight	Volunteer Coordinator	410-555-7890	Southeast
Jessie Samsonov	Marketing Director	410-555-4321	Mid West
Debra Whist	Public Relations	410-555-7654	Mid Atlantic
Justin Bachman	Fundraising	410-555-6534	Mid Atlantic

ON YOUR OWN

1. Think of a directory list that could be used by someone visiting your school. The list should include at least ten items, with three bits of information about each item. For example, a directory of teachers might include the teacher's name, classroom number, and subject. A directory of athletic teams might include the team name, season, and coach.

2. Start Word and create a new document.

3. Save the document at **OWD91_xx.**

4. Type the directory using tabs to separate each item of information.

5. In the same document, create a table in which you can type information in paragraph form about the directory. For example, in a directory of teachers, the first row might include the teacher's name and the second row might include information about a class he or she teaches, and a third might include a rating, such as four stars. In a directory of teams, the first row might include the team name and the second and third rows might include information about how the team has done in the past, such as a win and loss record.

6. When the document is complete, check the spelling and grammar.

7. Exchange the document with a classmate.

8. Working in the document created by your classmate, convert the table to paragraph text and the tabbed directory into a table.

9. AutoFit the table columns to fit the contents.

10. Adjust spacing and formatting as necessary. For example, center the table horizontally, and use shrink to fit to make the document fit on one page.

11. Preview the document and print it.

12. Give it back to the author.

13. In your original document, make changes or corrections that you think are necessary.

14. Save the document, close it, and exit Word.

Exercise | 92

Skills Covered

- Use the Research Tool
- Copy Data from a Web Page into a Word Document
- Set the View for Opening E-Mail Attachments

Software Skills Use Word's Research tool to locate information about a specific topic. You can select a reference source, or search all available sources, including the Internet. When a Web page is displayed on your computer, print it for future reference or to pass along to someone else. If you don't need to print the entire page, you can copy the data you need into a Word document to save or print for future use.

Application Skills The Horticultural Shop Owners Association has selected Cleveland, Ohio as the location for a national meeting. In this exercise, you will use Word's Research tool to look up information about the Rock and Roll Hall of Fame, which you will copy into a Word document.

TERMS

There are no new terms in this exercise.

NOTES

Use the Research Tool

- Use the Research task pane in Office 2007 programs such as Word to search through online reference sources, such as dictionaries, encyclopedias, and translation services.
- You can search for a keyword, term, or phrase.
- You can locate information such as definitions, synonyms, encyclopedia entries, and even links to relevant Web pages.
- You can select the specific reference tool or service to search from a list of available sources.
- Alternatively, you can select to search all available sources of a particular type, such as all reference books, or all research sites.
- The results of the search are displayed in the Research task pane.
- Some results also display a link to a relevant Web page; click a link to go to the destination.

Research task pane

517

- You can determine which reference sources are available in the Research task pane by adding or removing items from the Services list in the Research Options dialog box.
- You can also add new services to the list, remove services, and update current services.
- Note that some research services require that you sign up for a subscription.
- You can also view the properties for each available service. The properties include a description of the services, copyright information, the provider's name, and the path to the site.

Research Options dialog box

Copy Data from a Web Page to a Word Document

- You can use the Copy and Paste commands to copy data from a Web page into a Word document.
- Remember that copying someone else's work and using it without attribution is plagiarism.
- If you use Web page data in a report or other project, you must cite the source in a footnote, bibliography, or other list of sources.
- If you include a direct quote in your document, you can format it to stand out from the surrounding text using a double-indent and single line spacing.
- It is also important to know whether or not the source is reputable.
- You can copy a URL from an Address bar and paste it into a Word document. This is useful for recording a Web page address that you will need to use in a footnote or bibliography.

  ✓ *For information on Word and the World Wide Web, refer to the exercises in Lesson 5.*

Set the View for Opening E-Mail Attachments

- By default, when you open a document that you receive as an attachment to an e-mail message, it displays in Full Screen Reading view.
- You can use the Word Options dialog box to disable the feature so that the document opens in Print Layout view.

  ✓ *For more information on sending a document as an e-mail attachment, refer to Exercise 37.*

PROCEDURES

Copy Data from a Web Page into a Word Document (Ctrl + C/Ctrl + V)

To use shortcut menus:
1. Display the Web page in your Web browser.
2. Select data to copy.
3. Right-click selection.
4. Click **Copy** C

5. Open Word document.
6. Right-click position where you want to paste the data.
7. Click **Paste** .... P, ⏎Enter

To use menu commands:
1. Display the Web page in your Web browser.
2. Select data to copy.
3. Click **Edit** on your browser's menu bar .... Alt+E

4. Click **Copy** C
5. Open Word document.
6. Position insertion point where you want to paste the data.
7. Click **Home** tab .... Alt+H

   Clipboard Group

8. Click **Paste** button 📋 .... V, P

Use the Research Tool

1. Click the **Review** tab........ Alt+R

   ### Proofing Group

2. Click the **Research** button 🔍 .... R

   ✓ *The Research task pane opens.*

3. Type keyword or topic in Search for box.
4. Click the reference source drop-down arrow .... Tab↹, Tab↹, ↓
5. Click research tool or reference service to search .... ↓/↑
6. Click **Start Searching** button ➡.
7. Click link in Research task pane to display information.

Display Results of a Previous Search

1. Click the **Review** tab........ Alt+R

   ### Proofing Group

2. Click the **Research** button 🔍 .... R

   ✓ *The Research task pane opens.*

3. Click **Previous Search** button 🔙Back to display results of previous search.

   OR

   a. Click **Previous Search** drop-down arrow 🔙Back ▾
   b. Click previous search to display .... ↑/↓, ↵Enter

   OR

   ✓ *Click **Next Search** button 🔜 to display results of search displayed prior to the selected previous search.*

   OR

   a. Click **Next Search** drop-down arrow 🔜▾.
   b. Click search to display .... ↑/↓, ↵Enter

Select Research Services to Use

1. Click the **Review** tab........ Alt+R

   ### Proofing Group

2. Click the **Research** button 🔍 .... R

   ✓ *The Research task pane opens.*

3. Click **Research options** link.
4. Click to select or deselect services to use .... ↓/↑, Spacebar
5. Click **OK** .... ↵Enter

View Research Services Properties

1. Click the **Review** tab........ Alt+R

   ### Proofing Group

2. Click the **Research** button 🔍 .... R

   ✓ *The Research task pane opens.*

3. Click **Research options** link.
4. Click service to view .... ↓/↑
5. Click **Properties** .... Alt+E
6. Click **Close** .... ↵Enter
7. Click **OK**.

Add a Research Service to the Services List

1. Click the **Review** tab........ Alt+R

   ### Proofing Group

2. Click the **Research** button 🔍 .... R

   ✓ *The Research task pane opens.*

3. Click **Research options** link.
4. Click **Add Services** .... Alt+A
5. Type URL address of service to add.
6. Click **Add** .... Alt+D
7. Repeat steps 5 and 6 to add additional services.
8. Click **Close** .... Esc
9. Click **OK**.

Update or Remove a Research Service

1. Click the **Review** tab........ Alt+R

   ### Proofing Group

2. Click the **Research** button 🔍 .... R

   ✓ *The Research task pane opens.*

3. Click **Research options** link.
4. Click **Update/Remove** .... Alt+U
5. Select service or group to update or remove .... ↓/↑
6. Click **Update** .... Alt+U

   OR

   Click **Remove** .... Alt+U

7. Follow instructions to update or remove selected service or group.
8. Click **Close** .... Esc
9. Click **OK**.

Set the View for Opening E-Mail Attachments

1. Open a document.
2. Click the **Office Button** 🗎 .... Alt+F
3. Click **Word Options** I
4. Click to deselect **Open e-mail attachments in Full Screen Reading view** check box .... Alt+F

   ✓ *Select the check box to open e-mail attachments in Full Screen Reading view.*

5. Click **OK** .... ↵Enter

EXERCISE DIRECTIONS

Set Research Options

1. Start Word, if necessary.
2. Open the document ⊙ 92INVITE.
3. Save the file as **92INVITE_xx**.
4. Display the Research task pane.
5. Click the Research options link to display the Research Options dialog box.
6. Verify that the Encarta Dictionary: English (North America) source is selected. If not, select it.
7. Verify that at least one Research Site, such as MSN Search, is selected. If not, select it.
8. With the MSN Search site selected, click the Properties button to review the site's properties.
9. Close the Service Properties dialog box, and then click OK to close the dialog box.

Search for Information

✓ *The steps in this part of the exercise assume you have an Internet connection. If you do not, ask your instructor for more information.*

1. In the Research task pane, type the phrase **Rock Music** in the Search for text box.
2. Select to search the dictionary, and then start the search. The first item in the results list should be a definition of rock and roll music.
3. Click in the Search for text box and type **Rock and Roll Hall of Fame**.
4. Select to search using an available research site, such as MSN Search. The first item in the results list should include a link to the Rock and Roll Hall of Fame's Web site.
5. Click the link. Your Web browser should start and display the Home page of the Rock and Roll Hall of Fame.

✓ *If you cannot locate the link using the Research tool, or if it will not display the Web page, start your Web browser and go to the URL http://www.rockhall.com.*

6. Click the *Visitor Info* link in the links bar on the Web page.
7. Scroll down to view the location information.
8. Select the six lines of text starting with the line *Location* and copy the selection to the Clipboard.
9. Exit your Web browser.
10. Make the **92INVITE_xx** document active.
11. Position the insertion point on the blank line in the middle of the page (before the quotation) and paste the selection from the Clipboard.
12. Close the Research task pane.

Format the Quotation

1. Select the entire quotation and the name of the speaker (Billy Joel).
2. Format the paragraphs to apply a 1.0 inch indent from both the left and the right, and leave no space after the paragraph.
3. Justify the selection.
4. Position the insertion point at the beginning of the name of the speaker, and then set a left indent at 4" on the horizontal ruler.
5. Tab in to the new tab stop.
6. Check the spelling and grammar in the document.
7. Display the document in Print Preview. It should look similar to Illustration A.
8. Print the document.
9. Close the document, saving all changes, and exit Word.

Illustration A

Horticultural Shop Owners Association

452 Cathedral Street ✿ Baltimore, MD 21201

Horticultural Shop Owners Association Annual Meeting

Opening Reception

Rock and Roll Hall of Fame

Join fellow members of the association to start the annual meeting in style.

When: Friday, 6:30 p.m.

Dress: Casual

Tours will be available throughout the evening.

Location

Rock and Roll Hall of Fame and Museum
One Key Plaza
751 Erieside Ave
Cleveland, Ohio 44114
(East Ninth Street at Lake Erie)

"You can't go home with the Rock and Roll Hall of Fame.
You don't sleep with the Rock and Roll Hall of Fame. You
don't get hugged by the Rock and Roll Hall of Fame, and
you don't have children with the Rock and Roll Hall of
Fame. I want what everybody else wants: to love and to be
loved, and to have a family. Being in love has always been
the most important thing in my life."

Billy Joel

ON YOUR OWN

1. Start Word, if necessary.
2. Create a new document and save it with the name **OWD92_xx**.
3. Write a brief paragraph about a place in the world you would like to visit. It may be a city, a country, a landmark, a historic site, or a vacation destination.
4. Use the Research task pane to look up information in an encyclopedia about the place.
5. Use the Research task pane to search for links to Web sites about the destination.
6. Copy at least one paragraph of information about the destination to the Word document.
7. Record the source information and add it to your document.
8. Apply formatting as necessary. If there are any quotes in the content, format them with a double indent, justified.
9. Ask a classmate to review the document and make comments or suggestions.
10. Incorporate the comments and suggestions into the document.
11. Close the document, saving all changes.
12. Exit your Web browser.

Curriculum Connection: Science

Simple Machines

A simple machine is a machine that only requires the application of a single force to work. In general, they have no or few moving parts, and they were developed in order to make a task easier. Examples include a level, a wheel and axel, a pulley, a wedge, an inclined plane, and a screw. (A complex machine is made up or two or more simple machines.)

Research a Simple Machine

Pick one type of simple machine and then use Word's Research Tool to find out more about it. Look up definitions, encyclopedia entries, and links to relevant Web sites. Use a Word document to save notes, remembering to record your source information. Copy useful information from the sources and Web pages that you find into your Word document. If the data that you copy is formatted as a table, convert it into text. When you have completed your research, write a brief report about the machine. Include a bibliography, footnotes, or list of works cited.

Skills Covered

- **Use Smart Tags**

Software Skills   Use smart tags to perform actions in Word that you would otherwise have to open a different program to accomplish. For example, you can use a smart tag to look up an address in an Outlook contact list and then automatically enter the address into a letter in Word, or access the Internet to find stock quotes or street maps.

Application Skills   Long Shot, Inc. has signed an agreement to sponsor a golf tournament at a golf course in Myrtle Beach, South Carolina. You need to add the golf course manager to your contacts list. In this exercise, you will make sure all of your smart tags options are enabled. You will then open an existing letter to the golf course manager, and use a smart tag to add his information to your Outlook Contacts folder. You will then open another letter, and use the smart tag to automatically insert the address.

TERMS

Recognizer A type of data that Word identifies as a smart tag.

Smart tag A type of data that Word and other Microsoft Office 2007 programs recognizes and labels as available for use with other programs.

NOTES

Use Smart Tags

- **Smart tags** are a feature of Office 2007 that you can use to automatically integrate data entered in one program with another program.

  - ✓ *You have already used one type of smart tag—the Paste Options button lets you select from a list of possible formatting options. Refer to Exercise 19 for more information about the Paste Options button.*

- For example, you can use smart tags to integrate Outlook contact information with your Word documents:

  - If you type a person's name into a Word document, you can use a smart tag to add the person to your Outlook contact list, or to insert the person's address from your contact list into the letter.

- Word comes with a set of **recognizers** used to identify and label the following types of smart tags:

  - ✓ *You can download additional smart tags from Microsoft and other vendors.*

  - Addresses
  - Financial Symbols
  - Dates
  - Names
  - Places
  - Telephone Numbers
  - Times

- On the Smart Tags tab of the AutoCorrect dialog box, you can select which of the recognizers you want Word to mark as smart tags in your documents.

Smart Tags tab of the AutoCorrect dialog box

- Word marks smart tags in a document using a purple dotted underline.
- When you rest the mouse pointer over the smart tag, the Smart Tag Actions button displays.

Smart tag on a name

- Move the mouse pointer over the button to display a drop-down arrow. Click the arrow to display a menu of available actions.

Smart Tag Actions menu

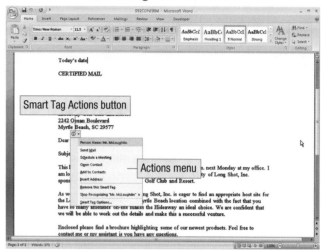

- The types of actions available on the menu depend on the type of recognizer.
- Smart tags are on by default, but you can turn them off on the Smart Tags tab of the AutoCorrect dialog box.
- On the Advanced page of the Word Options dialog box, you can select to hide the purple underline, and still use the smart tag feature.

  ✓ *You can hide the Smart Tags Actions buttons as well.*

- You can save smart tags with your documents if you want to retain a link between the data in your Word document and the source data.
- If you don't need the link, you don't need to save the smart tag—the data remains saved in the document.
- If you don't need all of the smart tags in a document, you can select the specific smart tags you want to retain and the ones you want to discard.
- Saving smart tags with your document increases document size.
- If you want to use smart tags on Web pages created with Word, you must set Word to save the smart tags in XML format.

PROCEDURES

Turn Smart Tags Off or On

1. Open a document.
2. Click the **Office Button** ⊞ .... Alt + F
3. Click **Word Options** I
4. Click **Proofing** .... P
5. Click **AutoCorrect Options** .... Alt + A
6. Click **Smart Tags** tab .... Ctrl + Tab↹
7. Click to select **Label text with smart tags** check box ...... Alt + L

   ✓ *A check mark in the check box indicates the option is on.*

8. Click **OK** .... ↵Enter
9. Click **OK** .... ↵Enter

Turn Display of Smart Tags Underlines Off or On

1. Open a document.
2. Click the **Office Button** ⊞ .... Alt + F
3. Click **Word Options** I
4. Click **Advanced** .... A
5. Click to deselect or select the **Show Smart Tags** check box .... Alt + A , A

   ✓ *A check mark in the check box indicates the option is on.*

6. Click **OK** .... ↵Enter

Select Smart Tag Recognizer(s)

1. Open a document.
2. Click the **Office Button** ⊞ .... Alt + F
3. Click **Word Options** I
4. Click **Proofing** .... P
5. Click **AutoCorrect Options** .... Alt + A
6. Click **Smart Tags** tab .... Ctrl + Tab↹

7. Click to select recognizer to display .... ↓ / ↑ , Spacebar

   ✓ *A check mark in the check box indicates that Word is set to recognize that Smart Tag type.*

8. Repeat step 7 to select or deselect additional recognizers.
9. Click **OK** .... ↵Enter
10. Click **OK** .... ↵Enter

Use a Smart Tag

1. Rest mouse pointer over smart tag in document.

   ✓ *Word displays the Smart Tag Actions button.*

2. Click the **Smart Tag Actions** button.
3. Click desired action.

Show/Hide Smart Tags Actions Buttons

1. Open a document.
2. Click the **Office Button** ⊞ .... Alt + F
3. Click **Word Options** I
4. Click **Proofing** .... P
5. Click **AutoCorrect Options** .... Alt + A
6. Click **Smart Tags** tab .... Ctrl + Tab↹
7. Click to select or deselect the **Show Smart Tag Actions buttons** check box .... Alt + B

   ✓ *A check mark in the check box indicates that the option is selected.*

8. Click **OK** .... ↵Enter
9. Click **OK** .... ↵Enter

Save Smart Tags with Document

1. Open a document.
2. Click the **Office Button** ⊞ .... Alt + F
3. Click **Word Options** I

4. Click **Advanced** .... A
5. Click to select the **Embed smart tags** check box .... Alt + M , Alt + M , Alt + M , Spacebar

   ✓ *A check mark in the check box indicates the option is on.*

6. Click **OK** .... ↵Enter

Save Smart Tags as XML in Web Pages

1. Open a document.
2. Click the **Office Button** ⊞ .... Alt + F
3. Click **Word Options** I
4. Click **Advanced** .... A
5. Click to select the **Save smart tags as XML properties in Web pages** check box ...... Alt + V , V , V , Spacebar

   ✓ *A check mark in the check box indicates the option is on.*

6. Click **OK** .... ↵Enter

Remove a Smart Tag from a Document

1. Rest mouse pointer over smart tag in document.

   ✓ *Word displays the Smart Tag Actions button.*

2. Click the **Smart Tag Actions** button.
3. Click **Remove this Smart Tag** ...... R

Remove all Smart Tags

1. Open a document.
2. Click the **Office Button** ⊞ .... Alt + F
3. Click **Word Options** I
4. Click **Proofing** .... P
5. Click **AutoCorrect Options** .... Alt + A
6. Click **Smart Tags** tab .... Ctrl + Tab↹
7. Click **Remove Smart Tags** .. Alt + R
8. Click **OK** .... ↵Enter
9. Click **OK** .... ↵Enter

EXERCISE DIRECTIONS

✓ *This exercise assumes you have Outlook 2007 installed.*

1. Start Word, if necessary.
2. Open the document 🔘 **93CONFIRM**.
3. Save the document as **93CONFIRM_xx**.
4. Open the Word Options box and set Word to display smart tag underlines.
5. Open the AutoCorrect dialog box and display the Smart Tags tab.
6. Enable smart tags, and select all available recognizers.
7. Close the AutoCorrect dialog box and the Word Options dialog box.
8. Move the mouse pointer over the smart tag under the recipient's name in the **93CONFIRM_xx** document.
9. Click the Smart Tags Actions button and select Add to Contacts.
10. Word displays a Contact card from your Outlook Contacts folder. Note that the name is already filled in.
11. Fill in additional information for Hugh McLaughlin by typing the data into the fields.

   ✓ *You can use the Copy and Paste commands to copy data from the Word document into the fields in the Contact card. You do not have to fill in every field on the card.*

12. Include the following information:

   Full Name: **Mr. Hugh McLaughlin**
   Job Title: **Manager**
   Company: **Hideaway Golf Club and Resort**
   Business Address: **2242 Ocean Boulevard**
   Myrtle Beach, SC 29577
   Business phone: **(843) 555-5432**
   Business fax: **(843) 555-5434**
   E-mail address: **hugh@hideaway.net**

13. When you are done, close the Contact card, saving the changes.
14. Close the **93CONFIRM_xx** document, saving all changes.
15. Open the 🔘 **93THANKS** document and save it as **93THANKS_xx**.
16. Replace the sample text Today's date with the current date, and then press ⏎Enter twice to insert a blank line.
17. Type **Mr. Hugh McLaughlin** and press ⏎Enter. Word should recognize the name as a smart tag.
18. Rest the mouse pointer on the smart tag to display the Smart Tag Actions button, click the button's drop-down arrow, and then click Insert Address. Word should insert the address that you entered on the Outlook Contact card.
19. If necessary, delete the extra blank line between the address and the salutation.
20. Check the spelling and grammar in the document.
21. Display the document in Print Preview. It should look similar to Illustration A.
22. Print the document.
23. Disable smart tags.
24. Close the document, saving all changes, and exit Word.

Illustration A

Today's date

Mr. Hugh McLaughlin
Hideaway Golf Club and Resort
2242 Ocean Boulevard
Myrtle Beach, SC 29577

Dear Hugh,

It was a pleasure meeting you yesterday to discuss the tournament. I know this will be a wonderful opportunity for both of our organizations.

Thank you very much for your time. I look forward to a successful partnership.

Sincerely,

Jason Hadid
Marketing Director
Long Shot, Inc.
234 Simsbury Drive
Ithaca, NY 14850

JH/yo

Copy to: M. Whitman

ON YOUR OWN

1. Make sure you have at least one person entered in your Outlook Contact list.

   ✓ *If necessary, consult your instructor for more information on using the Outlook Contact list.*

2. Start Word and create a new document.
3. Save the document as **OWD93_xx**.
4. Set Word to display smart tag underlines.
5. Enable smart tags, and select all available recognizers.
6. Type a letter to someone whose name is entered in your Outlook Contact list.

7. Use smart tags to insert the address.
8. When the letter is complete, check the spelling and grammar.
9. Preview the letter and print it.
10. Try using a different Smart Tag feature, such as looking up a map of an address, or sending an e-mail message.
11. Disable smart tags.
12. Close all open documents and exit all programs.

Exercise | 94

Skills Covered

- **Merge a Word Document with an Access Database**

Software Skills Creating a new data source document in Word for a mail merge is unnecessary if you already have a database stored in a database application, such as Microsoft Office Access. You can easily merge the Access data with a Word main document.

Application Skills As the Manager of in-house training at Long Shot, Inc., you want to send a letter to everyone who attended the Word 1 class last session to invite them to take the Word 2 class next session. The information for each student is already entered in an Access database. In this exercise, you will create a memo document in Word, and then merge it with data in the Access database.

TERMS

Access query An object containing a subset of records in an Access database.

Access table An object organized in rows and columns and used to store data in an Access database.

Database A file used to store records of data.

NOTES

Merge a Word Document with an Access Database

- If you have an existing Access **database** file, you can use it as a data source for a Mail Merge in Word.

    ✓ *For information on using Mail Merge, refer to the exercises in Lesson 7.*

- To conduct the merge, you simply select the Access file as the data source.

- If there is more than one **table** or **query** in the database file, Mail Merge prompts you to select the one you want to use.

- Complete the remaining steps to complete the merge.

- You can sort and filter records in the Access data source file using the same methods you use when you create the data source using Word.

- You cannot edit the records using Word. To make changes, open the database file in Access.

Select the table or query to use as the data source

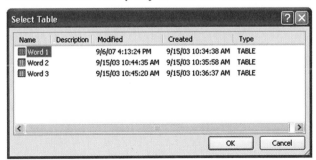

PROCEDURES

Use an Access Database as a Data Source File for a Mail Merge

1. Open a new blank document.
   OR
   Open an existing letter document.
2. Click the **Mailings** tab ..... `Alt`+`M`

   ### Start Mail Merge Group

3. Click the **Start Mail Merge** button 🗎 .... `S`
4. Click a document type:
   - **L**etters .... `L`
   - **E**-Mail Messages .... `E`
   - En**v**elopes .... `V`
   - L**a**bels .... `A`
   - **D**irectory .... `D`
5. Click the **Select Recipients** button 🗐 .... `Alt`+`M`, `R`
6. Click U**s**e Existing List .... `E`

   ✓ *The Select Data Source dialog box displays.*

7. Locate and select the Access database file.
8. Click **O**pen .... `Alt`+`O`

   ✓ *If there is more than one table or query, Word displays the Select Table dialog box.*

9. If necessary, click desired table or query .... `↓`/`↑`
10. Click **OK** .... `↵Enter`
11. Continue with steps for inserting merge fields and completing the merge.

    ✓ *For more information on merging documents with Word, refer to the exercises in Lesson 7.*

EXERCISE DIRECTIONS

1. Make a copy of the Access database file ⊙**94STUDENTS**, and name the copy **94STUDENTS_xx**.

   ✓ *To copy an Access database, right-click the file in the Window's Explorer window, and select Copy. Then go to where you wish to copy the file. Right-click on the destination folder, and select Paste. Right-click on the copied file and select Rename to rename the file.*

2. Start Word, and open ⊙**94MEMO**.
3. Save the document as **94MEMO_xx**.
4. Start Mail Merge.
5. Select to create letters, using the current document.
6. Locate and select **94STUDENTS_xx** as the data source file.
7. Select to use the Word 1 table as the data source table.
8. Use all records in the table.
9. Insert merge fields as shown in Illustration A.
10. Check the spelling and grammar in the document.
11. Preview the merge documents.
12. Complete the merge by merging all records to a new document.
13. Save the document as **94MERGE_xx**.
14. Print the merge documents.
15. Close all open files, saving all changes.

Illustration A

Long Shot, Inc.

INTERDEPARTMENT MEMORANDUM

To: «First_Name» «Last_Name», «Department»
From: Your Name
Date: Today's Date
Subject: In-house training

I hope you enjoyed participating in the «Course» class last session. The instructor told me that everyone who attended is now ready to move on to the next level. With that in mind, «First_Name», I want to let you know that we are planning to offer the Word 2 class on Thursday evenings starting in January. The course will run for eight weeks, and will cover the intermediate aspects of the software program. Please contact the training department to enroll for next session.

Best regards,

Your Name

P.S. Tell everyone in «Department» how much you learned from in-house training. We'd love them to sign up as well!

ON YOUR OWN

1. Create a form letter main document that you can send to relatives and friends thanking them for gifts you received recently for a birthday, holiday, or graduation. You can use graphics objects and formatting to make the document interesting to look at.

2. Save the document as **OWD94-1_xx**.

3. Create an Access database file named **OWD94-2_xx** that includes a table listing the names and addresses of the people you want to receive the letter. Include at least five records. Alternatively, make a copy of the Access database file ⊙**94GIFTLIST** and rename the copy **OWD94-2_xx**.

4. Use the table in the **OWD94-2_xx** database file as the data source for the **OWD94-1_xx** form letter.

5. Merge the letters to a new document named **OWD94-3_xx**.

6. Save and close all open files, and exit all open applications.

Skills Covered

- **Embed a PowerPoint Slide in a Word Document**
- **Export PowerPoint Slides and Notes to a Word Document**
- **Export PowerPoint Text to a Word Document**

Software Skills   Share information between two applications to save yourself work and to provide consistency between documents. If you have a PowerPoint presentation, for example, you can use the presentation information in a Word document. You can embed PowerPoint slides in a Word Document as graphics objects, and you can export text and graphics from a PowerPoint presentation into a Word document.

Application Skills   You have been asked to present information about the Blue Sky Dairy home delivery service at a company meeting. You already have a PowerPoint presentation about the study. You can use pieces of the presentation to create documents to distribute as a package at the meeting. In this exercise, you will create a cover for the package using a slide from the PowerPoint presentation. You will then export the entire presentation to a Word document to use as a handout, leaving blank lines for writing notes. Finally, you will export the text from the presentation as an outline to use as a table of contents for the handout package.

TERMS

Export To send text or data from one application to another application. The original data remains intact.

NOTES

Embed a PowerPoint Slide in a Word Document

- You can embed a slide in a Word document.
- The slide appears in Word in full color with graphics and text.
- Embedding a slide is similar to embedding an Excel object in a Word document.

  ✓ *See Exercise 89 for information on embedding an Excel object in a Word document.*

Export PowerPoint Slides and Notes to a Word Document

- You can **export** PowerPoint slides and notes to a Word document.
- When you export slides, miniatures of your slides are inserted in a table in the Word document.
- You can print slide notes with the slides, or leave blank lines for entering handwritten notes or comments.
- You can link the slides in the Word document to the source document so when you change the source document the linked document in Word updates automatically.

Export PowerPoint Text to a Word Document

- You can export PowerPoint text to a Word document.
- Text will be saved in rich text format (.rtf).
- The text will be formatted using Outline heading levels.
- When you open the .rtf file in Word, you can save it as a Word file.

PROCEDURES

Embed a PowerPoint Slide in Word

1. Open presentation in PowerPoint.
2. Select slide to copy.
3. Click **Home** tab .... Alt+H

   Clipboard Group

4. Click **Copy** button 🗐 C

   OR

   a. Right-click selection.
   b. Click **Copy** C
5. Make destination file active.
6. Position insertion point in the desired location.
7. Click **Home** tab .... Alt+H

   Clipboard Group

8. Click **Paste** button drop-down arrow 🗐 V
9. Click **Paste Special** .... S
10. Click **As** box, if necessary .... Alt+A
11. Click Microsoft Office PowerPoint Slide Object .... ↓/↑
12. Click **Paste** option button .... Alt+P
13. Click **OK** .... ↵Enter

Export PowerPoint Slides and Notes to Word

1. Open the presentation.
2. Click the **Office Button** 🗐 .... Alt+F
3. Click **Publish** .... U
4. Click **Create Handouts in Microsoft Office Word** .... H
5. Select option for page layout in Word:
   - **Notes next to slides** .... N
   - **Blank lines next to slides** ..... A
   - **Notes below slides** .... B
   - **Blank lines below slides** ..... K
   - **Outline only** .... O
6. Select one of the following:
   - **Paste** .... P
   - **Paste link** I
7. Click **OK** .... ↵Enter

Export PowerPoint Text to Word

1. Open the presentation.
2. Click the **Office Button** 🗐 .... Alt+F
3. Click **Save As** .... A
4. Type file name.
5. Select storage location.
6. Click **Save as type** drop-down arrow .... Alt+T
7. Select **Outline/RTF** .... ↓/↑, ↵Enter
8. Click **Save** .... Alt+S

Open RTF File in Word

1. Start Word.
2. Click the **Office Button** 🗐 .... Alt+F
3. Click **Open** .... O
4. Click **Save as type** drop-down arrow .... Alt+T
5. Select **All Files** ...... ↓/↑, ↵Enter
6. Select storage location.
7. Select file to open.
8. Click **Open** .... Alt+O

EXERCISE DIRECTIONS

✓ *The steps in this exercise assume you know how to use a PowerPoint presentation file. If you do not, ask your instructor for more information.*

Embed a Slide in a Word Document

1. Start Word, if necessary.
2. Open ◎95COVER.
3. Save the document as **95COVER_xx**.
4. Replace the sample text *Today's Date* with the current date.
5. Replace the sample text *Your Name* with your own name.
6. Start PowerPoint.
7. Open ◎95PRES.
8. Save it as **95PRES_xx**.
9. Select slide 1 and copy it to the Clipboard.

   ✓ *Click slide 1 to select it, and then click the Copy button* 🔲 *on the Home tab of the Ribbon.*

10. Switch to the **95COVER_xx** document in Word.
11. Embed the slide from the Clipboard onto the last line in the document.
12. Center the picture object horizontally on the page.

   ✓ *Click the object to select it, then click the Center button in the Paragraph group in the Home tab of the Ribbon.*

13. Check the spelling and grammar in the document.
14. Preview the document. It should look similar to Illustration A.
15. Close the document, saving all changes.

Export PowerPoint Data to Word

1. Switch back to the **95PRES_xx** PowerPoint presentation, and select to export the slides to a new Word document, selecting the Notes next to slides layout, and pasting the data.
2. Save the document as **95HANDOUT_xx**.
3. Preview both pages of the document. They should look similar to Illustration B.
4. Close the document, saving all changes.
5. Switch back to the **95PRES_xx** PowerPoint presentation.
6. Save the file in Outline/RTF format with the name **95OUT_xx.**
7. Close the **95PRES_xx** presentation file and exit PowerPoint. Do not save any changes.
8. Switch to Word and open the **95OUT_xx** file.
9. Change to Outline view.
10. Deselect the Show Text Formatting check box in the Outline Tools group on the Outlining tab of the Ribbon. The document should look similar to the one in Illustration C.
11. Close the document, saving all changes.

Illustration B

Slide 1 — Blue Sky Dairy Home Delivery Service / Fresh from Us to You

Slide 2 — Our Target Area
- Young families
- Middle to high income
- Long distance between markets
- Families always too busy

Slide 3 — What Are the Benefits?
- Reach customers where they live
- Create new profit center
- Opens market for new products
- Generates good will

Slide 4 — Estimated Startup Costs

Slide 5 — Estimated Monthly Expenses

Slide 6 — Conclusion
- There is a market for this service
- It creates a new profit center
- It generates good-will

Illustration C

⊕ Blue Sky Dairy
Home Delivery Service
  ⊖ Fresh from Us to You
  ⊖
⊕ Our Target Area
  ⊖ ■ Young families
  ⊖ ■ Middle to high income
  ⊖ ■ Long distance between markets
  ⊖ ■ Families always too busy
⊕ What Are the Benefits?
  ⊖ ■ Reach customers where they live
  ⊖ ■ Create new profit center
  ⊖ ■ Opens market for new products
  ⊖ ■ Generates good will
⊖ Estimated Startup Costs
⊖ Estimated Monthly Expenses
⊕ Conclusion
  ⊖ ■ There is a market for this service
  ⊖ ■ It creates a new profit center
  ⊖ ■ It generates good-will
  —

ON YOUR OWN

1. Create a PowerPoint presentation about yourself or about a club or organization to which you belong, or open the presentation ⊙ 95MYLIFE.

2. Save the presentation with the name OWD95-1_*xx*.

3. Create handouts in Word by exporting the entire presentation to a new document. Include notes if there are any, or leave blank lines for hand writing notes.

4. Save the document with the name OWD95-2_*xx*.

5. Insert a page break at the beginning of the document to create a new first page.

6. Enter and format text for a report title on the new first page.

7. Embed a slide from the presentation to illustrate the report cover.

8. Check the spelling and grammar in the document.

9. Print the document.

10. Ask a classmate to review the document and offer comments and suggestions.

11. Incorporate the suggestions and comments into the document.

12. Close all open documents, saving all changes.

13. Present the report along with the slide show to your class.

Exercise | 96

Critical Thinking

Application Skills The Horticultural Shop Owners' Association is sponsoring a trip to tour the Botanical Gardens in Montreal, Canada. The president of the association has asked you to create an information packet to send to members. She has sent you an Excel worksheet with financial information, a PowerPoint presentation about the trip, and an Access database that includes the names and addresses of the members. In this exercise, you will export the PowerPoint presentation to create a Word document. You will add a cover page to the document on which you will create a chart showing the satisfaction level of people who went on the trip last year, and you will add another page to the document on which you will embed financial information as an Excel worksheet object. Finally, you will use the Access database as a data source to create mailing labels so you can mail the packets to the members.

EXERCISE DIRECTIONS

✓ *The steps in this exercise assume you know how to use Excel, Access, and PowerPoint files. If you do not, ask your instructor for more information.*

Export a PowerPoint Presentation to Word

1. Start PowerPoint and open the presentation file ⊙**96MONTREAL**.
2. Publish the file as handouts in Word, pasting the slides, and using the layout that leaves blank lines next to each slide.
3. Save the Word document as **96PACKET_xx**.

Create and Format a Graph Object

1. Insert a page break at the beginning of the document to create a cover page.
2. Move the insertion point to the beginning of the document and type the title **Tour the Botanical Gardens of Montreal**, using a 48-point sans serif font, centered.
3. Leave 2.5" of space and type the following paragraph using a 12-point sans serif font, justified, with no spacing between lines:

   Join the Horticultural Shop Owners' Association on an exciting four-day trip to the Botanical Gardens in Montreal, Canada. Last year, twenty members of the association joined a similar

tour. When asked whether they were pleased with the experience, the overwhelming majority answered with a resounding "YES!"

4. Insert two blank lines, and then insert a new Clustered Column chart object.
5. Enter the following data in the worksheet:

	Responses
Happy	8
Unhappy	3
Ecstatic	14

6. Delete any remaining sample data from the worksheet (you cannot delete the default column labels), resize the data range to fit the data, and then minimize the worksheet.
7. Change the chart type to Exploded Pie in 3-D.
8. Hide the chart title and the legend.
9. Display data labels and format them to show the category name, percentages, and leader lines. Apply bold to the data label text.
10. Position the data labels so you can read them clearly.
11. Set text wrapping for the chart to square, and center it horizontally relative to the margins.
12. Save the changes.

Embed Excel Worksheet Data

1. Move the insertion point to the end of the document and insert a page break.
2. On the new last page of the document, type the following title in the Heading 1 style, centered:
   Breakdown of Costs for Montreal Trip
3. Leave 1.5" of space between the title and a blank line.
4. Start Excel and open the file ⊙**96COSTS**.
5. Select cells A4:D8 and copy the selection to the Clipboard.
6. Switch back to **96PACKET_xx** and embed the data as a Microsoft Excel Worksheet object on the last line of the document.
7. Double-click the object in Word to make the Excel commands available.
8. Apply 40% Accent 1 cell format to the data.
9. Increase the font size of the entire selection to 12 points.
10. Click outside the object to make the Word commands available again.
12. If necessary, center the object on the page.
14. Insert page numbers centered in the footer of all pages in the **96PACKET_xx** document.
15. Check the spelling and grammar in the document.
16. Preview the document, two pages at a time. Pages 1 and 2 should look similar to Illustration A, and Page 3 should look similar to Illustration B.
17. Print the document.
18. Close the document, saving all changes.
19. Close the **96COSTS** workbook without saving changes, and exit Excel.

Merge with an Access Database

1. Create a new blank Word document and save it as **96SETUP_xx**.
2. Use Mail Merge to generate mailing labels.
3. Select the Avery US Letter label number 5663.
4. Use the ⊙**96MEMBERS** Access database file as the data source.
5. Insert the Address Block field on the first label, and then update the labels.
6. Merge the labels to a new document.
7. Save the merge document as **96LABELS_xx**.
8. Print the document.
9. Close all open documents, saving all changes.
10. Exit all open applications.

Illustration A

Tour the Botanical Gardens of Montreal

Join the Horticultural Shop Owners' Association on an exciting four-day trip to the Botanical Gardens in Montreal, Canada. Last year, twenty members of the association joined a similar tour. When asked whether they were pleased with the experience, the overwhelming majority answered with a resounding "YES!"

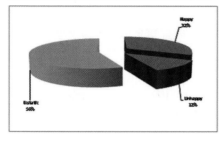

1

Slide 1

Slide 2

Slide 3

2

Illustration B

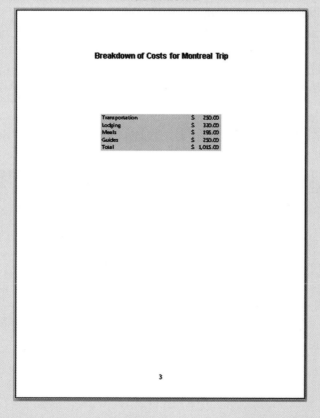

Breakdown of Costs for Montreal Trip

Transportation	$ 250.00
Lodging	$ 320.00
Meals	$ 195.00
Guides	$ 250.00
Total	$ 1,015.00

3

Exercise | 97

Curriculum Integration

Application Skills   For your language arts class, use the skills you have learned in Lesson 12 to create a multimedia presentation about a work of literature or an author. You can use the Research tool to locate information, pictures, and even sound. You can use the information you find to create a presentation. You can export the presentation to Word to create handouts for your class. If there is data that is suitable for charting, you can create a graph or chart, or use SmartArt to create a flowchart that illustrates plot development or a timeline of an author's life. Deliver your presentation to your class. Refer to Illustration A to see a sample of a SmartArt graphic.

EXERCISE DIRECTIONS

Pick a work of literature or an author that you have studied in class or at home.

Research the topic to find out more about it. You can look up definitions, encyclopedia entries, or Web pages that contain relevant information.

Take notes about the topic, or copy the information from the sources into a Word document. Always remember to record the source information so you can include it in a bibliography, footnotes, or a list of works cited.

When you have completed your research, use PowerPoint to create a presentation about the topic. Include text, graphics, and sound, if available. Save the presentation with a name such as **97PRES_xx**.

Test and proofread your presentation. Ask a classmate to view it and offer suggestions for how to improve it.

When you are satisfied with your presentation, export it to Word to create handouts. Save the handout document as **97HANDOUT_xx**.

Add one or more pages to the handout to create a cover page, a bibliography or list of works cited, and to add a SmartArt graphic or chart.

Check the spelling and grammar in the document.

Print the document.

Ask a classmate to review the document and offer comments and suggestions.

Incorporate the comments and suggestions into the document.

Save the document and close it. Exit all applications.

Pass out the handouts and deliver the presentation to your class.

Illustration A

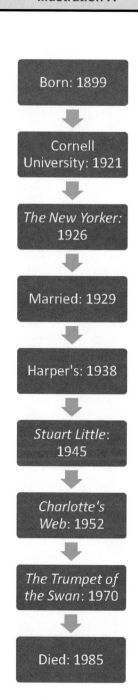

2

Lesson | 13

Challenge Exercises

Exercise | 98

Skills Covered

- Link a Worksheet into a Word Document
- Locate Data on the Internet
- Edit an Excel Worksheet
- Update a Linked Object in a Word Document

Application Skills   You have been asked to organize a four-day trip to the Botanical Gardens in Montreal, Canada for the Horticultural Shop Owners Association. You have an Excel worksheet listing lodging costs in Canadian dollars. In this exercise, you will link the worksheet to a Word memo, use the Research tool to locate current exchange rates on the Web, and then edit the Excel worksheet to convert the costs to U.S. dollars. Finally, you will update the link to the Word document, and format the data in Word.

If you do not have a live connection to the Internet, a Web page file with a currency exchange table is provided for use in this exercise.

EXERCISE DIRECTIONS

1. Start Word, if necessary, and create the document shown in Illustration A, or open ⊙ **98TRIP**.

2. Save the file as **98TRIP_xx**.

3. Start Excel and open the workbook ⊙ **98COSTS**.

4. Save the file as **98COSTS_xx**.

5. Copy the range A1:D10 to the Clipboard.

6. Switch back to Word and link the worksheet object on to the last line of the **98TRIP_xx** document.

7. Set the link for manual updating.

8. Use the Research tool to search for Web site pages with current currency exchange rates (such as www.X-rates.com), or open the Web page file ⊙ **98EXCHANGE** in Internet Explorer.

9. Locate the exchange rate for the number of Canadian dollars per one U.S dollar, and copy it to the Clipboard.

   ✓ Be careful to copy only the exchange rate with no additional spaces before it or after it. If you copy additional spaces you may see an error in the Excel worksheet when you paste the data. If so, delete the data from the cell and try again.

10. Switch to the **98COSTS_xx** workbook in Excel.

11. Paste the data from the Clipboard into cell C5, then copy it to cells C6, C7, and C8.

    ✓ If necessary, ask your instructor for information about working with Excel.

12. Disconnect from the Internet, if necessary.

13. In the **98COSTS_xx** workbook, create a formula in cell D5 to calculate the current cost in U.S. dollars of lodging in a four-star hotel.

    ✓ Hint: Divide the cost in Canadian dollars by the exchange rate.

14. Copy the formula to cells D6:D8.

15. Apply the Accent 2 cell style to cells A1:D2 and the 20% Accent 2 cell style to cells A3:D10.

16. Save the changes to the Excel workbook.

17. Switch to the **98TRIP_xx** document in Word.

18. Update the link.

19. Center the object horizontally.

20. Check the spelling and grammar in the document.

21. Preview the document. If should look similar to Illustration B.

22. Save and close all open documents and exit all open applications.

Illustration A

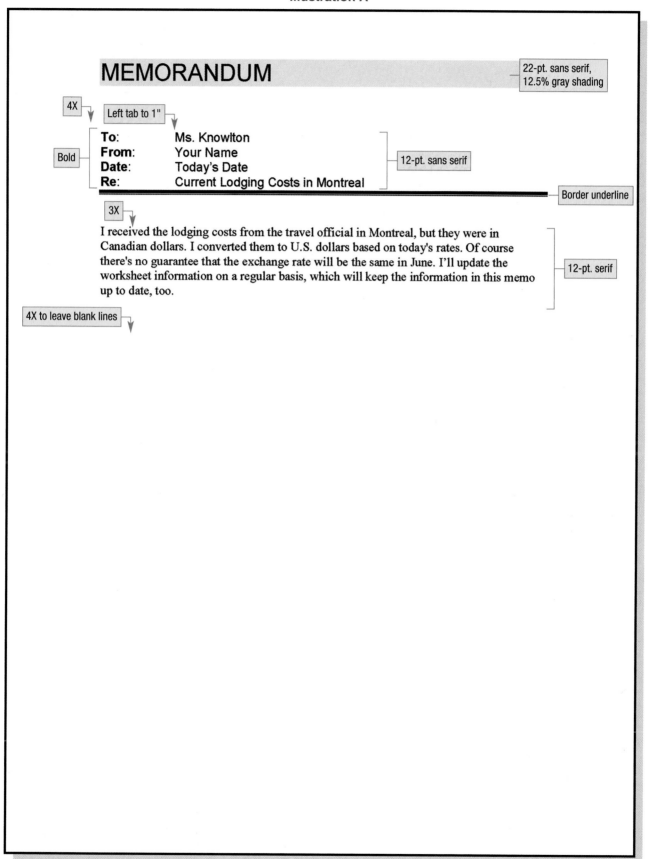

MEMORANDUM

22-pt. sans serif, 12.5% gray shading

4X

Left tab to 1"

Bold

To: Ms. Knowlton
From: Your Name
Date: Today's Date
Re: Current Lodging Costs in Montreal

12-pt. sans serif

Border underline

3X

I received the lodging costs from the travel official in Montreal, but they were in Canadian dollars. I converted them to U.S. dollars based on today's rates. Of course there's no guarantee that the exchange rate will be the same in June. I'll update the worksheet information on a regular basis, which will keep the information in this memo up to date, too.

12-pt. serif

4X to leave blank lines

MEMORANDUM

To: Ms. Knowlton
From: Your Name
Date: Today's Date
Re: Current Lodging Costs in Montreal

I received the lodging costs from the travel official in Montreal, but they were in Canadian dollars. I converted them to U.S. dollars based on today's rates. Of course there's no guarantee that the exchange rate will be the same in June. I'll update the worksheet information on a regular basis, which will keep the information in this memo up to date, too.

Lodging Packages; Four Days, Three Nights* Montreal, Canada			
Accommodations	Cost (CAD)	Exchange Rate	Cost (USD)
Four Star	$ 575.00	1.0546	$ 545.23
Three Star	$ 515.00	1.0546	$ 488.34
Economy	$ 465.00	1.0546	$ 440.93
Budget	$ 350.00	1.0546	$ 331.88

*Rates Based on Double Occupancy

Exercise | 99

Skills Covered

- Save a Word Document as a Web Page
- Download Clip Art and Insert it on a Web Page
- Link Excel Data with a Web Page
- Update Linked Data

Application Skills The President of the Horticultural Shop Owners Association wants you to make information about the trip to the botanical gardens in Montreal, Canada available on the organization's Web site. In this exercise, you will create a Word document about the trip and save it as a Web page. You will locate clip art and insert it on the Web page. You will also link worksheet information about lodging costs to the Web document, so if the conversion rate changes, the information on the Web site will remain current.

EXERCISE DIRECTIONS

1. Start Word, if necessary, and create the document shown in Illustration A, or open ⊙ **99TRIP**.

   ✓ Apply the styles as marked.

2. Save the document as a single file Web page with the title **Botanical Gardens Tour** and the file name **99TRIP_xx**.

3. Apply the Trek theme to the Web page, and apply the Light Yellow, Background 2 color to the page background.

4. Use the Clip Art task pane to locate a suitable clip art image and photo and insert them into the **99TRIP_xx** Web page document. Suitable images might include flowers, plants, gardens, travel, or Montreal.

   ✓ Alternatively, insert the graphics files ⊙ 99CITY and ⊙ 99GARDEN provided with this book.

5. Set the text wrap around both graphics to Square.

6. Resize and position the objects so that in Print Preview the document looks similar to Illustration B.

7. Save the changes.

8. Start Excel and open the workbook ⌨ **98COSTS_xx** that you used in Exercise 98, or open ⊙ **99COSTS**.

9. Save the file as **99COSTS_xx.**

10. Copy the range A1:D10 to the Clipboard.

11. Switch back to the **99TRIP_xx** Web page in Word and link the worksheet object on the last line of the document.

12. Switch back to the **99COSTS_xx** file in Excel.

13. Change the exchange rate in cells C5, C6, C7, and C8 to.1.15.

14. Increase the font size in cells A1:D10 to 12 points, and then adjust column widths as necessary.

15. Switch back to the Web page in Word, and update the link, if necessary.

16. Center the object horizontally on the Web page.

17. Check the spelling and grammar.

18. Preview the Web page document. It should look similar to Illustration B.

19. Print the document.

20. Save and close all open documents, and exit all open applications.

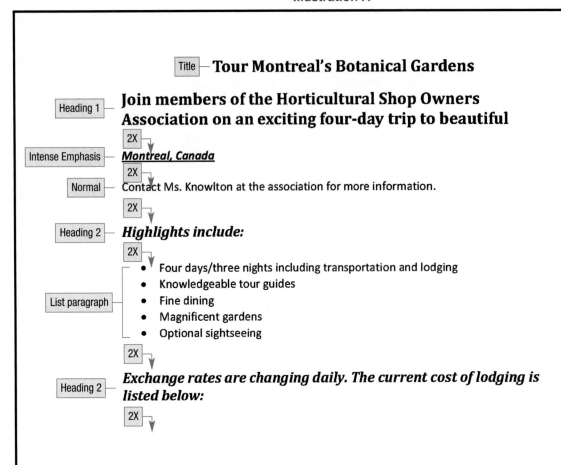

Title — **Tour Montreal's Botanical Gardens**

Heading 1 — **Join members of the Horticultural Shop Owners Association on an exciting four-day trip to beautiful**

2X

Intense Emphasis — ***Montreal, Canada***

2X

Normal — Contact Ms. Knowlton at the association for more information.

2X

Heading 2 — *Highlights include:*

2X

List paragraph —
- Four days/three nights including transportation and lodging
- Knowledgeable tour guides
- Fine dining
- Magnificent gardens
- Optional sightseeing

2X

Heading 2 — *Exchange rates are changing daily. The current cost of lodging is listed below:*

2X

Curriculum Connection: Social Studies

Student Organizations

Student organizations encourage leadership skills and teamwork. Many student organizations are specifically designed to provide business and technology students with education, job opportunities, community service, and real-world experience. Some are local groups, such as a Technology Club, which might teach classes at a senior center, and others are national organizations, such as Business Professionals of America, which sponsor conferences and competitions.

Promoting Club Membership

Develop a database of student organizations relating to the business and technology industries. Some might be local clubs available at your school and others might be national organizations. Include information such as the group's goals and objectives. If available, include contact information and club officers. Then, create a presentation to promote membership. List opportunities that these clubs sponsor, such as conferences, scholarships, or internships and explain how participation in such a group can promote a lifelong commitment to community service and professional development.

Illustration B

Tour Montreal's Botanical Gardens

Join members of the Horticultural Shop Owners Association on an exciting four-day trip to beautiful

Montreal, Canada

Contact Ms. Knowlton at the association for more information.

Highlights include:

- Four days/three nights including transportation and lodging
- Knowledgeable tour guides
- Fine dining
- Magnificent gardens
- Optional sightseeing

Exchange rates are changing daily. The current cost of lodging is listed below:

Lodging Packages; Four Days, Three Nights* Montreal, Canada				
Accommodations	Cost (CAD)		Exchange Rate	Cost (USD)
Four Star	$ 575.00		1.15	$ 500.00
Three Star	$ 515.00		1.15	$ 447.83
Economy	$ 465.00		1.15	$ 404.35
Budget	$ 350.00		1.15	$ 304.35

*Rates Based on Double Occupancy

Skills Covered

■ **Use an Access Database as a Merge Data Source**

■ **Change the Data Source for a Merge**

Application Skills You are a store manager for Liberty Blooms. You want to send out mailings to your customers about upcoming sales and events, but you want to customize the mailings for customers you know are interested in cut flowers and for customers you know are interested in gardening. You have all of the mailing information stored in an Access database, with queries that filter out the two groups. In this exercise, you will create a form letter document that can be customized, and then merge it first with one query and then again with the other query. You will then use all names in the database to generate envelopes.

EXERCISE DIRECTIONS

1. Use Windows to make a copy of the ◎100DATA Access database.

   ✓ *To copy an Access database, right-click the file in the Window's Explorer window, and select Copy. Navigate to the destination folder. Right-click the destination folder, and select Paste. Right-click on the copied file and select Rename to rename the file.*

2. Name the copied database file **100DATA_xx**.
3. Start Word, if necessary.
4. Create a new blank document and save it as **100CUTS_xx**.
5. Use Mail Merge to create a form letter that uses the *Cut Flowers* query in the **100DATA_xx** database as the data source.
6. Type the letter shown in Illustration A, inserting merge fields and merge blocks as necessary. Use a serif font, such as Times New Roman, and the No Spacing style to set the line spacing to single and the spacing after paragraphs to 0 pt.
7. Merge all of the letters to a new document and save it as **100CUTLETS_xx**.
8. Check the spelling and grammar in the document.

9. Print just the first letter.
10. Save the **100CUTS_xx** document, and then save it as a new document with the name **100GARDEN_xx**.
11. Change the recipient list to use the *Gardening* query in the **100DATA_xx** database.
12. Merge all of the letters to a new document and save it as **100GARDENLETS_xx**.
13. Check the spelling and grammar in the document.
14. Print just the first letter.
15. Close the document, saving all changes. Close the **100GARDEN_xx** document, saving all changes.
16. Create a new blank document and save it as **100MAIL_xx**.
18. Use Mail Merge to create envelopes for all of the letters, using the *Addresses* table in the **100DATA_xx** database as the data source.

    ✓ *You may type your own return address if you want.*

19. Merge the envelopes to a new document, and save it as **100ENV_xx**.
20. Print the first page.
21. Close all open documents, saving all changes.

Illustration A

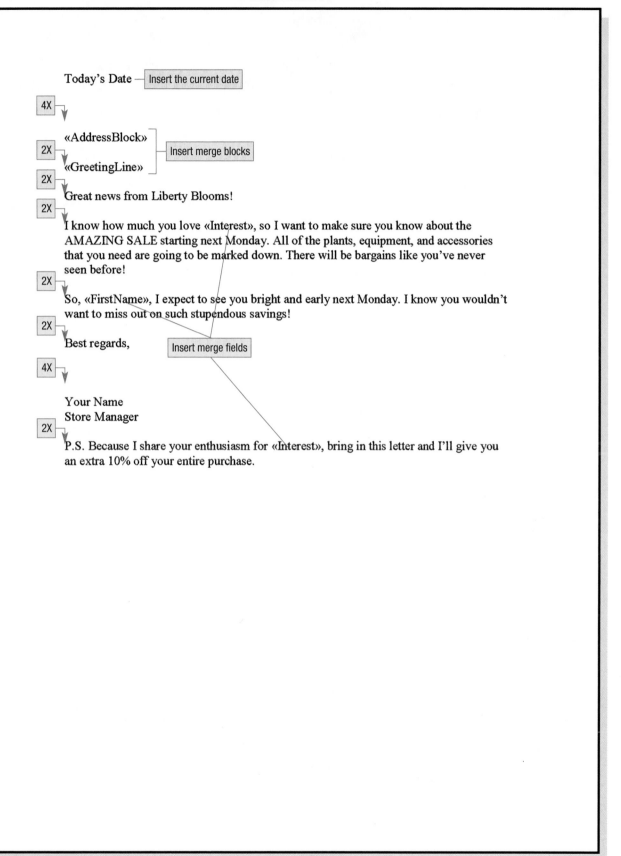

Today's Date — Insert the current date

4X

«AddressBlock»

2X — Insert merge blocks

«GreetingLine»

2X

Great news from Liberty Blooms!

2X

I know how much you love «Interest», so I want to make sure you know about the AMAZING SALE starting next Monday. All of the plants, equipment, and accessories that you need are going to be marked down. There will be bargains like you've never seen before!

2X

So, «FirstName», I expect to see you bright and early next Monday. I know you wouldn't want to miss out on such stupendous savings!

2X

Best regards,

Insert merge fields

4X

Your Name
Store Manager

2X

P.S. Because I share your enthusiasm for «Interest», bring in this letter and I'll give you an extra 10% off your entire purchase.

Exercise | 101

Skills Covered

- Locate Data on the Internet
- Copy Data from a Web Page to a Word Document
- Edit and Format a Table in a Word Document
- Send a Word Document as an E-Mail Attachment

Application Skills   To promote the home delivery service for Blue Sky Dairy, the owners want to take photos that can be used for publicity and marketing. They have asked you to research the features and prices of digital cameras, and then forward the information to them so they can review it and make a decision about which one to purchase. You will use the CNET Web site to locate information about digital camera devices. You will copy the information to a Word document, edit the document, and then e-mail the document to the company owners for review.

If you are connected to the Internet, use the suggested site to gather the required information, or select other appropriate Web sites. If you use a live connection, you may have to modify the steps to achieve the desired result, as the content of the live Web pages changes frequently.

The e-mail address supplied in this exercise is fictitious. If you are connected to the Internet and have an account with a mail service provider, you may substitute your own, your instructor's, or a classmate's email address. If you try to send the document to the fictitious address, you will receive a message that it is undeliverable.

EXERCISE DIRECTIONS

1. Start Word if necessary.
2. Create the document shown in Illustration A, or open ⊙101CAMERAS.
3. Save the file as **101CAMERAS_xx**.
4. Start your Web browser and go to the www.cnet.com Web site.
5. On the CNET home page, click the <u>Reviews</u> link.

   ✓ *If you are using a live connection, or a different Web site, the links may be different. For example, there may be a Cameras link directly on the home page.*

6. Click the <u>Digital camera reviews</u> link.
7. Under Find the Right Digital Cameras, click <u>$200-$300</u>.
8. In the Compare column on the right side of the table listing the camera information, click to select the check boxes for the first four cameras.

9. Click the Compare button at the top of the column.
10. On the Web page, select the data in the comparison table beginning with the Product name row and ending with the Price range row, and copy the selection to the Clipboard.
11. Switch to the **101CAMERAS_xx** document, and paste the data on to the last line.

    ✓ *If Word prompts you to use the Normal style, click Yes.*

12. Use the following steps to modify and format the table in the **101CAMERAS_xx** document as shown in Illustration B.
13. Select the entire table and apply the Table 3D effects 2 style.
14. Delete the pictures from the Product name row, along with the extra blank line.

15. Delete all rows except the following:
- Product name
- Editor's rating
- Digital zoom
- Still image format
- Optical zoom
- Memory storage capacity
- Flash memory form factor
- Battery technology

16. Center the table on the page.

17. Check the spelling and grammar in the document.

18. Preview the **101CAMERAS_xx** document. It should look similar to the one in Illustration B. If necessary, adjust column widths and row heights.

19. Send the document as an attachment to an e-mail message addressed to: mail@blueskydairy.net.

✓ *This is a fictitious email address. Ask your instructor if you should substitute an actual address in this step.*

20. Disconnect from the Internet.

21. Close all open documents, saving all changes.

Illustration A

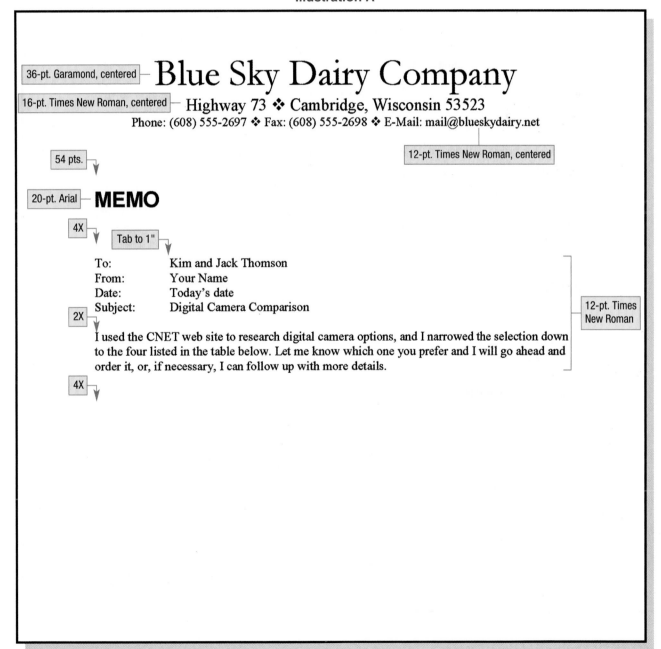

36-pt. Garamond, centered — **Blue Sky Dairy Company**

16-pt. Times New Roman, centered — Highway 73 ❖ Cambridge, Wisconsin 53523

Phone: (608) 555-2697 ❖ Fax: (608) 555-2698 ❖ E-Mail: mail@blueskydairy.net

12-pt. Times New Roman, centered

54 pts.

20-pt. Arial — **MEMO**

4X

Tab to 1"

To: Kim and Jack Thomson
From: Your Name
Date: Today's date
Subject: Digital Camera Comparison

2X

I used the CNET web site to research digital camera options, and I narrowed the selection down to the four listed in the table below. Let me know which one you prefer and I will go ahead and order it, or, if necessary, I can follow up with more details.

12-pt. Times New Roman

4X

Blue Sky Dairy Company

Highway 73 ❖ Cambridge, Wisconsin 53523
Phone: (608) 555-2697 ❖ Fax: (608) 555-2698 ❖ E-Mail: mail@blueskydairy.net

MEMO

To: Kim and Jack Thomson
From: Your Name
Date: Today's date
Subject: Digital Camera Comparison

I used the CNET web site to research digital camera options, and I narrowed the selection down to the four listed in the table below. Let me know which one you prefer and I will go ahead and order it, or, if necessary, I can follow up with more details.

Product name	Samsung S1050 (silver)	Samsung S1050 (black)	HP Photosmart R937	Casio Exilim EX-S880 (black)
Editors' rating (Editors' rating explained)	6.0 Good	6.0 Good	6.8 Good	6.4 Good
Digital zoom	5 x	5 x	8 x	4 x
Still image format	JPEG	JPEG	JPEG	JPEG
Optical zoom	5 x	5 x	3 x	3 x
Memory storage capacity	45 MB	48 MB	32 MB	10.8 MB
Flash memory form factor	Integrated	Integrated	Integrated	Integrated
Battery technology	Alkaline	Alkaline	Lithium ion	Lithium ion

Skills Covered

- **Create an Outline in Word**
- **Create a PowerPoint Presentation from a Word Outline**
- **Generate Presentation Handouts with Word**

Application Skills The Horticultural Shop Owners Association wants you to create a presentation to use at an informational meeting about the trip to the botanical gardens in Montreal. You will start with a Word outline. You will also use Word to create handouts for the meeting.

EXERCISE DIRECTIONS

1. Start Word, if necessary, and create the document shown in Illustration A, or open the file ⊚ 102OUT.

   ✓ *Use the Heading 1 and Heading 2 styles only.*

2. Save the document as **102OUT_xx**.

3. Check the spelling and grammar in the document, save the changes, and then close the document.

4. Start PowerPoint and save the new blank presentation file as **102PRES_xx**.

   ✓ *If necessary, ask your instructor for information on working in PowerPoint.*

5. Use the **102OUT_xx** document to create slides.

   a. On the Home tab in PowerPoint, click the New Slide button.

   b. Click Slides from Outline.

   c. Locate and select the **102OUT_xx** document.

   d. Click Insert.

6. Delete the blank title slide and apply the Title Slide layout to the new slide 1.

7. Apply the Trek theme to the presentation.

8. Apply the Split Horizontal In slide transition at slow speed to all slides in the presentation, set to advance on a mouse click or automatically after 10 seconds.

9. Preview the slide show from the beginning.

10. Save all changes.

11. Publish the presentation as handouts in Word. Select options to paste the slides into the document, and use the layout that displays blank lines to the right of the slides.

12. Save the new Word document as **102HAND_xx.**

13. Move the insertion point to the beginning of the document and insert a next page section break.

14. On the new first page, type the following lines of text in 20-point Arial, centered horizontally and vertically, with 12 points of space between each line (substitute your own name for the sample text Your Name):

    Horticultural Shop Owners Association
    Annual Garden Tour Presentation Handout
    Draft 1
    Prepared by
    Your Name

15. Create a footer on each page in the document with the page number flush left and today's date flush right.

16. Check the spelling and grammar in the document.

17. Preview the document, two pages at a time; it should look similar to Illustrations B and C.

18. Close all open documents, saving all changes.

- Tour the Montreal Botanical Gardens
  - Presented by
  - The Horticultural Shop Owners Association
- Join HSOA's Annual Garden Tour
  - Visit the world-renowned Montreal Botanical Gardens.
  - Spend four days and three nights in exciting Montreal, Canada.
  - See the early summer plants in bloom.
  - Enjoy free time to explore the city and its environs.
  - Travel in the company of fellow HSOA members.
- Tour Highlights
  - Travel by luxury coach
  - Experienced tour guides
  - Customized tour plans
  - Fine dining
  - Magnificent gardens
  - Exciting city
- Itinerary
  - June 15 a.m.: Depart Baltimore, Maryland
  - June 15 p.m.: Arrive Montreal, Canada
  - June 16 a.m.: Garden tour
  - June 16 p.m.: Free
  - June 17 a.m.: Garden tour and lecture
  - June 17 p.m.: Optional city tour
  - June 18 a.m.: Depart Montreal, Canada
  - June 18 p.m.: Arrive Baltimore, Maryland
- Registration and Pricing Information
  - Members: $1,195.00, inclusive
  - Non-members: $1,350, inclusive
  - Early bird rates available prior to May 15.

Illustration B

Horticultural Shop Owners Association

Annual Garden Tour Presentation Handout

Draft 1

Prepared by

Student's Name

Page 1

Today's Date

Slide 1

Presented by
The Horticultural Shop Owners Association
TOUR THE MONTREAL BOTANICAL GARDENS

Slide 2

JOIN HSOA'S ANNUAL GARDEN TOUR
- Visit the world-renowned Montreal Botanical Gardens.
- Spend four days and three nights in exciting Montreal, Canada.
- See the early summer plants in bloom.
- Enjoy free time to explore the city and its environs.
- Travel in the company of fellow HSOA members.

Slide 3

TOUR HIGHLIGHTS
- Travel by luxury coach
- Experienced tour guides
- Customized tour plans
- Fine dining
- Magnificent gardens
- Exciting city

Page 2

Today's Date

Illustration C

Slide 4

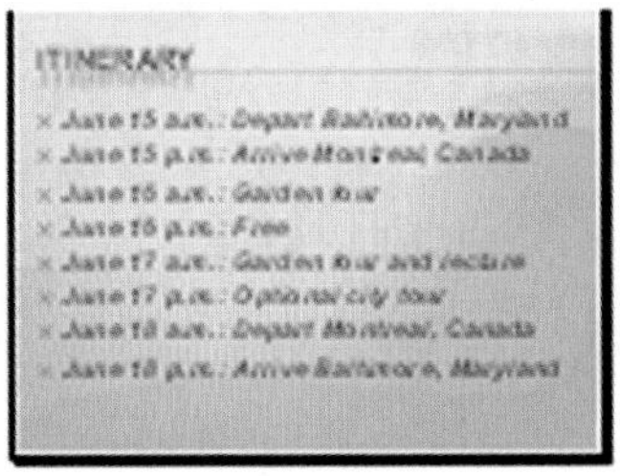

Slide 5

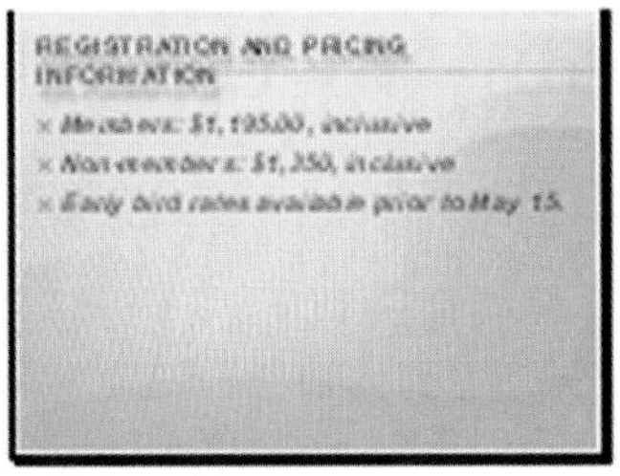

Page 3

Today's Date

Skills Covered

- **Create a Home Page Using a Table**
- **Link One Web Page to Another Web Page**
- **Link a Home Page to an Internet Site**
- **Add a Web Page to Your Favorites Folder**
- **Print a Web Page**

Application Skills The Horticultural Shop Owners Association has hired you to improve its Web site. In this exercise, you will create two Web pages in Word using tables. You will link the pages to each other. You will also provide links from the Home page to a site on the Internet about the botanical gardens. You will also save a Web page to your Favorites folder and print a Web page.

If you do not have a live connection to the Internet you may use the Web page files provided with this book.

EXERCISE DIRECTIONS

1. Start Word, if necessary, and create the document shown in Illustration A, or open the file ⊙ **103SITE**.

   a. Create a table with ten rows and two columns.

   b. Set row heights as follows:
   - Row 1: at least 1.75"
   - Rows 3 and 4: at least .5"
   - Rows 6 and 8: at least 1.5"
   - Rows 2, 5, 7, 9, and 10: at least .25"

   c. Set the width of column 1 to approximately 5" wide.

   d. Set the width of column 2 to approximately 2.25" wide.

   e. Merge the cells across row 3, and then merge the cells across row 4.

   f. Type all text in a sans serif font, using the font formatting and alignments specified in Illustration A.

   g. Use the Clip Art task pane to locate the three clip art pictures shown in Illustration A and insert them in the appropriate cells.

   ✓ If you cannot locate the same pictures, select others, or use the ⊙ 103GARDEN, ⊙ 103SUNFLOWER, and ⊙ 103CONFERENCE files supplied with this book.

   h. Set the height of each clip art picture to 1.5". Leave the aspect ratio locked so the width will adjust automatically.

   i. Center each picture horizontally and vertically within its cell.

   j. Apply borders as shown in Illustration A, and remove the table borders.

2. Save the document as a single file Web Page with the name **103SITE_xx** and the Web page title **HSOA Home Page**.

3. Apply the Blue Tissue paper background texture to the page.

4. Save the changes to the document.

5. Create a new document in Word and create the document shown in Illustration B, or open the file ⊙ **103MEETINGS**.

   a. Create a table with ten rows and two columns.

   b. Merge the cells in row 1, merge the cells in row 2, and then merge the cells in row 10.

   c. In column 1, merge the cells in rows 3 and 4, then merge the cells in rows 5 and 6, then merge the cells in rows 7 and 8.

   d. The rows in column 2 should not be merged.

   e. Set row height for rows 1 and 2 to at least 1" and for rows 3 through 10 to at least .5".

f. Type the 14-point sans serif font except where indicated, using the formatting and alignment shown on Illustration B.

g. Apply a 15% gray shade for the darker cells and a 5% gray shade for the lighter cells.

h. Use a 1 1/2 pt. double border as shown, or a 1/2 pt. single border, as shown.

6. Save the document as a single file Web Page with the name **103MEETINGS_xx** and the Web page title **Regional Meetings**.

7. Apply the Newsprint background texture to the document.

8. Insert a hyperlink from the text *HOME* on the **103MEETINGS_xx** to the **103SITE_xx** Web page file.

9. Check the spelling and grammar in the **103MEETINGS_xx** document.

10. Save the file and close it.

11. On the **103SITE_xx** page, link the text *Schedule* with the **103MEETINGS_xx** Web page file.

12. Link the clip art picture of the meeting to the **103MEETINGS_xx** file, as well.

13. Use the text *Montreal Botanical Gardens* to create a hyperlink to the official Web site, at the URL address **http://www2.ville.montreal.qc.ca/jardin/jardin.htm**.

14. Check the spelling and grammar in the **103SITE_xx** document.

15. Check the **103SITE_xx** Home page in your Web browser and test the links to the schedule page, then test the HOME link back to the **103SITE_xx** page.

16. If you have a live connection to the Internet, test the link to the Montreal Botanical Gardens Web site and browse the site.

17. Add a page from the site to your Favorites folder.

18. Print a page from the site.

✓ *If you do not have a live connection to the Internet, add the 103MEETINGS_xx page to your Favorites folder, and print it*

19. Disconnect from the Internet, if necessary.

20. Save and close all open documents and exit all open programs.

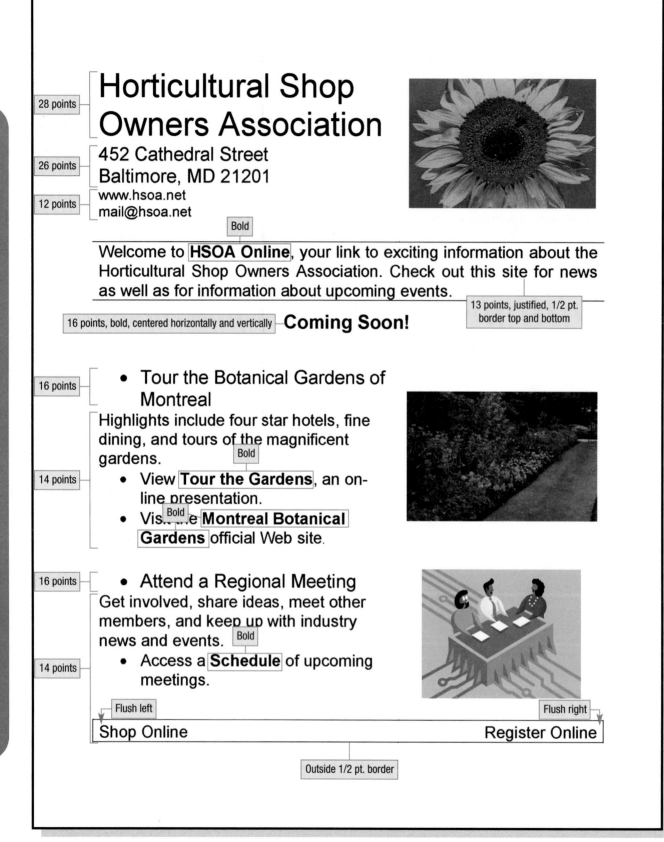

28 points

Horticultural Shop Owners Association

26 points

452 Cathedral Street
Baltimore, MD 21201

12 points

www.hsoa.net
mail@hsoa.net

Bold

Welcome to **HSOA Online**, your link to exciting information about the Horticultural Shop Owners Association. Check out this site for news as well as for information about upcoming events.

13 points, justified, 1/2 pt. border top and bottom

16 points, bold, centered horizontally and vertically — **Coming Soon!**

16 points

- Tour the Botanical Gardens of Montreal

Highlights include four star hotels, fine dining, and tours of the magnificent gardens.

Bold

14 points

- View **Tour the Gardens**, an on-line presentation.
- Vis..the **Montreal Botanical Gardens** official Web site.

Bold

16 points

- Attend a Regional Meeting

Get involved, share ideas, meet other members, and keep up with industry news and events.

Bold

14 points

- Access a **Schedule** of upcoming meetings.

Flush left

Flush right

Shop Online   Register Online

Outside 1/2 pt. border

Illustration B

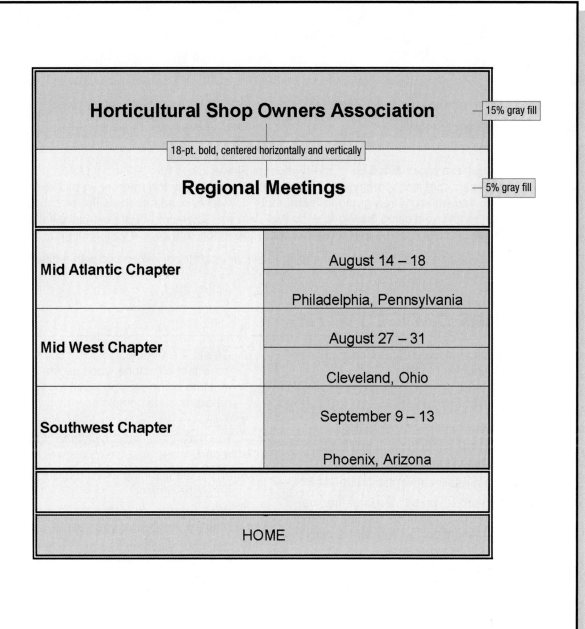

Exercise | 104

Skills Covered

- Plan a Team Project
- Complete a Research Report

Application Skills Liberty Blooms Flower Shop has asked you to be part of a team that is researching ways that the shop could use the Internet. In this exercise, you will work in a group to learn about how retail stores such as flower shops can benefit from using the World Wide Web. You will also learn about potential pitfalls. Finally, you will type up and present a one-page report that details your findings.

There is no sample solution file for this project, as each team will end up with a different result.

EXERCISE DIRECTIONS

1. Meet as a group to discuss the project and decide the approach you want to take.
2. Agree on a main thesis. Some ideas to consider include:
   - What makes an effective Web site?
   - Should online shopping be used in place of or in addition to in store shopping?
   - How can a retailer advertise on the Web?
3. Decide what sources you will use to gather the information you need. You might use the Internet, a library, or you might contact retailers directly to ask them about their experiences.
4. Set goals for the team as a whole.
5. Set individual goals so each team member understands his or her responsibility. You must decide how the work will be divided. For example, will all team members be involved in research? If so, one member might be responsible for research on the Internet, and another might be responsible for research at the library. Or, one might look for information about benefits of the Internet, and another might look for pitfalls. Another approach is to have each team member responsible for a different aspect of the project. For example, one might be responsible for managing and organizing the project, two might handle the research, and someone else might type the report.

6. Create a schedule, including deadlines for each important milestone, such as when all research must be complete and when a draft of the typed report must be complete.
7. Agree on the way to record source information so you have it available to include in the one-page report.
8. When the planning and organization are complete, begin the project.
9. Work together to complete the research, and meet regularly to discuss your results.
10. Use your research to organize and create the one-page report. Format the report correctly, including margins, headings, headers or footers, and footnotes or endnotes.
11. When the report is complete, check the spelling and grammar.
12. Correct errors as necessary.
13. Display the document in Print Preview.
14. Print the document and have someone proofread it.
15. Make changes and corrections as necessary.
16. Display the document in Print Preview again, and then print the document.
17. Close the file, saving all changes.
18. Present your report to the other teams.

Skills Covered

- **Use Smart Tags to Locate Financial Data on the Internet**
- **Copy Data from the Internet into an Excel Worksheet**

- **Use Excel Worksheet Data to Create a Word Table**
- **Attach a Word Document to an E-Mail Message**

Application Skills   A group of employees at Long Shot, Inc. has formed an investment club. As the club treasurer you have been tracking the portfolio. You believe it is time to sell some stock in order to spread the investments into other market segments. In this exercise, you will use smart tags to access the Internet to look up the current trading prices of the stocks. You will copy the information into an Excel worksheet you have already prepared, then copy the entire worksheet into a Word document. Finally, you will attach the Word document to an e-mail message and send it to the club president.

If you use a live connection the links and data may not be quite the same as those used in the exercise steps, as the information changes frequently. The e-mail address supplied in this exercise is fictitious. If you try to send the message it will come back as undeliverable. If you have an Internet connection and a mail service provider, your instructor may want you to substitute a real e-mail address.

EXERCISE DIRECTIONS

1. Start Word if necessary and create the memo document shown in Illustration A, or open the document ◉ 105INVEST.

2. Save the file as **105INVEST_xx**.

3. Enable smart tags, if necessary.

4. Start Excel and open the workbook ◉ 105STOCKS.

5. Save the file as **105STOCKS_xx**.

6. Replace the sample text *Today's Date* with the current date.

7. Enable smart tags, if necessary.

8. Move the mouse pointer over the ticker symbol for Amazon.com.

    ✓ *The Smart Tag Actions button is displayed. If smart tags are not displayed in the worksheet, make sure the Label data with smart tags option is selected on the Smart Tags tab of the AutoCorrect Options dialog box, and that all recognizers are selected. (Using smart tags in Excel is similar to using them in Word.)*

9. Click the Smart Tag Actions button, and then click Financial symbol on the drop-down menu.

10. On the Actions menu, click Stock quote on MSN MoneyCentral.

11. Sign in to your Internet Service Provider if prompted.

12. On the MoneyCentral stock quote page that is displayed, select the current trading stock price and copy it to the Clipboard.

    ✓ *Be careful to copy only the stock price with no additional spaces before it or after it. If you copy additional spaces you may see an error in the Excel worksheet when you paste the data. If so, delete the data from the cell and try again.*

13. Switch to the Excel worksheet and paste it into cell F6. If necessary, adjust column widths to display all data.

✓ *The worksheet is set up to calculate the current value and the return on investment, and display the results in the appropriate cells.*

14. Repeat steps 9 through 13 to gather the current trading information for the other companies in the Excel worksheet.

✓ *Use the smart tag for each ticker symbol to get a stock quote, and then copy and paste the data into the appropriate cells in column F.*

15. In the **105STOCKS_*xx*** worksheet, copy the range A1:H9 to the Clipboard.

16. Close the Excel file, saving all changes, and exit Excel.

17. Switch to the **105INVEST_*xx*** Word document, and paste the worksheet on the last line of the memo.

18. Apply the Table List 1 style to the table in the Word document.

19. Delete all unnecessary space(s) in the table, such as those before and after the dollar signs in the *Original Investment*, *Value*, and *Return* columns.

20. Adjust column widths as necessary so the data wraps correctly and is easy to read. If necessary, change the font size to 10 points.

21. Merge and center the data in the first two rows.

22. Center the entire table horizontally on the page.

23. Check the spelling and grammar in the document.

24. Preview the Word document. It should look similar to Illustration B.

✓ *The current prices will vary.*

25. Print the document.

26. Send the document as an attachment to an email message addressed to **mail@longshotinc.net**.

✓ *This is a fictitious e-mail address. Your instructor may ask you to use a different address.*

27. Type the subject: **Stock Prices**, and type the message: **Here's the information I promised. Get back to me ASAP – these stocks are volatile and we have to act fast.**

28. Close the **105INVEST_*xx*** file, saving all changes.

29. Exit all open programs.

Illustration A

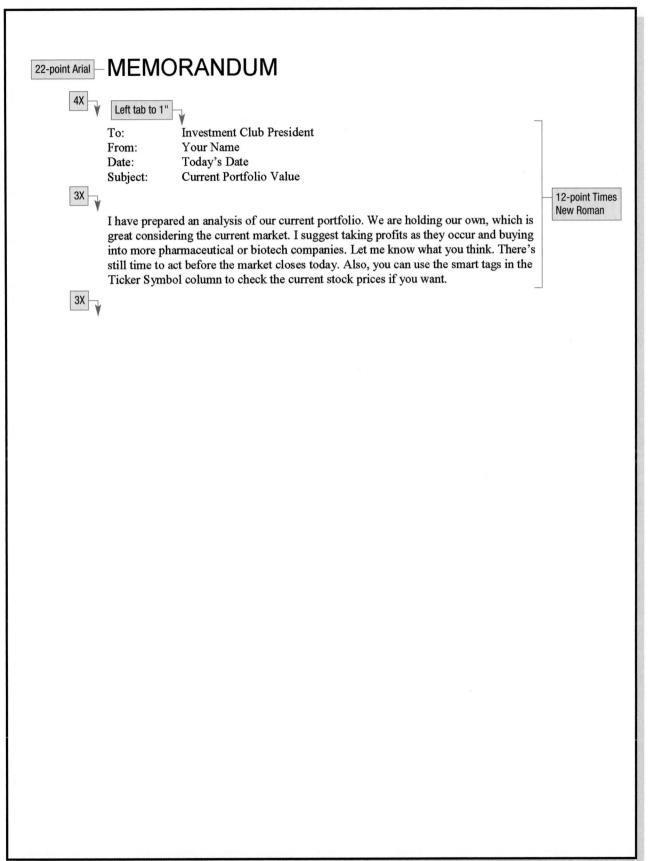

22-point Arial

MEMORANDUM

4X

Left tab to 1"

To: Investment Club President
From: Your Name
Date: Today's Date
Subject: Current Portfolio Value

3X

12-point Times New Roman

I have prepared an analysis of our current portfolio. We are holding our own, which is great considering the current market. I suggest taking profits as they occur and buying into more pharmaceutical or biotech companies. Let me know what you think. There's still time to act before the market closes today. Also, you can use the smart tags in the Ticker Symbol column to check the current stock prices if you want.

3X

MEMORANDUM

To: Investment Club President
From: Your Name
Date: Today's Date
Subject: Current Portfolio Value

I have prepared an analysis of our current portfolio. We are holding our own, which is great considering the current market. I suggest taking profits as they occur and buying into more pharmaceutical or biotech companies. Let me know what you think. There's still time to act before the market closes today. Also, you can use the smart tags in the Ticker Symbol column to check the current stock prices if you want.

Long Shot, Inc.							
Investment Club							
Date:	Today's Date						
Company	Ticker Symbol	Shares Owned	Purchase Price	Original Investment	Last Trade	Value	Return
Amazon.com	AMZN	100	31.45	$3,145.00	**83.38**	$8,338.00	$5,193.00
Cisco Systems, Inc.	CSCO	100	22.33	$2,233.00	**31.62**	$3,162.00	$929.00
Eli Lilly and Company	LLY	125	61.48	$7,685.00	**55.98**	$6,997.50	$(687.50)
Intel Corp	INTC	100	44.48	$4,448.00	**25.47**	$2,547.00	$(1,901.00)

Exercise | 106

Skills Covered

- ■ **Import Data from Excel into Word**
- ■ **Import Data from Access into Word**

Application Skills   As the Director of Training at Long Shot, Inc., you want to send a memo to the Director of Human Resources with information about three new instructors you would like to hire. You already have their names and addresses stored in an Access database file, and you have information about the courses they will teach in an Excel worksheet file. In this exercise, you import the information from the Excel file and the Access file into a Word memo document.

EXERCISE DIRECTIONS

✓ *Before starting this exercise, copy the Access database* 🔘 106HIRES. *Rename the copy* 106HIRES_xx.

1. Start Word and Access, if necessary.
2. Open the Access database file **106HIRES_xx.**
3. Open the *New Hires* table.
4. Select the three records in the table and copy them to the Clipboard.
5. Open the Word document 🔘 **106MEMO.**
6. Save the document as **106MEMO_xx.**
7. Replace the sample text *Your Name* with your own name, and the sample date *Today's date* with the current date.
8. Position the insertion point on the last line of the document.
9. Paste the Access data from the Clipboard into the Word memo.
10. Close the **106HIRES_xx** database file.
11. In the **106MEMO_xx** document, delete the first row in the table (*New Hires*).

12. Delete the three blank columns from the table (*Company Name*, *Address Line 2*, and *Country*).
13. Move the insertion point to the end of the document and insert a blank line.
14. Save the changes to the **106MEMO_xx** document.
15. Open the Excel worksheet file 🔘 **106COURSES.**
16. Save the file as **106COURSES_xx.**
17. Select the range A2:C8 and copy the selection to the Clipboard.
18. Switch to the **106MEMO_xx** document.
19. Paste the Excel data from the Clipboard on to the last line of the **106MEMO_xx** document.
20. In the **106MEMO_xx** document, and then center the table horizontally on the page.
21. Display the document in Print Preview. It should look similar to Illustration A.
22. Print the document.
23. Close all open programs and documents, saving all changes.

Long Shot, Inc.

INTERDEPARTMENT MEMORANDUM

To: Director of Human Resources
From: Student's Name
Date: Today's date
Re: Training Department Expenses

I have made a decision regarding the hiring of three new instructors for the training department. Below you will find their contact information as well as a schedule detailing the courses I would like them to teach. Please tender their offers as soon as possible. Please give me a call if you have any questions. Thanks.

Title	First Name	Last Name	Address Line 1	City	State	ZIP Code	Home Phone	Work Phone	E-mail Address
Mr.	George	Kaplan	980 Main Street	Ithaca	NY	14850	607-555-1234	607-555-4321	gkaplan@mail.com
Ms.	Patricia	Boyd	65 Blueberry Lane	Ithaca	NY	14850	607-555-5678	607-555-8765	pboyd@mail.com
Mrs.	Hannah	Thompson	3232 Chestnut Street	Ithaca	NY	14850	607-555-9012	607-555-2109	hthomspon@mail.com

COURSE NAME	SESSIONS OFFERED	INSTRUCTOR
Word Processing 1	Fall	H. Thompson
Word Processing 2	Fall	G. Kaplan
Word Processing 3	Winter	G. Kaplan
Using the Internet	Spring	P. Boyd
Database Management	Winter	P. Boyd
Spreadsheet Basics	Spring	H. Thompson

- **Use Graphics Objects to Create a Double-Sided Flyer**
- **Insert a File**
- **Apply Newsletter Formatting**
- **Use Mail Merge to Generate Mailing Labels**

Application Skills   Blue Sky Dairy has asked you to create a flyer suitable for mailing to let customers know about the essay contest and the home delivery service. In this exercise, you will create a two-page document that can be printed as a double-sided flyer, folded in half, sealed, and mailed. To set up the document you will use columns, sections, text boxes, and clip art. When the flyer is complete, you will use a mail merge to create mailing labels to use to send the flyer to customers.

EXERCISE DIRECTIONS

✓ Before starting this exercise, copy the Access database ⊙107DATA. Rename the copy 107DATA_xx.

1. Start Word, if necessary, and create a new blank document.
2. Save the document as **107FLYER_xx**.
3. Insert a blank line, and then insert a page break. This creates a document with two pages with a blank line on each page.
4. Position the insertion point at the top of the document and create the page shown in Illustration A. This will be the outside of the flyer when it is folded for mailing:
   a. Insert a text box for entering the return address.
   b. Size the text box to .75" high and 2.5" wide.
   c. Make sure there is no border around the box.
   d. Position the text box in the upper-left corner of the page, .5" to the right of the page and .25" below the page.
   e. Enter the text shown in Illustration A. Use a sans serif font. Type the company name in 14 points and the address in 12 points.
   f. Insert another text box to mark where the mailing label will go.

g. Size the second text box to accommodate your mailing labels. For the default label (Avery Standard 2160 Mini-Address) make the box 1.25" high by 2.75" wide, and apply a dotted border.
h. Center the text box horizontally on the page, and set the vertical absolute position to 2.31" below the paragraph.
i. Enter the text shown in Illustration A. Use a 12-point serif font, centered.
j. Insert a clip art picture of a cow below the return address box.

   ✓ If necessary, use the graphics file ⊙107COW supplied with this book.

k. Size the picture to 1.5" high (the width should adjust automatically).
l. Set text wrapping to Tight.
m. Position the picture -.5" to the right of the margin and 0" below the paragraph.
n. Insert the Explosion 2 AutoShape. This shape will be printed on the back of the outside of the flyer when it is folded for mailing.
o. Format the AutoShape in the 3-D Style 2, with a Light Turquoise fill.
p. Size the AutoShape to 4.2" high by 6.5" wide.

q. Position the AutoShape horizontally centered on the page and vertically 6" below the page.

r. Add the text shown in Illustration A to the shape, using a 26-point bold, sans serif font, centered.

5. Save the document.

6. Preview the document. Page 1 should look similar to Illustration A.

7. Position the insertion point on the second page of the document.

8. Insert the file 🔘107SIDEB. This is the text for the inside of the flyer.

   ✓ *Alternatively, type the text as shown in Illustration B.*

9. Format the page as shown in Illustration B:

   a. Use 14-point Arial unless otherwise marked.

   b. Center the first three lines, the two headlines, and the last paragraph, and leave all other paragraphs flush left.

   c. Apply a border under the second line, as shown in the illustration.

   d. Leave 6 points of space after the second line, then 3 points of space after all other paragraphs.

   e. Insert a continuous section break at the beginning of the fourth line.

   f. Insert a continuous section break at the beginning of the last paragraph on the page.

   g. Leave 12 points of space before the last paragraph on the page.

   h. Format Section 2 into two columns of equal width.

   i. Apply bullet lists as shown in Illustration B.

   j. Apply dropped capitals as shown in Illustration B.

k. If necessary, insert a column break after the first bulleted list.

l. Insert clip art pictures as shown in Illustration B.

   ✓ *If necessary, use the 🔘 107DELIVERY and 🔘 107PEN graphics files supplied with this book.*

m. Set text wrap for the clip art to Square.

n. Size both pictures to 1.5" high, and leave the aspect ratio locked so the width will adjust automatically.

o. Position the clip art pictures as shown in Illustration B.

10. Check the spelling and grammar in the document.

11. Preview page 2. It should look similar to the one in Illustration B.

12. Print page 1 of the document.

13. Reload the printed document in the printer so that you can print on the other side.

    ✓ *Ask your instructor for information on loading paper into the printer for double-sided printing. Often, the side that has already been printed is inserted printed side up, with the top pointing in.*

14. Print page 2 of the document.

15. Create a new blank document and save it as **107LABELS_xx**.

16. Use Mail Merge to generate mailing labels, using the **107DATA_xx** database as the data source.

17. Use the default mailing label format.

18. Merge the labels to a new document and save it as **107LABELSa_xx**.

19. Close all open documents, saving all changes.

Curriculum Connection: Social Studies

Job Safety

Whether you work in an office or on an assembly line, safety is an important workplace issue. The Occupational Safety & Health Administration (OSHA) is a branch of the U.S. Department of Labor, responsible for assuring the safety and health of America's workers. OSHA sets the standards for on the job safety that every business in the United States is required to follow. Many companies have their own safety standards, and provide education for employees on proper behavior and precautions. They also institute plans and procedures to follow in case of an emergency.

Accident Prevention

Create a worksheet or table that lists primary causes of work-related accidents and injuries in offices. You may be able to locate statistics on the Internet or in your library, or you can try to imagine possibilities, such as falls, repetitive stress injuries, or back strain. You may also be able to locate information about the costs of such accidents to businesses, in terms of lost productivity, worker's compensation, or insurance claims. When the worksheet is complete, write a report that a human resources department could distribute to company employees explaining ways to prevent accidents. Include information about good work attitudes, such as being alert and cooperative, as well as specific situations to avoid. Also provide instructions for the company's emergency plan. Use the worksheet or table to illustrate the report.

Illustration A

Blue Sky Dairy Co.
Highway 73
Cambridge, WI 53523

Attach mailing label here

**EXCITING
NEWS FROM
BLUE SKY
DAIRY!**

Blue Sky Dairy Co.
"Where Quality is Our Middle Name"

Don't Miss Out on All the Fun

Essay Contest

Participate in the first ever Blue Sky Dairy Essay Contest! We are thrilled to sponsor an essay contest specifically for teens. The topic for the first contest is Break Away from the Herd. There will be four divisions for four age groups: Junior Division includes students in grades 1 through 4; Middle Division includes students in grades 5 through 9; and Senior Division includes students in grades 10 through 12.

Prizes include:

- Scholarships
- Computer equipment
- Gift certificates
- Travel vouchers

Home Delivery Service

Blue Sky Dairy is pleased to announce that it is starting a home delivery service. At first, Blue Sky trucks will provide delivery to subscribers in the local area, but we hope to expand the program soon to all areas. Home delivery insures that you receive the best quality products when you need them, without having to make a trip to the store.

Products that can be ordered for home delivery include:

- Milk
- Butter
- Cream
- Half and Half
- Ice Cream

For more information about the essay contest, the home delivery service, or any of the other exciting happenings at Blue Sky, call: 608-555-2697. Or visit our website at: www.blueskydairy.net.

Index